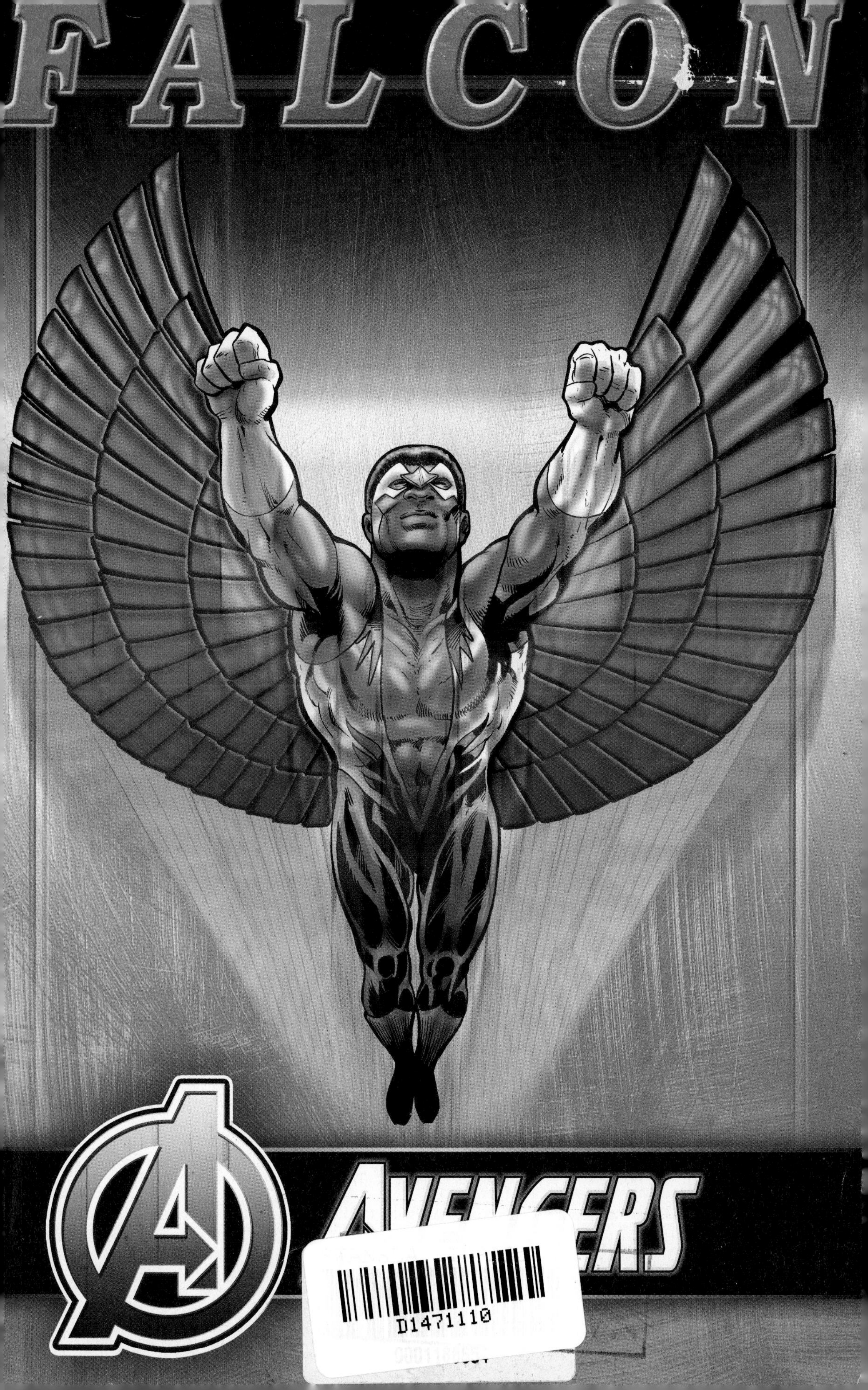
FALCON
AVENGERS

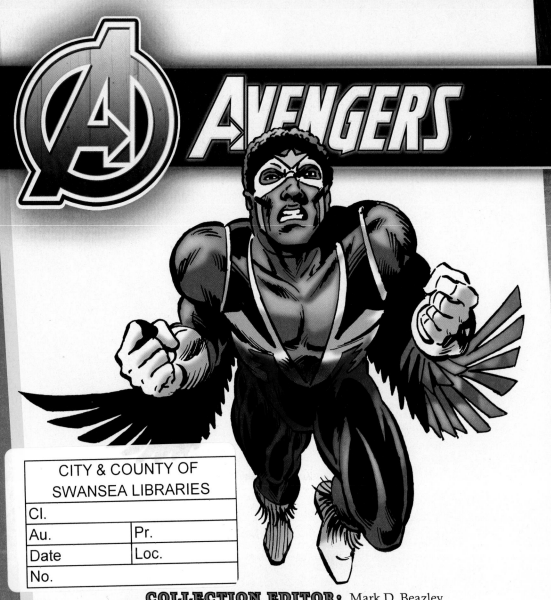

COLLECTION EDITOR: Mark D. Beazley
ASSOCIATE MANAGING EDITOR: Alex Starbuck
EDITOR, SPECIAL PROJECTS: Jennifer Grünwald
SENIOR EDITOR, SPECIAL PROJECTS: Jeff Youngquist
RESEARCH: Gary Henderson & Jeph York
LAYOUT: Jeph York **PRODUCTION:** ColorTek & Joe Frontirre
BOOK DESIGNER: Nelson Ribeiro
SVP PRINT, SALES & MARKETING: David Gabriel

EDITOR IN CHIEF: Axel Alonso
CHIEF CREATIVE OFFICER: Joe Quesada
PUBLISHER: Dan Buckley
EXECUTIVE PRODUCER: Alan Fine

Special Thanks to Gregory Hecht

AVENGERS: FALCON. Contains material originally published in magazine form as FALCON #1-4; MARVEL PREMIERE #49; and CAPTAIN AMERICA #117-119, #220 and #276-278. First printing
2014. ISBN# 978-0-7851-8826-1. Published by MARVEL WORLDWIDE, INC., a subsidiary of MARVEL ENTERTAINMENT, LLC. OFFICE OF PUBLICATION: 135 West 50th Street, New York, NY 10020.
Copyright © 1969, 1978, 1979, 1982, 1983, 1984 and 2014 Marvel Characters, Inc. All rights reserved. All characters featured in this issue and the distinctive names and likenesses thereof,
and all related indicia are trademarks of Marvel Characters, Inc. No similarity between any of the names, characters, persons, and/or institutions in this magazine with those of any living or dead
person or institution is intended, and any such similarity which may exist is purely coincidental. **Printed in the U.S.A.** ALAN FINE, EVP - Office of the President, Marvel Worldwide, Inc. and EVP &
CMO Marvel Characters B.V.; DAN BUCKLEY, Publisher & President - Print, Animation & Digital Divisions; JOE QUESADA, Chief Creative Officer; TOM BREVOORT, SVP of Publishing; DAVID BOGART,
SVP of Operations & Procurement, Publishing; C.B. CEBULSKI, SVP of Creator & Content Development; DAVID GABRIEL, SVP of Print & Digital Publishing Sales; JIM O'KEEFE, VP of Operations &
Logistics; DAN CARR, Executive Director of Publishing Technology; SUSAN CRESPI, Editorial Operations Manager; ALEX MORALES, Publishing Operations Manager; STAN LEE, Chairman Emeritus.
For information regarding advertising in Marvel Comics or on Marvel.com, please contact Niza Disla, Director of Marvel Partnerships, at ndisla@marvel.com. For Marvel subscription inquiries, please
call 800-217-9158. **Manufactured between 1/10/2014 and 2/17/2014 by R.R. DONNELLEY, INC., SALEM, VA, USA.**

10 9 8 7 6 5 4 3 2 1

FALCON

WRITERS
Jim Owsley, Stan Lee, Mark Evanier
& J.M. DeMatteis with Scott Edelman

PENCILERS
Paul Smith, Mark Bright, Gene Colan,
Sal Buscema & Mike Zeck with Bob Budiansky

INKERS
Vince Colletta, Mike Gustovich, Joe Sinnott
& Dave Simons with Al Gordon,
John Beatty & Josef Rubinstein

COLORISTS
Christie Scheele, Stephen Mellor,
Ben Sean & Bob Sharen

LETTERERS
Rick Parker, Clem Robins, Sam Rosen & Jim Novak with Michael Higgins
& Jack Morelli

ASSISTANT EDITORS
Jim Owsley, Jim Salicrup & Michael Carlin

EDITORS
Larry Hama, Stan Lee, Roger Stern
& Mark Gruenwald with Archie Goodwin

FRONT COVER ARTISTS
Frank Miller, Klaus Janson & Thomas Mason

BACK COVER ARTISTS
Gene Colan, Joe Sinnott & Tom Smith

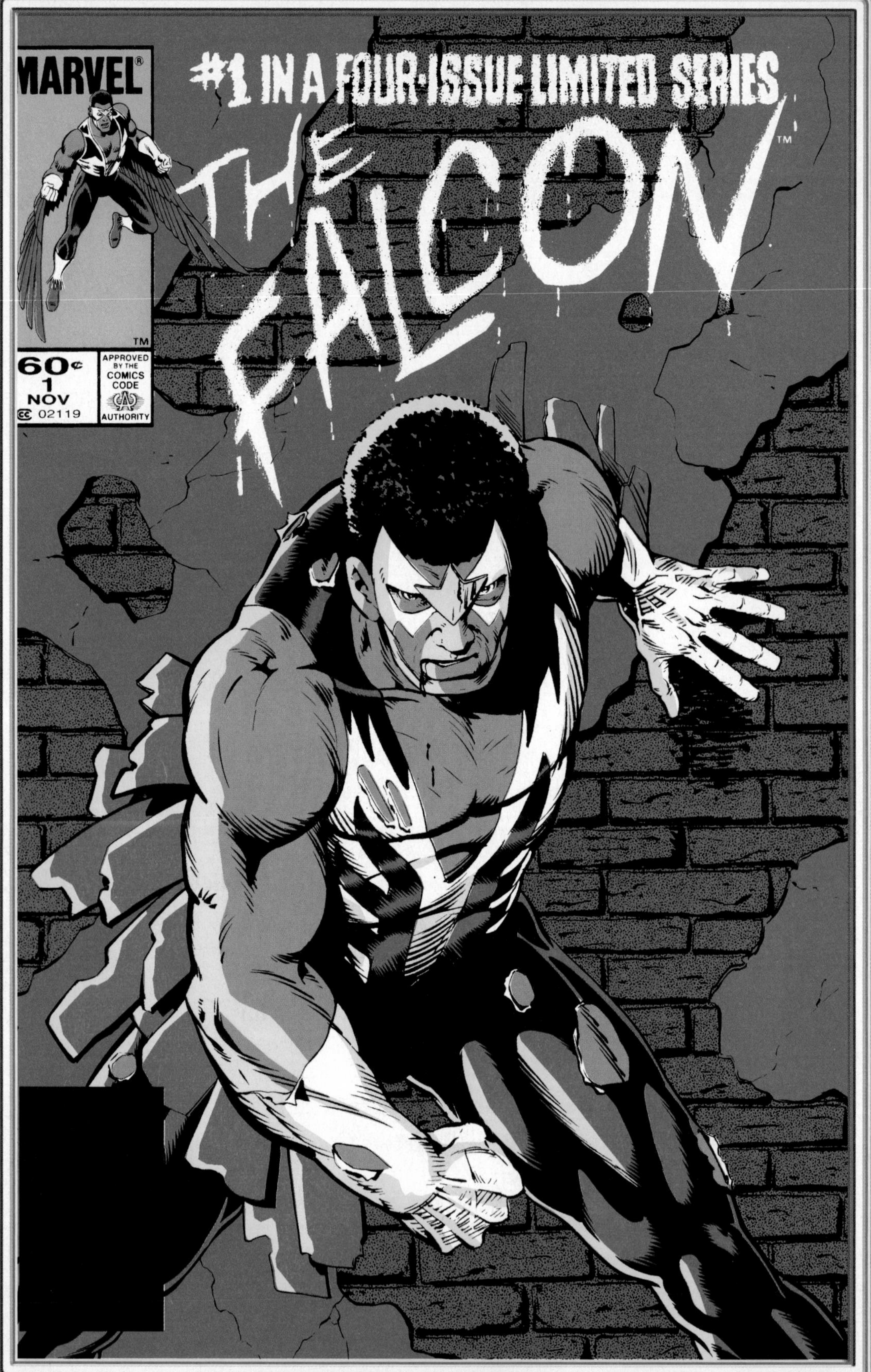
MARVEL®
#1 IN A FOUR-ISSUE LIMITED SERIES
THE FALCON™
TM
60¢
1
NOV
02119
APPROVED BY THE COMICS CODE AUTHORITY

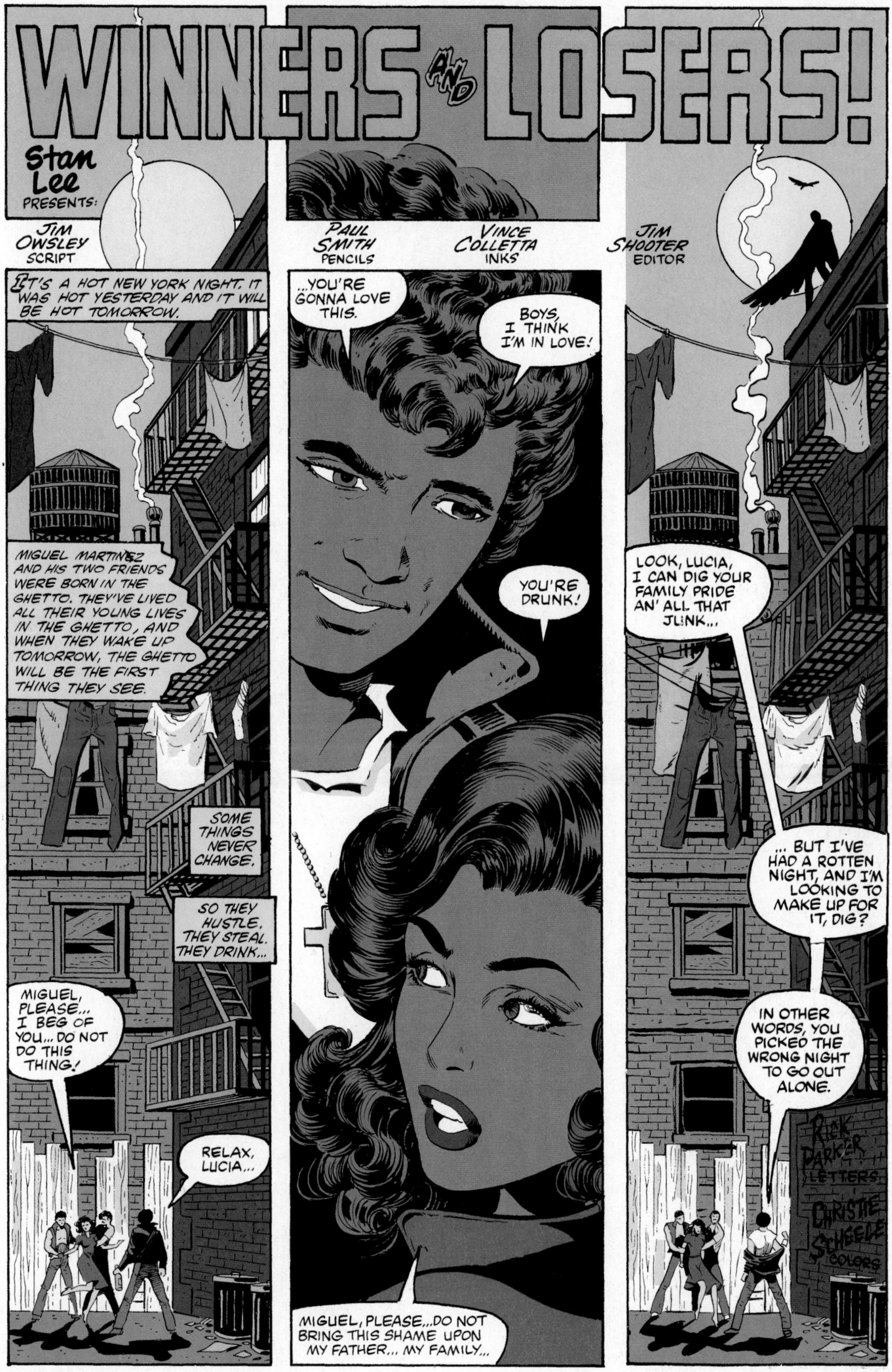
WINNERS AND LOSERS!
Stan Lee PRESENTS:
JIM OWSLEY SCRIPT
PAUL SMITH PENCILS
VINCE COLLETTA INKS
JIM SHOOTER EDITOR
IT'S A HOT NEW YORK NIGHT. IT WAS HOT YESTERDAY AND IT WILL BE HOT TOMORROW.
MIGUEL MARTINEZ AND HIS TWO FRIENDS WERE BORN IN THE GHETTO. THEY'VE LIVED ALL THEIR YOUNG LIVES IN THE GHETTO, AND WHEN THEY WAKE UP TOMORROW, THE GHETTO WILL BE THE FIRST THING THEY SEE.
SOME THINGS NEVER CHANGE.
SO THEY HUSTLE. THEY STEAL. THEY DRINK...
MIGUEL, PLEASE... I BEG OF YOU... DO NOT DO THIS THING!
RELAX, LUCIA...
...YOU'RE GONNA LOVE THIS.
BOYS, I THINK I'M IN LOVE!
YOU'RE DRUNK!
MIGUEL, PLEASE... DO NOT BRING THIS SHAME UPON MY FATHER... MY FAMILY...
LOOK, LUCIA, I CAN DIG YOUR FAMILY PRIDE AN' ALL THAT JUNK...
... BUT I'VE HAD A ROTTEN NIGHT, AND I'M LOOKING TO MAKE UP FOR IT, DIG?
IN OTHER WORDS, YOU PICKED THE WRONG NIGHT TO GO OUT ALONE.
RICK PARKER LETTERS
CHRISTIE SCHEELE COLORS

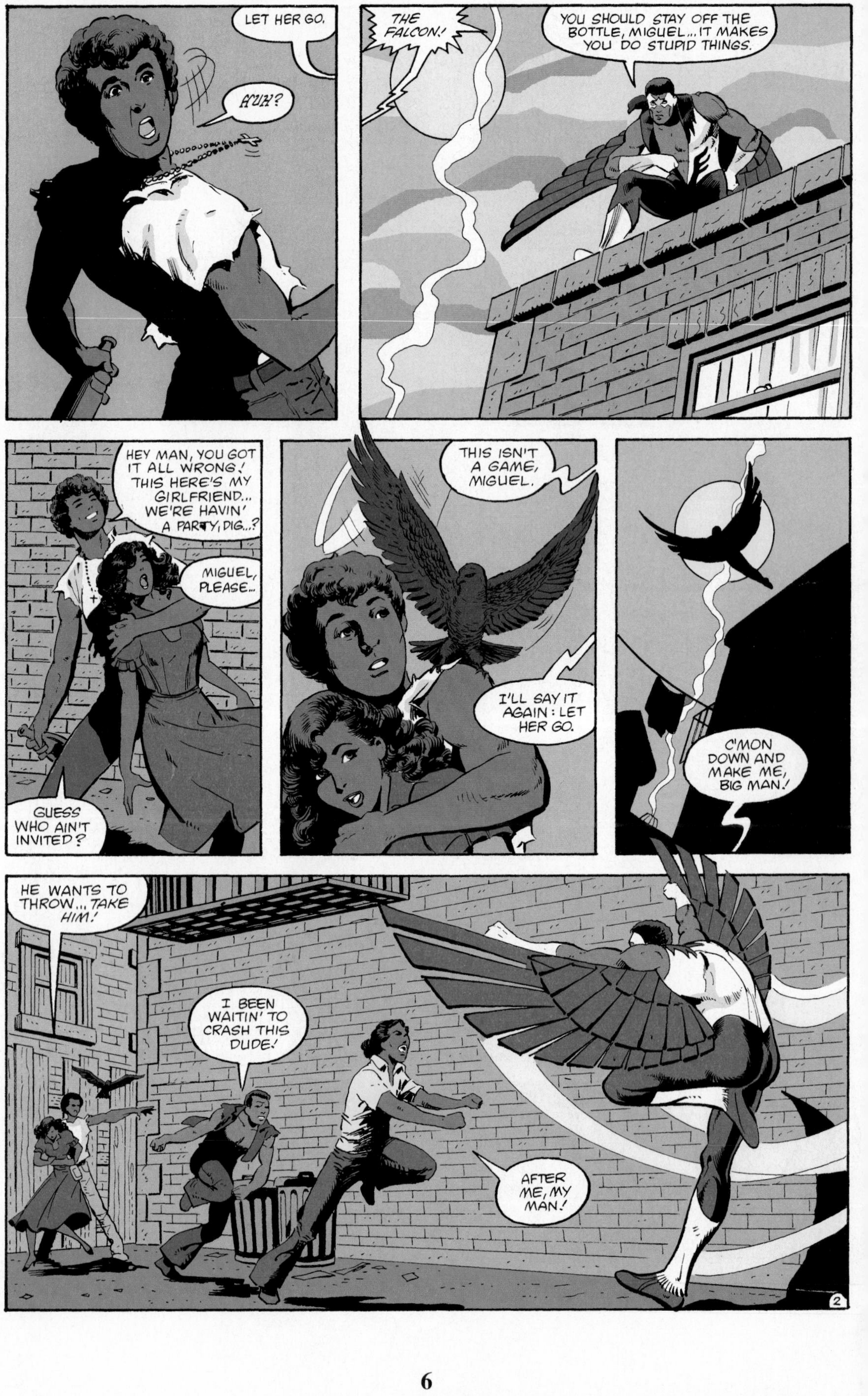
LET HER GO.
HUH?
THE FALCON!
YOU SHOULD STAY OFF THE BOTTLE, MIGUEL... IT MAKES YOU DO STUPID THINGS.
HEY MAN, YOU GOT IT ALL WRONG! THIS HERE'S MY GIRLFRIEND... WE'RE HAVIN' A PARTY, DIG...?
MIGUEL, PLEASE...
GUESS WHO AIN'T INVITED?
THIS ISN'T A GAME, MIGUEL.
I'LL SAY IT AGAIN: LET HER GO.
C'MON DOWN AND MAKE ME, BIG MAN!
HE WANTS TO THROW... TAKE HIM!
I BEEN WAITIN' TO CRASH THIS DUDE!
AFTER ME, MY MAN!
2

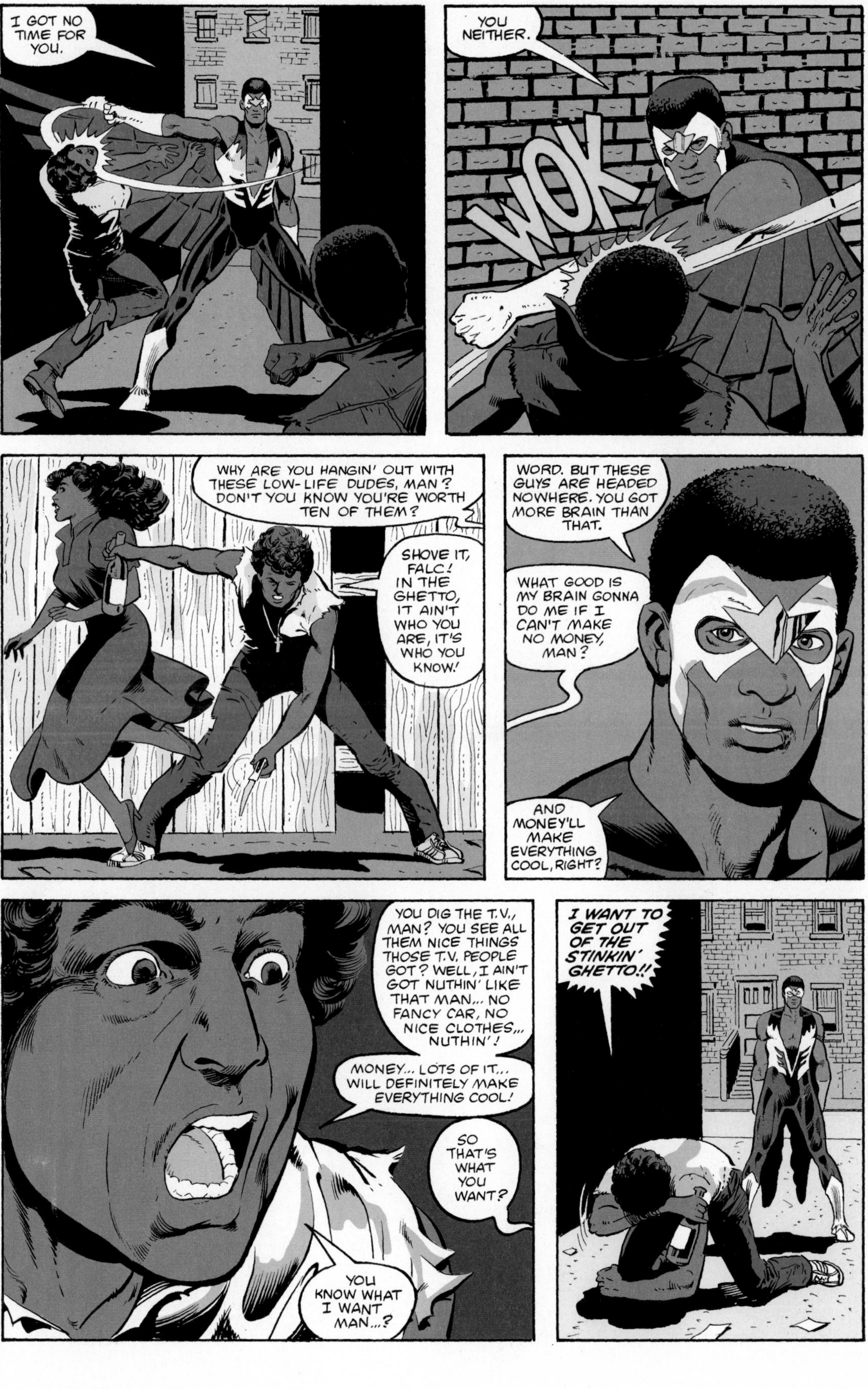
I GOT NO TIME FOR YOU.
YOU NEITHER.
WOK
WHY ARE YOU HANGIN' OUT WITH THESE LOW-LIFE DUDES, MAN? DON'T YOU KNOW YOU'RE WORTH TEN OF THEM?
SHOVE IT, FALC! IN THE GHETTO, IT AIN'T WHO YOU ARE, IT'S WHO YOU KNOW!
WORD. BUT THESE GUYS ARE HEADED NOWHERE. YOU GOT MORE BRAIN THAN THAT.
WHAT GOOD IS MY BRAIN GONNA DO ME IF I CAN'T MAKE NO MONEY, MAN?
AND MONEY'LL MAKE EVERYTHING COOL, RIGHT?
YOU DIG THE T.V., MAN? YOU SEE ALL THEM NICE THINGS THOSE T.V. PEOPLE GOT? WELL, I AIN'T GOT NUTHIN' LIKE THAT MAN... NO FANCY CAR, NO NICE CLOTHES... NUTHIN'!
MONEY... LOTS OF IT... WILL DEFINITELY MAKE EVERYTHING COOL!
SO THAT'S WHAT YOU WANT?
YOU KNOW WHAT I WANT MAN...?
I WANT TO GET OUT OF THE STINKIN' GHETTO!!

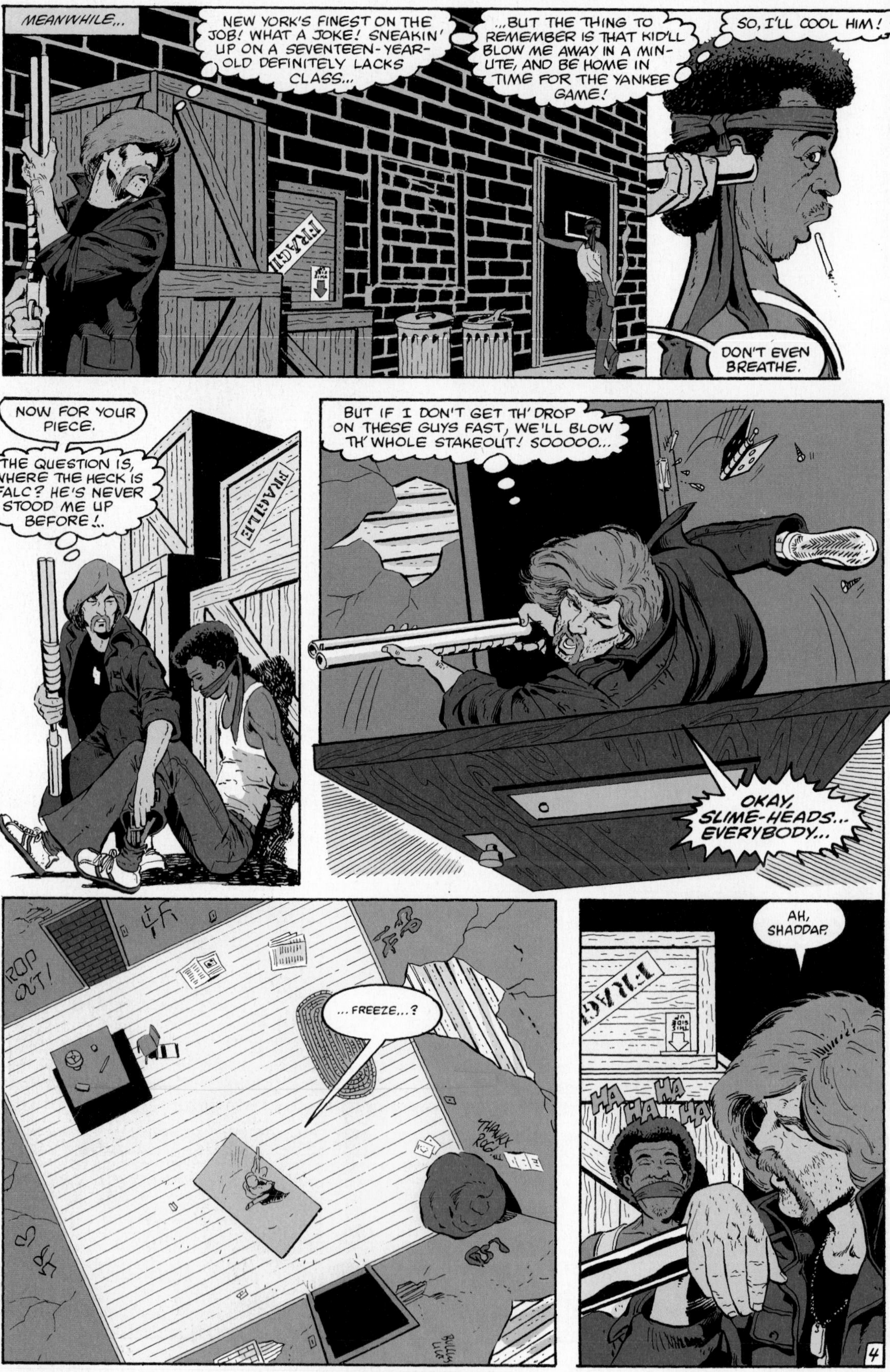
MEANWHILE...
NEW YORK'S FINEST ON THE JOB! WHAT A JOKE! SNEAKIN' UP ON A SEVENTEEN-YEAR-OLD DEFINITELY LACKS CLASS...
...BUT THE THING TO REMEMBER IS THAT KID'LL BLOW ME AWAY IN A MINUTE, AND BE HOME IN TIME FOR THE YANKEE GAME!
SO, I'LL COOL HIM!
FRAGILE
DON'T EVEN BREATHE.
NOW FOR YOUR PIECE.
THE QUESTION IS, WHERE THE HECK IS FALC? HE'S NEVER STOOD ME UP BEFORE!..
FRAGILE
BUT IF I DON'T GET TH' DROP ON THESE GUYS FAST, WE'LL BLOW TH' WHOLE STAKEOUT! SOOOOO...
OKAY, SLIME-HEADS... EVERYBODY...
...FREEZE...?
AH, SHADDAP.
HA HA HA HA
4

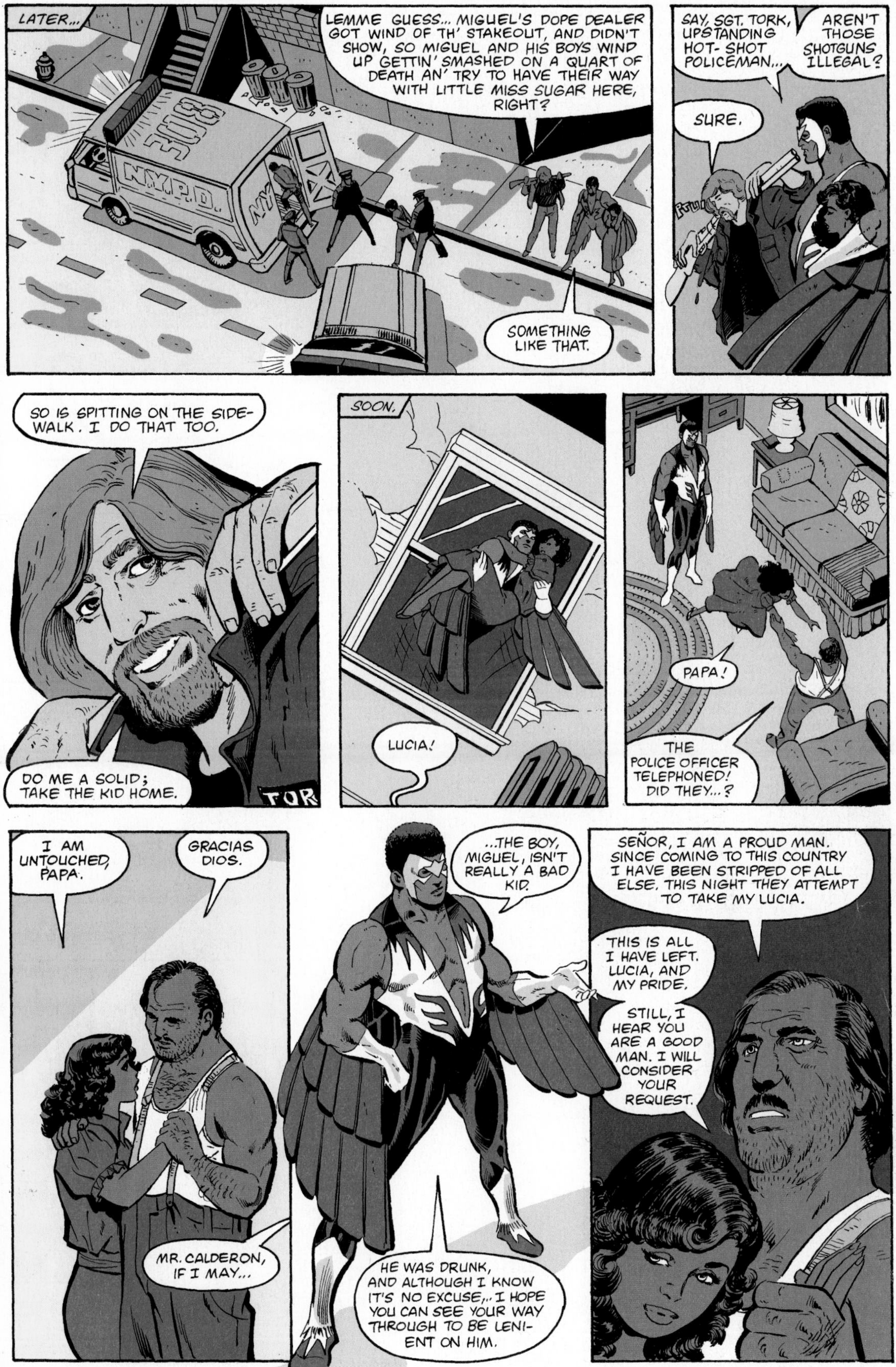
LATER...
LEMME GUESS... MIGUEL'S DOPE DEALER GOT WIND OF TH' STAKEOUT, AND DIDN'T SHOW, SO MIGUEL AND HIS BOYS WIND UP GETTIN' SMASHED ON A QUART OF DEATH AN' TRY TO HAVE THEIR WAY WITH LITTLE MISS SUGAR HERE, RIGHT?
SOMETHING LIKE THAT.
SAY, SGT. TORK, UPSTANDING HOT-SHOT POLICEMAN...
AREN'T THOSE SHOTGUNS ILLEGAL?
SURE.
SO IS SPITTING ON THE SIDE-WALK. I DO THAT TOO.
DO ME A SOLID; TAKE THE KID HOME.
SOON.
LUCIA!
PAPA!
THE POLICE OFFICER TELEPHONED! DID THEY...?
I AM UNTOUCHED, PAPA.
GRACIAS DIOS.
MR. CALDERON, IF I MAY...
...THE BOY, MIGUEL, ISN'T REALLY A BAD KID.
HE WAS DRUNK, AND ALTHOUGH I KNOW IT'S NO EXCUSE,.. I HOPE YOU CAN SEE YOUR WAY THROUGH TO BE LENI-ENT ON HIM.
SEÑOR, I AM A PROUD MAN. SINCE COMING TO THIS COUNTRY I HAVE BEEN STRIPPED OF ALL ELSE. THIS NIGHT THEY ATTEMPT TO TAKE MY LUCIA.
THIS IS ALL I HAVE LEFT. LUCIA, AND MY PRIDE.
STILL, I HEAR YOU ARE A GOOD MAN. I WILL CONSIDER YOUR REQUEST.

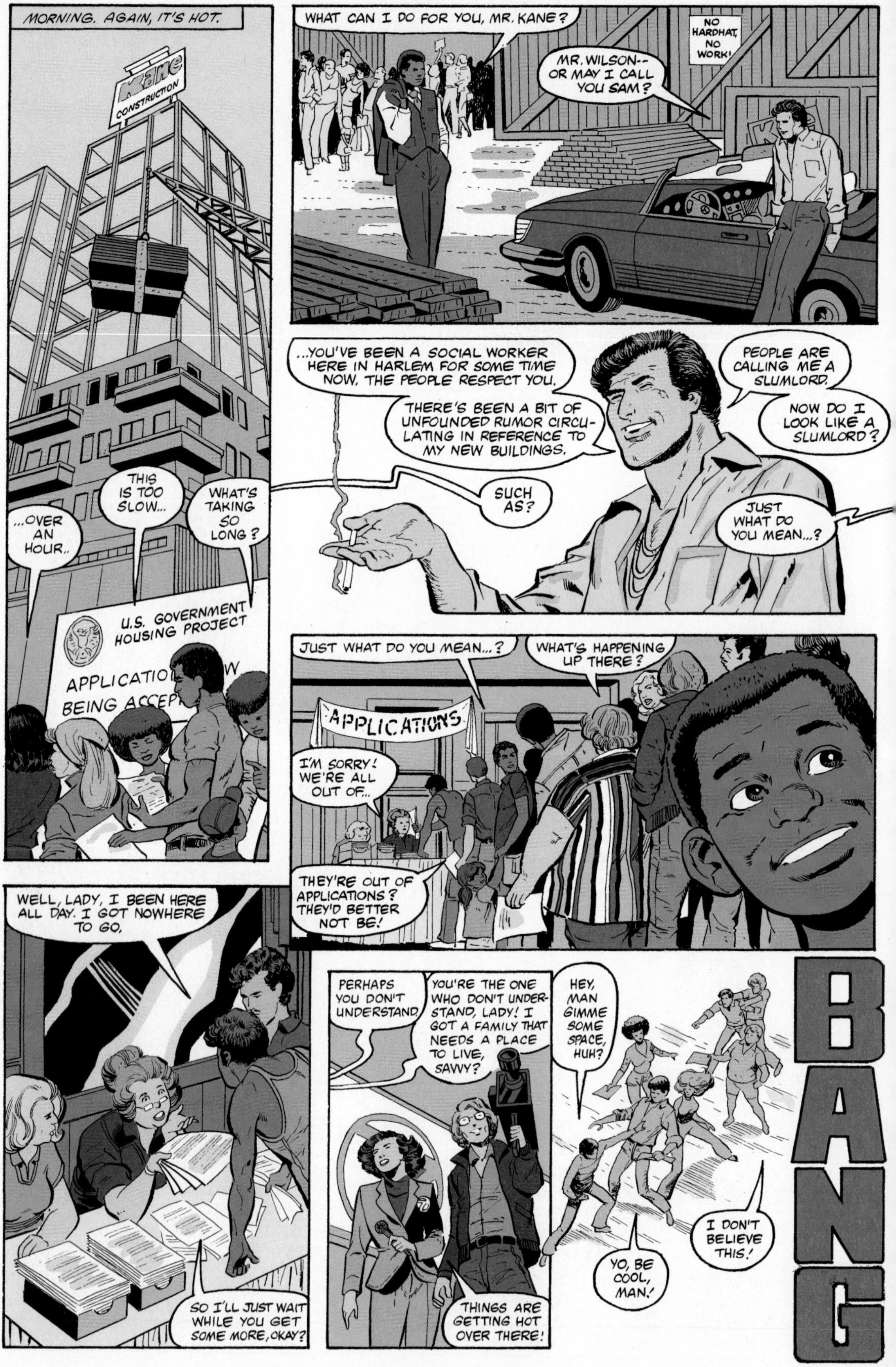
MORNING. AGAIN, IT'S HOT.
Kane CONSTRUCTION
...OVER AN HOUR..
THIS IS TOO SLOW...
WHAT'S TAKING SO LONG?
U.S. GOVERNMENT HOUSING PROJECT
APPLICATIO W BEING ACCEP
WHAT CAN I DO FOR YOU, MR. KANE?
NO HARDHAT, NO WORK!
MR. WILSON-- OR MAY I CALL YOU SAM?
...YOU'VE BEEN A SOCIAL WORKER HERE IN HARLEM FOR SOME TIME NOW. THE PEOPLE RESPECT YOU.
THERE'S BEEN A BIT OF UNFOUNDED RUMOR CIRCULATING IN REFERENCE TO MY NEW BUILDINGS.
PEOPLE ARE CALLING ME A SLUMLORD.
NOW DO I LOOK LIKE A SLUMLORD?
SUCH AS?
JUST WHAT DO YOU MEAN...?
JUST WHAT DO YOU MEAN...?
WHAT'S HAPPENING UP THERE?
APPLICATIONS
I'M SORRY! WE'RE ALL OUT OF...
THEY'RE OUT OF APPLICATIONS? THEY'D BETTER NOT BE!
WELL, LADY, I BEEN HERE ALL DAY. I GOT NOWHERE TO GO.
SO I'LL JUST WAIT WHILE YOU GET SOME MORE, OKAY?
PERHAPS YOU DON'T UNDERSTAND.
YOU'RE THE ONE WHO DON'T UNDERSTAND, LADY! I GOT A FAMILY THAT NEEDS A PLACE TO LIVE, SAVVY?
THINGS ARE GETTING HOT OVER THERE!
HEY, MAN GIMME SOME SPACE, HUH?
YO, BE COOL, MAN!
I DON'T BELIEVE THIS!
BANG

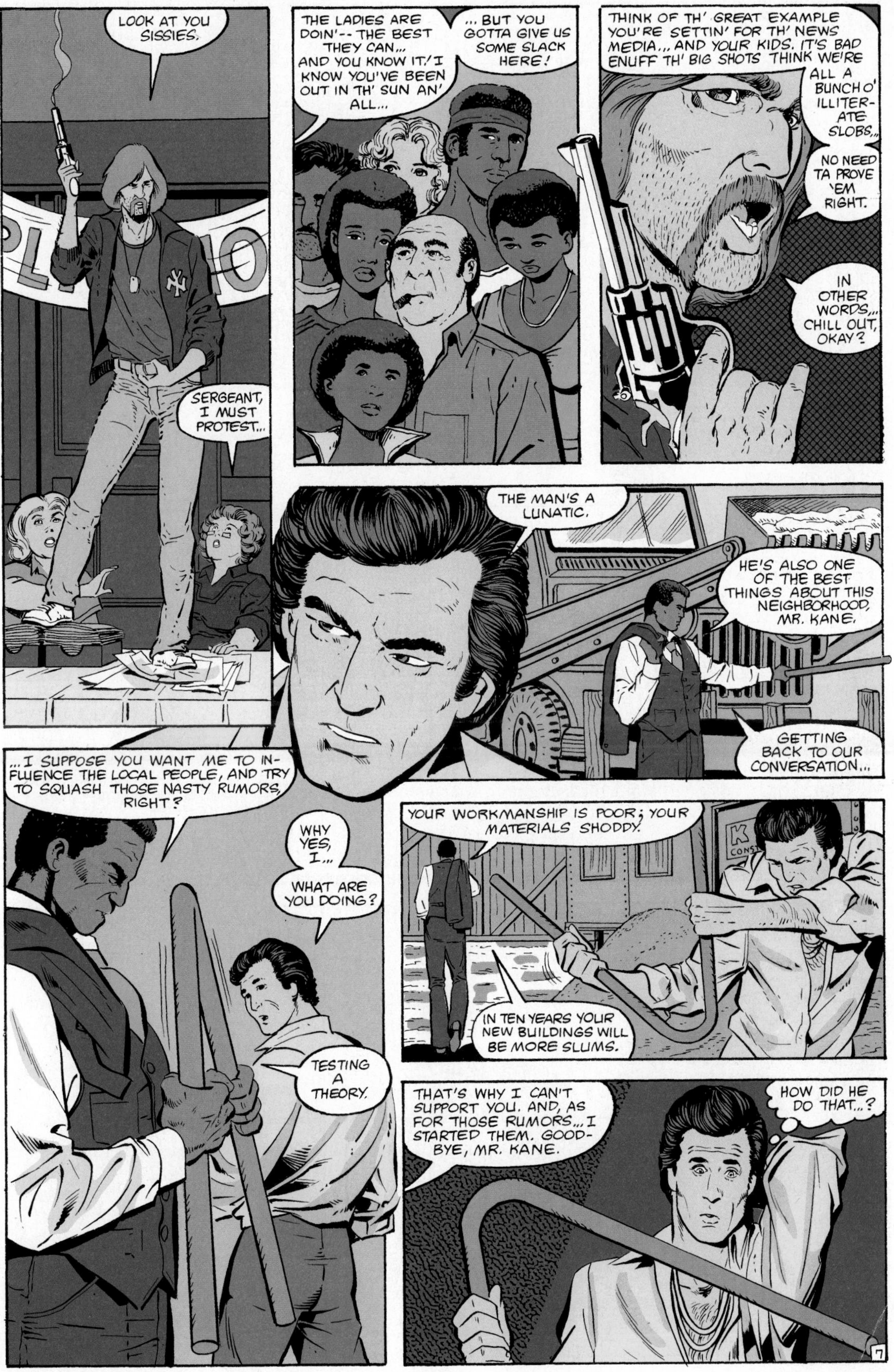
LOOK AT YOU SISSIES.
SERGEANT, I MUST PROTEST...
THE LADIES ARE DOIN'-- THE BEST THEY CAN... AND YOU KNOW IT! I KNOW YOU'VE BEEN OUT IN TH' SUN AN' ALL...
...BUT YOU GOTTA GIVE US SOME SLACK HERE!
THINK OF TH' GREAT EXAMPLE YOU'RE SETTIN' FOR TH' NEWS MEDIA... AND YOUR KIDS. IT'S BAD ENUFF TH' BIG SHOTS THINK WE'RE ALL A BUNCH O' ILLITER-ATE SLOBS...
NO NEED TA PROVE 'EM RIGHT.
IN OTHER WORDS... CHILL OUT, OKAY?
THE MAN'S A LUNATIC.
HE'S ALSO ONE OF THE BEST THINGS ABOUT THIS NEIGHBORHOOD, MR. KANE.
GETTING BACK TO OUR CONVERSATION...
...I SUPPOSE YOU WANT ME TO IN-FLUENCE THE LOCAL PEOPLE, AND TRY TO SQUASH THOSE NASTY RUMORS, RIGHT?
WHY YES, I...
WHAT ARE YOU DOING?
TESTING A THEORY.
YOUR WORKMANSHIP IS POOR; YOUR MATERIALS SHODDY.
IN TEN YEARS YOUR NEW BUILDINGS WILL BE MORE SLUMS.
THAT'S WHY I CAN'T SUPPORT YOU. AND, AS FOR THOSE RUMORS... I STARTED THEM. GOOD-BYE, MR. KANE.
HOW DID HE DO THAT...?
7

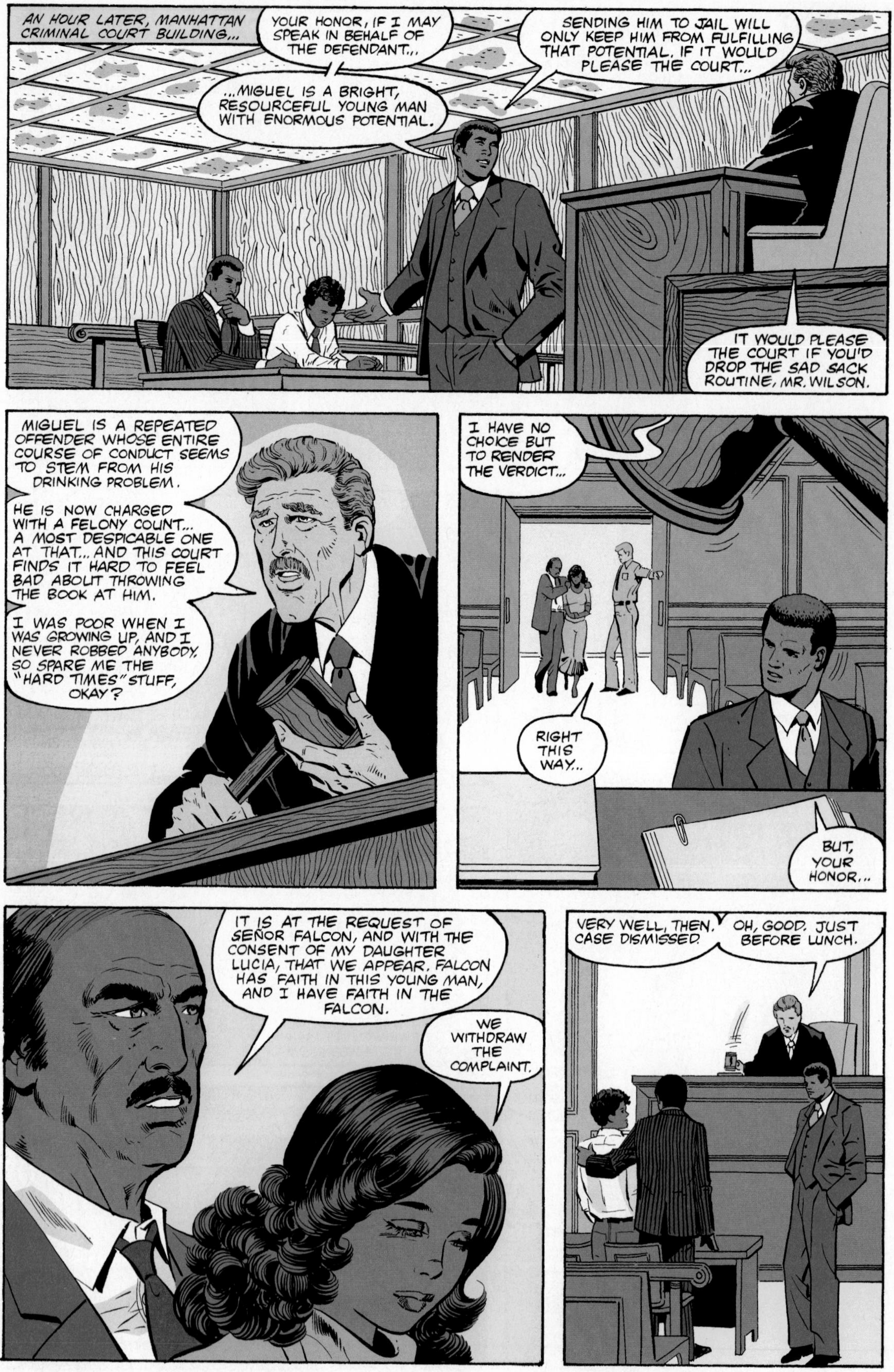
AN HOUR LATER, MANHATTAN CRIMINAL COURT BUILDING...
YOUR HONOR, IF I MAY SPEAK IN BEHALF OF THE DEFENDANT...
...MIGUEL IS A BRIGHT, RESOURCEFUL YOUNG MAN WITH ENORMOUS POTENTIAL.
SENDING HIM TO JAIL WILL ONLY KEEP HIM FROM FULFILLING THAT POTENTIAL. IF IT WOULD PLEASE THE COURT...
IT WOULD PLEASE THE COURT IF YOU'D DROP THE SAD SACK ROUTINE, MR. WILSON.
MIGUEL IS A REPEATED OFFENDER WHOSE ENTIRE COURSE OF CONDUCT SEEMS TO STEM FROM HIS DRINKING PROBLEM.
HE IS NOW CHARGED WITH A FELONY COUNT... A MOST DESPICABLE ONE AT THAT... AND THIS COURT FINDS IT HARD TO FEEL BAD ABOUT THROWING THE BOOK AT HIM.
I WAS POOR WHEN I WAS GROWING UP, AND I NEVER ROBBED ANYBODY, SO SPARE ME THE "HARD TIMES" STUFF, OKAY?
I HAVE NO CHOICE BUT TO RENDER THE VERDICT...
RIGHT THIS WAY...
BUT, YOUR HONOR...
IT IS AT THE REQUEST OF SEÑOR FALCON, AND WITH THE CONSENT OF MY DAUGHTER LUCIA, THAT WE APPEAR. FALCON HAS FAITH IN THIS YOUNG MAN, AND I HAVE FAITH IN THE FALCON.
WE WITHDRAW THE COMPLAINT.
VERY WELL, THEN. CASE DISMISSED.
OH, GOOD. JUST BEFORE LUNCH.

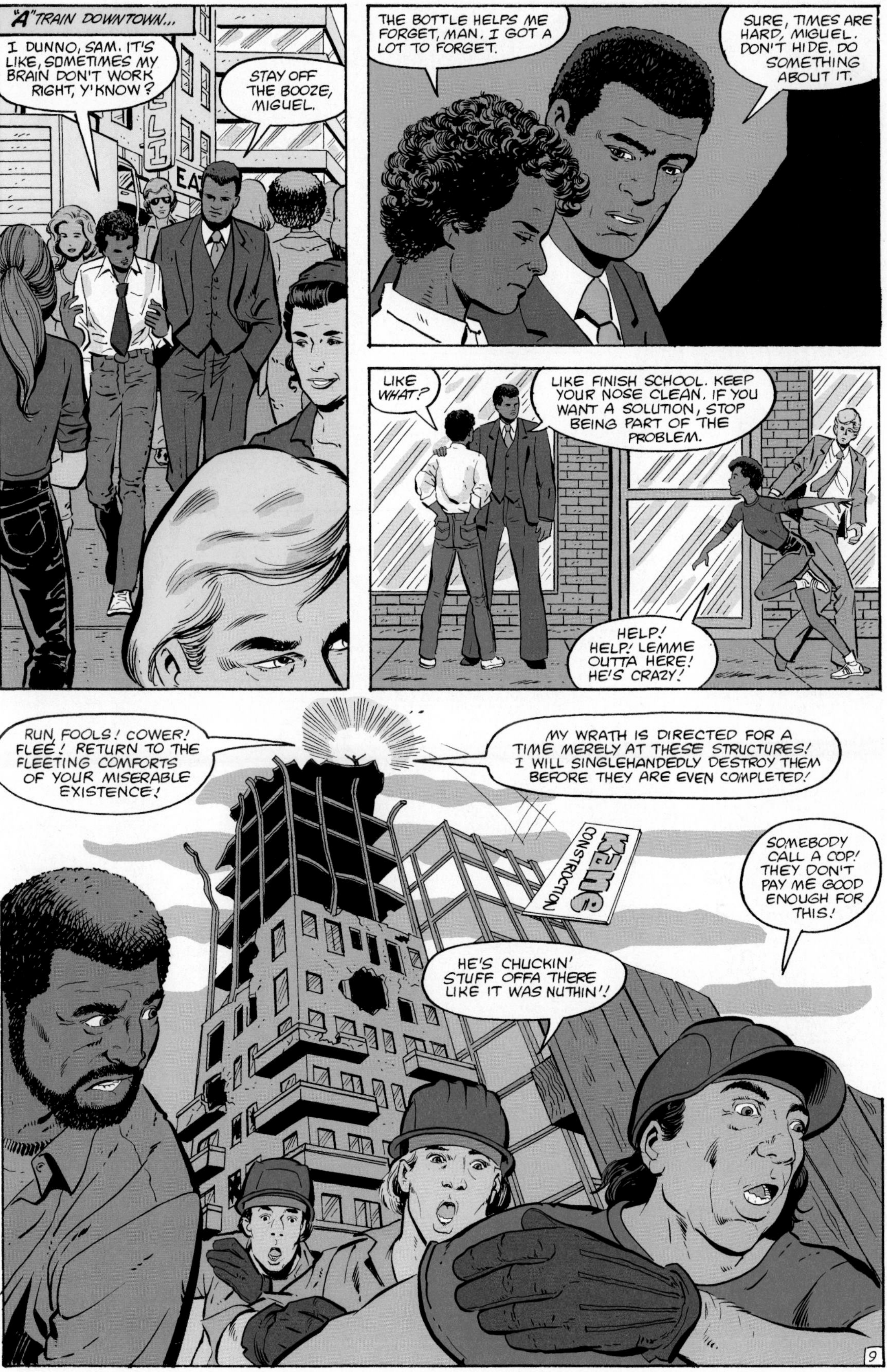
"A" TRAIN DOWNTOWN...
I DUNNO, SAM. IT'S LIKE, SOMETIMES MY BRAIN DON'T WORK RIGHT, Y'KNOW?
STAY OFF THE BOOZE, MIGUEL.
THE BOTTLE HELPS ME FORGET, MAN. I GOT A LOT TO FORGET.
SURE, TIMES ARE HARD, MIGUEL. DON'T HIDE. DO SOMETHING ABOUT IT.
LIKE WHAT?
LIKE FINISH SCHOOL. KEEP YOUR NOSE CLEAN. IF YOU WANT A SOLUTION, STOP BEING PART OF THE PROBLEM.
HELP! HELP! LEMME OUTTA HERE! HE'S CRAZY!
RUN, FOOLS! COWER! FLEE! RETURN TO THE FLEETING COMFORTS OF YOUR MISERABLE EXISTENCE!
MY WRATH IS DIRECTED FOR A TIME MERELY AT THESE STRUCTURES! I WILL SINGLEHANDEDLY DESTROY THEM BEFORE THEY ARE EVEN COMPLETED!
KANE CONSTRUCTION
SOMEBODY CALL A COP! THEY DON'T PAY ME GOOD ENOUGH FOR THIS!
HE'S CHUCKIN' STUFF OFFA THERE LIKE IT WAS NUTHIN'!
9

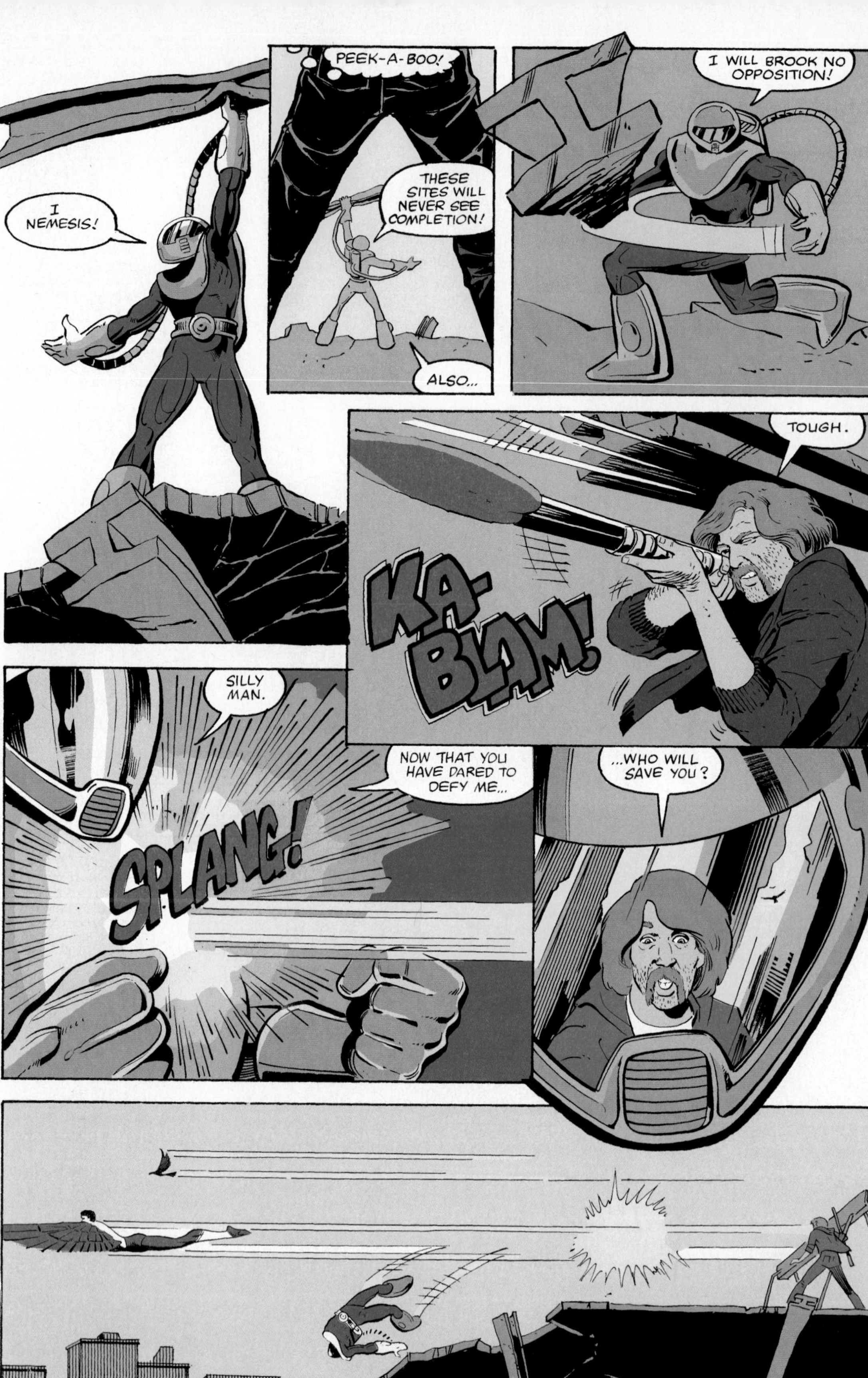
I NEMESIS!
PEEK-A-BOO!
THESE SITES WILL NEVER SEE COMPLETION!
ALSO...
I WILL BROOK NO OPPOSITION!
TOUGH.
KA-BLAM!
SILLY MAN.
NOW THAT YOU HAVE DARED TO DEFY ME...
SPLANG!
...WHO WILL SAVE YOU?

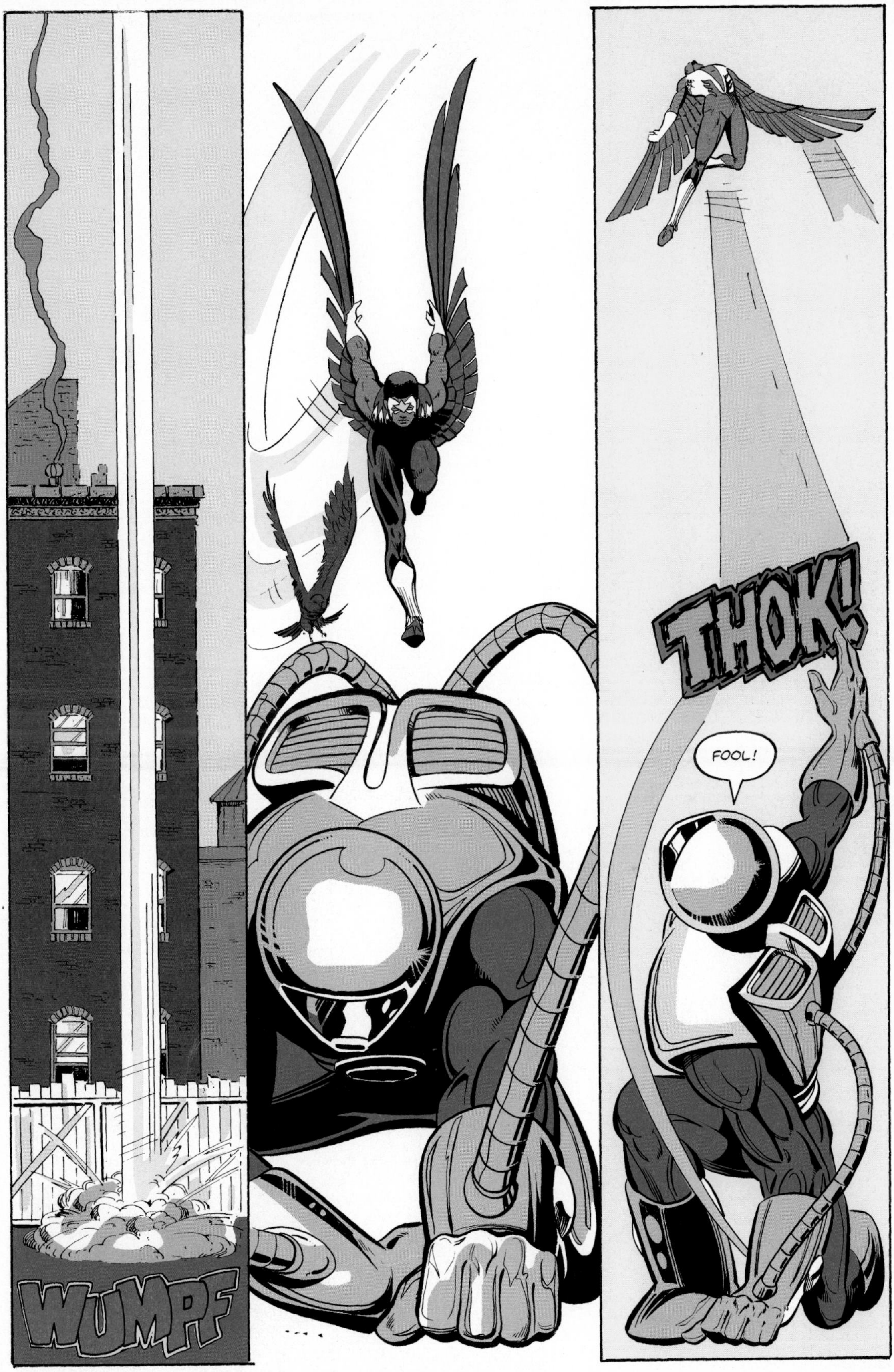
WUMPF
THOK!
FOOL!

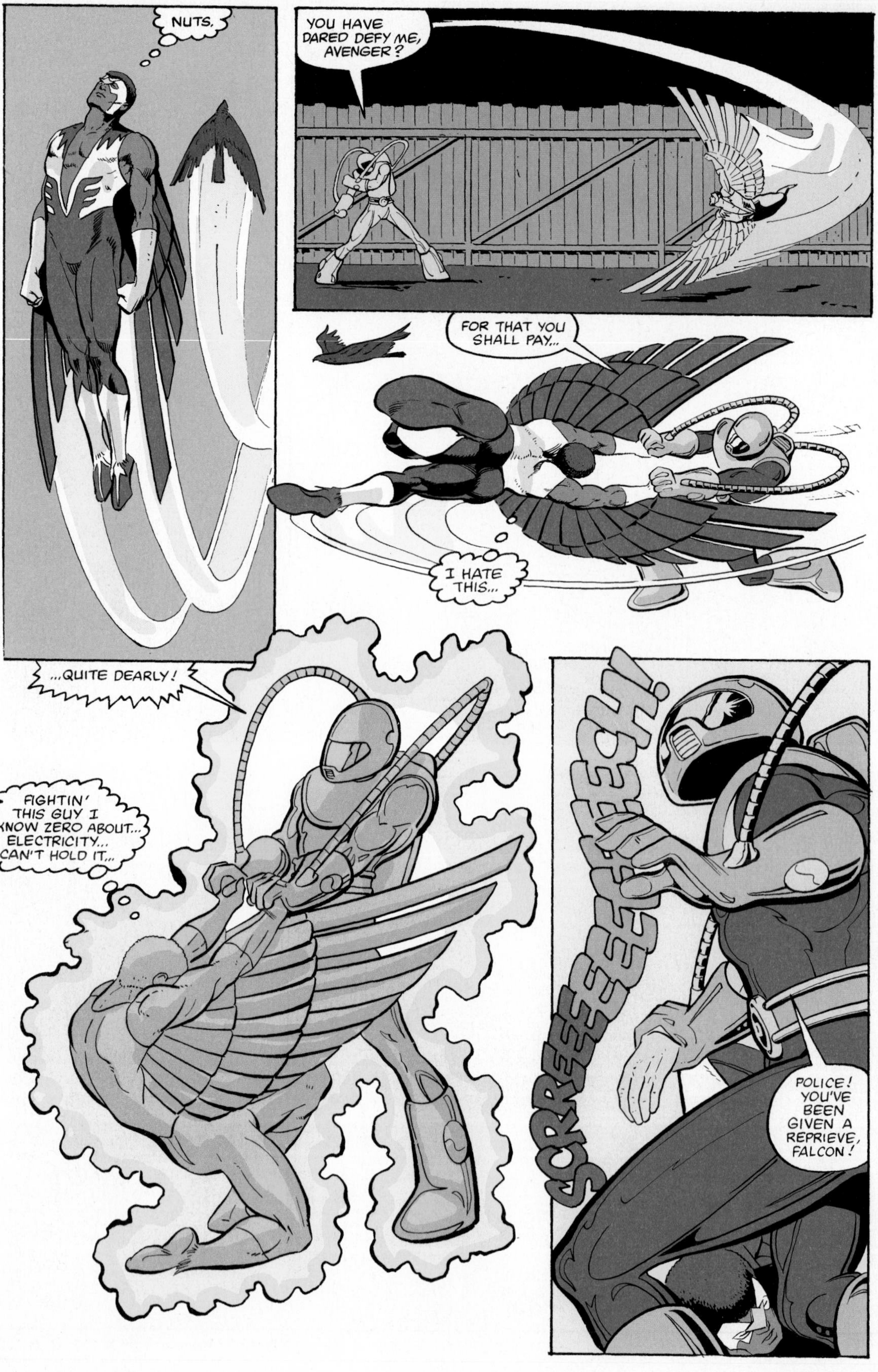
NUTS.
YOU HAVE DARED DEFY ME, AVENGER?
FOR THAT YOU SHALL PAY...
I HATE THIS...
...QUITE DEARLY!
FIGHTIN' THIS GUY I KNOW ZERO ABOUT... ELECTRICITY... CAN'T HOLD IT...
SCRREEEEEEEEECH!
POLICE! YOU'VE BEEN GIVEN A REPRIEVE, FALCON!

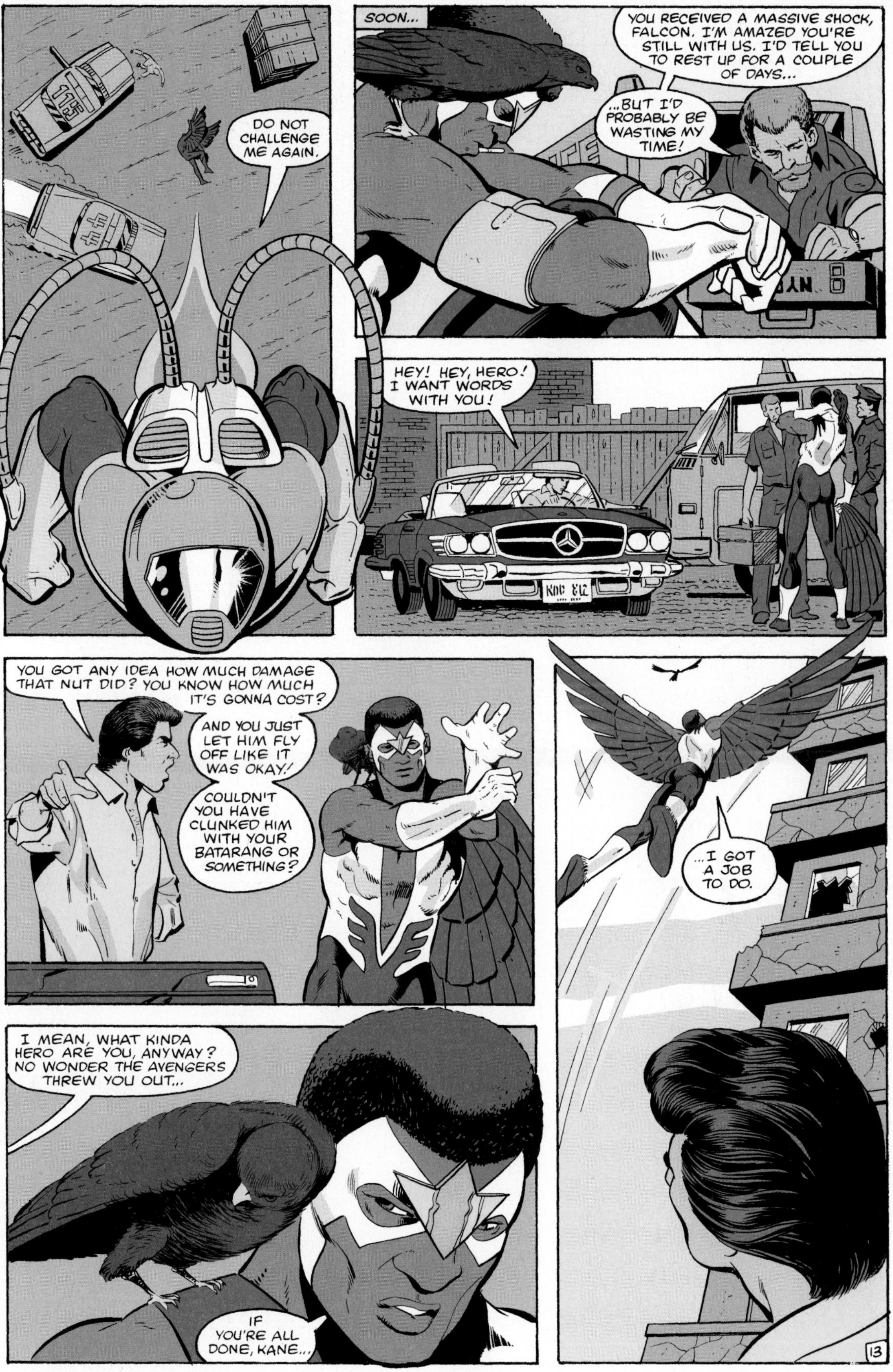
DO NOT CHALLENGE ME AGAIN.
SOON...
YOU RECEIVED A MASSIVE SHOCK, FALCON. I'M AMAZED YOU'RE STILL WITH US. I'D TELL YOU TO REST UP FOR A COUPLE OF DAYS...
...BUT I'D PROBABLY BE WASTING MY TIME!
HEY! HEY, HERO! I WANT WORDS WITH YOU!
YOU GOT ANY IDEA HOW MUCH DAMAGE THAT NUT DID? YOU KNOW HOW MUCH IT'S GONNA COST?
AND YOU JUST LET HIM FLY OFF LIKE IT WAS OKAY!
COULDN'T YOU HAVE CLUNKED HIM WITH YOUR BATARANG OR SOMETHING?
I MEAN, WHAT KINDA HERO ARE YOU, ANYWAY? NO WONDER THE AVENGERS THREW YOU OUT...
IF YOU'RE ALL DONE, KANE...
...I GOT A JOB TO DO.
13

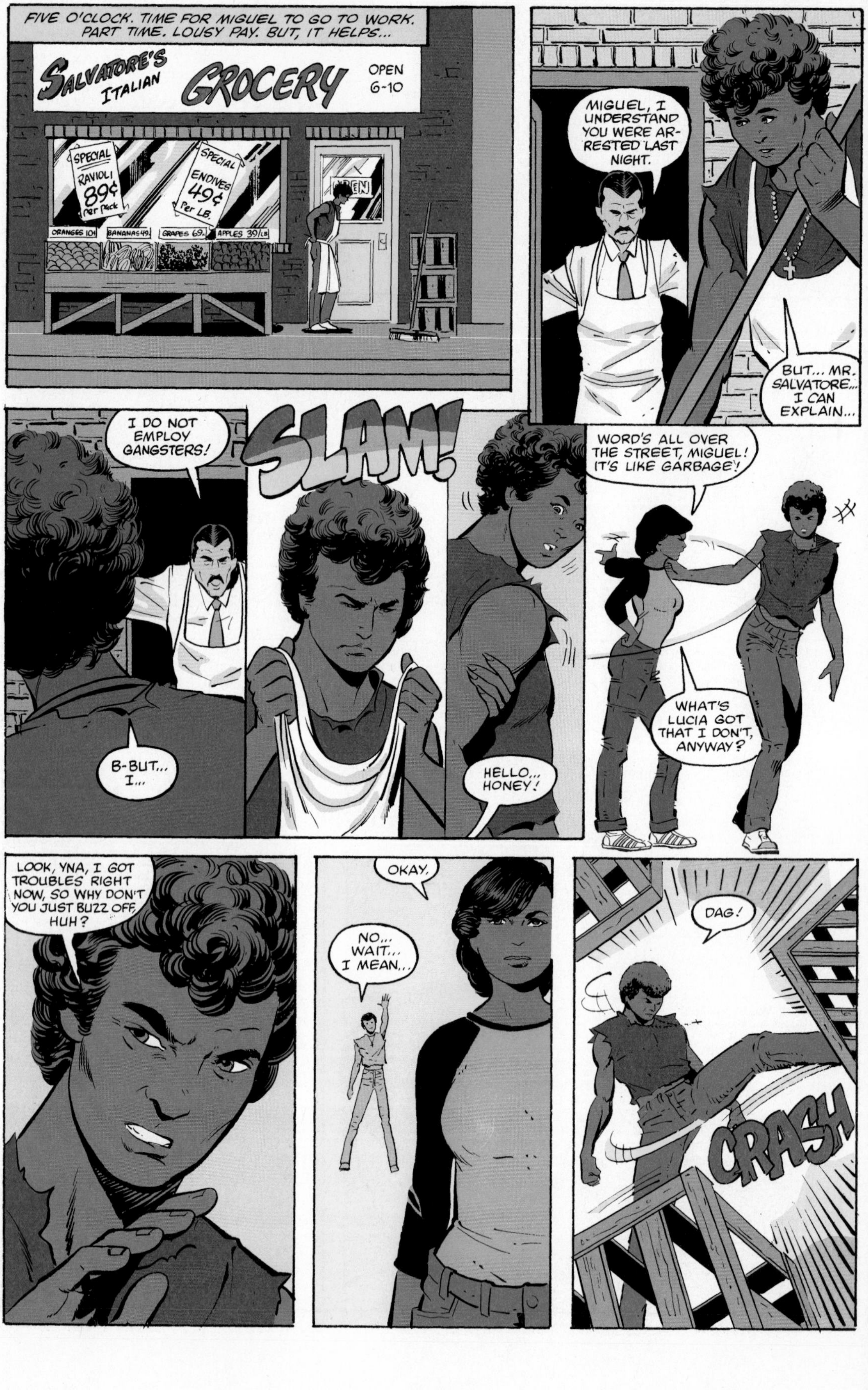
FIVE O'CLOCK. TIME FOR MIGUEL TO GO TO WORK. PART TIME. LOUSY PAY. BUT, IT HELPS...
SALVATORE'S ITALIAN GROCERY
OPEN 6-10
SPECIAL RAVIOLI 89¢ Per Pack
SPECIAL ENDIVES 49¢ Per LB.
ORANGES 10¢
BANANAS 49¢
GRAPES 69¢
APPLES 39¢/LB
MIGUEL, I UNDERSTAND YOU WERE AR-RESTED LAST NIGHT.
BUT... MR. SALVATORE... I CAN EXPLAIN...
I DO NOT EMPLOY GANGSTERS!
B-BUT... I...
SLAM!
HELLO... HONEY!
WORD'S ALL OVER THE STREET, MIGUEL! IT'S LIKE GARBAGE!
WHAT'S LUCIA GOT THAT I DON'T, ANYWAY?
LOOK, YNA, I GOT TROUBLES RIGHT NOW, SO WHY DON'T YOU JUST BUZZ OFF, HUH?
OKAY.
NO... WAIT... I MEAN...
DAG!
CRASH

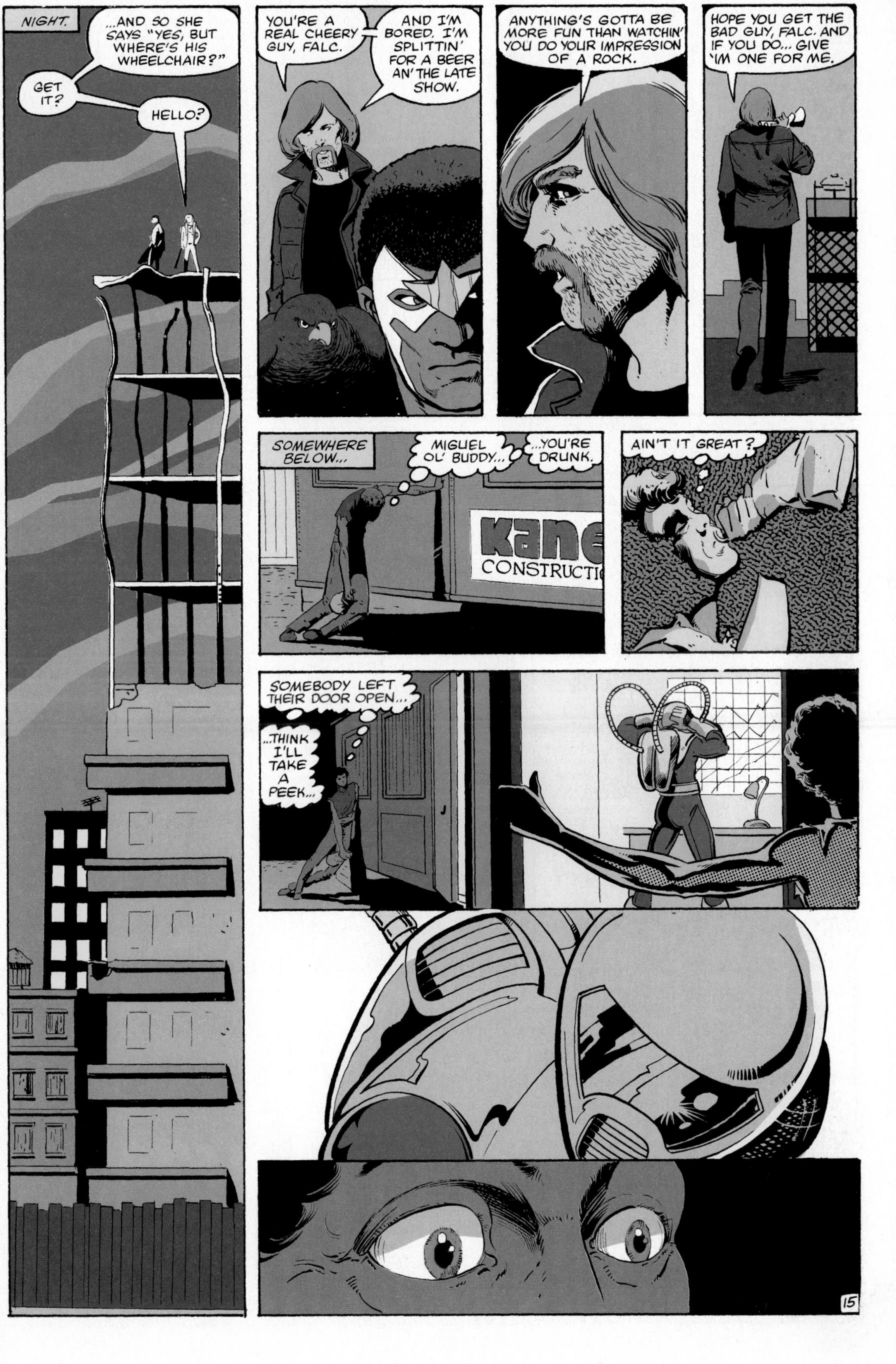

NIGHT.
...AND SO SHE SAYS "YES, BUT WHERE'S HIS WHEELCHAIR?"
GET IT?
HELLO?
YOU'RE A REAL CHEERY GUY, FALC.
AND I'M BORED. I'M SPLITTIN' FOR A BEER AN' THE LATE SHOW.
ANYTHING'S GOTTA BE MORE FUN THAN WATCHIN' YOU DO YOUR IMPRESSION OF A ROCK.
HOPE YOU GET THE BAD GUY, FALC. AND IF YOU DO... GIVE 'IM ONE FOR ME.
SOMEWHERE BELOW...
MIGUEL OL' BUDDY...
...YOU'RE DRUNK.
kane CONSTRUCTI
AIN'T IT GREAT?
SOMEBODY LEFT THEIR DOOR OPEN...
...THINK I'LL TAKE A PEEK...
15

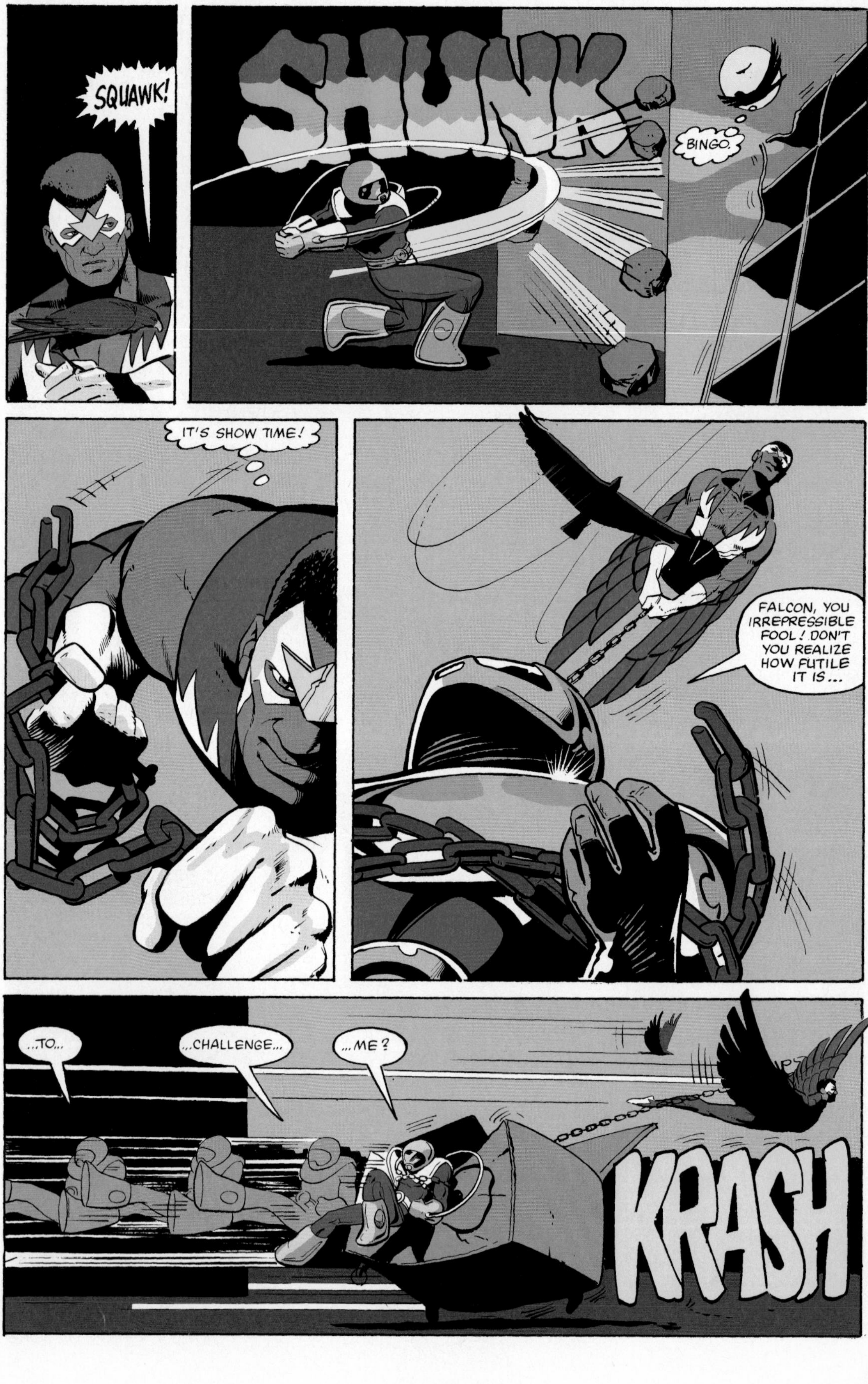
SQUAWK!
SHUNK
BINGO.
IT'S SHOW TIME!
FALCON, YOU IRREPRESSIBLE FOOL! DON'T YOU REALIZE HOW FUTILE IT IS...
...TO...
...CHALLENGE...
...ME?
KRASH

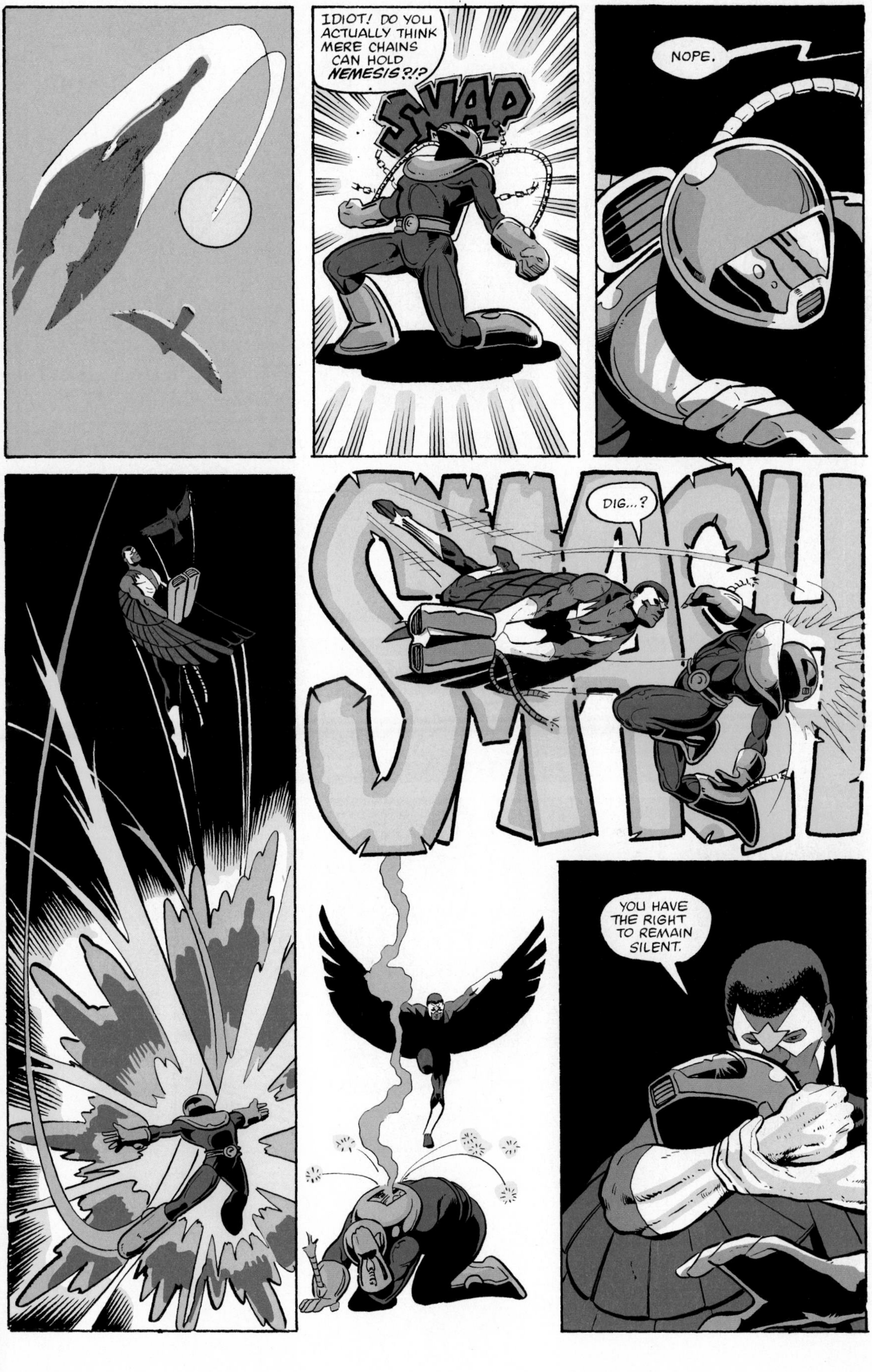
IDIOT! DO YOU ACTUALLY THINK MERE CHAINS CAN HOLD NEMESIS?!?
SNAP
NOPE.
DIG...?
SMASH!
YOU HAVE THE RIGHT TO REMAIN SILENT.

FALC!

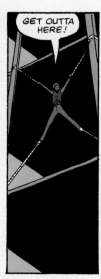
GET OUTTA HERE!

THE WHOLE THING'S GONNA COME DOWN!

GET AWAY BEFORE THE DYNAMITE BLOWS!

LORD.

STAY COOL, MIGUEL.

FALC... NO! DON'T TRY IT, MAN... THE FUSE IS ALMOST GONE.

DON'T WASTE YOURSELF ON ME, MAN! I'M NOT WORTH IT!

I'LL JUST SCREW UP AGAIN!

FALC... NO!!

I KNOW JUST WHERE TO PUT THIS!

HEY, NEMESIS! HEADS UP!

18

KABOOM!

18

22

YOU SHOULD LET ME DIE. I DESERVE IT.

I GOT HALF A DOZEN PEOPLE STICKIN' THEIR NECKS OUT FOR ME, AND I KEEP MESSIN' UP.

I GOT NOTHIN' TO LIVE FOR.

HEY, MAN... STOP SWIMMIN' IN SELF-PITY. YOU'LL MAKE IT.

AND, BECAUSE YOU'LL MAKE IT, OTHERS WILL.

AND, WHILE WE WERE COOLIN' OUT, NEMESIS APPEARED.

NOW, WHERE?

WHERE INDEED...?

WHAT TH--?

OUT OF MY WAY, CRETINS!

WHAT'S UP? HEY!

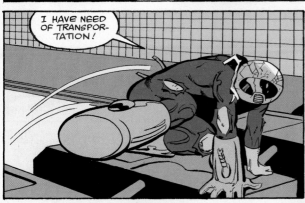

I HAVE NEED OF TRANSPORTATION!

THE TRAIN! WHERE IS THE TRAIN!

I MUST KEEP MOVING! I WILL NOT BE CAPTURED!

STOP! I COMMAND IT!

19

23

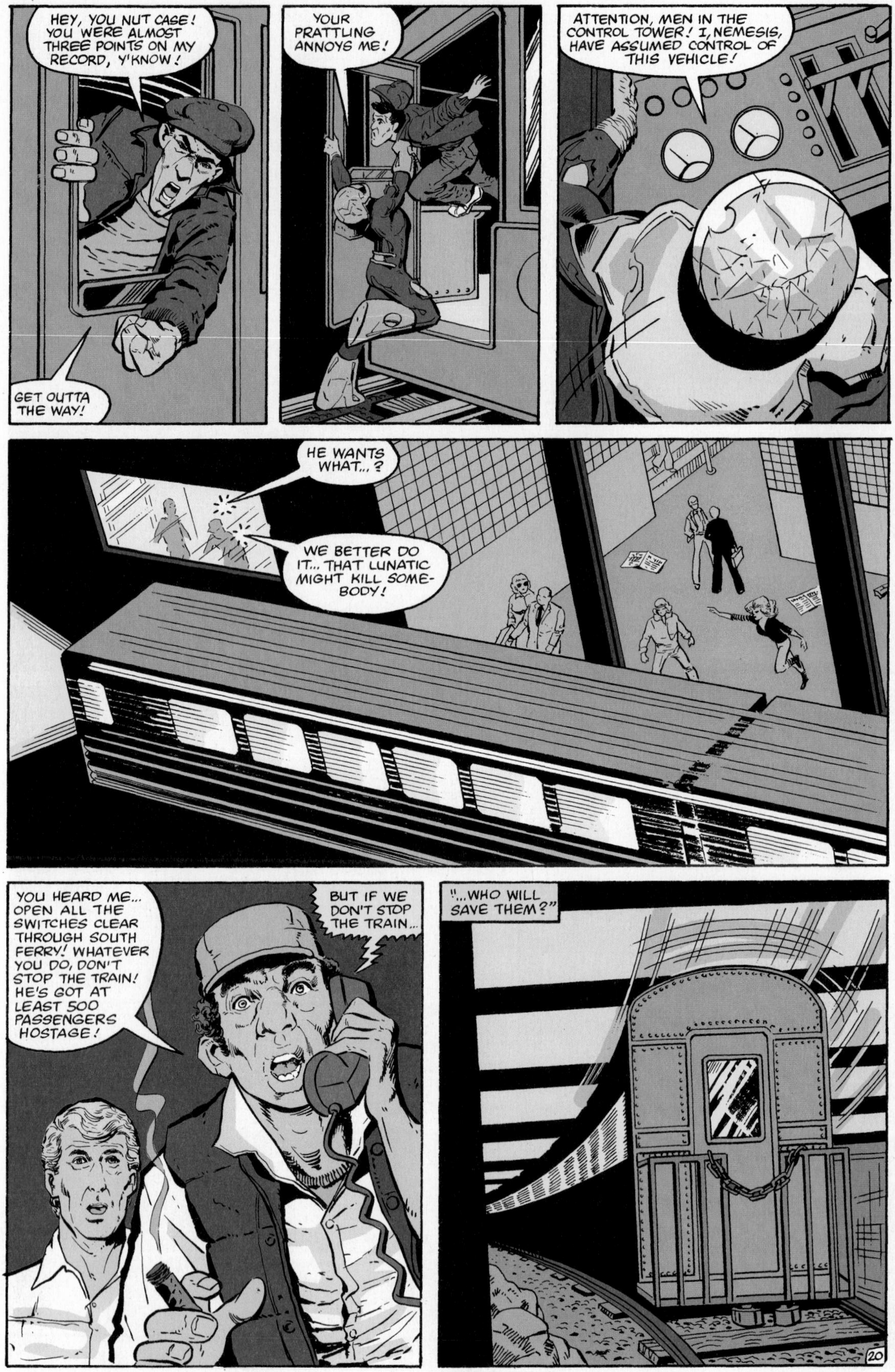
HEY, YOU NUT CASE! YOU WERE ALMOST THREE POINTS ON MY RECORD, Y'KNOW!
GET OUTTA THE WAY!
YOUR PRATTLING ANNOYS ME!
ATTENTION, MEN IN THE CONTROL TOWER! I, NEMESIS, HAVE ASSUMED CONTROL OF THIS VEHICLE!
HE WANTS WHAT...?
WE BETTER DO IT... THAT LUNATIC MIGHT KILL SOMEBODY!
YOU HEARD ME... OPEN ALL THE SWITCHES CLEAR THROUGH SOUTH FERRY! WHATEVER YOU DO, DON'T STOP THE TRAIN! HE'S GOT AT LEAST 500 PASSENGERS HOSTAGE!
BUT IF WE DON'T STOP THE TRAIN...
"...WHO WILL SAVE THEM?"
20

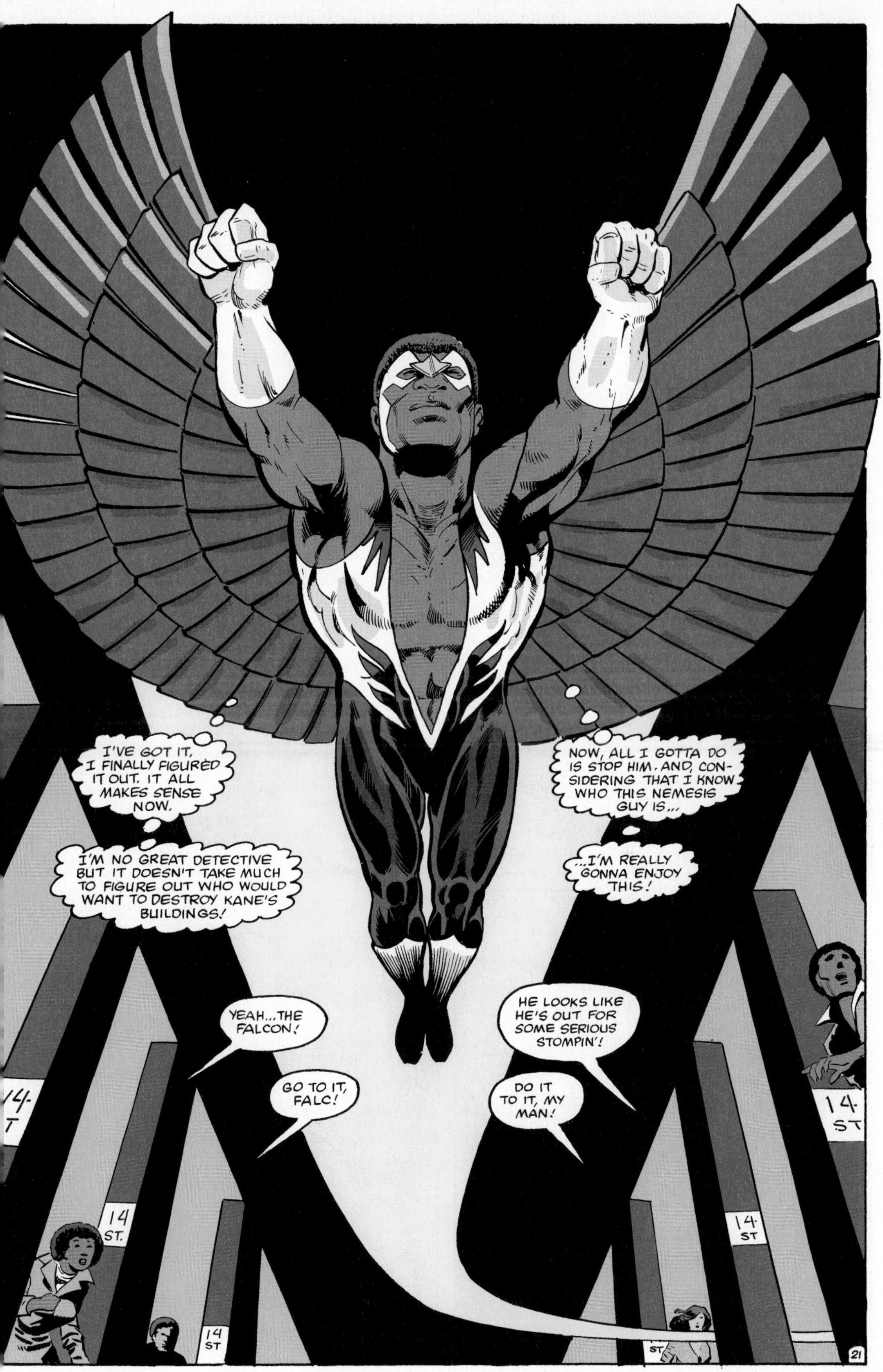
I'VE GOT IT, I FINALLY FIGURED IT OUT. IT ALL MAKES SENSE NOW.
I'M NO GREAT DETECTIVE BUT IT DOESN'T TAKE MUCH TO FIGURE OUT WHO WOULD WANT TO DESTROY KANE'S BUILDINGS!
NOW, ALL I GOTTA DO IS STOP HIM. AND, CONSIDERING THAT I KNOW WHO THIS NEMESIS GUY IS...
...I'M REALLY GONNA ENJOY THIS!
YEAH... THE FALCON!
GO TO IT, FALC!
HE LOOKS LIKE HE'S OUT FOR SOME SERIOUS STOMPIN'!
DO IT TO IT, MY MAN!
14 ST
14 ST.
14 ST
14 ST
14 ST
21

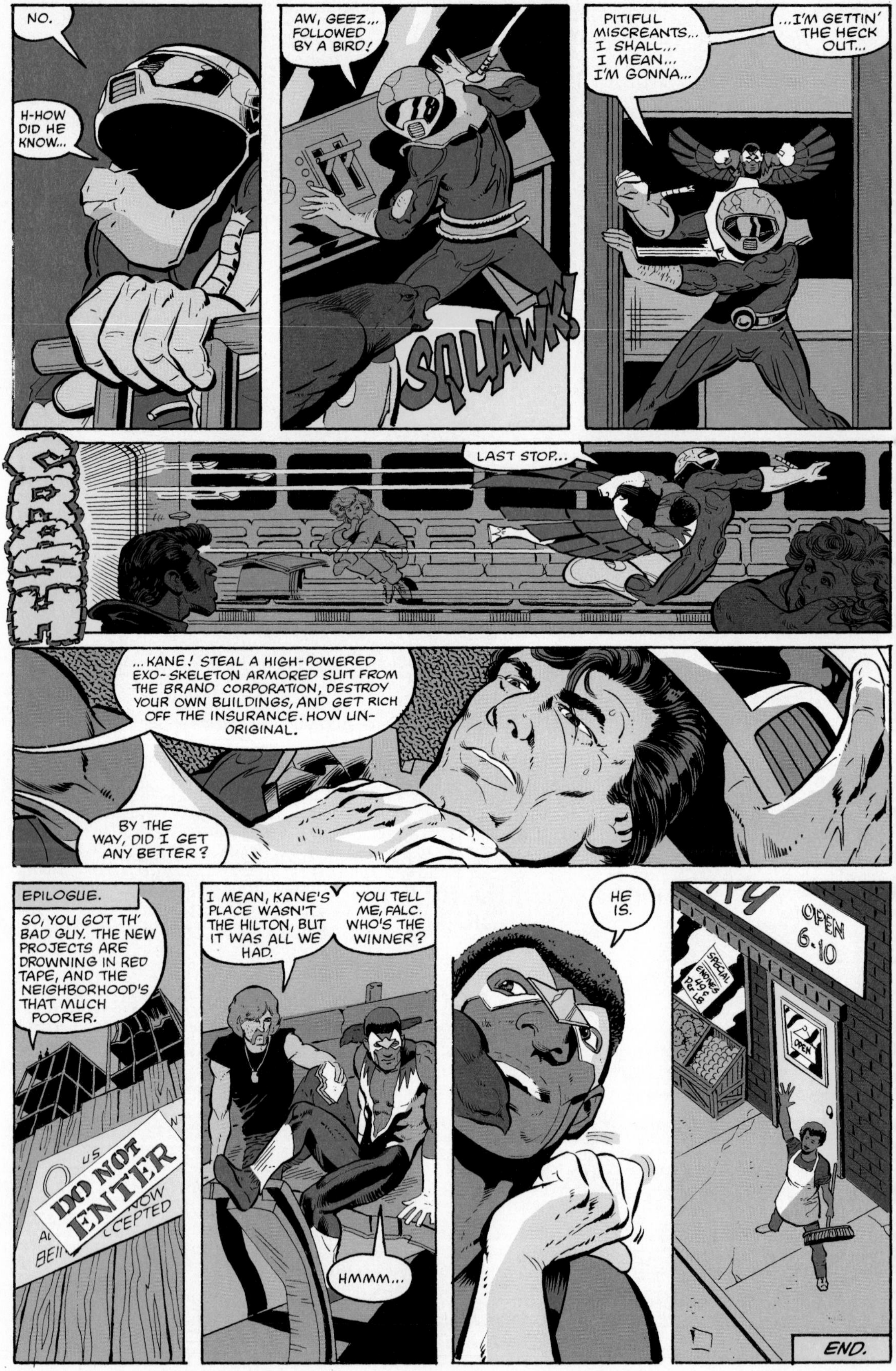
NO.
H-HOW DID HE KNOW...
AW, GEEZ... FOLLOWED BY A BIRD!
SQUAWK!
PITIFUL MISCREANTS... I SHALL... I MEAN... I'M GONNA...
...I'M GETTIN' THE HECK OUT...
CRASH
LAST STOP...
...KANE! STEAL A HIGH-POWERED EXO-SKELETON ARMORED SUIT FROM THE BRAND CORPORATION, DESTROY YOUR OWN BUILDINGS, AND GET RICH OFF THE INSURANCE. HOW UN-ORIGINAL.
BY THE WAY, DID I GET ANY BETTER?
EPILOGUE.
SO, YOU GOT TH' BAD GUY. THE NEW PROJECTS ARE DROWNING IN RED TAPE, AND THE NEIGHBORHOOD'S THAT MUCH POORER.
DO NOT ENTER
I MEAN, KANE'S PLACE WASN'T THE HILTON, BUT IT WAS ALL WE HAD.
YOU TELL ME, FALC. WHO'S THE WINNER?
HMMM...
HE IS.
OPEN 6-10
OPEN
END.

CRIB NOTES

% MARVEL COMICS GROUP
387 Park Avenue South
New York, New York 10016

LARRY HAMA
EDITOR
JIM OWSLEY
ASSISTANT EDITOR

IT'S ABOUT TIME

How long has it been now? Was it June or July of 1981 that I got this great idea for a Falcon story. I went scurrying down the Marvel halls to the palatial east wing where Jim Shooter, Editor-In-Chief, hangs his hat. He wasn't there.

Gritting my teeth, I settled into the traditional "where's Jim *now?*" treasure hunt, and began turning over the Marvel offices looking for him. Hmmm... not in the jacuzzi... not on the tennis courts ... not up in the pent-house with **Stan...**

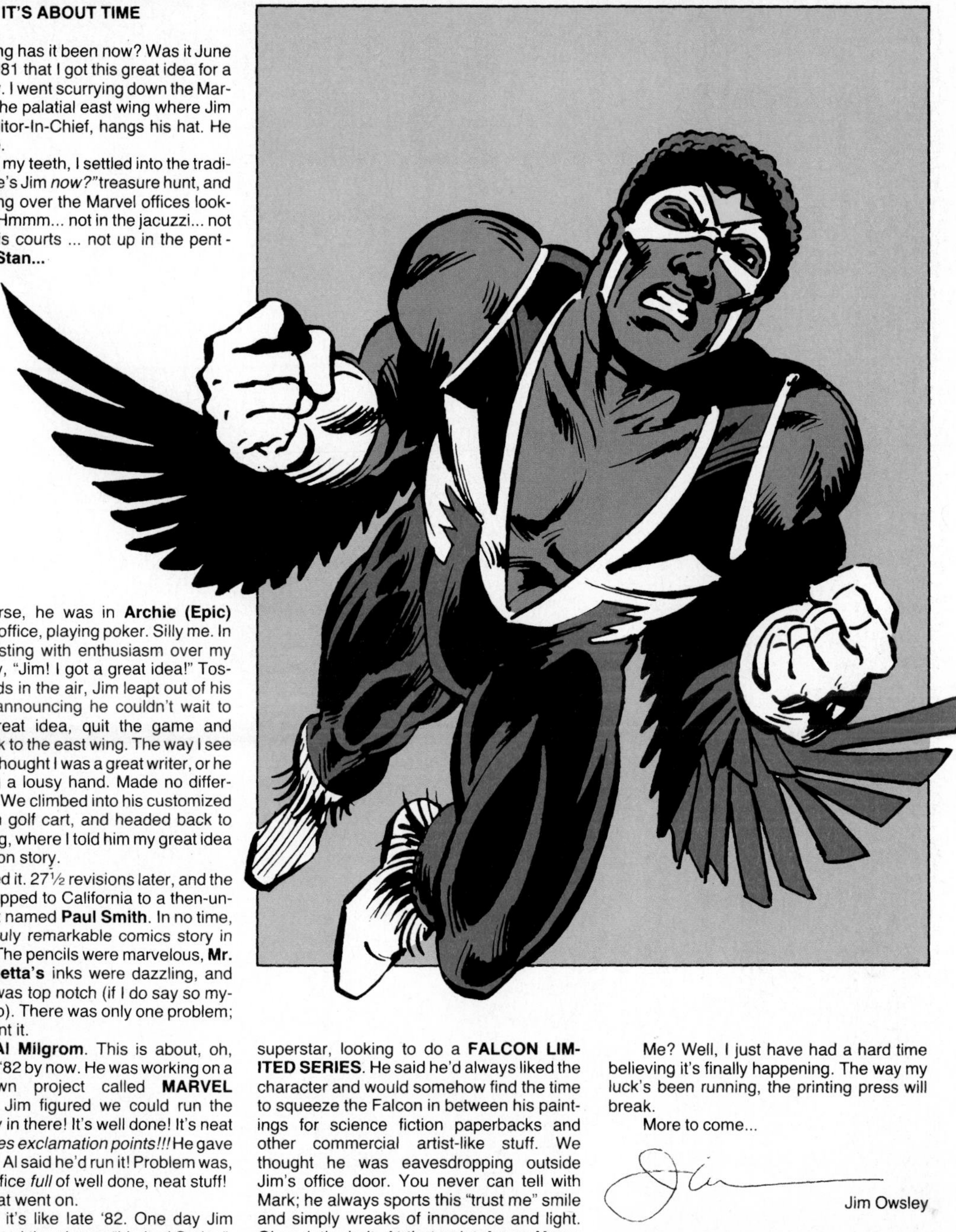

Of course, he was in **Archie (Epic) Goodwin**'s office, playing poker. Silly me. In I came, bursting with enthusiasm over my Falcon story, "Jim! I got a great idea!" Tossing his cards in the air, Jim leapt out of his chair and, announcing he couldn't wait to hear my great idea, quit the game and headed back to the east wing. The way I see it, either he thought I was a great writer, or he was holding a lousy hand. Made no difference to me. We climbed into his customized **Spider-Man** golf cart, and headed back to the east wing, where I told him my great idea for this Falcon story.

He loved it. 27½ revisions later, and the plot was shipped to California to a then-unknown artist named **Paul Smith**. In no time, we had a truly remarkable comics story in our hands. The pencils were marvelous, **Mr. Vinnie Colletta's** inks were dazzling, and the writing was top notch (if I do say so myself, and I do). There was only one problem; where to print it.

Enter **Al Milgrom**. This is about, oh, February of '82 by now. He was working on a then-unknown project called **MARVEL FANFARE**. Jim figured we could run the Falcon story in there! It's well done! It's neat stuff! *Jim likes exclamation points!!!* He gave the job to Al! Al said he'd run it! Problem was, Al had an office *full* of well done, neat stuff!

The beat went on.

Finally, it's like late '82. One day Jim Shooter coined the phrase "Limited Series", and a light went on in his head. "Let's do a **FALCON LIMITED SERIES** based on the original Falcon story you did umpteen years ago!" Okay, but who do we get to draw it since Paul Smith was then committed to the **X-MEN** Institution of Mental Illness and Deadline Crunches?

As if on cue, in walks **Mark Bright**, aspiring new artist and professional future superstar, looking to do a **FALCON LIMITED SERIES**. He said he'd always liked the character and would somehow find the time to squeeze the Falcon in between his paintings for science fiction paperbacks and other commercial artist-like stuff. We thought he was eavesdropping outside Jim's office door. You never can tell with Mark; he always sports this "trust me" smile and simply wreaks of innocence and light. Okay, let's do it. At that point, **Larry Hama** sauntered in and demanded to edit the series (I'm paraphrasing a bit here). Jim saw the light, and the three of us left the east wing's putting green, and went on to further greatness.

So, here we are. I can't believe it. It's finally being published. Jim's happy. Paul's happy. Larry's happy. Mark – well, he'll be happy next month when he takes over.

Me? Well, I just have had a hard time believing it's finally happening. The way my luck's been running, the printing press will break.

More to come...

Jim Owsley

NEXT: It is 50 tons of walking solid steel. It is armed with the deadliest offensive weaponry known to man. It can think. It can *kill*. It's called a **SENTINEL,** and it's out to destroy **THE FALCON.** In thirty days.

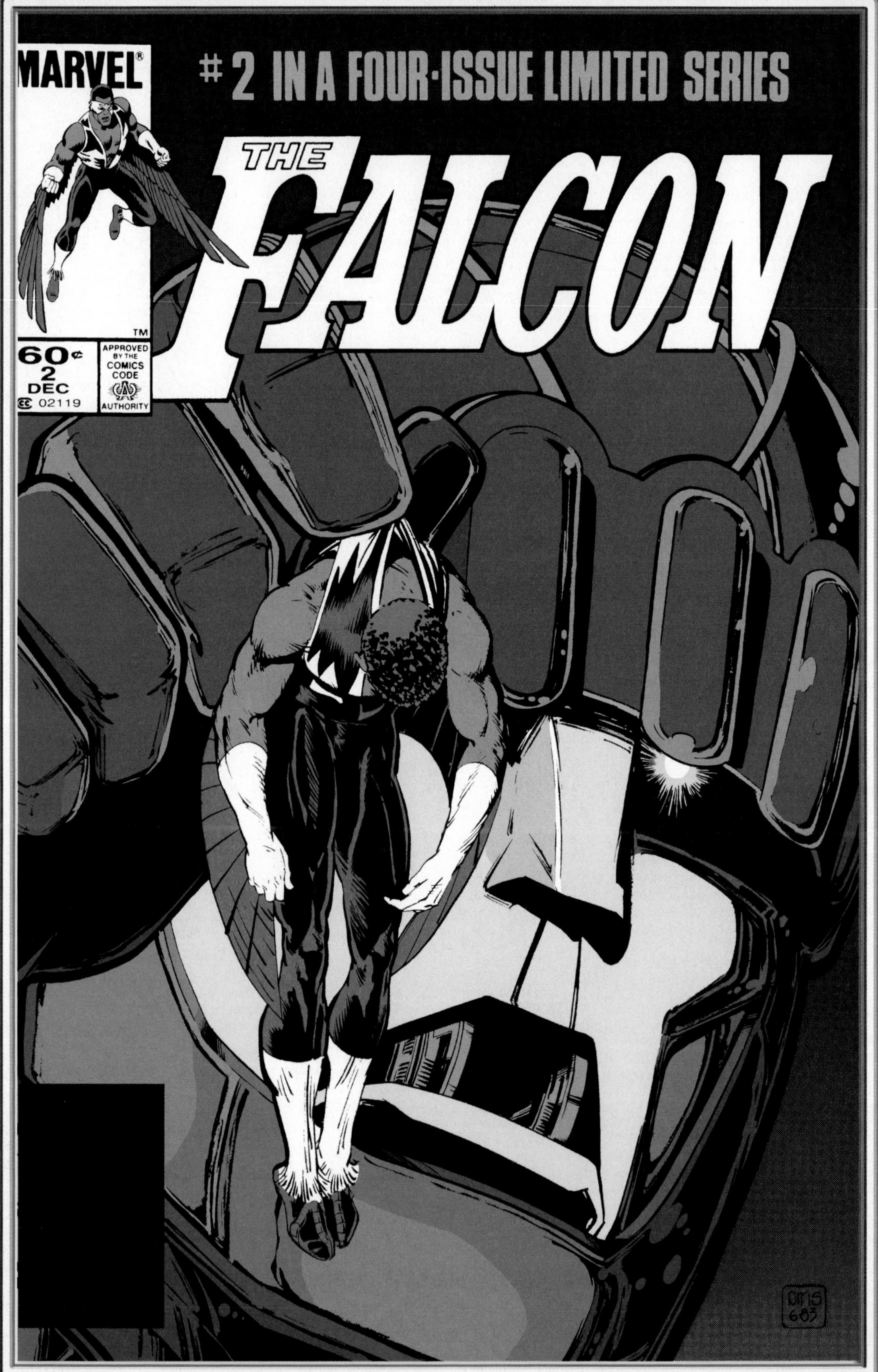
MARVEL®
#2 IN A FOUR-ISSUE LIMITED SERIES
THE FALCON
TM
60¢
2
DEC
02119
APPROVED BY THE COMICS CODE AUTHORITY

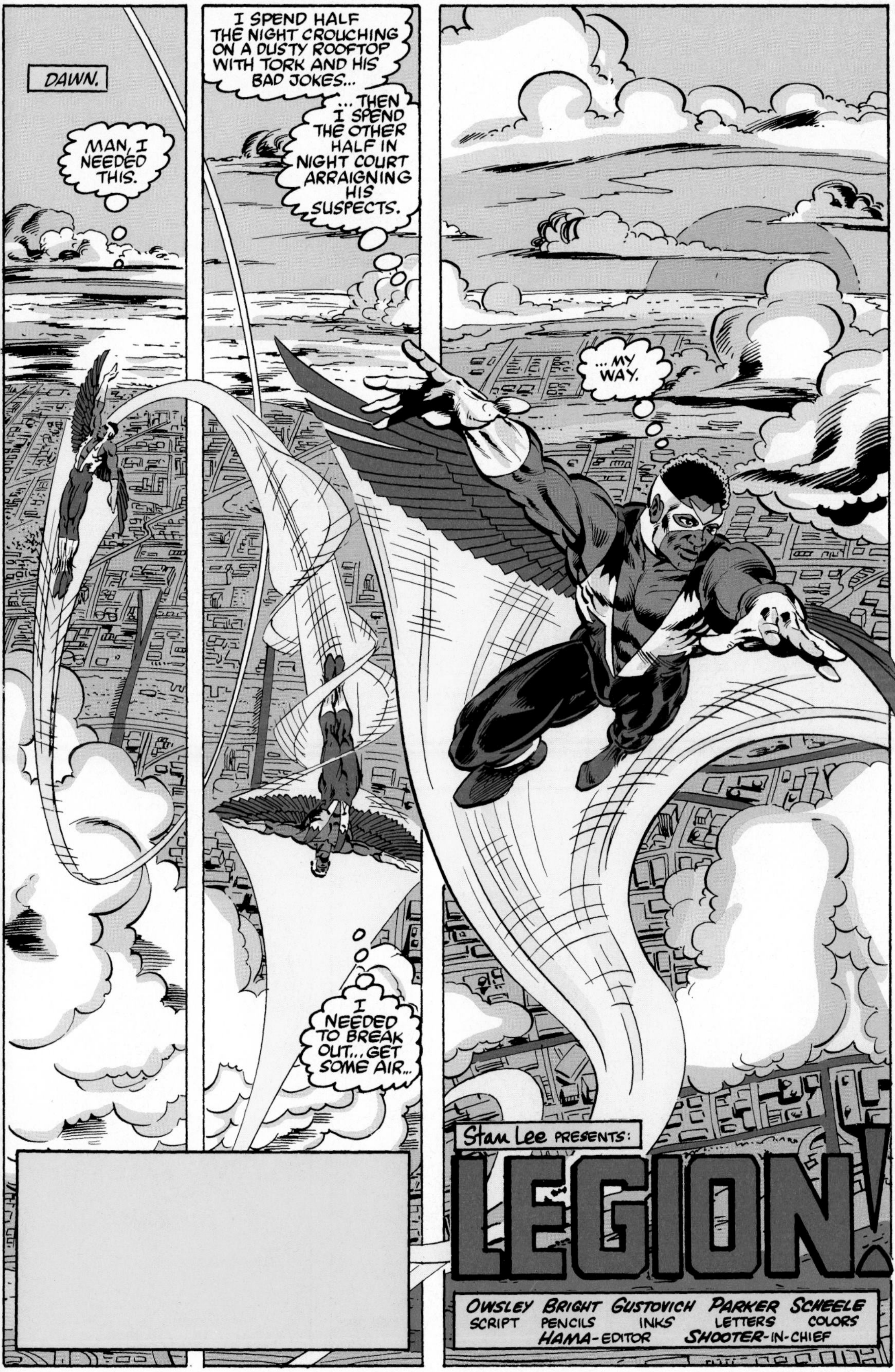

DAWN.
MAN, I NEEDED THIS.
I SPEND HALF THE NIGHT CROUCHING ON A DUSTY ROOFTOP WITH TORK AND HIS BAD JOKES...
...THEN I SPEND THE OTHER HALF IN NIGHT COURT ARRAIGNING HIS SUSPECTS.
I NEEDED TO BREAK OUT...GET SOME AIR...
...MY WAY.
Stan Lee PRESENTS:
LEGION!
OWSLEY SCRIPT
BRIGHT PENCILS
GUSTOVICH INKS
PARKER LETTERS
SCHEELE COLORS
HAMA-EDITOR
SHOOTER-IN-CHIEF

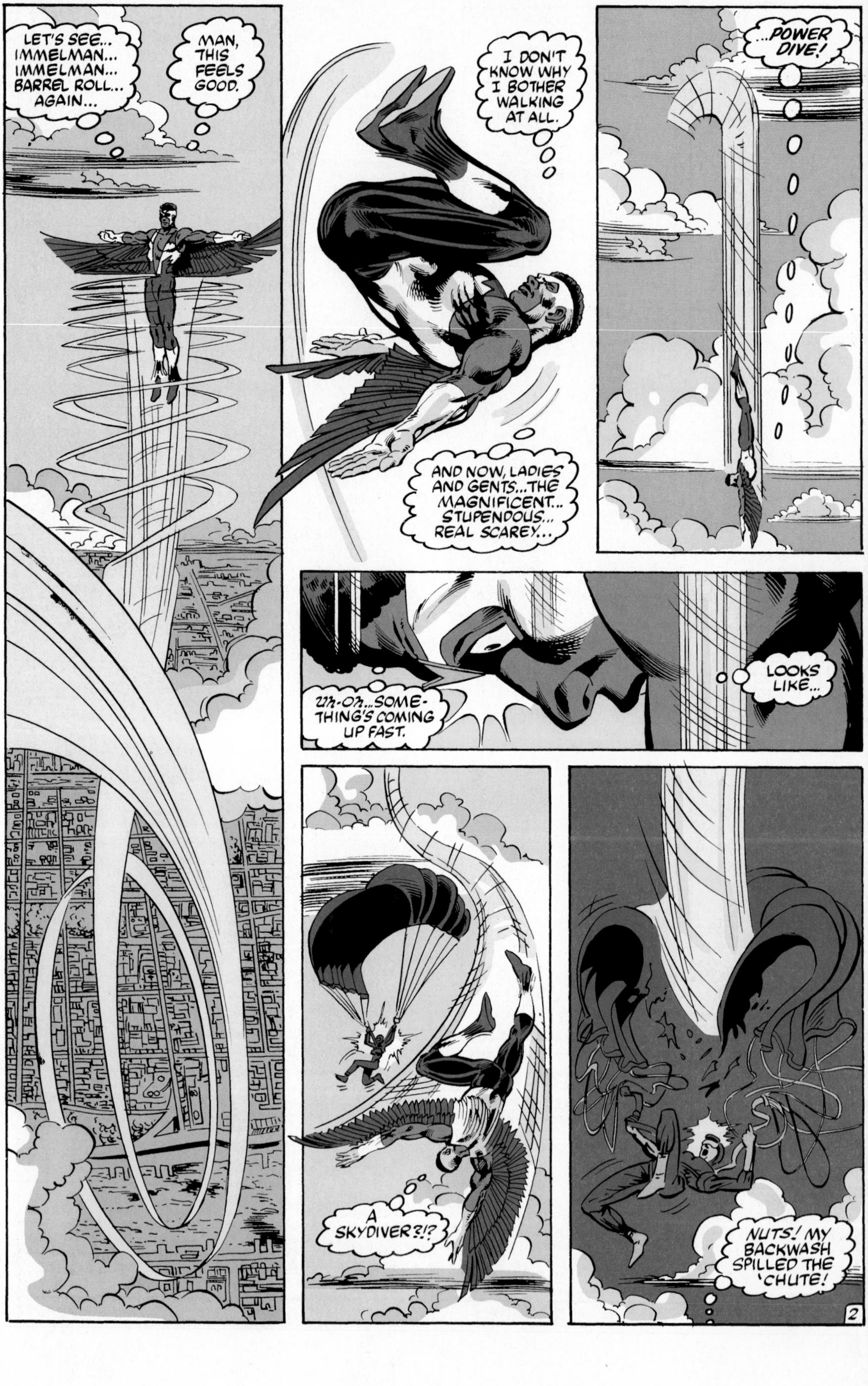
LET'S SEE... IMMELMAN... IMMELMAN... BARREL ROLL... AGAIN...
MAN, THIS FEELS GOOD.
I DON'T KNOW WHY I BOTHER WALKING AT ALL.
AND NOW, LADIES AND GENTS...THE MAGNIFICENT... STUPENDOUS... REAL SCAREY...
...POWER DIVE!
UH-OH...SOMETHING'S COMING UP FAST.
LOOKS LIKE...
A SKYDIVER?!?
NUTS! MY BACKWASH SPILLED THE 'CHUTE!
2

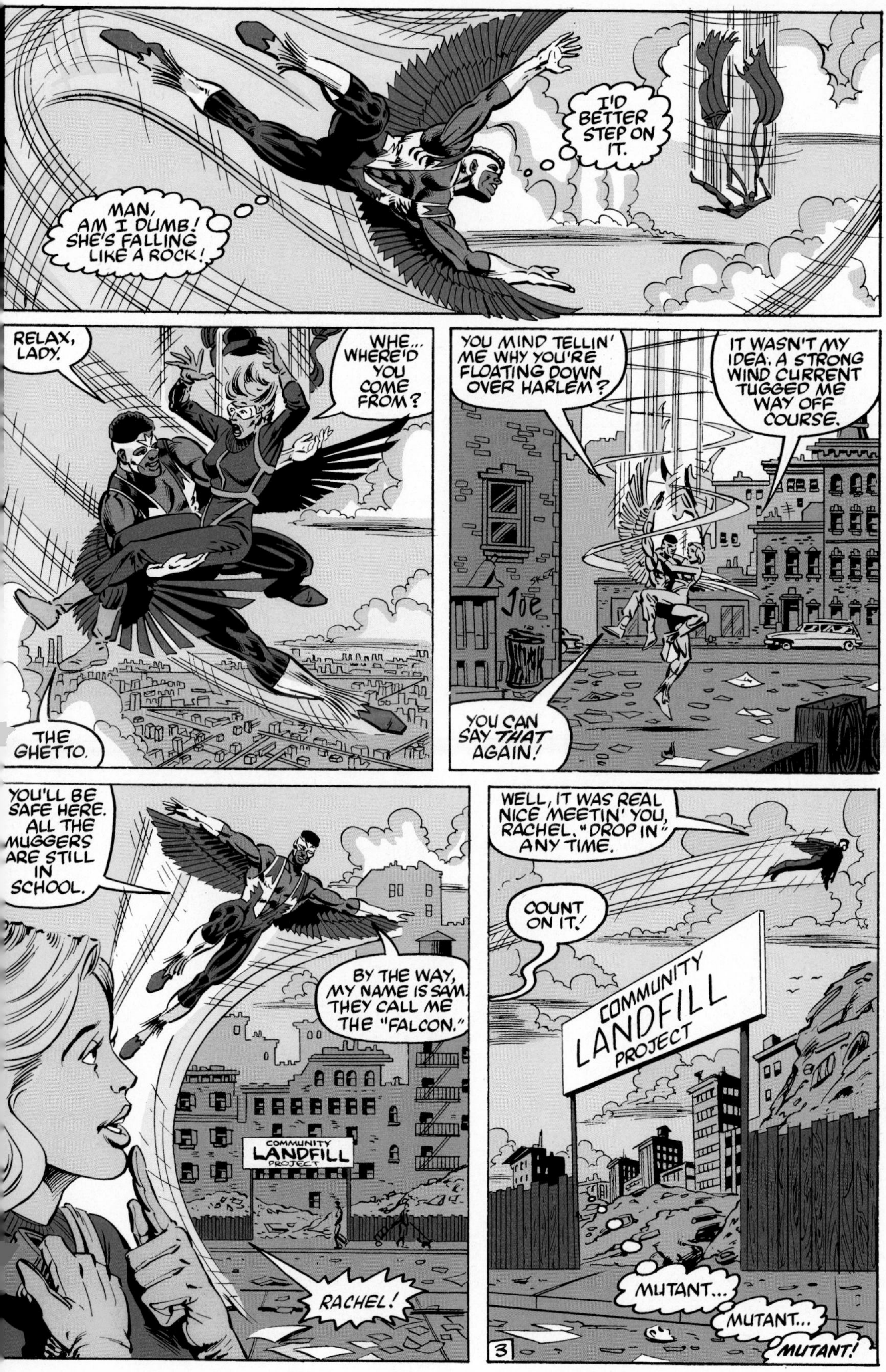
MAN, AM I DUMB! SHE'S FALLING LIKE A ROCK!
I'D BETTER STEP ON IT.
RELAX, LADY.
WHE... WHERE'D YOU COME FROM?
THE GHETTO.
YOU MIND TELLIN' ME WHY YOU'RE FLOATING DOWN OVER HARLEM?
IT WASN'T MY IDEA. A STRONG WIND CURRENT TUGGED ME WAY OFF COURSE.
YOU CAN SAY THAT AGAIN!
JOE
YOU'LL BE SAFE HERE. ALL THE MUGGERS ARE STILL IN SCHOOL.
BY THE WAY, MY NAME IS SAM. THEY CALL ME THE "FALCON."
COMMUNITY LANDFILL PROJECT
RACHEL!
WELL, IT WAS REAL NICE MEETIN' YOU, RACHEL. "DROP IN" ANY TIME.
COUNT ON IT!
COMMUNITY LANDFILL PROJECT
MUTANT...
MUTANT...
MUTANT!
3

210TH STREET OFF BROADWAY...

OHH SAMMEE-- SAMMEEE--

♪ RIIISE N' SHIIIINE! ♪

C'MON, LUNKHEAD! ON YA FEET! WE GOT STUFF TO DO.

WHY, GOOD MORNING, SGT. TORK...AND HOW ARE YOU...?

CHERRY, FALC. JUST CHEERY.

TORK, ANYBODY EVER TELL YOU DISTURBIN' THE PEACE IS AGAINST THE LAW?

I'M A COP, FALC. I CAN BREAK THE LAW IF I WANNA.

YOU'RE SICK.

SICK, HUH?

YEAH, I'M SICK, O.K. YOU BET I AM. IT'S A SICKNESS THAT COMES FROM HAVIN' A MAGNUM TAPED TO YOUR BACK AN TH' TRIGGER TO A DOUBLE-BARREL 12-GUAGE GLUED TO YOUR HOT SWEATY HANDS...

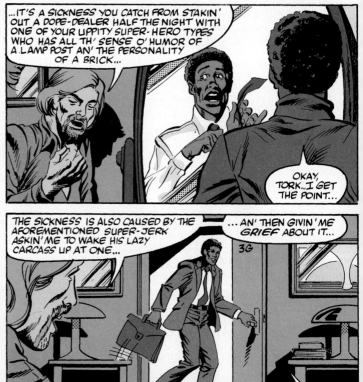

...IT'S A SICKNESS YOU CATCH FROM STAKIN' OUT A DOPE-DEALER HALF THE NIGHT WITH ONE OF YOUR UPPITY SUPER-HERO TYPES WHO HAS ALL TH' SENSE O' HUMOR OF A LAMP POST AN' THE PERSONALITY OF A BRICK...

OKAY, TORK...I GET THE POINT...

THE SICKNESS IS ALSO CAUSED BY THE AFOREMENTIONED SUPER-JERK ASKIN' ME TO WAKE HIS LAZY CARCASS UP AT ONE...

...AN' THEN GIVIN' ME GRIEF ABOUT IT...

GOOD-BYE, TORK.

4

32

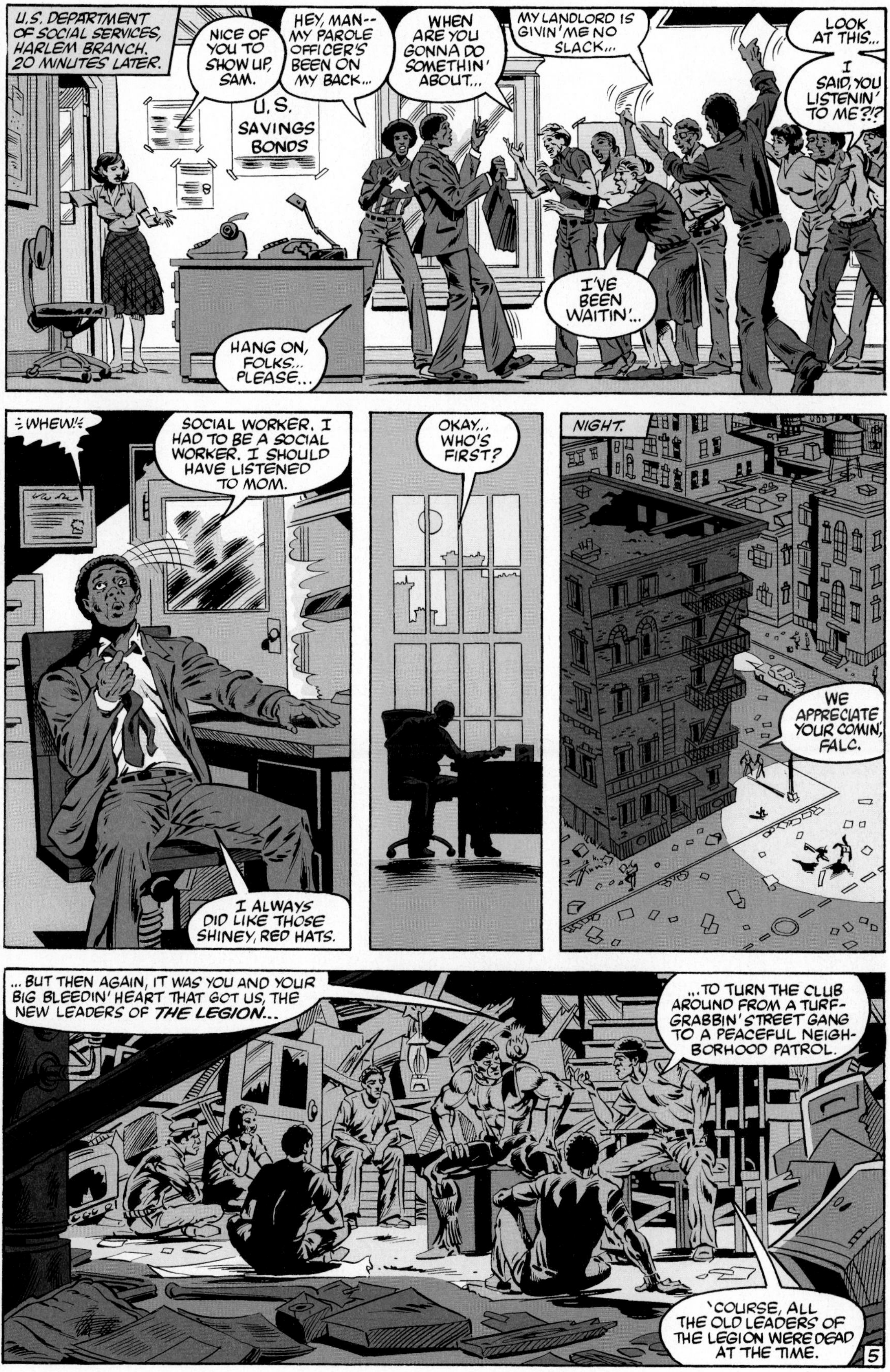
U.S. DEPARTMENT OF SOCIAL SERVICES, HARLEM BRANCH. 20 MINUTES LATER.
NICE OF YOU TO SHOW UP, SAM.
HEY, MAN-- MY PAROLE OFFICER'S BEEN ON MY BACK...
WHEN ARE YOU GONNA DO SOMETHIN' ABOUT...
MY LANDLORD IS GIVIN' ME NO SLACK...
LOOK AT THIS...
I SAID, YOU LISTENIN' TO ME?!?
U.S. SAVINGS BONDS
I'VE BEEN WAITIN'...
HANG ON, FOLKS... PLEASE...
WHEW!
SOCIAL WORKER. I HAD TO BE A SOCIAL WORKER. I SHOULD HAVE LISTENED TO MOM.
I ALWAYS DID LIKE THOSE SHINEY, RED HATS.
OKAY... WHO'S FIRST?
NIGHT.
WE APPRECIATE YOUR COMIN', FALC.
...BUT THEN AGAIN, IT WAS YOU AND YOUR BIG BLEEDIN' HEART THAT GOT US, THE NEW LEADERS OF THE LEGION...
...TO TURN THE CLUB AROUND FROM A TURF-GRABBIN' STREET GANG TO A PEACEFUL NEIGHBORHOOD PATROL.
'COURSE, ALL THE OLD LEADERS OF THE LEGION WERE DEAD AT THE TIME.
5

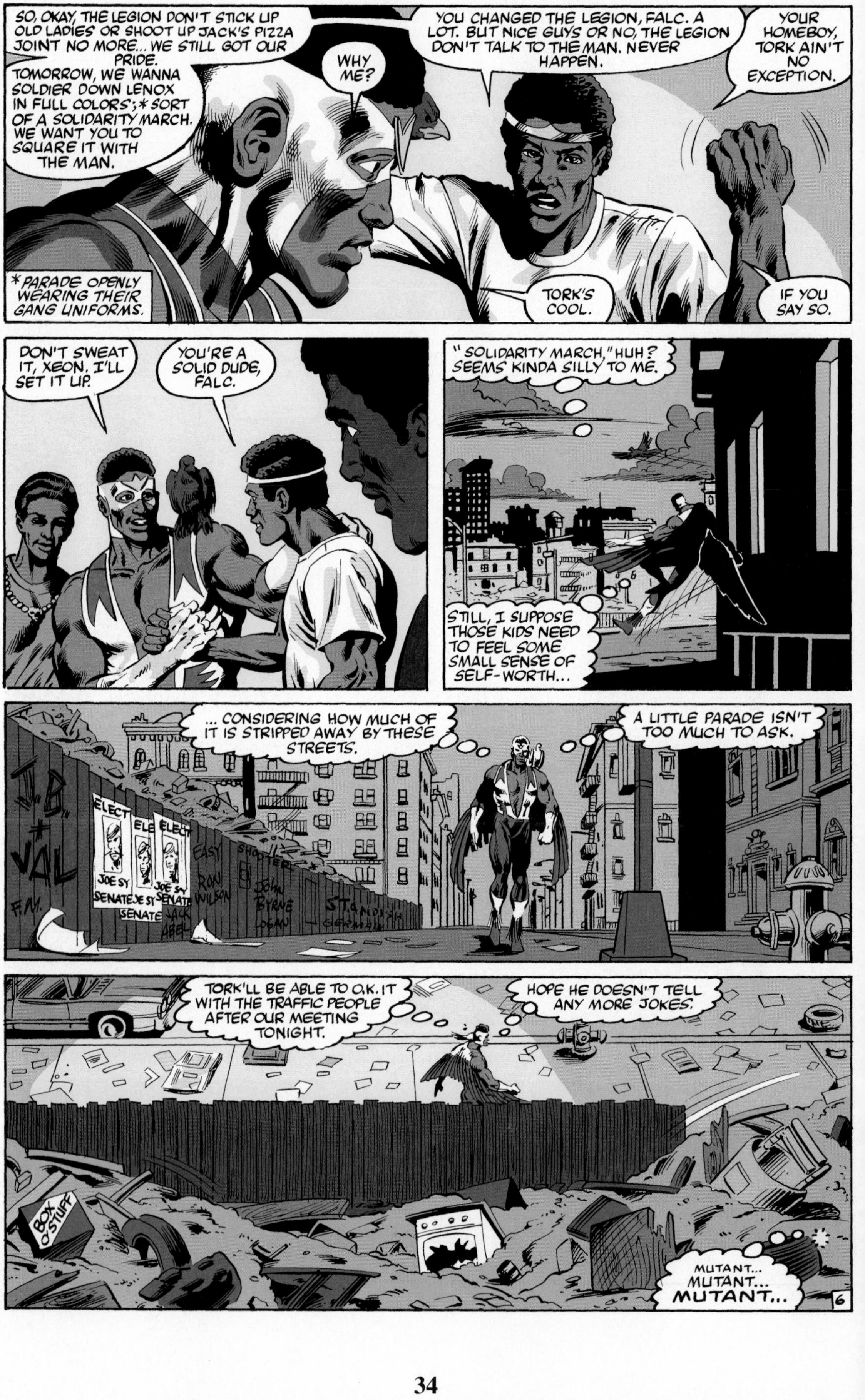

SO, OKAY, THE LEGION DON'T STICK UP OLD LADIES OR SHOOT UP JACK'S PIZZA JOINT NO MORE... WE STILL GOT OUR PRIDE.
TOMORROW, WE WANNA SOLDIER DOWN LENOX IN FULL COLORS;* SORT OF A SOLIDARITY MARCH. WE WANT YOU TO SQUARE IT WITH THE MAN.
WHY ME?
YOU CHANGED THE LEGION, FALC. A LOT. BUT NICE GUYS OR NO, THE LEGION DON'T TALK TO THE MAN. NEVER HAPPEN.
YOUR HOMEBOY, TORK AIN'T NO EXCEPTION.
*PARADE OPENLY WEARING THEIR GANG UNIFORMS.
TORK'S COOL.
IF YOU SAY SO.
DON'T SWEAT IT, XEON. I'LL SET IT UP.
YOU'RE A SOLID DUDE, FALC.
"SOLIDARITY MARCH," HUH? SEEMS KINDA SILLY TO ME.
STILL, I SUPPOSE THOSE KIDS NEED TO FEEL SOME SMALL SENSE OF SELF-WORTH...
... CONSIDERING HOW MUCH OF IT IS STRIPPED AWAY BY THESE STREETS.
A LITTLE PARADE ISN'T TOO MUCH TO ASK.
ELECT
JOE SY
SENATE
EASY
SHOOTER
RON WILSON
JOHN BYRNE
JACK ABEL
TORK'LL BE ABLE TO O.K. IT WITH THE TRAFFIC PEOPLE AFTER OUR MEETING TONIGHT.
HOPE HE DOESN'T TELL ANY MORE JOKES.
BOX O' STUFF
MUTANT... MUTANT... MUTANT...
6

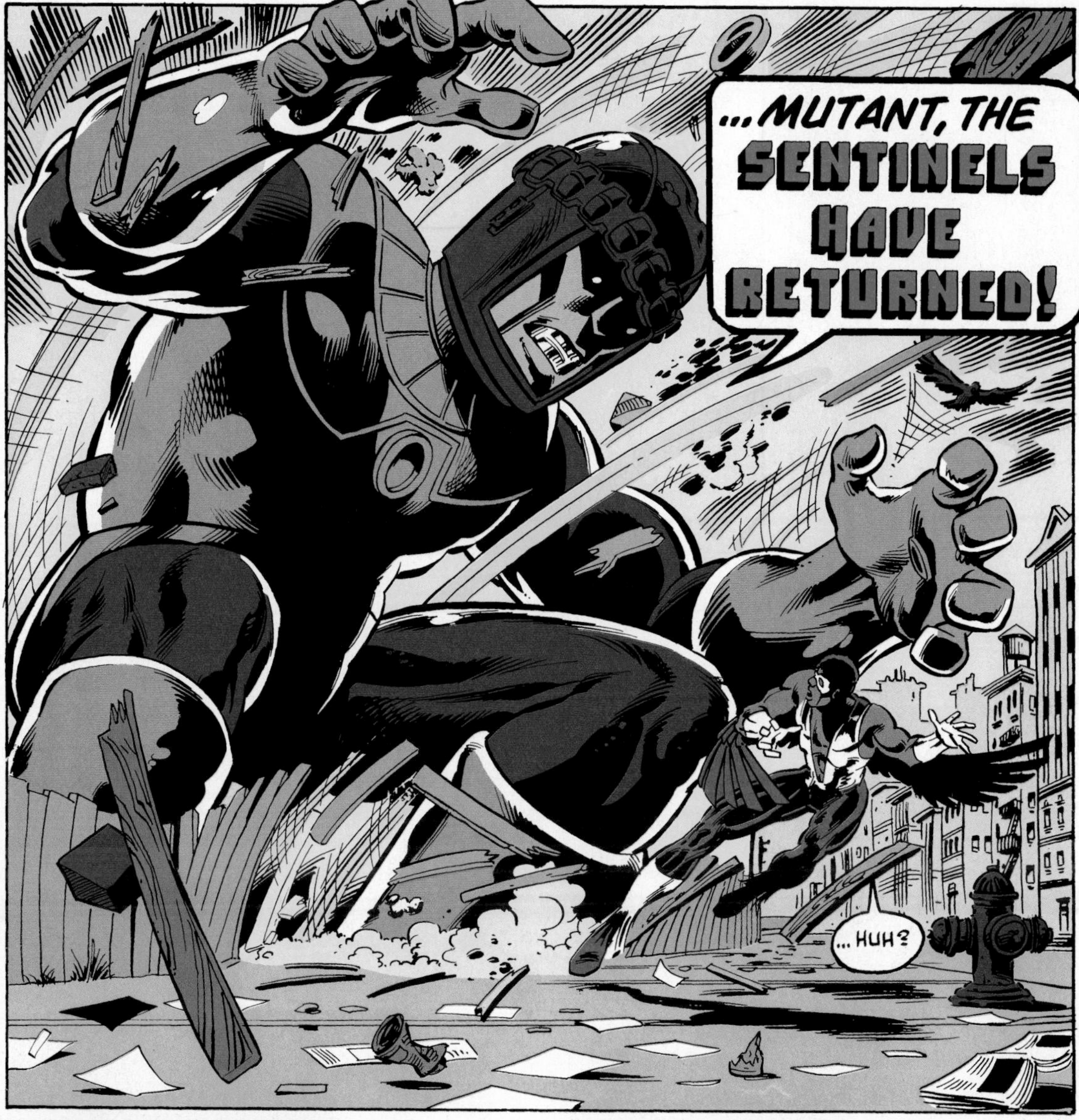
...MUTANT, THE SENTINELS HAVE RETURNED!
...HUH?

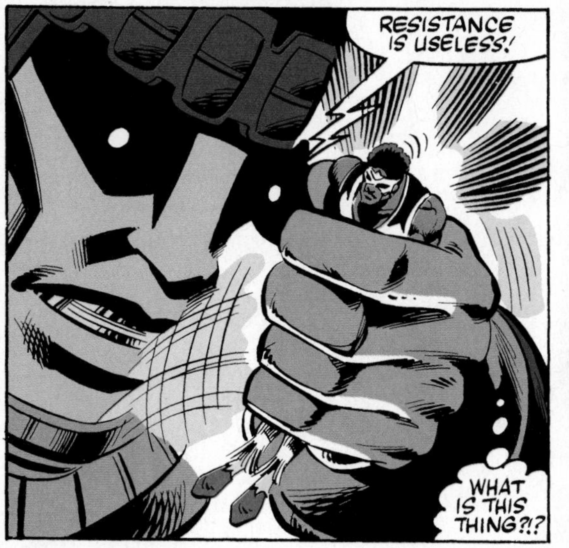
RESISTANCE IS USELESS!
WHAT IS THIS THING?!?

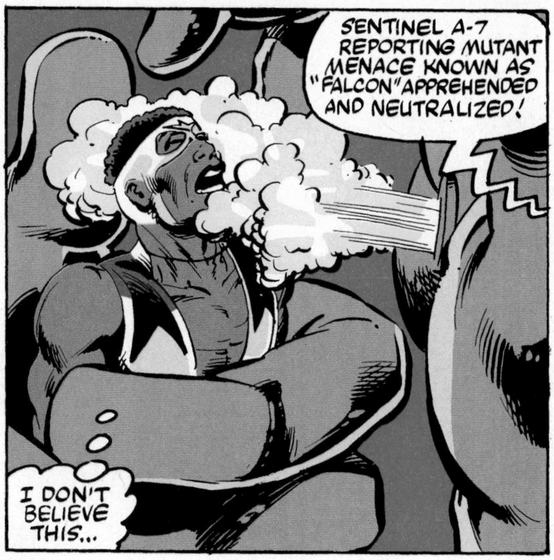
SENTINEL A-7 REPORTING MUTANT MENACE KNOWN AS "FALCON" APPREHENDED AND NEUTRALIZED!
I DON'T BELIEVE THIS...

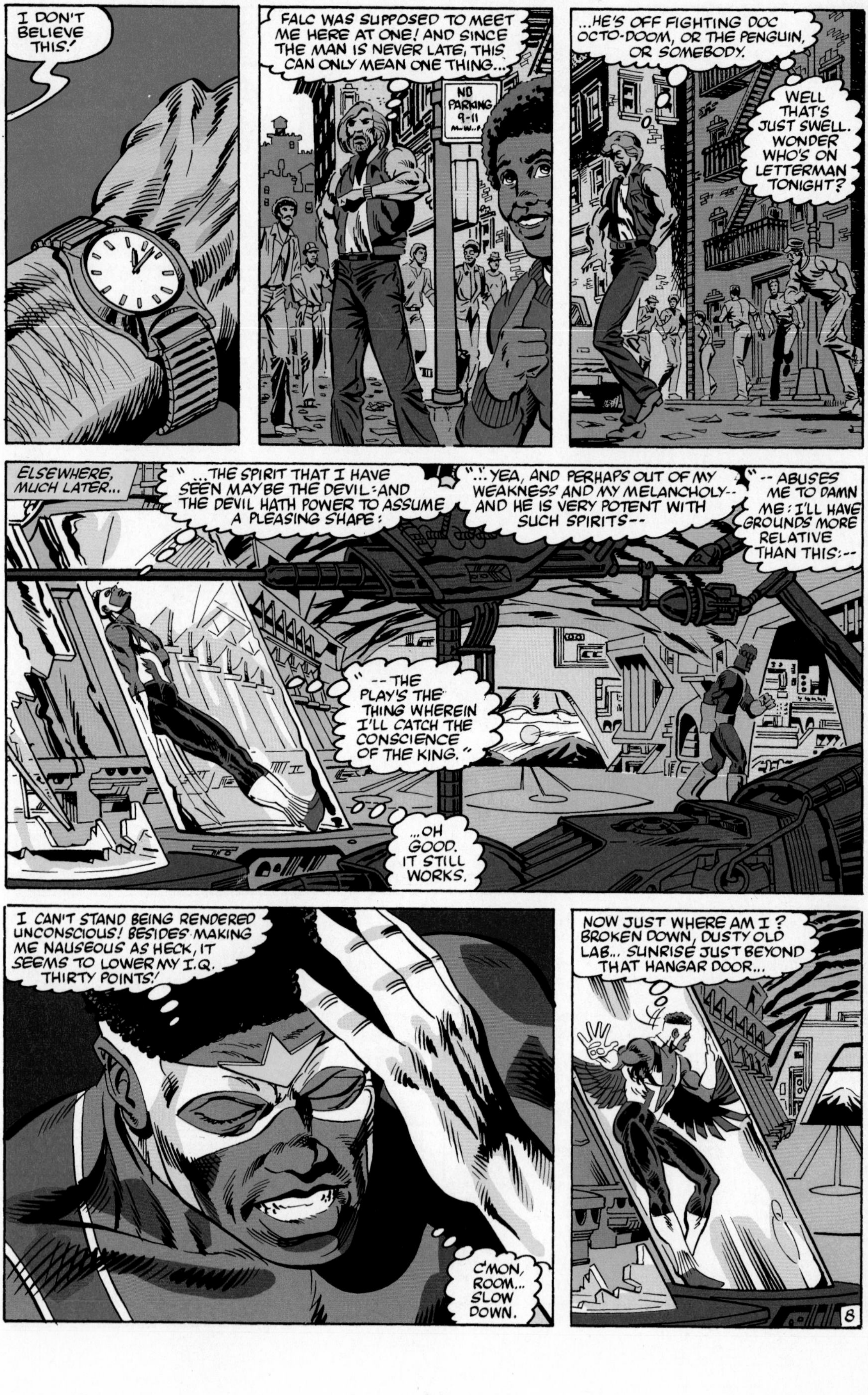
I DON'T BELIEVE THIS!
FALC WAS SUPPOSED TO MEET ME HERE AT ONE! AND SINCE THE MAN IS NEVER LATE, THIS CAN ONLY MEAN ONE THING...
NO PARKING 9-11
...HE'S OFF FIGHTING DOC OCTO-DOOM, OR THE PENGUIN, OR SOMEBODY.
WELL THAT'S JUST SWELL. WONDER WHO'S ON LETTERMAN TONIGHT?
ELSEWHERE, MUCH LATER...
"...THE SPIRIT THAT I HAVE SEEN MAY BE THE DEVIL: AND THE DEVIL HATH POWER TO ASSUME A PLEASING SHAPE:
"...YEA, AND PERHAPS OUT OF MY WEAKNESS AND MY MELANCHOLY-- AND HE IS VERY POTENT WITH SUCH SPIRITS--
"--ABUSES ME TO DAMN ME: I'LL HAVE GROUNDS MORE RELATIVE THAN THIS:--
"--THE PLAY'S THE THING WHEREIN I'LL CATCH THE CONSCIENCE OF THE KING."
...OH GOOD. IT STILL WORKS.
I CAN'T STAND BEING RENDERED UNCONSCIOUS! BESIDES MAKING ME NAUSEOUS AS HECK, IT SEEMS TO LOWER MY I.Q. THIRTY POINTS!
C'MON, ROOM... SLOW DOWN.
NOW JUST WHERE AM I? BROKEN DOWN, DUSTY OLD LAB... SUNRISE JUST BEYOND THAT HANGAR DOOR...
8

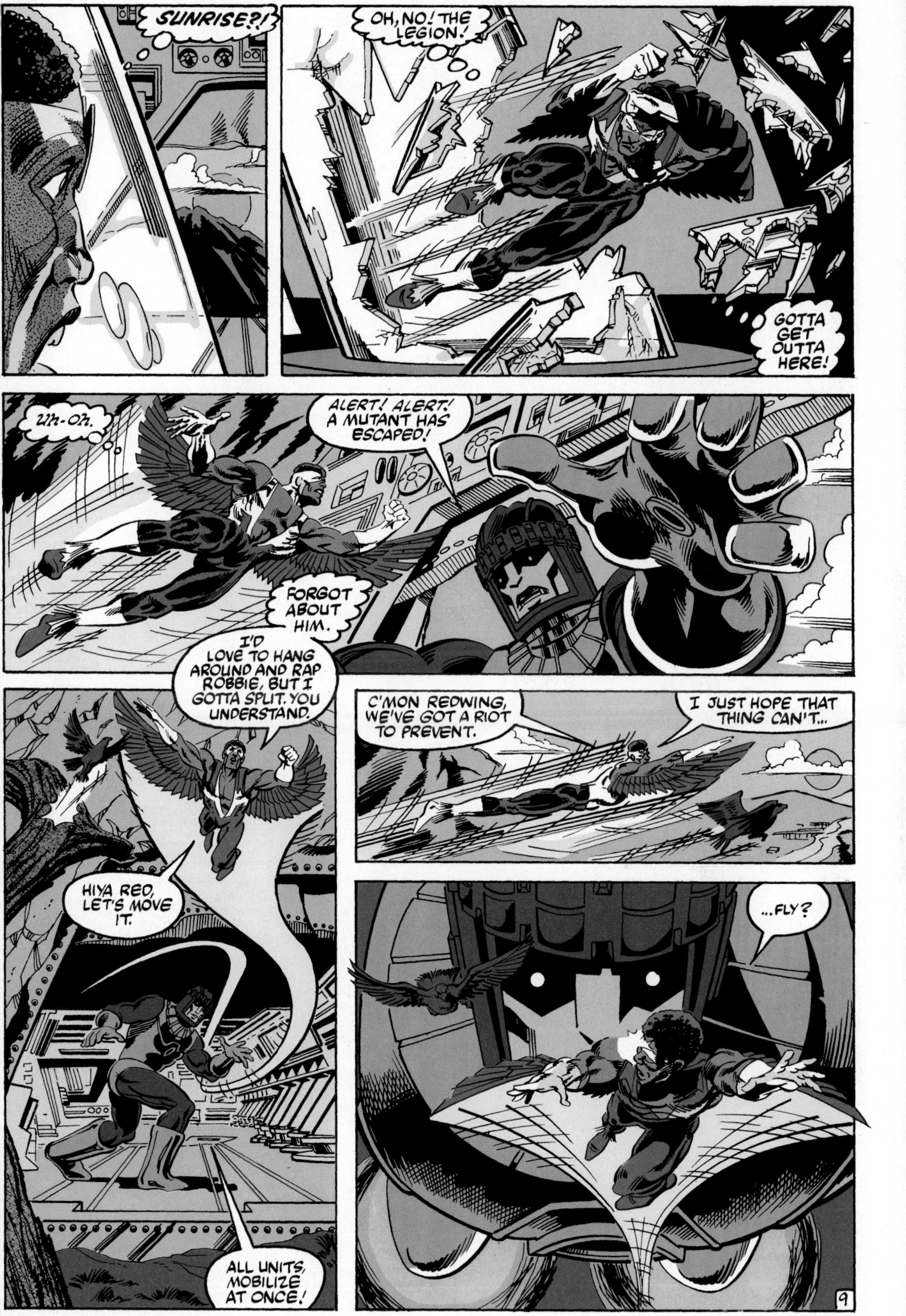
SUNRISE?!
OH, NO! THE LEGION!
GOTTA GET OUTTA HERE!
Uh-Oh.
ALERT! ALERT! A MUTANT HAS ESCAPED!
FORGOT ABOUT HIM.
I'D LOVE TO HANG AROUND AND RAP ROBBIE, BUT I GOTTA SPLIT. YOU UNDERSTAND.
HIYA RED, LET'S MOVE IT.
ALL UNITS, MOBILIZE AT ONCE!
C'MON REDWING, WE'VE GOT A RIOT TO PREVENT.
I JUST HOPE THAT THING CAN'T...
...FLY?
9

MEANWHILE, BACK IN THE CITY...

OKAY... OKAY... "XEROX" OR WHATEVER... WHAT THE HECK'S GOIN' ON?

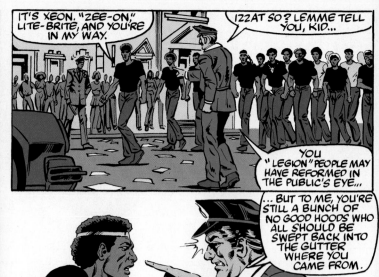

IT'S XEON. "ZEE-ON," LITE-BRITE, AND YOU'RE IN MY WAY.

IZZAT SO? LEMME TELL YOU, KID...

YOU "LEGION" PEOPLE MAY HAVE REFORMED IN THE PUBLIC'S EYE...

...BUT TO ME, YOU'RE STILL A BUNCH OF NO GOOD HOODS WHO ALL SHOULD BE SWEPT BACK INTO THE GUTTER WHERE YOU CAME FROM.

IN OTHER WORDS... MOVE YER PARADE BEFORE I RAIN ON IT!

XEON!

LAY OFF 'IM, MAN!

LEGION... WE GOT STATIC!

GREAT! THREE WEEKS OUT OF THE ACADEMY AND I DRAW RIOT DUTY! OH, NO... THAT KID'S GOING TO TRASH ARNIE!

HEY... F-FREEZE...

WHAT THE... HEY, YOU STUPID ROOKIE...

...DON'T...

BLAM

38

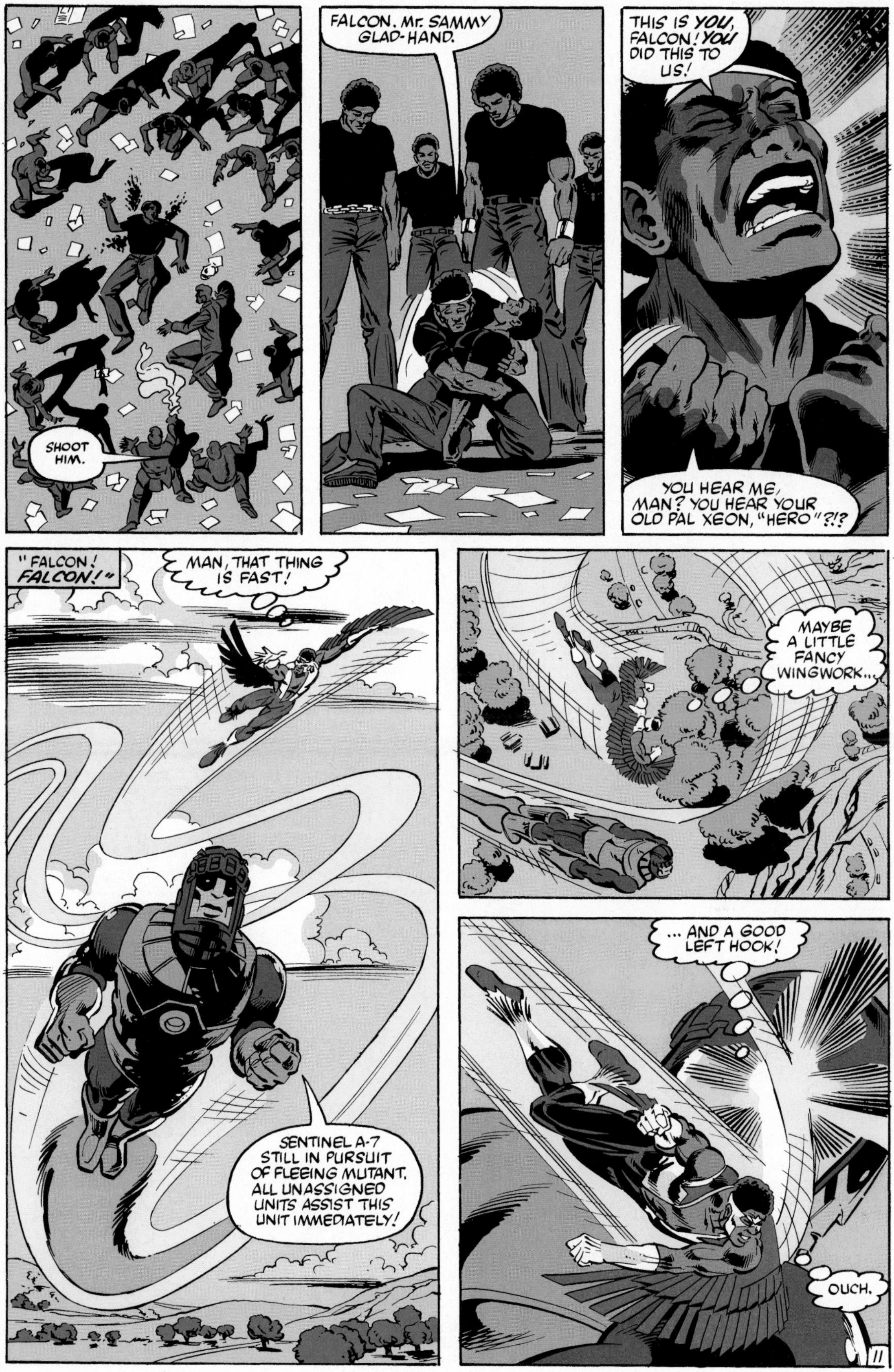
SHOOT HIM.
FALCON. Mr. SAMMY GLAD-HAND.
THIS IS YOU, FALCON! YOU DID THIS TO US!
YOU HEAR ME, MAN? YOU HEAR YOUR OLD PAL XEON, "HERO"?!?
"FALCON! FALCON!"
MAN, THAT THING IS FAST!
SENTINEL A-7 STILL IN PURSUIT OF FLEEING MUTANT. ALL UNASSIGNED UNITS ASSIST THIS UNIT IMMEDIATELY!
MAYBE A LITTLE FANCY WINGWORK...
... AND A GOOD LEFT HOOK!
OUCH.
11

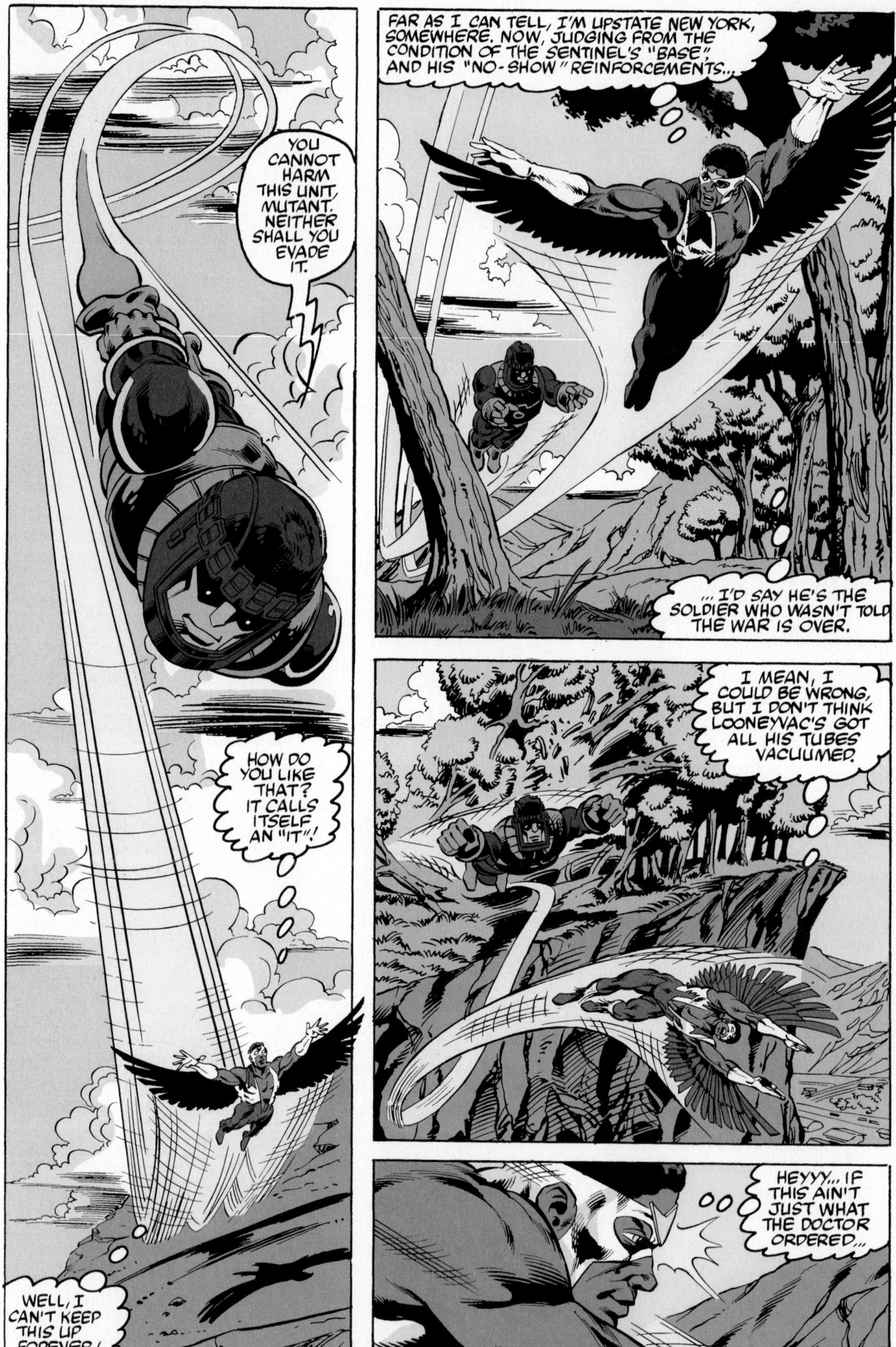
YOU CANNOT HARM THIS UNIT, MUTANT. NEITHER SHALL YOU EVADE IT.
HOW DO YOU LIKE THAT? IT CALLS ITSELF AN "IT"!
WELL, I CAN'T KEEP THIS UP FOREVER!
FAR AS I CAN TELL, I'M UPSTATE NEW YORK, SOMEWHERE. NOW, JUDGING FROM THE CONDITION OF THE SENTINEL'S "BASE" AND HIS "NO-SHOW" REINFORCEMENTS...
...I'D SAY HE'S THE SOLDIER WHO WASN'T TOLD THE WAR IS OVER.
I MEAN, I COULD BE WRONG, BUT I DON'T THINK LOONEYVAC'S GOT ALL HIS TUBES VACUUMED.
HEYYY... IF THIS AIN'T JUST WHAT THE DOCTOR ORDERED...
12

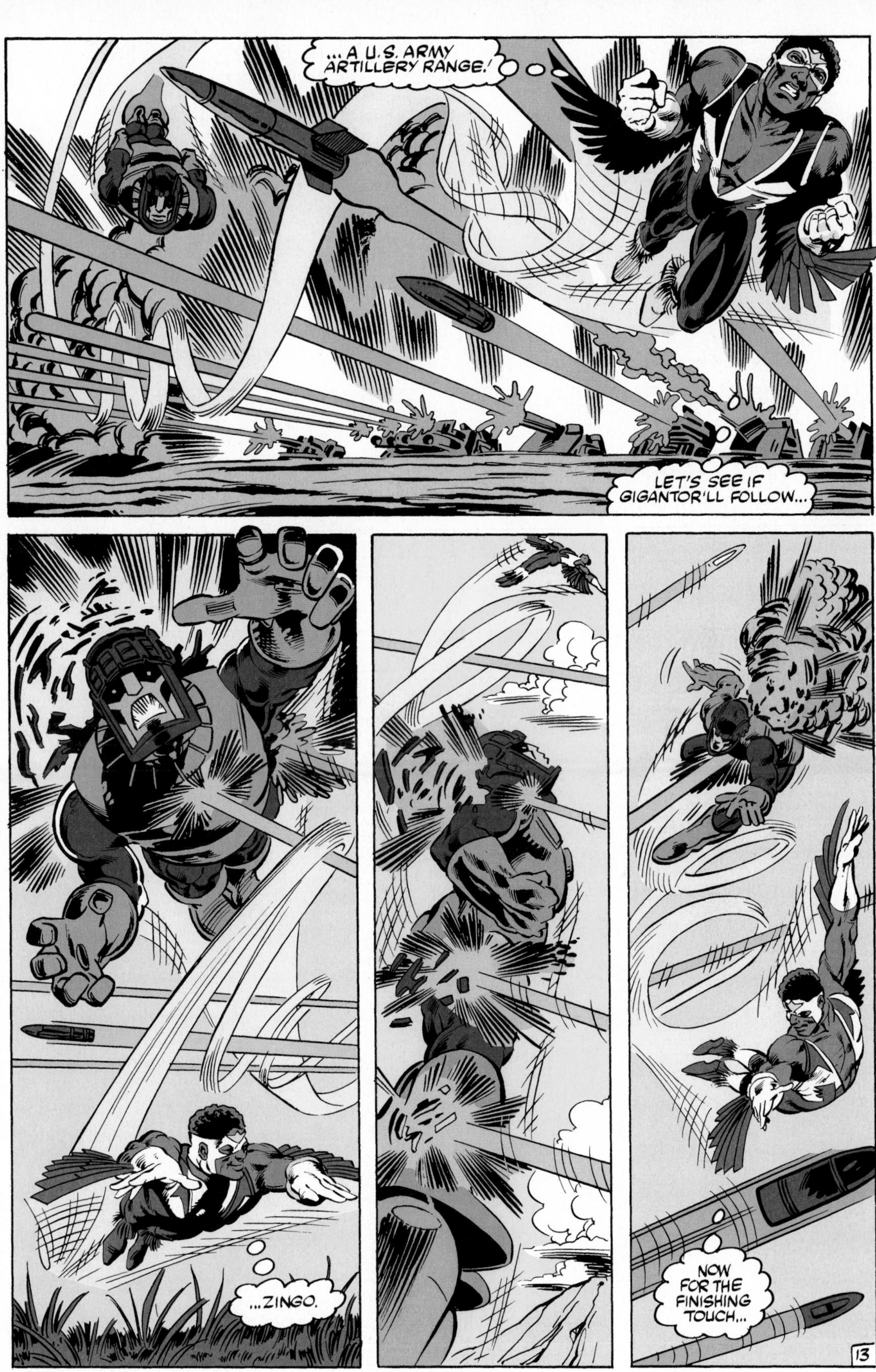
...A U.S. ARMY ARTILLERY RANGE!
LET'S SEE IF GIGANTOR'LL FOLLOW...
...ZINGO.
NOW FOR THE FINISHING TOUCH...
13

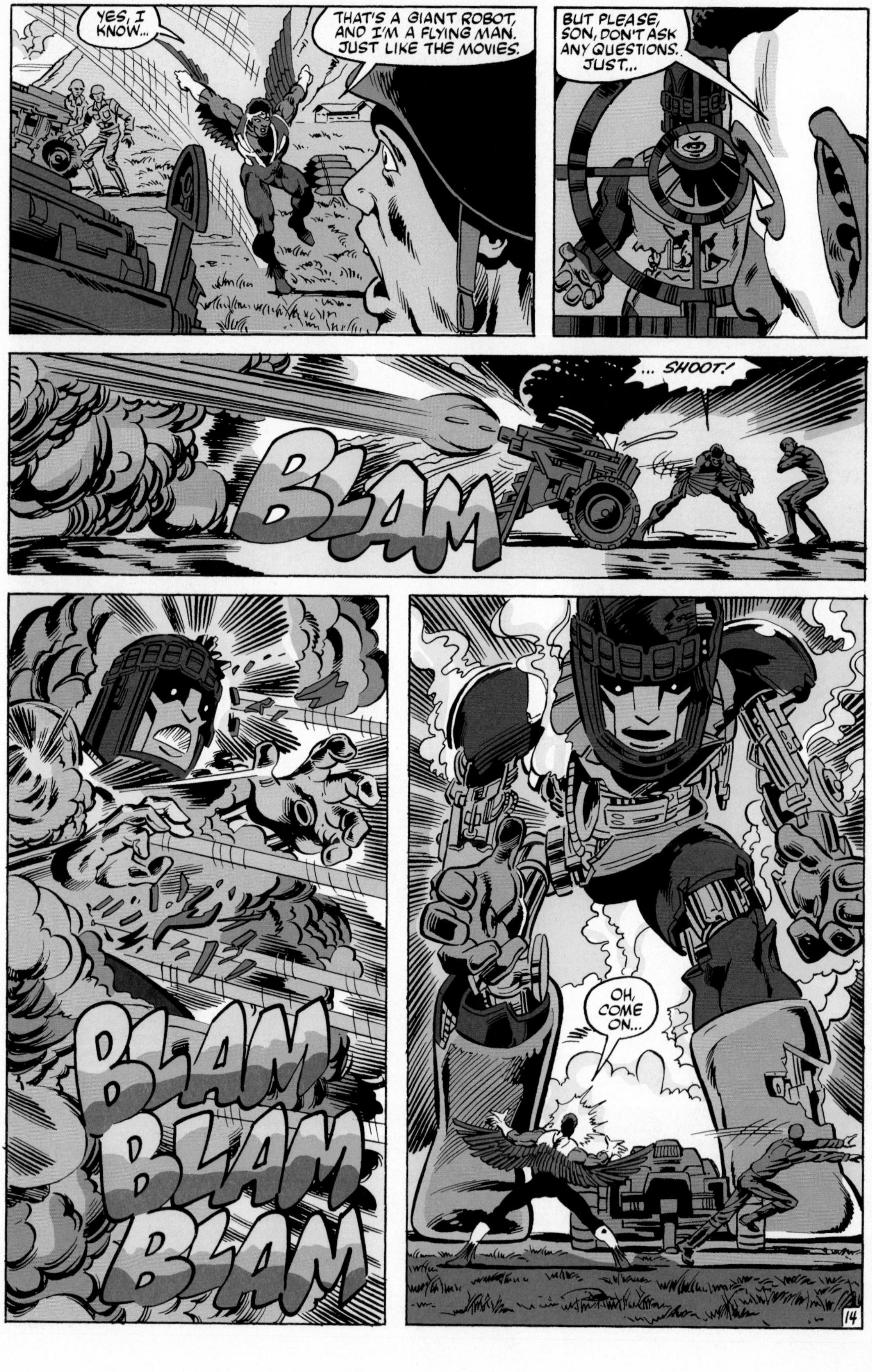
YES, I KNOW...
THAT'S A GIANT ROBOT, AND I'M A FLYING MAN. JUST LIKE THE MOVIES.
BUT PLEASE, SON, DON'T ASK ANY QUESTIONS. JUST...
... SHOOT!
BLAM
BLAM
BLAM
BLAM
OH, COME ON...
14

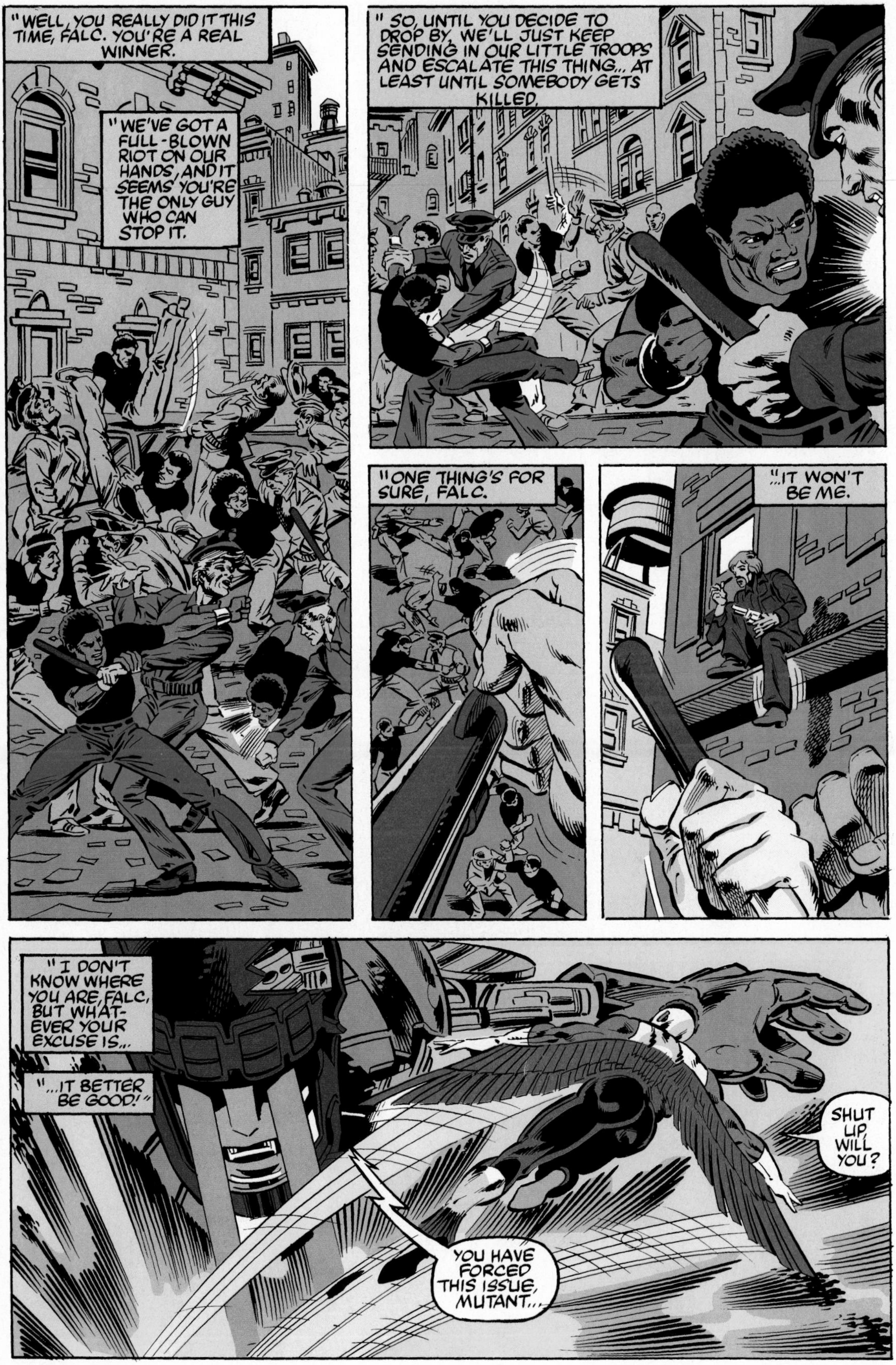
"WELL, YOU REALLY DID IT THIS TIME, FALC. YOU'RE A REAL WINNER.
"WE'VE GOT A FULL-BLOWN RIOT ON OUR HANDS, AND IT SEEMS YOU'RE THE ONLY GUY WHO CAN STOP IT.
" SO, UNTIL YOU DECIDE TO DROP BY, WE'LL JUST KEEP SENDING IN OUR LITTLE TROOPS AND ESCALATE THIS THING... AT LEAST UNTIL SOMEBODY GETS KILLED.
"ONE THING'S FOR SURE, FALC.
...IT WON'T BE ME.
"I DON'T KNOW WHERE YOU ARE, FALC, BUT WHATEVER YOUR EXCUSE IS...
"...IT BETTER BE GOOD!"
SHUT UP, WILL YOU?
YOU HAVE FORCED THIS ISSUE, MUTANT...

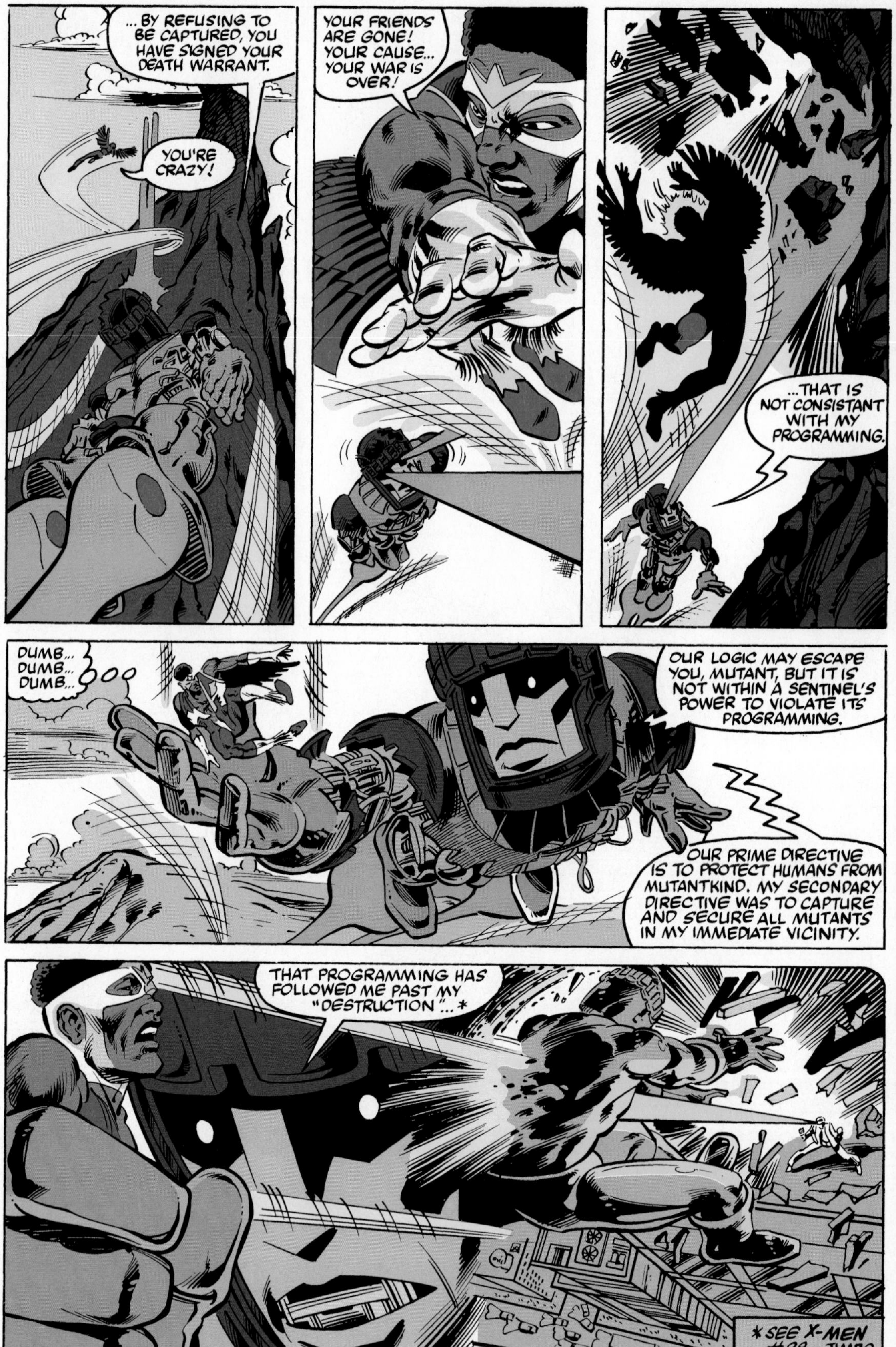
...BY REFUSING TO BE CAPTURED, YOU HAVE SIGNED YOUR DEATH WARRANT.
YOU'RE CRAZY!
YOUR FRIENDS ARE GONE! YOUR CAUSE... YOUR WAR IS OVER!
...THAT IS NOT CONSISTANT WITH MY PROGRAMMING.
DUMB... DUMB... DUMB...
OUR LOGIC MAY ESCAPE YOU, MUTANT, BUT IT IS NOT WITHIN A SENTINEL'S POWER TO VIOLATE ITS PROGRAMMING.
OUR PRIME DIRECTIVE IS TO PROTECT HUMANS FROM MUTANTKIND. MY SECONDARY DIRECTIVE WAS TO CAPTURE AND SECURE ALL MUTANTS IN MY IMMEDIATE VICINITY.
THAT PROGRAMMING HAS FOLLOWED ME PAST MY "DESTRUCTION"...*
*SEE X-MEN #98--JIMBO.

THE MUTANT CALLED CYCLOPS OF THE ASSOCIATION REFERRED TO AS THE X-MEN CAUGHT THIS UNIT OFF-BALANCE WITH A HIGH-INTENSITY OPTIC BLAST.

THIS UNIT TOPPLED 112 STORIES TO THE STREET.

THIS UNIT'S DISMEMBERED STRUCTURE WAS THEN PLACED INTO A LAND RECLAMATION SITE.

THE SANITATION CREW THAT TRANSPORTED THIS UNIT WERE WOEFULLY IGNORANT OF THE FACT...

...THAT THIS UNIT'S ELECTRONIC BRAIN WAS STILL FUNCTIONAL.

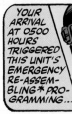

YOUR ARRIVAL AT 0500 HOURS TRIGGERED THIS UNIT'S EMERGENCY RE-ASSEM-BLING* PRO-GRAMMING...

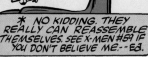

* NO KIDDING. THEY REALLY CAN REASSEMBLE THEMSELVES. SEE X-MEN #59 IF YOU DON'T BELIEVE ME.--Ed.

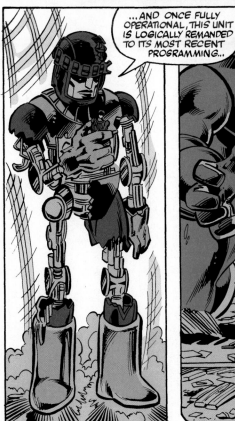

...AND ONCE FULLY OPERATIONAL, THIS UNIT IS LOGICALLY REMANDED TO ITS MOST RECENT PROGRAMMING...

...WHICH PRECLUDED YOUR CAPTURE.

HOWEVER, SINCE YOU WISH TO WAIVE CAPTURE...

...THIS UNIT IS LEFT ONLY ONE OPTION.

HIS FIST... HE'S TIGHTENING HIS FIST...

17

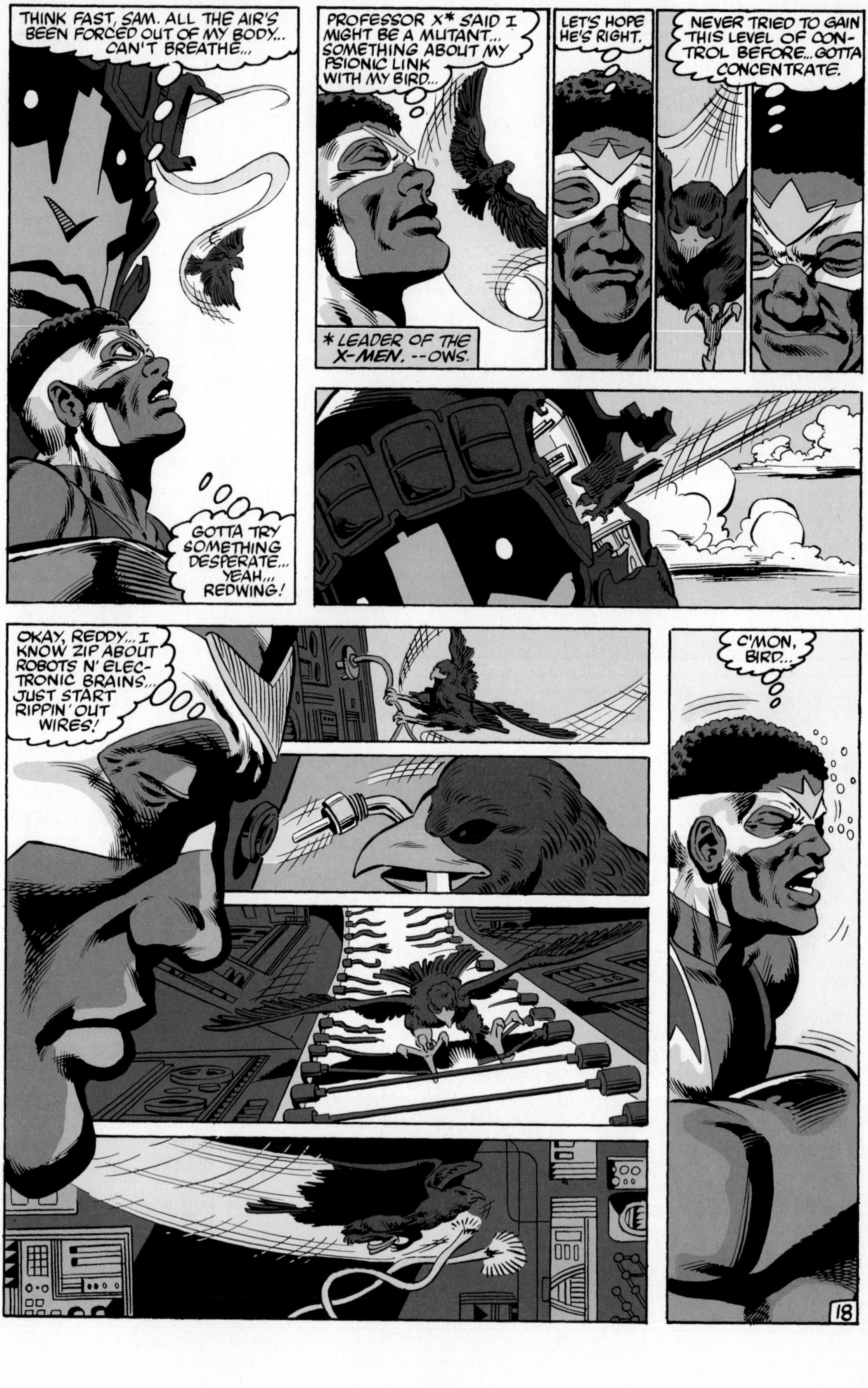
THINK FAST, SAM. ALL THE AIR'S BEEN FORCED OUT OF MY BODY... CAN'T BREATHE...
GOTTA TRY SOMETHING DESPERATE... YEAH... REDWING!
PROFESSOR X* SAID I MIGHT BE A MUTANT... SOMETHING ABOUT MY PSIONIC LINK WITH MY BIRD...
* LEADER OF THE X-MEN. --OWS.
LET'S HOPE HE'S RIGHT.
NEVER TRIED TO GAIN THIS LEVEL OF CONTROL BEFORE... GOTTA CONCENTRATE.
OKAY, REDDY... I KNOW ZIP ABOUT ROBOTS N' ELECTRONIC BRAINS... JUST START RIPPIN' OUT WIRES!
C'MON, BIRD...
18

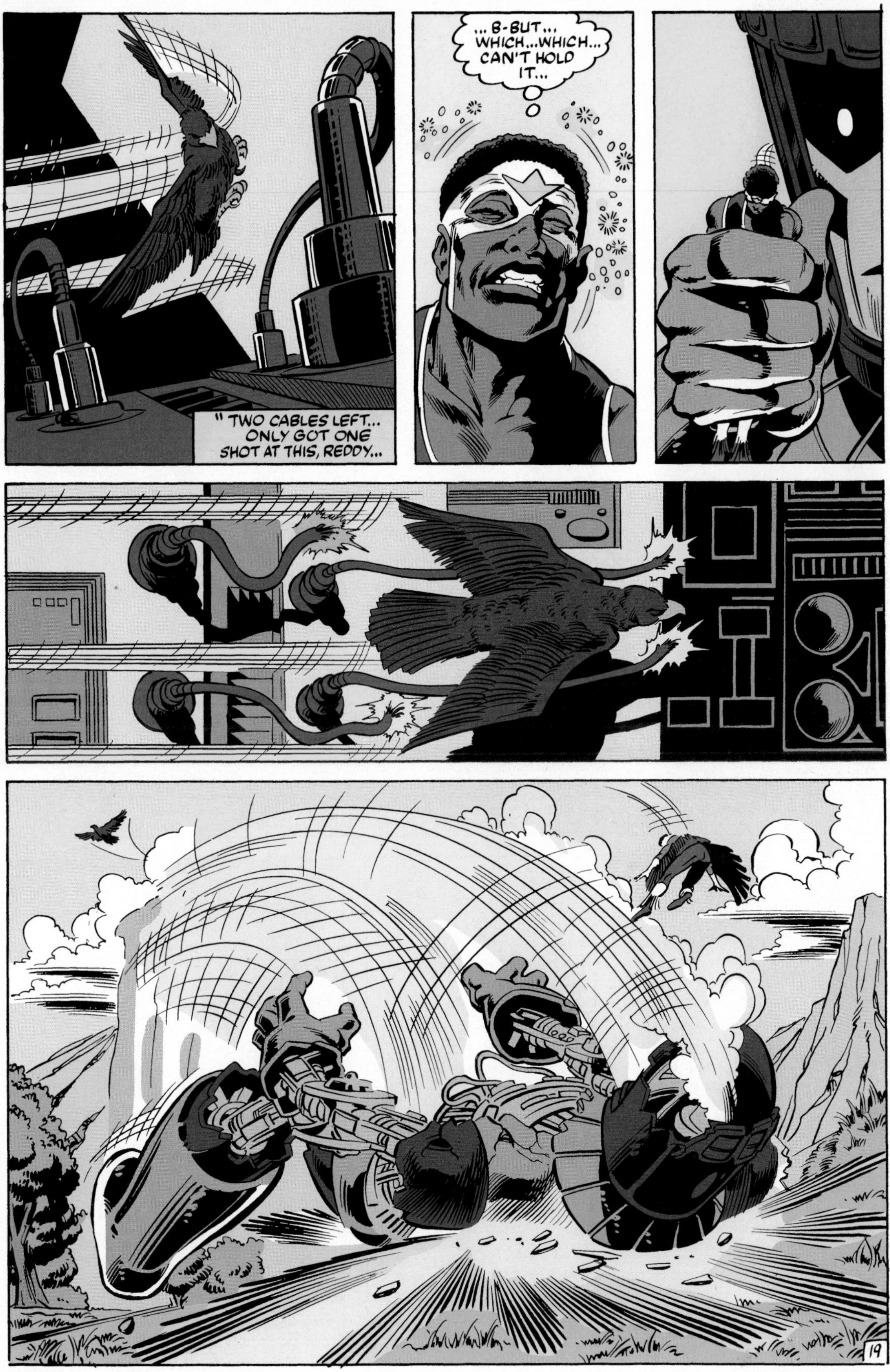
"TWO CABLES LEFT... ONLY GOT ONE SHOT AT THIS, REDDY...
...B-BUT... WHICH...WHICH... CAN'T HOLD IT...
19

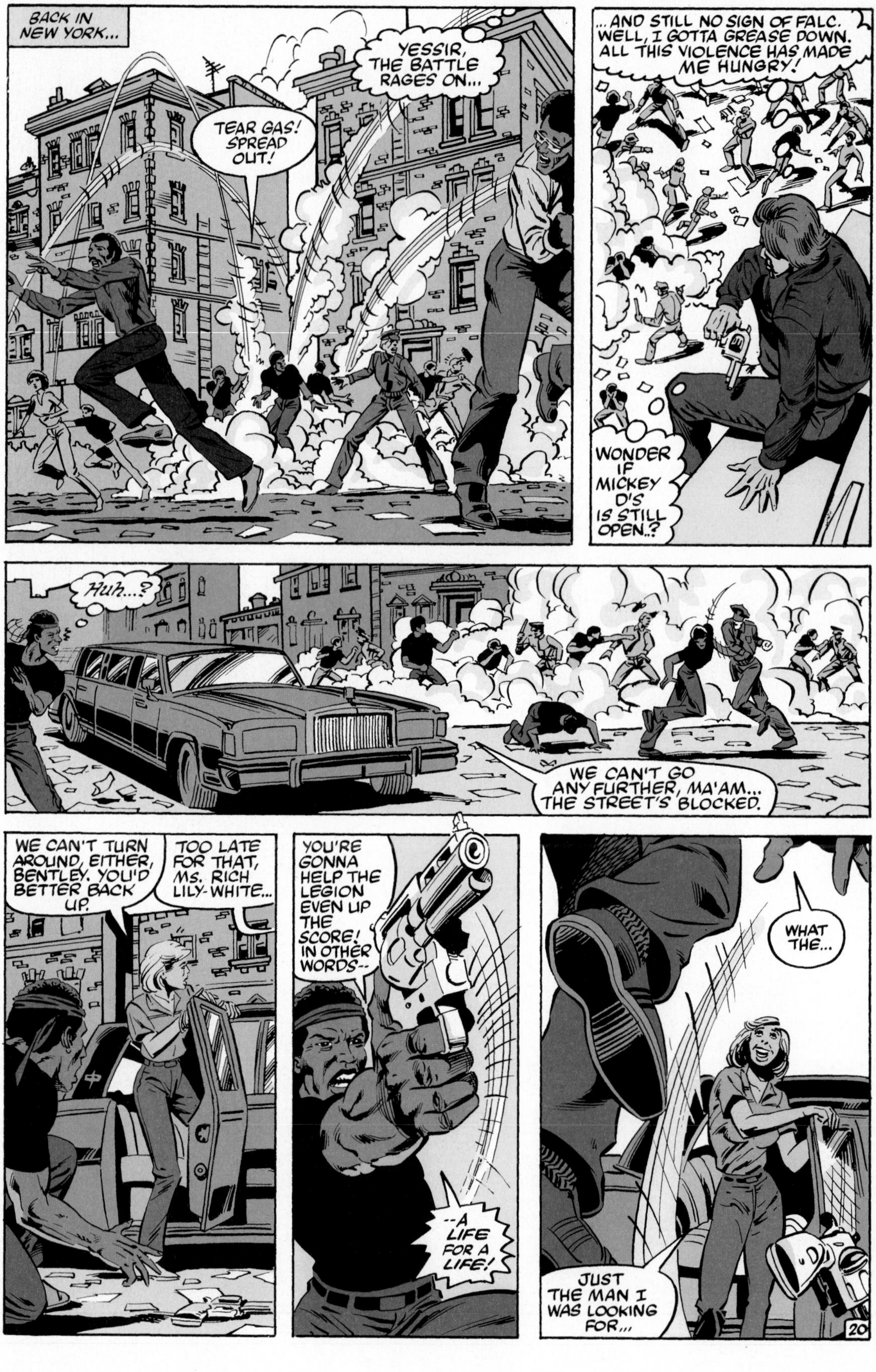
BACK IN NEW YORK...
YESSIR, THE BATTLE RAGES ON...
TEAR GAS! SPREAD OUT!
...AND STILL NO SIGN OF FALC. WELL, I GOTTA GREASE DOWN. ALL THIS VIOLENCE HAS MADE ME HUNGRY!
WONDER IF MICKEY D'S IS STILL OPEN..?
Huh...?
WE CAN'T GO ANY FURTHER, MA'AM... THE STREET'S BLOCKED.
WE CAN'T TURN AROUND, EITHER, BENTLEY. YOU'D BETTER BACK UP.
TOO LATE FOR THAT, MS. RICH LILY-WHITE...
YOU'RE GONNA HELP THE LEGION EVEN UP THE SCORE! IN OTHER WORDS--
--A LIFE FOR A LIFE!
WHAT THE...
JUST THE MAN I WAS LOOKING FOR...
20

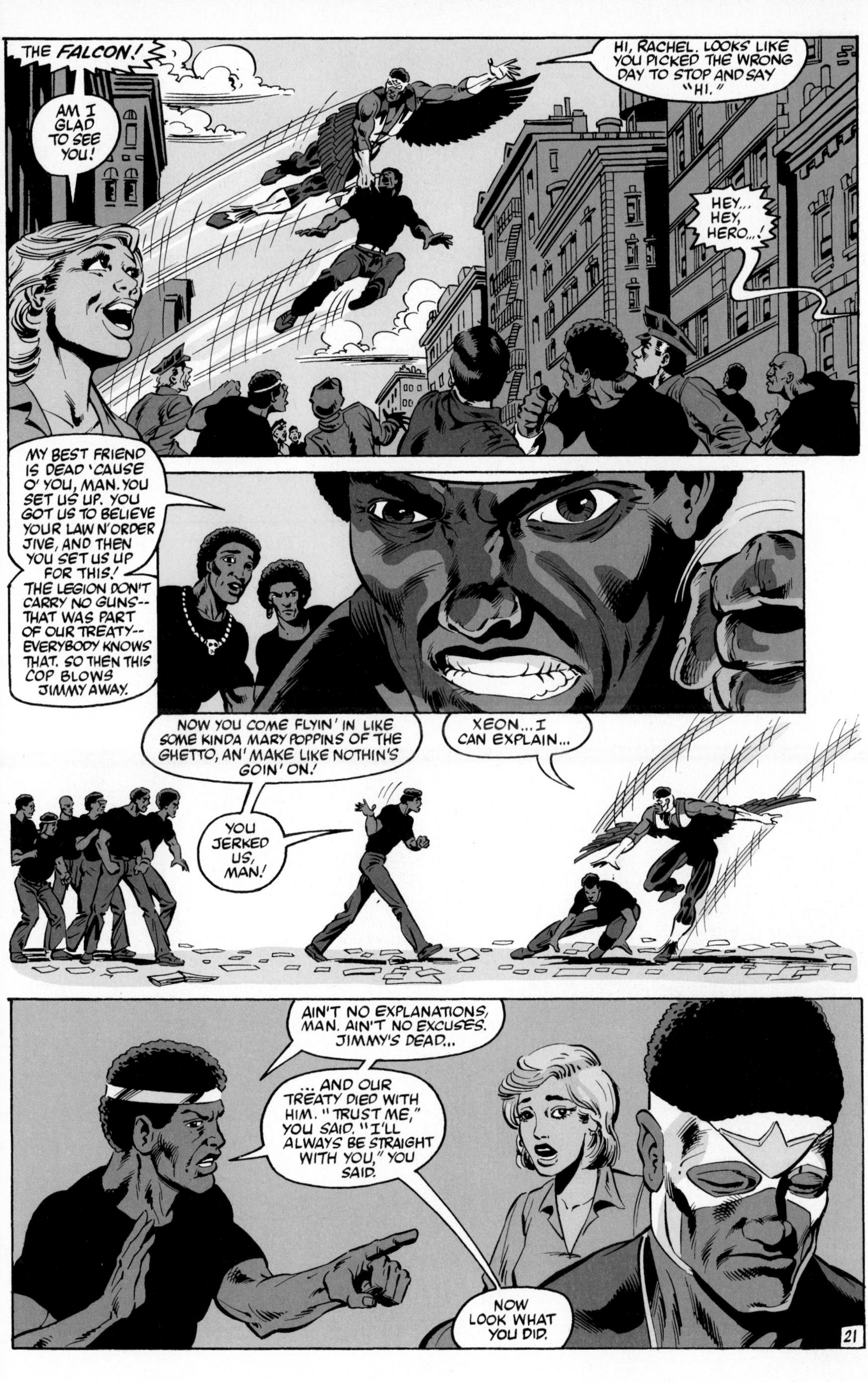
THE FALCON!
AM I GLAD TO SEE YOU!
HI, RACHEL. LOOKS LIKE YOU PICKED THE WRONG DAY TO STOP AND SAY "HI."
HEY... HEY, HERO...!
MY BEST FRIEND IS DEAD 'CAUSE O' YOU, MAN. YOU SET US UP. YOU GOT US TO BELIEVE YOUR LAW N'ORDER JIVE, AND THEN YOU SET US UP FOR THIS! THE LEGION DON'T CARRY NO GUNS-- THAT WAS PART OF OUR TREATY-- EVERYBODY KNOWS THAT. SO THEN THIS COP BLOWS JIMMY AWAY.
NOW YOU COME FLYIN' IN LIKE SOME KINDA MARY POPPINS OF THE GHETTO, AN' MAKE LIKE NOTHIN'S GOIN' ON!
YOU JERKED US, MAN!
XEON... I CAN EXPLAIN...
AIN'T NO EXPLANATIONS, MAN. AIN'T NO EXCUSES. JIMMY'S DEAD...
... AND OUR TREATY DIED WITH HIM. "TRUST ME," YOU SAID. "I'LL ALWAYS BE STRAIGHT WITH YOU," YOU SAID.
NOW LOOK WHAT YOU DID.
21

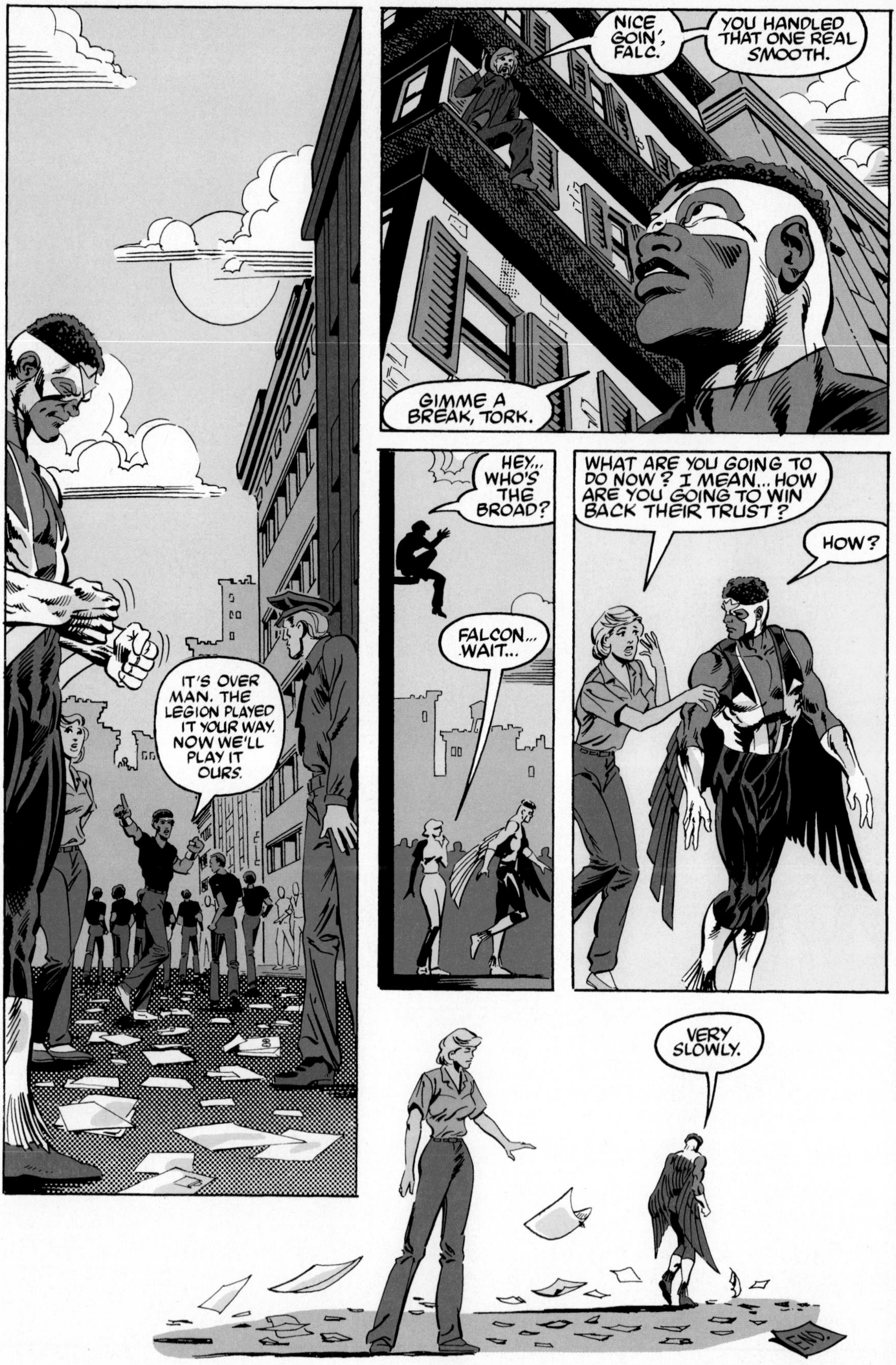
IT'S OVER MAN. THE LEGION PLAYED IT YOUR WAY. NOW WE'LL PLAY IT OURS.
NICE GOIN', FALC.
YOU HANDLED THAT ONE REAL SMOOTH.
GIMME A BREAK, TORK.
HEY... WHO'S THE BROAD?
FALCON... WAIT...
WHAT ARE YOU GOING TO DO NOW? I MEAN... HOW ARE YOU GOING TO WIN BACK THEIR TRUST?
HOW?
VERY SLOWLY.
END.

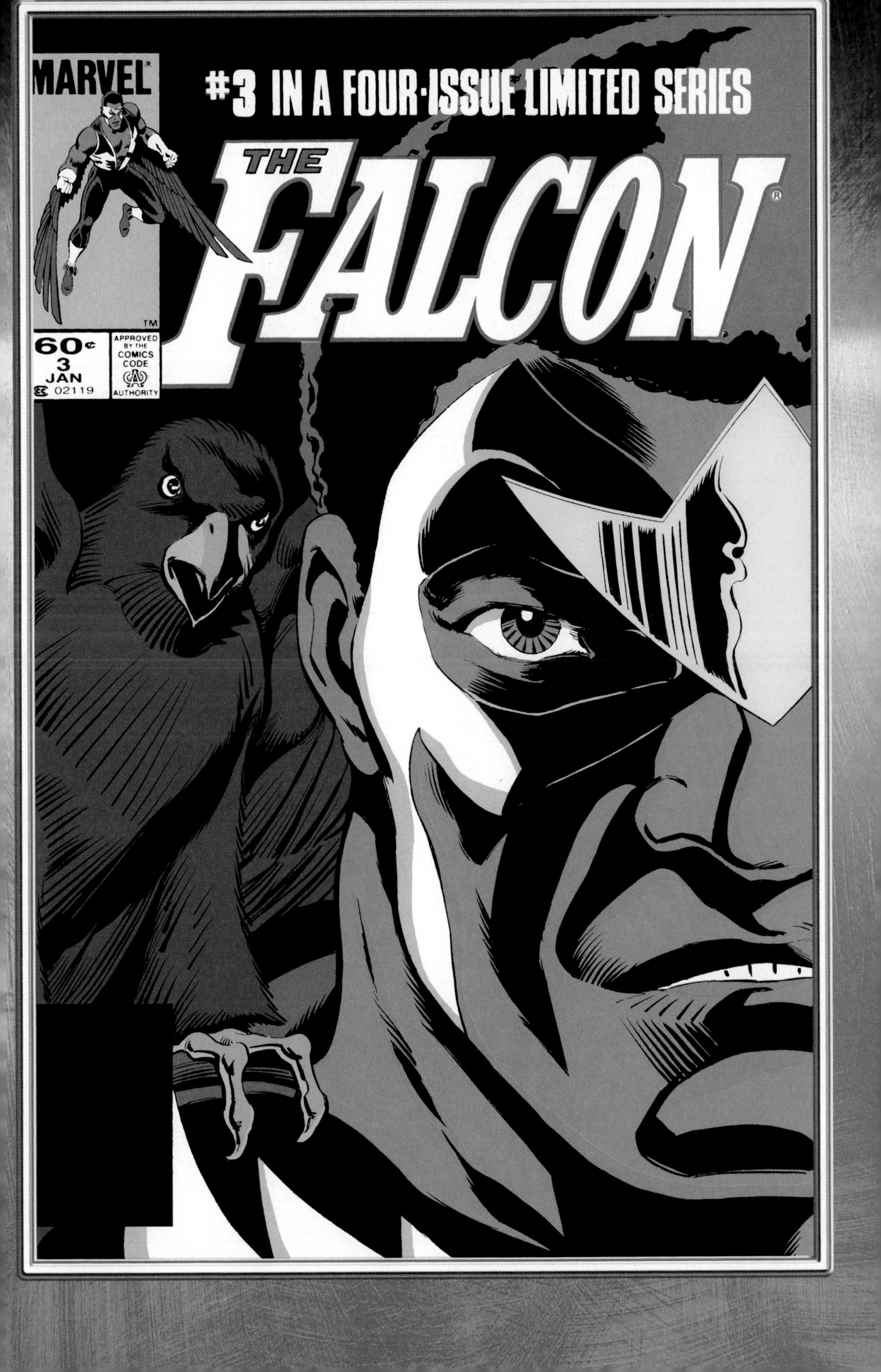
MARVEL
#3 IN A FOUR-ISSUE LIMITED SERIES
THE FALCON
TM
60¢
3
JAN
02119
APPROVED BY THE COMICS CODE AUTHORITY

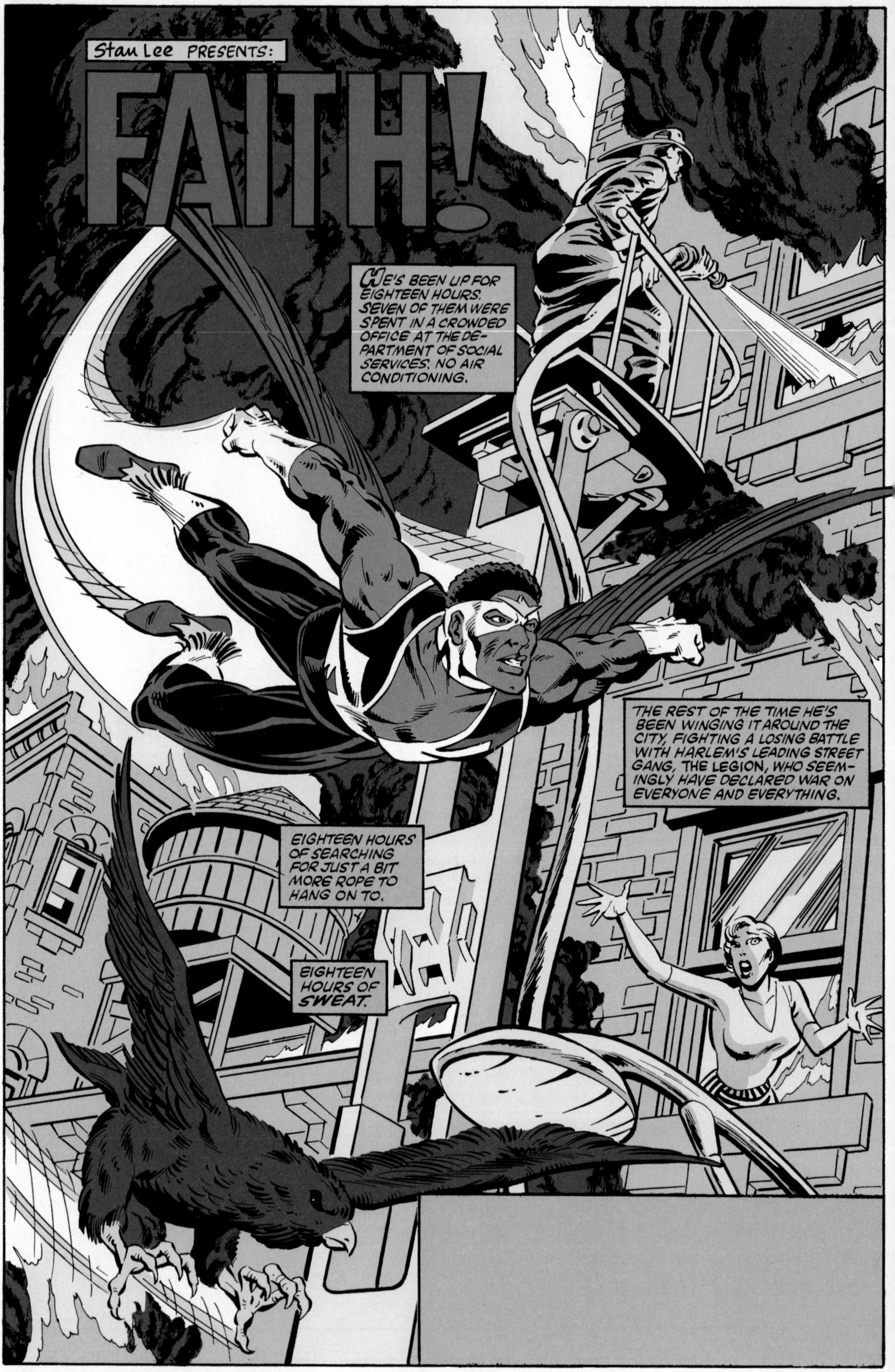

Stan Lee PRESENTS:
FAITH!
HE'S BEEN UP FOR EIGHTEEN HOURS. SEVEN OF THEM WERE SPENT IN A CROWDED OFFICE AT THE DEPARTMENT OF SOCIAL SERVICES. NO AIR CONDITIONING.
THE REST OF THE TIME HE'S BEEN WINGING IT AROUND THE CITY, FIGHTING A LOSING BATTLE WITH HARLEM'S LEADING STREET GANG, THE LEGION, WHO SEEMINGLY HAVE DECLARED WAR ON EVERYONE AND EVERYTHING.
EIGHTEEN HOURS OF SEARCHING FOR JUST A BIT MORE ROPE TO HANG ON TO.
EIGHTEEN HOURS OF SWEAT.

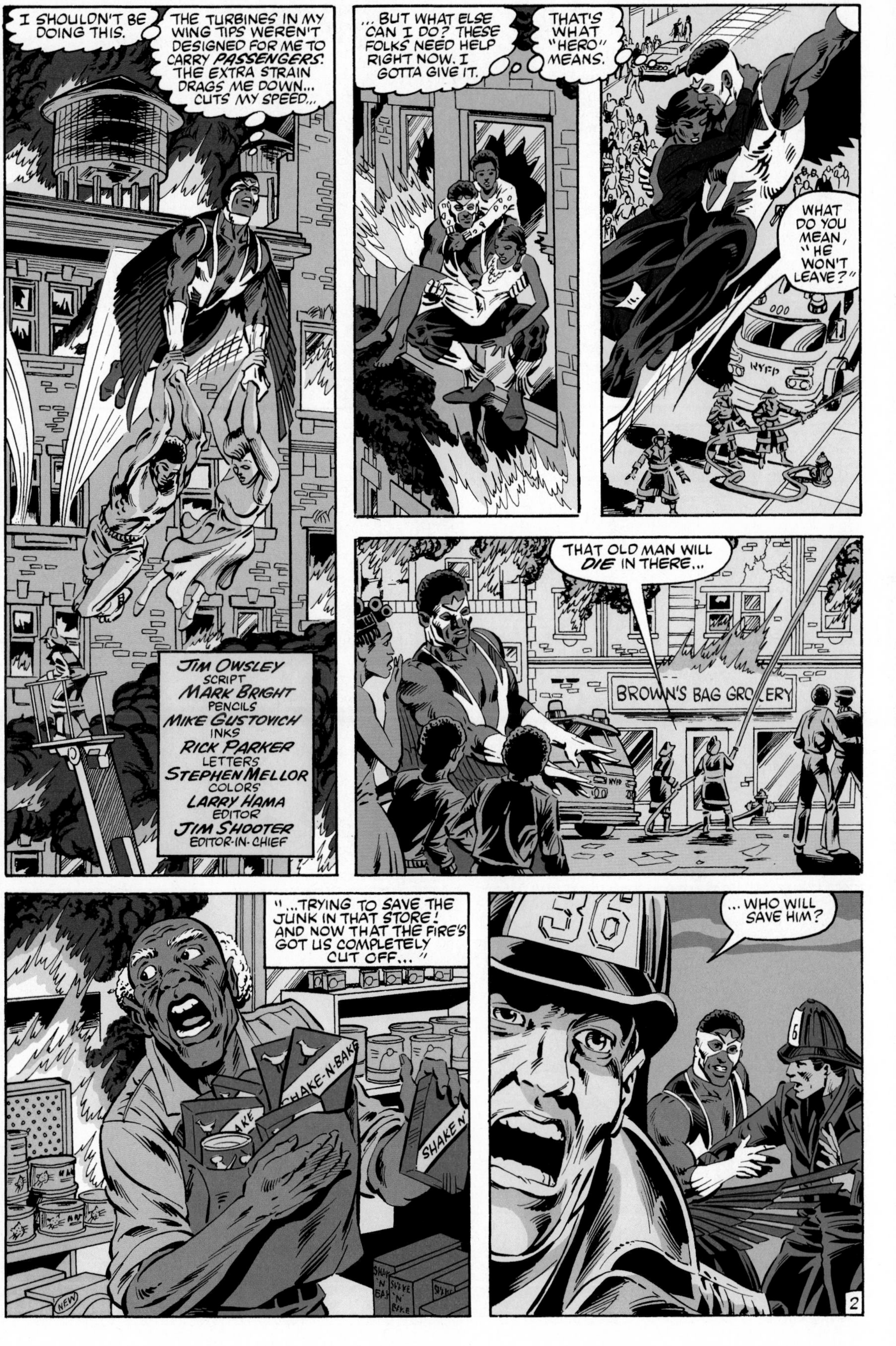
I SHOULDN'T BE DOING THIS.
THE TURBINES IN MY WING TIPS WEREN'T DESIGNED FOR ME TO CARRY *PASSENGERS*. THE EXTRA STRAIN DRAGS ME DOWN... CUTS MY SPEED...
JIM OWSLEY SCRIPT
MARK BRIGHT PENCILS
MIKE GUSTOVICH INKS
RICK PARKER LETTERS
STEPHEN MELLOR COLORS
LARRY HAMA EDITOR
JIM SHOOTER EDITOR-IN-CHIEF
...BUT WHAT ELSE CAN I DO? THESE FOLKS NEED HELP RIGHT NOW. I GOTTA GIVE IT.
THAT'S WHAT "HERO" MEANS.
WHAT DO YOU MEAN, "HE WON'T LEAVE?"
NYFD
THAT OLD MAN WILL *DIE* IN THERE...
BROWN'S BAG GROCERY
"...TRYING TO SAVE THE JUNK IN THAT STORE! AND NOW THAT THE FIRE'S GOT US COMPLETELY CUT OFF..."
SHAKE-N-BAKE
SHAKE N'
...WHO WILL SAVE HIM?
36
2

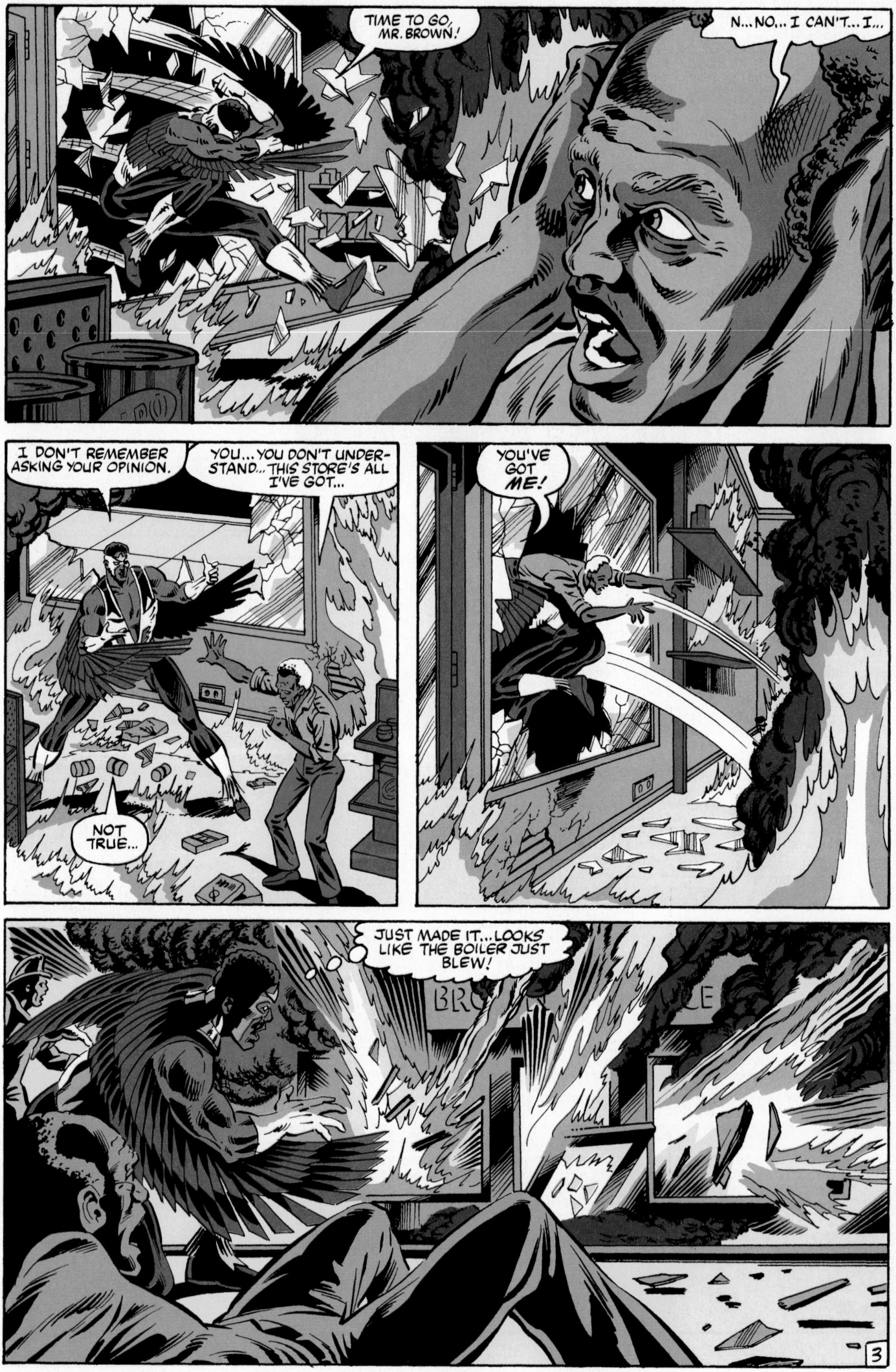
TIME TO GO, MR. BROWN!
N... NO... I CAN'T... I...
I DON'T REMEMBER ASKING YOUR OPINION.
YOU... YOU DON'T UNDERSTAND... THIS STORE'S ALL I'VE GOT...
NOT TRUE...
YOU'VE GOT ME!
JUST MADE IT... LOOKS LIKE THE BOILER JUST BLEW!
3

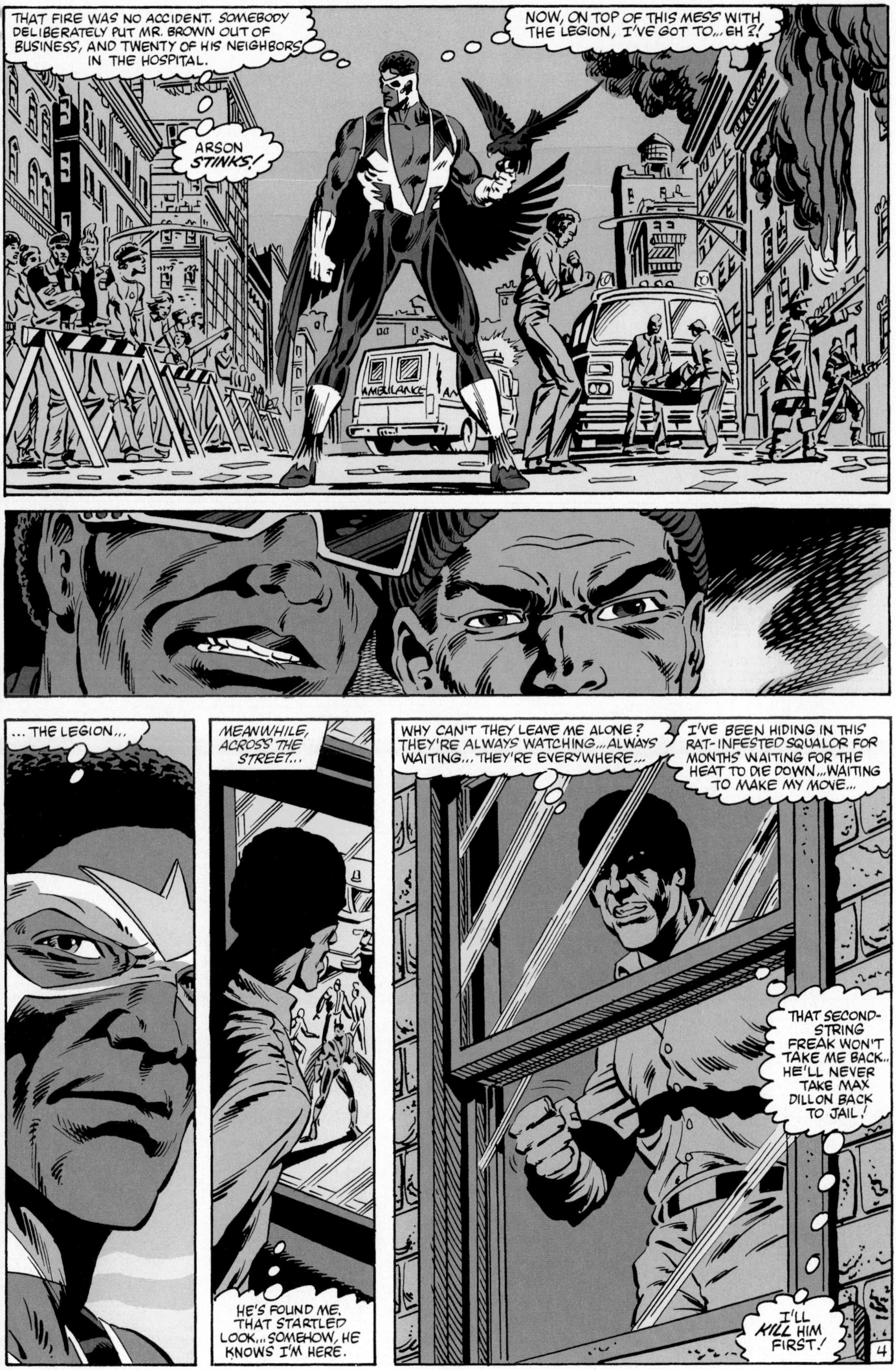
THAT FIRE WAS NO ACCIDENT. SOMEBODY DELIBERATELY PUT MR. BROWN OUT OF BUSINESS, AND TWENTY OF HIS NEIGHBORS IN THE HOSPITAL.
ARSON STINKS!
NOW, ON TOP OF THIS MESS WITH THE LEGION, I'VE GOT TO... EH?!
... THE LEGION...
MEANWHILE, ACROSS THE STREET...
HE'S FOUND ME. THAT STARTLED LOOK... SOMEHOW, HE KNOWS I'M HERE.
WHY CAN'T THEY LEAVE ME ALONE? THEY'RE ALWAYS WATCHING... ALWAYS WAITING... THEY'RE EVERYWHERE...
I'VE BEEN HIDING IN THIS RAT-INFESTED SQUALOR FOR MONTHS WAITING FOR THE HEAT TO DIE DOWN... WAITING TO MAKE MY MOVE...
THAT SECOND-STRING FREAK WON'T TAKE ME BACK.. HE'LL NEVER TAKE MAX DILLON BACK TO JAIL!
I'LL KILL HIM FIRST!
4

TWENTY-ONE HOURS AND COUNTING. SAM WILSON ARRIVES HOME.

TORK!

WHAT ARE YOU DOING IN MY APARTMENT?

GIVE IT UP, MAN.

"WHY, SGT. TORK! WHAT A PLEASANT SURPRISE! WHAT BRINGS N.Y.'S FINEST TO MY HUMBLE ABODE, HMMM?" YOU GOT NO CLASS, FALC.

CLOCK *THIS*, FALC!

HUH? R.C.! DRAGON!

YUP, TWO BONA-FIDE LEGION-AIRES--JUNIOR WOOD-CHUCKS OF THE GHETTO-- ALL TRUSSED-UP AND READY TO BE BOOKED!

I'M WATCHIN' LETTERMAN! WHAT'S IT LOOK LIKE I'M DOIN'?

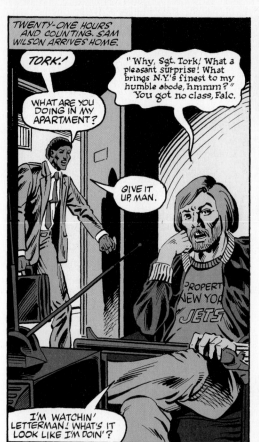

TORK, HOW COULD--

RELAX, FALC...AT LEAST I FOUND A USE FOR THESE SORRY-LOOKIN' TIES OF YOURS!

I FOUND THESE LITTLE DARLINGS TRYING TO REDECORATE YOUR PLACE WITH A SPRAY CAN.

ATE NIGHT WITH ETTERMAN

WHAT SAY YOU AN' ME KICK THE STINK OUT OF THESE TWO SNOTS?

TORK!

5

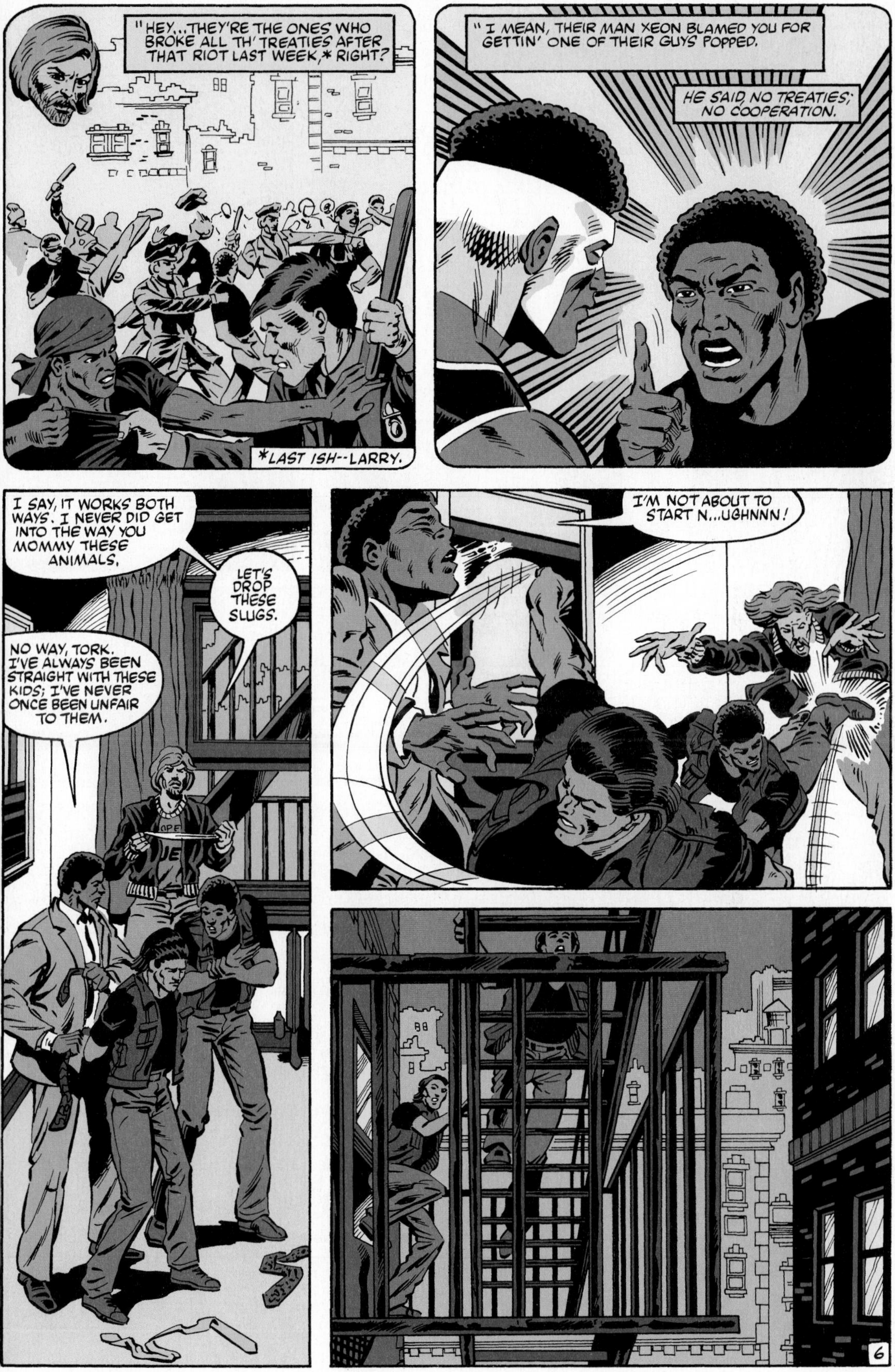
"HEY...THEY'RE THE ONES WHO BROKE ALL TH' TREATIES AFTER THAT RIOT LAST WEEK,* RIGHT?
*LAST ISH--LARRY.
"I MEAN, THEIR MAN XEON BLAMED YOU FOR GETTIN' ONE OF THEIR GUYS POPPED.
HE SAID NO TREATIES; NO COOPERATION.
I SAY, IT WORKS BOTH WAYS. I NEVER DID GET INTO THE WAY YOU MOMMY THESE ANIMALS.
LET'S DROP THESE SLUGS.
NO WAY, TORK. I'VE ALWAYS BEEN STRAIGHT WITH THESE KIDS; I'VE NEVER ONCE BEEN UNFAIR TO THEM.
I'M NOT ABOUT TO START N...UGHNNN!
6

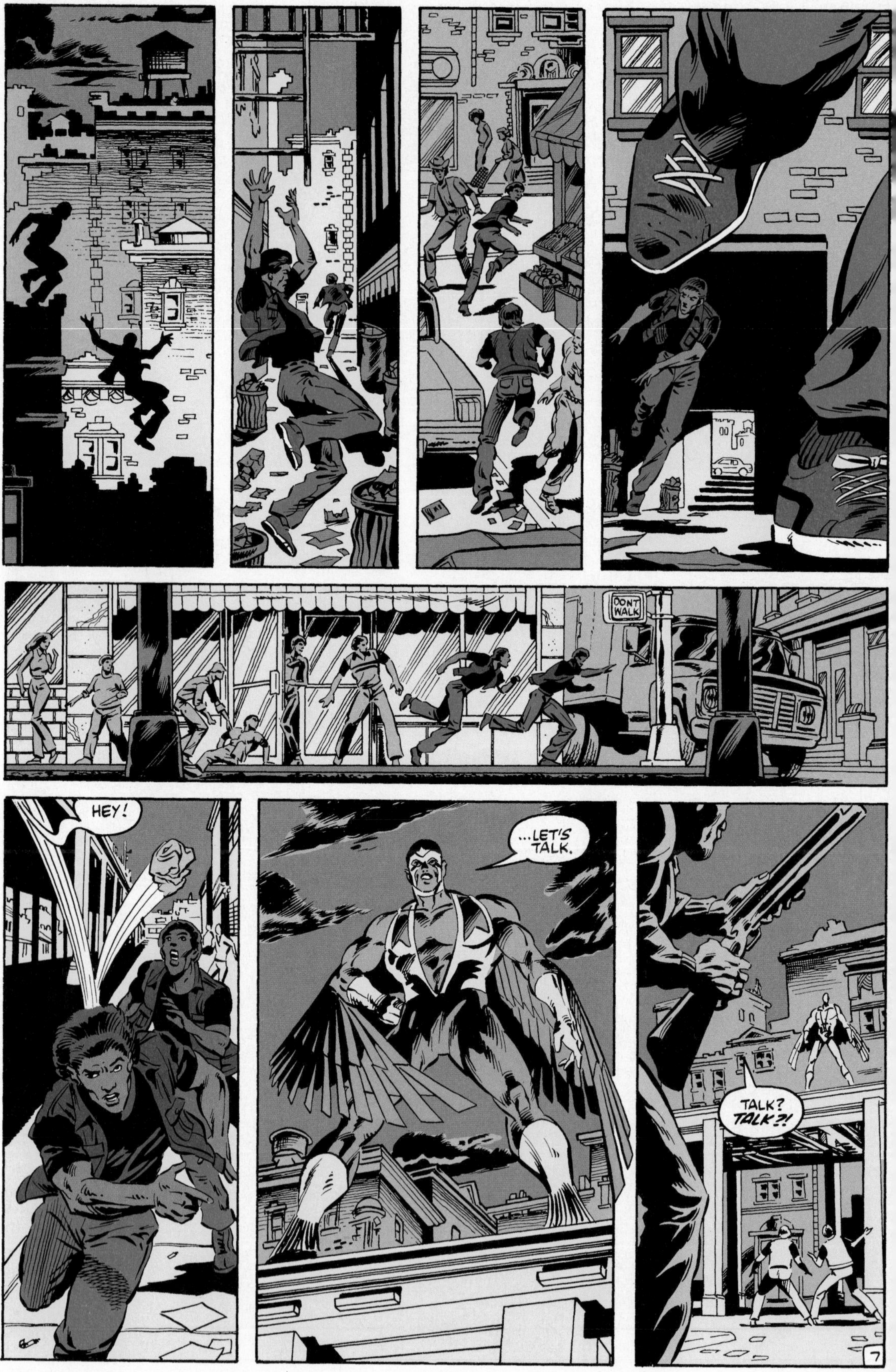

DONT WALK
HEY!
...LET'S TALK.
TALK? TALK?!
7

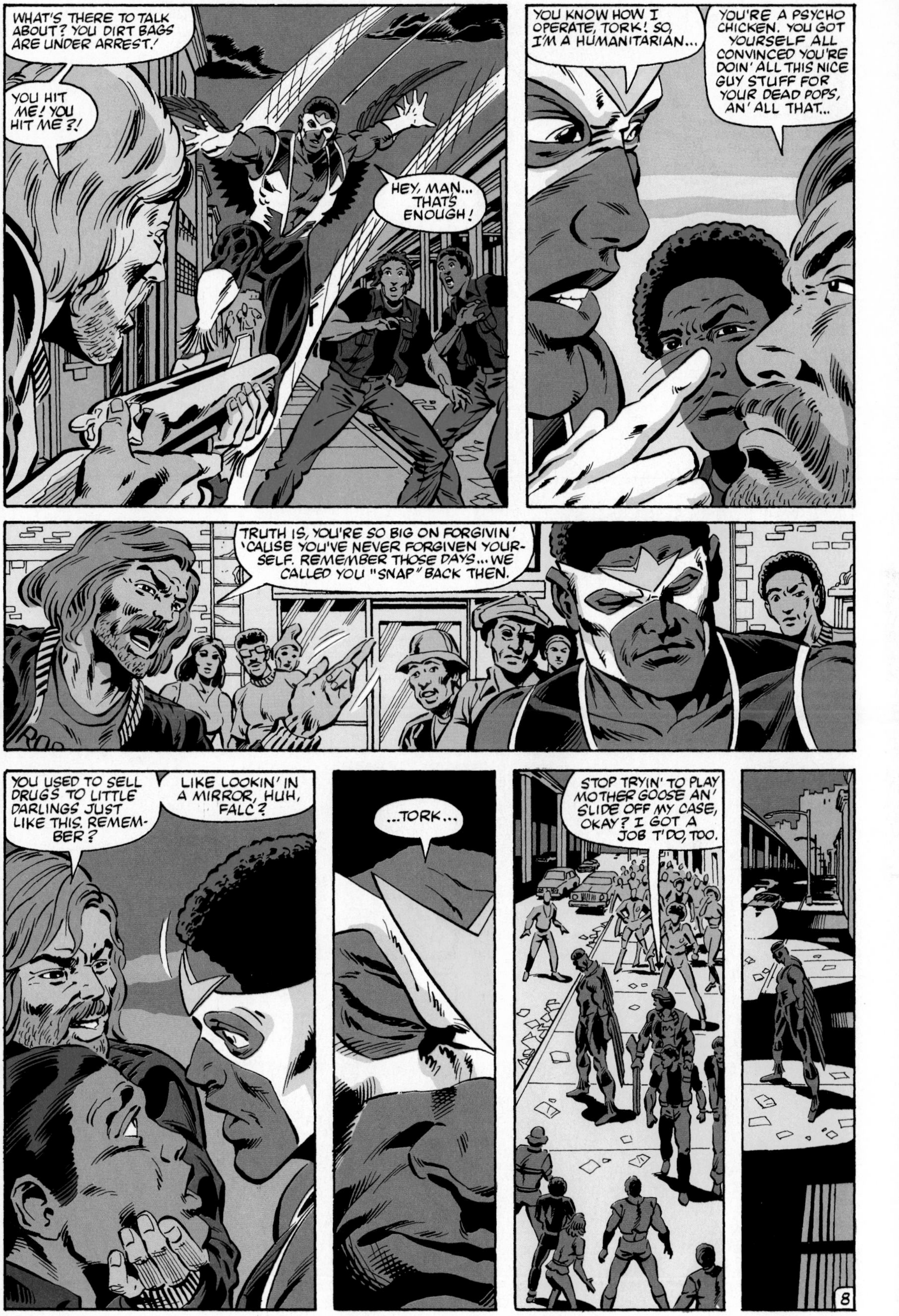
WHAT'S THERE TO TALK ABOUT? YOU DIRT BAGS ARE UNDER ARREST!
YOU HIT ME! YOU HIT ME?!
HEY, MAN... THAT'S ENOUGH!
YOU KNOW HOW I OPERATE, TORK! SO, I'M A HUMANITARIAN...
YOU'RE A PSYCHO CHICKEN. YOU GOT YOURSELF ALL CONVINCED YOU'RE DOIN' ALL THIS NICE GUY STUFF FOR YOUR DEAD POPS, AN' ALL THAT...
TRUTH IS, YOU'RE SO BIG ON FORGIVIN' 'CAUSE YOU'VE NEVER FORGIVEN YOURSELF. REMEMBER THOSE DAYS... WE CALLED YOU "SNAP" BACK THEN.
YOU USED TO SELL DRUGS TO LITTLE DARLINGS JUST LIKE THIS. REMEMBER?
LIKE LOOKIN' IN A MIRROR, HUH, FALC?
...TORK...
STOP TRYIN' TO PLAY MOTHER GOOSE AN' SLIDE OFF MY CASE, OKAY? I GOT A JOB T'DO, TOO.
8

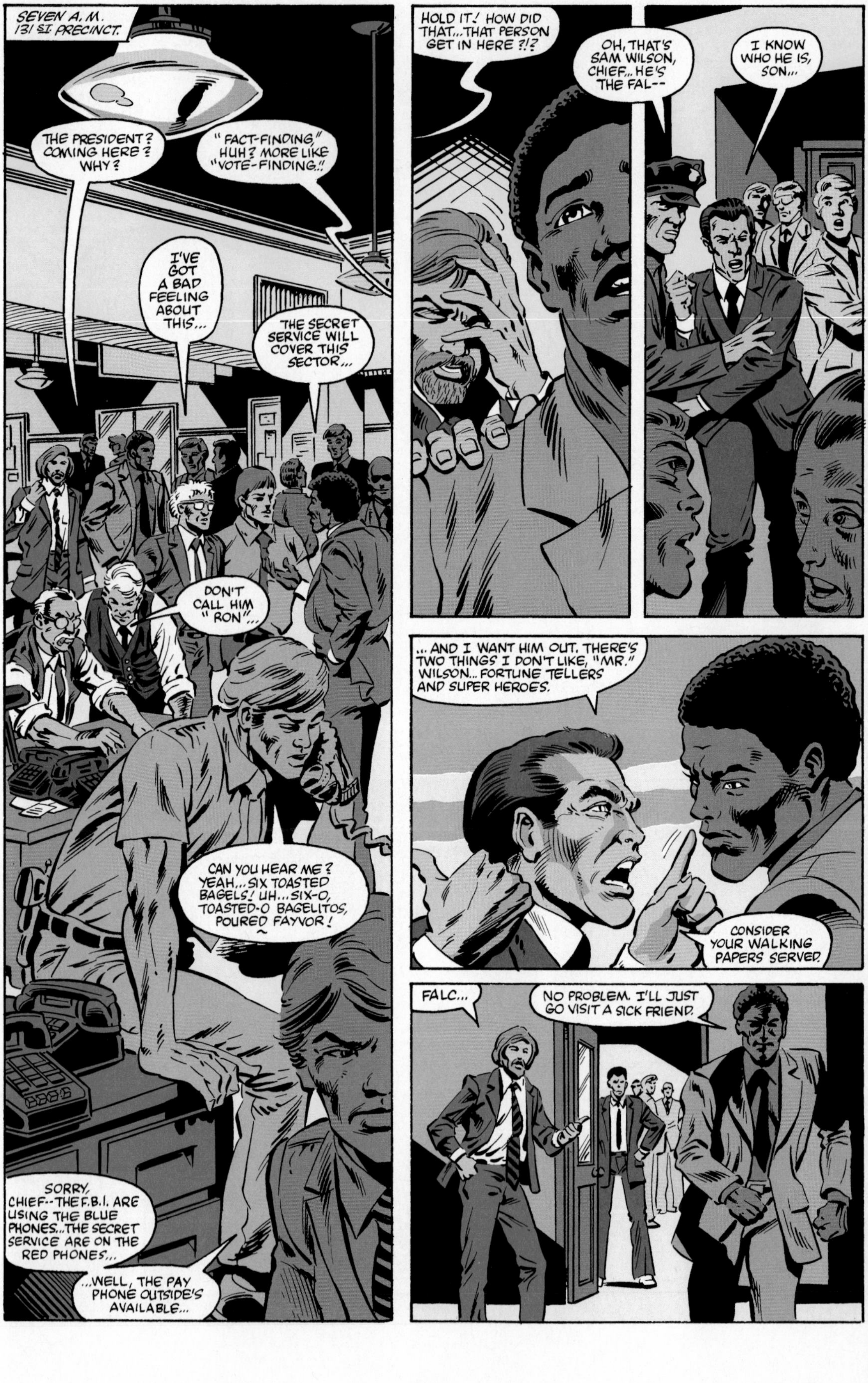
SEVEN A.M. 131 ST. PRECINCT.
THE PRESIDENT? COMING HERE? WHY?
"FACT-FINDING," HUH? MORE LIKE "VOTE-FINDING."
I'VE GOT A BAD FEELING ABOUT THIS...
THE SECRET SERVICE WILL COVER THIS SECTOR...
DON'T CALL HIM "RON"...
CAN YOU HEAR ME? YEAH... SIX TOASTED BAGELS! UH... SIX-O, TOASTED-O BAGELITOS, POURED FAYVOR!
SORRY, CHIEF--THE F.B.I. ARE USING THE BLUE PHONES... THE SECRET SERVICE ARE ON THE RED PHONES...
...WELL, THE PAY PHONE OUTSIDE'S AVAILABLE...
HOLD IT! HOW DID THAT... THAT PERSON GET IN HERE?!?
OH, THAT'S SAM WILSON, CHIEF... HE'S THE FAL--
I KNOW WHO HE IS, SON...
...AND I WANT HIM OUT. THERE'S TWO THINGS I DON'T LIKE, "MR." WILSON... FORTUNE TELLERS AND SUPER HEROES.
CONSIDER YOUR WALKING PAPERS SERVED.
FALC...
NO PROBLEM. I'LL JUST GO VISIT A SICK FRIEND.

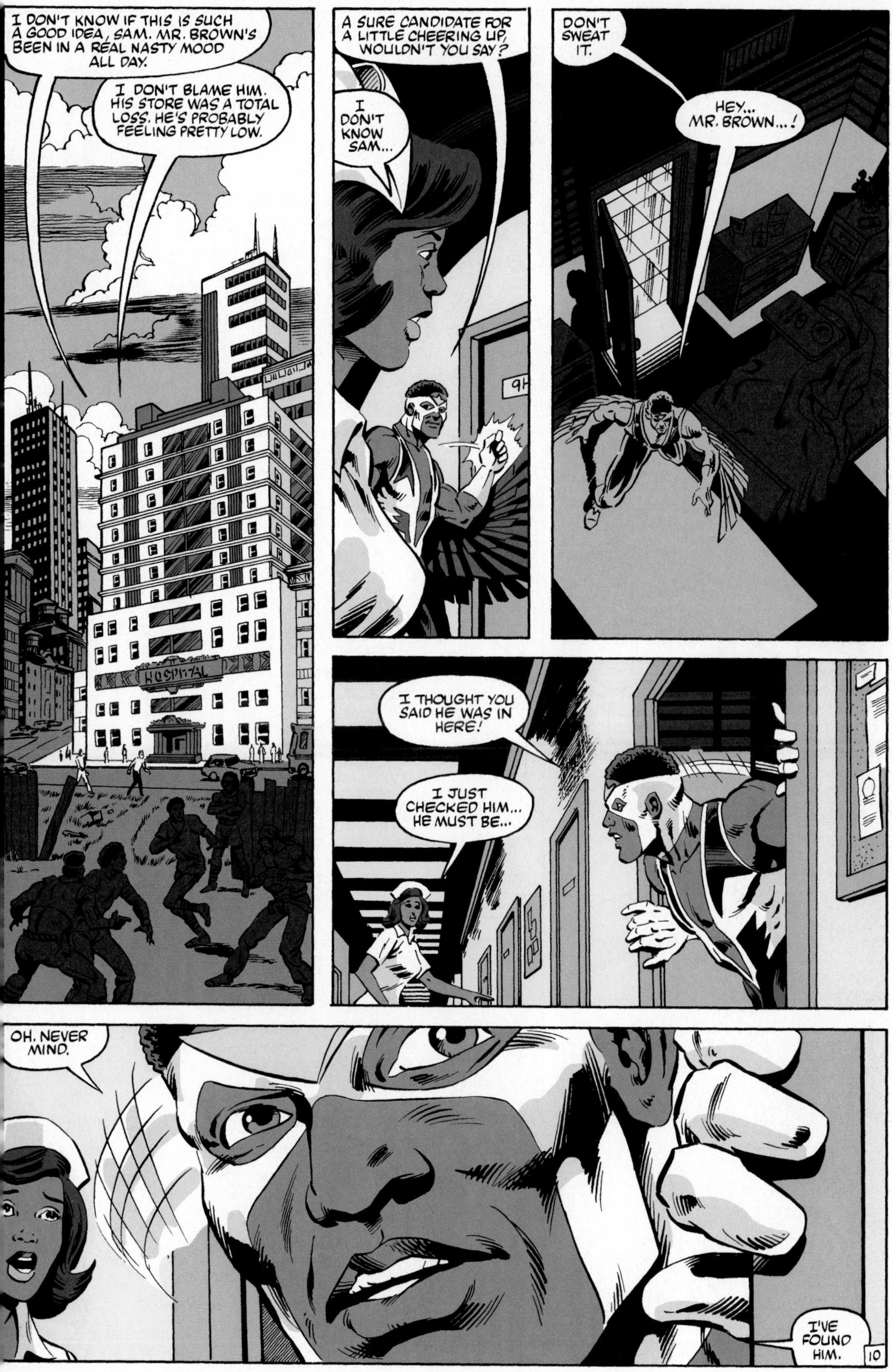

I DON'T KNOW IF THIS IS SUCH A GOOD IDEA, SAM. MR. BROWN'S BEEN IN A REAL NASTY MOOD ALL DAY.
I DON'T BLAME HIM. HIS STORE WAS A TOTAL LOSS. HE'S PROBABLY FEELING PRETTY LOW.
HOSPITAL
A SURE CANDIDATE FOR A LITTLE CHEERING UP, WOULDN'T YOU SAY?
I DON'T KNOW SAM...
DON'T SWEAT IT.
HEY... MR. BROWN...!
I THOUGHT YOU SAID HE WAS IN HERE!
I JUST CHECKED HIM... HE MUST BE...
OH. NEVER MIND.
I'VE FOUND HIM.
10

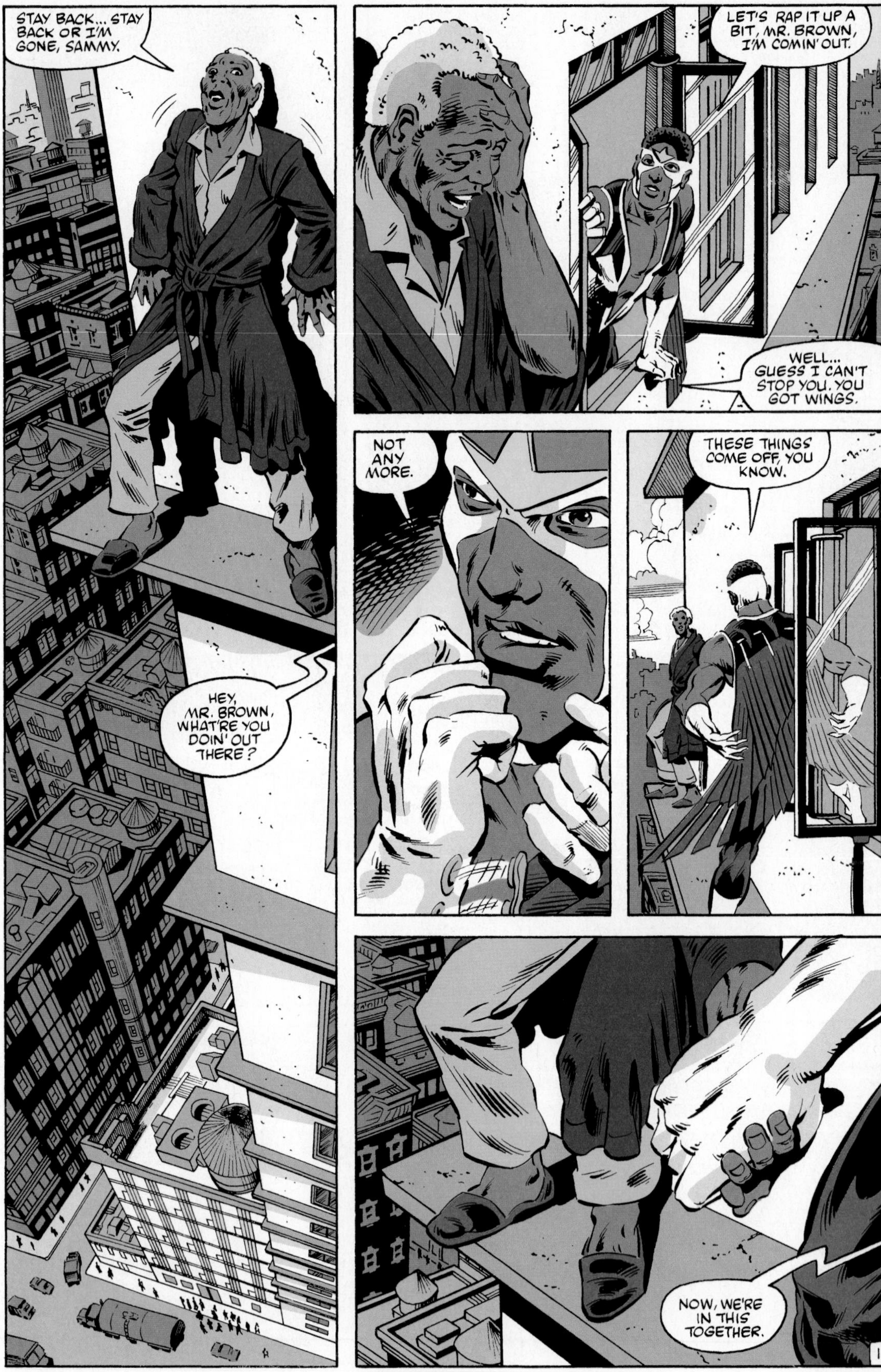
STAY BACK... STAY BACK OR I'M GONE, SAMMY.
HEY, MR. BROWN, WHAT'RE YOU DOIN' OUT THERE?
LET'S RAP IT UP A BIT, MR. BROWN, I'M COMIN' OUT.
WELL... GUESS I CAN'T STOP YOU. YOU GOT WINGS.
NOT ANY MORE.
THESE THINGS COME OFF, YOU KNOW.
NOW, WE'RE IN THIS TOGETHER.
11

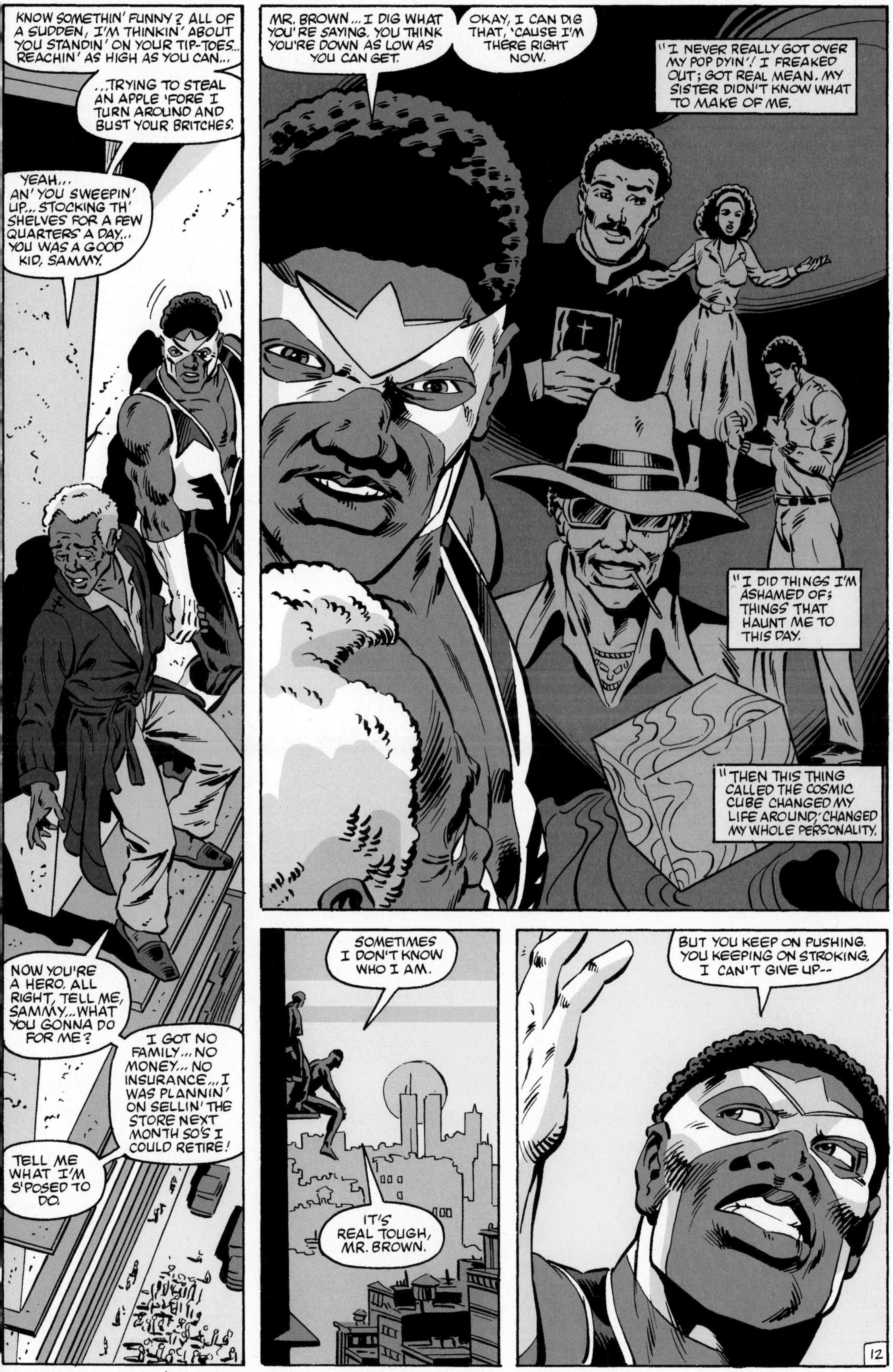
KNOW SOMETHIN' FUNNY? ALL OF A SUDDEN, I'M THINKIN' ABOUT YOU STANDIN' ON YOUR TIP-TOES... REACHIN' AS HIGH AS YOU CAN...
...TRYING TO STEAL AN APPLE 'FORE I TURN AROUND AND BUST YOUR BRITCHES.
YEAH... AN' YOU SWEEPIN' UP... STOCKING TH' SHELVES FOR A FEW QUARTERS A DAY... YOU WAS A GOOD KID, SAMMY.
NOW YOU'RE A HERO. ALL RIGHT, TELL ME, SAMMY... WHAT YOU GONNA DO FOR ME?
I GOT NO FAMILY... NO MONEY... NO INSURANCE... I WAS PLANNIN' ON SELLIN' THE STORE NEXT MONTH SO'S I COULD RETIRE!
TELL ME WHAT I'M S'POSED TO DO.
MR. BROWN... I DIG WHAT YOU'RE SAYING. YOU THINK YOU'RE DOWN AS LOW AS YOU CAN GET.
OKAY, I CAN DIG THAT, 'CAUSE I'M THERE RIGHT NOW.
"I NEVER REALLY GOT OVER MY POP DYIN'. I FREAKED OUT; GOT REAL MEAN. MY SISTER DIDN'T KNOW WHAT TO MAKE OF ME.
"I DID THINGS I'M ASHAMED OF; THINGS THAT HAUNT ME TO THIS DAY.
"THEN THIS THING CALLED THE COSMIC CUBE CHANGED MY LIFE AROUND; CHANGED MY WHOLE PERSONALITY.
SOMETIMES I DON'T KNOW WHO I AM.
IT'S REAL TOUGH, MR. BROWN.
BUT YOU KEEP ON PUSHING. YOU KEEPING ON STROKING. I CAN'T GIVE UP--
12

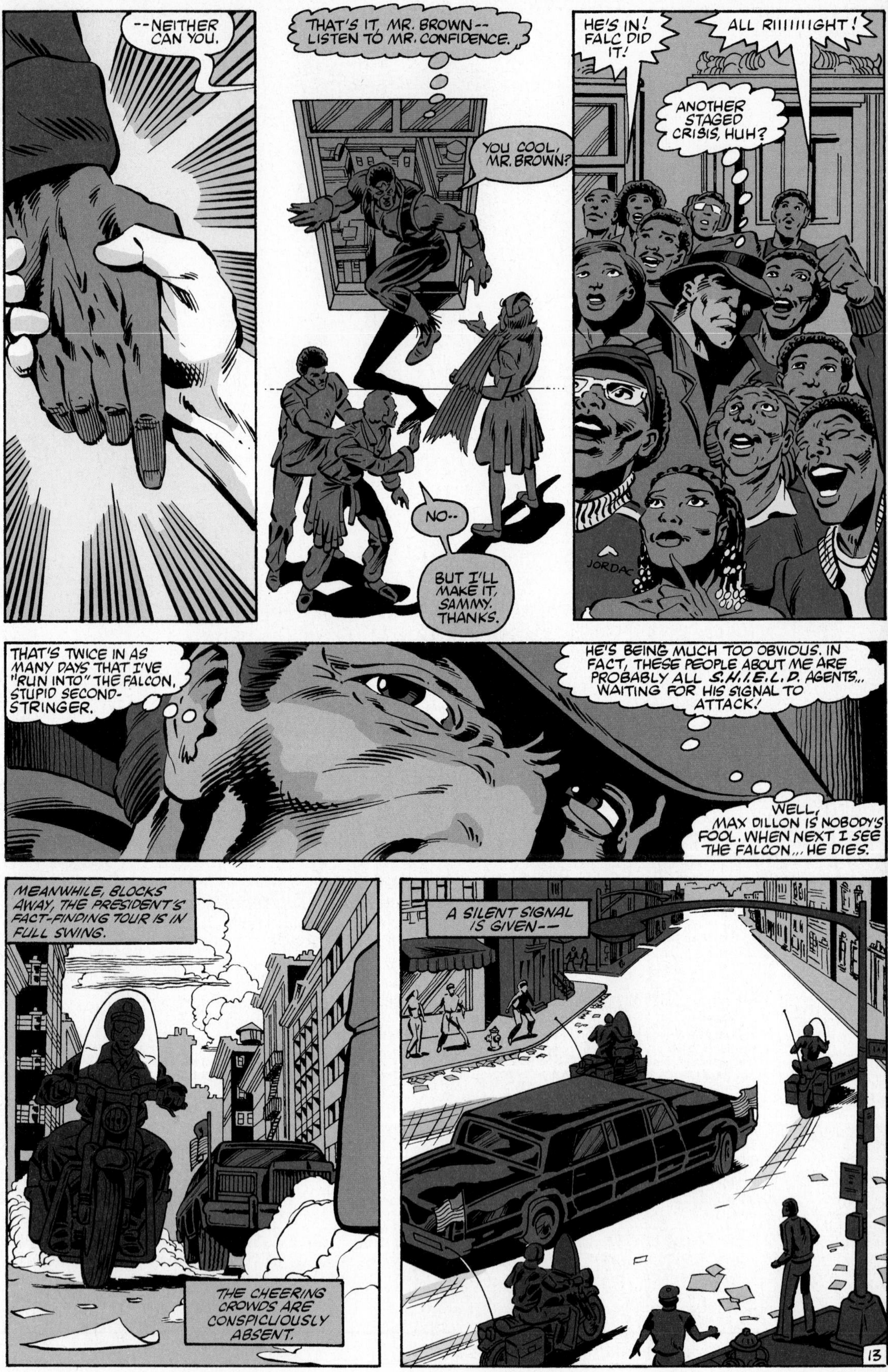
--NEITHER CAN YOU.
THAT'S IT, MR. BROWN-- LISTEN TO MR. CONFIDENCE.
YOU COOL, MR. BROWN?
NO--
BUT I'LL MAKE IT, SAMMY. THANKS.
HE'S IN! FALC DID IT!
ALL RIIIIIIIGHT!
ANOTHER STAGED CRISIS, HUH?
THAT'S TWICE IN AS MANY DAYS THAT I'VE "RUN INTO" THE FALCON, STUPID SECOND-STRINGER.
HE'S BEING MUCH TOO OBVIOUS. IN FACT, THESE PEOPLE ABOUT ME ARE PROBABLY ALL S.H.I.E.L.D. AGENTS... WAITING FOR HIS SIGNAL TO ATTACK!
WELL, MAX DILLON IS NOBODY'S FOOL. WHEN NEXT I SEE THE FALCON... HE DIES.
MEANWHILE, BLOCKS AWAY, THE PRESIDENT'S FACT-FINDING TOUR IS IN FULL SWING.
THE CHEERING CROWDS ARE CONSPICUOUSLY ABSENT.
A SILENT SIGNAL IS GIVEN--
13

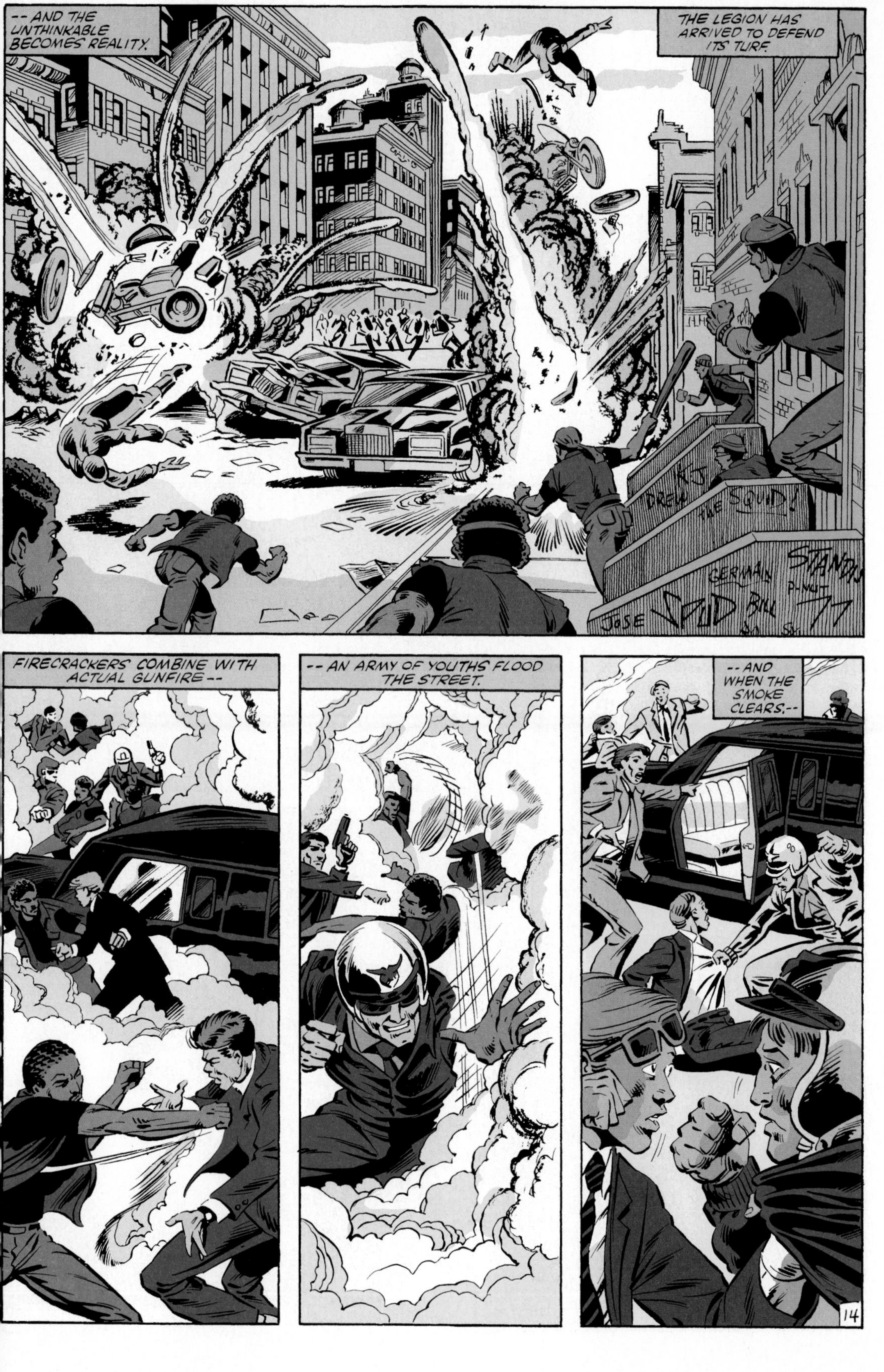
--AND THE UNTHINKABLE BECOMES REALITY.
THE LEGION HAS ARRIVED TO DEFEND ITS TURF.
FIRECRACKERS COMBINE WITH ACTUAL GUNFIRE--
--AN ARMY OF YOUTHS FLOOD THE STREET.
--AND WHEN THE SMOKE CLEARS.--
14

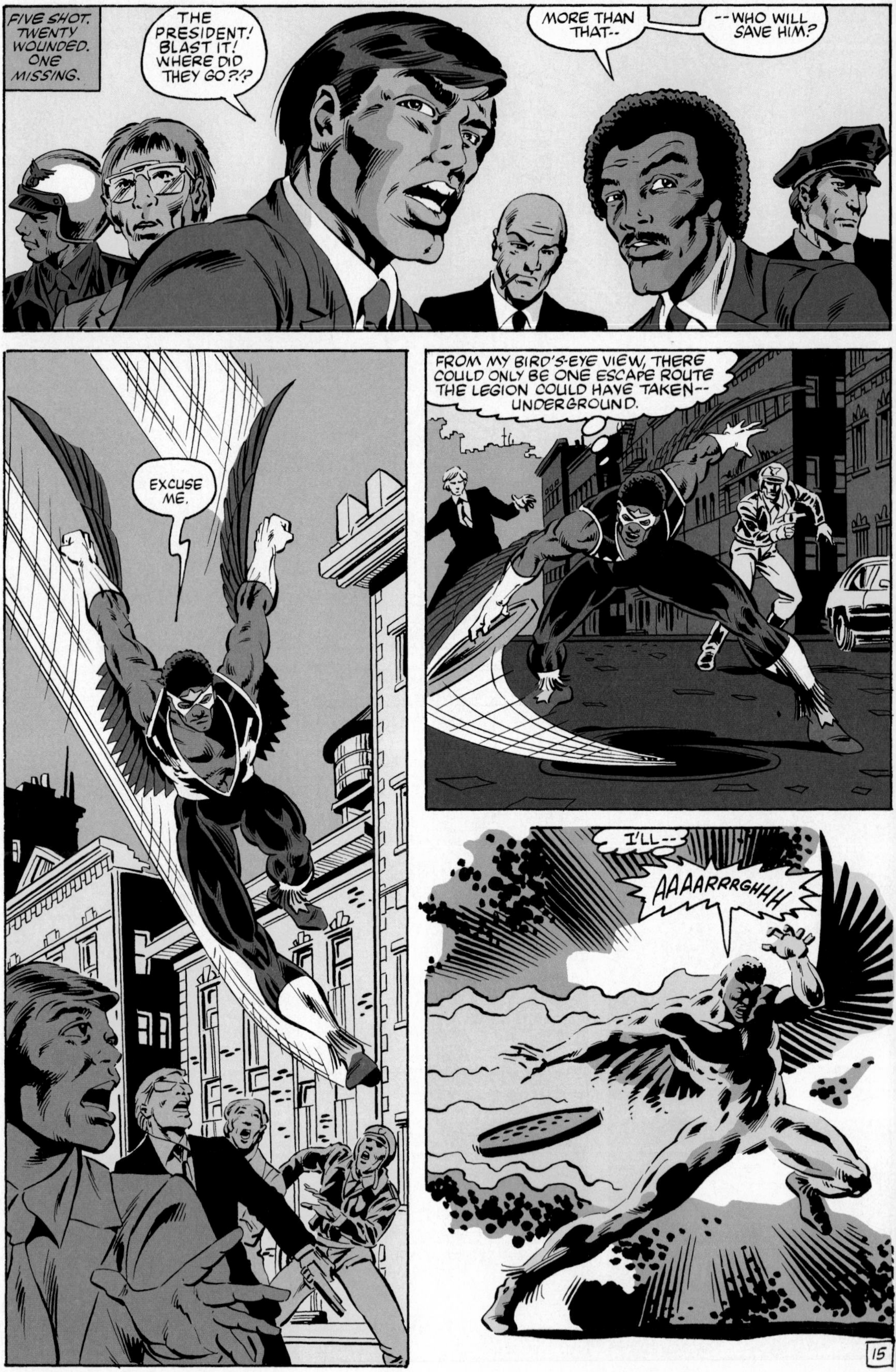
FIVE SHOT. TWENTY WOUNDED. ONE MISSING.
THE PRESIDENT! BLAST IT! WHERE DID THEY GO?!?
MORE THAN THAT--
--WHO WILL SAVE HIM?
EXCUSE ME.
FROM MY BIRD'S-EYE VIEW, THERE COULD ONLY BE ONE ESCAPE ROUTE THE LEGION COULD HAVE TAKEN-- UNDERGROUND.
I'LL--
AAAARRRGHHH
15

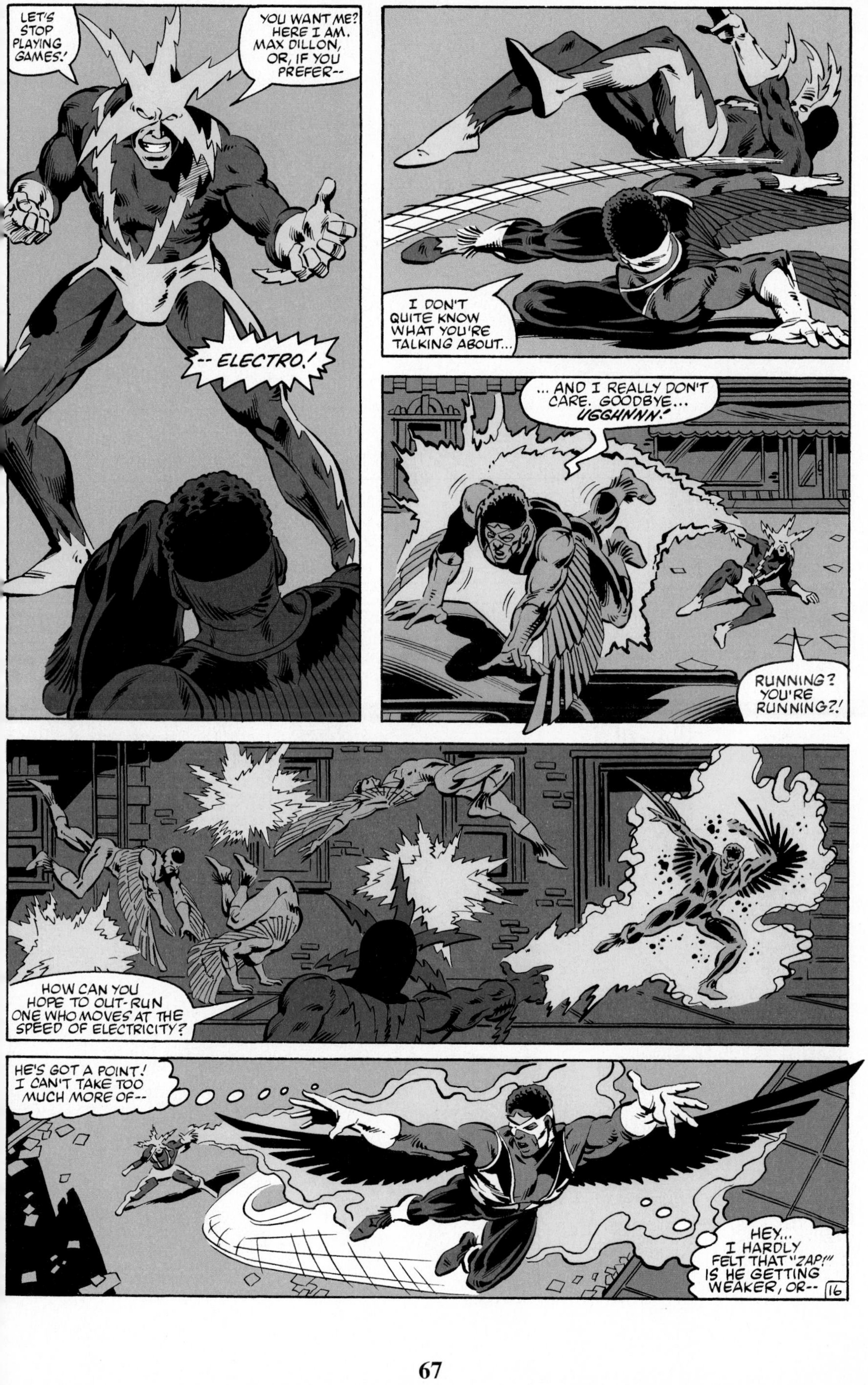
LET'S STOP PLAYING GAMES!
YOU WANT ME? HERE I AM. MAX DILLON, OR, IF YOU PREFER--
-- ELECTRO!
I DON'T QUITE KNOW WHAT YOU'RE TALKING ABOUT...
... AND I REALLY DON'T CARE. GOODBYE... UGGHNNN!
RUNNING? YOU'RE RUNNING?!
HOW CAN YOU HOPE TO OUT-RUN ONE WHO MOVES AT THE SPEED OF ELECTRICITY?
HE'S GOT A POINT! I CAN'T TAKE TOO MUCH MORE OF--
HEY... I HARDLY FELT THAT "ZAP!" IS HE GETTING WEAKER, OR--
16

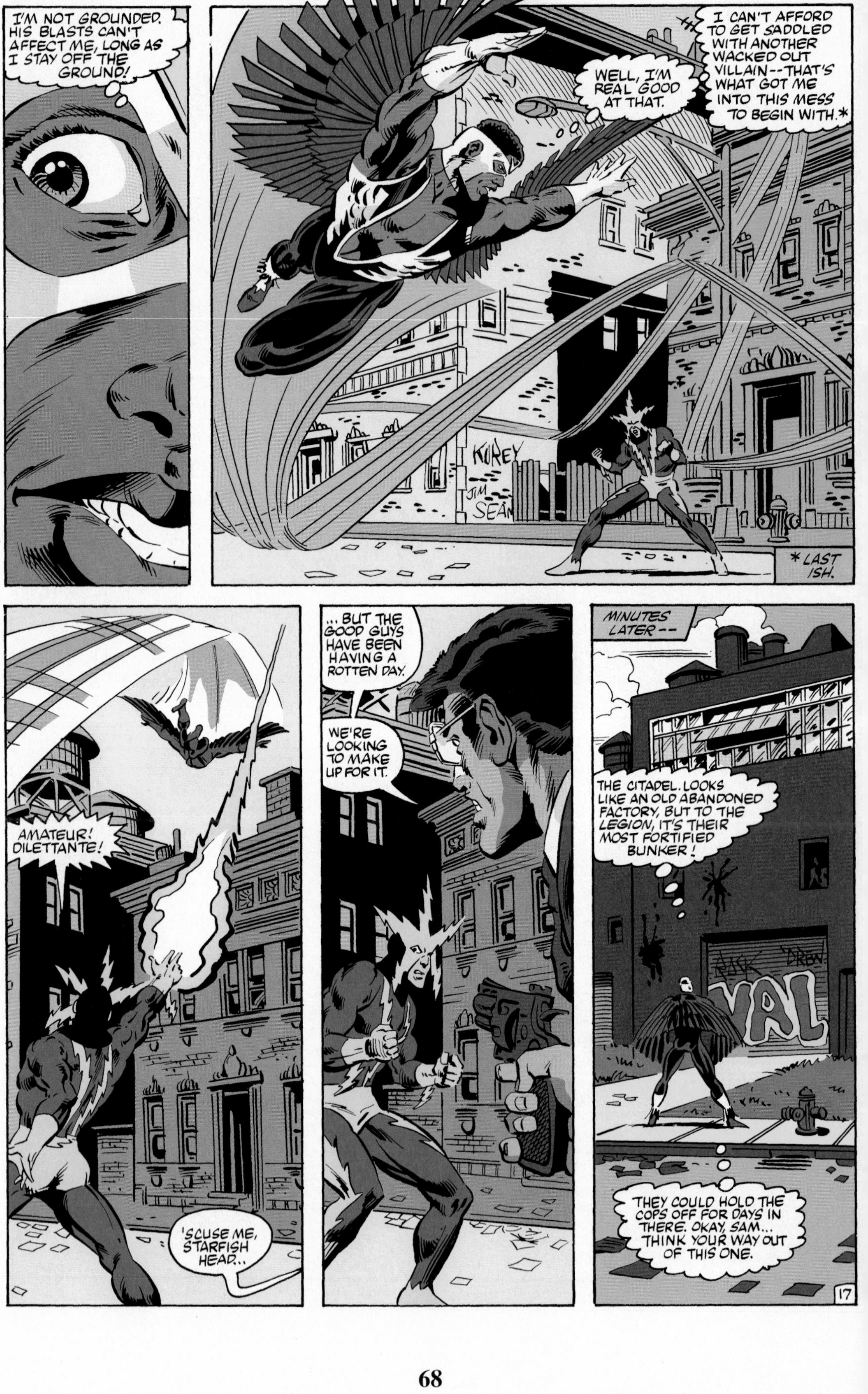

I'M NOT GROUNDED. HIS BLASTS CAN'T AFFECT ME, LONG AS I STAY OFF THE GROUND!
WELL, I'M REAL GOOD AT THAT.
I CAN'T AFFORD TO GET SADDLED WITH ANOTHER WACKED OUT VILLAIN--THAT'S WHAT GOT ME INTO THIS MESS TO BEGIN WITH.*
KOREY
JIM
SEAN
*LAST ISH.
AMATEUR! DILETTANTE!
'SCUSE ME, STARFISH HEAD...
...BUT THE GOOD GUYS HAVE BEEN HAVING A ROTTEN DAY.
WE'RE LOOKING TO MAKE UP FOR IT.
MINUTES LATER--
THE CITADEL. LOOKS LIKE AN OLD ABANDONED FACTORY, BUT TO THE LEGION, IT'S THEIR MOST FORTIFIED BUNKER!
DREW
VAL
THEY COULD HOLD THE COPS OFF FOR DAYS IN THERE. OKAY, SAM... THINK YOUR WAY OUT OF THIS ONE.
17

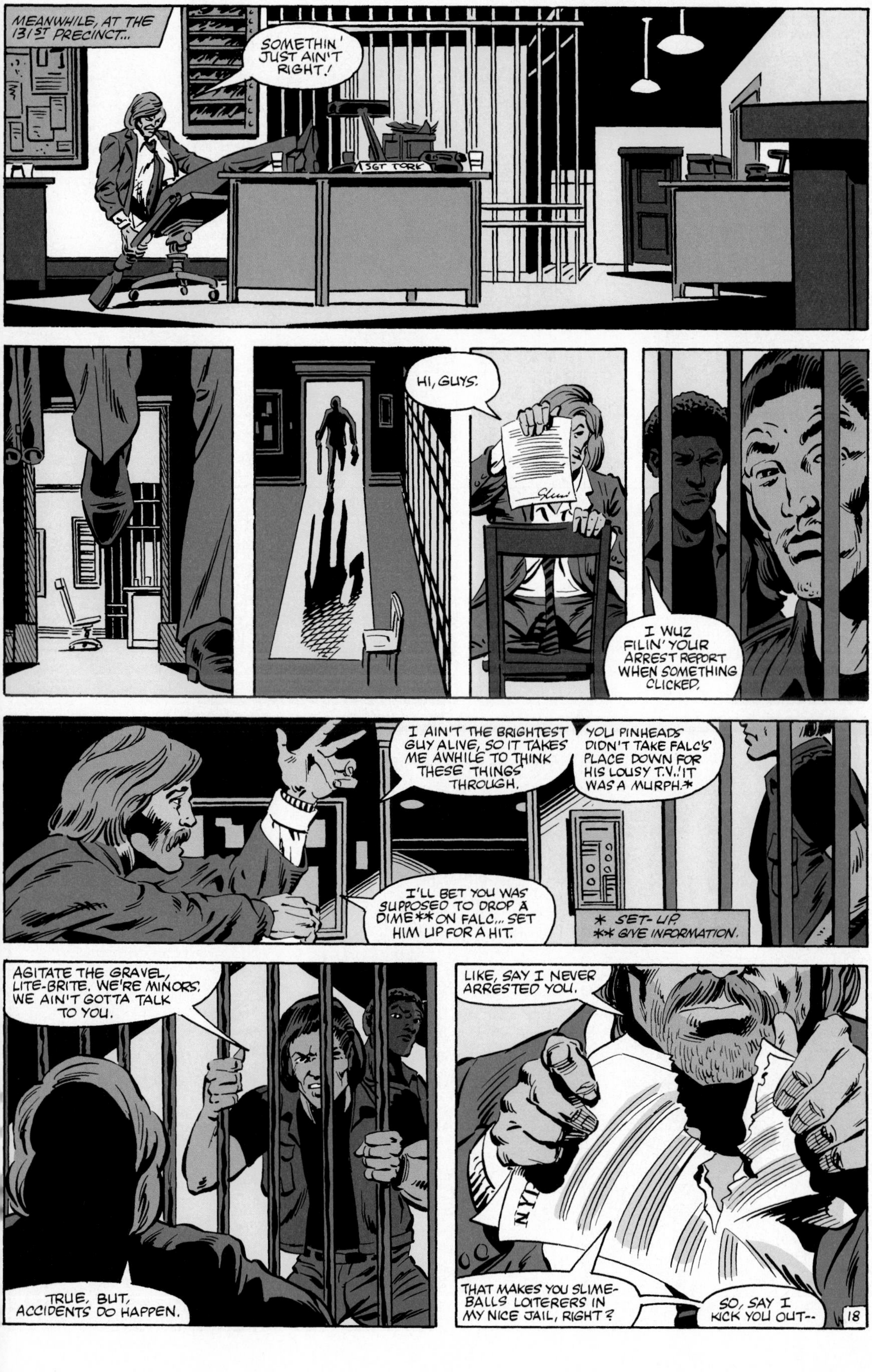
MEANWHILE, AT THE 131ST PRECINCT...
SOMETHIN' JUST AIN'T RIGHT!
SGT TORK
HI, GUYS.
I WUZ FILIN' YOUR ARREST REPORT WHEN SOMETHING CLICKED.
I AIN'T THE BRIGHTEST GUY ALIVE, SO IT TAKES ME AWHILE TO THINK THESE THINGS THROUGH.
YOU PINHEADS DIDN'T TAKE FALC'S PLACE DOWN FOR HIS LOUSY T.V.! IT WAS A MURPH.*
I'LL BET YOU WAS SUPPOSED TO DROP A DIME** ON FALC... SET HIM UP FOR A HIT.
* SET-UP.
** GIVE INFORMATION.
AGITATE THE GRAVEL, LITE-BRITE. WE'RE MINORS. WE AIN'T GOTTA TALK TO YOU.
TRUE, BUT, ACCIDENTS DO HAPPEN.
LIKE, SAY I NEVER ARRESTED YOU.
THAT MAKES YOU SLIME-BALLS LOITERERS IN MY NICE JAIL, RIGHT?
SO, SAY I KICK YOU OUT--
18

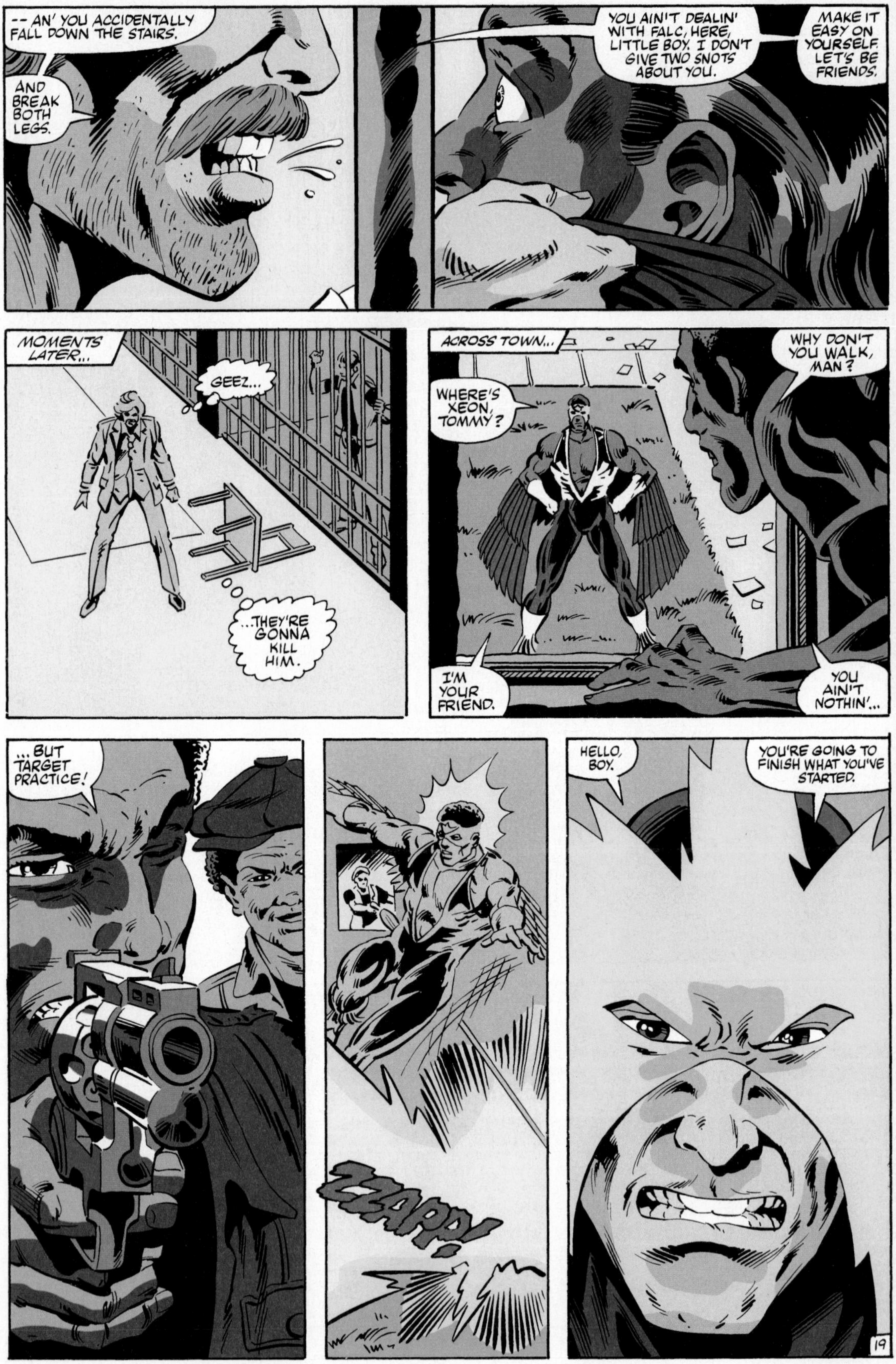
-- AN' YOU ACCIDENTALLY FALL DOWN THE STAIRS.
AND BREAK BOTH LEGS.
YOU AIN'T DEALIN' WITH FALC, HERE, LITTLE BOY. I DON'T GIVE TWO SNOTS ABOUT YOU.
MAKE IT EASY ON YOURSELF. LET'S BE FRIENDS.
MOMENTS LATER...
GEEZ...
...THEY'RE GONNA KILL HIM.
ACROSS TOWN...
WHERE'S XEON, TOMMY?
WHY DON'T YOU WALK, MAN?
I'M YOUR FRIEND.
YOU AIN'T NOTHIN'...
... BUT TARGET PRACTICE!
ZZAPP!
HELLO, BOY.
YOU'RE GOING TO FINISH WHAT YOU'VE STARTED.
19

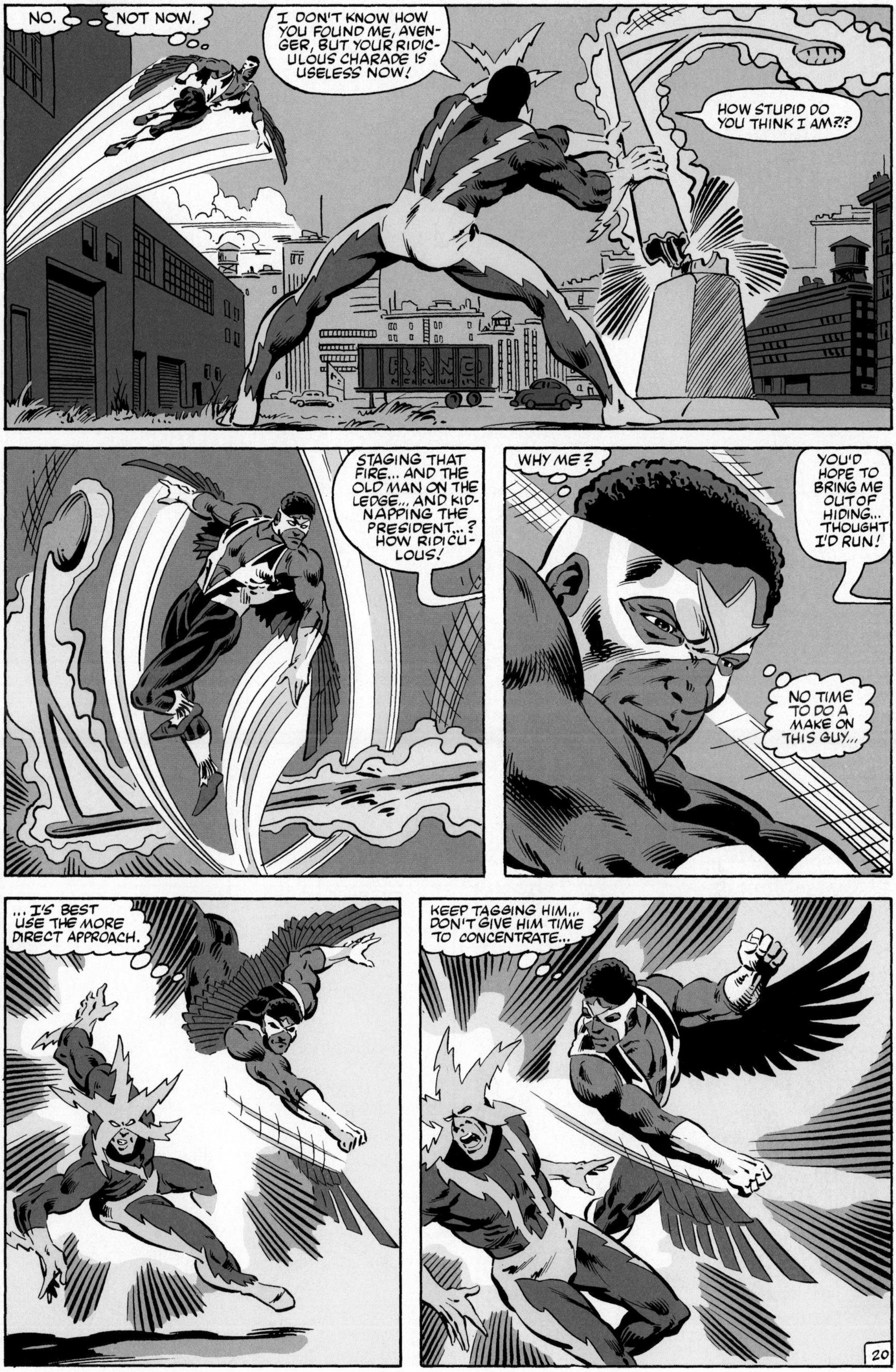
NO. NOT NOW.
I DON'T KNOW HOW YOU FOUND ME, AVENGER, BUT YOUR RIDICULOUS CHARADE IS USELESS NOW!
HOW STUPID DO YOU THINK I AM?!?
STAGING THAT FIRE... AND THE OLD MAN ON THE LEDGE... AND KIDNAPPING THE PRESIDENT...? HOW RIDICULOUS!
WHY ME?
YOU'D HOPE TO BRING ME OUT OF HIDING... THOUGHT I'D RUN!
NO TIME TO DO A MAKE ON THIS GUY...
...I'S BEST USE THE MORE DIRECT APPROACH.
KEEP TAGGING HIM... DON'T GIVE HIM TIME TO CONCENTRATE...
20

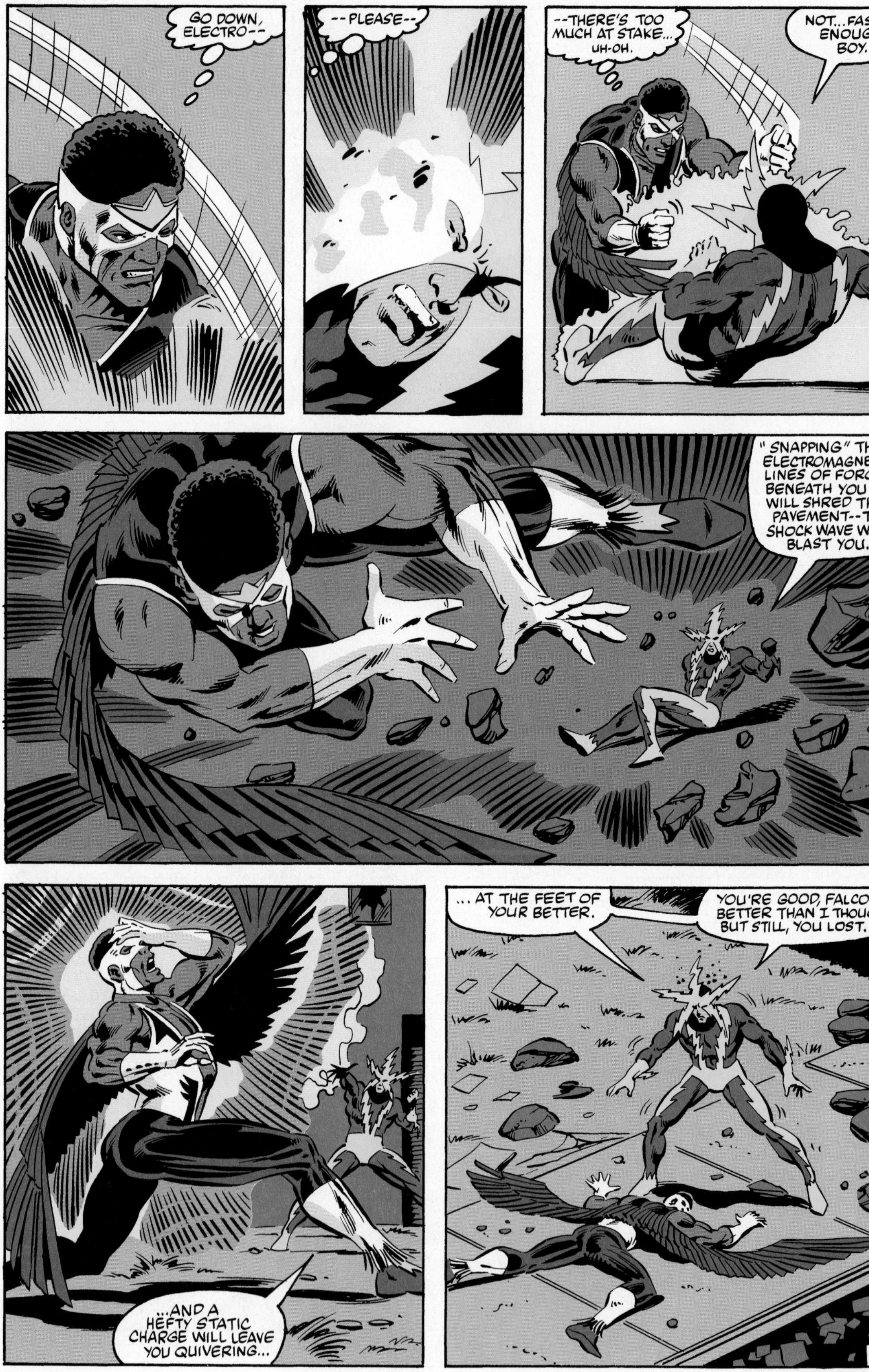
GO DOWN, ELECTRO--
--PLEASE--
--THERE'S TOO MUCH AT STAKE... UH-OH.
NOT...FAST ENOUGH... BOY.
"SNAPPING" THE ELECTROMAGNETIC LINES OF FORCE BENEATH YOU WILL SHRED THE PAVEMENT--THE SHOCK WAVE WILL BLAST YOU...
...AND A HEFTY STATIC CHARGE WILL LEAVE YOU QUIVERING...
... AT THE FEET OF YOUR BETTER.
YOU'RE GOOD, FALCON. BETTER THAN I THOUGHT. BUT STILL, YOU LOST.
21

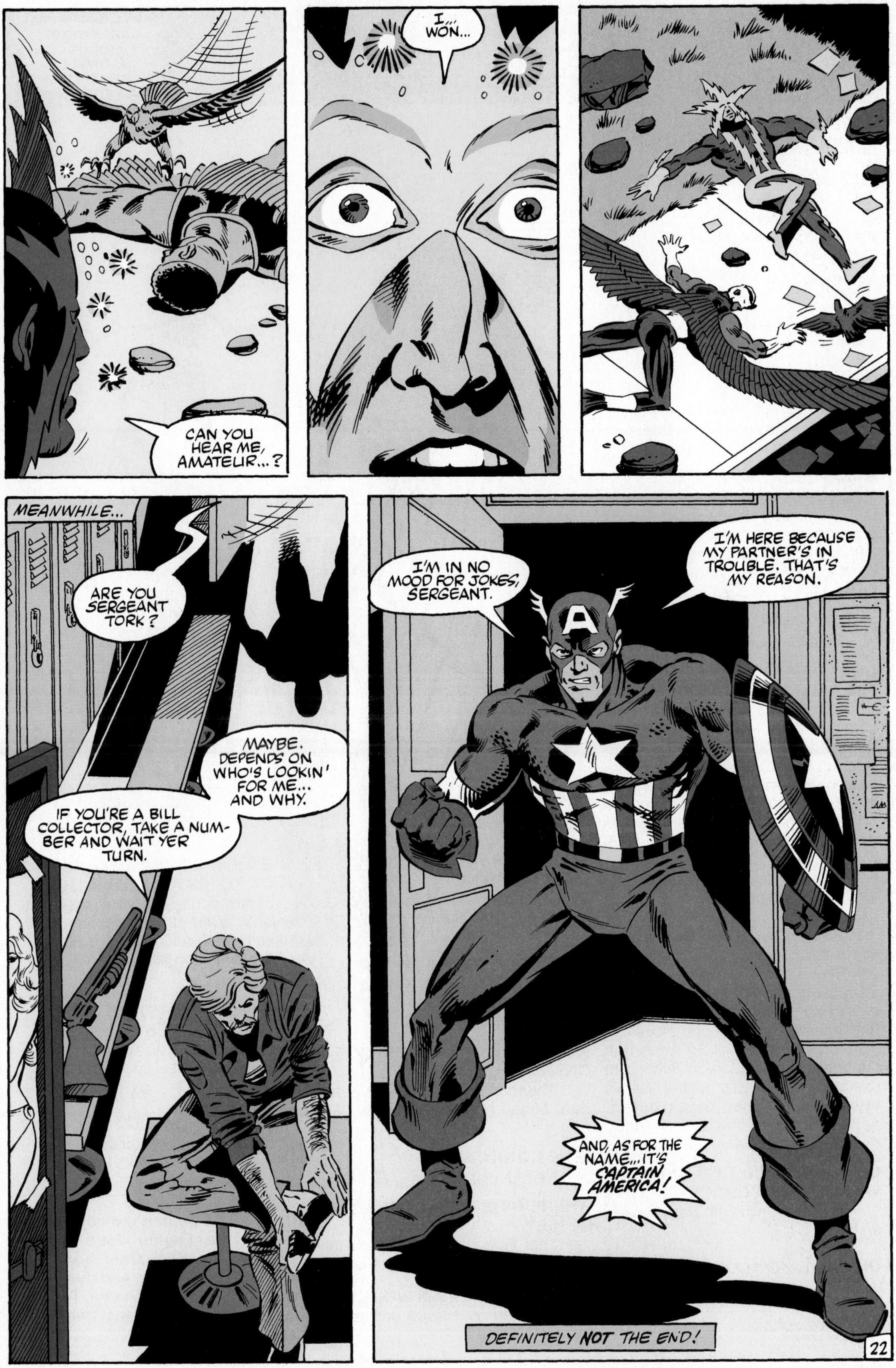
CAN YOU HEAR ME, AMATEUR...?
I... WON...
MEANWHILE...
ARE YOU SERGEANT TORK?
MAYBE. DEPENDS ON WHO'S LOOKIN' FOR ME... AND WHY.
IF YOU'RE A BILL COLLECTOR, TAKE A NUMBER AND WAIT YER TURN.
I'M IN NO MOOD FOR JOKES, SERGEANT.
I'M HERE BECAUSE MY PARTNER'S IN TROUBLE. THAT'S MY REASON.
AND, AS FOR THE NAME... IT'S CAPTAIN AMERICA!
DEFINITELY NOT THE END!
22

CRIB NOTES

% MARVEL COMICS GROUP
387 Park Avenue South
New York, New York 10016

LARRY HAMA
EDITOR
JIM OWSLEY
ASSISTANT EDITOR

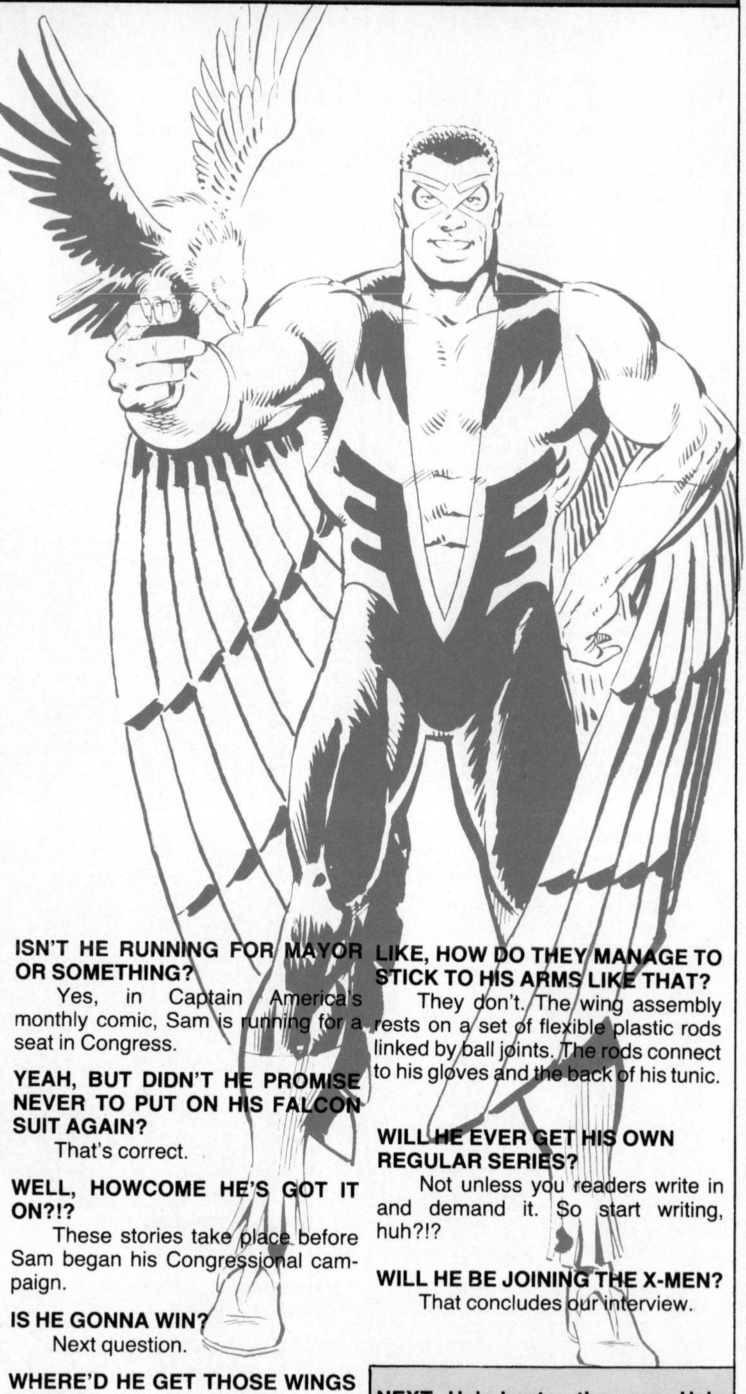

EVERYTHING YOU WANTED TO KNOW ABOUT THE FALCON:

LIKE, HOWCOME EVERYBODY CALLS HIM "SAM"?

The Falcon's secret identity – that of social worker Sam Wilson – is public record.

YEAH? WHY?

Due to the well-publicized trial for his past offenses as "Snap" Wilson, the Falcon's secret identity was revealed.

HUH?

Prior to his becoming the Falcon, Sam was a small-time racketeer who called himself "Snap" Wilson.

RACKETEER? WHAT'S A RACKETEER?

"Racketeer" is a word they used to use to describe undesireable characters who were into illegal business dealings. Like running numbers. Like drugs. Like "protection" operations.

YOU MEAN, HE WAS A CROOK.

Something like that.

OKAY, SO HOW'D HE GET TO BE THE FALCON?

Sam, or "Snap", was en route from a mob assignment in Rio, when his plane crashed on a Caribbean island run by the Exiles, a group of professional killers who were working for the Red Skull. The Skull used the powers of the cosmic cube to evolve Sam's psionic link with his bird, Redwing, and change Sam's entire personna around to make him appealing to Captain America, whom the Skull had imprisoned on the island. Cap met Sam, and eventually trained Sam as his partner. It was much later that the Skull's true rationale for using Sam came to light; in a subsequent battle with Captain America, the Skull forced the Falcon, through a cosmic-cube-created mindlink, to aid him in his battle against Cap. In fighting to overcome the Skull's control, Sam's memory of his "Snap" days returned, and he confessed that he was indeed this "Snap" Wilson.

BUT, DIDN'T YOU JUST SAY SNAP WILSON WAS A CROOK?

Yes, that's why the Falcon went on trial.

OH. WELL, HOWCOME HE ISN'T IN JAIL?

He was released in Captain America's custody.

ISN'T HE RUNNING FOR MAYOR OR SOMETHING?

Yes, in Captain America's monthly comic, Sam is running for a seat in Congress.

YEAH, BUT DIDN'T HE PROMISE NEVER TO PUT ON HIS FALCON SUIT AGAIN?

That's correct.

WELL, HOWCOME HE'S GOT IT ON?!?

These stories take place before Sam began his Congressional campaign.

IS HE GONNA WIN?

Next question.

WHERE'D HE GET THOSE WINGS OF HIS?

The Falcon's wings were designed and built by the Black Panther.

HOW DO THE WINGS WORK?

Buy the next issue and see for yourself.

LIKE, HOW DO THEY MANAGE TO STICK TO HIS ARMS LIKE THAT?

They don't. The wing assembly rests on a set of flexible plastic rods linked by ball joints. The rods connect to his gloves and the back of his tunic.

WILL HE EVER GET HIS OWN REGULAR SERIES?

Not unless you readers write in and demand it. So start writing, huh?!?

WILL HE BE JOINING THE X-MEN?

That concludes our interview.

NEXT: He's beaten the cops. He's beaten the Legion. He's beaten Captain America. Only one man stands between him and the president of the United States. Electro vs. the Falcon. The Final battle. Be here.

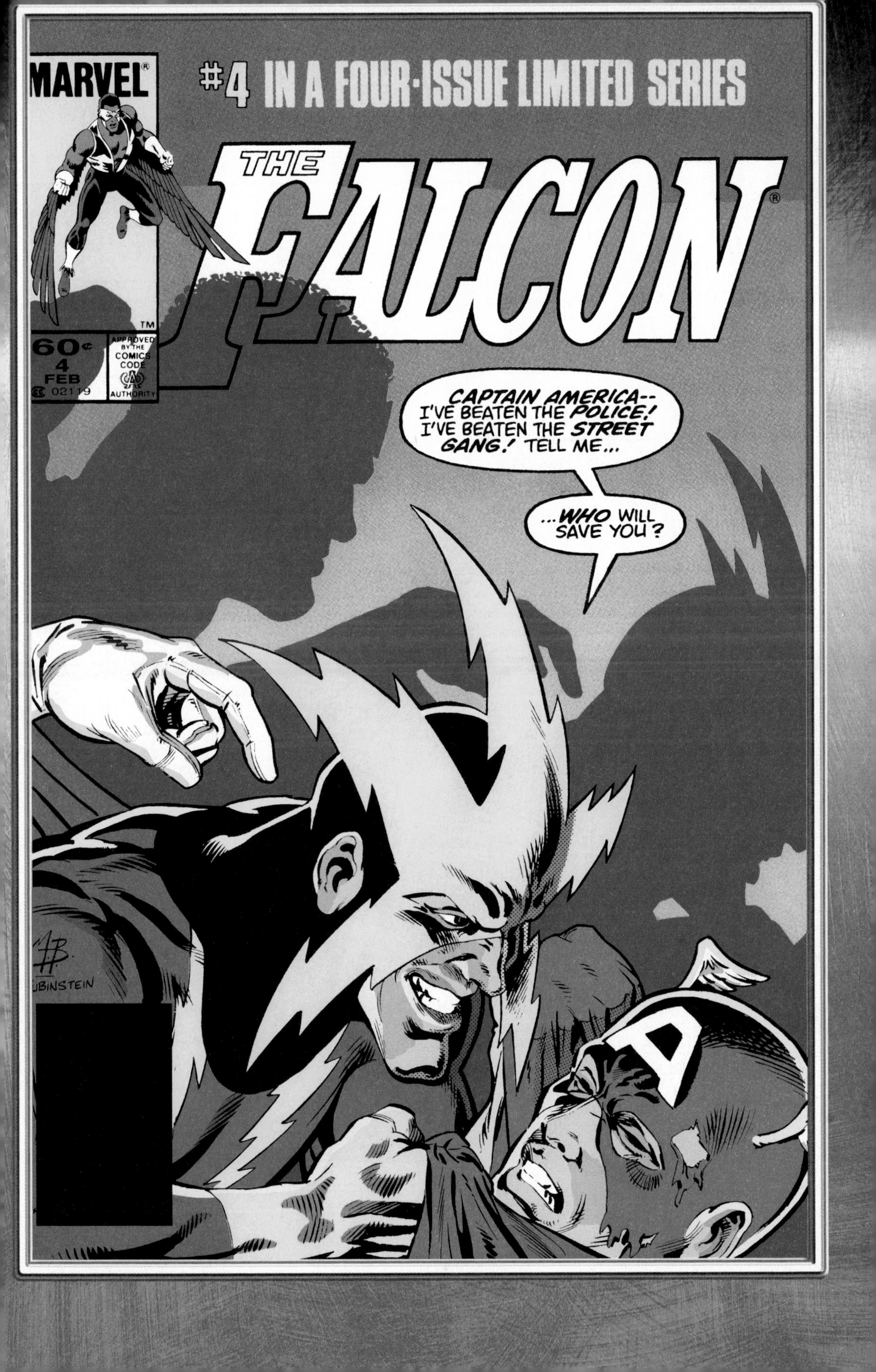
MARVEL
#4 IN A FOUR-ISSUE LIMITED SERIES
THE FALCON
60¢ 4 FEB
02119
APPROVED BY THE COMICS CODE AUTHORITY
CAPTAIN AMERICA-- I'VE BEATEN THE POLICE! I'VE BEATEN THE STREET GANG! TELL ME...
...WHO WILL SAVE YOU?

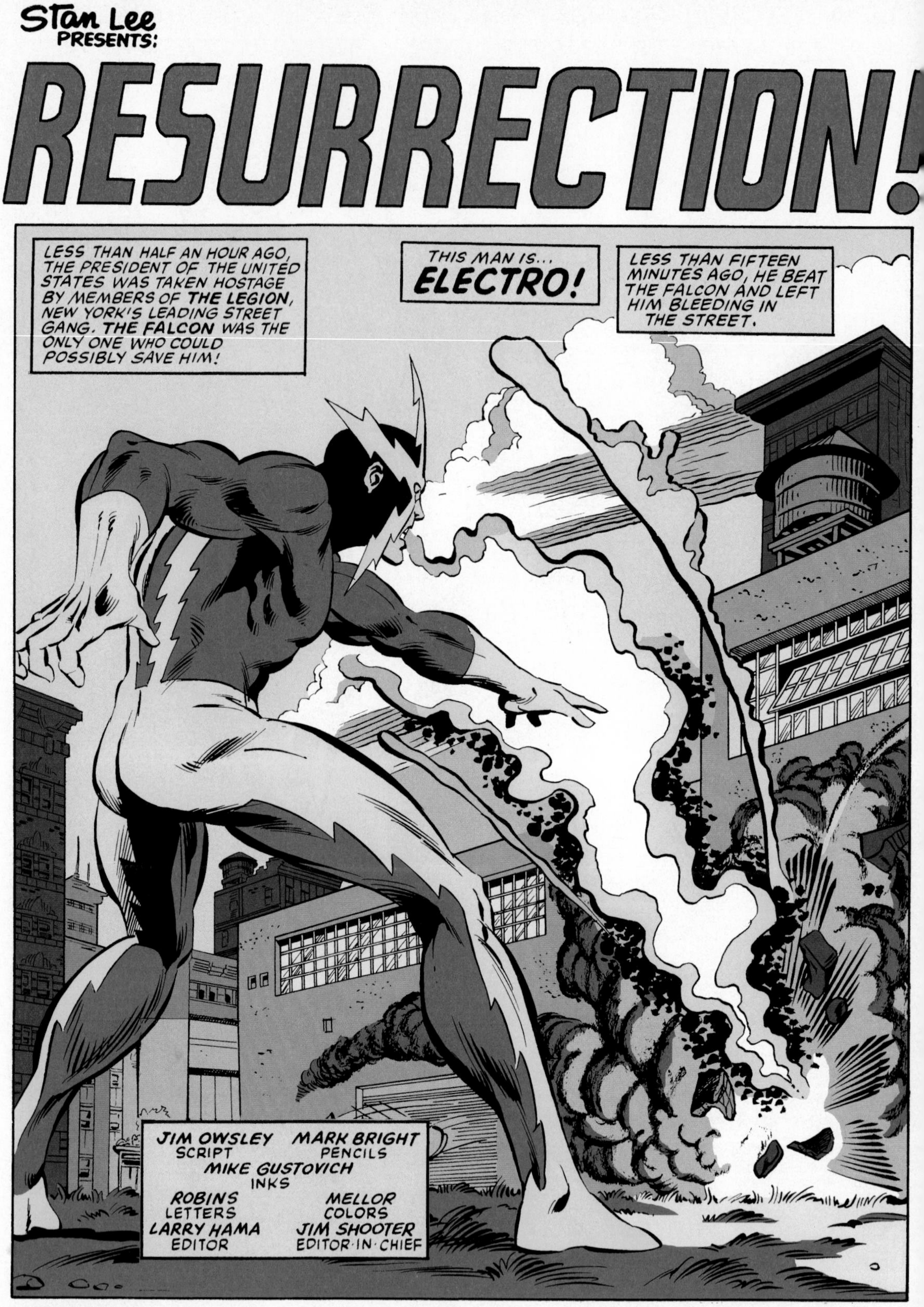
Stan Lee PRESENTS:
RESURRECTION!
LESS THAN HALF AN HOUR AGO, THE PRESIDENT OF THE UNITED STATES WAS TAKEN HOSTAGE BY MEMBERS OF THE LEGION, NEW YORK'S LEADING STREET GANG. THE FALCON WAS THE ONLY ONE WHO COULD POSSIBLY SAVE HIM!
THIS MAN IS... ELECTRO!
LESS THAN FIFTEEN MINUTES AGO, HE BEAT THE FALCON AND LEFT HIM BLEEDING IN THE STREET.
JIM OWSLEY SCRIPT
MARK BRIGHT PENCILS
MIKE GUSTOVICH INKS
ROBINS LETTERS
MELLOR COLORS
LARRY HAMA EDITOR
JIM SHOOTER EDITOR-IN-CHIEF

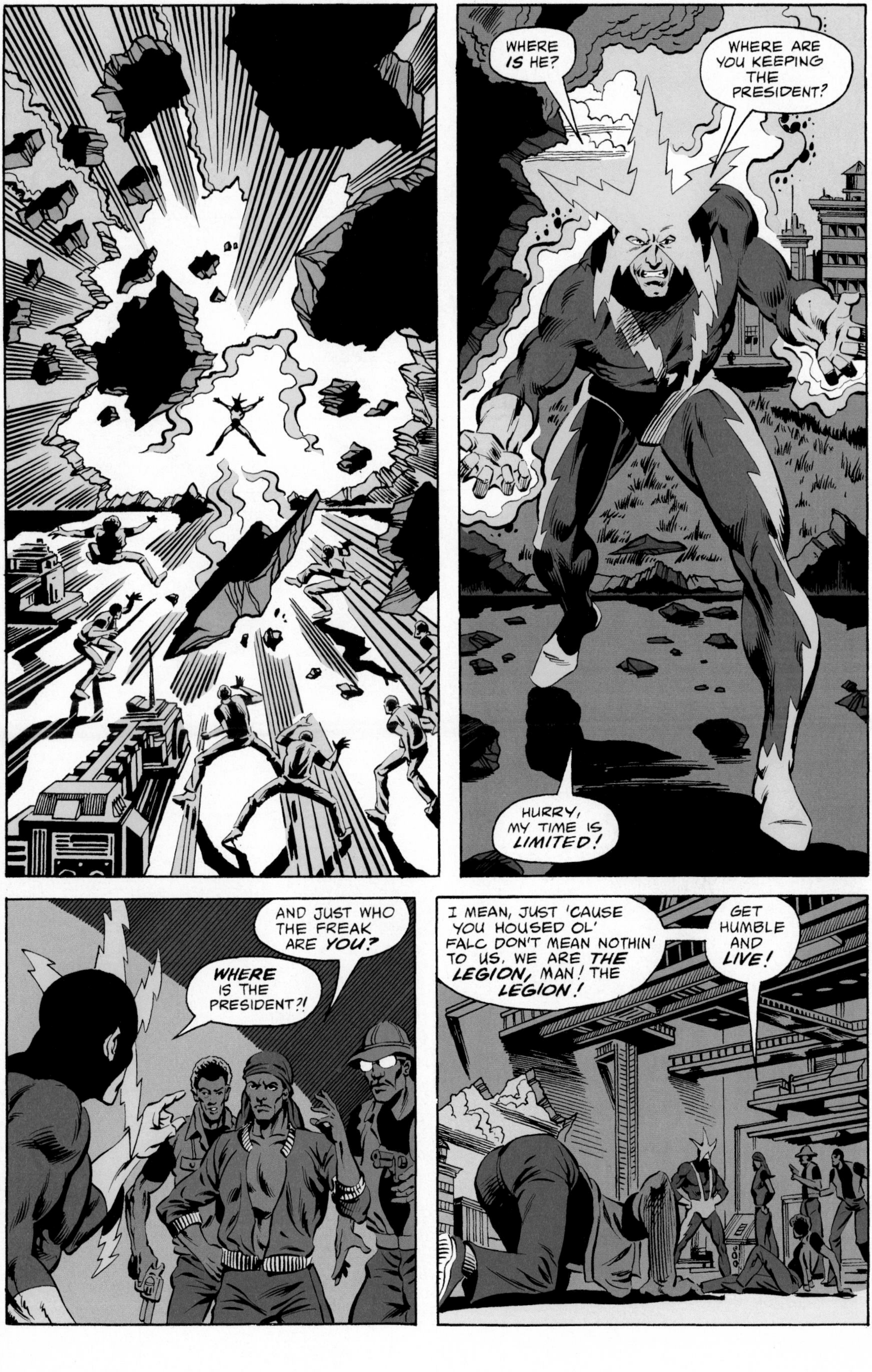
WHERE IS HE?
WHERE ARE YOU KEEPING THE PRESIDENT?
HURRY, MY TIME IS LIMITED!
AND JUST WHO THE FREAK ARE YOU?
WHERE IS THE PRESIDENT?!
I MEAN, JUST 'CAUSE YOU HOUSED OL' FALC DON'T MEAN NOTHIN' TO US. WE ARE THE LEGION, MAN! THE LEGION!
GET HUMBLE AND LIVE!

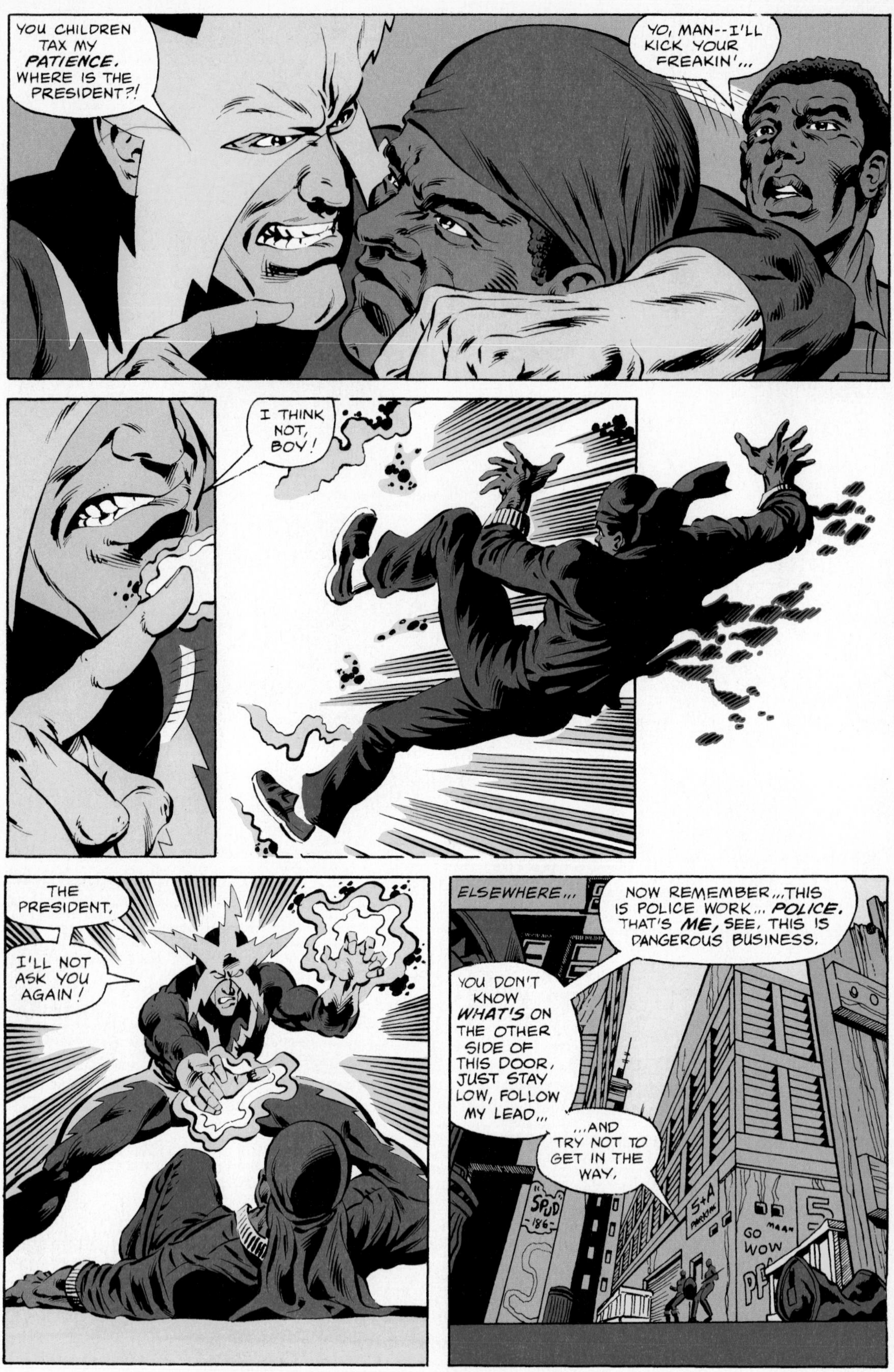
YOU CHILDREN TAX MY PATIENCE. WHERE IS THE PRESIDENT?!
YO, MAN--I'LL KICK YOUR FREAKIN'...
I THINK NOT, BOY!
THE PRESIDENT.
I'LL NOT ASK YOU AGAIN!
ELSEWHERE...
NOW REMEMBER...THIS IS POLICE WORK... POLICE. THAT'S ME, SEE. THIS IS DANGEROUS BUSINESS.
YOU DON'T KNOW WHAT'S ON THE OTHER SIDE OF THIS DOOR. JUST STAY LOW, FOLLOW MY LEAD...
...AND TRY NOT TO GET IN THE WAY.

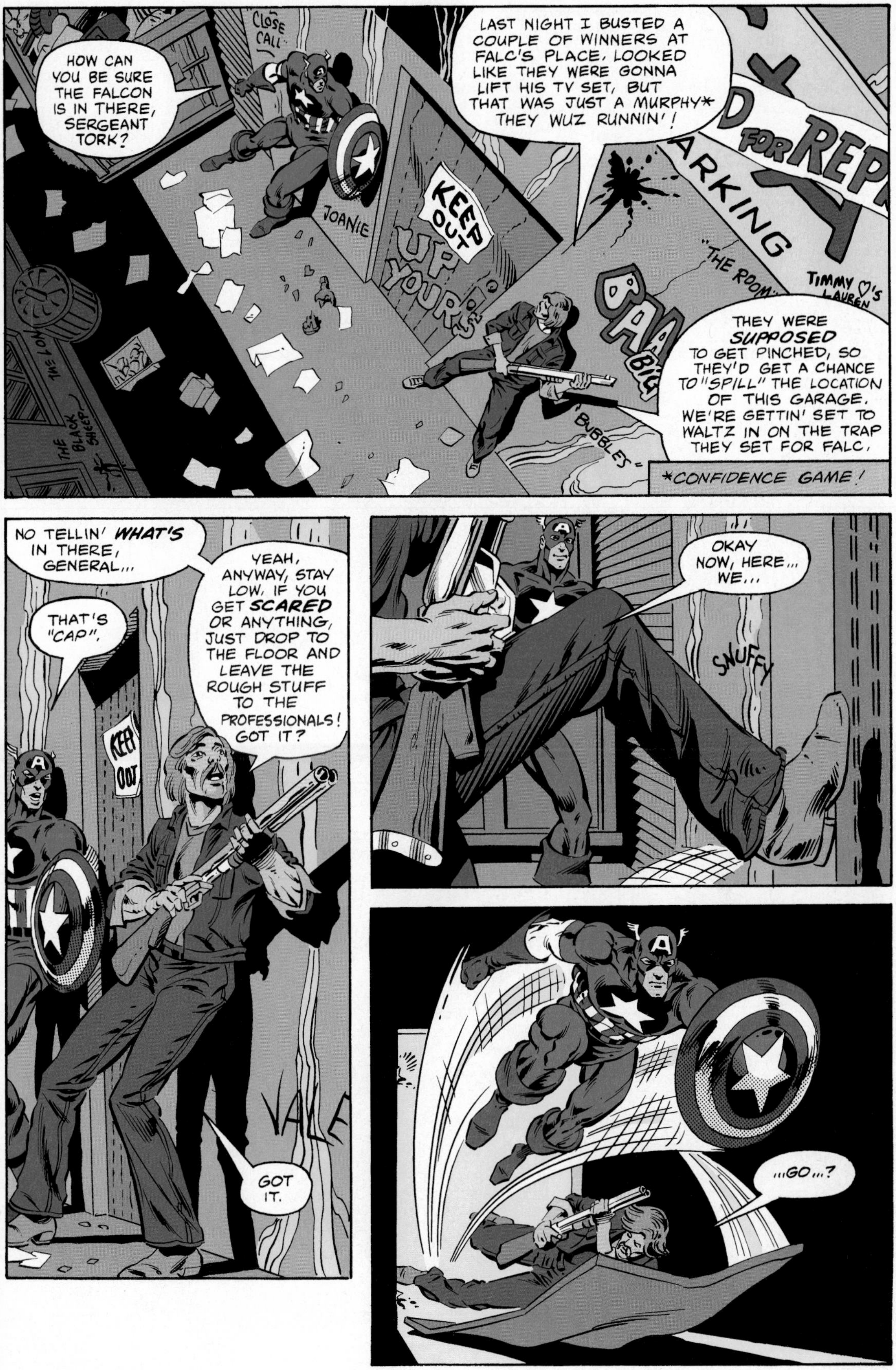
CLOSE CALL
HOW CAN YOU BE SURE THE FALCON IS IN THERE, SERGEANT TORK?
LAST NIGHT I BUSTED A COUPLE OF WINNERS AT FALC'S PLACE. LOOKED LIKE THEY WERE GONNA LIFT HIS TV SET, BUT THAT WAS JUST A MURPHY* THEY WUZ RUNNIN'!
KEEP OUT
JOANIE
UP YOURS
ARKING
FOR REP
"THE ROOM"
TIMMY ♡'S LAUREN
BAA
BIG
THEY WERE SUPPOSED TO GET PINCHED, SO THEY'D GET A CHANCE TO "SPILL" THE LOCATION OF THIS GARAGE. WE'RE GETTIN' SET TO WALTZ IN ON THE TRAP THEY SET FOR FALC.
"BUBBLES"
THE BLACK SHEEP
*CONFIDENCE GAME!
NO TELLIN' WHAT'S IN THERE, GENERAL...
YEAH, ANYWAY, STAY LOW. IF YOU GET SCARED OR ANYTHING, JUST DROP TO THE FLOOR AND LEAVE THE ROUGH STUFF TO THE PROFESSIONALS! GOT IT?
THAT'S "CAP".
KEEP OUT
GOT IT.
OKAY NOW, HERE... WE...
SNUFFY
...GO...?

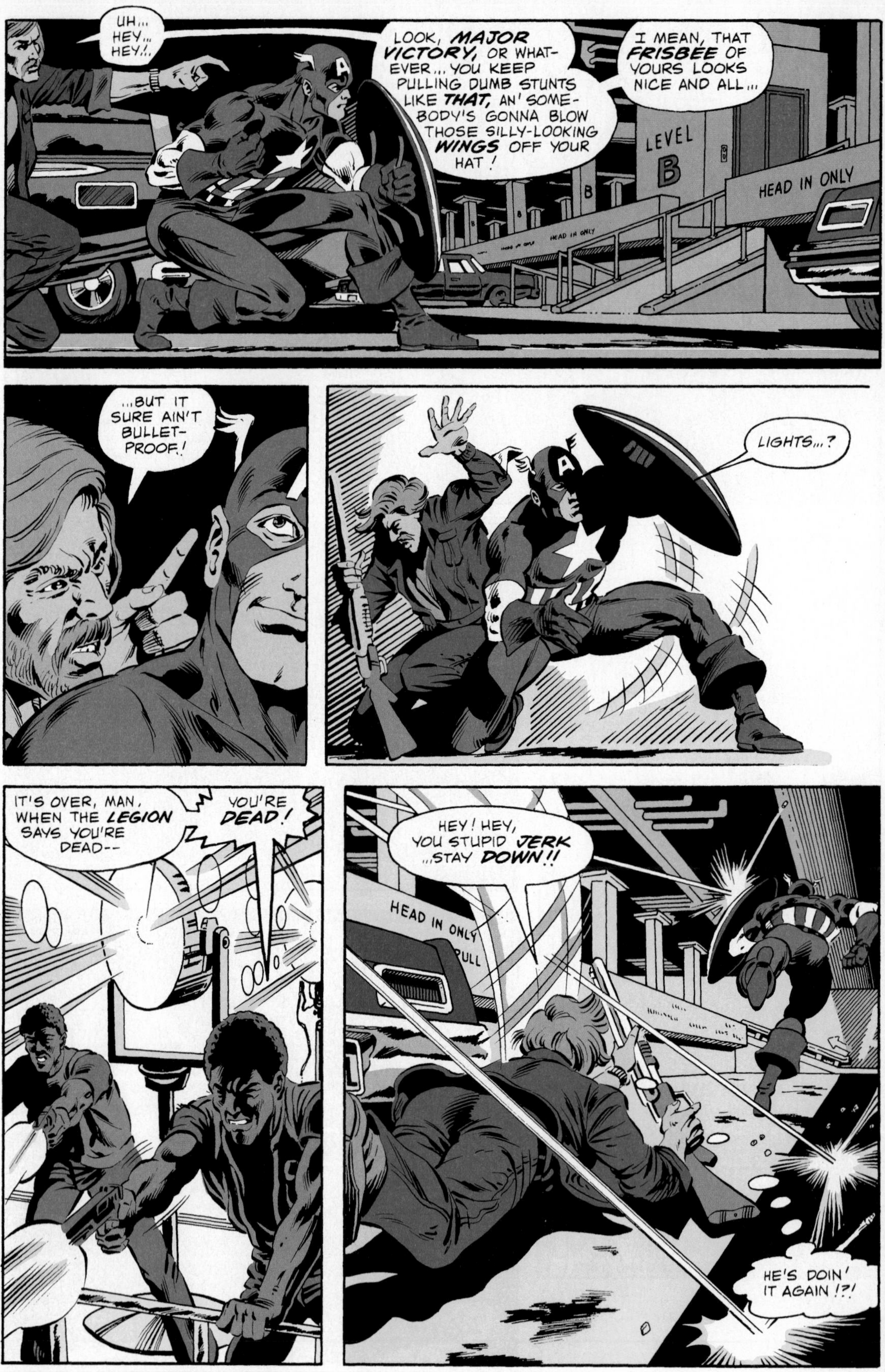

UH... HEY... HEY!..
LOOK, MAJOR VICTORY, OR WHAT-EVER... YOU KEEP PULLING DUMB STUNTS LIKE THAT, AN' SOME-BODY'S GONNA BLOW THOSE SILLY-LOOKING WINGS OFF YOUR HAT!
I MEAN, THAT FRISBEE OF YOURS LOOKS NICE AND ALL...
LEVEL B
HEAD IN ONLY
...BUT IT SURE AIN'T BULLET-PROOF!
LIGHTS...?
IT'S OVER, MAN, WHEN THE LEGION SAYS YOU'RE DEAD--
YOU'RE DEAD!
HEY! HEY, YOU STUPID JERK ...STAY DOWN!!
HEAD IN ONLY
PULL
HE'S DOIN' IT AGAIN!?!

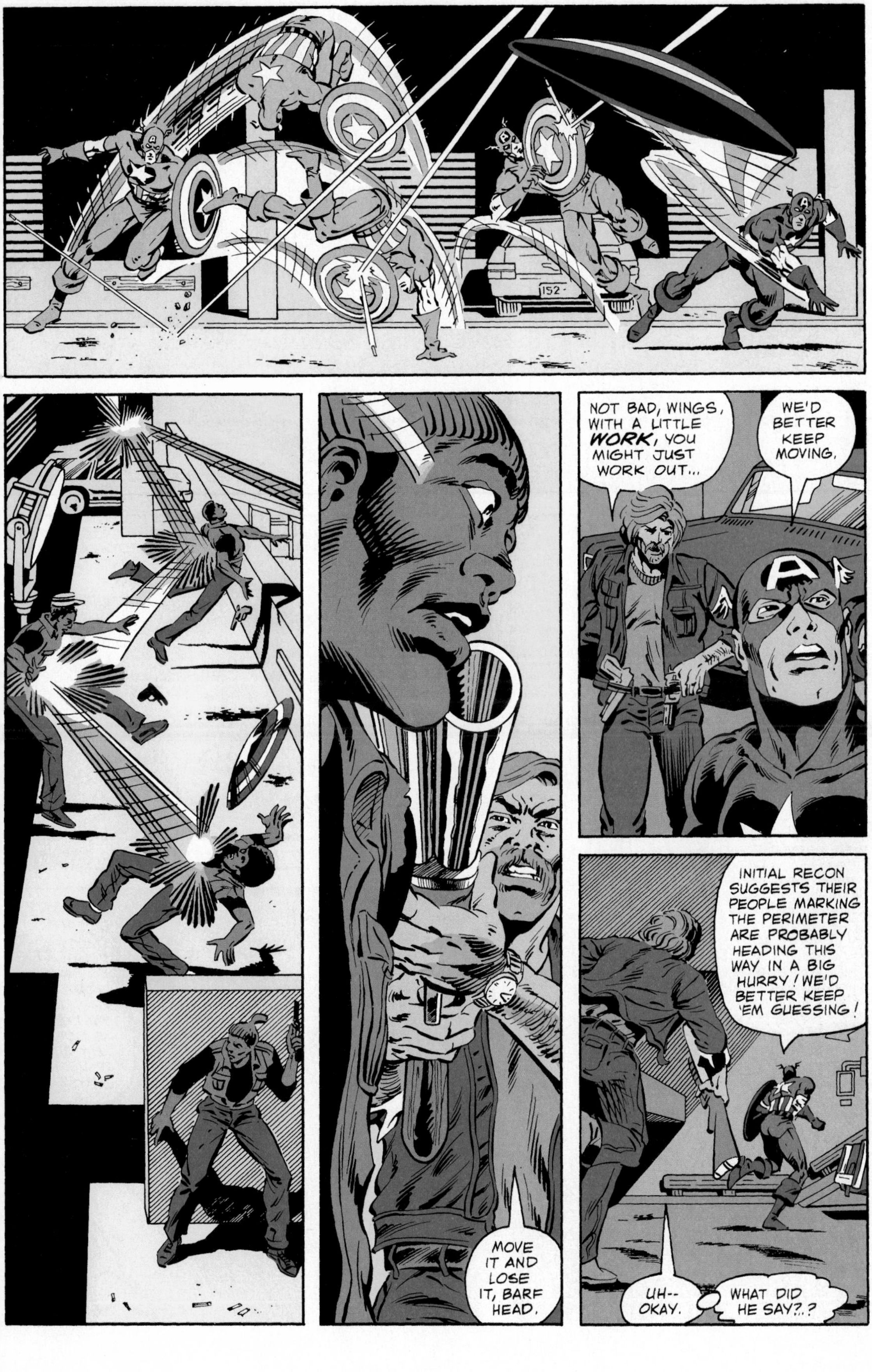
MOVE IT AND LOSE IT, BARF HEAD.
NOT BAD, WINGS, WITH A LITTLE **WORK**, YOU MIGHT JUST WORK OUT...
WE'D BETTER KEEP MOVING.
INITIAL RECON SUGGESTS THEIR PEOPLE MARKING THE PERIMETER ARE PROBABLY HEADING THIS WAY IN A BIG HURRY! WE'D BETTER KEEP 'EM GUESSING!
UH-- OKAY.
WHAT DID HE SAY?..?

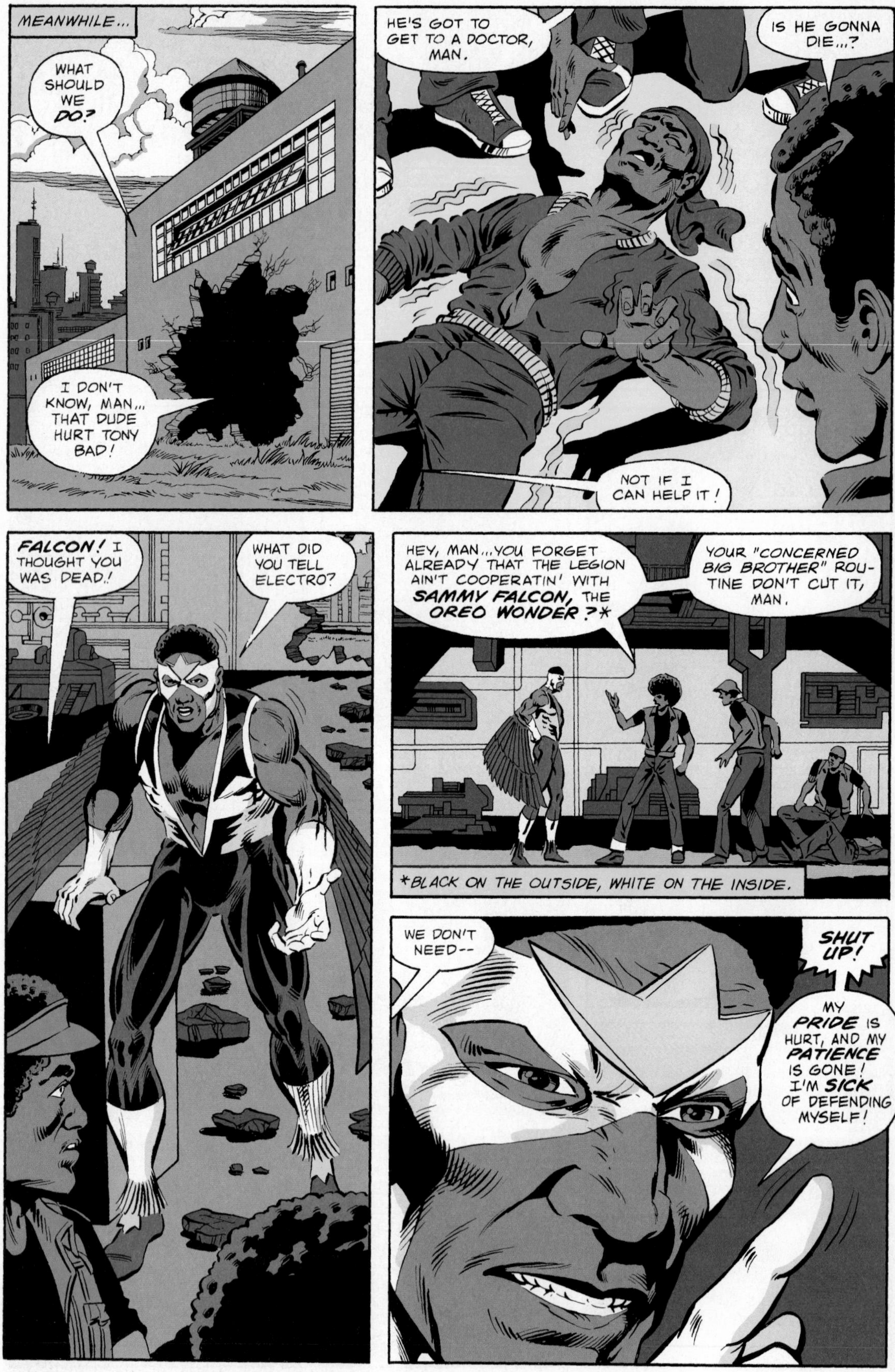
MEANWHILE...
WHAT SHOULD WE DO?
I DON'T KNOW, MAN... THAT DUDE HURT TONY BAD!
HE'S GOT TO GET TO A DOCTOR, MAN.
IS HE GONNA DIE...?
NOT IF I CAN HELP IT!
FALCON! I THOUGHT YOU WAS DEAD!
WHAT DID YOU TELL ELECTRO?
HEY, MAN... YOU FORGET ALREADY THAT THE LEGION AIN'T COOPERATIN' WITH SAMMY FALCON, THE OREO WONDER?*
YOUR "CONCERNED BIG BROTHER" ROU-TINE DON'T CUT IT, MAN.
*BLACK ON THE OUTSIDE, WHITE ON THE INSIDE.
WE DON'T NEED--
SHUT UP!
MY PRIDE IS HURT, AND MY PATIENCE IS GONE! I'M SICK OF DEFENDING MYSELF!

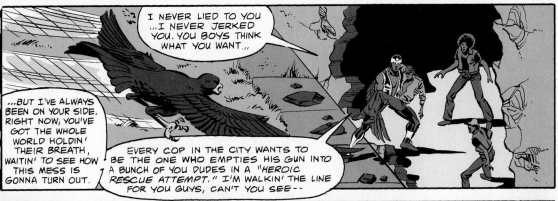

I NEVER LIED TO YOU ...I NEVER JERKED YOU. YOU BOYS THINK WHAT YOU WANT...

...BUT I'VE ALWAYS BEEN ON YOUR SIDE. RIGHT NOW, YOU'VE GOT THE WHOLE WORLD HOLDIN' THEIR BREATH, WAITIN' TO SEE HOW THIS MESS IS GONNA TURN OUT.

EVERY COP IN THE CITY WANTS TO BE THE ONE WHO EMPTIES HIS GUN INTO A BUNCH OF YOU DUDES IN A "HEROIC RESCUE ATTEMPT." I'M WALKIN' THE LINE FOR YOU GUYS, CAN'T YOU SEE--

IT'S NO USE. THEY DON'T TRUST ME. THEY DON'T EVEN LIKE ME.

GREAT.

OKAY, FIRST I GET TONY TO THE HOSPITAL. THEN, MR. ELECTRO, I'M COMIN' FOR YOU!

IT'S A GOOD THING I HAD REDWING TAIL ELECTRO. SINCE REDDY'S BACK NOW THAT MEANS ELECTRO'S SETTLED DOWN SOMEPLACE, AND ALL I'VE GOTTA DO IS FOLLOW THE BIRD.

MEANWHILE, AT THE GARAGE...

I DON'T BELIEVE IT! THESE YOUNG FOOLS ACTUALLY *ARE* HOLDING THE PRESIDENT CAPTIVE! AND I THOUGHT THIS WAS ALL JUST A HOAX.*

MY BATTLE WITH THE FALCON DRAINED ALMOST ALL OF MY ENERGY. THE POWER LINES UP HERE SHOULD FIX THAT.

*LAST ISH--LARRY.

YES...POWER ...SWEET, HYPNOTIC POWER...I AM ELECTRO...

...AND *ELECTRO IS POWER!!!*

83

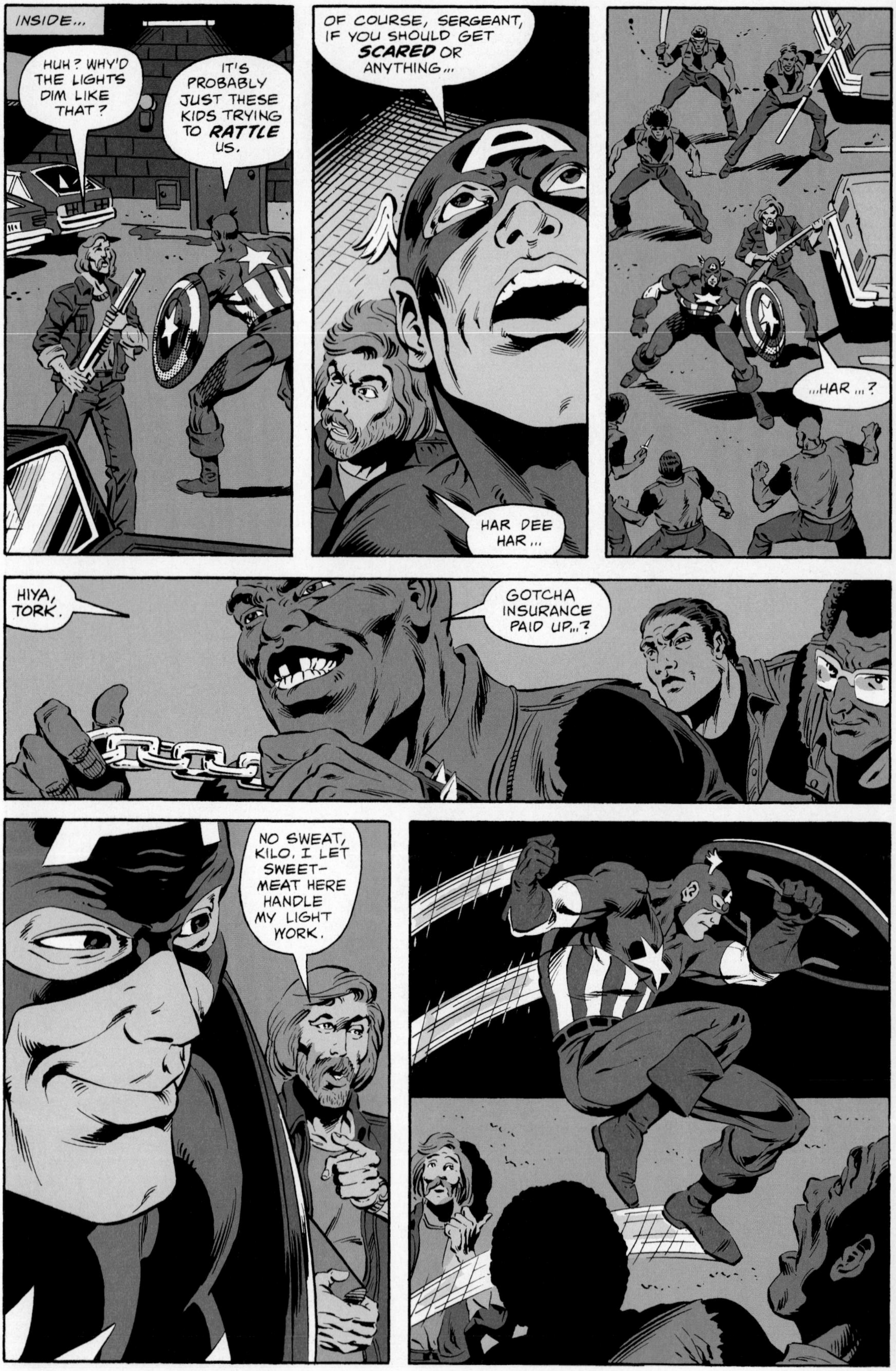
INSIDE...
HUH? WHY'D THE LIGHTS DIM LIKE THAT?
IT'S PROBABLY JUST THESE KIDS TRYING TO RATTLE US.
OF COURSE, SERGEANT, IF YOU SHOULD GET SCARED OR ANYTHING...
HAR DEE HAR...
...HAR...?
HIYA, TORK.
GOTCHA INSURANCE PAID UP...?
NO SWEAT, KILO. I LET SWEET-MEAT HERE HANDLE MY LIGHT WORK.

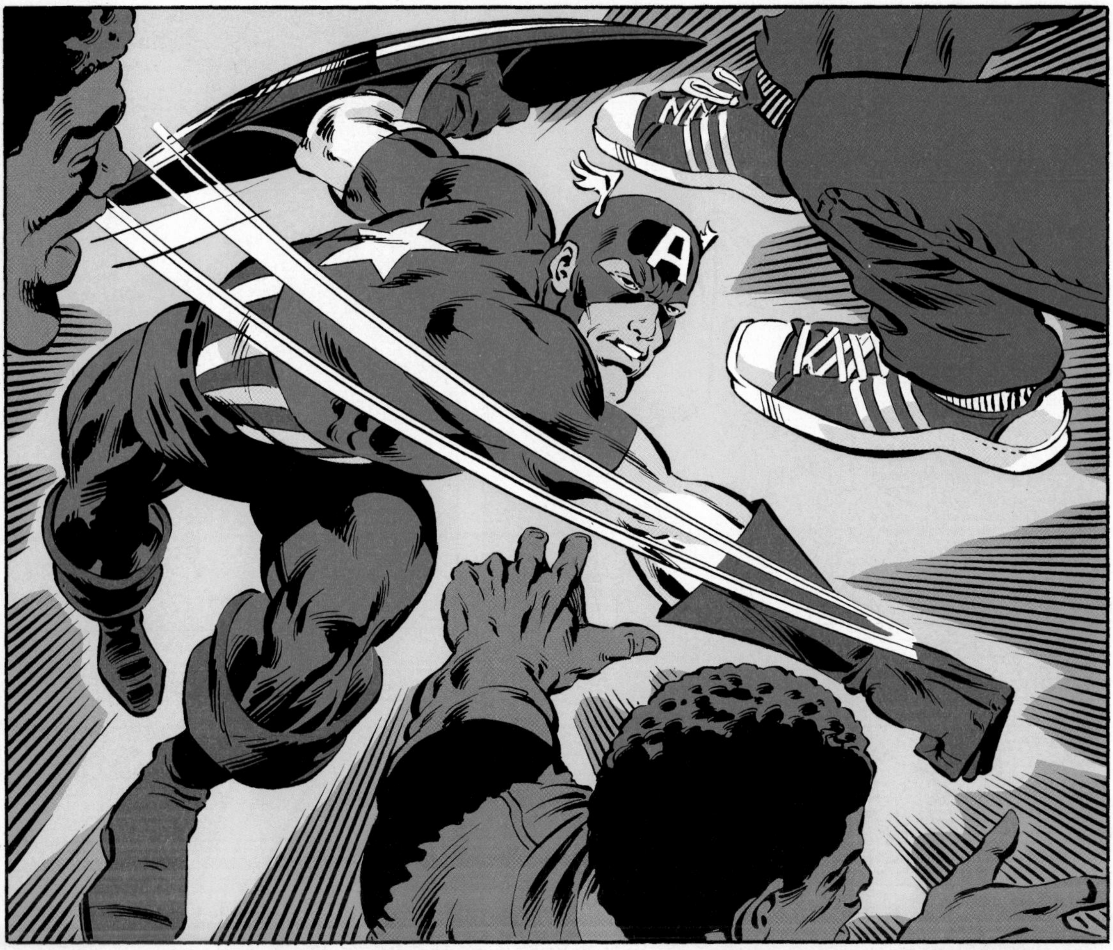

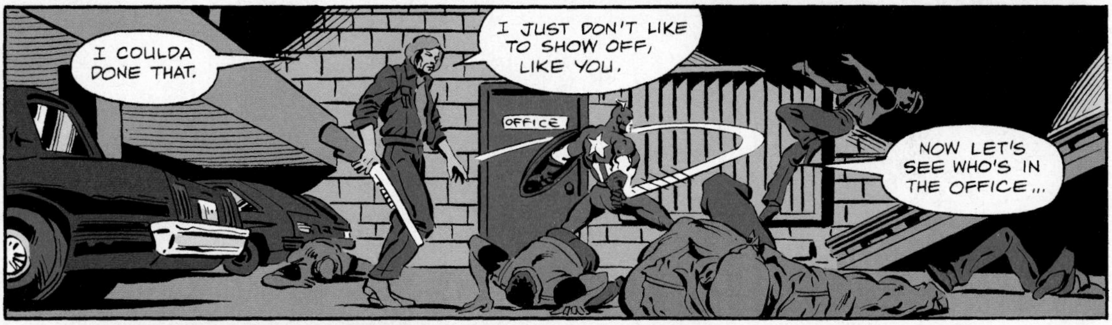
I COULDA DONE THAT.
I JUST DON'T LIKE TO SHOW OFF, LIKE YOU.
OFFICE
NOW LET'S SEE WHO'S IN THE OFFICE...

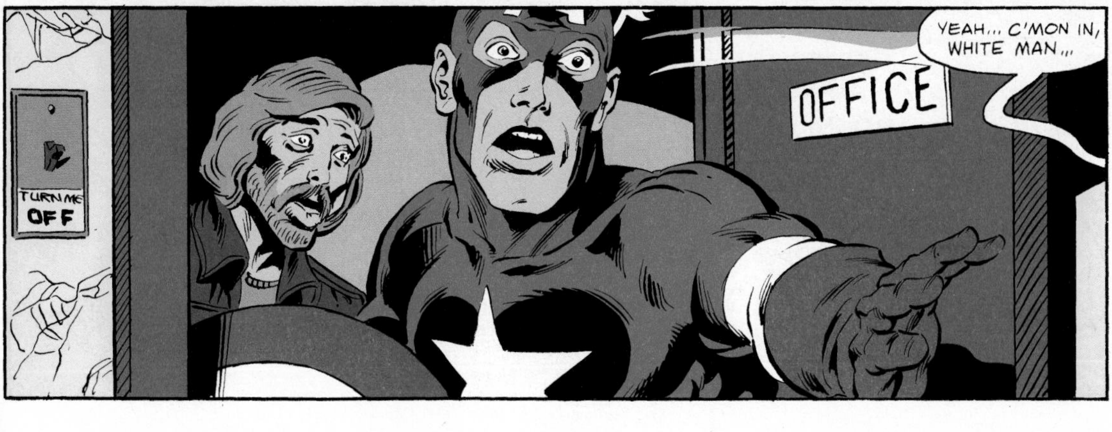
TURN ME OFF
OFFICE
YEAH... C'MON IN, WHITE MAN...

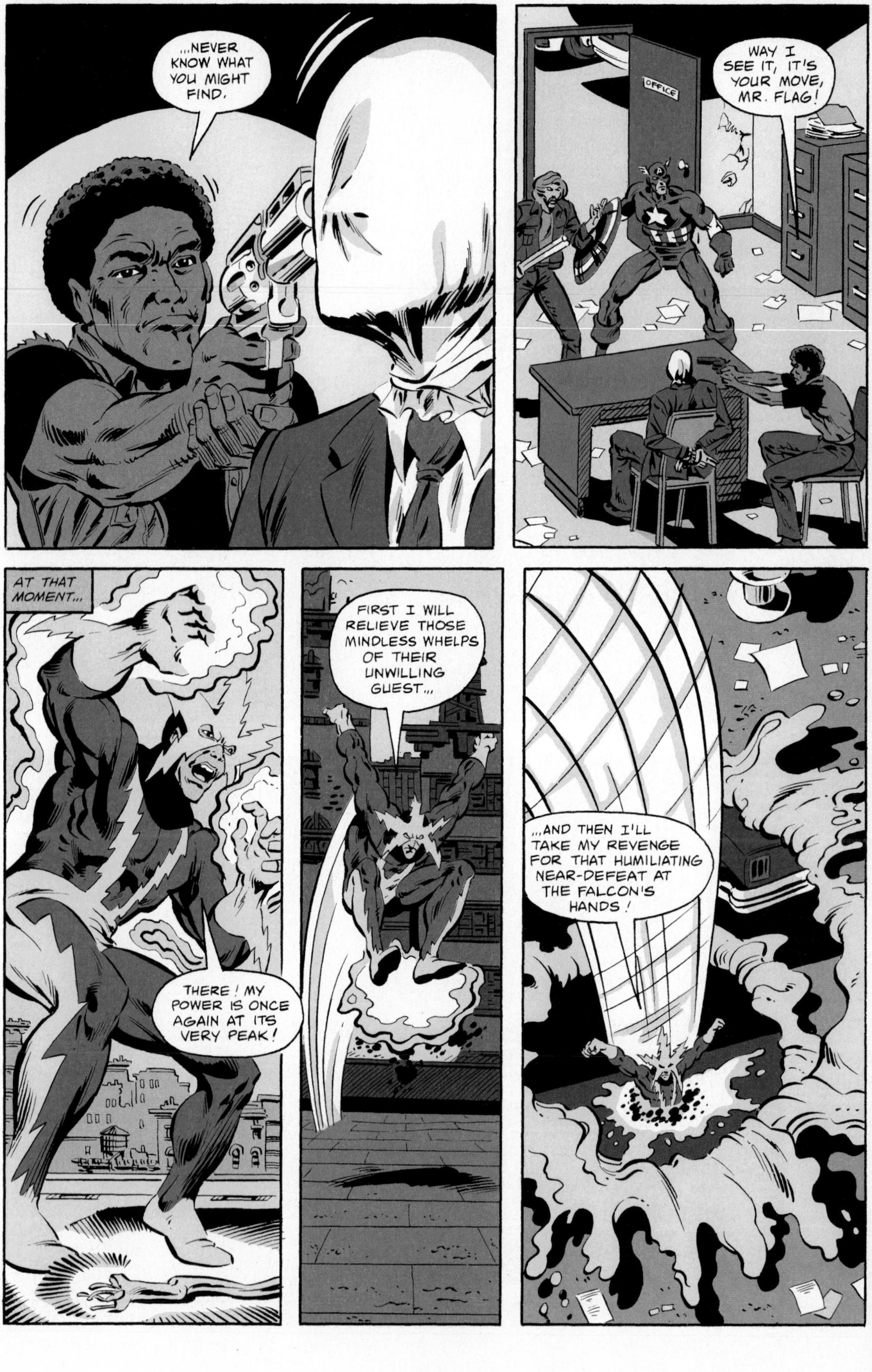
...NEVER KNOW WHAT YOU MIGHT FIND.
OFFICE
WAY I SEE IT, IT'S YOUR MOVE, MR. FLAG!
AT THAT MOMENT...
THERE! MY POWER IS ONCE AGAIN AT ITS VERY PEAK!
FIRST I WILL RELIEVE THOSE MINDLESS WHELPS OF THEIR UNWILLING GUEST...
...AND THEN I'LL TAKE MY REVENGE FOR THAT HUMILIATING NEAR-DEFEAT AT THE FALCON'S HANDS!

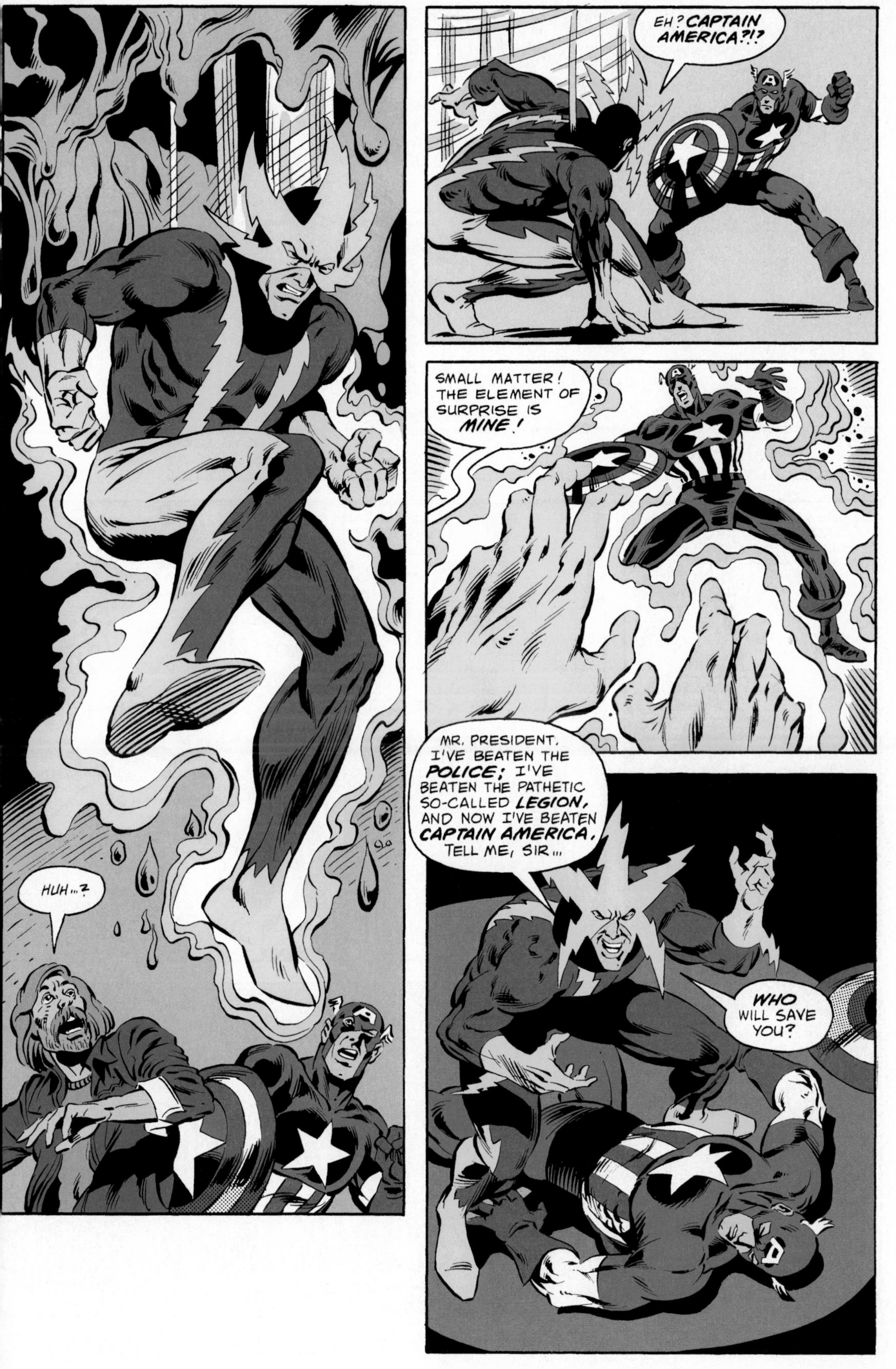
HUH...?
EH? CAPTAIN AMERICA?!?
SMALL MATTER! THE ELEMENT OF SURPRISE IS MINE!
MR. PRESIDENT, I'VE BEATEN THE POLICE; I'VE BEATEN THE PATHETIC SO-CALLED LEGION, AND NOW I'VE BEATEN CAPTAIN AMERICA. TELL ME, SIR...
WHO WILL SAVE YOU?

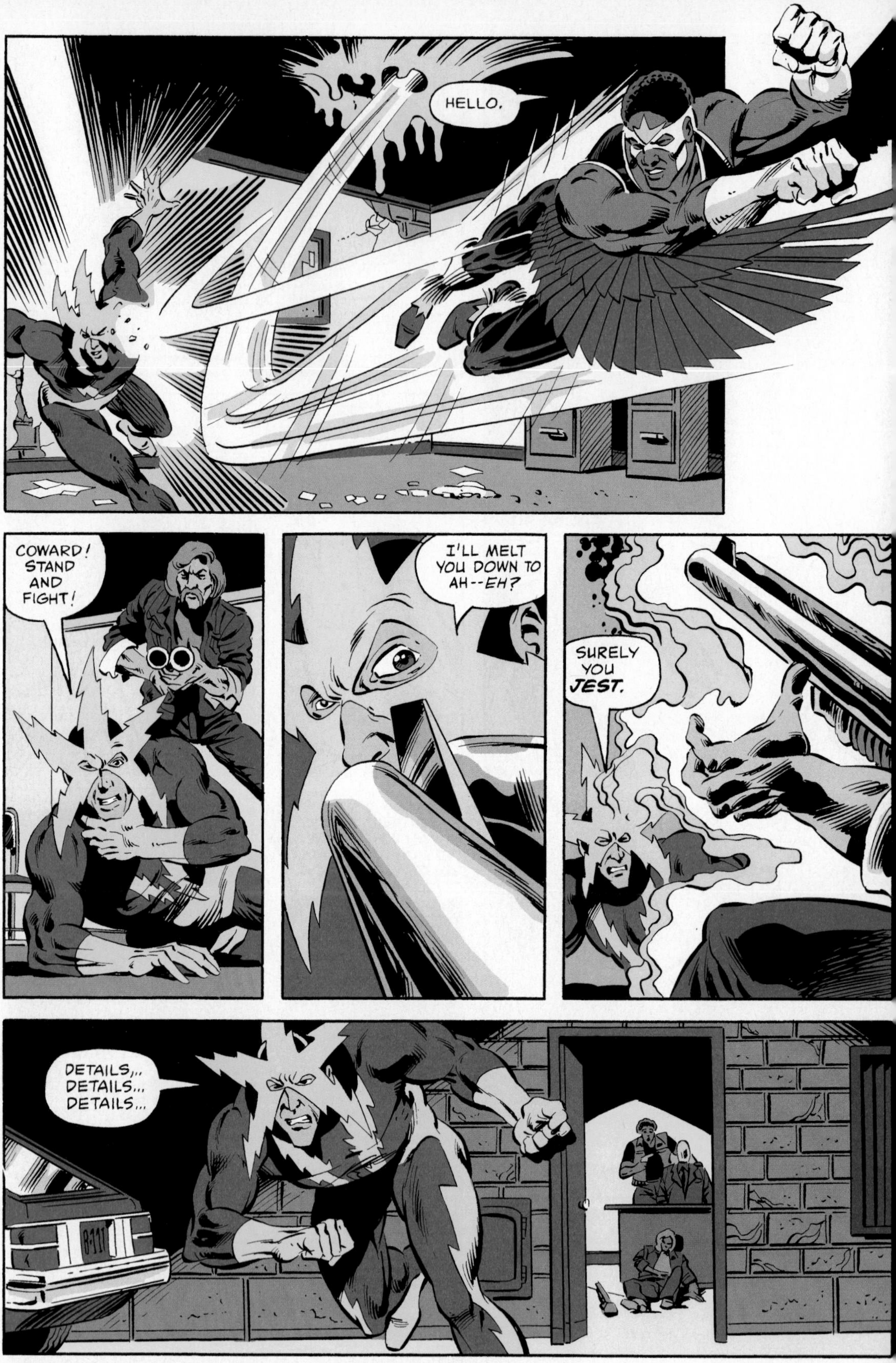
HELLO.
COWARD! STAND AND FIGHT!
I'LL MELT YOU DOWN TO AH--EH?
SURELY YOU JEST.
DETAILS... DETAILS... DETAILS...

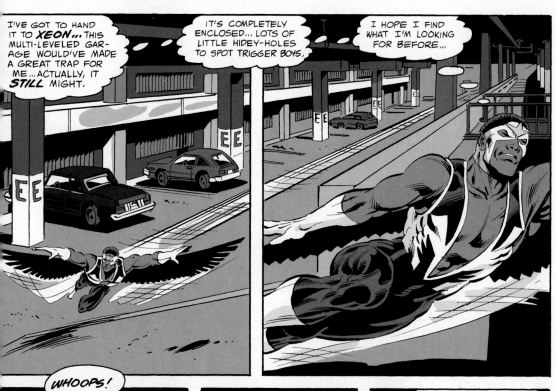

I'VE GOT TO HAND IT TO *XEON*... THIS MULTI-LEVELED GARAGE WOULD'VE MADE A GREAT TRAP FOR ME...ACTUALLY, IT **STILL** MIGHT.

IT'S COMPLETELY ENCLOSED... LOTS OF LITTLE HIDEY-HOLES TO SPOT TRIGGER BOYS.

I HOPE I FIND WHAT I'M LOOKING FOR BEFORE...

WHOOPS!

HEAD IN PARKING

PULL UP TO

HOW DID HE CATCH UP TO ME SO FAST...?

SO...THAT'S HOW HE'S BEEN FOLLOWING ME... "SKATING" ALONG ON AN ELECTROMAGNETIC FORCE FIELD!

HEAD IN

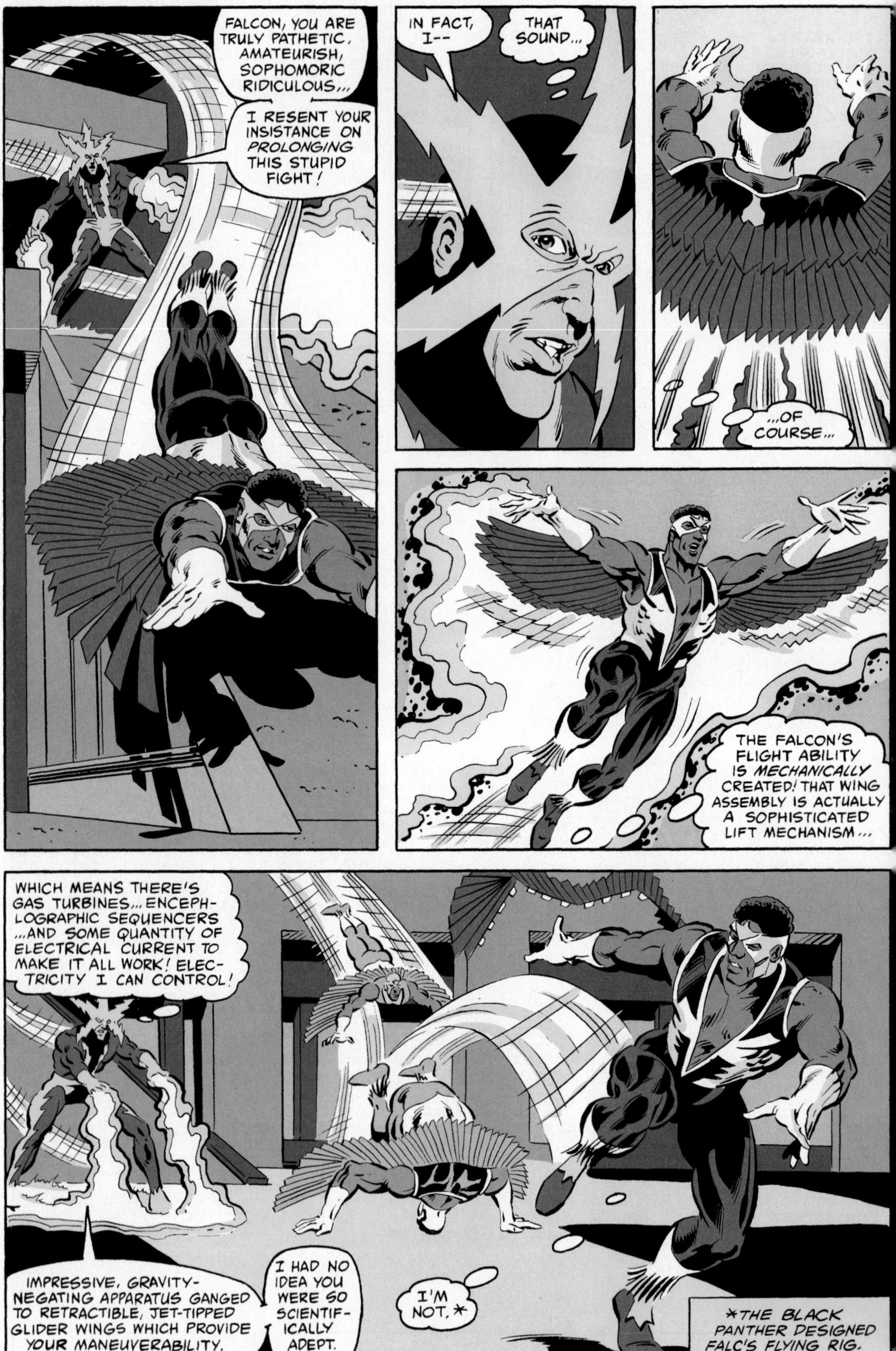
FALCON, YOU ARE TRULY PATHETIC, AMATEURISH, SOPHOMORIC RIDICULOUS...
I RESENT YOUR INSISTANCE ON PROLONGING THIS STUPID FIGHT!
IN FACT, I--
THAT SOUND...
...OF COURSE...
THE FALCON'S FLIGHT ABILITY IS MECHANICALLY CREATED! THAT WING ASSEMBLY IS ACTUALLY A SOPHISTICATED LIFT MECHANISM...
WHICH MEANS THERE'S GAS TURBINES... ENCEPH-LOGRAPHIC SEQUENCERS ...AND SOME QUANTITY OF ELECTRICAL CURRENT TO MAKE IT ALL WORK! ELEC-TRICITY I CAN CONTROL!
IMPRESSIVE, GRAVITY-NEGATING APPARATUS GANGED TO RETRACTIBLE, JET-TIPPED GLIDER WINGS WHICH PROVIDE YOUR MANEUVERABILITY.
I HAD NO IDEA YOU WERE SO SCIENTIF-ICALLY ADEPT.
I'M NOT. *
*THE BLACK PANTHER DESIGNED FALC'S FLYING RIG.

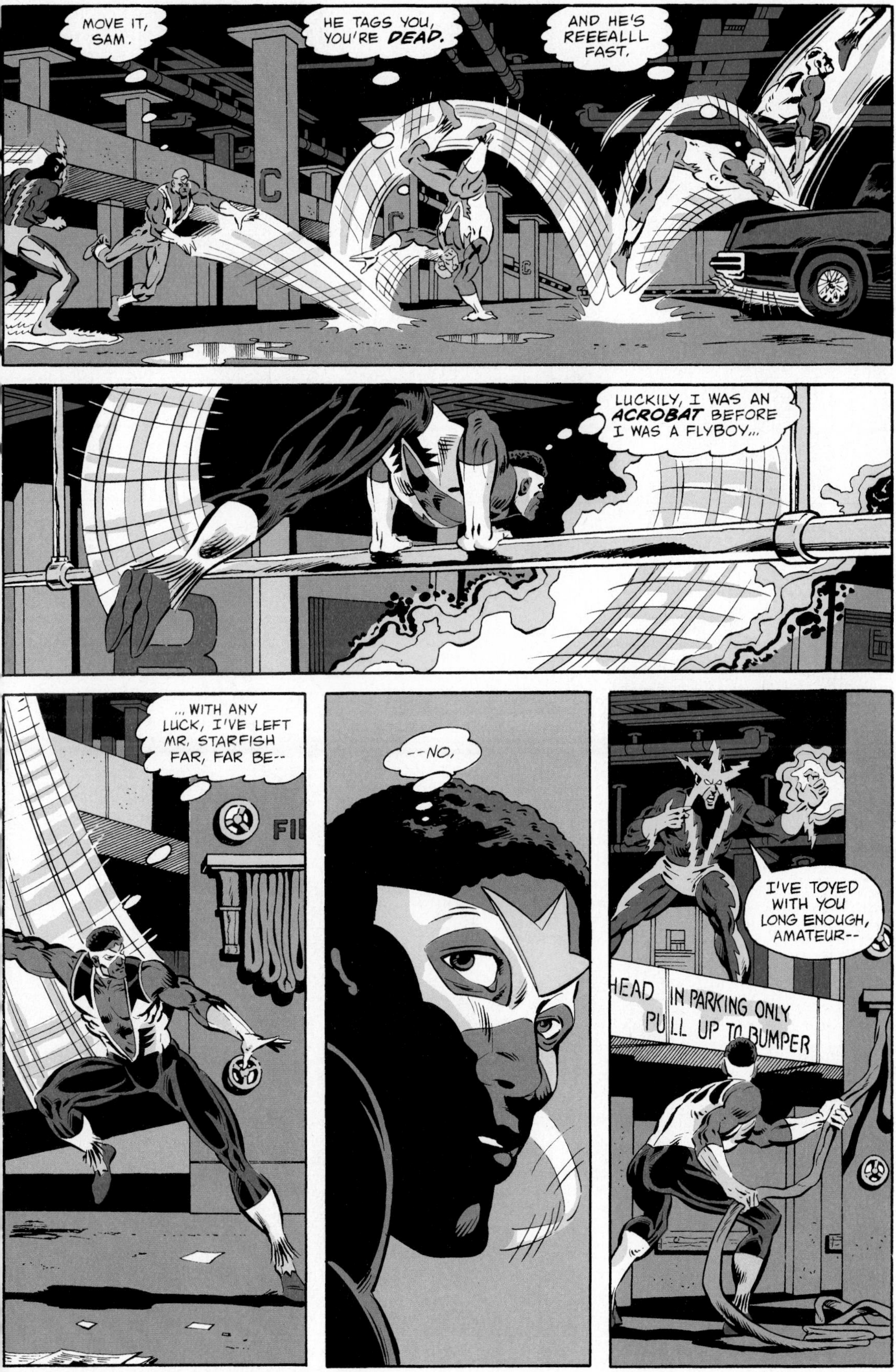
MOVE IT, SAM.
HE TAGS YOU, YOU'RE DEAD.
AND HE'S REEEALLL FAST.
LUCKILY, I WAS AN ACROBAT BEFORE I WAS A FLYBOY...
...WITH ANY LUCK, I'VE LEFT MR. STARFISH FAR, FAR BE--
FI
--NO.
I'VE TOYED WITH YOU LONG ENOUGH, AMATEUR--
HEAD IN PARKING ONLY
PULL UP TO BUMPER

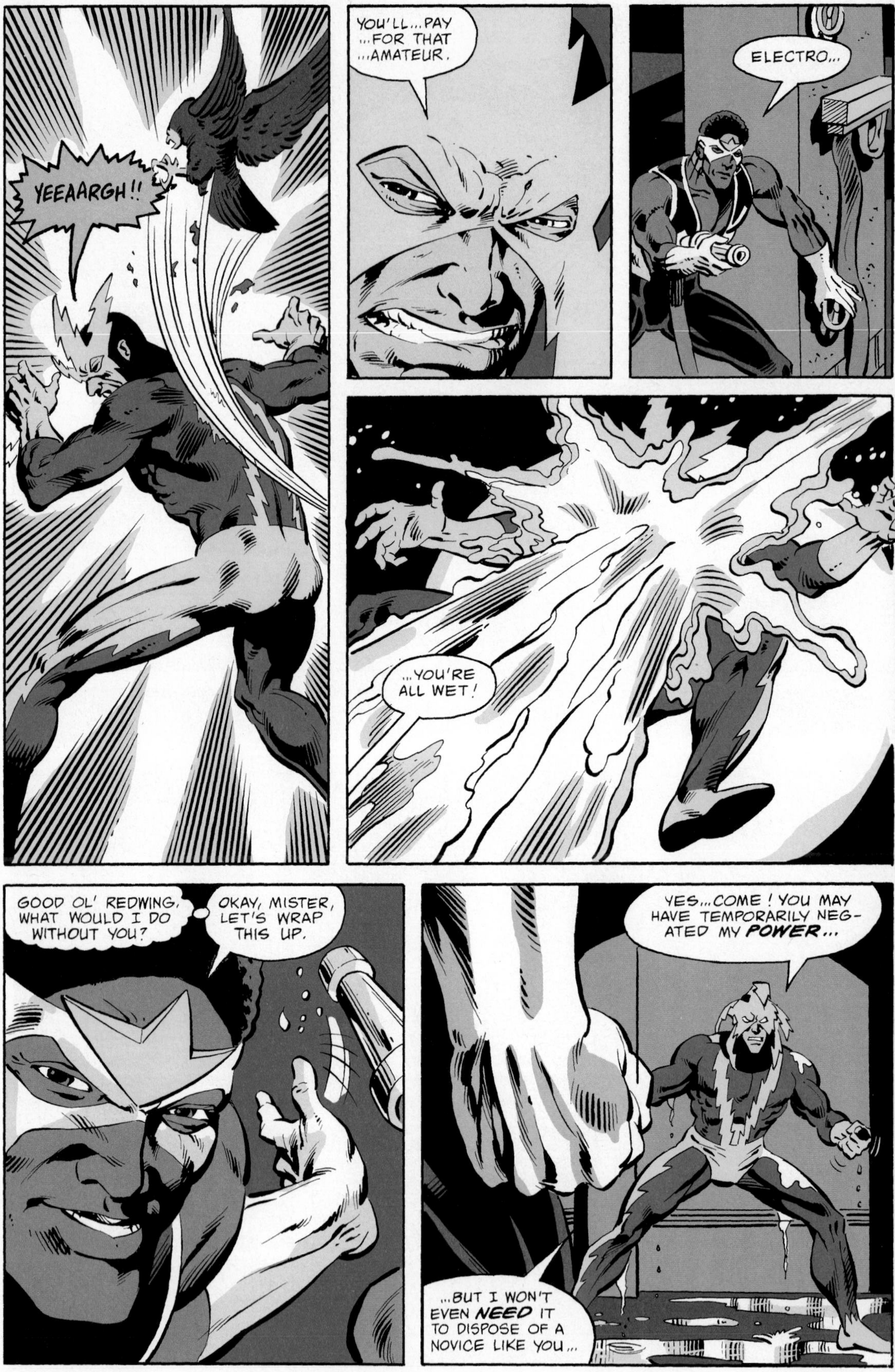
YEEAARGH!!
YOU'LL...PAY ...FOR THAT ...AMATEUR.
ELECTRO...
...YOU'RE ALL WET!
GOOD OL' REDWING, WHAT WOULD I DO WITHOUT YOU?
OKAY, MISTER, LET'S WRAP THIS UP.
YES...COME! YOU MAY HAVE TEMPORARILY NEG-ATED MY POWER...
...BUT I WON'T EVEN NEED IT TO DISPOSE OF A NOVICE LIKE YOU...

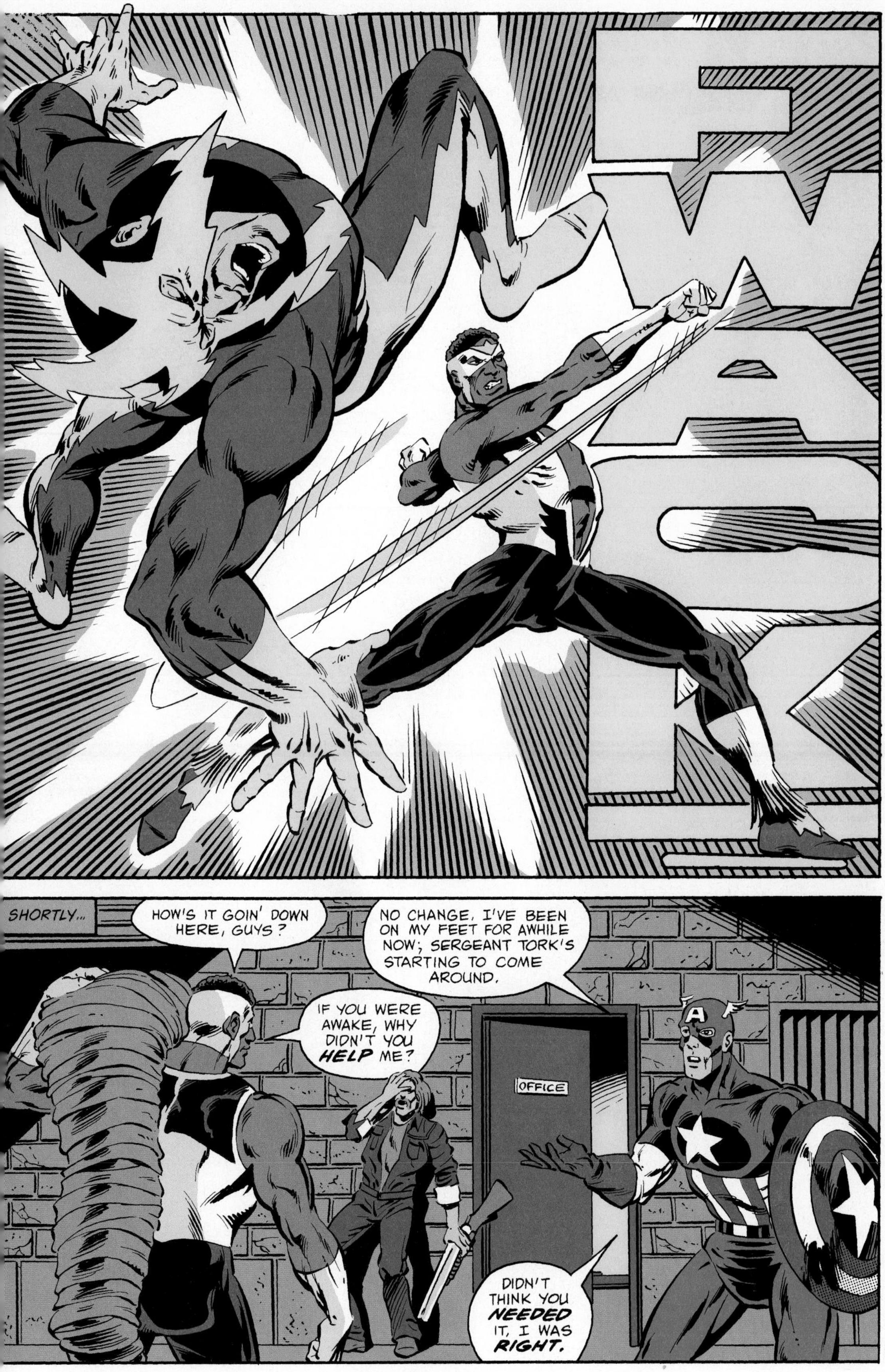
FWACK
SHORTLY...
HOW'S IT GOIN' DOWN HERE, GUYS?
NO CHANGE. I'VE BEEN ON MY FEET FOR AWHILE NOW; SERGEANT TORK'S STARTING TO COME AROUND.
IF YOU WERE AWAKE, WHY DIDN'T YOU HELP ME?
OFFICE
DIDN'T THINK YOU NEEDED IT. I WAS RIGHT.

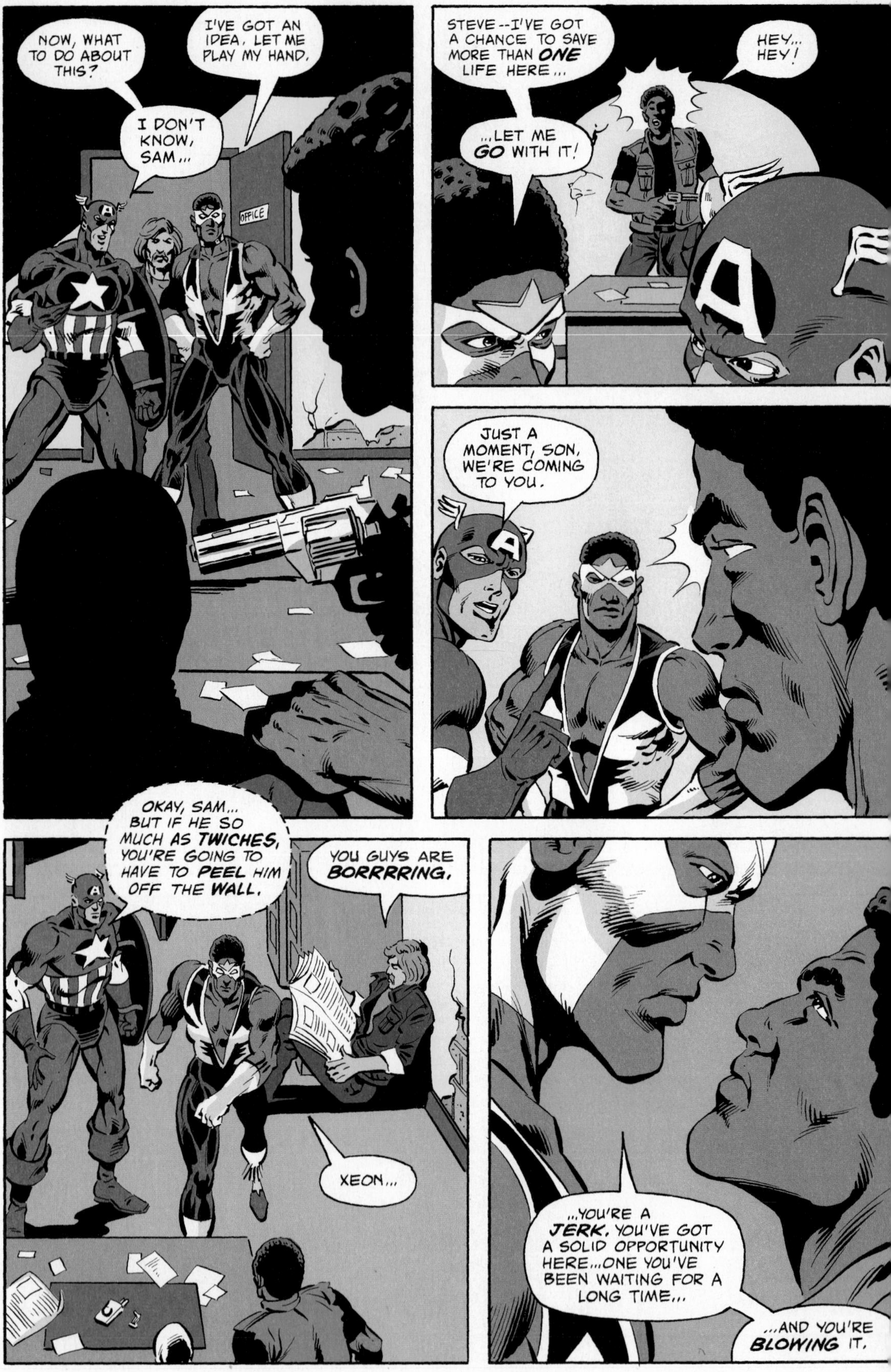
NOW, WHAT TO DO ABOUT THIS?
I DON'T KNOW, SAM...
I'VE GOT AN IDEA. LET ME PLAY MY HAND.
OFFICE
STEVE--I'VE GOT A CHANCE TO SAVE MORE THAN ONE LIFE HERE...
...LET ME GO WITH IT!
HEY... HEY!
JUST A MOMENT, SON. WE'RE COMING TO YOU.
OKAY, SAM... BUT IF HE SO MUCH AS TWICHES, YOU'RE GOING TO HAVE TO PEEL HIM OFF THE WALL.
YOU GUYS ARE BORRRRING.
XEON...
...YOU'RE A JERK. YOU'VE GOT A SOLID OPPORTUNITY HERE...ONE YOU'VE BEEN WAITING FOR A LONG TIME...
...AND YOU'RE BLOWING IT.

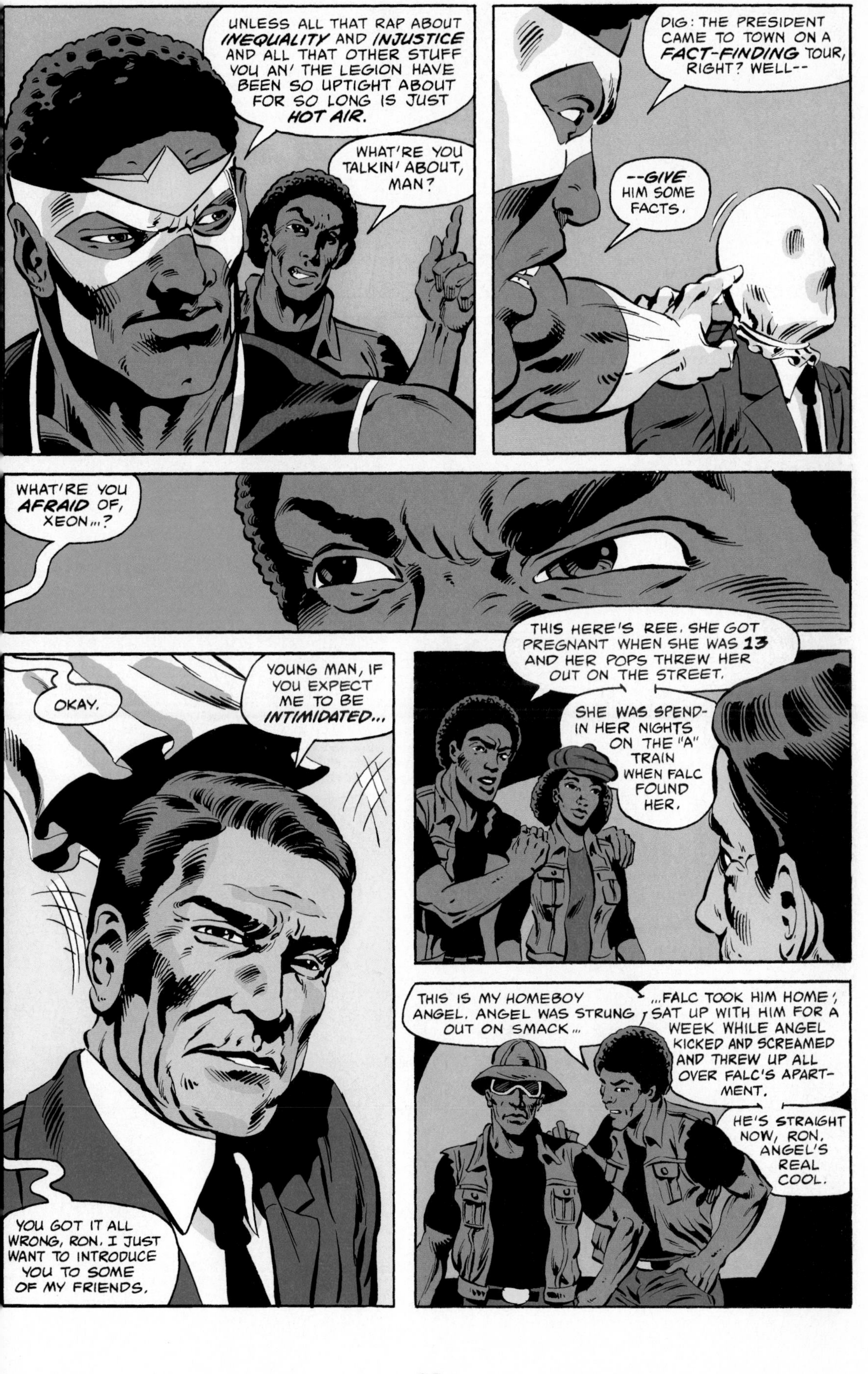
UNLESS ALL THAT RAP ABOUT INEQUALITY AND INJUSTICE AND ALL THAT OTHER STUFF YOU AN' THE LEGION HAVE BEEN SO UPTIGHT ABOUT FOR SO LONG IS JUST HOT AIR.
WHAT'RE YOU TALKIN' ABOUT, MAN?
DIG: THE PRESIDENT CAME TO TOWN ON A FACT-FINDING TOUR, RIGHT? WELL--
--GIVE HIM SOME FACTS.
WHAT'RE YOU AFRAID OF, XEON...?
OKAY.
YOUNG MAN, IF YOU EXPECT ME TO BE INTIMIDATED...
YOU GOT IT ALL WRONG, RON. I JUST WANT TO INTRODUCE YOU TO SOME OF MY FRIENDS.
THIS HERE'S REE. SHE GOT PREGNANT WHEN SHE WAS 13 AND HER POPS THREW HER OUT ON THE STREET.
SHE WAS SPEND-IN HER NIGHTS ON THE "A" TRAIN WHEN FALC FOUND HER.
THIS IS MY HOMEBOY ANGEL. ANGEL WAS STRUNG OUT ON SMACK...
...FALC TOOK HIM HOME; SAT UP WITH HIM FOR A WEEK WHILE ANGEL KICKED AND SCREAMED AND THREW UP ALL OVER FALC'S APART-MENT.
HE'S STRAIGHT NOW, RON. ANGEL'S REAL COOL.

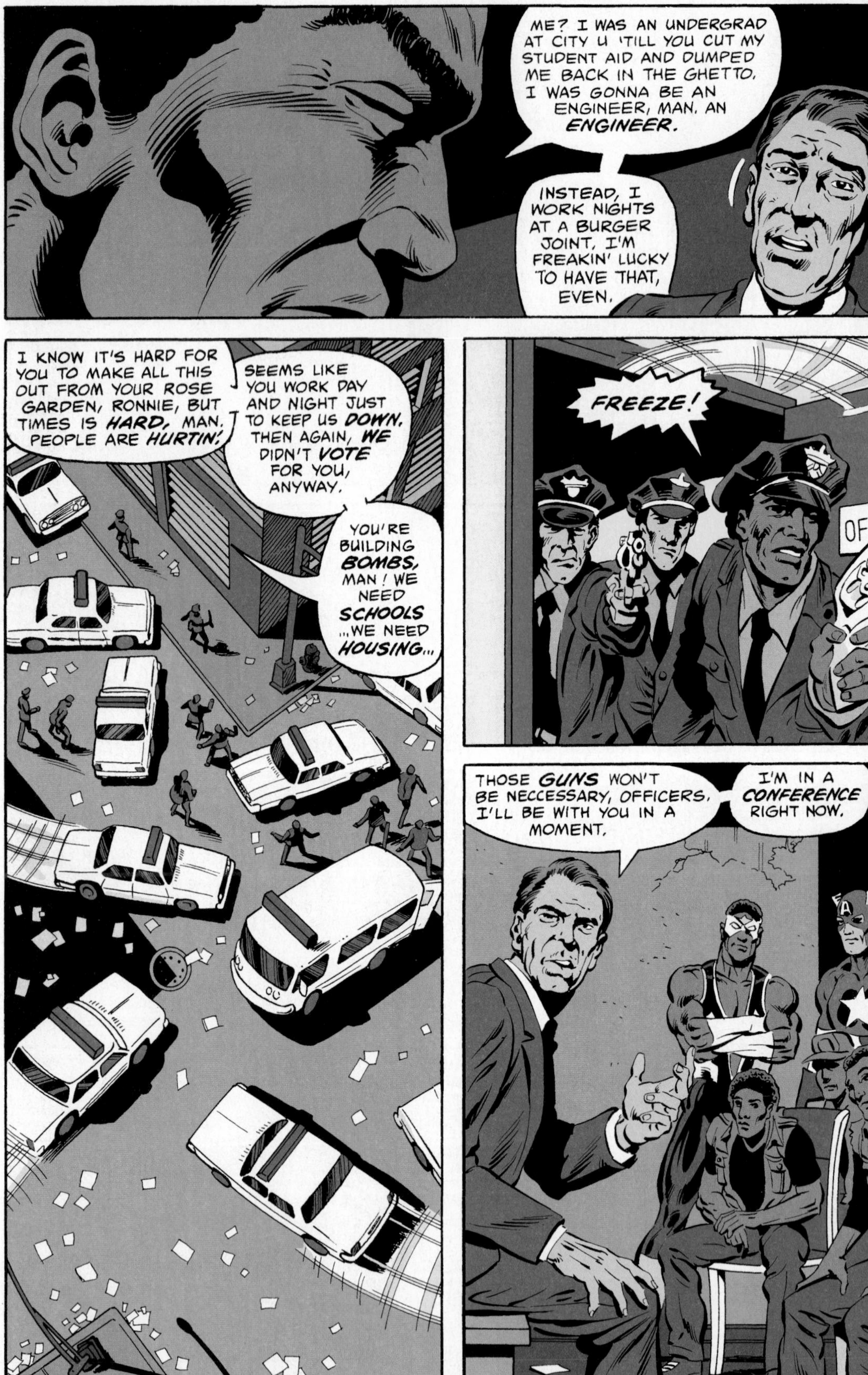
ME? I WAS AN UNDERGRAD AT CITY U 'TILL YOU CUT MY STUDENT AID AND DUMPED ME BACK IN THE GHETTO. I WAS GONNA BE AN ENGINEER, MAN. AN ENGINEER.
INSTEAD, I WORK NIGHTS AT A BURGER JOINT. I'M FREAKIN' LUCKY TO HAVE THAT, EVEN.
I KNOW IT'S HARD FOR YOU TO MAKE ALL THIS OUT FROM YOUR ROSE GARDEN, RONNIE, BUT TIMES IS HARD, MAN. PEOPLE ARE HURTIN'!
SEEMS LIKE YOU WORK DAY AND NIGHT JUST TO KEEP US DOWN. THEN AGAIN, WE DIDN'T VOTE FOR YOU, ANYWAY.
YOU'RE BUILDING BOMBS, MAN! WE NEED SCHOOLS ...WE NEED HOUSING...
FREEZE!
THOSE GUNS WON'T BE NECCESSARY, OFFICERS. I'LL BE WITH YOU IN A MOMENT.
I'M IN A CONFERENCE RIGHT NOW.

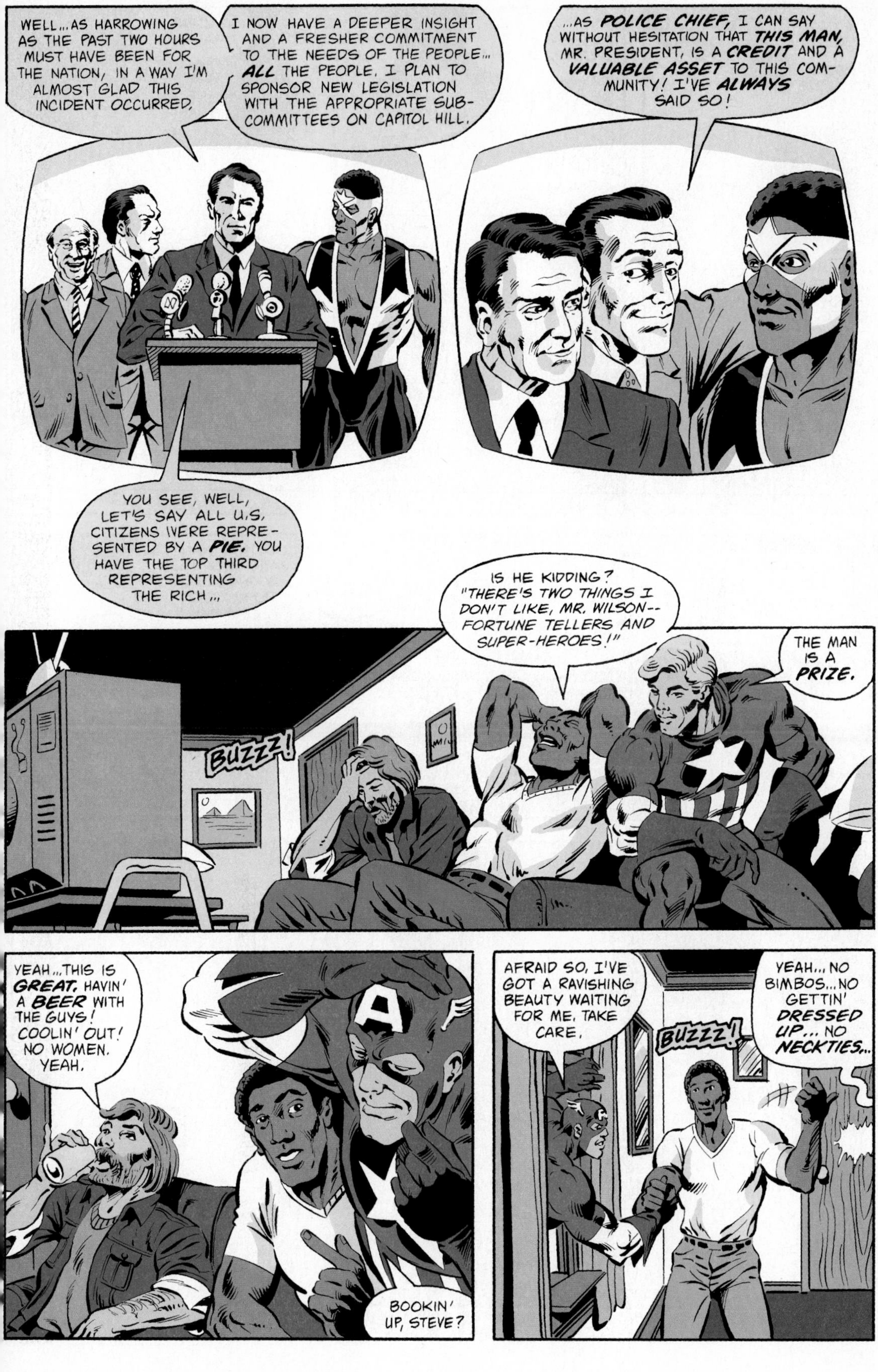
WELL... AS HARROWING AS THE PAST TWO HOURS MUST HAVE BEEN FOR THE NATION, IN A WAY I'M ALMOST GLAD THIS INCIDENT OCCURRED,
I NOW HAVE A DEEPER INSIGHT AND A FRESHER COMMITMENT TO THE NEEDS OF THE PEOPLE... ALL THE PEOPLE. I PLAN TO SPONSOR NEW LEGISLATION WITH THE APPROPRIATE SUB-COMMITTEES ON CAPITOL HILL.
YOU SEE, WELL, LET'S SAY ALL U.S. CITIZENS WERE REPRESENTED BY A PIE. YOU HAVE THE TOP THIRD REPRESENTING THE RICH...
...AS POLICE CHIEF, I CAN SAY WITHOUT HESITATION THAT THIS MAN, MR. PRESIDENT, IS A CREDIT AND A VALUABLE ASSET TO THIS COMMUNITY! I'VE ALWAYS SAID SO!
BUZZZ!
IS HE KIDDING? "THERE'S TWO THINGS I DON'T LIKE, MR. WILSON-- FORTUNE TELLERS AND SUPER-HEROES!"
THE MAN IS A PRIZE.
YEAH... THIS IS GREAT. HAVIN' A BEER WITH THE GUYS! COOLIN' OUT! NO WOMEN. YEAH.
BOOKIN' UP, STEVE?
AFRAID SO, I'VE GOT A RAVISHING BEAUTY WAITING FOR ME. TAKE CARE.
BUZZZ!
YEAH... NO BIMBOS... NO GETTIN' DRESSED UP... NO NECKTIES...

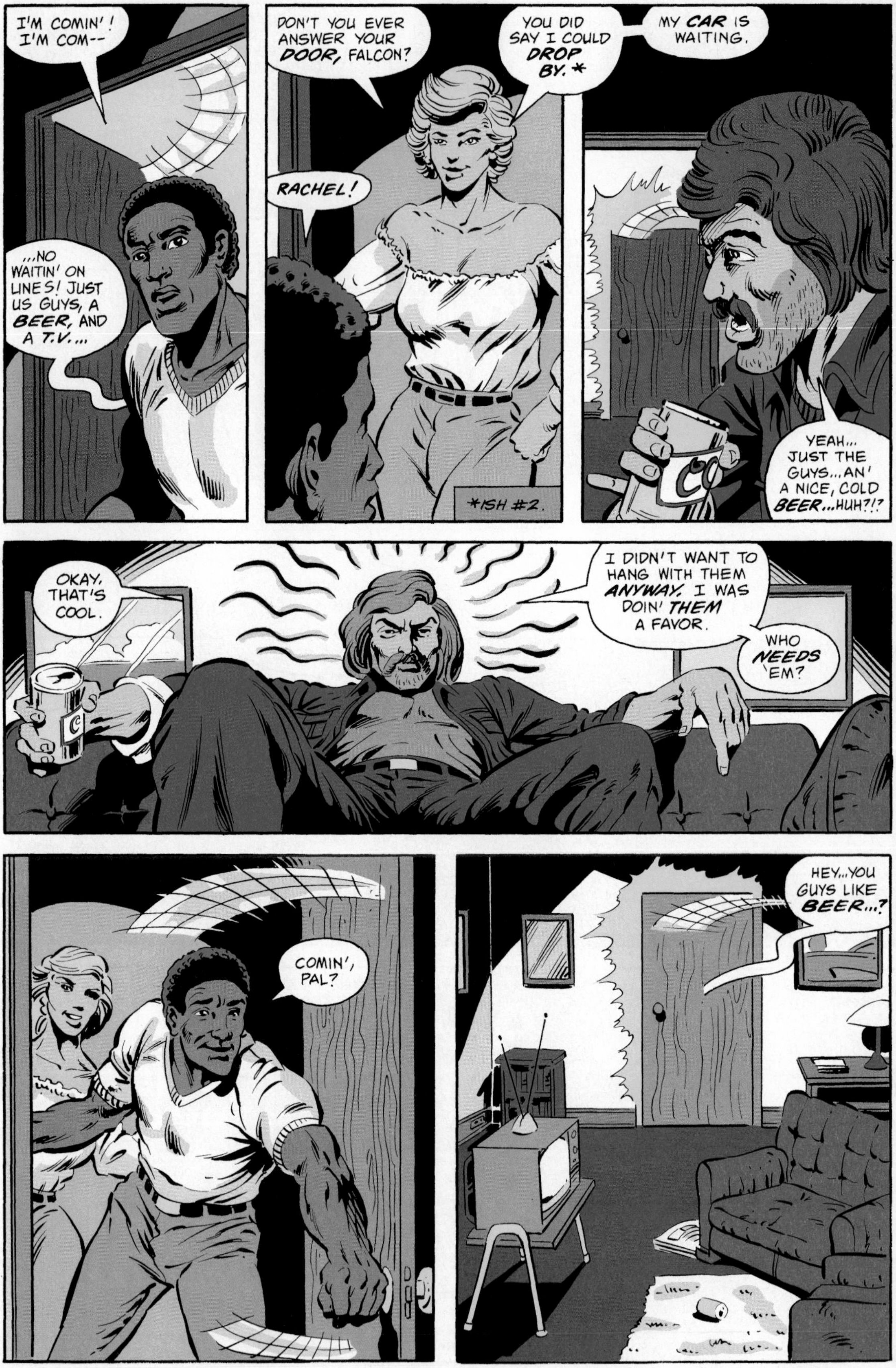
I'M COMIN'! I'M COM--
...NO WAITIN' ON LINES! JUST US GUYS, A BEER, AND A T.V. ...
DON'T YOU EVER ANSWER YOUR DOOR, FALCON?
RACHEL!
YOU DID SAY I COULD DROP BY.*
*ISH #2.
MY CAR IS WAITING.
YEAH... JUST THE GUYS... AN' A NICE, COLD BEER... HUH?!?
OKAY. THAT'S COOL.
I DIDN'T WANT TO HANG WITH THEM ANYWAY. I WAS DOIN' THEM A FAVOR.
WHO NEEDS 'EM?
COMIN', PAL?
HEY... YOU GUYS LIKE BEER...?

WHO IS THE FALCON?

Who is the Falcon? How did Sam Wilson meet Captain America, take on the mantle of a superhero, and become Cap's trusted partner — and later an Avenger?

Years before, the villainous Red Skull lost the all-powerful Cosmic Cube in a battle with Captain America. The Skull's motley crew of minions, the Exiles, eventually located the Cube — but when they returned it to their master, the Red Skull betrayed them and banished the group back to their island home.

The Skull used the Cube's limitless power to torment Captain America, sending his arch-foe to strange dimensions and forcing him to battle hordes of creatures. When this failed to break Cap's spirit, the Skull changed tactics — and used the cube to switch bodies with Captain America!

The Red Skull arranged to have Cap, now trapped in the Skull's villainous form, pursued by police and his own teammates, the mighty Avengers. Meanwhile, the Skull publicly posed as Captain America, basking in the hero-worshipping adulation of the masses — and alienating young Rick Jones, who had been trying to convince the real Cap to take him on as his sidekick.

When even this did not cause Captain America to despair, the Skull used the Cube to banish Cap — still in the form of the Red Skull — to the Exiles' island…hoping that his enraged former minions would tear the "Red Skull" limb from limb!

CAPT. AMERICA
12¢ 115 IND. JULY
CAPTAIN AMERICA
NOW BEGINS THE NIGHTMARE!
MARVEL COMICS GROUP

CAPT. AMERICA
15¢ 116 IND AUG
CAPTAIN AMERICA
MARVEL COMICS GROUP
GUEST STARRING:
THE MIGHTY AVENGERS!

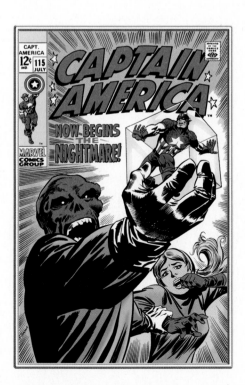

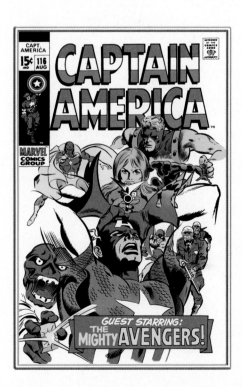

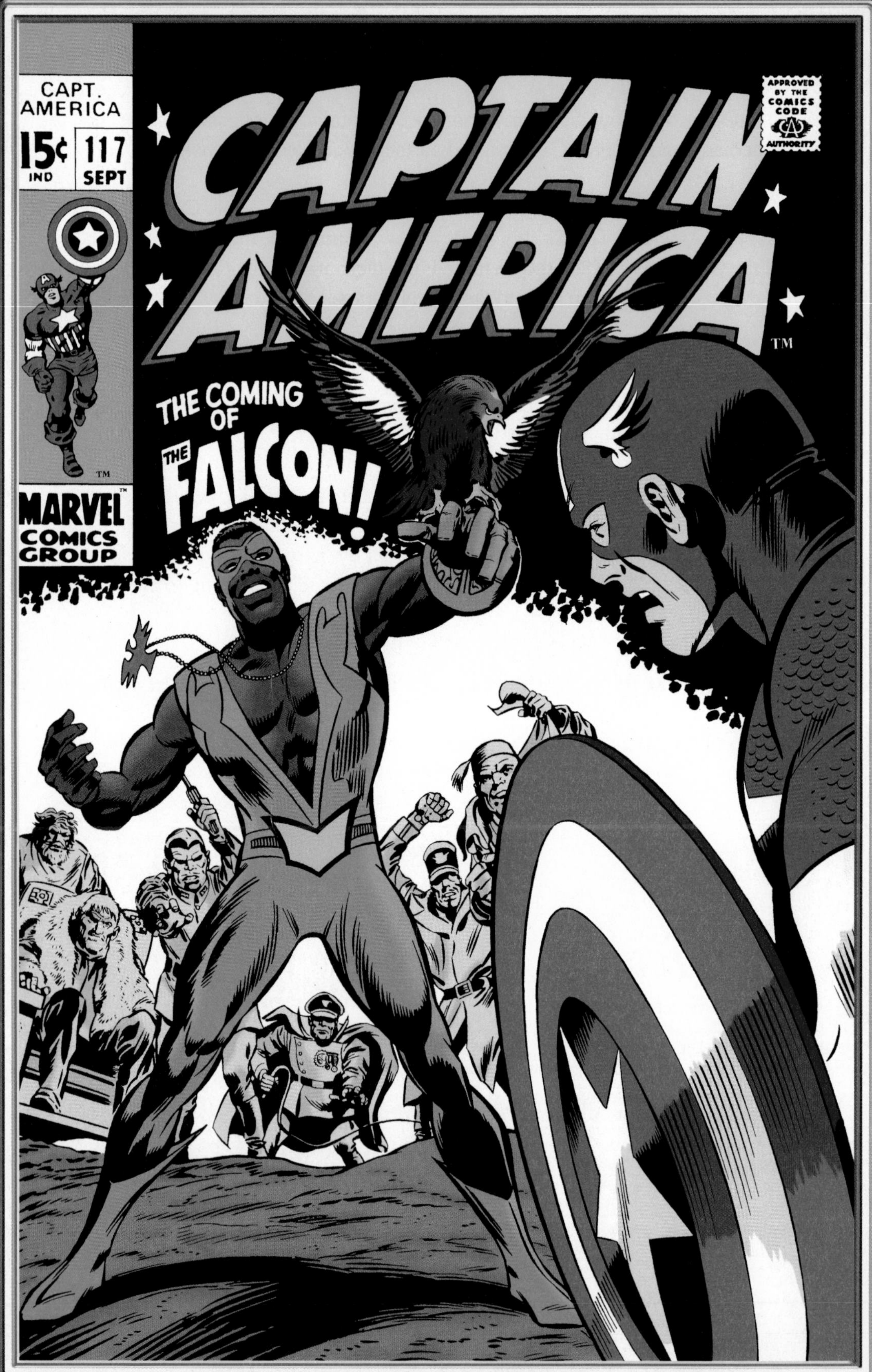
CAPT. AMERICA
15¢ IND
117 SEPT
APPROVED BY THE COMICS CODE AUTHORITY
CAPTAIN AMERICA™
THE COMING OF THE FALCON!
MARVEL™ COMICS GROUP

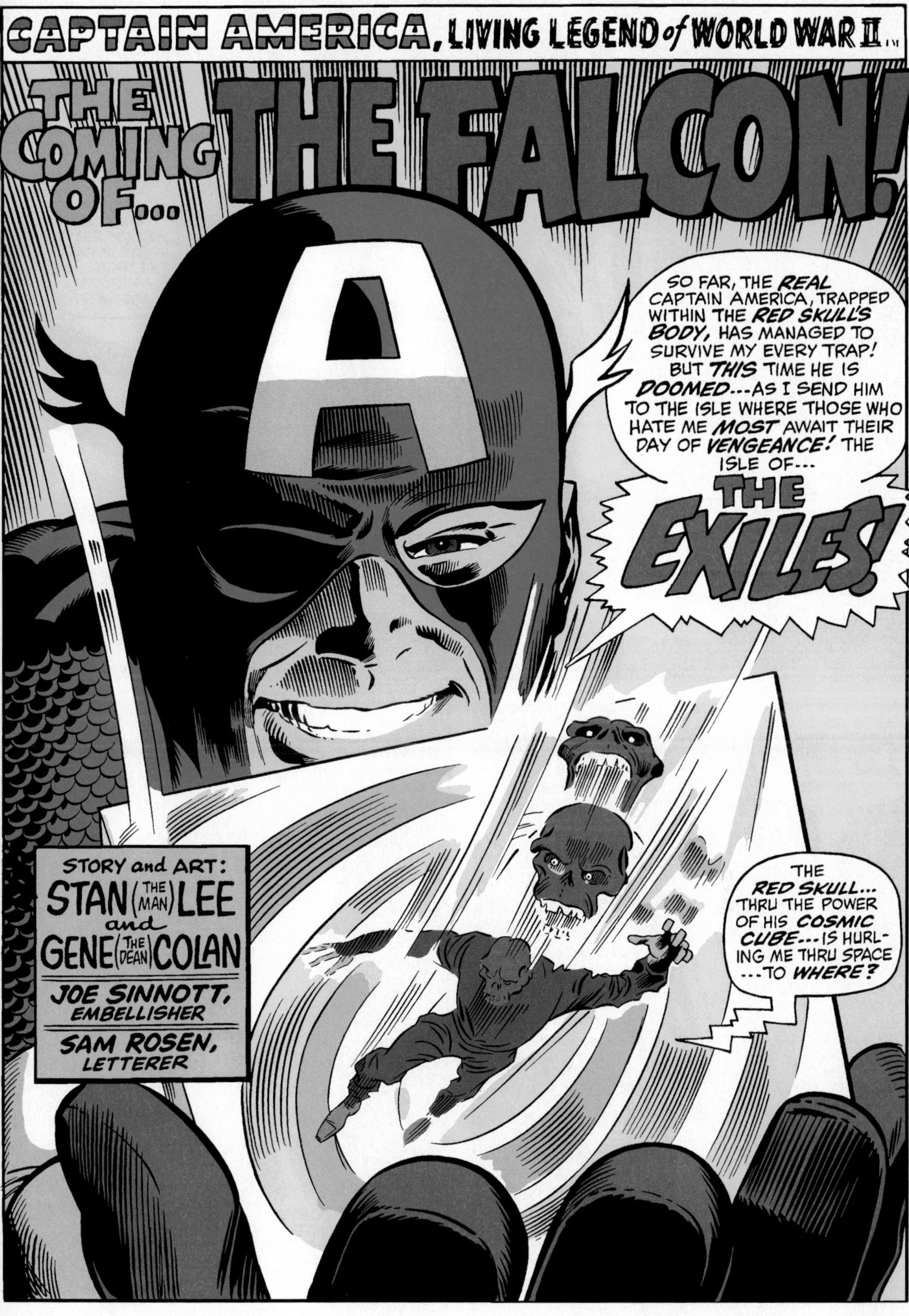
CAPTAIN AMERICA, LIVING LEGEND of WORLD WAR II.
THE COMING OF... THE FALCON!
SO FAR, THE REAL CAPTAIN AMERICA, TRAPPED WITHIN THE RED SKULL'S BODY, HAS MANAGED TO SURVIVE MY EVERY TRAP! BUT THIS TIME HE IS DOOMED--AS I SEND HIM TO THE ISLE WHERE THOSE WHO HATE ME MOST AWAIT THEIR DAY OF VENGEANCE! THE ISLE OF...
THE EXILES!
STORY and ART: STAN (THE MAN) LEE and GENE (THE DEAN) COLAN
JOE SINNOTT, EMBELLISHER
SAM ROSEN, LETTERER
THE RED SKULL... THRU THE POWER OF HIS COSMIC CUBE--IS HURLING ME THRU SPACE --TO WHERE?

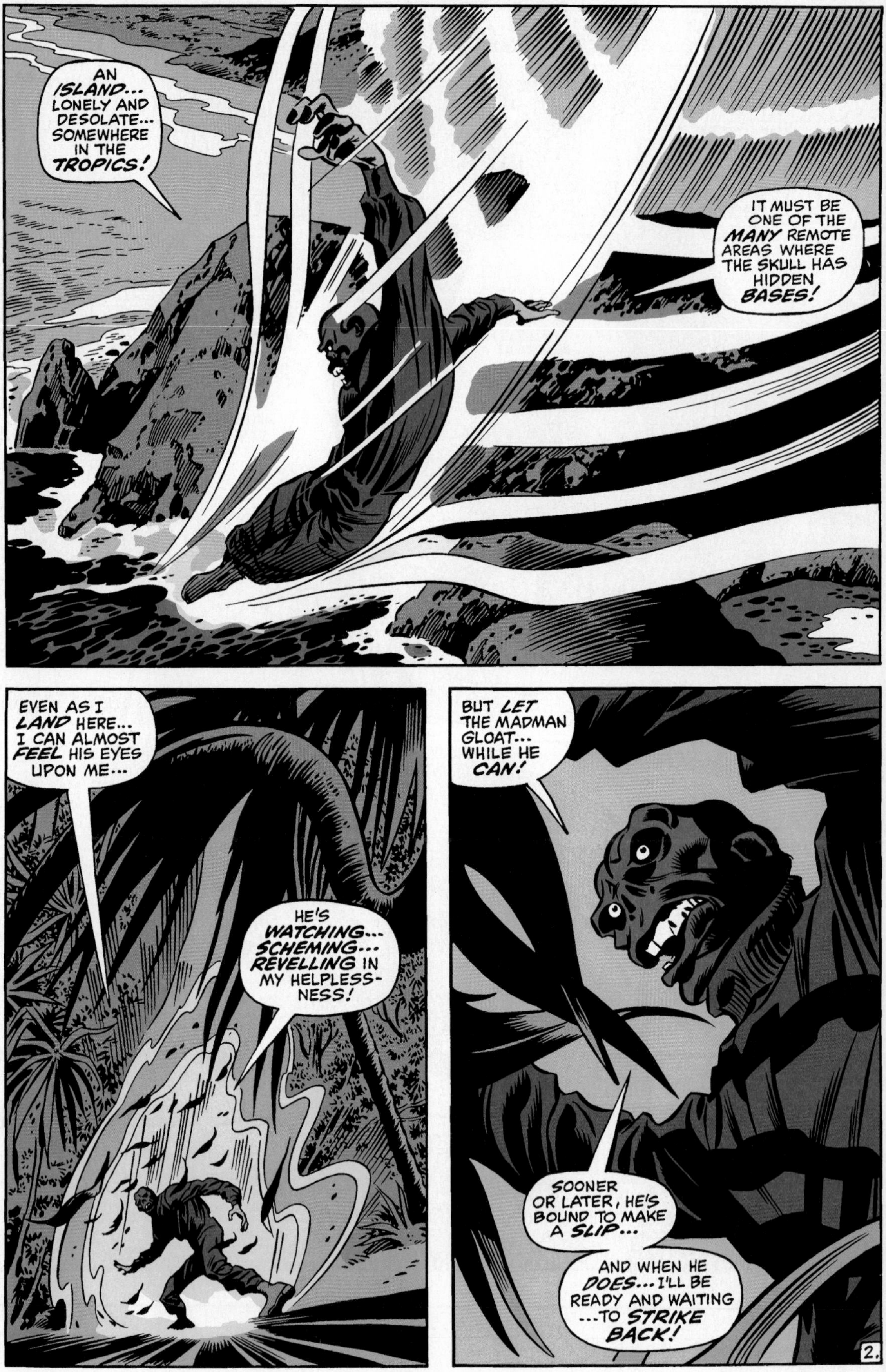
AN ISLAND... LONELY AND DESOLATE... SOMEWHERE IN THE TROPICS!
IT MUST BE ONE OF THE MANY REMOTE AREAS WHERE THE SKULL HAS HIDDEN BASES!
EVEN AS I LAND HERE... I CAN ALMOST FEEL HIS EYES UPON ME...
HE'S WATCHING... SCHEMING... REVELLING IN MY HELPLESS-NESS!
BUT LET THE MADMAN GLOAT... WHILE HE CAN!
SOONER OR LATER, HE'S BOUND TO MAKE A SLIP...
AND WHEN HE DOES... I'LL BE READY AND WAITING ...TO STRIKE BACK!
2.

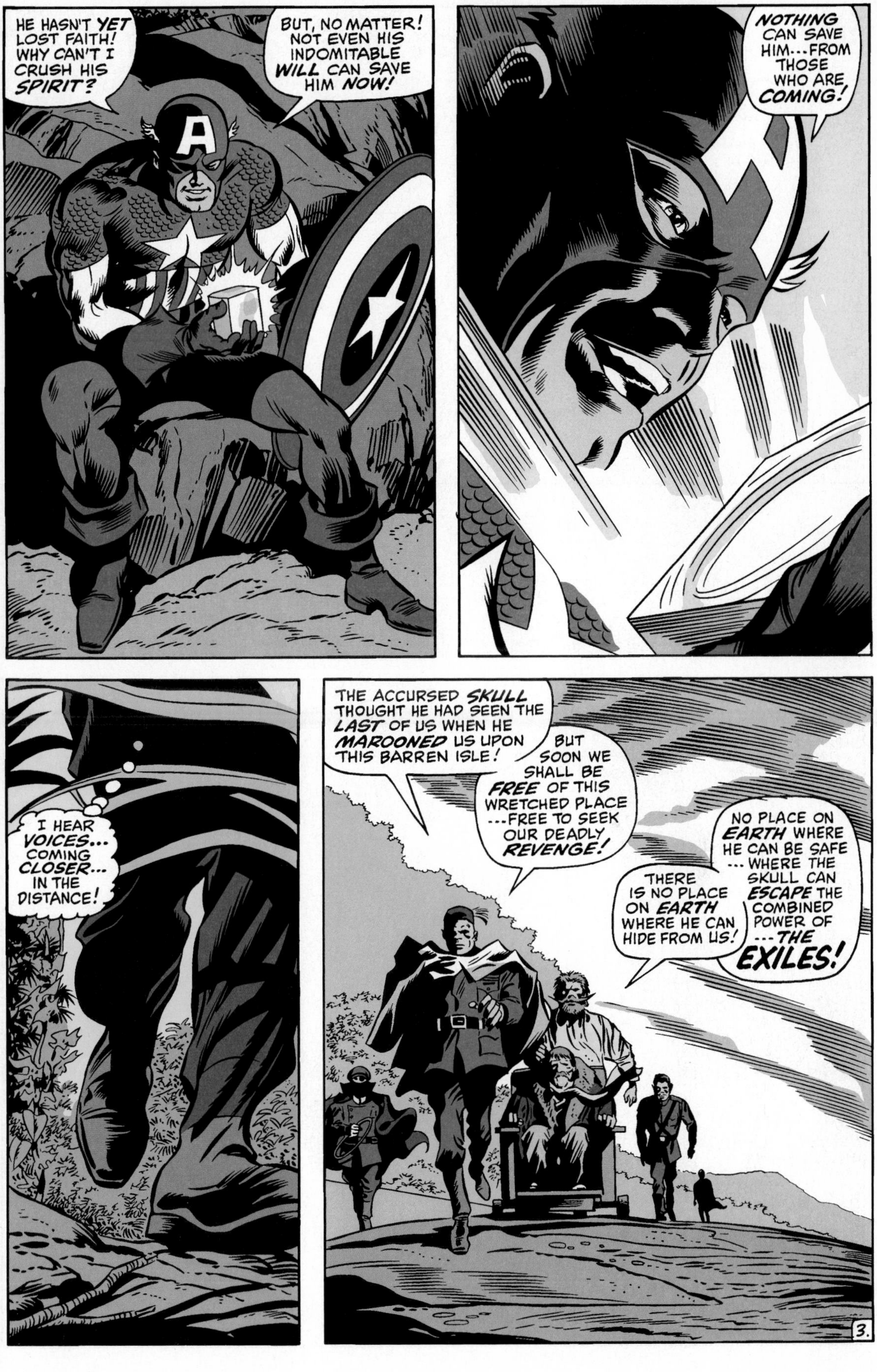

HE HASN'T YET LOST FAITH! WHY CAN'T I CRUSH HIS SPIRIT?
BUT, NO MATTER! NOT EVEN HIS INDOMITABLE WILL CAN SAVE HIM NOW!
NOTHING CAN SAVE HIM...FROM THOSE WHO ARE COMING!
I HEAR VOICES... COMING CLOSER... IN THE DISTANCE!
THE ACCURSED SKULL THOUGHT HE HAD SEEN THE LAST OF US WHEN HE MAROONED US UPON THIS BARREN ISLE!
BUT SOON WE SHALL BE FREE OF THIS WRETCHED PLACE ---FREE TO SEEK OUR DEADLY REVENGE!
THERE IS NO PLACE ON EARTH WHERE HE CAN HIDE FROM US!
NO PLACE ON EARTH WHERE HE CAN BE SAFE ... WHERE THE SKULL CAN ESCAPE THE COMBINED POWER OF ---THE EXILES!
3.

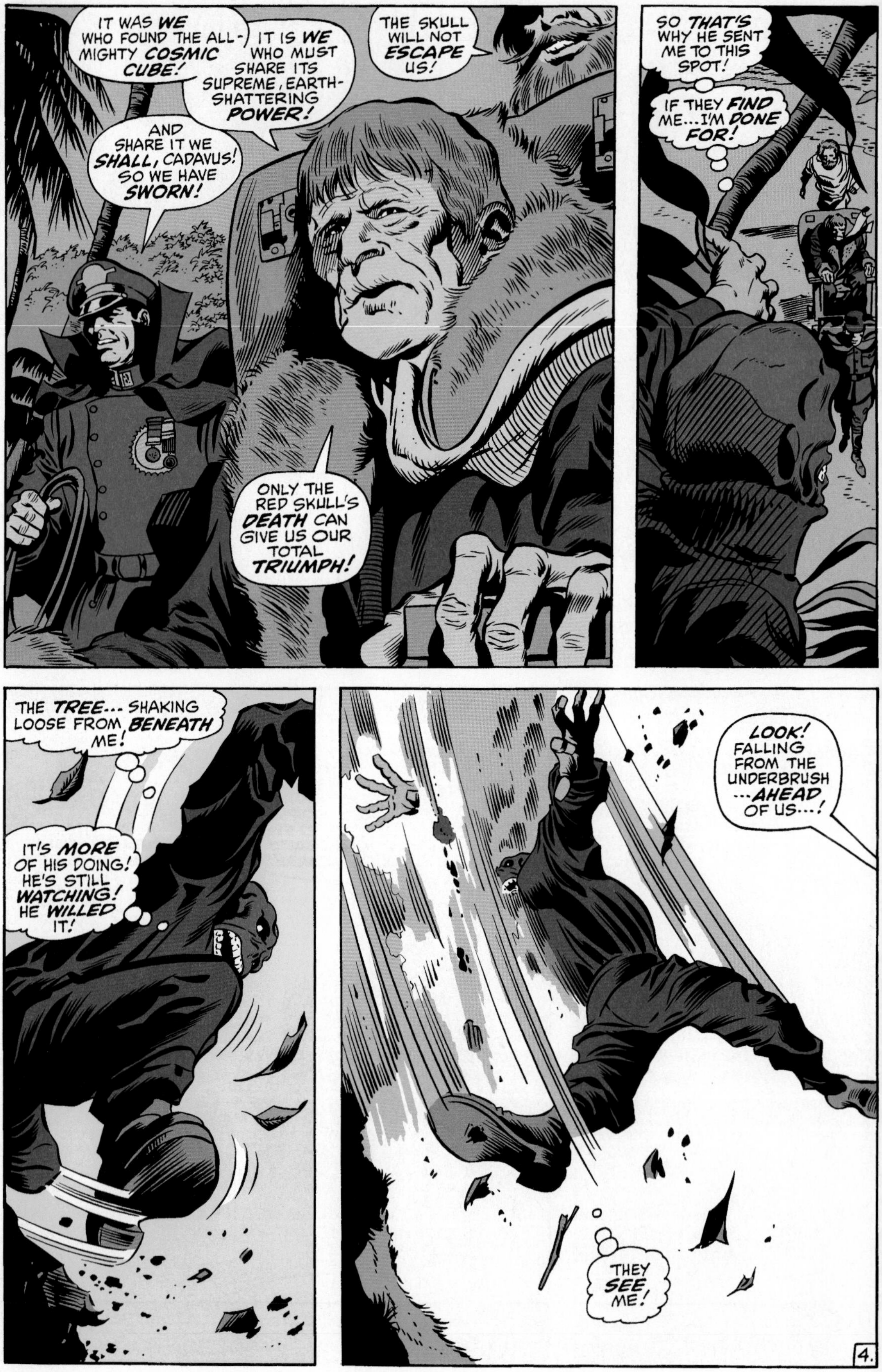
IT WAS WE WHO FOUND THE ALL-MIGHTY COSMIC CUBE!
IT IS WE WHO MUST SHARE ITS SUPREME, EARTH-SHATTERING POWER!
THE SKULL WILL NOT ESCAPE US!
AND SHARE IT WE SHALL, CADAVUS! SO WE HAVE SWORN!
ONLY THE RED SKULL'S DEATH CAN GIVE US OUR TOTAL TRIUMPH!
SO THAT'S WHY HE SENT ME TO THIS SPOT!
IF THEY FIND ME...I'M DONE FOR!
THE TREE... SHAKING LOOSE FROM BENEATH ME!
IT'S MORE OF HIS DOING! HE'S STILL WATCHING! HE WILLED IT!
LOOK! FALLING FROM THE UNDERBRUSH ...AHEAD OF US...!
THEY SEE ME!
4.

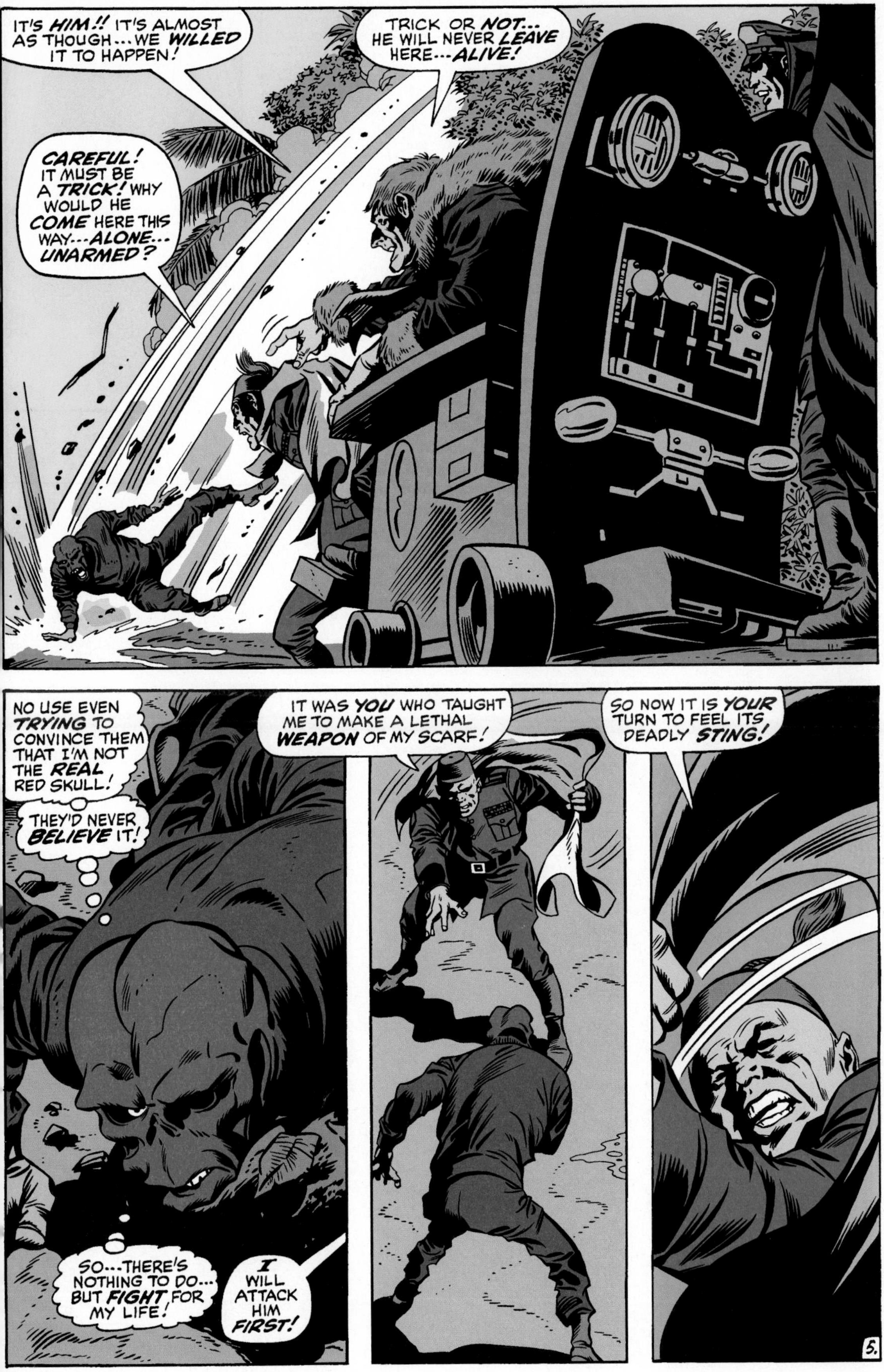
IT'S HIM!! IT'S ALMOST AS THOUGH... WE WILLED IT TO HAPPEN!
TRICK OR NOT... HE WILL NEVER LEAVE HERE... ALIVE!
CAREFUL! IT MUST BE A TRICK! WHY WOULD HE COME HERE THIS WAY... ALONE... UNARMED?
NO USE EVEN TRYING TO CONVINCE THEM THAT I'M NOT THE REAL RED SKULL!
THEY'D NEVER BELIEVE IT!
SO... THERE'S NOTHING TO DO... BUT FIGHT FOR MY LIFE!
I WILL ATTACK HIM FIRST!
IT WAS YOU WHO TAUGHT ME TO MAKE A LETHAL WEAPON OF MY SCARF!
SO NOW IT IS YOUR TURN TO FEEL ITS DEADLY STING!
5.

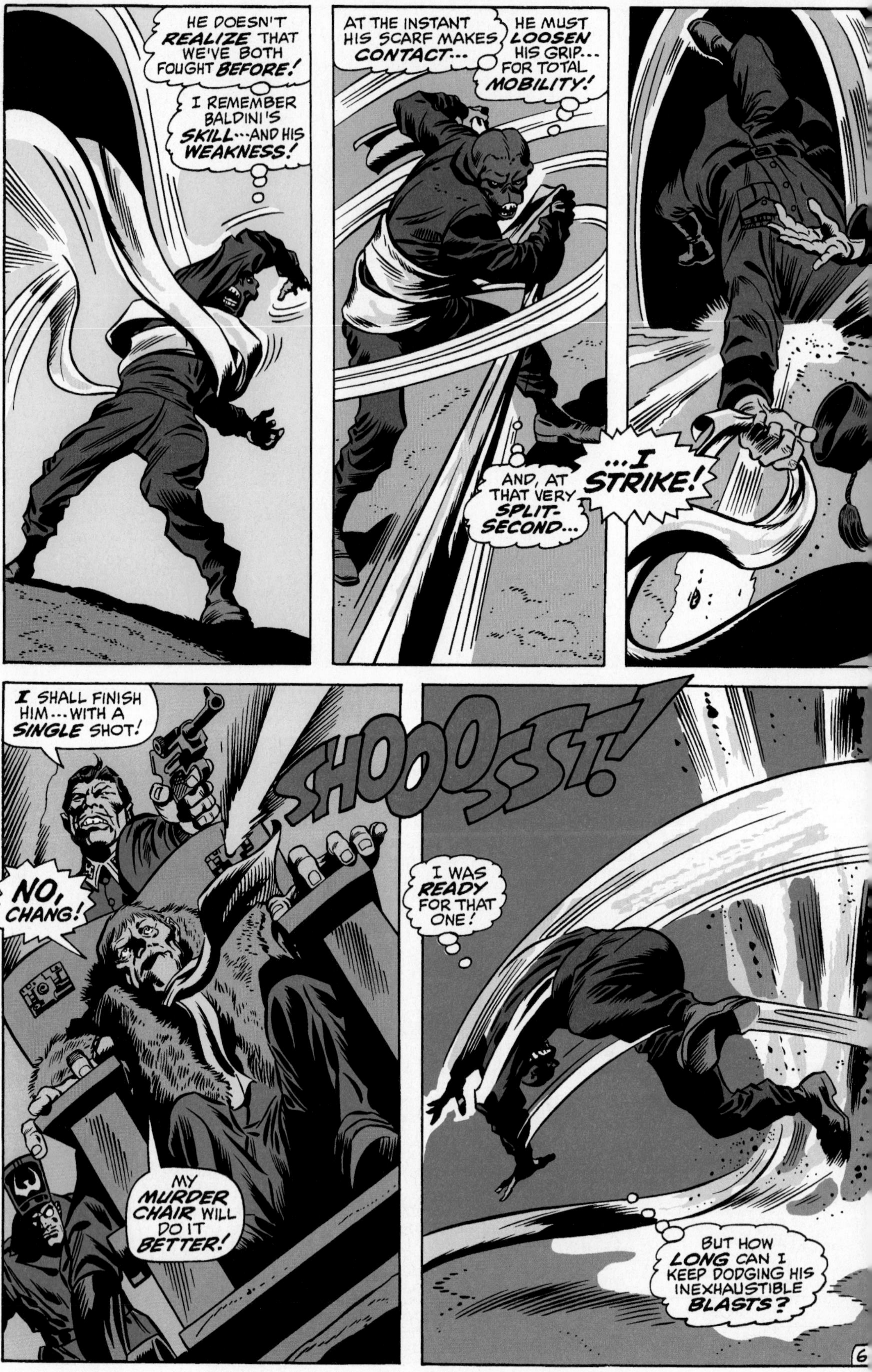
HE DOESN'T REALIZE THAT WE'VE BOTH FOUGHT BEFORE!
I REMEMBER BALDINI'S SKILL···AND HIS WEAKNESS!
AT THE INSTANT HIS SCARF MAKES CONTACT...
HE MUST LOOSEN HIS GRIP... FOR TOTAL MOBILITY!
AND, AT THAT VERY SPLIT-SECOND...
...I STRIKE!
I SHALL FINISH HIM···WITH A SINGLE SHOT!
NO, CHANG!
MY MURDER CHAIR WILL DO IT BETTER!
SHOOOSSST!
I WAS READY FOR THAT ONE!
BUT HOW LONG CAN I KEEP DODGING HIS INEXHAUSTIBLE BLASTS?
6

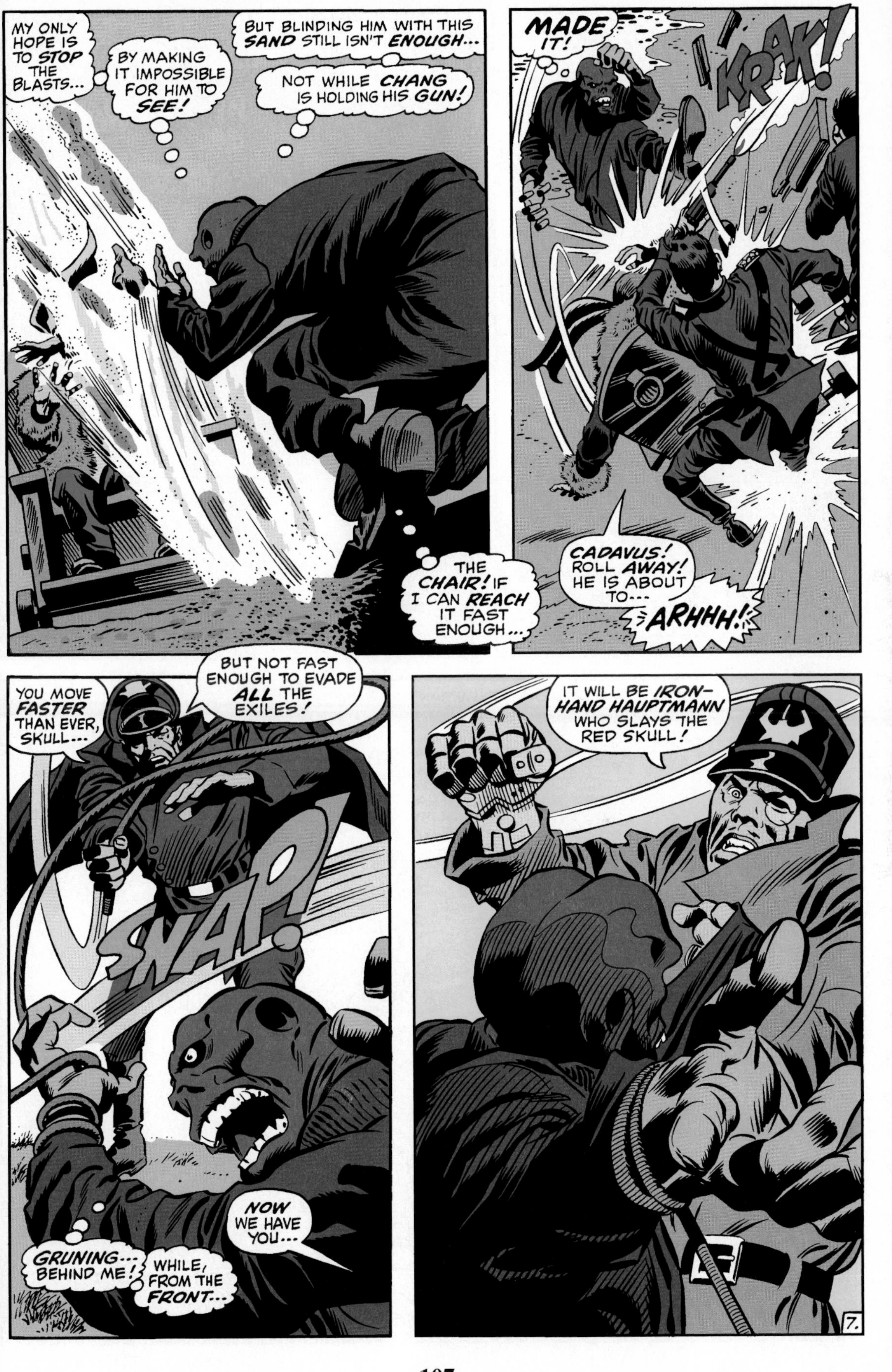
MY ONLY HOPE IS TO STOP THE BLASTS...
BY MAKING IT IMPOSSIBLE FOR HIM TO SEE!
BUT BLINDING HIM WITH THIS SAND STILL ISN'T ENOUGH...
NOT WHILE CHANG IS HOLDING HIS GUN!
THE CHAIR! IF I CAN REACH IT FAST ENOUGH...
MADE IT!
KRAK!
CADAVUS! ROLL AWAY! HE IS ABOUT TO---
ARHHH!
YOU MOVE FASTER THAN EVER, SKULL...
BUT NOT FAST ENOUGH TO EVADE ALL THE EXILES!
SNAP!
NOW WE HAVE YOU...
GRUNING... BEHIND ME!
WHILE, FROM THE FRONT...
IT WILL BE IRON-HAND HAUPTMANN WHO SLAYS THE RED SKULL!
7.

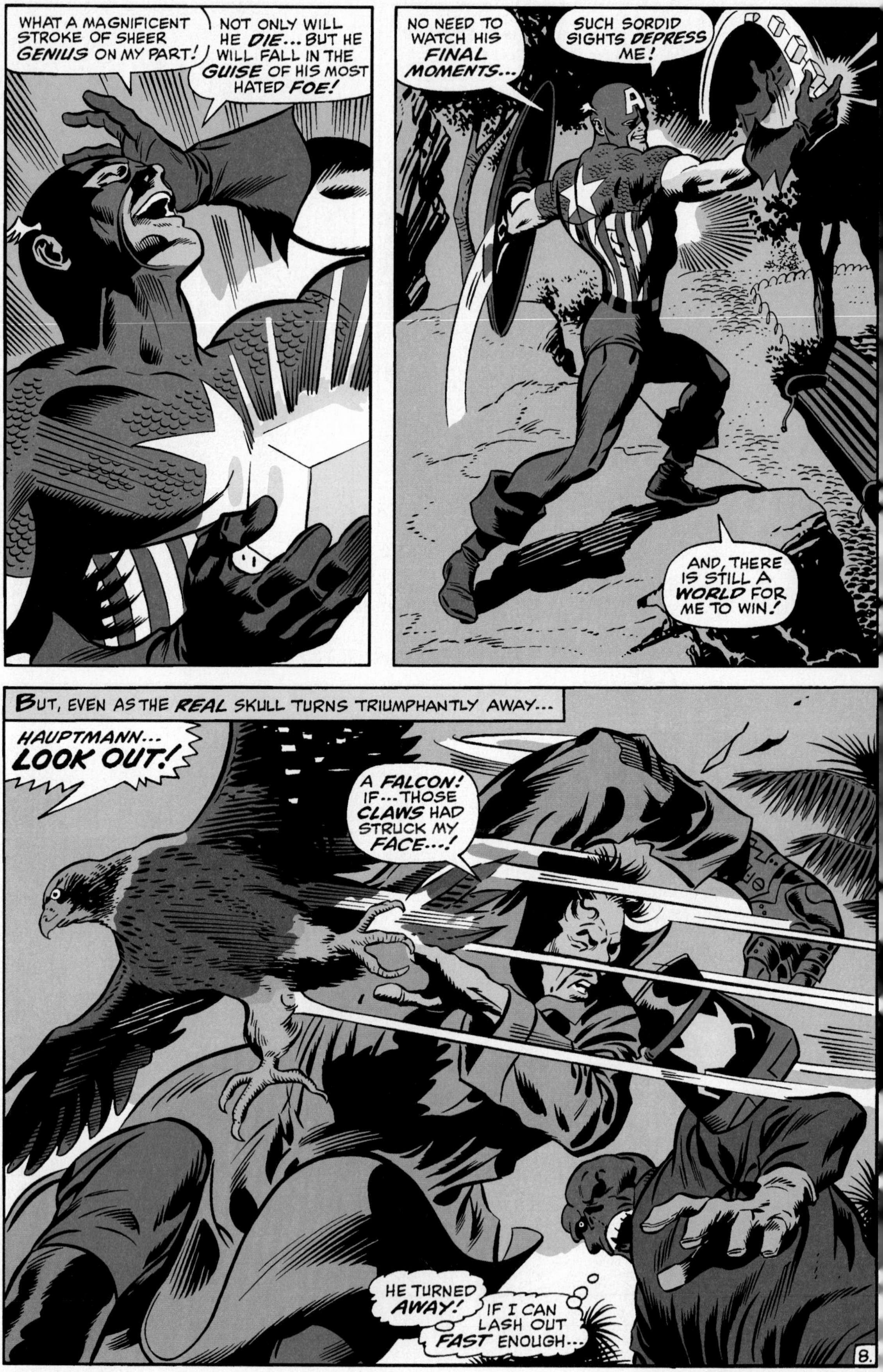
WHAT A MAGNIFICENT STROKE OF SHEER GENIUS ON MY PART!
NOT ONLY WILL HE DIE... BUT HE WILL FALL IN THE GUISE OF HIS MOST HATED FOE!
NO NEED TO WATCH HIS FINAL MOMENTS...
SUCH SORDID SIGHTS DEPRESS ME!
AND, THERE IS STILL A WORLD FOR ME TO WIN!
BUT, EVEN AS THE REAL SKULL TURNS TRIUMPHANTLY AWAY...
HAUPTMANN... LOOK OUT!
A FALCON! IF... THOSE CLAWS HAD STRUCK MY FACE...!
HE TURNED AWAY!
IF I CAN LASH OUT FAST ENOUGH...
8.

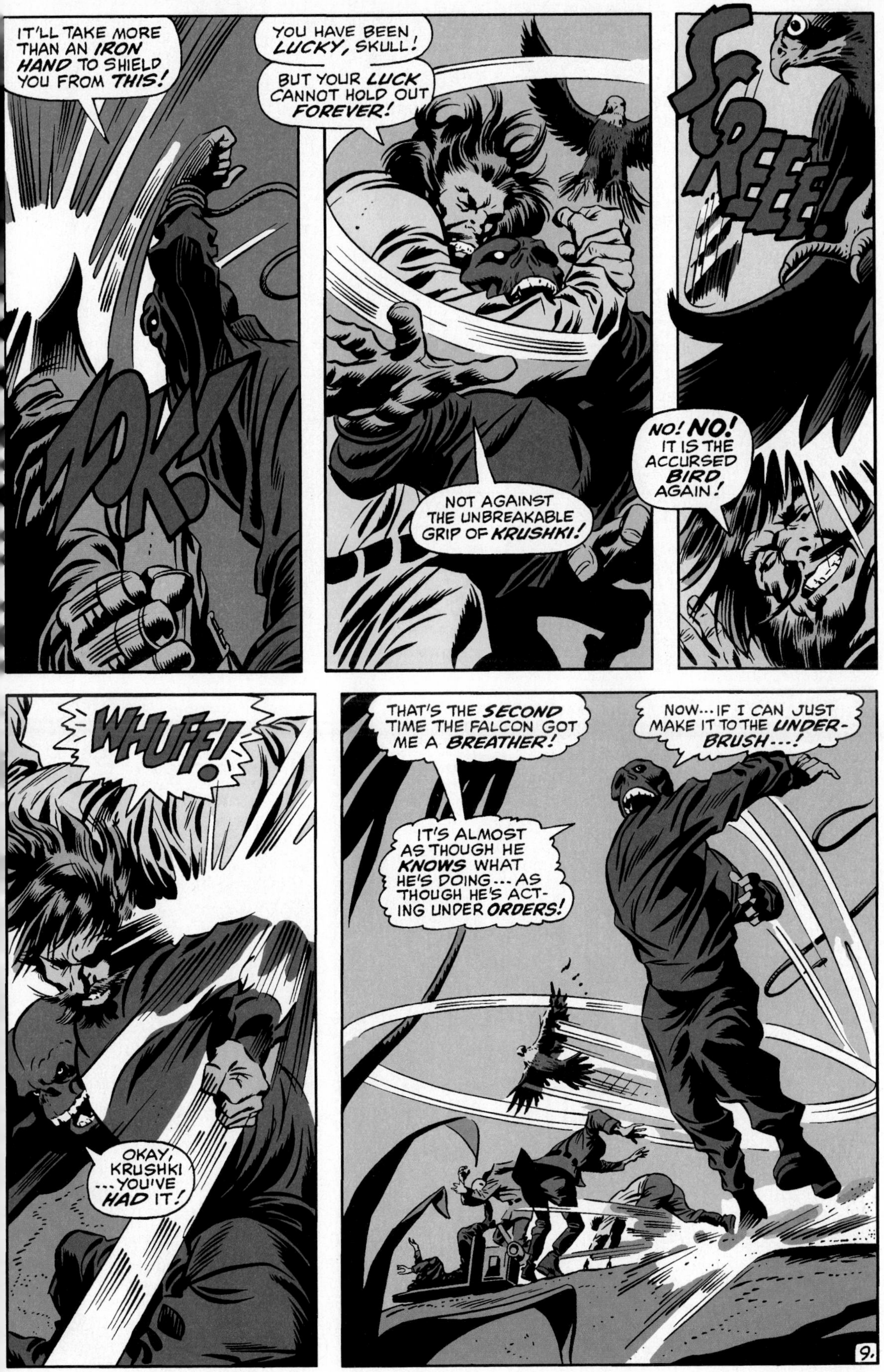
IT'LL TAKE MORE THAN AN IRON HAND TO SHIELD YOU FROM THIS!
YOU HAVE BEEN LUCKY, SKULL!
BUT YOUR LUCK CANNOT HOLD OUT FOREVER!
NOT AGAINST THE UNBREAKABLE GRIP OF KRUSHKI!
NO! NO! IT IS THE ACCURSED BIRD AGAIN!
WHUFF!
OKAY, KRUSHKI ...YOU'VE HAD IT!
THAT'S THE SECOND TIME THE FALCON GOT ME A BREATHER!
IT'S ALMOST AS THOUGH HE KNOWS WHAT HE'S DOING... AS THOUGH HE'S ACTING UNDER ORDERS!
NOW... IF I CAN JUST MAKE IT TO THE UNDER-BRUSH...!
9.

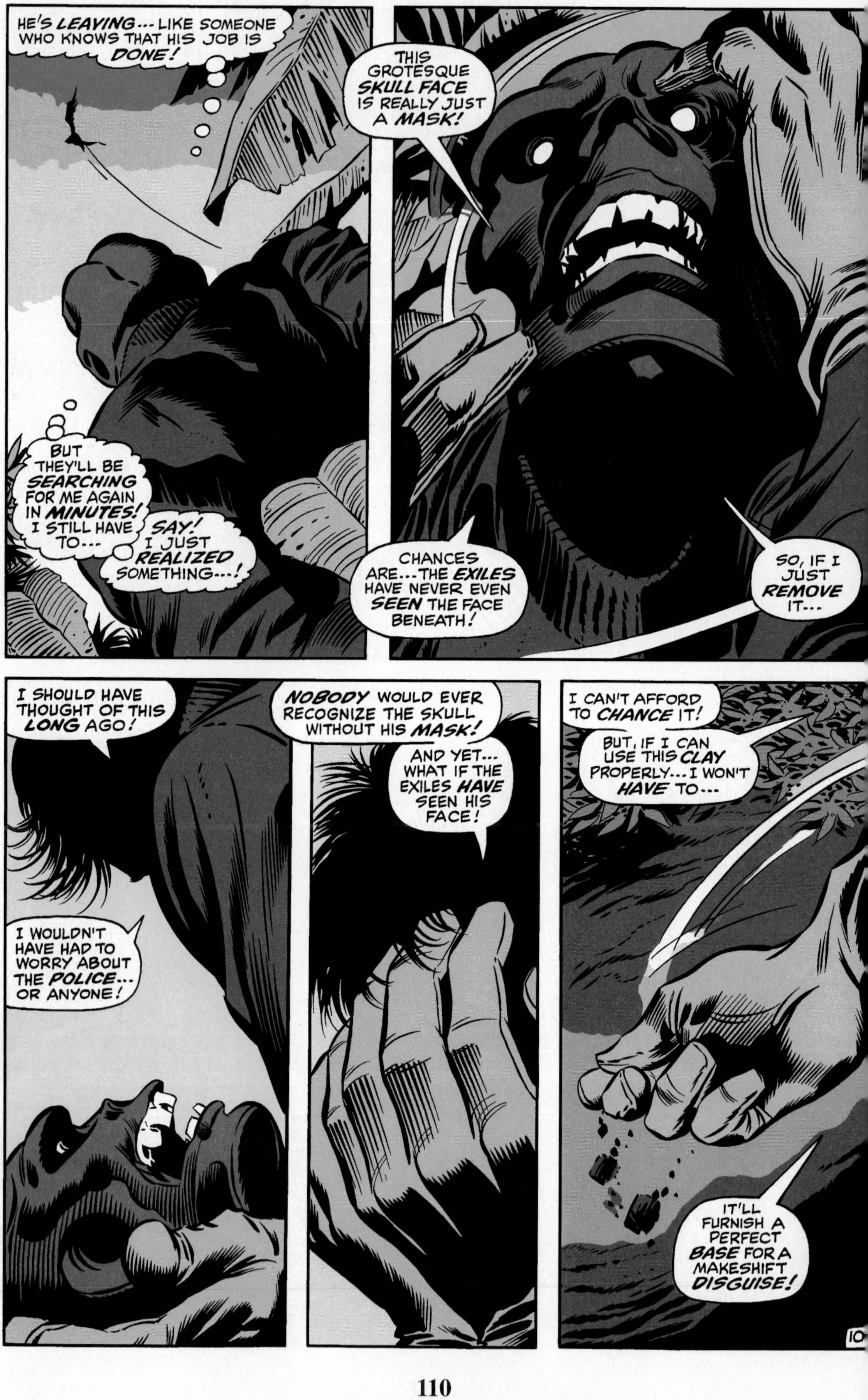
HE'S LEAVING... LIKE SOMEONE WHO KNOWS THAT HIS JOB IS DONE!
BUT THEY'LL BE SEARCHING FOR ME AGAIN IN MINUTES! I STILL HAVE TO...
SAY! I JUST REALIZED SOMETHING...!
THIS GROTESQUE SKULL FACE IS REALLY JUST A MASK!
CHANCES ARE... THE EXILES HAVE NEVER EVEN SEEN THE FACE BENEATH!
SO, IF I JUST REMOVE IT...
I SHOULD HAVE THOUGHT OF THIS LONG AGO!
I WOULDN'T HAVE HAD TO WORRY ABOUT THE POLICE... OR ANYONE!
NOBODY WOULD EVER RECOGNIZE THE SKULL WITHOUT HIS MASK!
AND YET... WHAT IF THE EXILES HAVE SEEN HIS FACE!
I CAN'T AFFORD TO CHANCE IT!
BUT, IF I CAN USE THIS CLAY PROPERLY... I WON'T HAVE TO...
IT'LL FURNISH A PERFECT BASE FOR A MAKESHIFT DISGUISE!
10

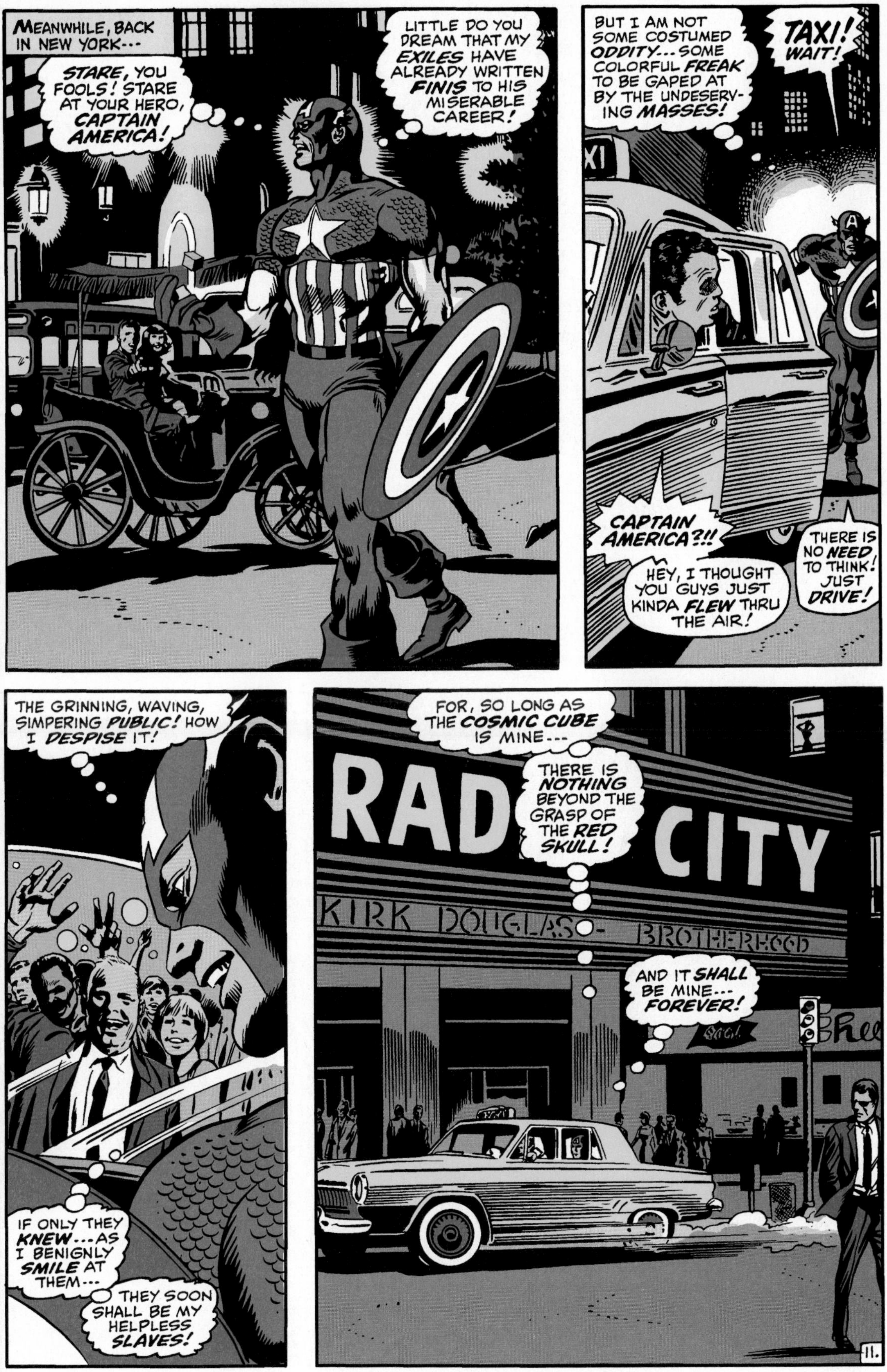
MEANWHILE, BACK IN NEW YORK---
STARE, YOU FOOLS! STARE AT YOUR HERO, CAPTAIN AMERICA!
LITTLE DO YOU DREAM THAT MY EXILES HAVE ALREADY WRITTEN FINIS TO HIS MISERABLE CAREER!
BUT I AM NOT SOME COSTUMED ODDITY... SOME COLORFUL FREAK TO BE GAPED AT BY THE UNDESERVING MASSES!
TAXI! WAIT!
XI
CAPTAIN AMERICA?!!
HEY, I THOUGHT YOU GUYS JUST KINDA FLEW THRU THE AIR!
THERE IS NO NEED TO THINK! JUST DRIVE!
THE GRINNING, WAVING, SIMPERING PUBLIC! HOW I DESPISE IT!
IF ONLY THEY KNEW...AS I BENIGNLY SMILE AT THEM...
THEY SOON SHALL BE MY HELPLESS SLAVES!
FOR, SO LONG AS THE COSMIC CUBE IS MINE---
RAD
CITY
THERE IS NOTHING BEYOND THE GRASP OF THE RED SKULL!
KIRK DOUGLAS - BROTHERHOOD
AND IT SHALL BE MINE--- FOREVER!
11.

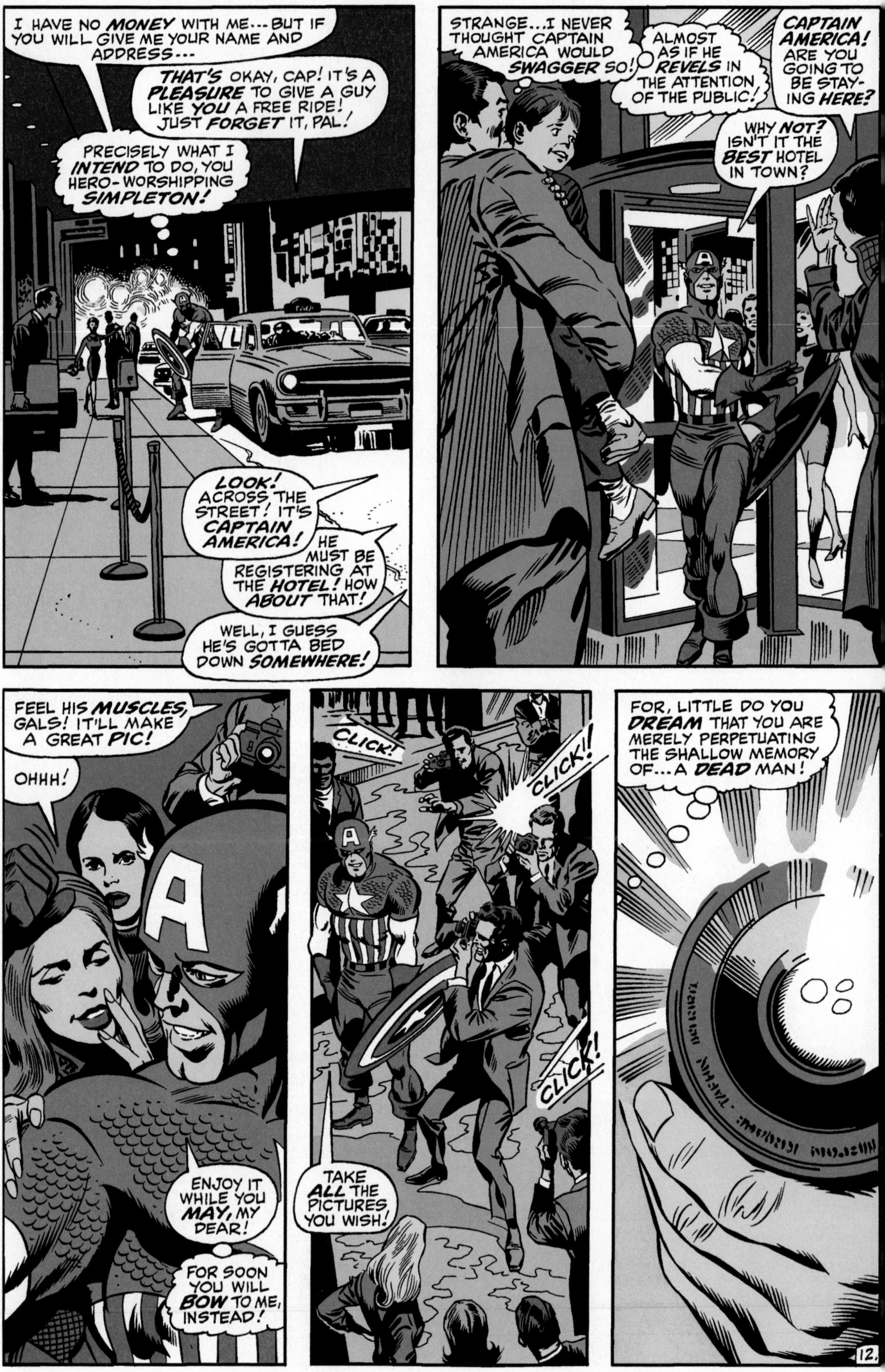
I HAVE NO MONEY WITH ME... BUT IF YOU WILL GIVE ME YOUR NAME AND ADDRESS...
THAT'S OKAY, CAP! IT'S A PLEASURE TO GIVE A GUY LIKE YOU A FREE RIDE! JUST FORGET IT, PAL!
PRECISELY WHAT I INTEND TO DO, YOU HERO-WORSHIPPING SIMPLETON!
LOOK! ACROSS THE STREET! IT'S CAPTAIN AMERICA!
HE MUST BE REGISTERING AT THE HOTEL! HOW ABOUT THAT!
WELL, I GUESS HE'S GOTTA BED DOWN SOMEWHERE!
STRANGE...I NEVER THOUGHT CAPTAIN AMERICA WOULD SWAGGER SO!
ALMOST AS IF HE REVELS IN THE ATTENTION OF THE PUBLIC!
CAPTAIN AMERICA! ARE YOU GOING TO BE STAYING HERE?
WHY NOT? ISN'T IT THE BEST HOTEL IN TOWN?
FEEL HIS MUSCLES, GALS! IT'LL MAKE A GREAT PIC!
OHHH!
ENJOY IT WHILE YOU MAY, MY DEAR!
FOR SOON YOU WILL BOW TO ME, INSTEAD!
CLICK!
CLICK!!
CLICK!
TAKE ALL THE PICTURES YOU WISH!
FOR, LITTLE DO YOU DREAM THAT YOU ARE MERELY PERPETUATING THE SHALLOW MEMORY OF... A DEAD MAN!
12.

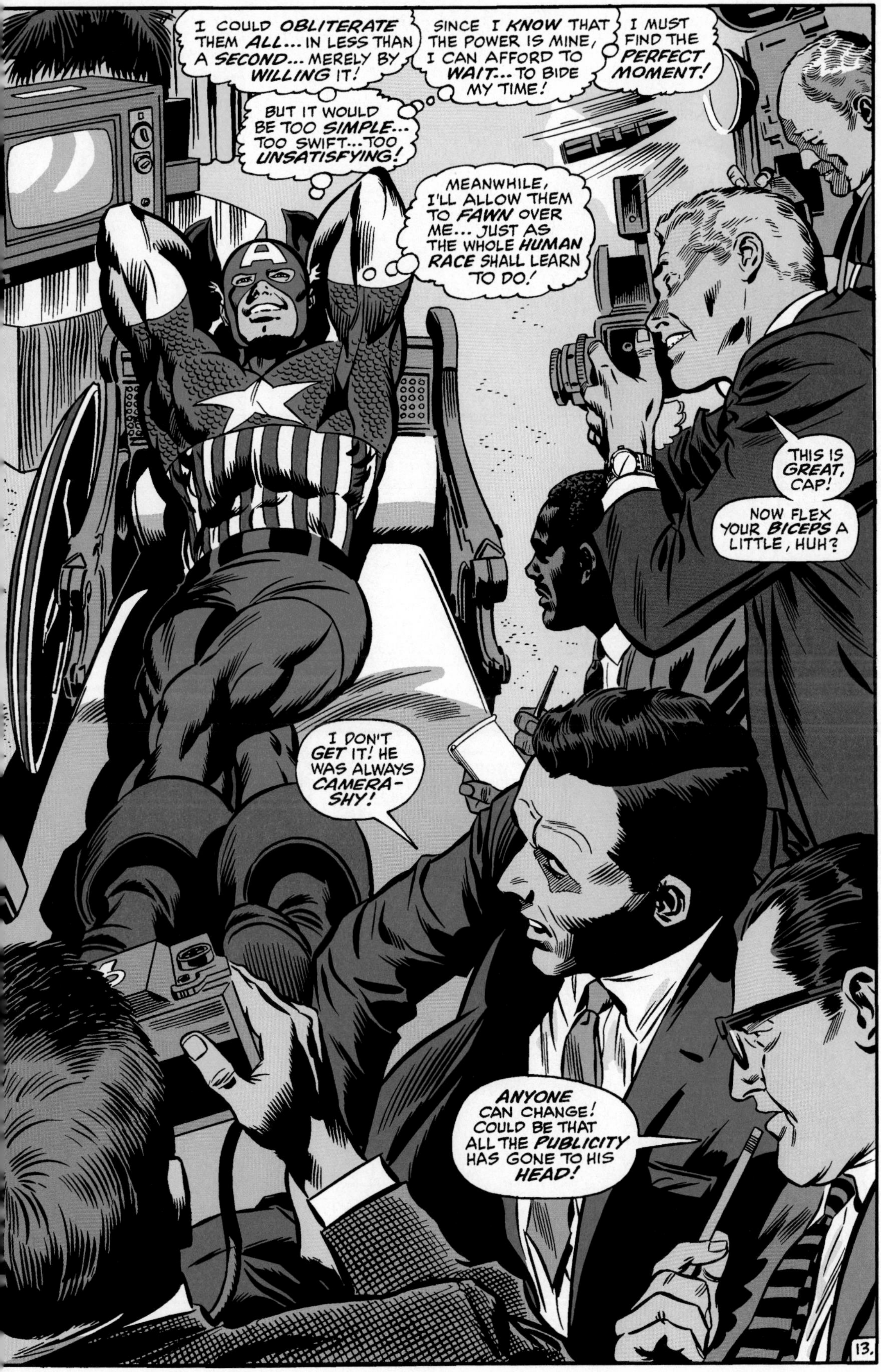
I COULD OBLITERATE THEM ALL... IN LESS THAN A SECOND... MERELY BY WILLING IT!
SINCE I KNOW THAT THE POWER IS MINE, I CAN AFFORD TO WAIT... TO BIDE MY TIME!
I MUST FIND THE PERFECT MOMENT!
BUT IT WOULD BE TOO SIMPLE... TOO SWIFT... TOO UNSATISFYING!
MEANWHILE, I'LL ALLOW THEM TO FAWN OVER ME... JUST AS THE WHOLE HUMAN RACE SHALL LEARN TO DO!
THIS IS GREAT, CAP!
NOW FLEX YOUR BICEPS A LITTLE, HUH?
I DON'T GET IT! HE WAS ALWAYS CAMERA-SHY!
ANYONE CAN CHANGE! COULD BE THAT ALL THE PUBLICITY HAS GONE TO HIS HEAD!
13.

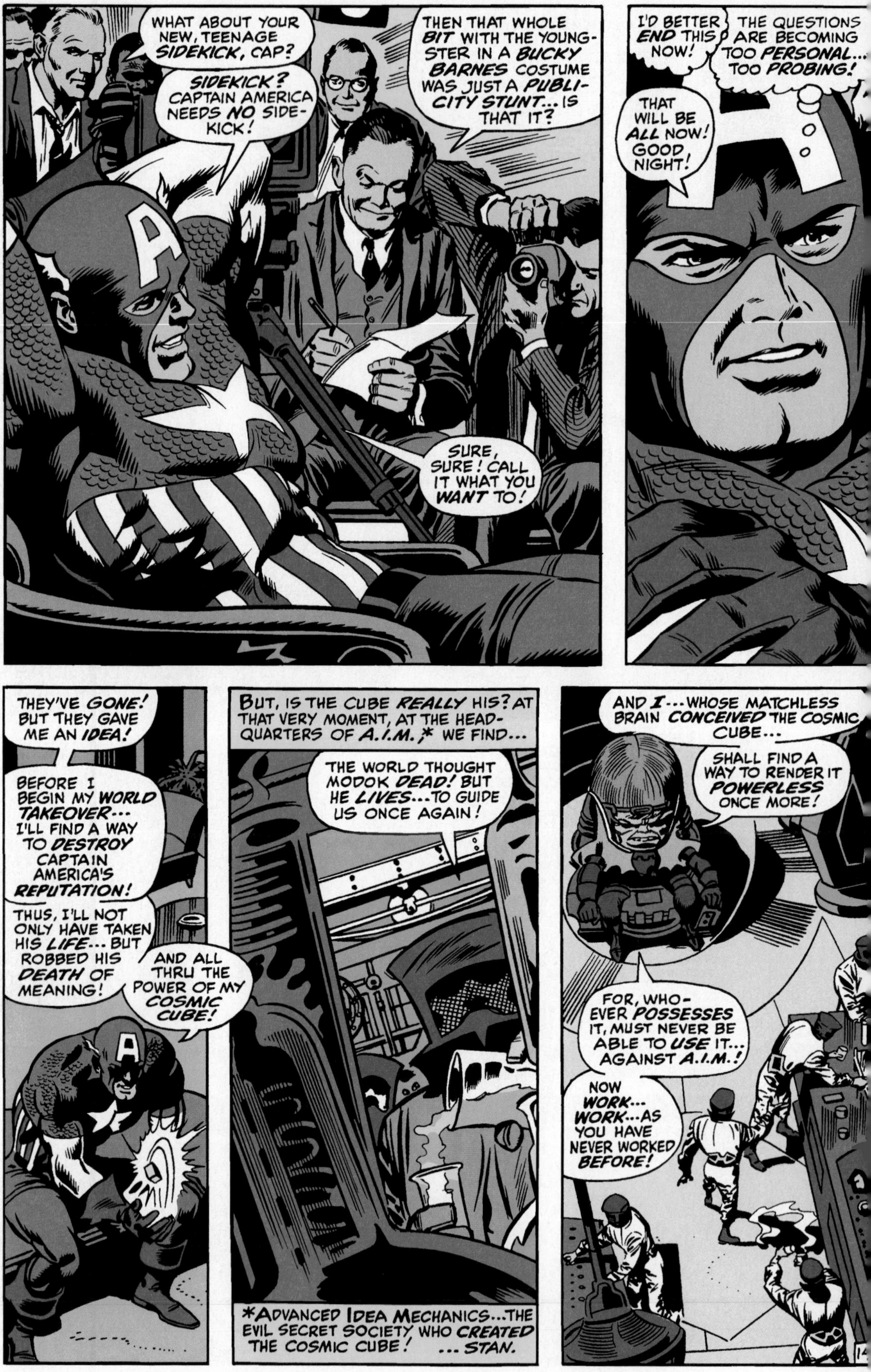
WHAT ABOUT YOUR NEW, TEENAGE SIDEKICK, CAP?
SIDEKICK? CAPTAIN AMERICA NEEDS NO SIDE-KICK!
THEN THAT WHOLE BIT WITH THE YOUNG-STER IN A BUCKY BARNES COSTUME WAS JUST A PUBLI-CITY STUNT... IS THAT IT?
SURE, SURE! CALL IT WHAT YOU WANT TO!
I'D BETTER END THIS NOW!
THE QUESTIONS ARE BECOMING TOO PERSONAL... TOO PROBING!
THAT WILL BE ALL NOW! GOOD NIGHT!
THEY'VE GONE! BUT THEY GAVE ME AN IDEA!
BEFORE I BEGIN MY WORLD TAKEOVER... I'LL FIND A WAY TO DESTROY CAPTAIN AMERICA'S REPUTATION!
THUS, I'LL NOT ONLY HAVE TAKEN HIS LIFE... BUT ROBBED HIS DEATH OF MEANING!
AND ALL THRU THE POWER OF MY COSMIC CUBE!
BUT, IS THE CUBE REALLY HIS? AT THAT VERY MOMENT, AT THE HEAD-QUARTERS OF A.I.M.,* WE FIND...
THE WORLD THOUGHT MODOK DEAD! BUT HE LIVES... TO GUIDE US ONCE AGAIN!
*ADVANCED IDEA MECHANICS... THE EVIL SECRET SOCIETY WHO CREATED THE COSMIC CUBE! ... STAN.
AND I... WHOSE MATCHLESS BRAIN CONCEIVED THE COSMIC CUBE...
SHALL FIND A WAY TO RENDER IT POWERLESS ONCE MORE!
FOR, WHO-EVER POSSESSES IT, MUST NEVER BE ABLE TO USE IT... AGAINST A.I.M.!
NOW WORK... WORK... AS YOU HAVE NEVER WORKED BEFORE!

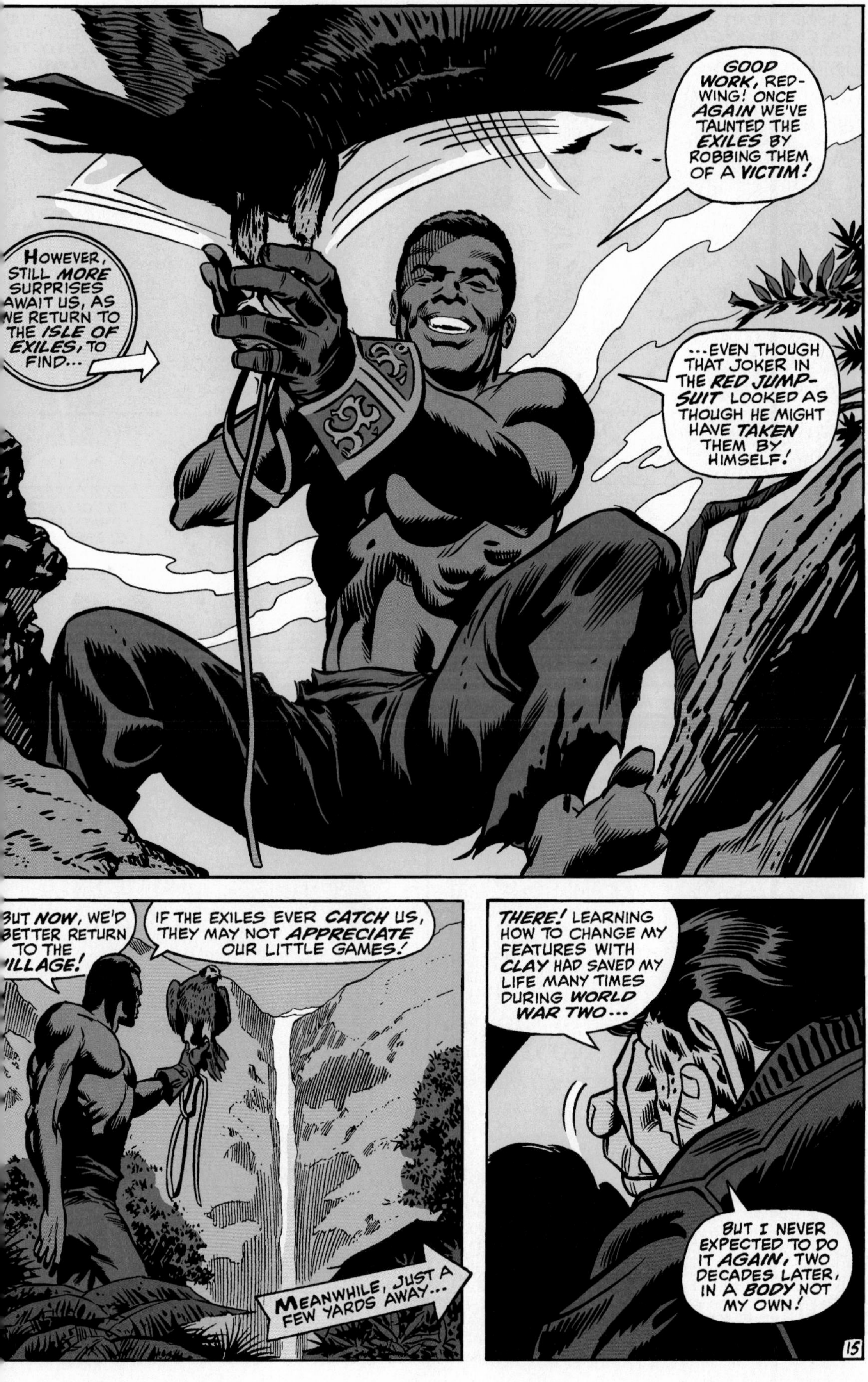
GOOD WORK, RED-WING! ONCE AGAIN WE'VE TAUNTED THE EXILES BY ROBBING THEM OF A VICTIM!
HOWEVER, STILL MORE SURPRISES AWAIT US, AS WE RETURN TO THE ISLE OF EXILES, TO FIND...
...EVEN THOUGH THAT JOKER IN THE RED JUMP-SUIT LOOKED AS THOUGH HE MIGHT HAVE TAKEN THEM BY HIMSELF!
BUT NOW, WE'D BETTER RETURN TO THE ILLAGE!
IF THE EXILES EVER CATCH US, THEY MAY NOT APPRECIATE OUR LITTLE GAMES!
MEANWHILE, JUST A FEW YARDS AWAY...
THERE! LEARNING HOW TO CHANGE MY FEATURES WITH CLAY HAD SAVED MY LIFE MANY TIMES DURING WORLD WAR TWO...
BUT I NEVER EXPECTED TO DO IT AGAIN, TWO DECADES LATER, IN A BODY NOT MY OWN!
15

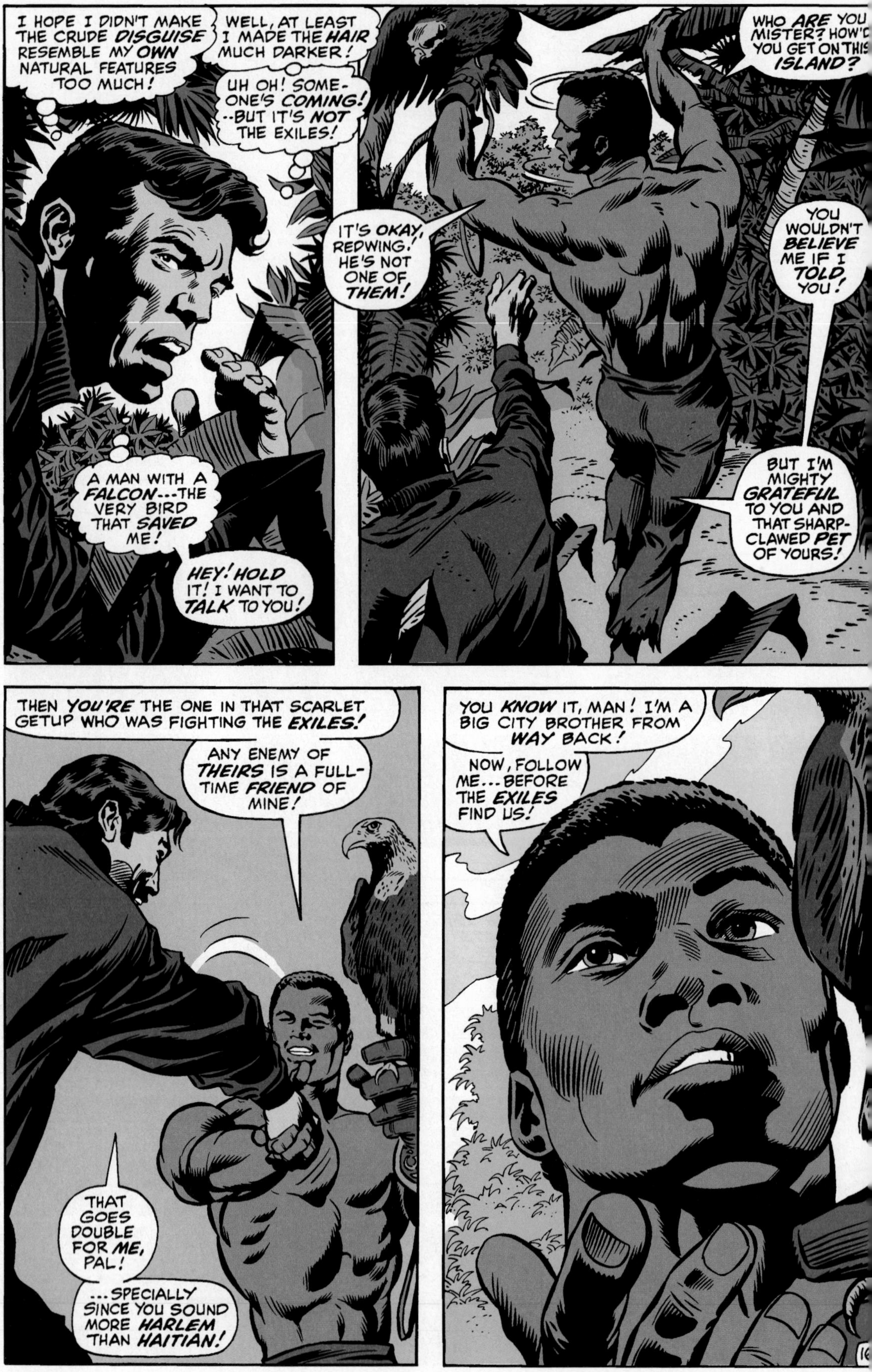
I HOPE I DIDN'T MAKE THE CRUDE DISGUISE RESEMBLE MY OWN NATURAL FEATURES TOO MUCH!
WELL, AT LEAST I MADE THE HAIR MUCH DARKER!
UH OH! SOME-ONE'S COMING! --BUT IT'S NOT THE EXILES!
A MAN WITH A FALCON---THE VERY BIRD THAT SAVED ME!
HEY! HOLD IT! I WANT TO TALK TO YOU!
WHO ARE YOU MISTER? HOW'D YOU GET ON THIS ISLAND?
IT'S OKAY, REDWING! HE'S NOT ONE OF THEM!
YOU WOULDN'T BELIEVE ME IF I TOLD YOU!
BUT I'M MIGHTY GRATEFUL TO YOU AND THAT SHARP-CLAWED PET OF YOURS!
THEN YOU'RE THE ONE IN THAT SCARLET GETUP WHO WAS FIGHTING THE EXILES!
ANY ENEMY OF THEIRS IS A FULL-TIME FRIEND OF MINE!
THAT GOES DOUBLE FOR ME, PAL!
...SPECIALLY SINCE YOU SOUND MORE HARLEM THAN HAITIAN!
YOU KNOW IT, MAN! I'M A BIG CITY BROTHER FROM WAY BACK!
NOW, FOLLOW ME... BEFORE THE EXILES FIND US!
16

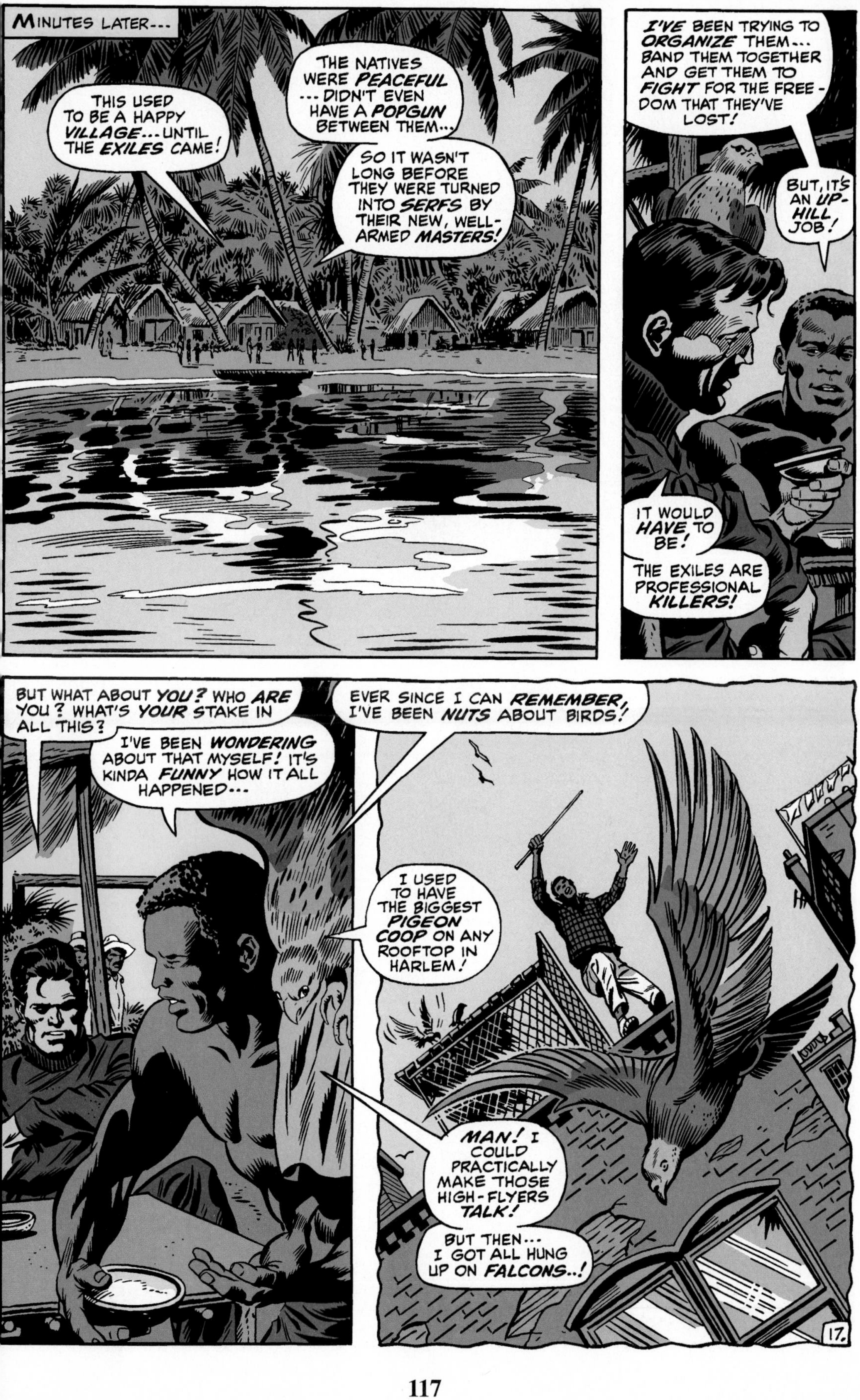
MINUTES LATER---
THIS USED TO BE A HAPPY VILLAGE... UNTIL THE EXILES CAME!
THE NATIVES WERE PEACEFUL ---DIDN'T EVEN HAVE A POPGUN BETWEEN THEM...
SO IT WASN'T LONG BEFORE THEY WERE TURNED INTO SERFS BY THEIR NEW, WELL-ARMED MASTERS!
I'VE BEEN TRYING TO ORGANIZE THEM... BAND THEM TOGETHER AND GET THEM TO FIGHT FOR THE FREE-DOM THAT THEY'VE LOST!
BUT, IT'S AN UP-HILL JOB!
IT WOULD HAVE TO BE!
THE EXILES ARE PROFESSIONAL KILLERS!
BUT WHAT ABOUT YOU? WHO ARE YOU? WHAT'S YOUR STAKE IN ALL THIS?
I'VE BEEN WONDERING ABOUT THAT MYSELF! IT'S KINDA FUNNY HOW IT ALL HAPPENED---
EVER SINCE I CAN REMEMBER, I'VE BEEN NUTS ABOUT BIRDS!
I USED TO HAVE THE BIGGEST PIGEON COOP ON ANY ROOFTOP IN HARLEM!
MAN! I COULD PRACTICALLY MAKE THOSE HIGH-FLYERS TALK!
BUT THEN... I GOT ALL HUNG UP ON FALCONS..!
17.

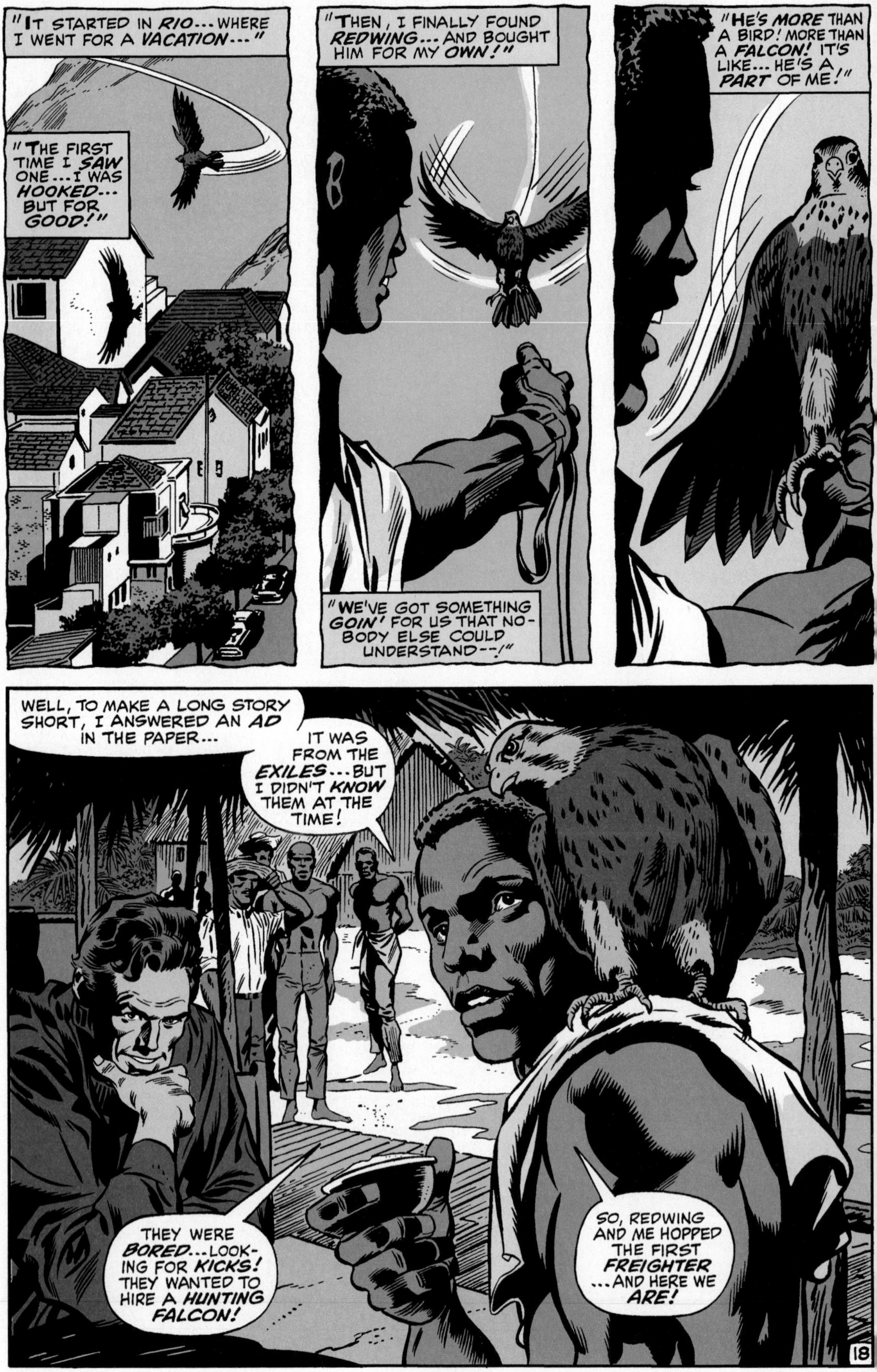
"IT STARTED IN RIO... WHERE I WENT FOR A VACATION..."
"THE FIRST TIME I SAW ONE... I WAS HOOKED... BUT FOR GOOD!"
"THEN, I FINALLY FOUND REDWING... AND BOUGHT HIM FOR MY OWN!"
"WE'VE GOT SOMETHING GOIN' FOR US THAT NOBODY ELSE COULD UNDERSTAND--!"
"HE'S MORE THAN A BIRD! MORE THAN A FALCON! IT'S LIKE... HE'S A PART OF ME!"
WELL, TO MAKE A LONG STORY SHORT, I ANSWERED AN AD IN THE PAPER...
IT WAS FROM THE EXILES...BUT I DIDN'T KNOW THEM AT THE TIME!
THEY WERE BORED...LOOKING FOR KICKS! THEY WANTED TO HIRE A HUNTING FALCON!
SO, REDWING AND ME HOPPED THE FIRST FREIGHTER ...AND HERE WE ARE!
18

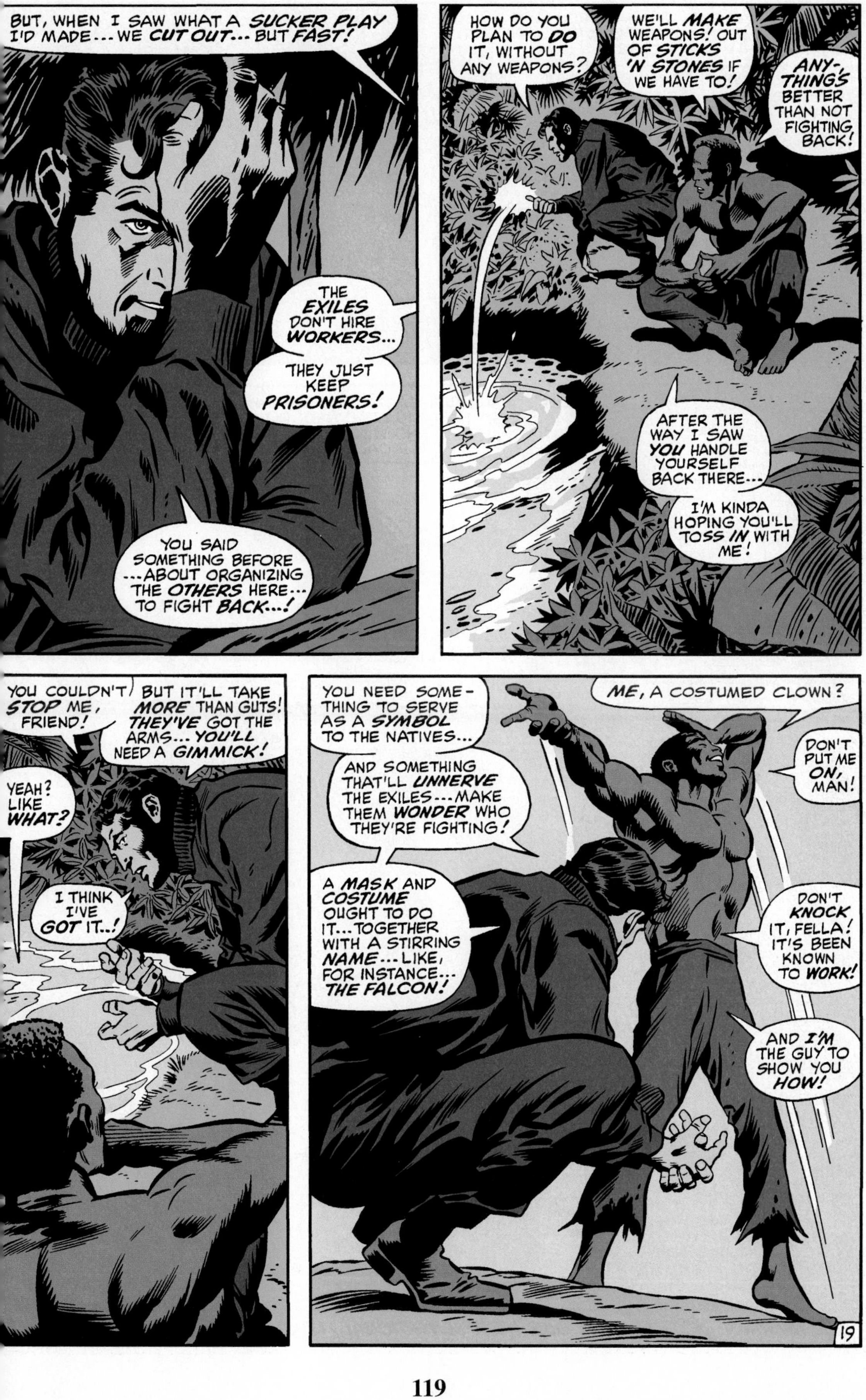
BUT, WHEN I SAW WHAT A SUCKER PLAY I'D MADE... WE CUT OUT... BUT FAST!
THE EXILES DON'T HIRE WORKERS...
THEY JUST KEEP PRISONERS!
YOU SAID SOMETHING BEFORE ...ABOUT ORGANIZING THE OTHERS HERE... TO FIGHT BACK...!
HOW DO YOU PLAN TO DO IT, WITHOUT ANY WEAPONS?
WE'LL MAKE WEAPONS! OUT OF STICKS 'N STONES IF WE HAVE TO!
ANY-THING'S BETTER THAN NOT FIGHTING BACK!
AFTER THE WAY I SAW YOU HANDLE YOURSELF BACK THERE...
I'M KINDA HOPING YOU'LL TOSS IN WITH ME!
YOU COULDN'T STOP ME, FRIEND!
BUT IT'LL TAKE MORE THAN GUTS! THEY'VE GOT THE ARMS... YOU'LL NEED A GIMMICK!
YEAH? LIKE WHAT?
I THINK I'VE GOT IT..!
YOU NEED SOME-THING TO SERVE AS A SYMBOL TO THE NATIVES...
AND SOMETHING THAT'LL UNNERVE THE EXILES... MAKE THEM WONDER WHO THEY'RE FIGHTING!
A MASK AND COSTUME OUGHT TO DO IT... TOGETHER WITH A STIRRING NAME... LIKE, FOR INSTANCE... THE FALCON!
ME, A COSTUMED CLOWN?
DON'T PUT ME ON, MAN!
DON'T KNOCK IT, FELLA! IT'S BEEN KNOWN TO WORK!
AND I'M THE GUY TO SHOW YOU HOW!
19

PATIENTLY, THE MAN WHO HAD BEEN *CAPTAIN AMERICA* TALKS ON... SLOWLY *CONVINCING* HIS ATTENTIVE COMPANION... WHILE, NEARBY...

WE'LL *COMB* THE ISLAND TILL WE *FIND* HIM!

THE LONGER IT *TAKES*, THE GREATER *PRICE* HE'LL PAY!

PATIENCE! PATIENCE! HE CANNOT *ESCAPE* US!

THERE ARE *NONE* ON THIS ISLE WHO WILL DARE TO *AID* HIM!

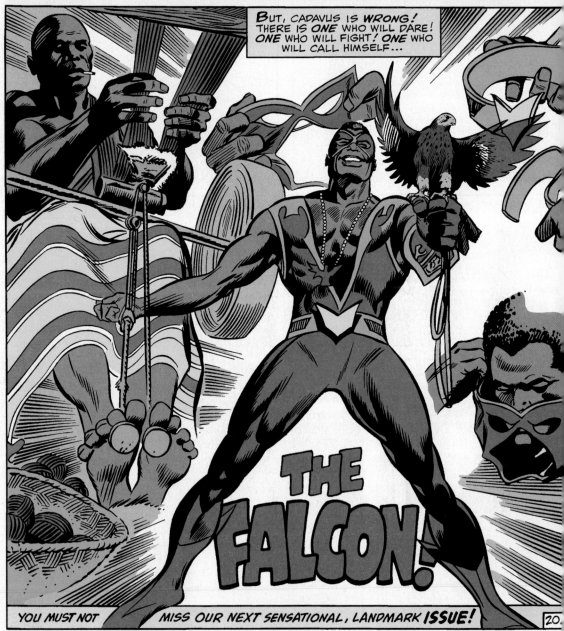

BUT, CADAVUS IS *WRONG!* THERE IS *ONE* WHO WILL DARE! *ONE* WHO WILL FIGHT! *ONE* WHO WILL CALL HIMSELF...

THE FALCON!

YOU MUST NOT MISS OUR NEXT SENSATIONAL, LANDMARK *ISSUE!*

20.

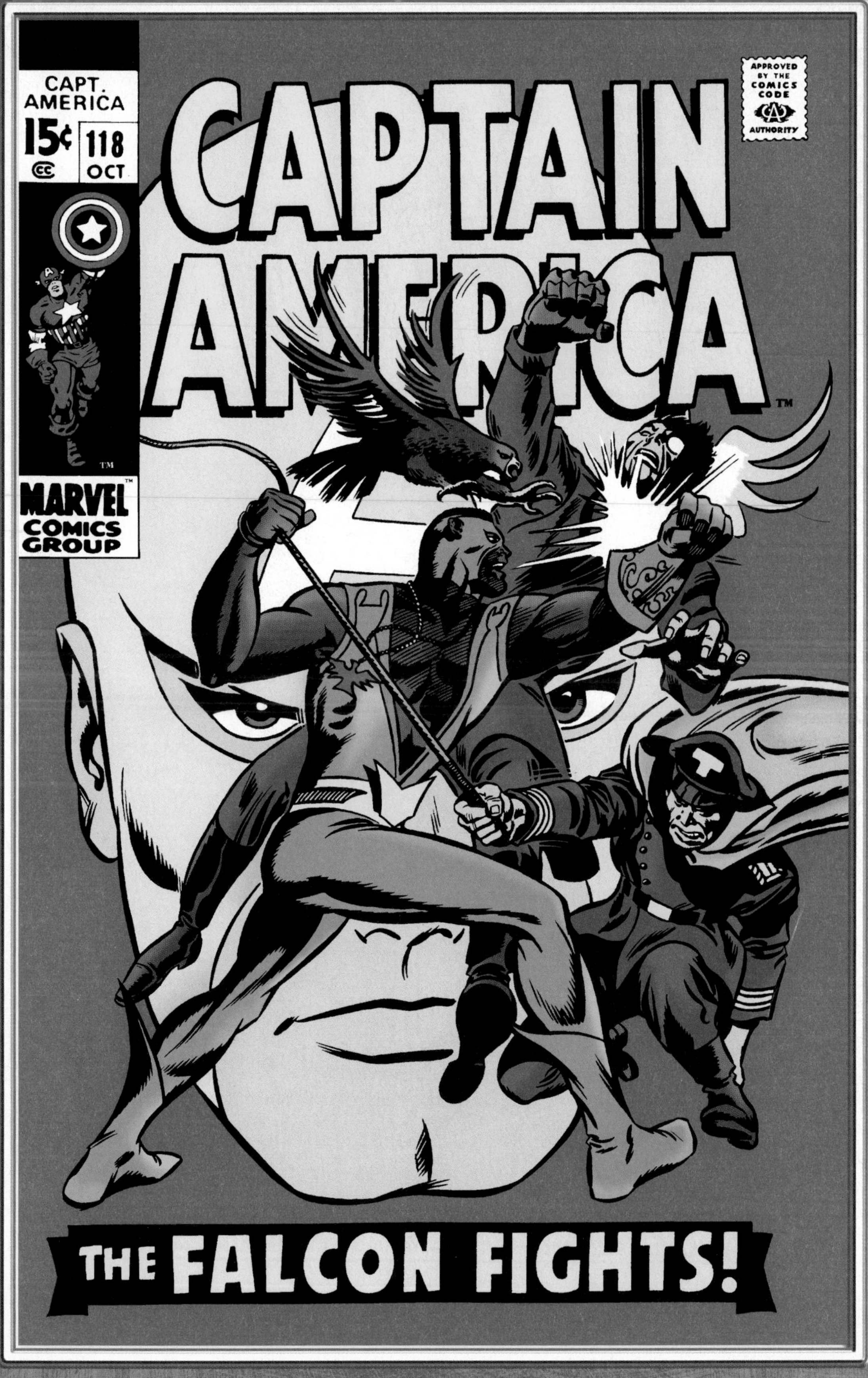
CAPT. AMERICA
15¢
118
OCT
MARVEL COMICS GROUP
APPROVED BY THE COMICS CODE AUTHORITY
CAPTAIN AMERICA
THE FALCON FIGHTS!

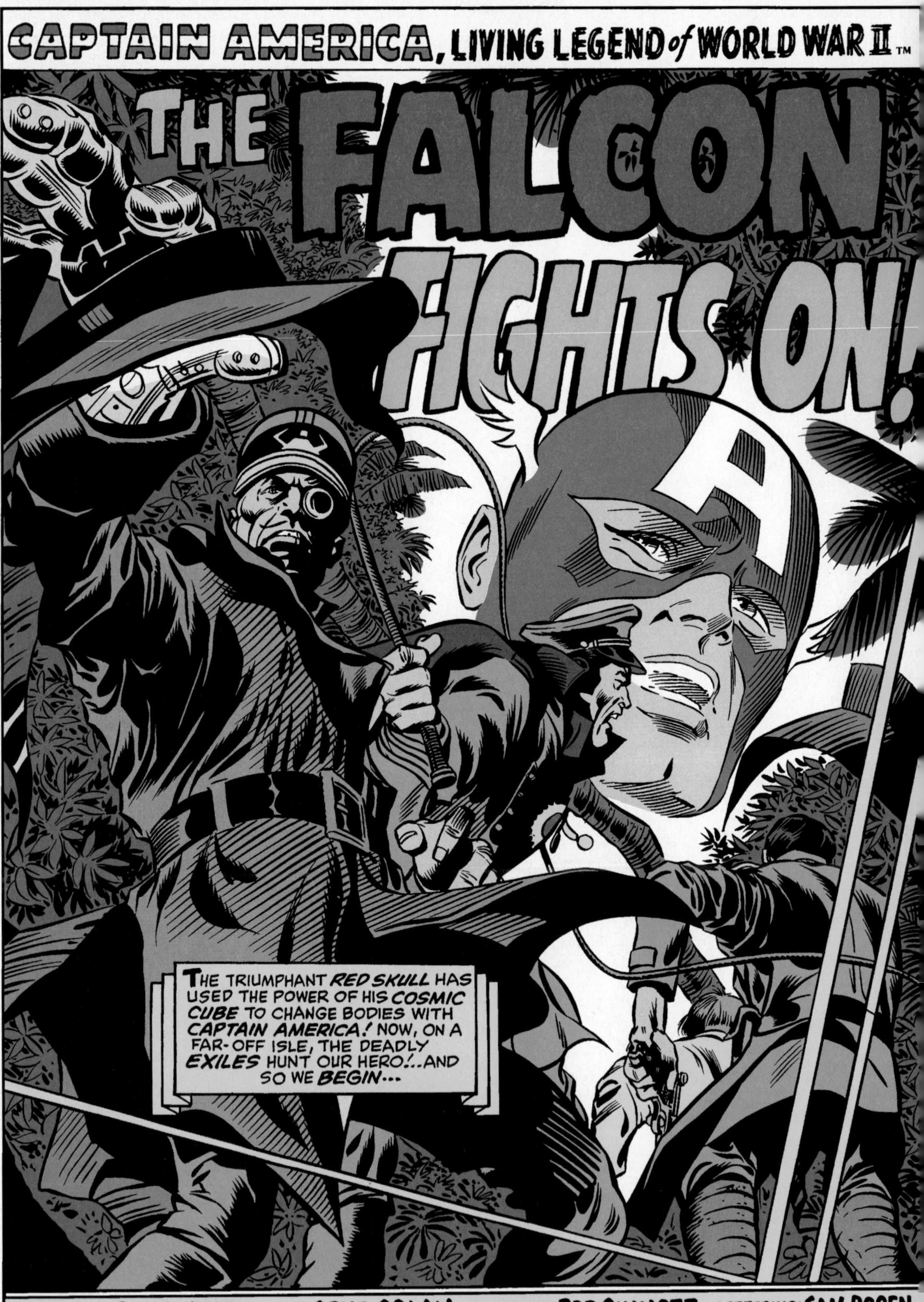

CAPTAIN AMERICA, LIVING LEGEND of WORLD WAR II ™
THE FALCON FIGHTS ON!
THE TRIUMPHANT RED SKULL HAS USED THE POWER OF HIS COSMIC CUBE TO CHANGE BODIES WITH CAPTAIN AMERICA! NOW, ON A FAR-OFF ISLE, THE DEADLY EXILES HUNT OUR HERO!..AND SO WE BEGIN...
SCRIPT: STAN LEE...ART: GENE COLAN...INKING: JOE SINNOTT...LETTERING: SAM ROSEN

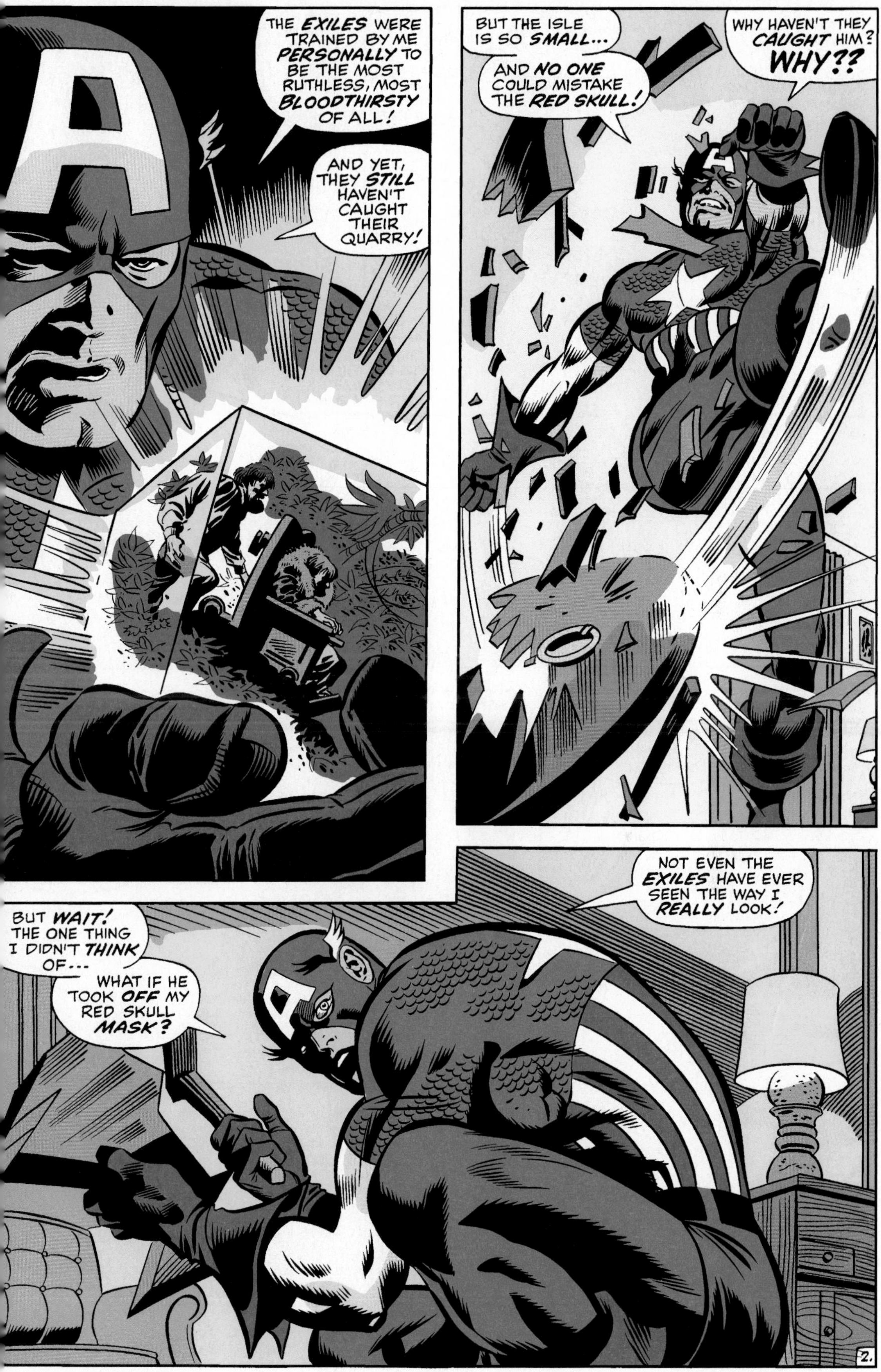
THE EXILES WERE TRAINED BY ME PERSONALLY TO BE THE MOST RUTHLESS, MOST BLOODTHIRSTY OF ALL!
AND YET, THEY STILL HAVEN'T CAUGHT THEIR QUARRY!
BUT THE ISLE IS SO SMALL...
AND NO ONE COULD MISTAKE THE RED SKULL!
WHY HAVEN'T THEY CAUGHT HIM? WHY??
NOT EVEN THE EXILES HAVE EVER SEEN THE WAY I REALLY LOOK!
BUT WAIT! THE ONE THING I DIDN'T THINK OF...
WHAT IF HE TOOK OFF MY RED SKULL MASK?
2.

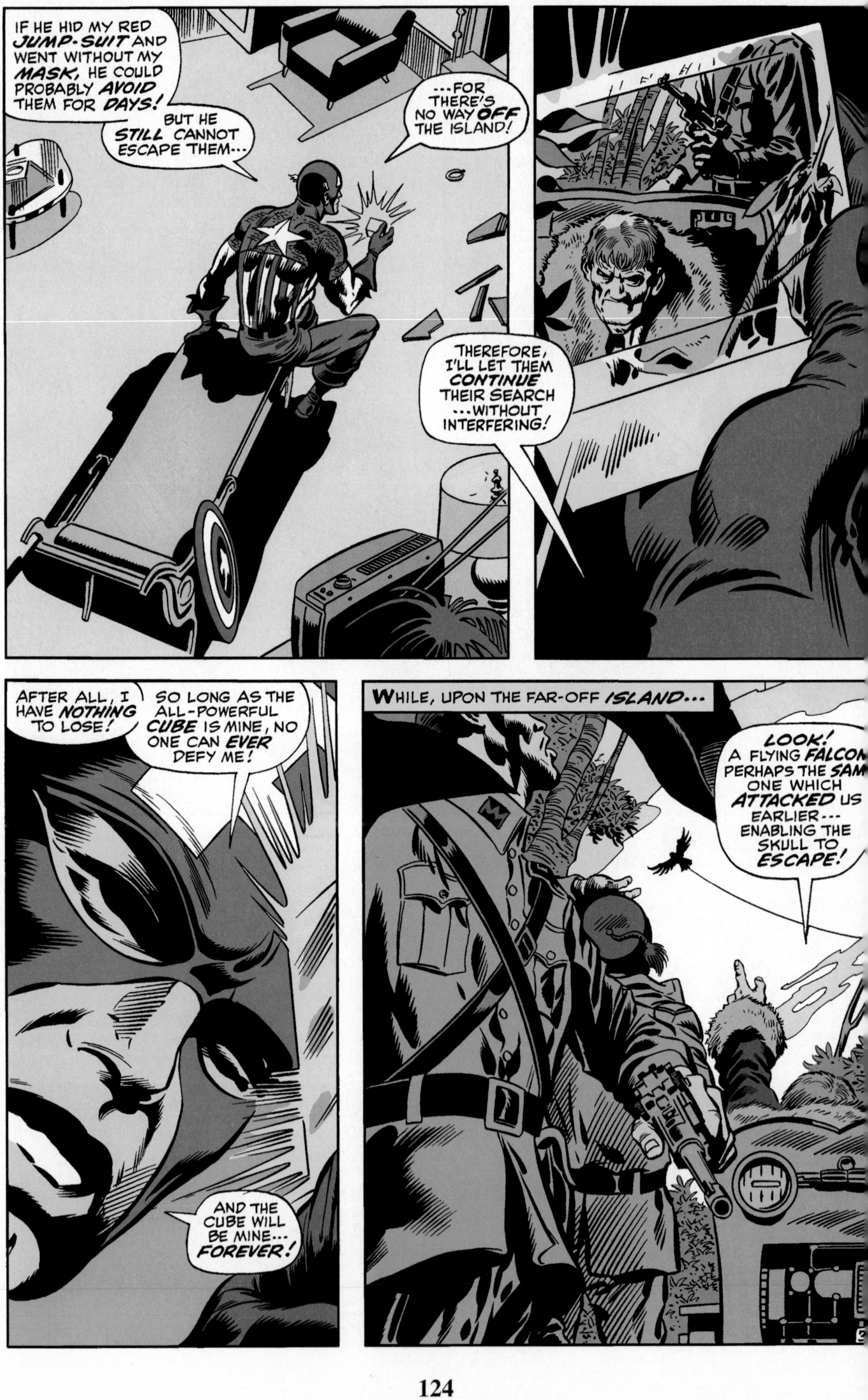
IF HE HID MY RED JUMP-SUIT AND WENT WITHOUT MY MASK, HE COULD PROBABLY AVOID THEM FOR DAYS!
BUT HE STILL CANNOT ESCAPE THEM...
...FOR THERE'S NO WAY OFF THE ISLAND!
THEREFORE, I'LL LET THEM CONTINUE THEIR SEARCH ...WITHOUT INTERFERING!
AFTER ALL, I HAVE NOTHING TO LOSE!
SO LONG AS THE ALL-POWERFUL CUBE IS MINE, NO ONE CAN EVER DEFY ME!
AND THE CUBE WILL BE MINE... FOREVER!
WHILE, UPON THE FAR-OFF ISLAND...
LOOK! A FLYING FALCON PERHAPS THE SAM ONE WHICH ATTACKED US EARLIER... ENABLING THE SKULL TO ESCAPE!

STAND BACK! THE ACCURSED BIRD WILL *BOTHER* US NO MORE!

KRAK! KRAK!

KRAK! KRAK!

YOU *MISSED* HIM, YOU *BUNGLER!*

KRAK KRAK KRAK KRAK KRAK KRAK

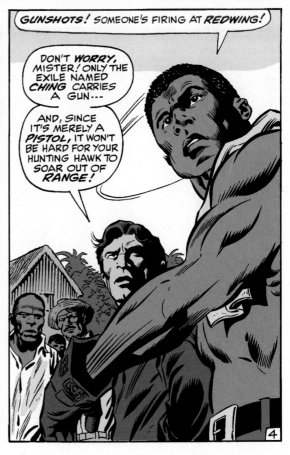

GUNSHOTS! SOMEONE'S FIRING AT *REDWING!*

DON'T *WORRY,* MISTER! ONLY THE EXILE NAMED *CHING* CARRIES A GUN...

AND, SINCE IT'S MERELY A *PISTOL,* IT WON'T BE HARD FOR YOUR HUNTING HAWK TO SOAR OUT OF *RANGE!*

4

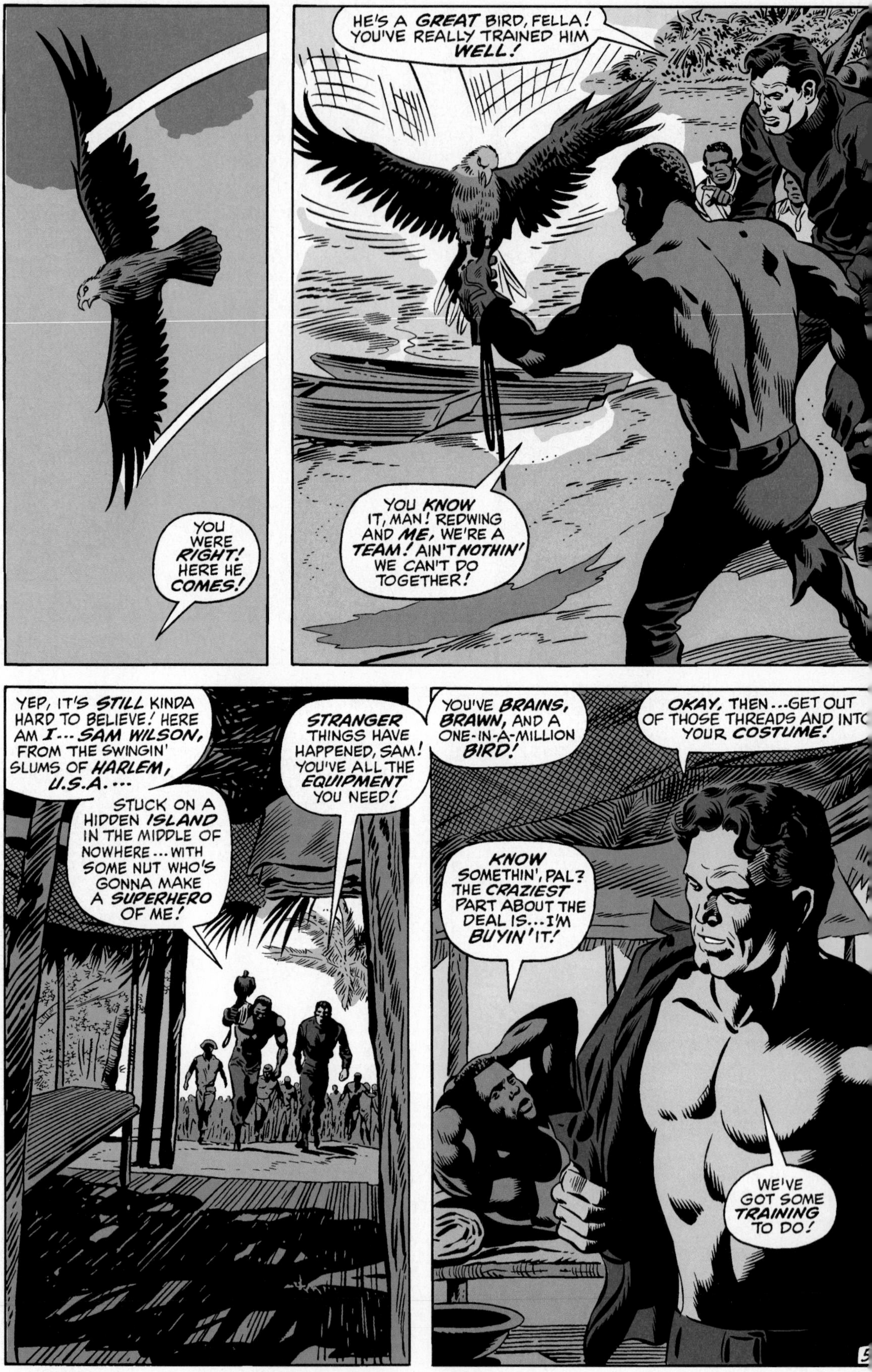

YOU WERE RIGHT! HERE HE COMES!
HE'S A GREAT BIRD, FELLA! YOU'VE REALLY TRAINED HIM WELL!
YOU KNOW IT, MAN! REDWING AND ME, WE'RE A TEAM! AIN'T NOTHIN' WE CAN'T DO TOGETHER!
YEP, IT'S STILL KINDA HARD TO BELIEVE! HERE AM I... SAM WILSON, FROM THE SWINGIN' SLUMS OF HARLEM, U.S.A. ...
STUCK ON A HIDDEN ISLAND IN THE MIDDLE OF NOWHERE... WITH SOME NUT WHO'S GONNA MAKE A SUPERHERO OF ME!
STRANGER THINGS HAVE HAPPENED, SAM! YOU'VE ALL THE EQUIPMENT YOU NEED!
YOU'VE BRAINS, BRAWN, AND A ONE-IN-A-MILLION BIRD!
OKAY. THEN...GET OUT OF THOSE THREADS AND INTO YOUR COSTUME!
KNOW SOMETHIN', PAL? THE CRAZIEST PART ABOUT THE DEAL IS... I'M BUYIN' IT!
WE'VE GOT SOME TRAINING TO DO!

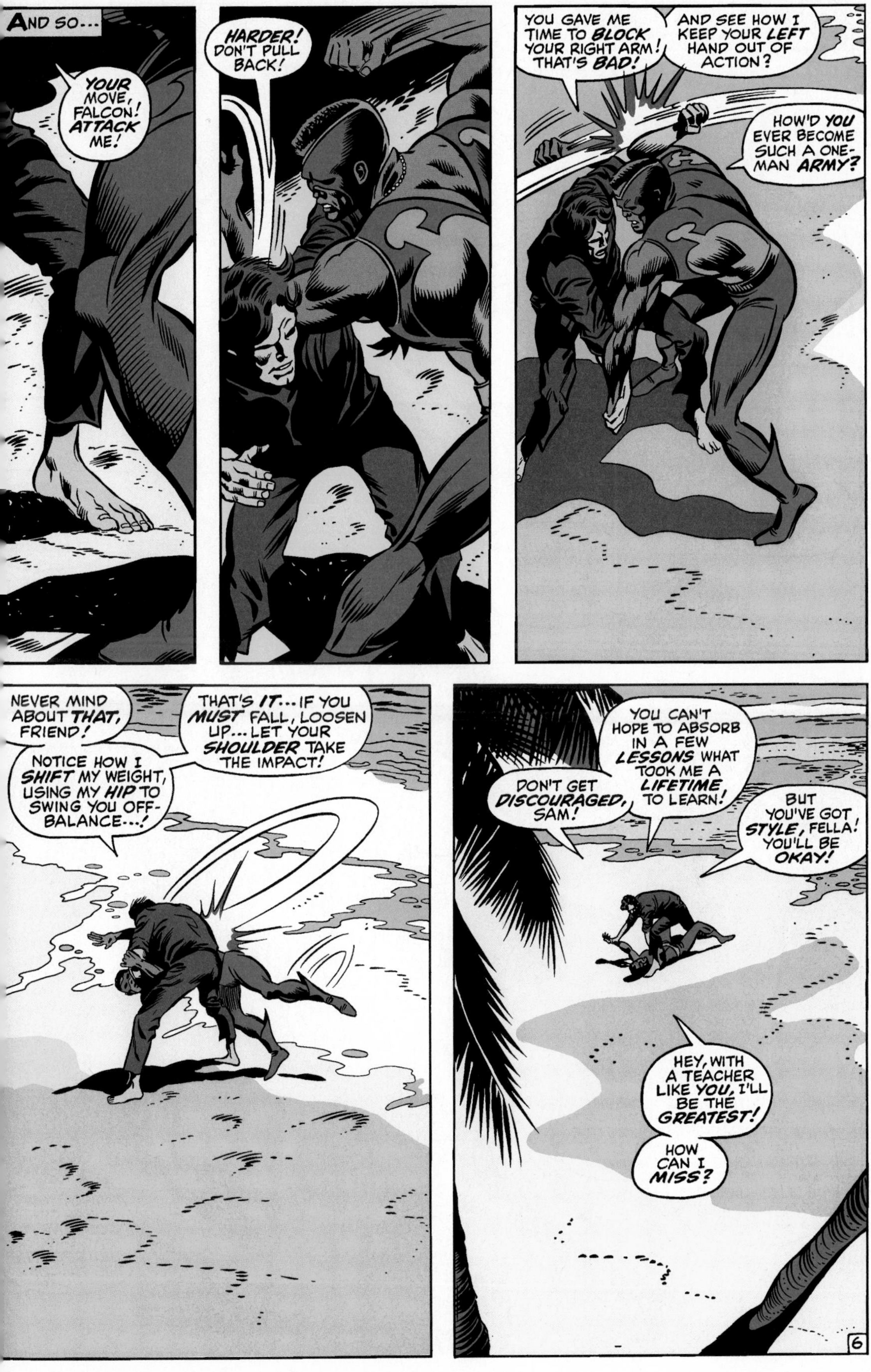
AND SO...
YOUR MOVE, FALCON! ATTACK ME!
HARDER! DON'T PULL BACK!
YOU GAVE ME TIME TO BLOCK YOUR RIGHT ARM! THAT'S BAD!
AND SEE HOW I KEEP YOUR LEFT HAND OUT OF ACTION?
HOW'D YOU EVER BECOME SUCH A ONE-MAN ARMY?
NEVER MIND ABOUT THAT, FRIEND!
NOTICE HOW I SHIFT MY WEIGHT, USING MY HIP TO SWING YOU OFF-BALANCE...!
THAT'S IT... IF YOU MUST FALL, LOOSEN UP... LET YOUR SHOULDER TAKE THE IMPACT!
DON'T GET DISCOURAGED, SAM!
YOU CAN'T HOPE TO ABSORB IN A FEW LESSONS WHAT TOOK ME A LIFETIME TO LEARN!
BUT YOU'VE GOT STYLE, FELLA! YOU'LL BE OKAY!
HEY, WITH A TEACHER LIKE YOU, I'LL BE THE GREATEST!
HOW CAN I MISS?
6

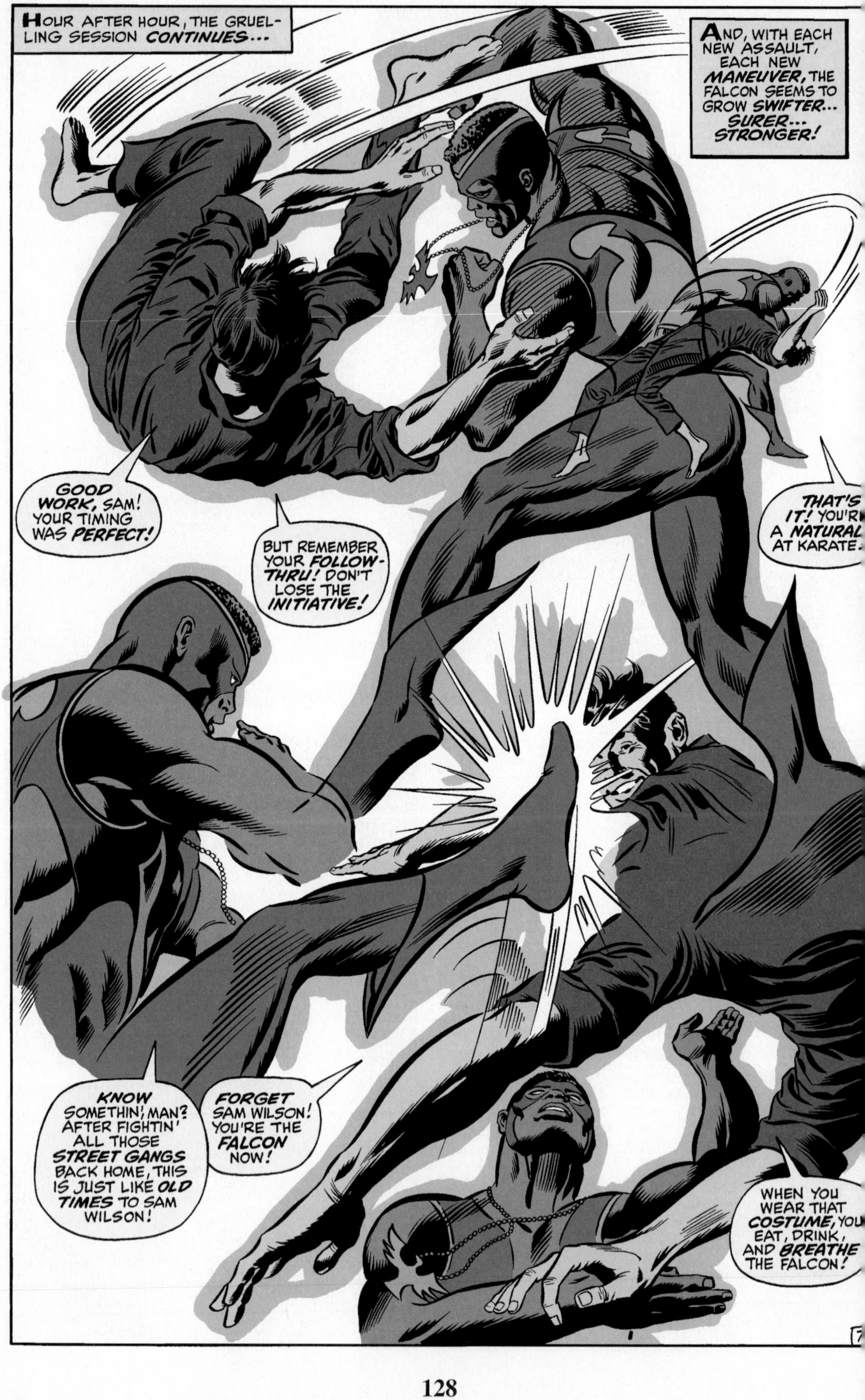
HOUR AFTER HOUR, THE GRUELLING SESSION CONTINUES...
AND, WITH EACH NEW ASSAULT, EACH NEW MANEUVER, THE FALCON SEEMS TO GROW SWIFTER... SURER... STRONGER!
GOOD WORK, SAM! YOUR TIMING WAS PERFECT!
BUT REMEMBER YOUR FOLLOW-THRU! DON'T LOSE THE INITIATIVE!
THAT'S IT! YOU'R A NATURAL AT KARATE.
KNOW SOMETHIN', MAN? AFTER FIGHTIN' ALL THOSE STREET GANGS BACK HOME, THIS IS JUST LIKE OLD TIMES TO SAM WILSON!
FORGET SAM WILSON! YOU'RE THE FALCON NOW!
WHEN YOU WEAR THAT COSTUME, YOU EAT, DRINK, AND BREATHE THE FALCON!

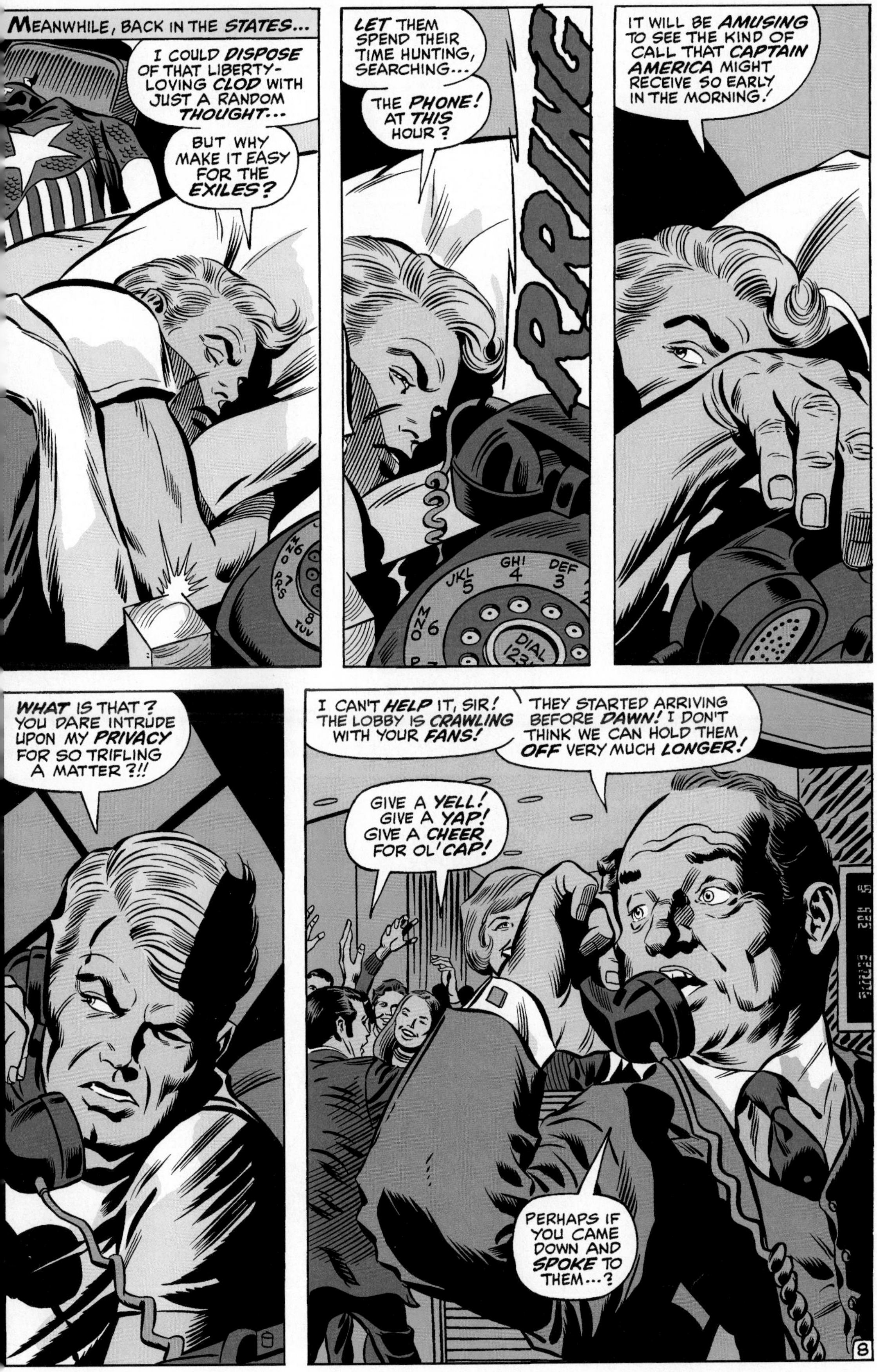
MEANWHILE, BACK IN THE STATES...
I COULD DISPOSE OF THAT LIBERTY-LOVING CLOD WITH JUST A RANDOM THOUGHT...
BUT WHY MAKE IT EASY FOR THE EXILES?
LET THEM SPEND THEIR TIME HUNTING, SEARCHING...
THE PHONE! AT THIS HOUR?
RRING
IT WILL BE AMUSING TO SEE THE KIND OF CALL THAT CAPTAIN AMERICA MIGHT RECEIVE SO EARLY IN THE MORNING!
WHAT IS THAT? YOU DARE INTRUDE UPON MY PRIVACY FOR SO TRIFLING A MATTER?!!
I CAN'T HELP IT, SIR! THE LOBBY IS CRAWLING WITH YOUR FANS!
THEY STARTED ARRIVING BEFORE DAWN! I DON'T THINK WE CAN HOLD THEM OFF VERY MUCH LONGER!
GIVE A YELL! GIVE A YAP! GIVE A CHEER FOR OL' CAP!
PERHAPS IF YOU CAME DOWN AND SPOKE TO THEM...?
8

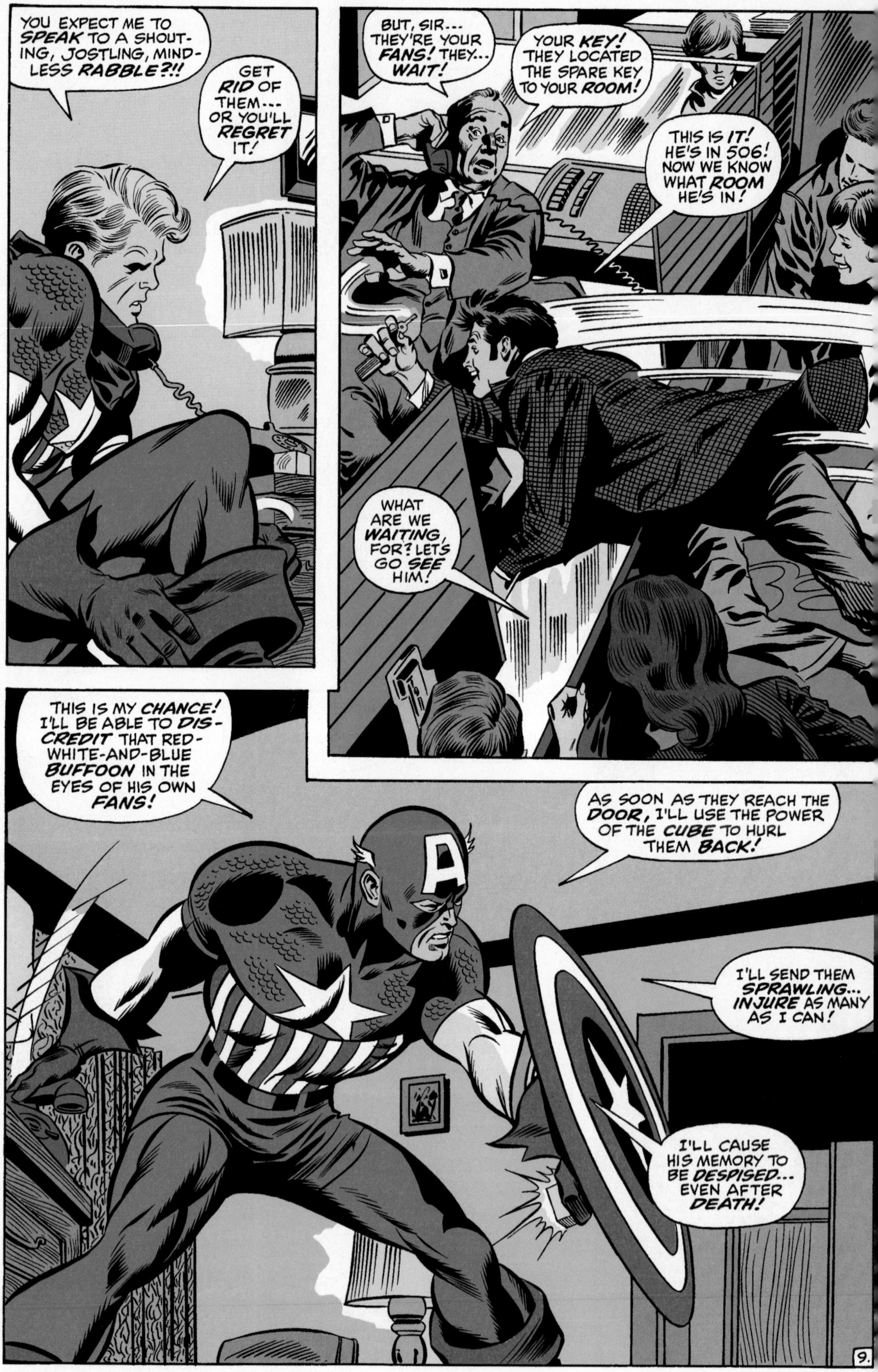
YOU EXPECT ME TO SPEAK TO A SHOUTING, JOSTLING, MINDLESS RABBLE?!!
GET RID OF THEM--- OR YOU'LL REGRET IT!
BUT, SIR... THEY'RE YOUR FANS! THEY... WAIT!
YOUR KEY! THEY LOCATED THE SPARE KEY TO YOUR ROOM!
THIS IS IT! HE'S IN 506! NOW WE KNOW WHAT ROOM HE'S IN!
WHAT ARE WE WAITING FOR? LET'S GO SEE HIM!
THIS IS MY CHANCE! I'LL BE ABLE TO DISCREDIT THAT RED-WHITE-AND-BLUE BUFFOON IN THE EYES OF HIS OWN FANS!
AS SOON AS THEY REACH THE DOOR, I'LL USE THE POWER OF THE CUBE TO HURL THEM BACK!
I'LL SEND THEM SPRAWLING... INJURE AS MANY AS I CAN!
I'LL CAUSE HIS MEMORY TO BE DESPISED... EVEN AFTER DEATH!
9.

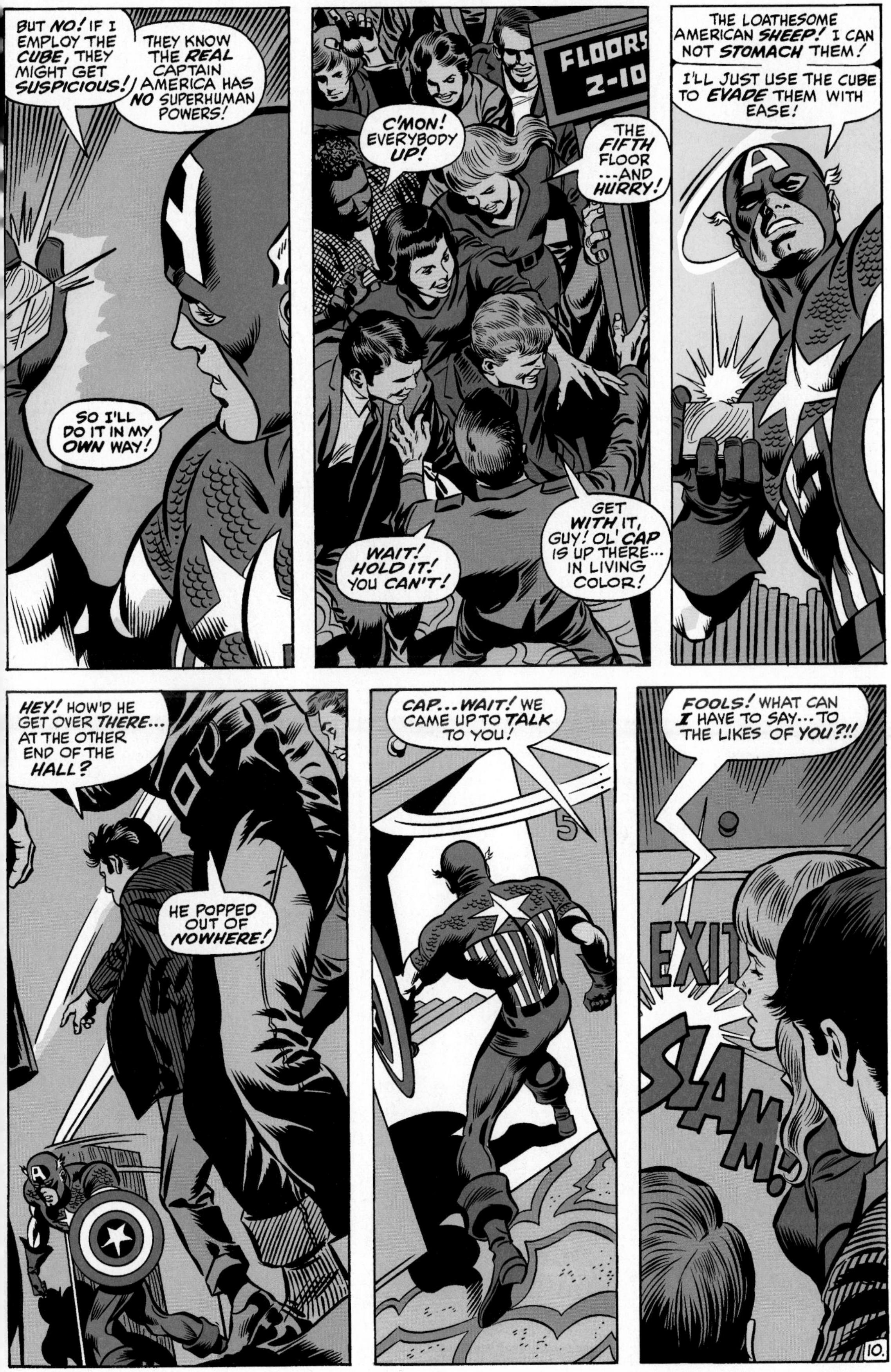
BUT NO! IF I EMPLOY THE CUBE, THEY MIGHT GET SUSPICIOUS!
THEY KNOW THE REAL CAPTAIN AMERICA HAS NO SUPERHUMAN POWERS!
SO I'LL DO IT IN MY OWN WAY!
FLOORS 2-10
C'MON! EVERYBODY UP!
THE FIFTH FLOOR ...AND HURRY!
WAIT! HOLD IT! YOU CAN'T!
GET WITH IT, GUY! OL' CAP IS UP THERE... IN LIVING COLOR!
THE LOATHESOME AMERICAN SHEEP! I CAN NOT STOMACH THEM!
I'LL JUST USE THE CUBE TO EVADE THEM WITH EASE!
HEY! HOW'D HE GET OVER THERE... AT THE OTHER END OF THE HALL?
HE POPPED OUT OF NOWHERE!
CAP... WAIT! WE CAME UP TO TALK TO YOU!
5
FOOLS! WHAT CAN I HAVE TO SAY... TO THE LIKES OF YOU?!!
EXIT
SLAM!
10.

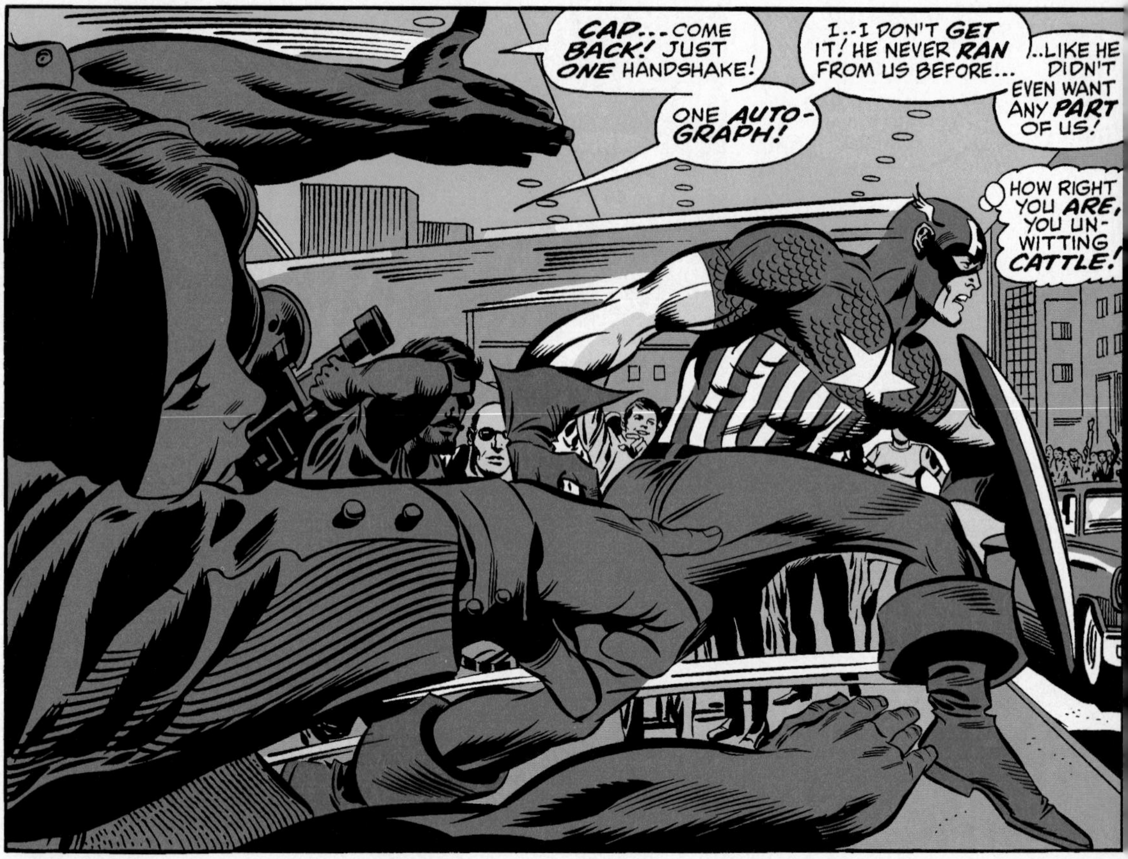
CAP... COME BACK! JUST ONE HANDSHAKE!
ONE AUTO-GRAPH!
I..-I DON'T GET IT! HE NEVER RAN FROM US BEFORE...
..LIKE HE DIDN'T EVEN WANT ANY PART OF US!
HOW RIGHT YOU ARE, YOU UN-WITTING CATTLE!

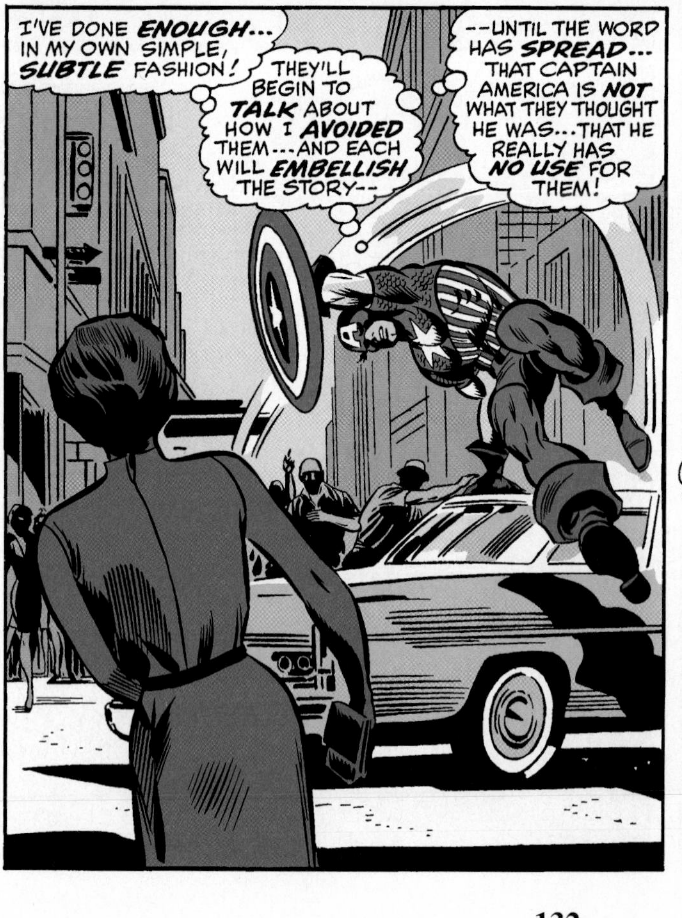
I'VE DONE ENOUGH... IN MY OWN SIMPLE, SUBTLE FASHION!
THEY'LL BEGIN TO TALK ABOUT HOW I AVOIDED THEM... AND EACH WILL EMBELLISH THE STORY--
--UNTIL THE WORD HAS SPREAD... THAT CAPTAIN AMERICA IS NOT WHAT THEY THOUGHT HE WAS... THAT HE REALLY HAS NO USE FOR THEM!

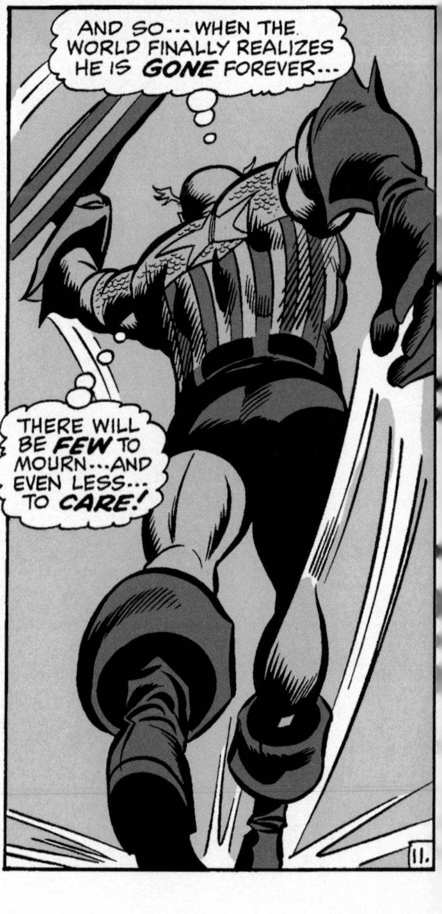
AND SO... WHEN THE WORLD FINALLY REALIZES HE IS GONE FOREVER...
THERE WILL BE FEW TO MOURN... AND EVEN LESS... TO CARE!
11.

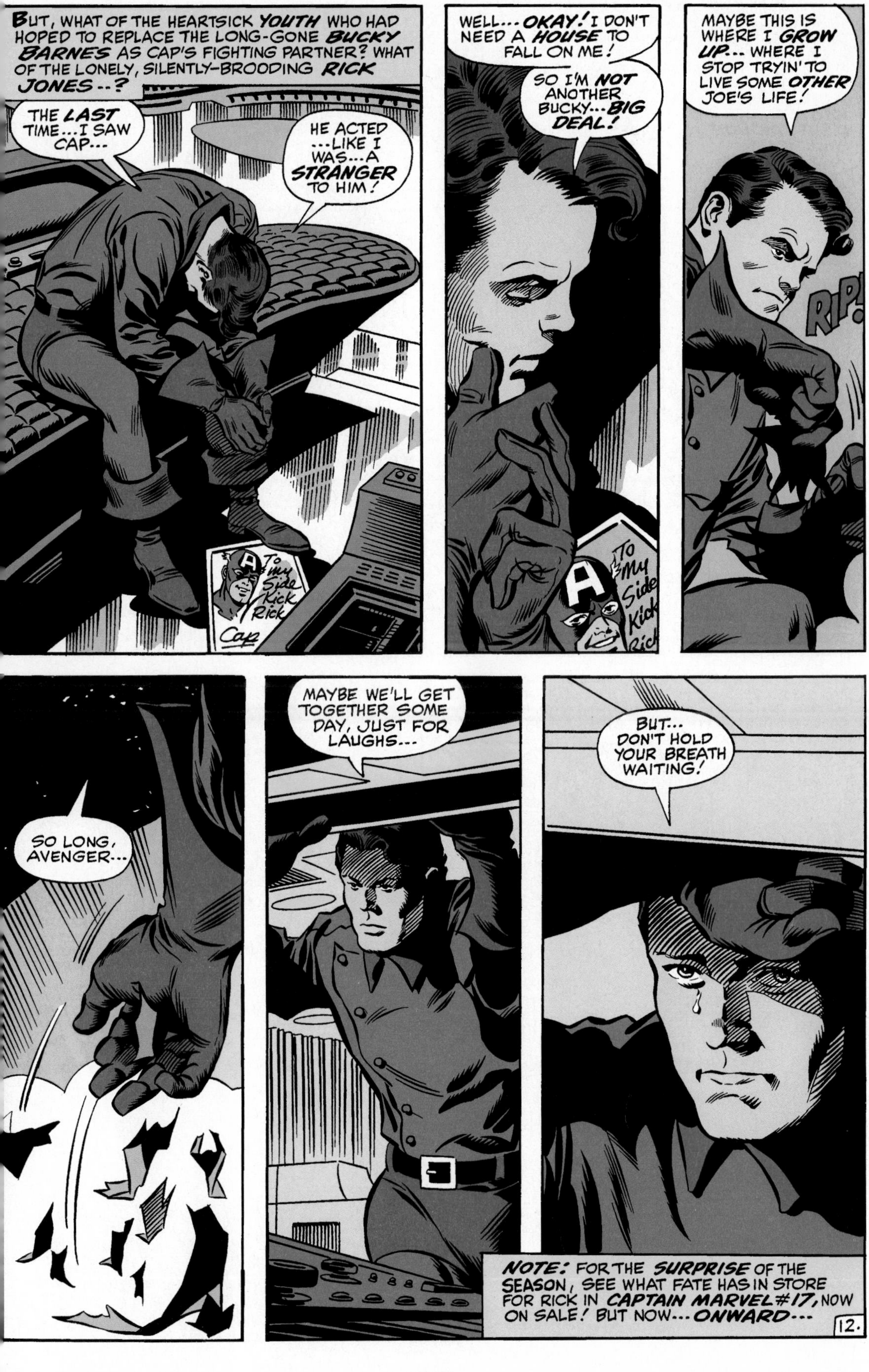

BUT, WHAT OF THE HEARTSICK YOUTH WHO HAD HOPED TO REPLACE THE LONG-GONE BUCKY BARNES AS CAP'S FIGHTING PARTNER? WHAT OF THE LONELY, SILENTLY-BROODING RICK JONES--?
THE LAST TIME...I SAW CAP...
HE ACTED ...LIKE I WAS...A STRANGER TO HIM!
To my Side Kick Rick Cap
WELL...OKAY! I DON'T NEED A HOUSE TO FALL ON ME!
SO I'M NOT ANOTHER BUCKY...BIG DEAL!
MAYBE THIS IS WHERE I GROW UP... WHERE I STOP TRYIN' TO LIVE SOME OTHER JOE'S LIFE!
RIP!
SO LONG, AVENGER...
MAYBE WE'LL GET TOGETHER SOME DAY, JUST FOR LAUGHS...
BUT... DON'T HOLD YOUR BREATH WAITING!
NOTE: FOR THE SURPRISE OF THE SEASON, SEE WHAT FATE HAS IN STORE FOR RICK IN CAPTAIN MARVEL #17, NOW ON SALE! BUT NOW... ONWARD...
12.

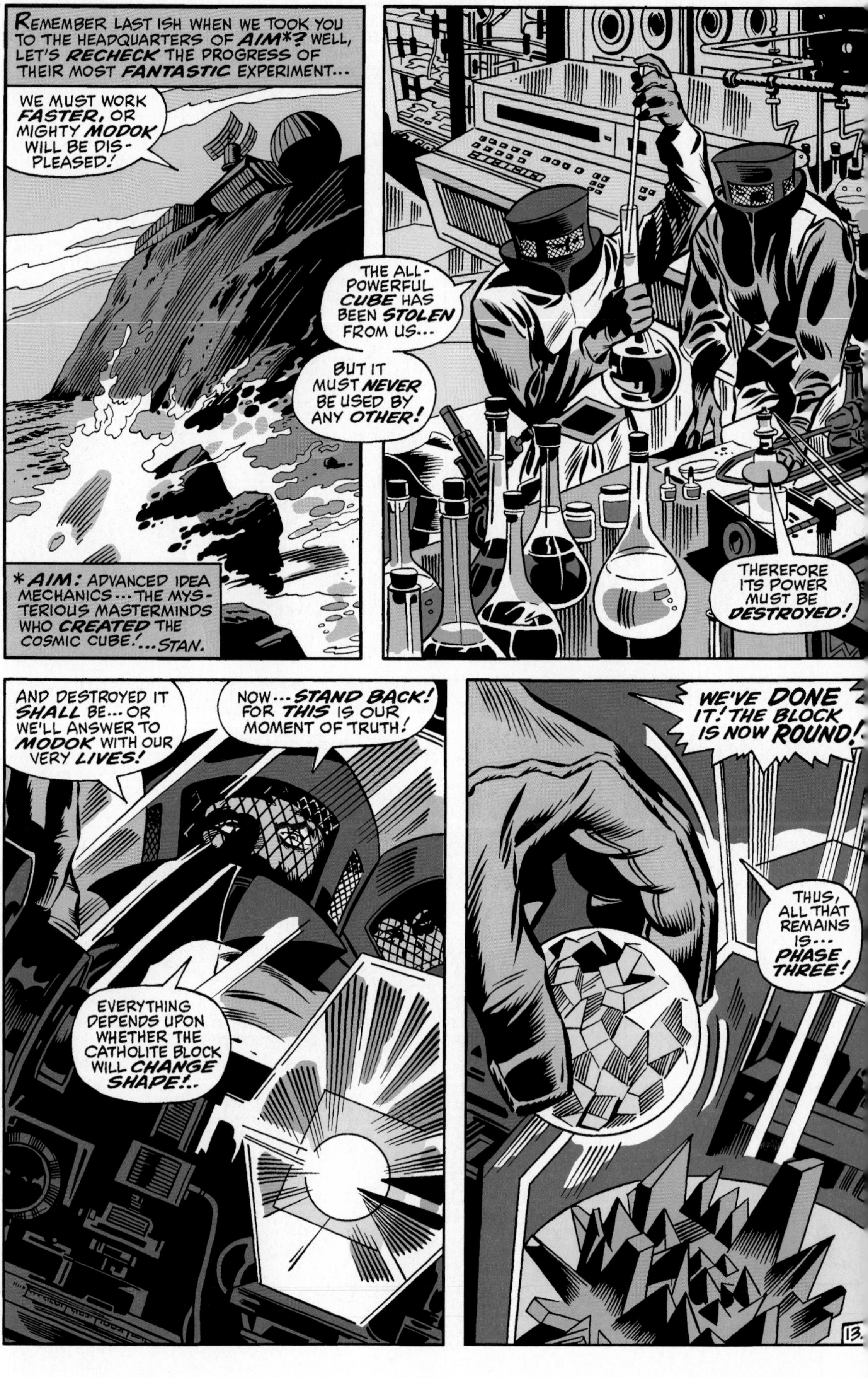
REMEMBER LAST ISH WHEN WE TOOK YOU TO THE HEADQUARTERS OF AIM*? WELL, LET'S RECHECK THE PROGRESS OF THEIR MOST FANTASTIC EXPERIMENT...
WE MUST WORK FASTER, OR MIGHTY MODOK WILL BE DIS-PLEASED!
*AIM: ADVANCED IDEA MECHANICS... THE MYS-TERIOUS MASTERMINDS WHO CREATED THE COSMIC CUBE!...STAN.
THE ALL-POWERFUL CUBE HAS BEEN STOLEN FROM US...
BUT IT MUST NEVER BE USED BY ANY OTHER!
THEREFORE ITS POWER MUST BE DESTROYED!
AND DESTROYED IT SHALL BE... OR WE'LL ANSWER TO MODOK WITH OUR VERY LIVES!
NOW... STAND BACK! FOR THIS IS OUR MOMENT OF TRUTH!
EVERYTHING DEPENDS UPON WHETHER THE CATHOLITE BLOCK WILL CHANGE SHAPE!..
WE'VE DONE IT! THE BLOCK IS NOW ROUND!
THUS, ALL THAT REMAINS IS... PHASE THREE!
13

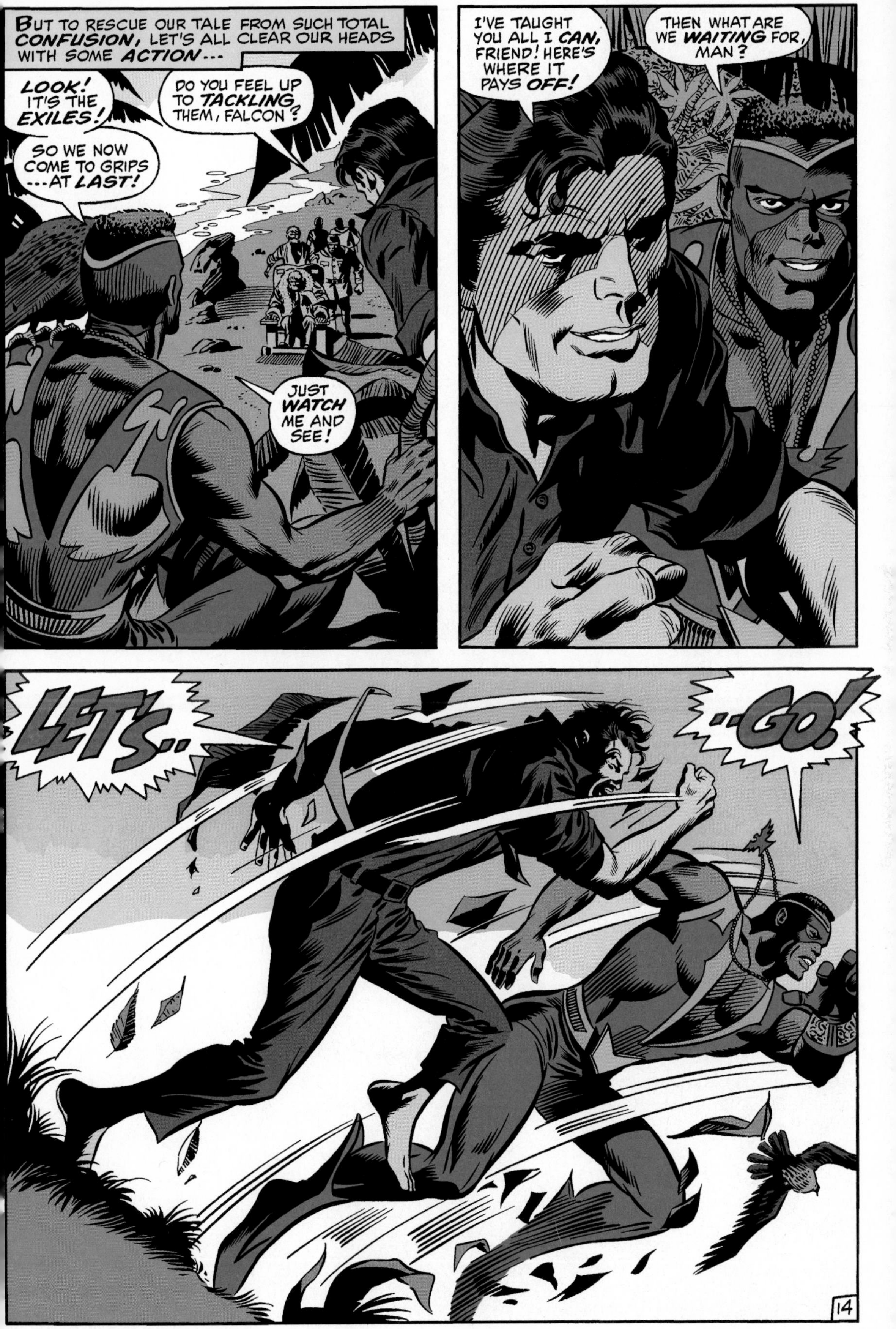

BUT TO RESCUE OUR TALE FROM SUCH TOTAL CONFUSION, LET'S ALL CLEAR OUR HEADS WITH SOME ACTION---
LOOK! IT'S THE EXILES!
DO YOU FEEL UP TO TACKLING THEM, FALCON?
SO WE NOW COME TO GRIPS---AT LAST!
JUST WATCH ME AND SEE!
I'VE TAUGHT YOU ALL I CAN, FRIEND! HERE'S WHERE IT PAYS OFF!
THEN WHAT ARE WE WAITING FOR, MAN?
LET'S..
..GO!
14

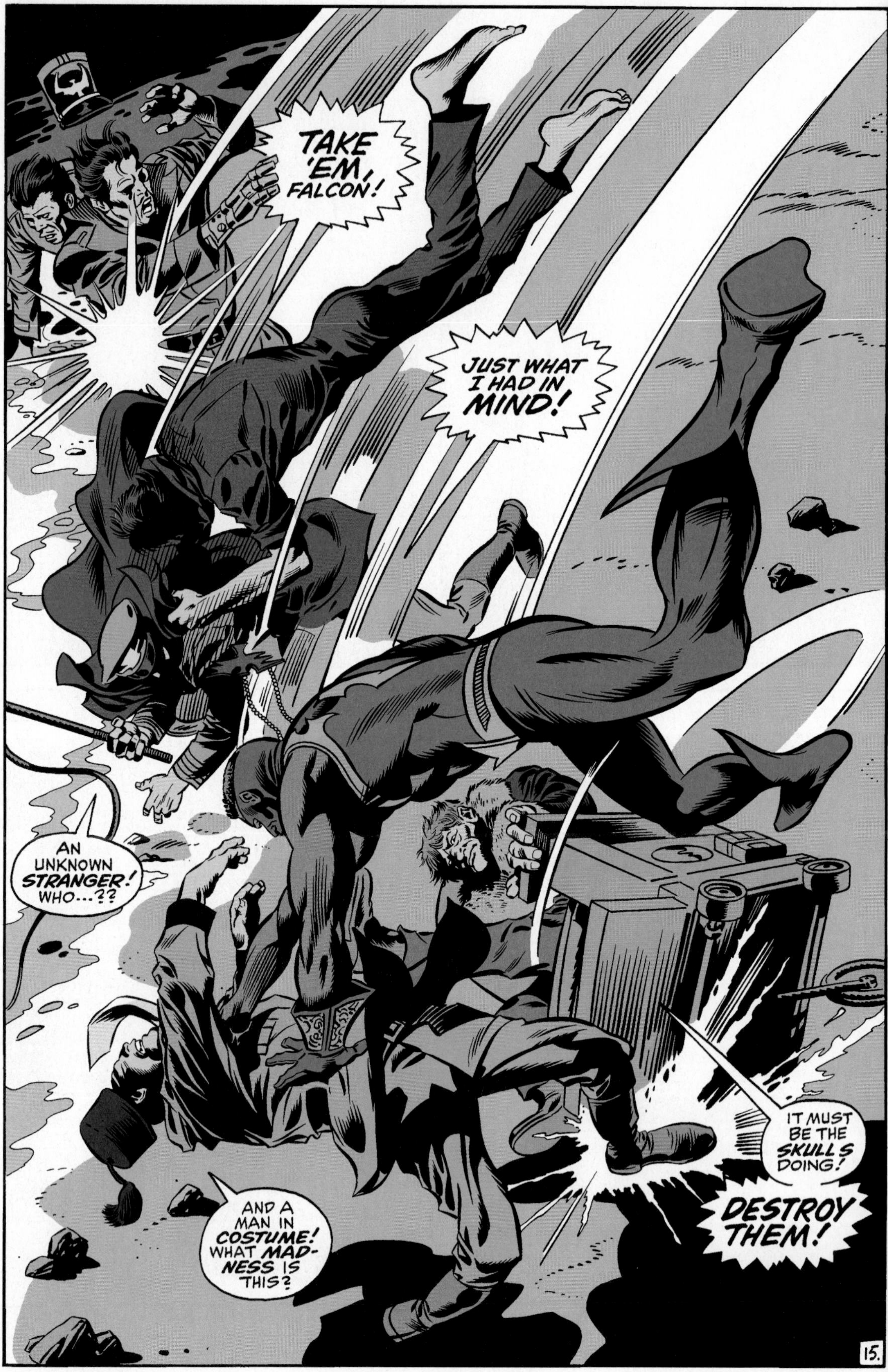
TAKE 'EM, FALCON!
JUST WHAT I HAD IN MIND!
AN UNKNOWN STRANGER! WHO...??
AND A MAN IN COSTUME! WHAT MADNESS IS THIS?
IT MUST BE THE SKULL'S DOING!
DESTROY THEM!
15.

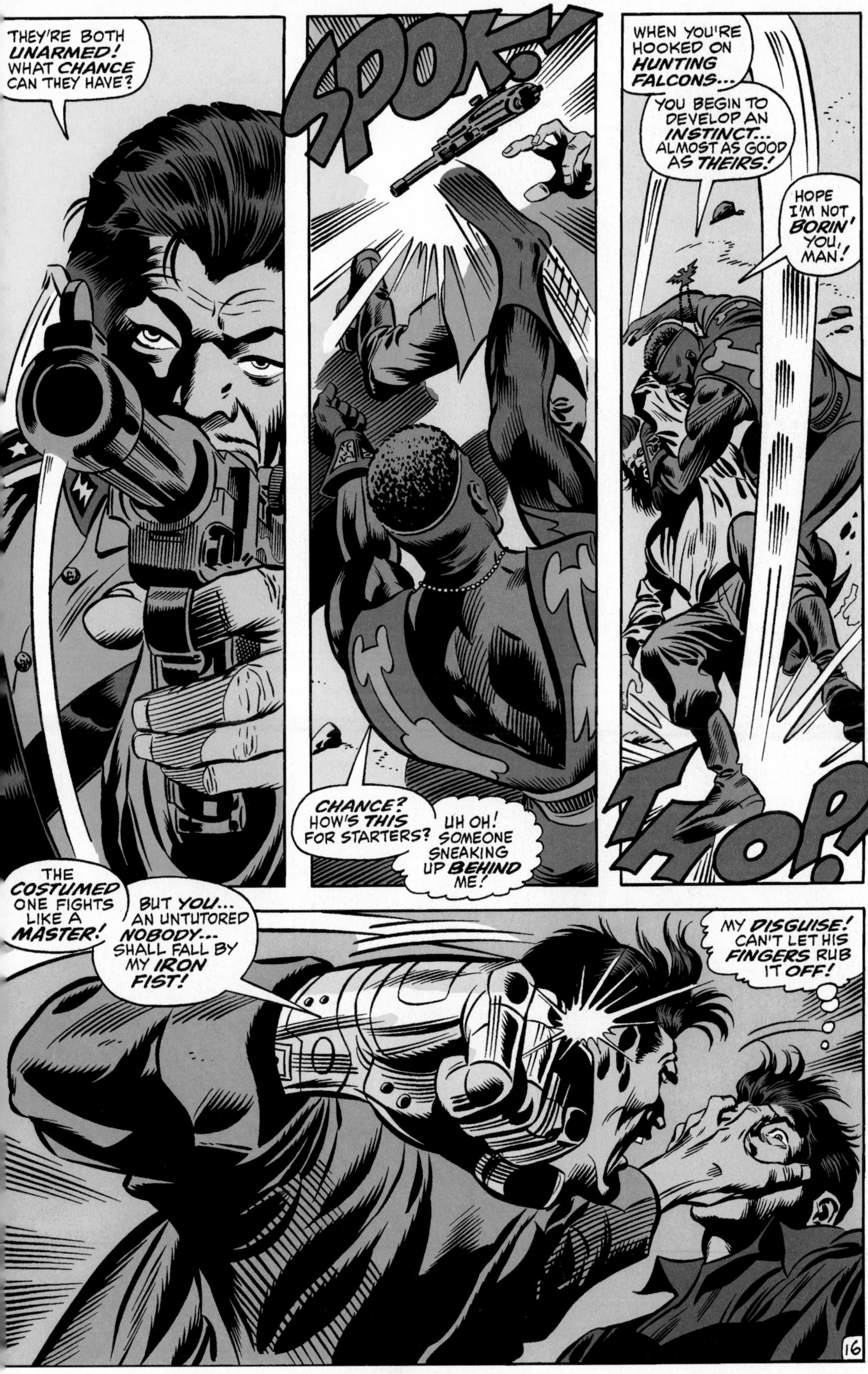
THEY'RE BOTH UNARMED! WHAT CHANCE CAN THEY HAVE?
SPOK!
CHANCE? HOW'S THIS FOR STARTERS?
UH OH! SOMEONE SNEAKING UP BEHIND ME!
WHEN YOU'RE HOOKED ON HUNTING FALCONS...
YOU BEGIN TO DEVELOP AN INSTINCT... ALMOST AS GOOD AS THEIRS!
HOPE I'M NOT BORIN' YOU, MAN!
THOP!
THE COSTUMED ONE FIGHTS LIKE A MASTER!
BUT YOU... AN UNTUTORED NOBODY... SHALL FALL BY MY IRON FIST!
MY DISGUISE! CAN'T LET HIS FINGERS RUB IT OFF!
16

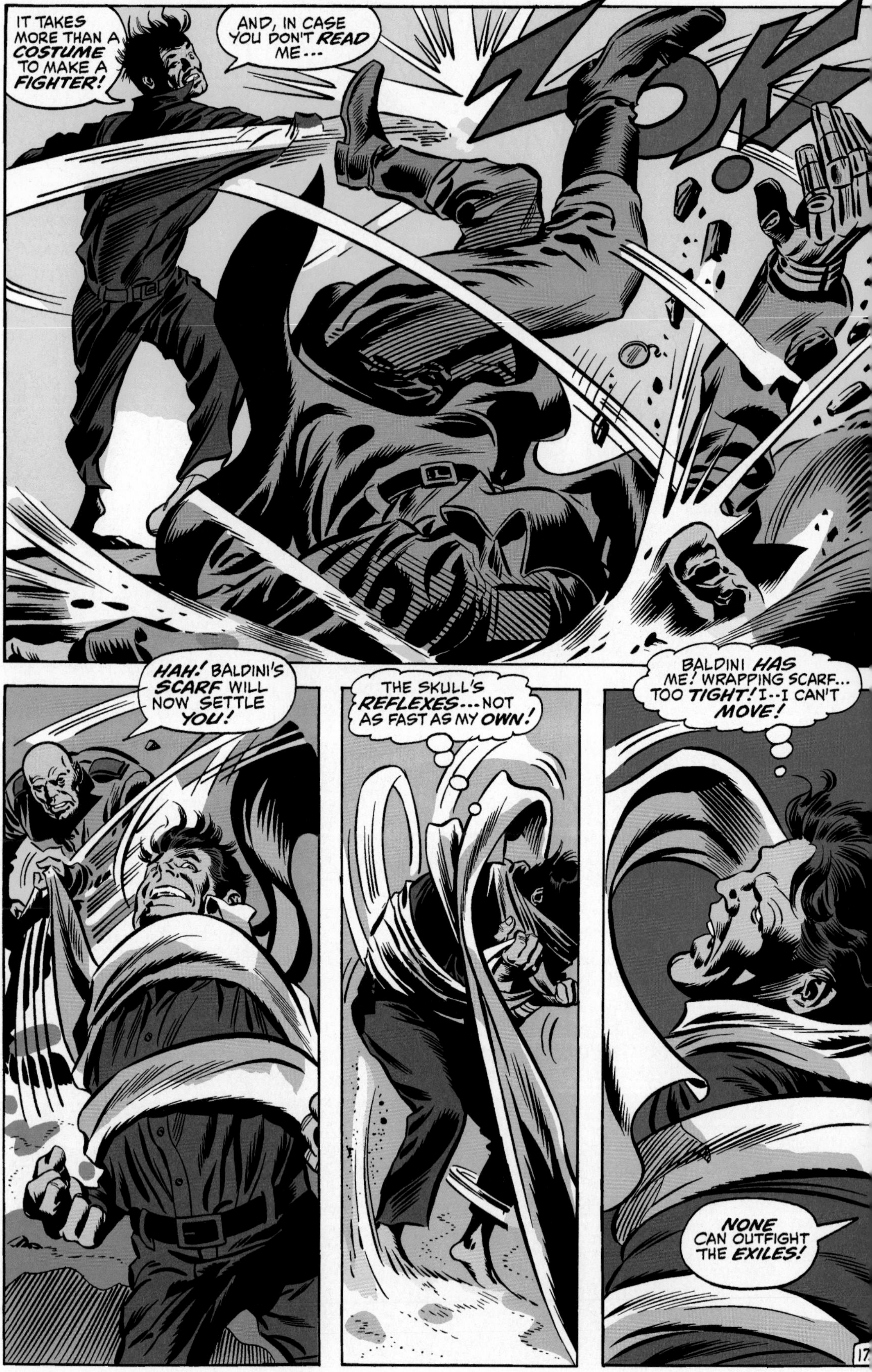
IT TAKES MORE THAN A COSTUME TO MAKE A FIGHTER!
AND, IN CASE YOU DON'T READ ME---
ZOK!
HAH! BALDINI'S SCARF WILL NOW SETTLE YOU!
THE SKULL'S REFLEXES--- NOT AS FAST AS MY OWN!
BALDINI HAS ME! WRAPPING SCARF... TOO TIGHT! I--I CAN'T MOVE!
NONE CAN OUTFIGHT THE EXILES!
17

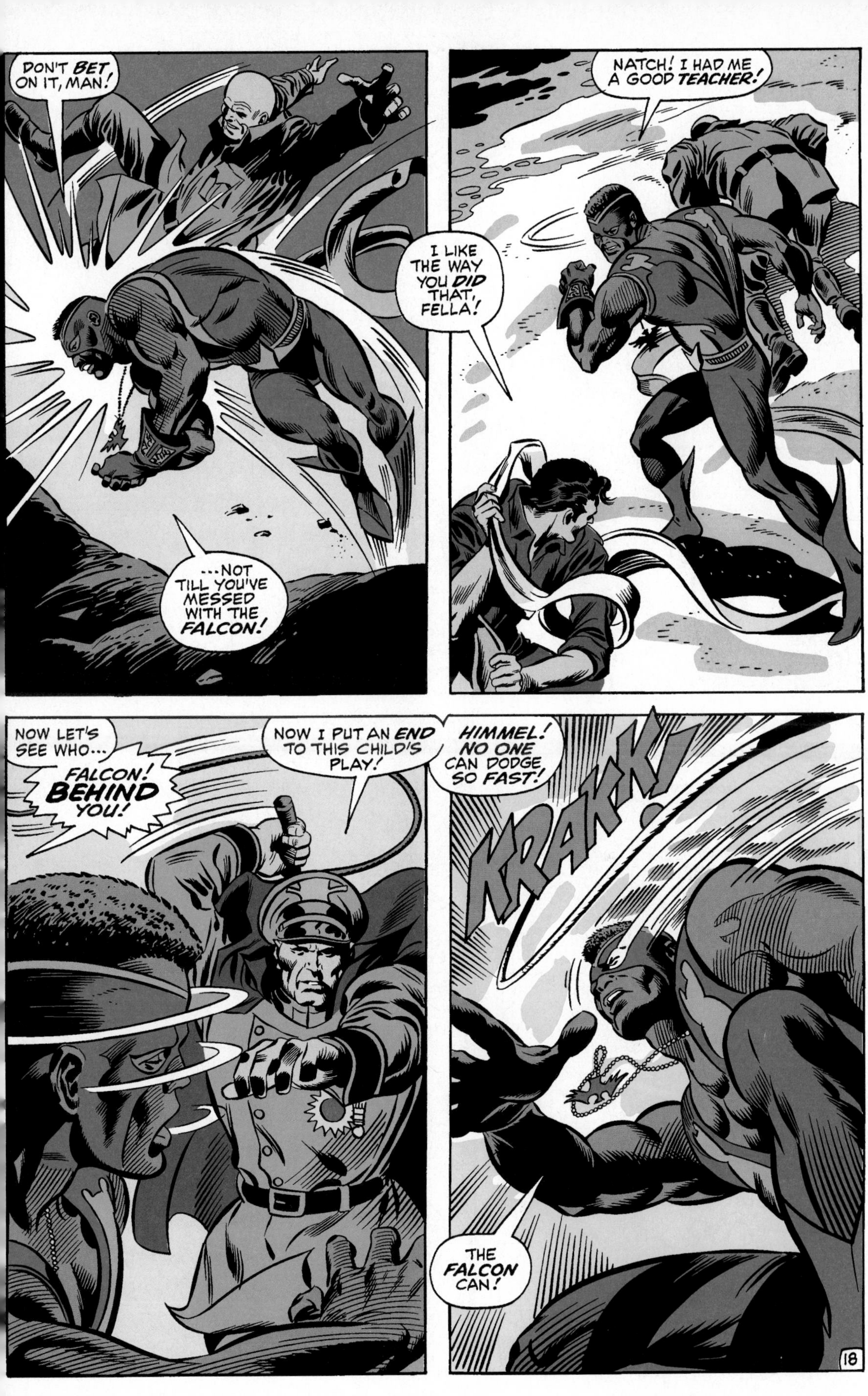
DON'T BET ON IT, MAN!
...NOT TILL YOU'VE MESSED WITH THE FALCON!
NATCH! I HAD ME A GOOD TEACHER!
I LIKE THE WAY YOU DID THAT, FELLA!
NOW LET'S SEE WHO...
FALCON! BEHIND YOU!
NOW I PUT AN END TO THIS CHILD'S PLAY!
HIMMEL! NO ONE CAN DODGE SO FAST!
KRAKK!
THE FALCON CAN!
18

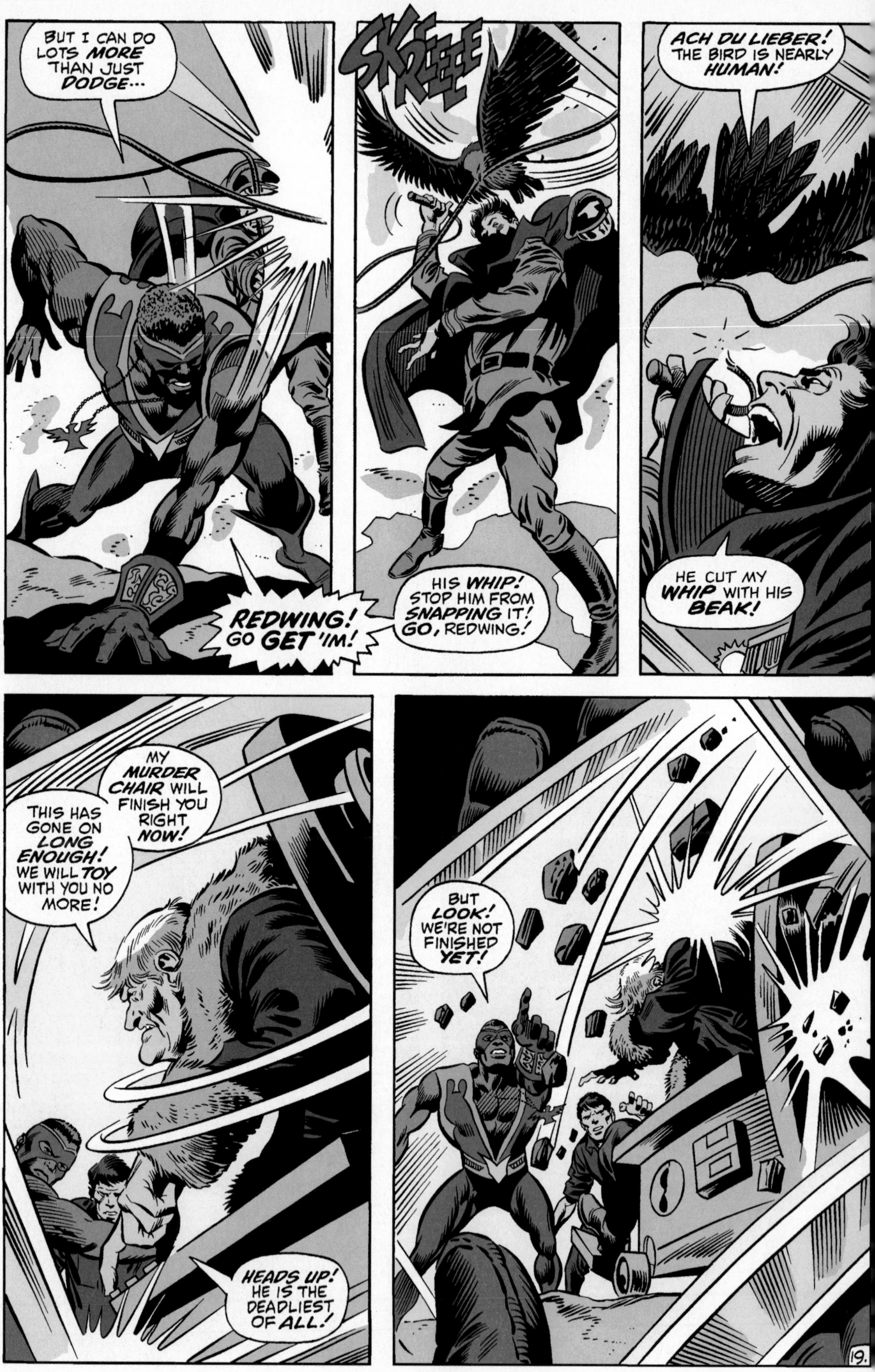
BUT I CAN DO LOTS MORE THAN JUST DODGE...
REDWING! GO GET 'IM!
SKREEEEE
HIS WHIP! STOP HIM FROM SNAPPING IT! GO, REDWING!
ACH DU LIEBER! THE BIRD IS NEARLY HUMAN!
HE CUT MY WHIP WITH HIS BEAK!
THIS HAS GONE ON LONG ENOUGH! WE WILL TOY WITH YOU NO MORE!
MY MURDER CHAIR WILL FINISH YOU RIGHT NOW!
HEADS UP! HE IS THE DEADLIEST OF ALL!
BUT LOOK! WE'RE NOT FINISHED YET!
19.

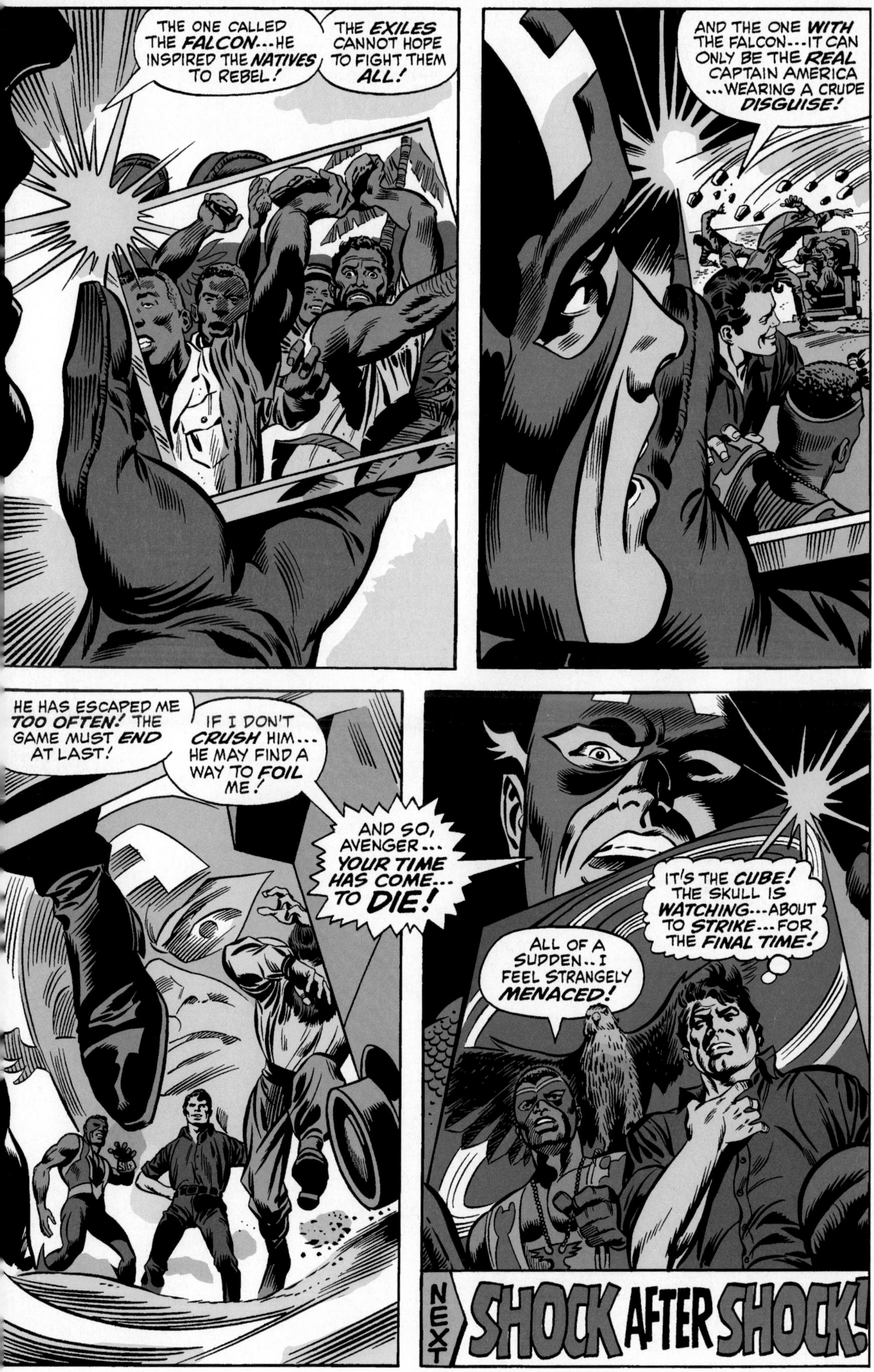
THE ONE CALLED THE FALCON--HE INSPIRED THE NATIVES TO REBEL!
THE EXILES CANNOT HOPE TO FIGHT THEM ALL!
AND THE ONE WITH THE FALCON---IT CAN ONLY BE THE REAL CAPTAIN AMERICA ...WEARING A CRUDE DISGUISE!
HE HAS ESCAPED ME TOO OFTEN! THE GAME MUST END AT LAST!
IF I DON'T CRUSH HIM... HE MAY FIND A WAY TO FOIL ME!
AND SO, AVENGER... YOUR TIME HAS COME... TO DIE!
IT'S THE CUBE! THE SKULL IS WATCHING---ABOUT TO STRIKE...FOR THE FINAL TIME!
ALL OF A SUDDEN..I FEEL STRANGELY MENACED!
NEXT
SHOCK AFTER SHOCK!

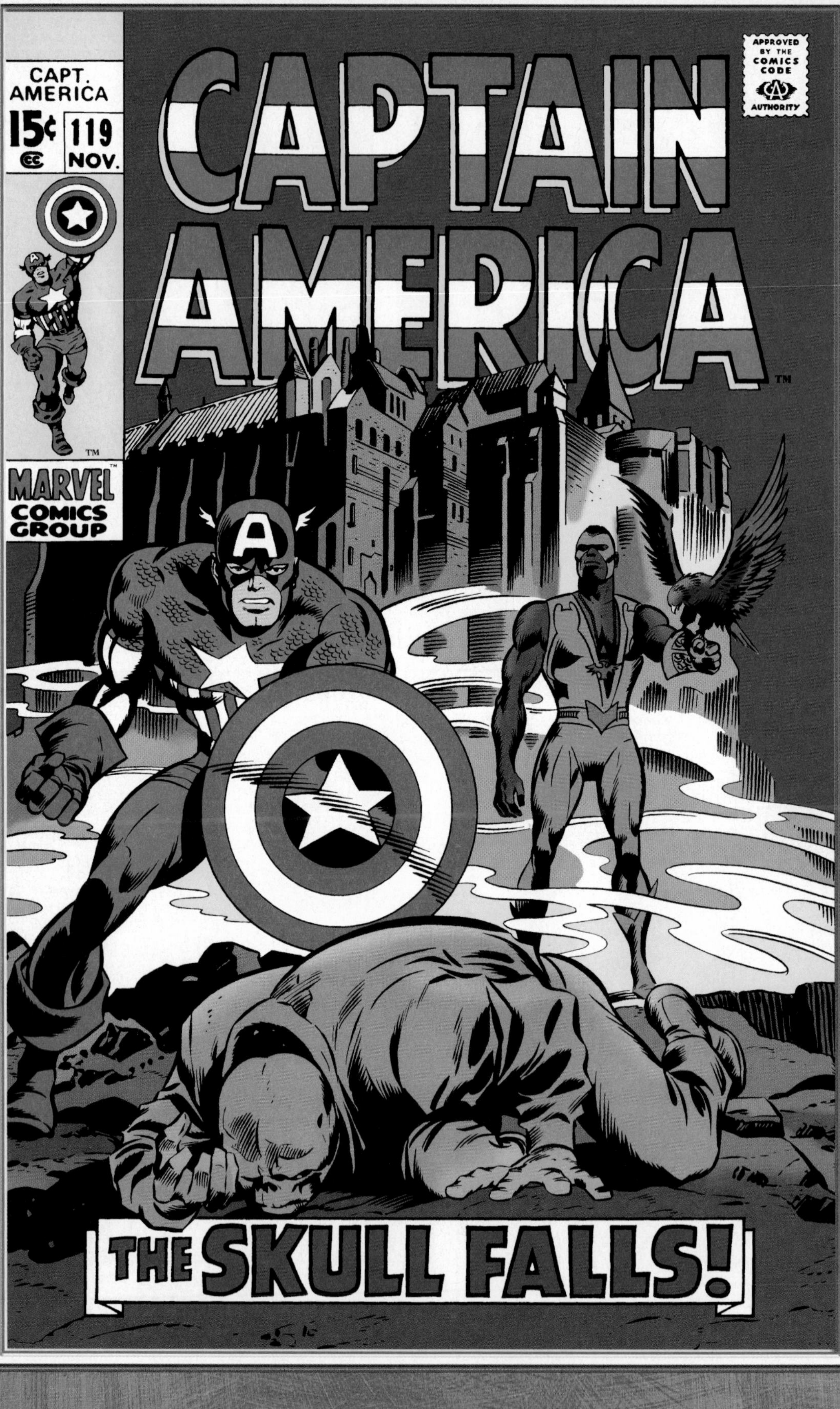

CAPT. AMERICA
15¢
119
NOV.
APPROVED BY THE COMICS CODE AUTHORITY
CAPTAIN AMERICA
MARVEL COMICS GROUP
THE SKULL FALLS!

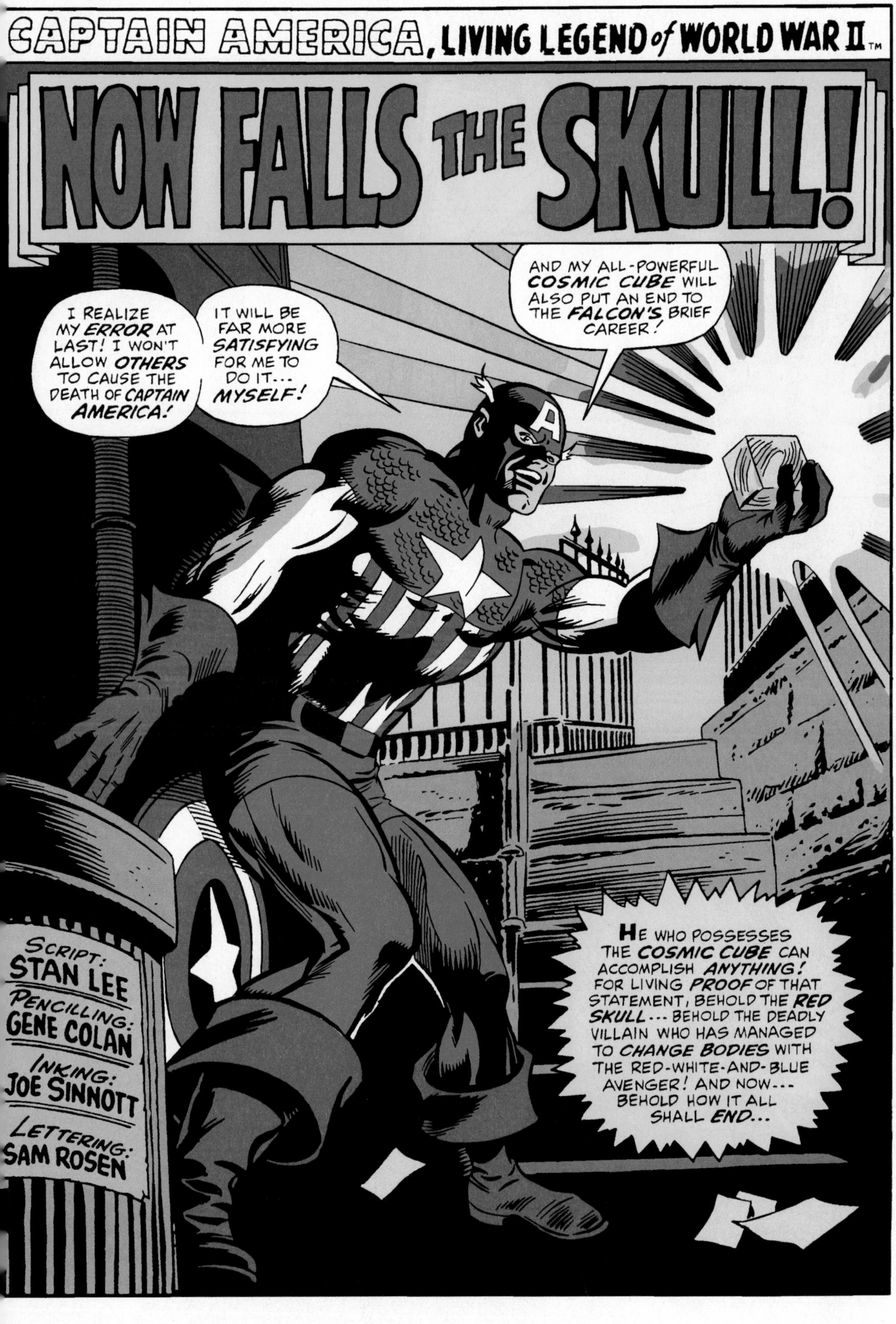
CAPTAIN AMERICA, LIVING LEGEND of WORLD WAR II™
NOW FALLS THE SKULL!
I REALIZE MY ERROR AT LAST! I WON'T ALLOW OTHERS TO CAUSE THE DEATH OF CAPTAIN AMERICA!
IT WILL BE FAR MORE SATISFYING FOR ME TO DO IT... MYSELF!
AND MY ALL-POWERFUL COSMIC CUBE WILL ALSO PUT AN END TO THE FALCON'S BRIEF CAREER!
HE WHO POSSESSES THE COSMIC CUBE CAN ACCOMPLISH ANYTHING! FOR LIVING PROOF OF THAT STATEMENT, BEHOLD THE RED SKULL... BEHOLD THE DEADLY VILLAIN WHO HAS MANAGED TO CHANGE BODIES WITH THE RED-WHITE-AND-BLUE AVENGER! AND NOW... BEHOLD HOW IT ALL SHALL END...
SCRIPT: STAN LEE
PENCILLING: GENE COLAN
INKING: JOE SINNOTT
LETTERING: SAM ROSEN

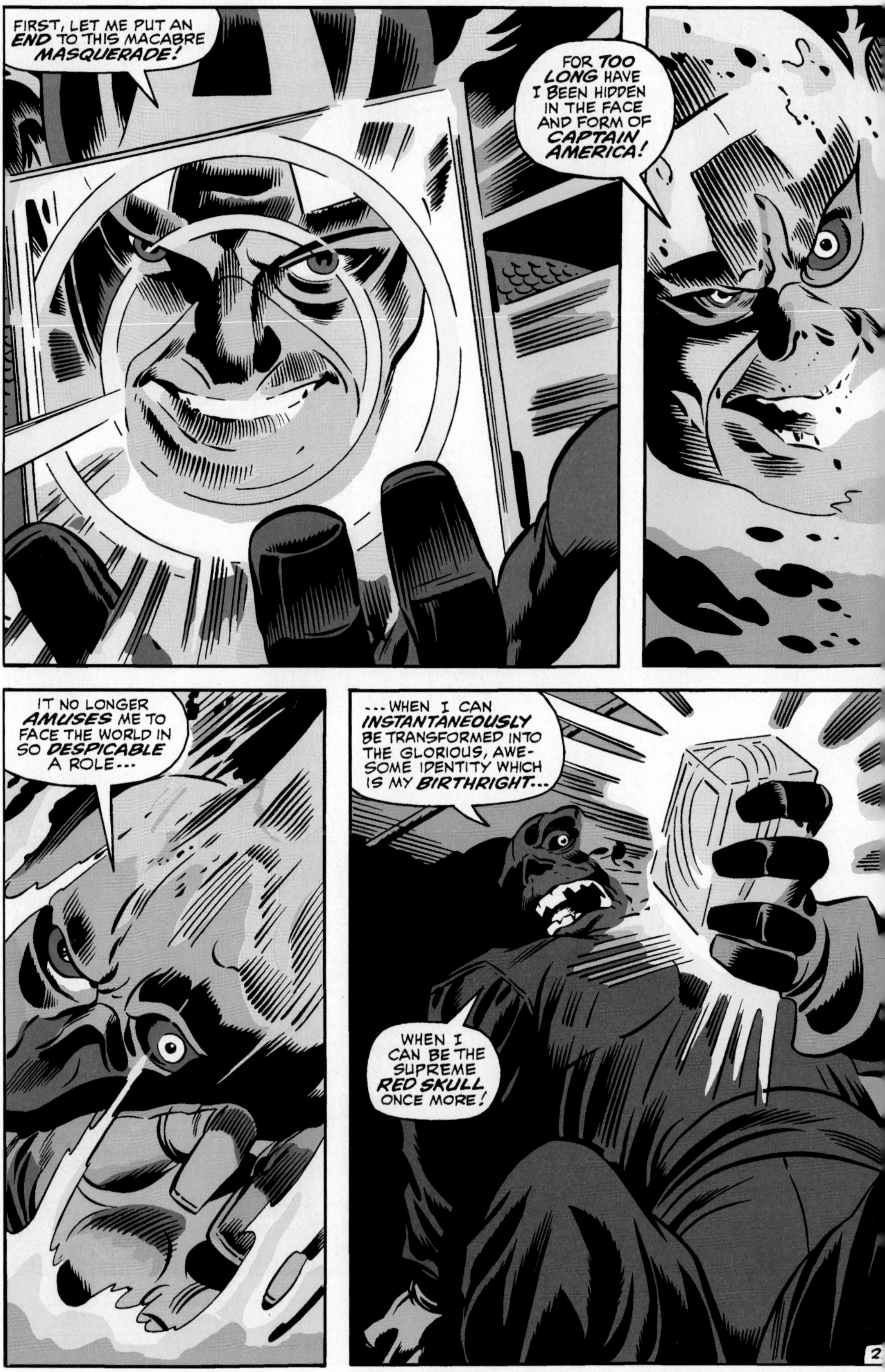
FIRST, LET ME PUT AN END TO THIS MACABRE MASQUERADE!
FOR TOO LONG HAVE I BEEN HIDDEN IN THE FACE AND FORM OF CAPTAIN AMERICA!
IT NO LONGER AMUSES ME TO FACE THE WORLD IN SO DESPICABLE A ROLE---
---WHEN I CAN INSTANTANEOUSLY BE TRANSFORMED INTO THE GLORIOUS, AWE-SOME IDENTITY WHICH IS MY BIRTHRIGHT---
WHEN I CAN BE THE SUPREME RED SKULL ONCE MORE!
2

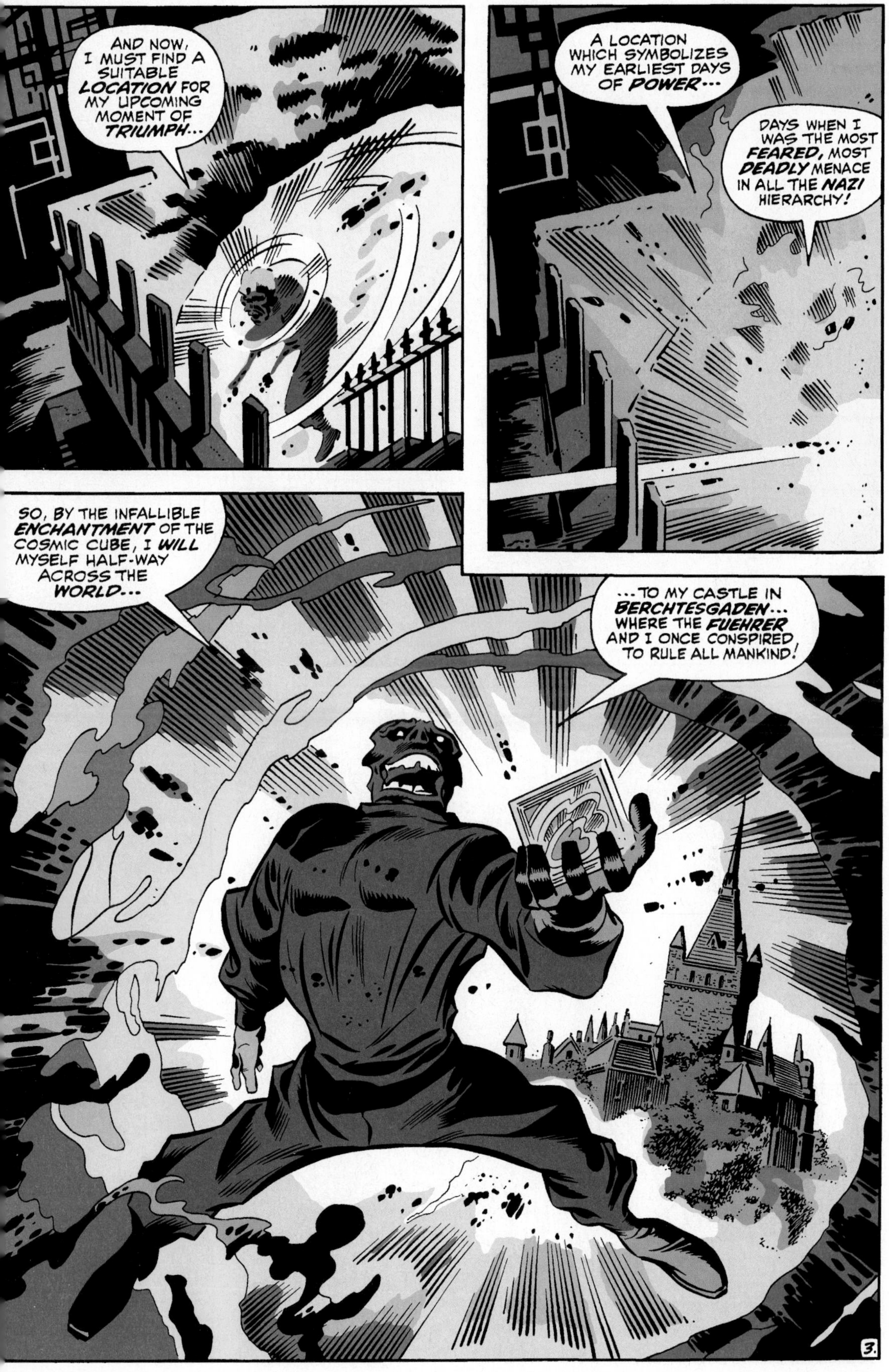
AND NOW, I MUST FIND A SUITABLE LOCATION FOR MY UPCOMING MOMENT OF TRIUMPH...
A LOCATION WHICH SYMBOLIZES MY EARLIEST DAYS OF POWER---
DAYS WHEN I WAS THE MOST FEARED, MOST DEADLY MENACE IN ALL THE NAZI HIERARCHY!
SO, BY THE INFALLIBLE ENCHANTMENT OF THE COSMIC CUBE, I WILL MYSELF HALF-WAY ACROSS THE WORLD...
...TO MY CASTLE IN BERCHTESGADEN... WHERE THE FUEHRER AND I ONCE CONSPIRED TO RULE ALL MANKIND!
3.

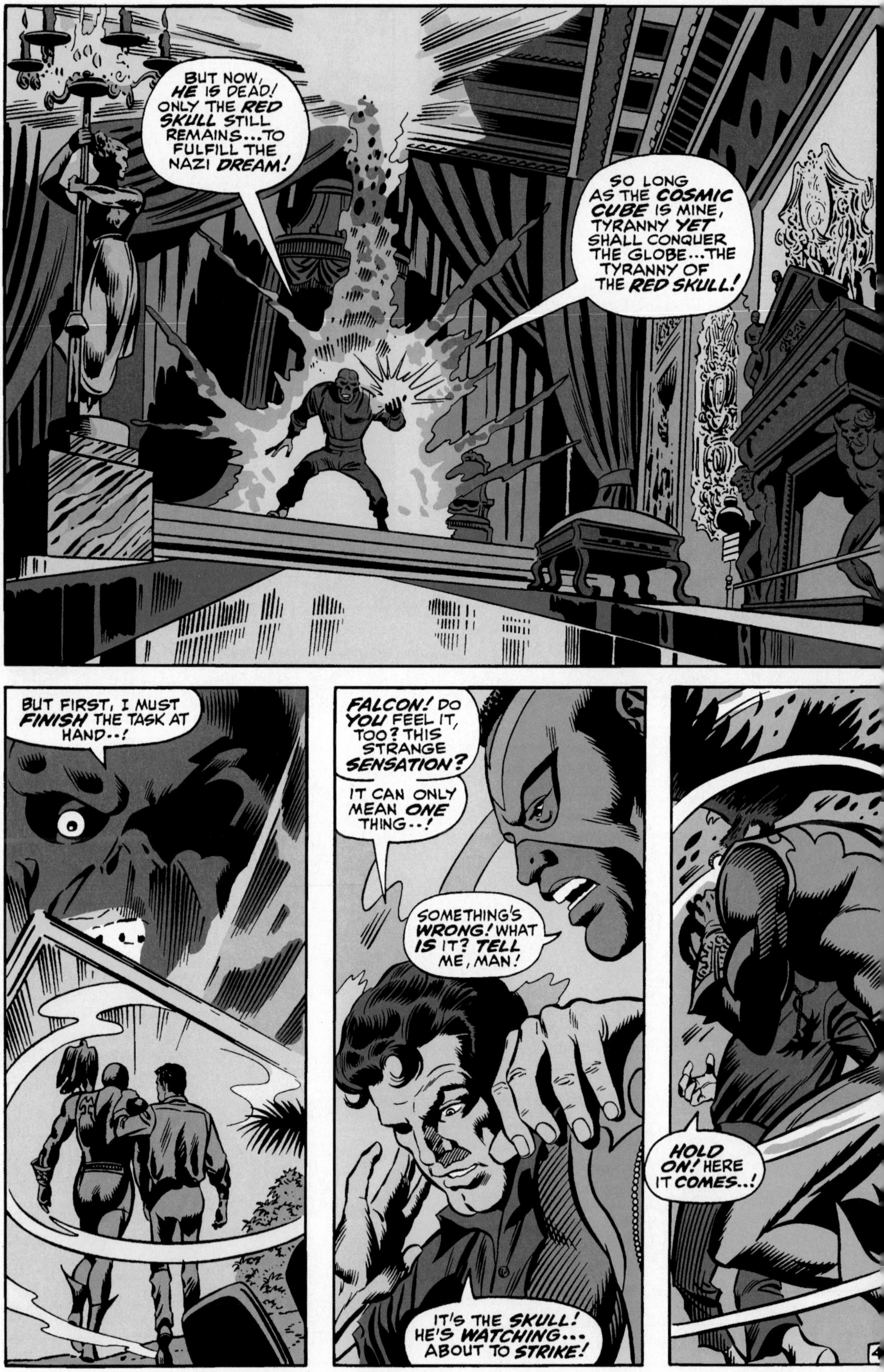
BUT NOW, HE IS DEAD! ONLY THE RED SKULL STILL REMAINS...TO FULFILL THE NAZI DREAM!
SO LONG AS THE COSMIC CUBE IS MINE, TYRANNY YET SHALL CONQUER THE GLOBE...THE TYRANNY OF THE RED SKULL!
BUT FIRST, I MUST FINISH THE TASK AT HAND--!
FALCON! DO YOU FEEL IT, TOO? THIS STRANGE SENSATION?
IT CAN ONLY MEAN ONE THING--!
SOMETHING'S WRONG! WHAT IS IT? TELL ME, MAN!
IT'S THE SKULL! HE'S WATCHING... ABOUT TO STRIKE!
HOLD ON! HERE IT COMES..!

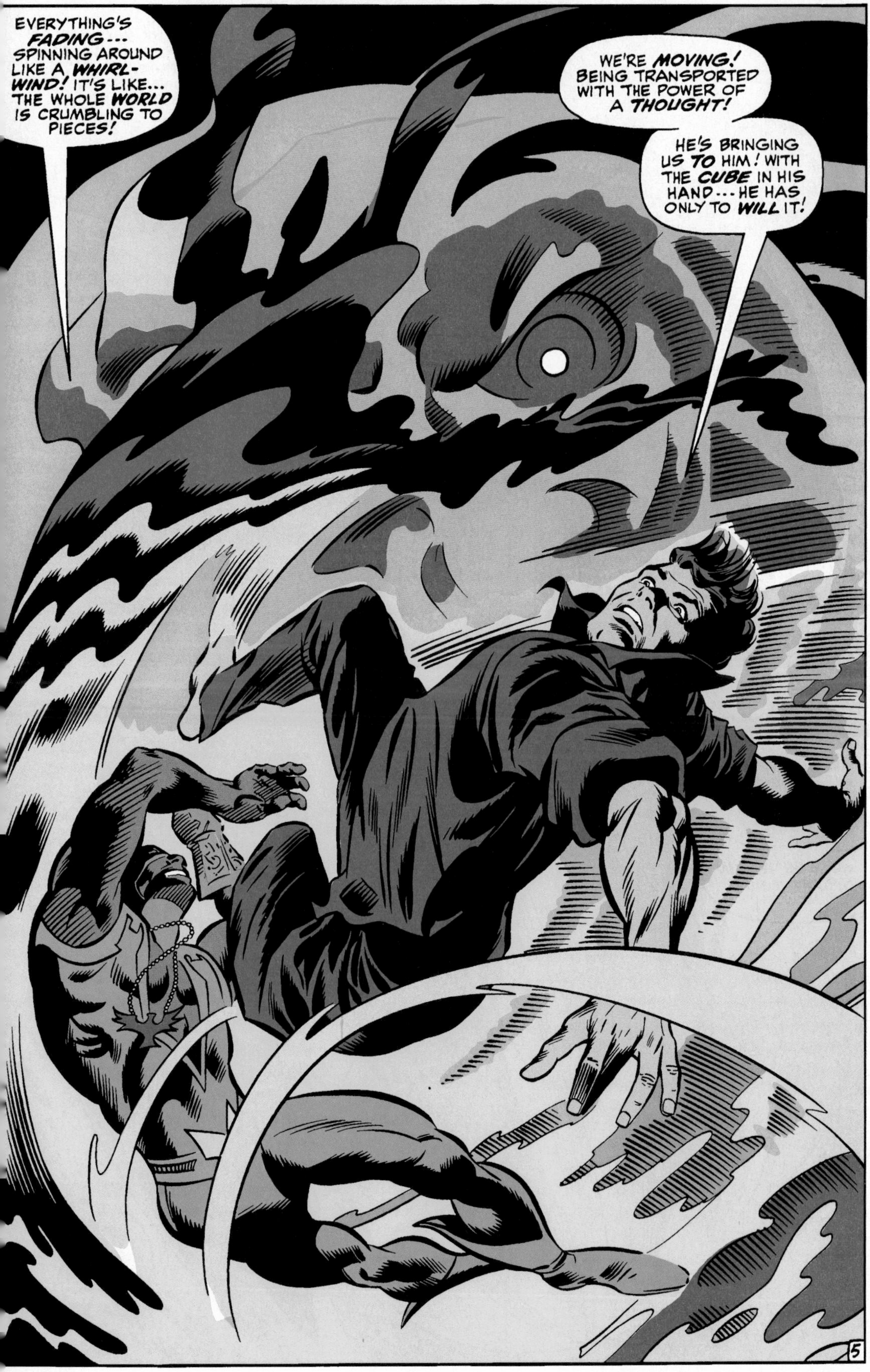
EVERYTHING'S FADING--- SPINNING AROUND LIKE A WHIRL-WIND! IT'S LIKE... THE WHOLE WORLD IS CRUMBLING TO PIECES!
WE'RE MOVING! BEING TRANSPORTED WITH THE POWER OF A THOUGHT!
HE'S BRINGING US TO HIM! WITH THE CUBE IN HIS HAND--- HE HAS ONLY TO WILL IT!
5

IT...IT ISN'T *POSSIBLE!* WE MUST...BE *DREAMING!*

IT'S *MY FAULT,* FALCON!

HE'S AFTER *ME!* YOU'RE JUST...AN INNOCENT *BYSTANDER!*

WHEN WE *LAND...* GET *AWAY* FROM ME! *RUN!* THE SKULL MAY LET *YOU* GO!

I'M HIS ENEMY! *I'M* THE ONE HE'S WAITING TO *DESTROY!*

THE WHOLE THING'S *CRAZY!* BUT WHAT-EVER HAPPENS...I'M NOT RUNNING *OUT!* WE'LL FACE IT *TO-GETHER!*

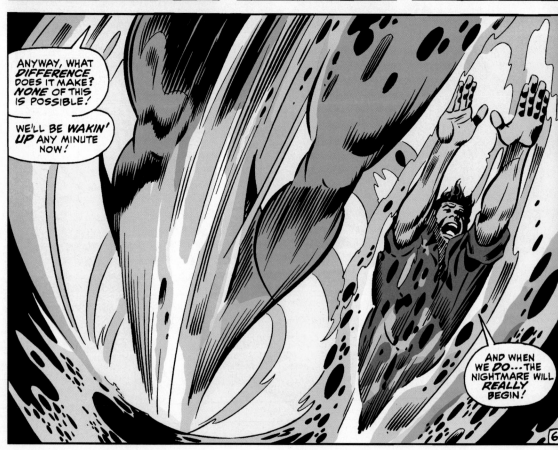

ANYWAY, WHAT *DIFFERENCE* DOES IT MAKE? *NONE* OF THIS IS POSSIBLE!

WE'LL BE *WAKIN'* UP ANY MINUTE NOW!

AND WHEN WE *DO*...THE NIGHTMARE WILL *REALLY* BEGIN!

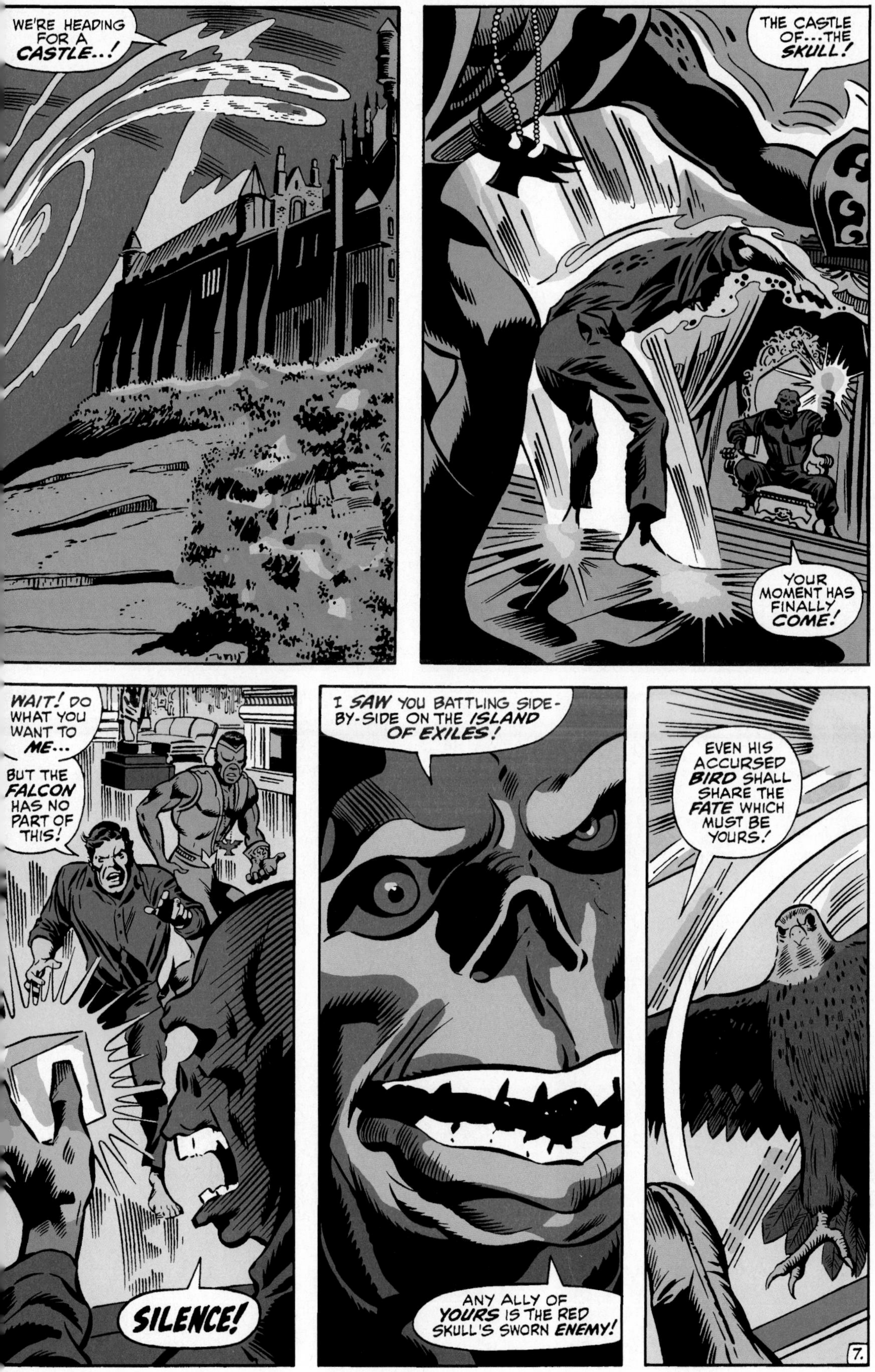
WE'RE HEADING FOR A CASTLE..!
THE CASTLE OF...THE SKULL!
YOUR MOMENT HAS FINALLY COME!
WAIT! DO WHAT YOU WANT TO ME...
BUT THE FALCON HAS NO PART OF THIS!
SILENCE!
I SAW YOU BATTLING SIDE-BY-SIDE ON THE ISLAND OF EXILES!
ANY ALLY OF YOURS IS THE RED SKULL'S SWORN ENEMY!
EVEN HIS ACCURSED BIRD SHALL SHARE THE FATE WHICH MUST BE YOURS!
7.

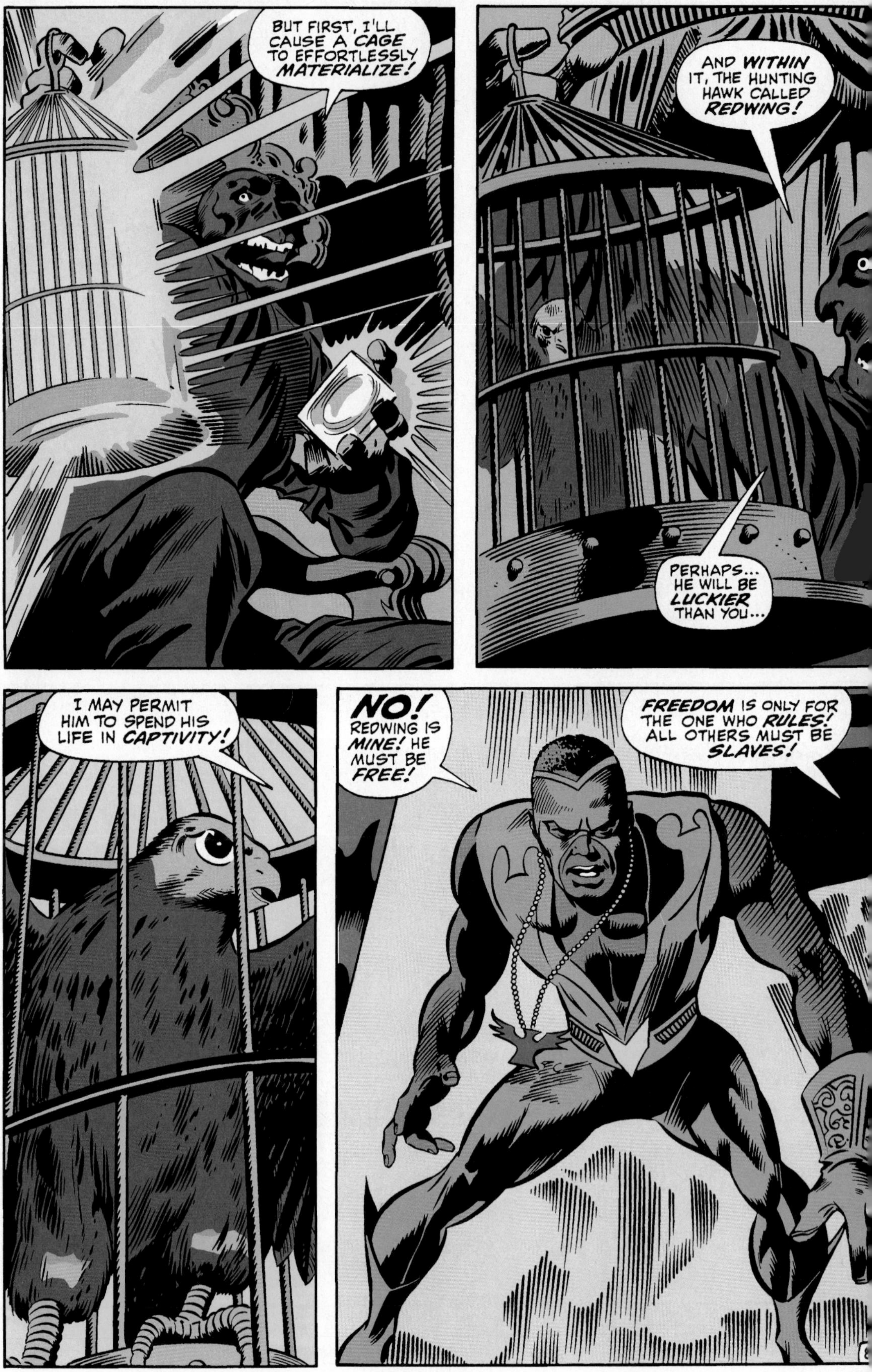
BUT FIRST, I'LL CAUSE A CAGE TO EFFORTLESSLY MATERIALIZE!
AND WITHIN IT, THE HUNTING HAWK CALLED REDWING!
PERHAPS... HE WILL BE LUCKIER THAN YOU...
I MAY PERMIT HIM TO SPEND HIS LIFE IN CAPTIVITY!
NO! REDWING IS MINE! HE MUST BE FREE!
FREEDOM IS ONLY FOR THE ONE WHO RULES! ALL OTHERS MUST BE SLAVES!

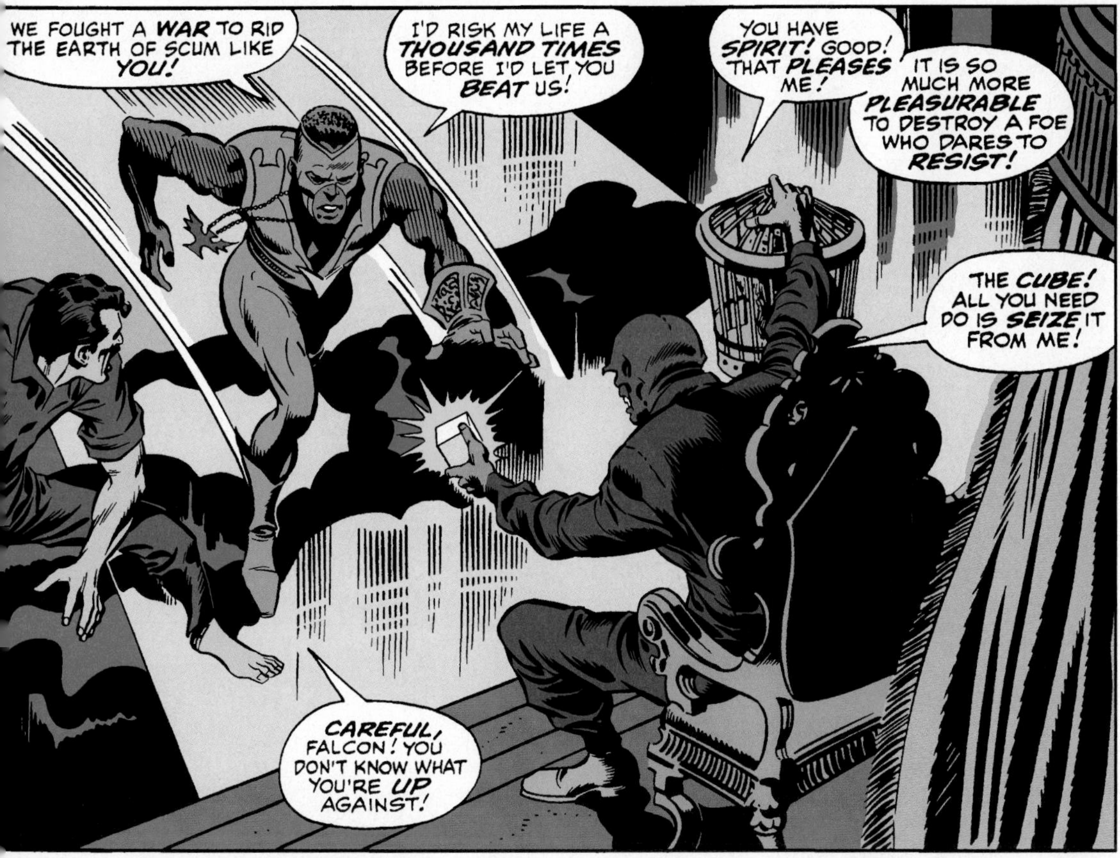
WE FOUGHT A WAR TO RID THE EARTH OF SCUM LIKE YOU!
I'D RISK MY LIFE A THOUSAND TIMES BEFORE I'D LET YOU BEAT US!
YOU HAVE SPIRIT! GOOD! THAT PLEASES ME!
IT IS SO MUCH MORE PLEASURABLE TO DESTROY A FOE WHO DARES TO RESIST!
THE CUBE! ALL YOU NEED DO IS SEIZE IT FROM ME!
CAREFUL, FALCON! YOU DON'T KNOW WHAT YOU'RE UP AGAINST!

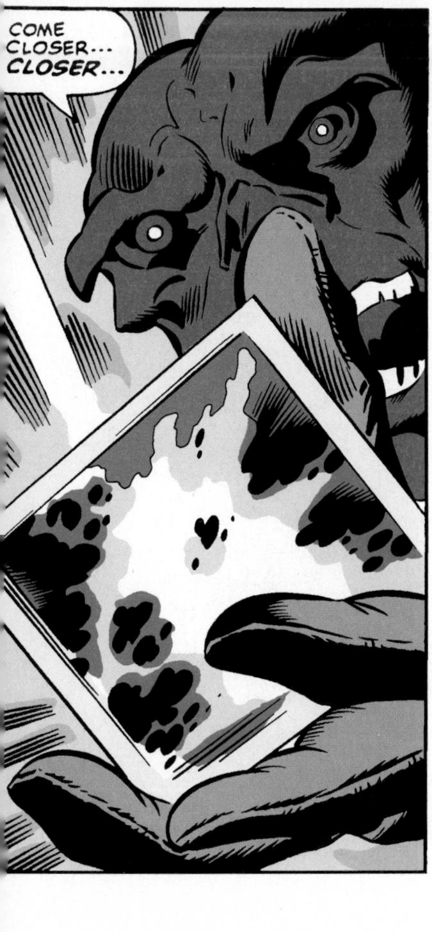
COME CLOSER... CLOSER...

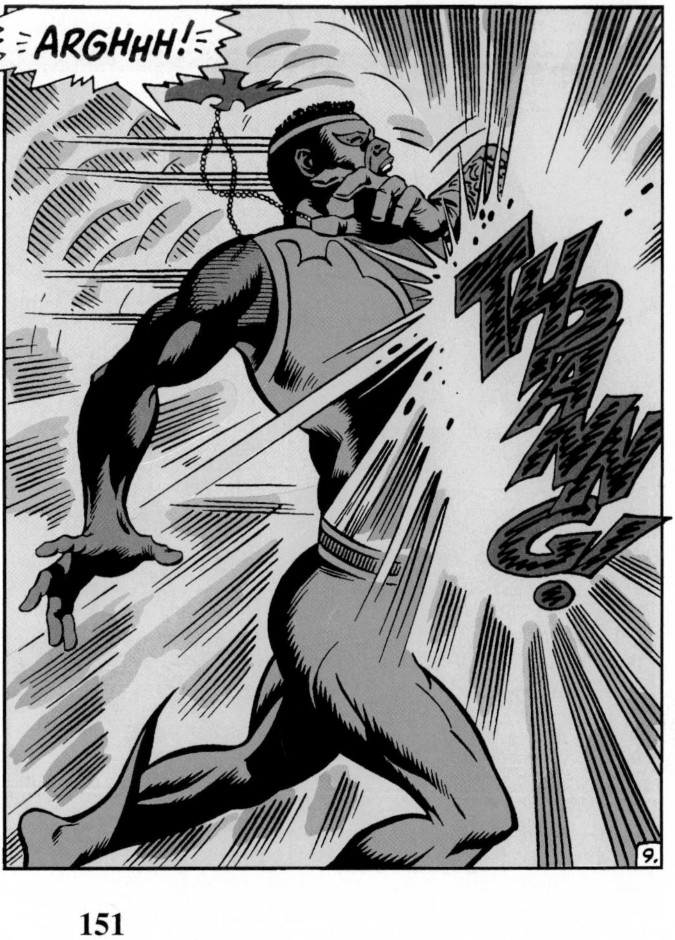
ARGHHH!
THANNG!
9.

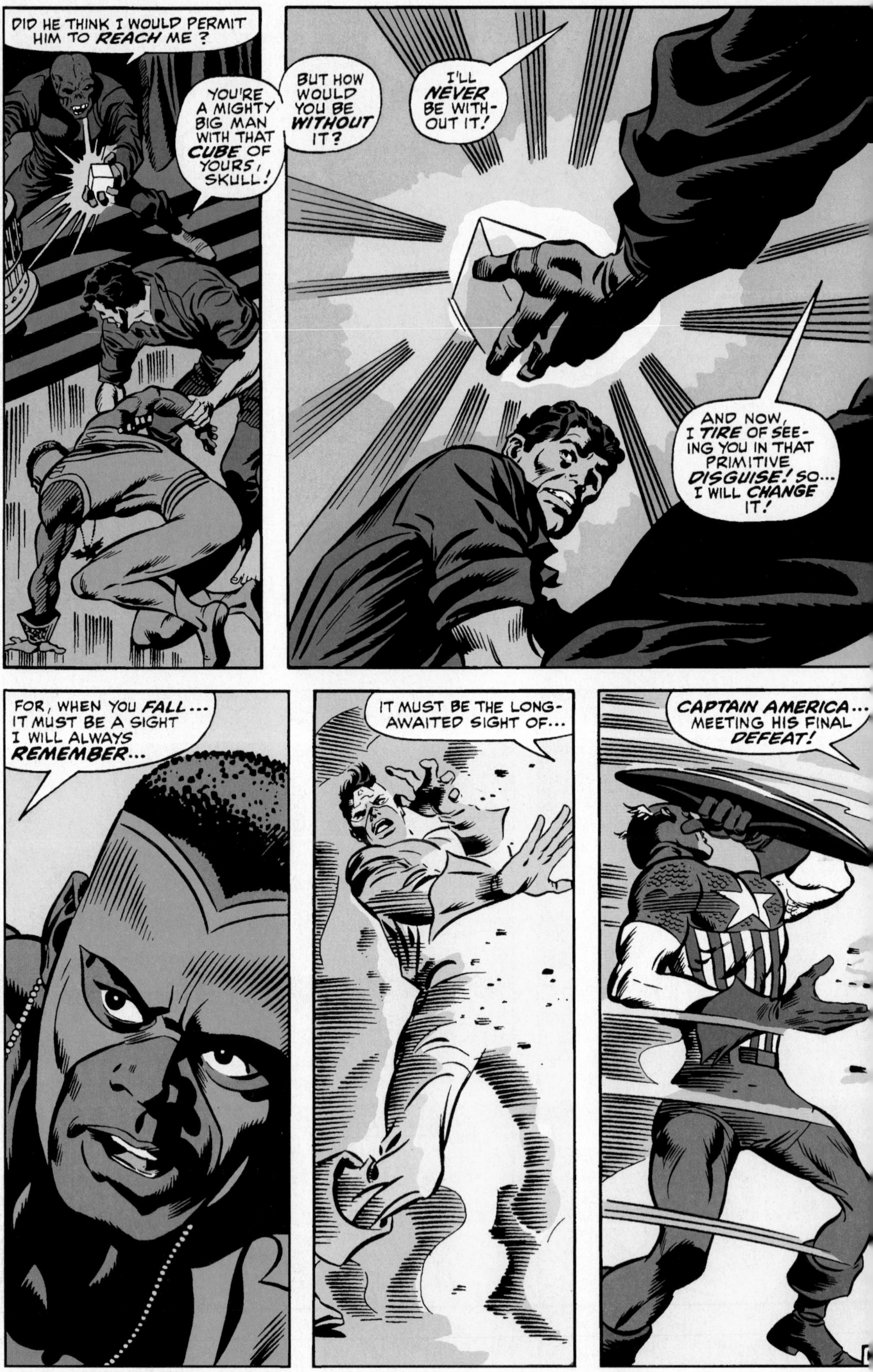
DID HE THINK I WOULD PERMIT HIM TO REACH ME?
YOU'RE A MIGHTY BIG MAN WITH THAT CUBE OF YOURS, SKULL!
BUT HOW WOULD YOU BE WITHOUT IT?
I'LL NEVER BE WITHOUT IT!
AND NOW, I TIRE OF SEEING YOU IN THAT PRIMITIVE DISGUISE! SO... I WILL CHANGE IT!
FOR, WHEN YOU FALL... IT MUST BE A SIGHT I WILL ALWAYS REMEMBER...
IT MUST BE THE LONG-AWAITED SIGHT OF...
CAPTAIN AMERICA... MEETING HIS FINAL DEFEAT!

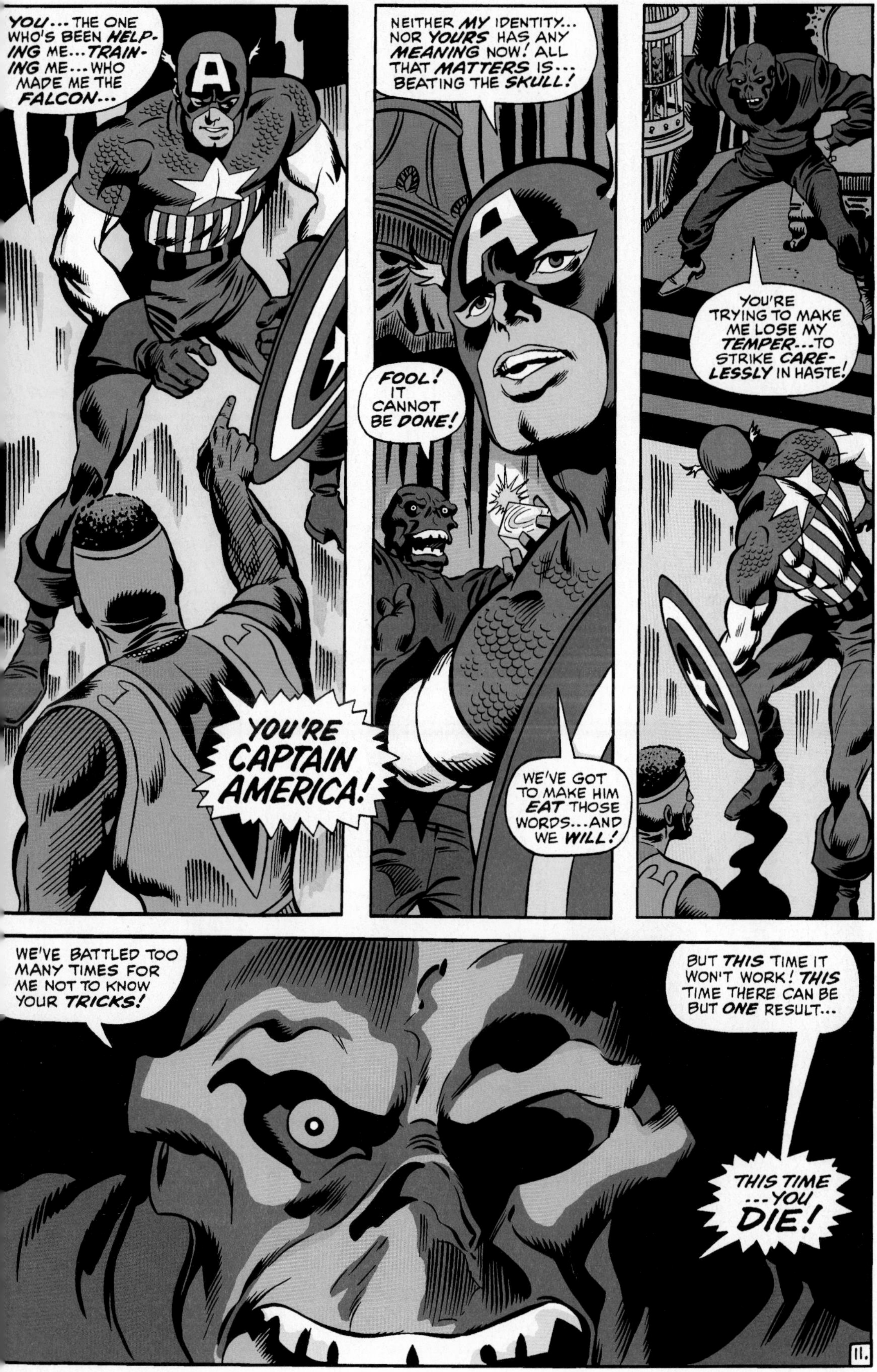
YOU... THE ONE WHO'S BEEN HELPING ME... TRAINING ME... WHO MADE ME THE FALCON...
YOU'RE CAPTAIN AMERICA!
NEITHER MY IDENTITY... NOR YOURS HAS ANY MEANING NOW! ALL THAT MATTERS IS... BEATING THE SKULL!
FOOL! IT CANNOT BE DONE!
WE'VE GOT TO MAKE HIM EAT THOSE WORDS... AND WE WILL!
YOU'RE TRYING TO MAKE ME LOSE MY TEMPER... TO STRIKE CARELESSLY IN HASTE!
WE'VE BATTLED TOO MANY TIMES FOR ME NOT TO KNOW YOUR TRICKS!
BUT THIS TIME IT WON'T WORK! THIS TIME THERE CAN BE BUT ONE RESULT...
THIS TIME ...YOU DIE!
11.

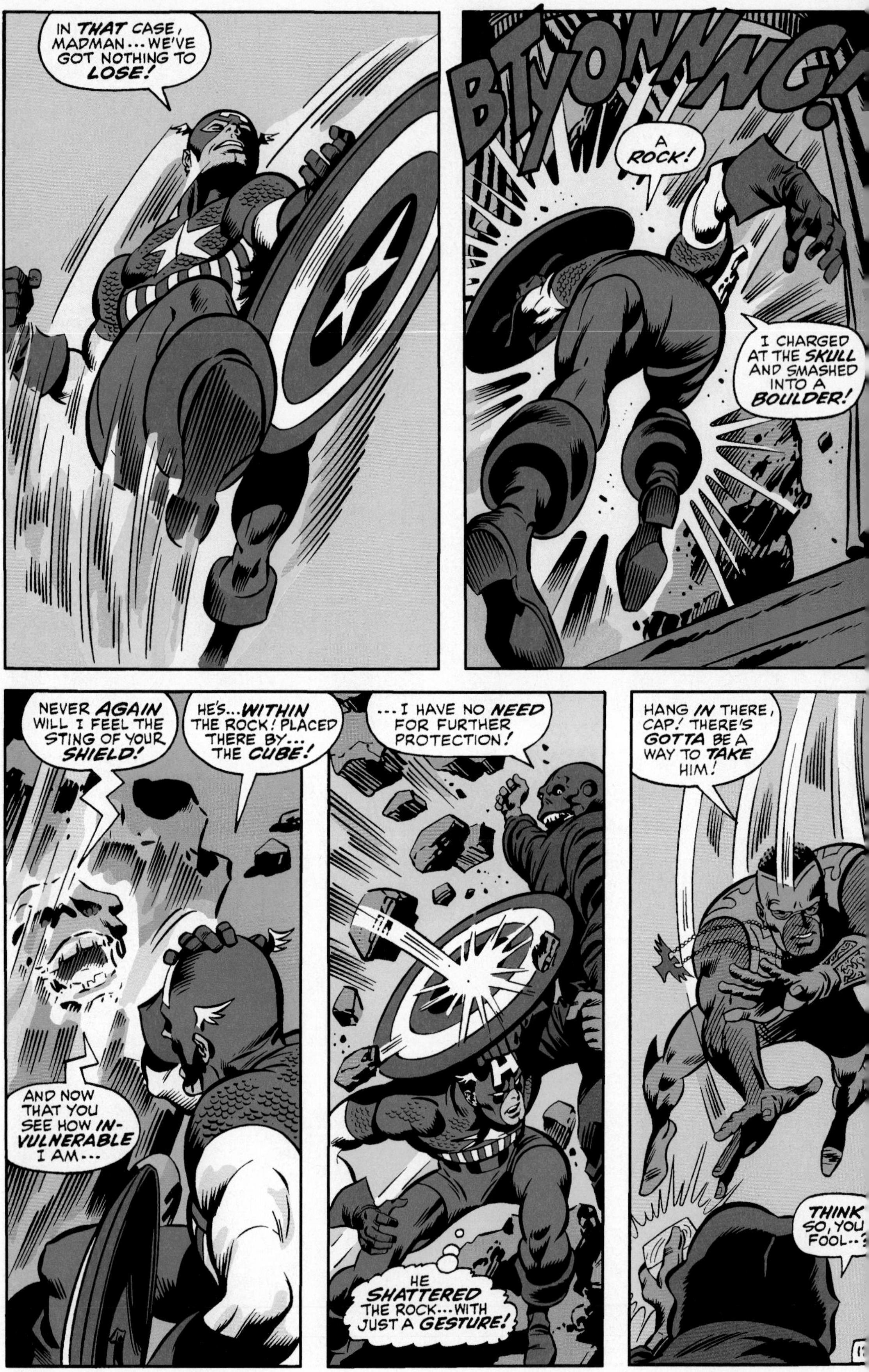

IN THAT CASE, MADMAN... WE'VE GOT NOTHING TO LOSE!
BTYONNNG!
A ROCK!
I CHARGED AT THE SKULL AND SMASHED INTO A BOULDER!
NEVER AGAIN WILL I FEEL THE STING OF YOUR SHIELD!
HE'S...WITHIN THE ROCK! PLACED THERE BY... THE CUBE!
AND NOW THAT YOU SEE HOW IN-VULNERABLE I AM...
...I HAVE NO NEED FOR FURTHER PROTECTION!
HE SHATTERED THE ROCK...WITH JUST A GESTURE!
HANG IN THERE, CAP! THERE'S GOTTA BE A WAY TO TAKE HIM!
THINK SO, YOU FOOL--?

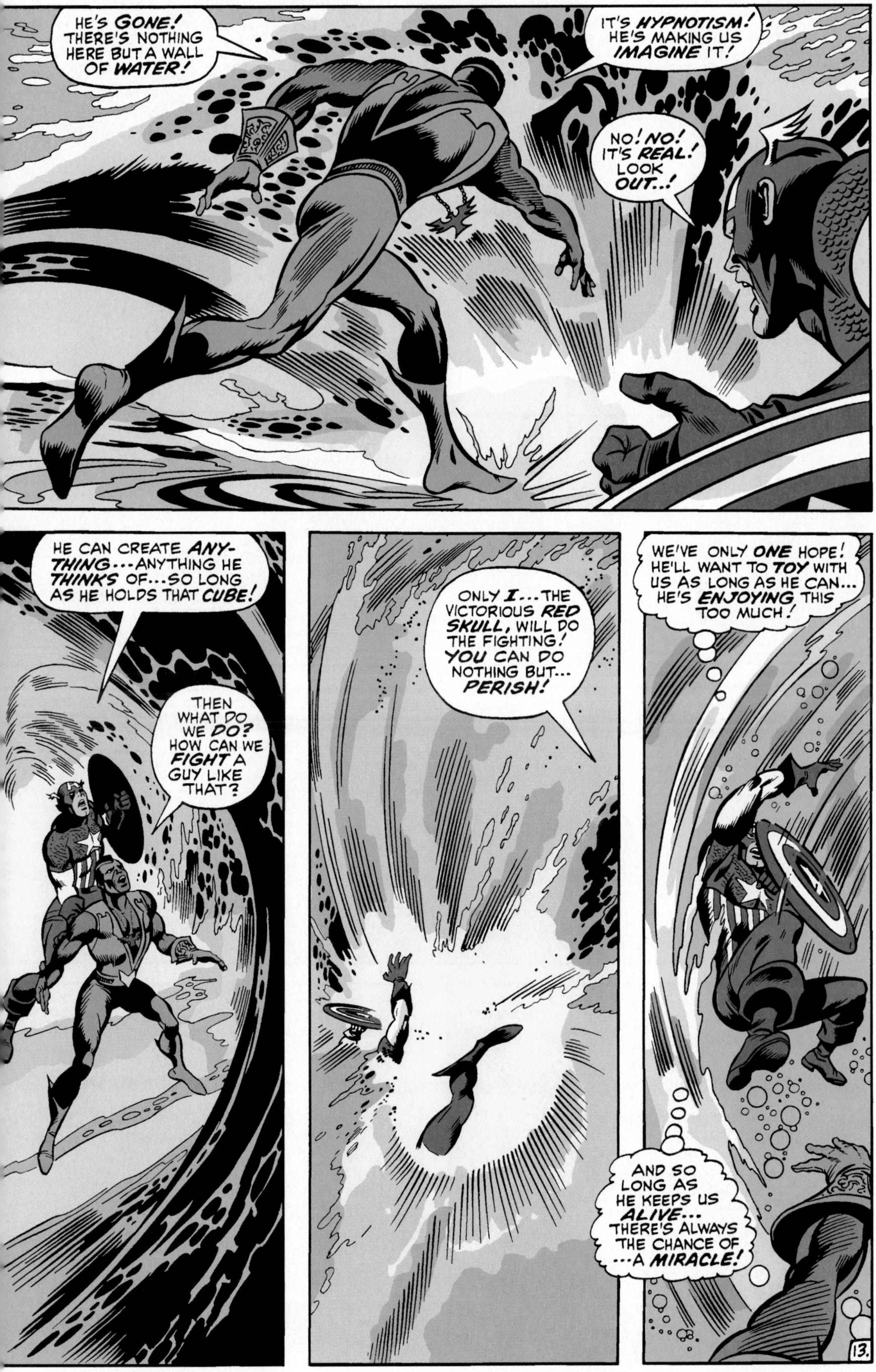
HE'S GONE! THERE'S NOTHING HERE BUT A WALL OF WATER!
IT'S HYPNOTISM! HE'S MAKING US IMAGINE IT!
NO! NO! IT'S REAL! LOOK OUT..!
HE CAN CREATE ANYTHING...ANYTHING HE THINKS OF...SO LONG AS HE HOLDS THAT CUBE!
THEN WHAT DO WE DO? HOW CAN WE FIGHT A GUY LIKE THAT?
ONLY I...THE VICTORIOUS RED SKULL, WILL DO THE FIGHTING! YOU CAN DO NOTHING BUT... PERISH!
WE'VE ONLY ONE HOPE! HE'LL WANT TO TOY WITH US AS LONG AS HE CAN... HE'S ENJOYING THIS TOO MUCH!
AND SO LONG AS HE KEEPS US ALIVE... THERE'S ALWAYS THE CHANCE OF ...A MIRACLE!
13.

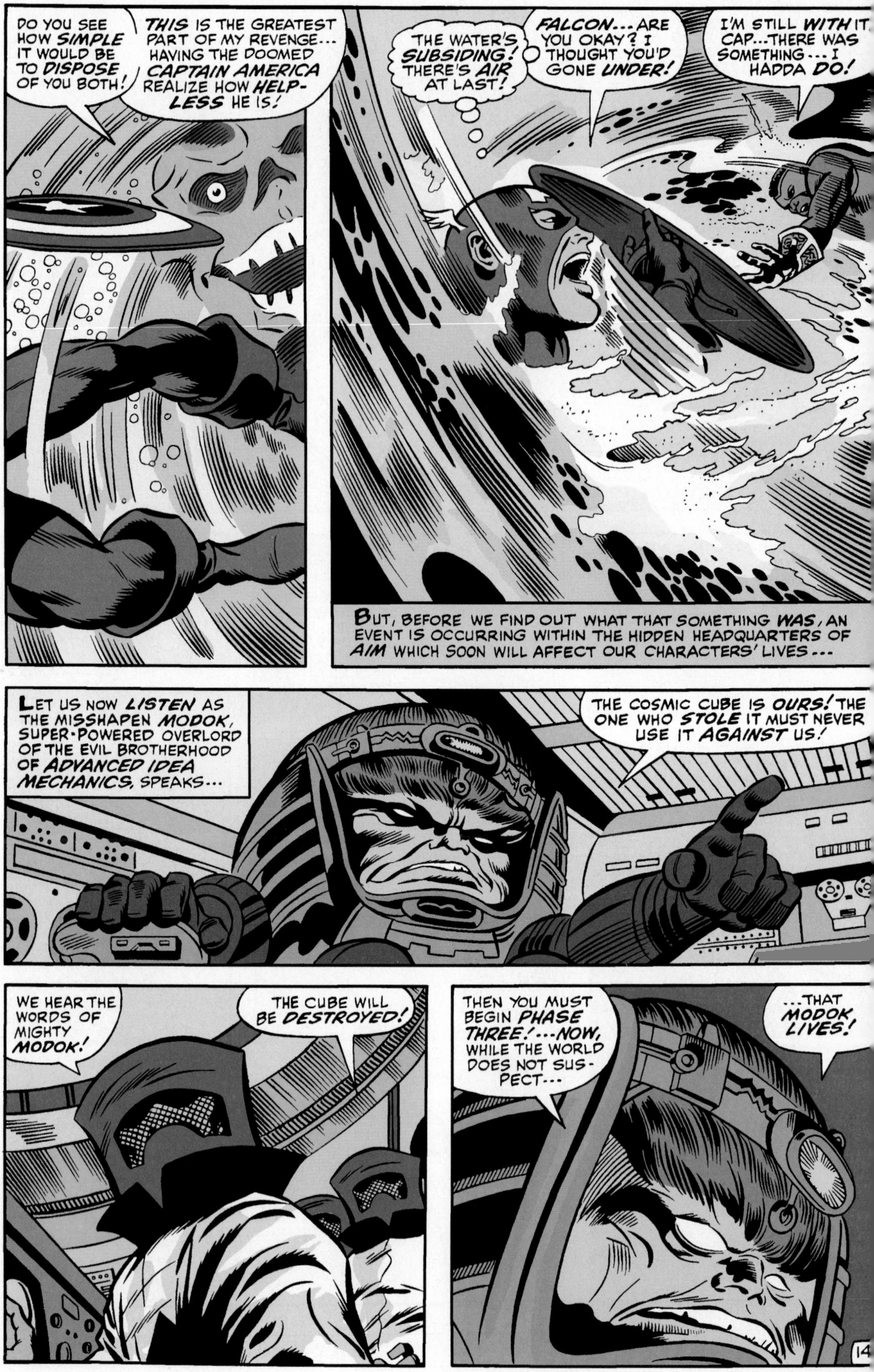

DO YOU SEE HOW SIMPLE IT WOULD BE TO DISPOSE OF YOU BOTH!
THIS IS THE GREATEST PART OF MY REVENGE... HAVING THE DOOMED CAPTAIN AMERICA REALIZE HOW HELP-LESS HE IS!
THE WATER'S SUBSIDING! THERE'S AIR AT LAST!
FALCON... ARE YOU OKAY? I THOUGHT YOU'D GONE UNDER!
I'M STILL WITH IT CAP... THERE WAS SOMETHING... I HADDA DO!
BUT, BEFORE WE FIND OUT WHAT THAT SOMETHING WAS, AN EVENT IS OCCURRING WITHIN THE HIDDEN HEADQUARTERS OF AIM WHICH SOON WILL AFFECT OUR CHARACTERS' LIVES...
LET US NOW LISTEN AS THE MISSHAPEN MODOK, SUPER-POWERED OVERLORD OF THE EVIL BROTHERHOOD OF ADVANCED IDEA MECHANICS, SPEAKS...
THE COSMIC CUBE IS OURS! THE ONE WHO STOLE IT MUST NEVER USE IT AGAINST US!
WE HEAR THE WORDS OF MIGHTY MODOK!
THE CUBE WILL BE DESTROYED!
THEN YOU MUST BEGIN PHASE THREE! ... NOW, WHILE THE WORLD DOES NOT SUS-PECT...
...THAT MODOK LIVES!
14

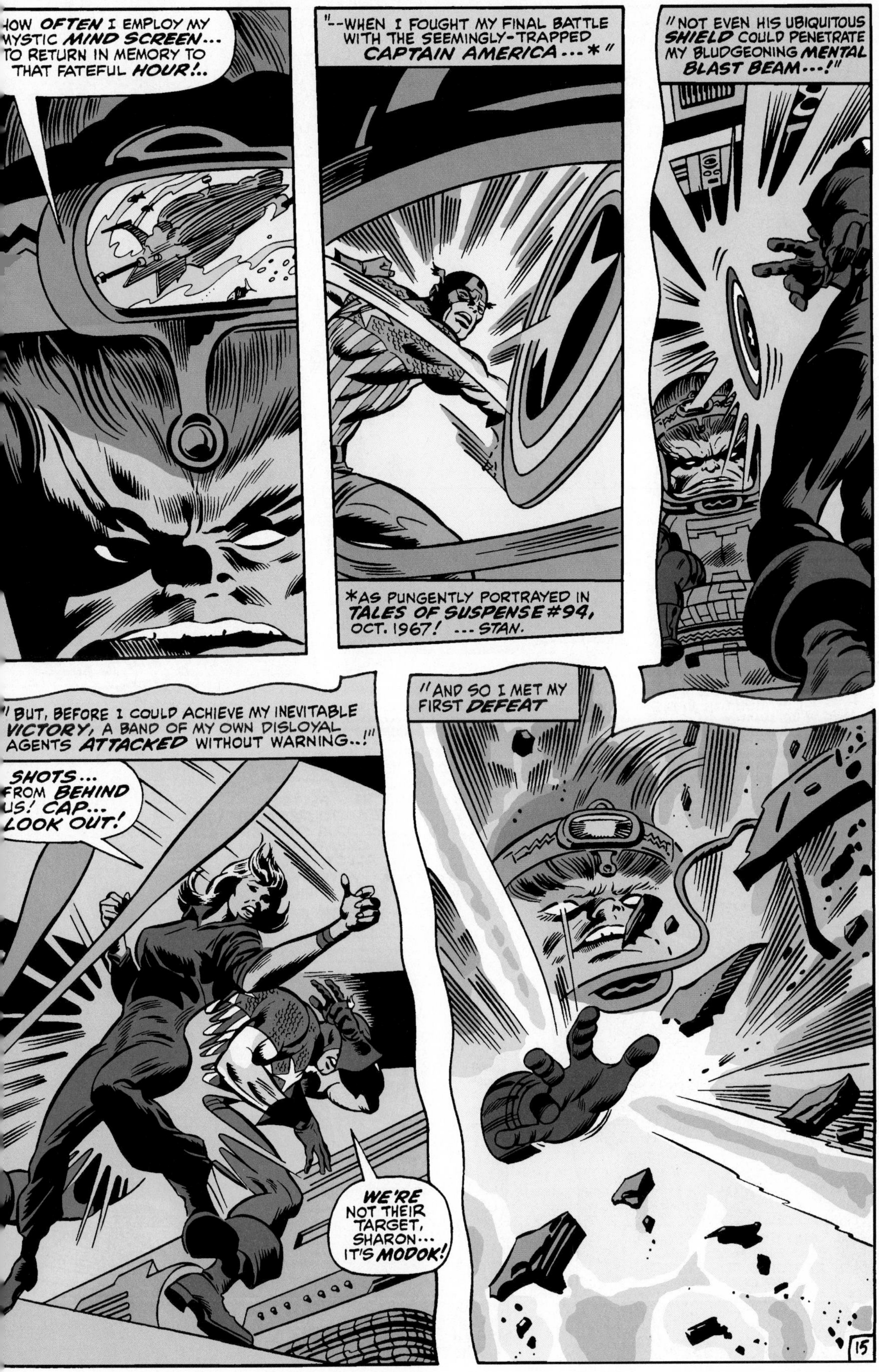
HOW OFTEN I EMPLOY MY MYSTIC MIND SCREEN... TO RETURN IN MEMORY TO THAT FATEFUL HOUR!..
"--WHEN I FOUGHT MY FINAL BATTLE WITH THE SEEMINGLY-TRAPPED CAPTAIN AMERICA...*"
*AS PUNGENTLY PORTRAYED IN TALES OF SUSPENSE #94, OCT. 1967! ...STAN.
"NOT EVEN HIS UBIQUITOUS SHIELD COULD PENETRATE MY BLUDGEONING MENTAL BLAST BEAM...!"
"BUT, BEFORE I COULD ACHIEVE MY INEVITABLE VICTORY, A BAND OF MY OWN DISLOYAL AGENTS ATTACKED WITHOUT WARNING..!"
SHOTS... FROM BEHIND US! CAP... LOOK OUT!
WE'RE NOT THEIR TARGET, SHARON... IT'S MODOK!
"AND SO I MET MY FIRST DEFEAT
15

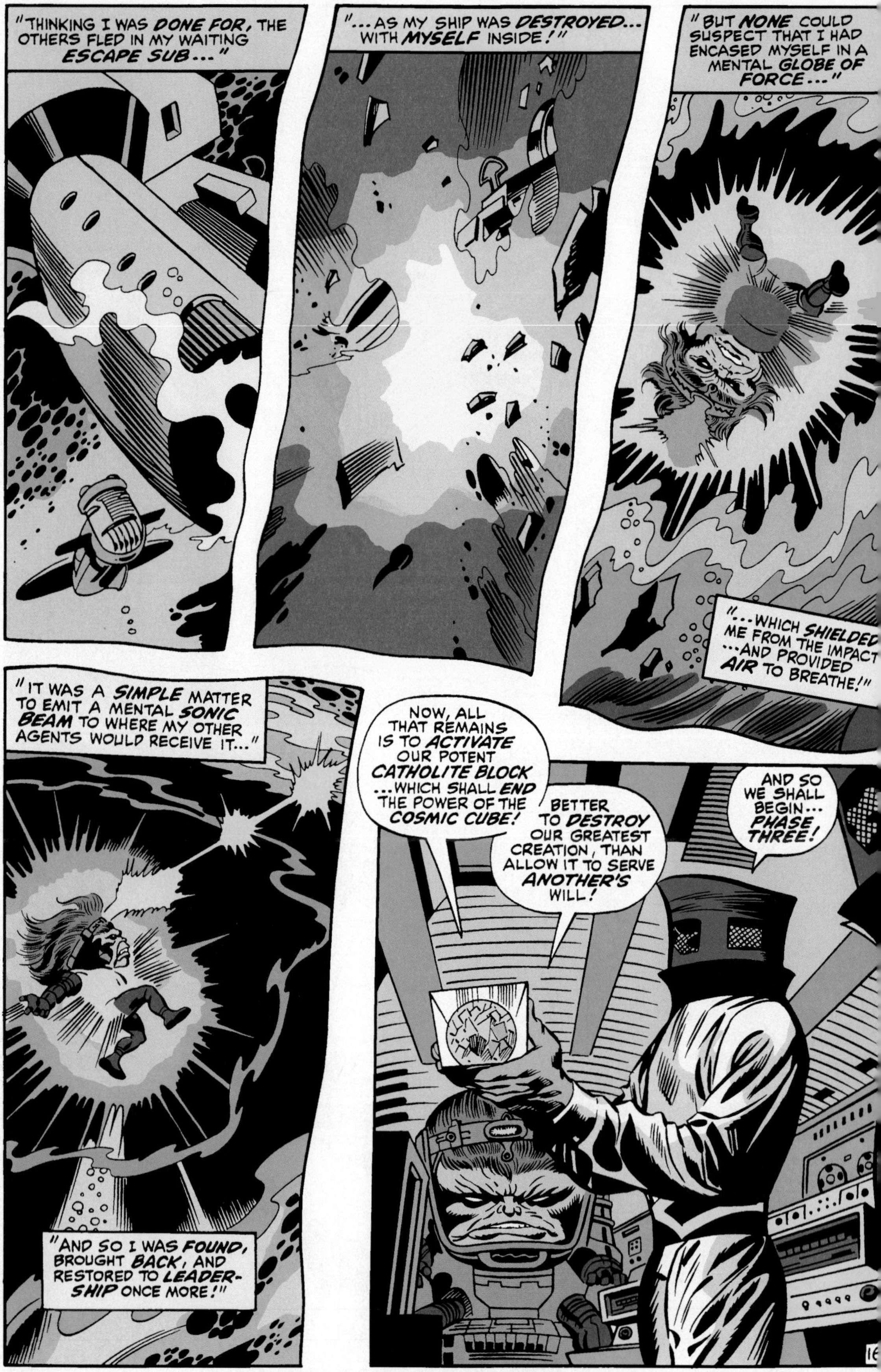
"THINKING I WAS DONE FOR, THE OTHERS FLED IN MY WAITING ESCAPE SUB..."
"...AS MY SHIP WAS DESTROYED... WITH MYSELF INSIDE!"
"BUT NONE COULD SUSPECT THAT I HAD ENCASED MYSELF IN A MENTAL GLOBE OF FORCE..."
"...WHICH SHIELDED ME FROM THE IMPACT ...AND PROVIDED AIR TO BREATHE!"
"IT WAS A SIMPLE MATTER TO EMIT A MENTAL SONIC BEAM TO WHERE MY OTHER AGENTS WOULD RECEIVE IT..."
"AND SO I WAS FOUND, BROUGHT BACK, AND RESTORED TO LEADER-SHIP ONCE MORE!"
NOW, ALL THAT REMAINS IS TO ACTIVATE OUR POTENT CATHOLITE BLOCK ...WHICH SHALL END THE POWER OF THE COSMIC CUBE!
BETTER TO DESTROY OUR GREATEST CREATION, THAN ALLOW IT TO SERVE ANOTHER'S WILL!
AND SO WE SHALL BEGIN... PHASE THREE!
16

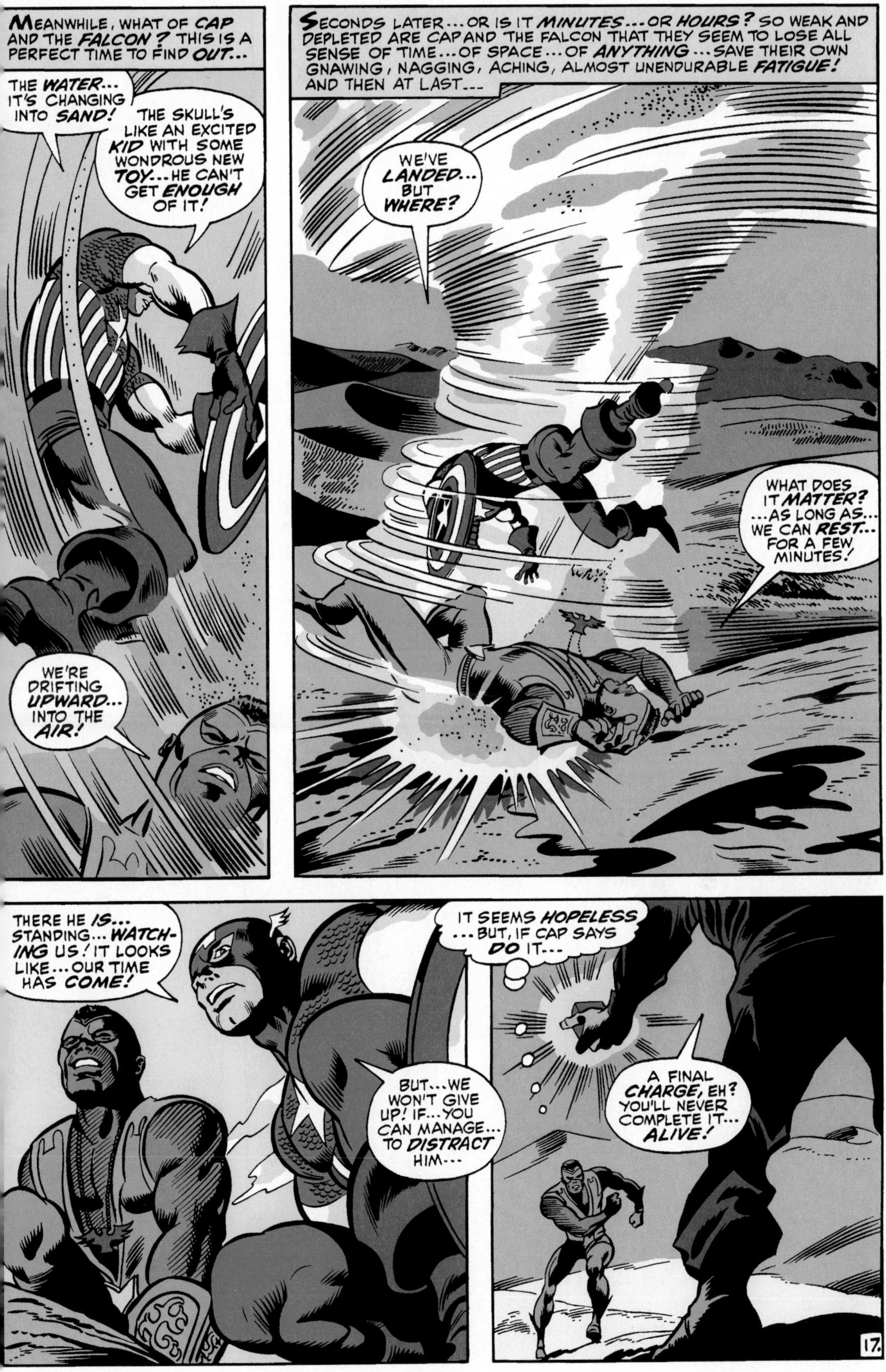
MEANWHILE, WHAT OF CAP AND THE FALCON? THIS IS A PERFECT TIME TO FIND OUT...
THE WATER... IT'S CHANGING INTO SAND!
THE SKULL'S LIKE AN EXCITED KID WITH SOME WONDROUS NEW TOY... HE CAN'T GET ENOUGH OF IT!
WE'RE DRIFTING UPWARD... INTO THE AIR!
SECONDS LATER... OR IS IT MINUTES... OR HOURS? SO WEAK AND DEPLETED ARE CAP AND THE FALCON THAT THEY SEEM TO LOSE ALL SENSE OF TIME... OF SPACE... OF ANYTHING... SAVE THEIR OWN GNAWING, NAGGING, ACHING, ALMOST UNENDURABLE FATIGUE! AND THEN AT LAST...
WE'VE LANDED... BUT WHERE?
WHAT DOES IT MATTER? ...AS LONG AS... WE CAN REST... FOR A FEW MINUTES!
THERE HE IS... STANDING... WATCHING US! IT LOOKS LIKE... OUR TIME HAS COME!
BUT... WE WON'T GIVE UP! IF... YOU CAN MANAGE... TO DISTRACT HIM...
IT SEEMS HOPELESS ...BUT, IF CAP SAYS DO IT...
A FINAL CHARGE, EH? YOU'LL NEVER COMPLETE IT... ALIVE!
17.

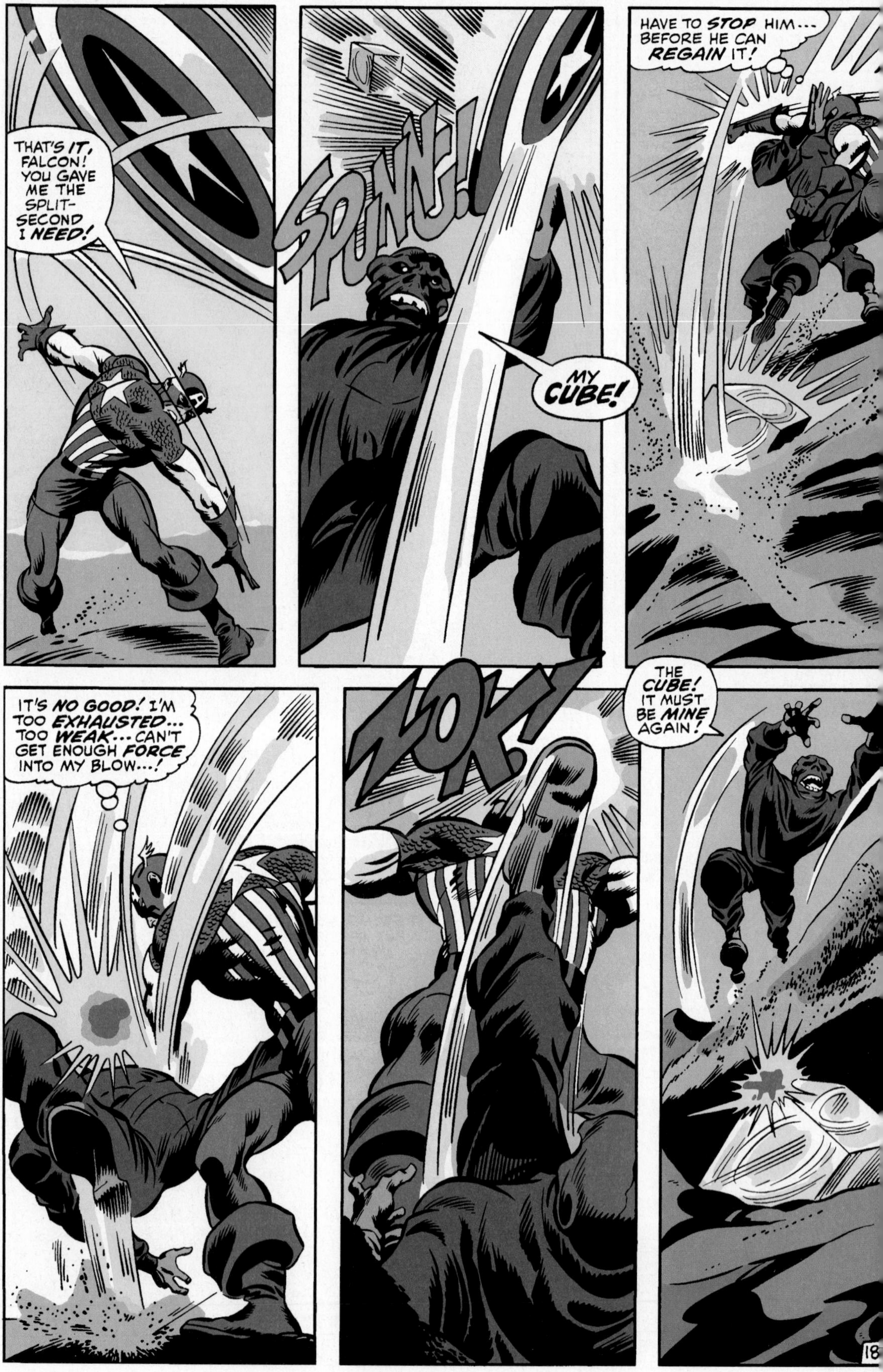
THAT'S IT, FALCON! YOU GAVE ME THE SPLIT-SECOND I NEED!
SPANNG!
MY CUBE!
HAVE TO STOP HIM--- BEFORE HE CAN REGAIN IT!
IT'S NO GOOD! I'M TOO EXHAUSTED... TOO WEAK... CAN'T GET ENOUGH FORCE INTO MY BLOW...!
ZOK!
THE CUBE! IT MUST BE MINE AGAIN!
18

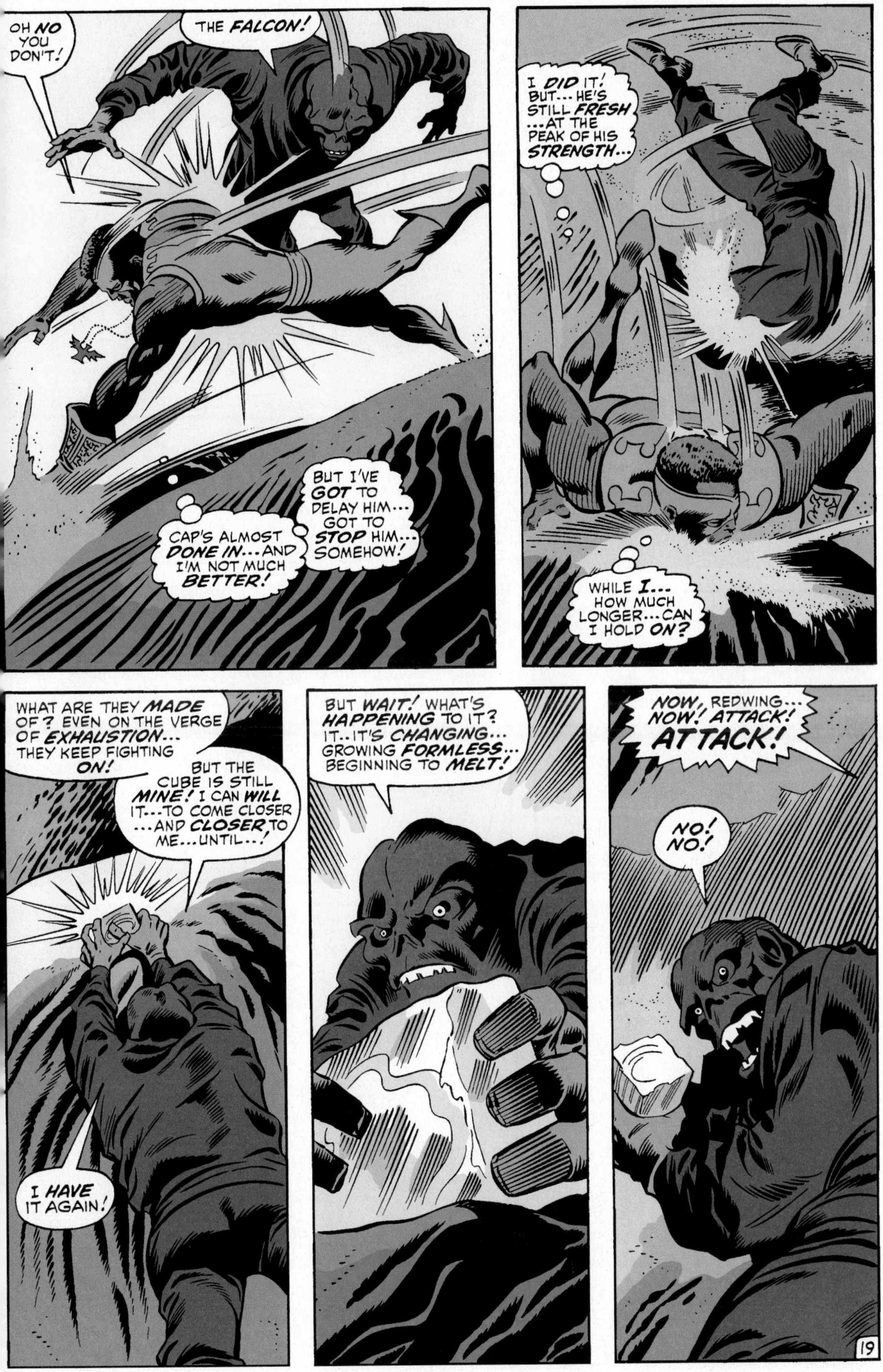
OH NO YOU DON'T!
THE FALCON!
I DID IT! BUT... HE'S STILL FRESH ...AT THE PEAK OF HIS STRENGTH...
BUT I'VE GOT TO DELAY HIM... GOT TO STOP HIM... SOMEHOW!
CAP'S ALMOST DONE IN... AND I'M NOT MUCH BETTER!
WHILE I... HOW MUCH LONGER... CAN I HOLD ON?
WHAT ARE THEY MADE OF? EVEN ON THE VERGE OF EXHAUSTION... THEY KEEP FIGHTING ON!
BUT THE CUBE IS STILL MINE! I CAN WILL IT---TO COME CLOSER ...AND CLOSER, TO ME...UNTIL..!
I HAVE IT AGAIN!
BUT WAIT! WHAT'S HAPPENING TO IT? IT..IT'S CHANGING... GROWING FORMLESS... BEGINNING TO MELT!
NOW, REDWING... NOW! ATTACK! ATTACK!
NO! NO!
19

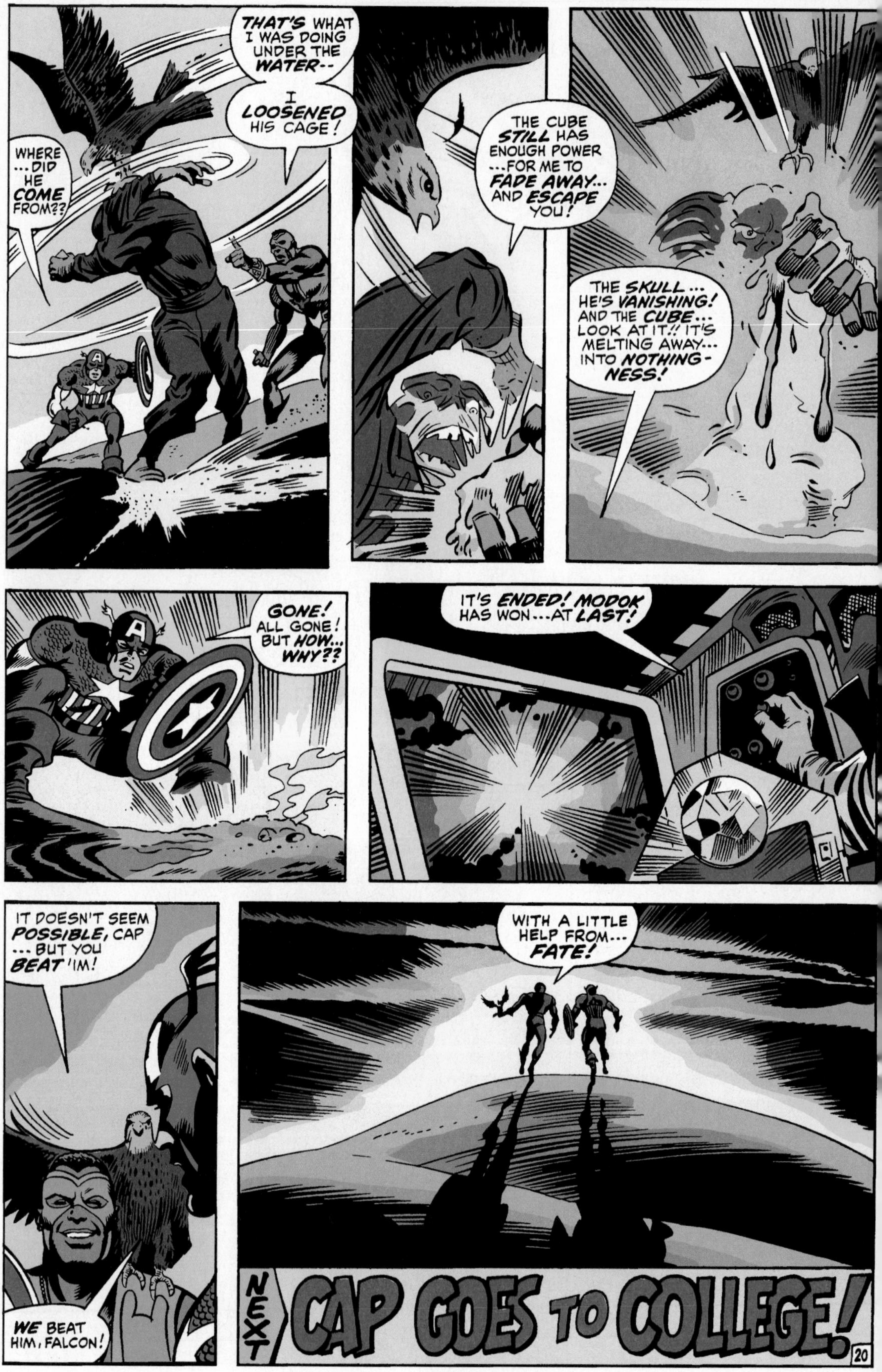
THAT'S WHAT I WAS DOING UNDER THE WATER--
I LOOSENED HIS CAGE!
WHERE ...DID HE COME FROM??
THE CUBE STILL HAS ENOUGH POWER ...FOR ME TO FADE AWAY... AND ESCAPE YOU!
THE SKULL ... HE'S VANISHING! AND THE CUBE... LOOK AT IT!! IT'S MELTING AWAY... INTO NOTHING-NESS!
GONE! ALL GONE! BUT HOW... WHY??
IT'S ENDED! MODOK HAS WON...AT LAST!
IT DOESN'T SEEM POSSIBLE, CAP ... BUT YOU BEAT 'IM!
WE BEAT HIM, FALCON!
WITH A LITTLE HELP FROM... FATE!
NEXT CAP GOES TO COLLEGE!
20

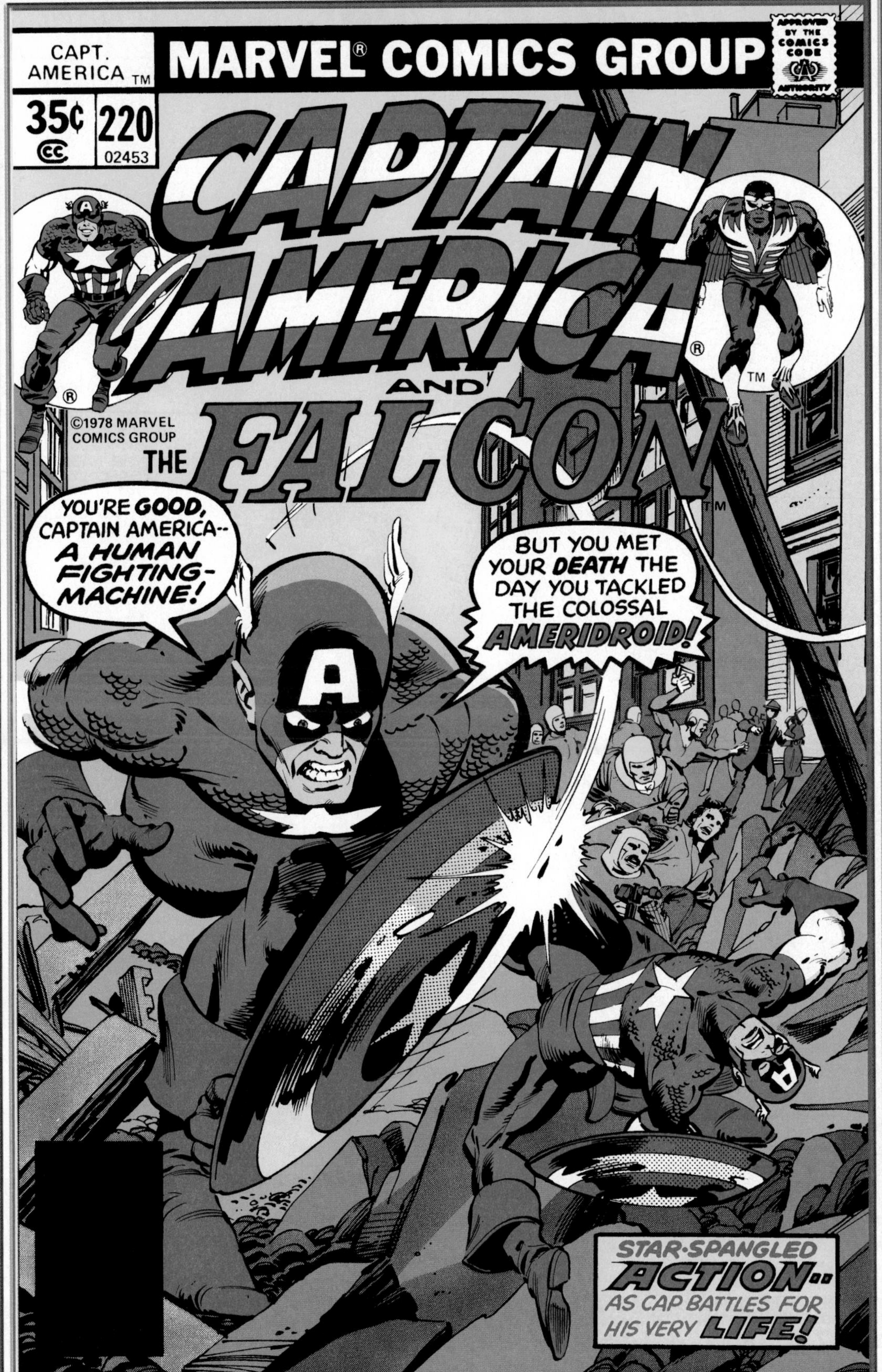
CAPT. AMERICA TM
MARVEL® COMICS GROUP
APPROVED BY THE COMICS CODE AUTHORITY
35¢ CC
220
02453
CAPTAIN AMERICA®
AND
THE FALCON™
©1978 MARVEL COMICS GROUP
YOU'RE GOOD, CAPTAIN AMERICA-- A HUMAN FIGHTING-MACHINE!
BUT YOU MET YOUR DEATH THE DAY YOU TACKLED THE COLOSSAL AMERIDROID!
STAR-SPANGLED ACTION.. AS CAP BATTLES FOR HIS VERY LIFE!

Captain America #220 (April 1978) featured the Falcon's first solo backup story.

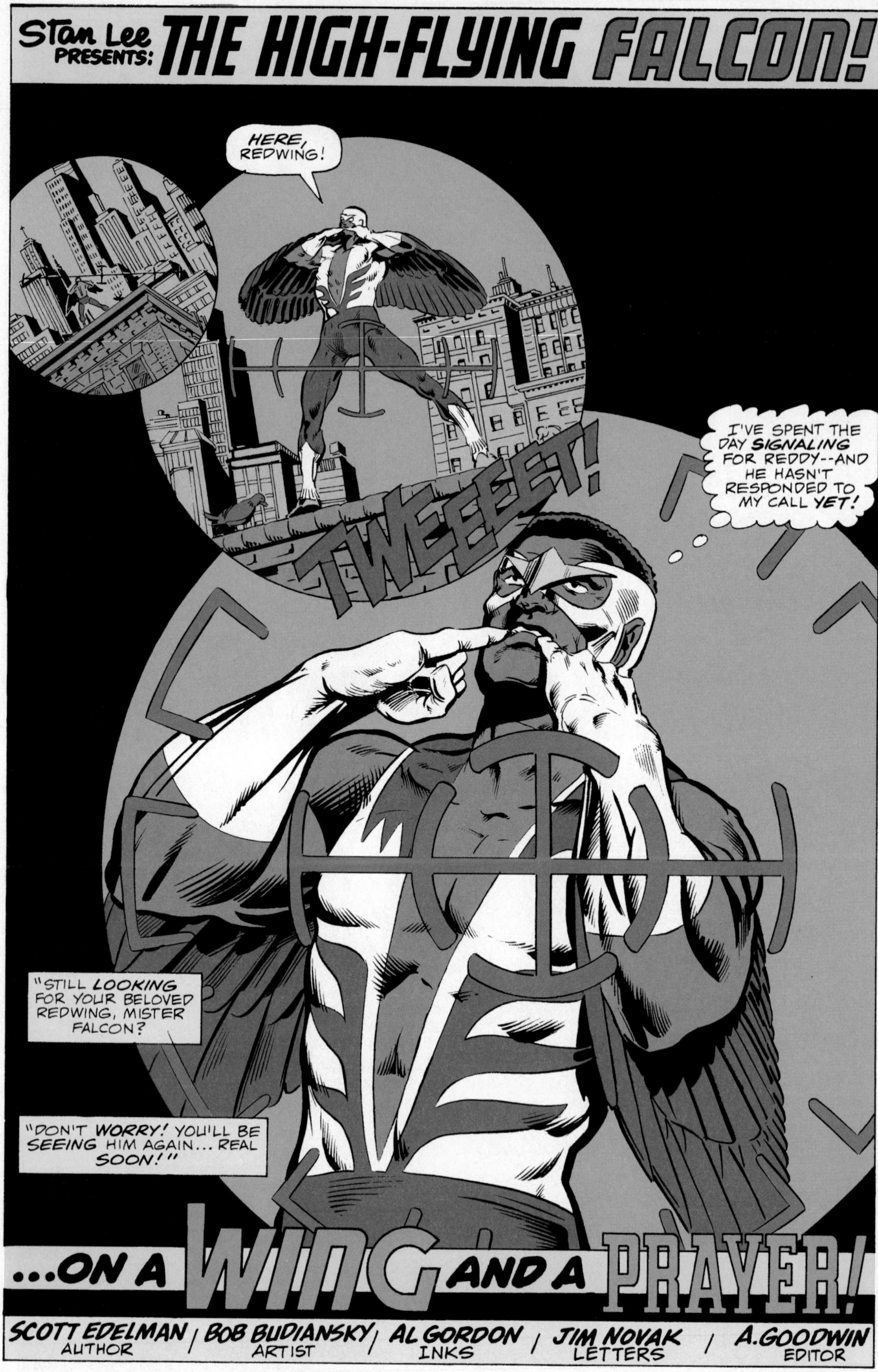
Stan Lee PRESENTS: THE HIGH-FLYING FALCON!
HERE, REDWING!
TWEEEET!
I'VE SPENT THE DAY SIGNALING FOR REDDY--AND HE HASN'T RESPONDED TO MY CALL YET!
"STILL LOOKING FOR YOUR BELOVED REDWING, MISTER FALCON?
"DON'T WORRY! YOU'LL BE SEEING HIM AGAIN... REAL SOON!"
...ON A WING AND A PRAYER!
SCOTT EDELMAN AUTHOR / BOB BUDIANSKY ARTIST / AL GORDON INKS / JIM NOVAK LETTERS / A.GOODWIN EDITOR

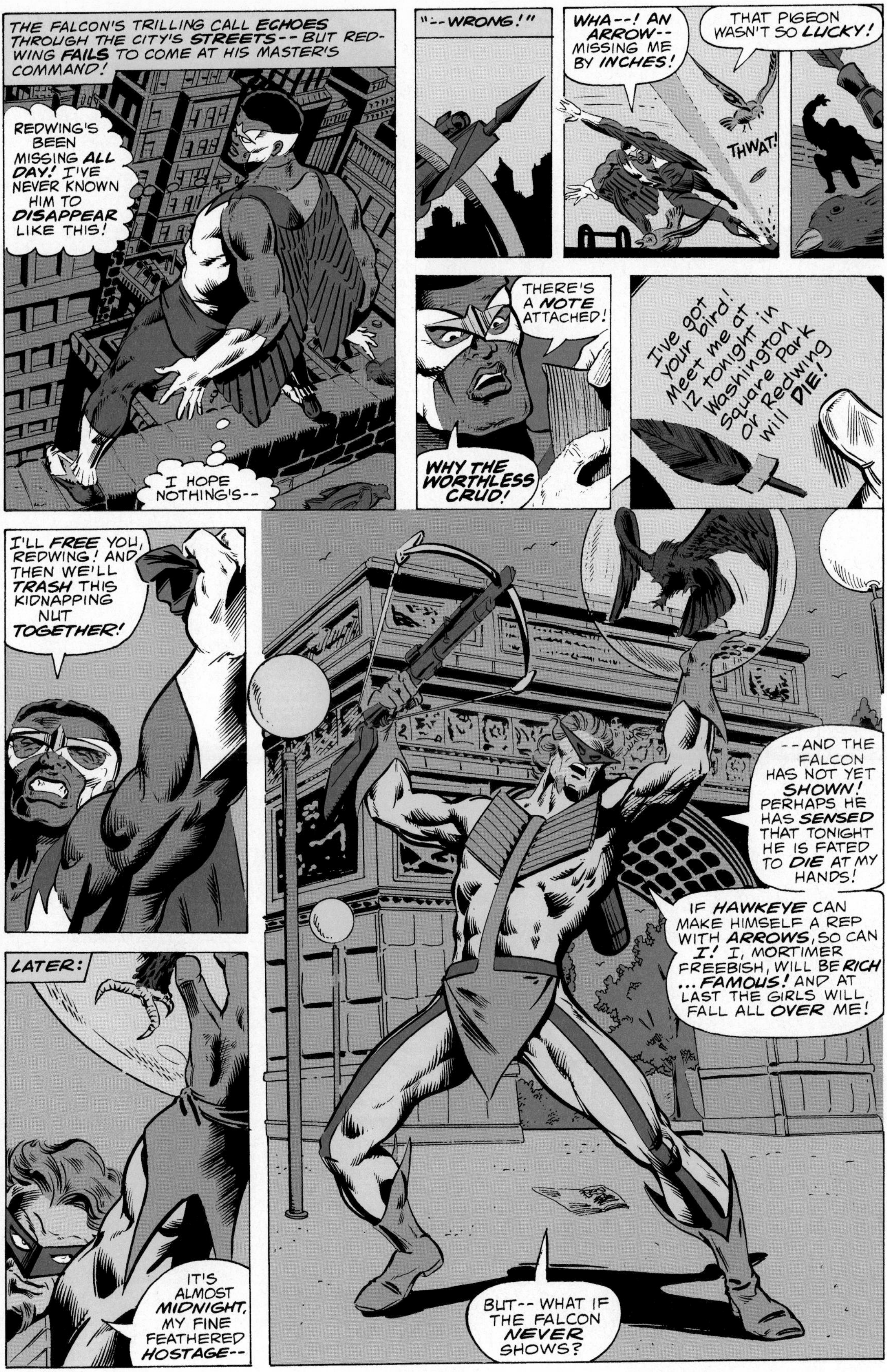
THE FALCON'S TRILLING CALL ECHOES THROUGH THE CITY'S STREETS-- BUT REDWING FAILS TO COME AT HIS MASTER'S COMMAND!
REDWING'S BEEN MISSING ALL DAY! I'VE NEVER KNOWN HIM TO DISAPPEAR LIKE THIS!
I HOPE NOTHING'S--
"--WRONG!"
WHA--! AN ARROW-- MISSING ME BY INCHES!
THWAT!
THAT PIGEON WASN'T SO LUCKY!
THERE'S A NOTE ATTACHED!
WHY THE WORTHLESS CRUD!
I've got your bird! Meet me at 12 tonight in Washington Square Park or Redwing will DIE!
I'LL FREE YOU, REDWING! AND THEN WE'LL TRASH THIS KIDNAPPING NUT TOGETHER!
LATER:
IT'S ALMOST MIDNIGHT, MY FINE FEATHERED HOSTAGE--
--AND THE FALCON HAS NOT YET SHOWN! PERHAPS HE HAS SENSED THAT TONIGHT HE IS FATED TO DIE AT MY HANDS!
IF HAWKEYE CAN MAKE HIMSELF A REP WITH ARROWS, SO CAN I! I, MORTIMER FREEBISH, WILL BE RICH ...FAMOUS! AND AT LAST THE GIRLS WILL FALL ALL OVER ME!
BUT-- WHAT IF THE FALCON NEVER SHOWS?

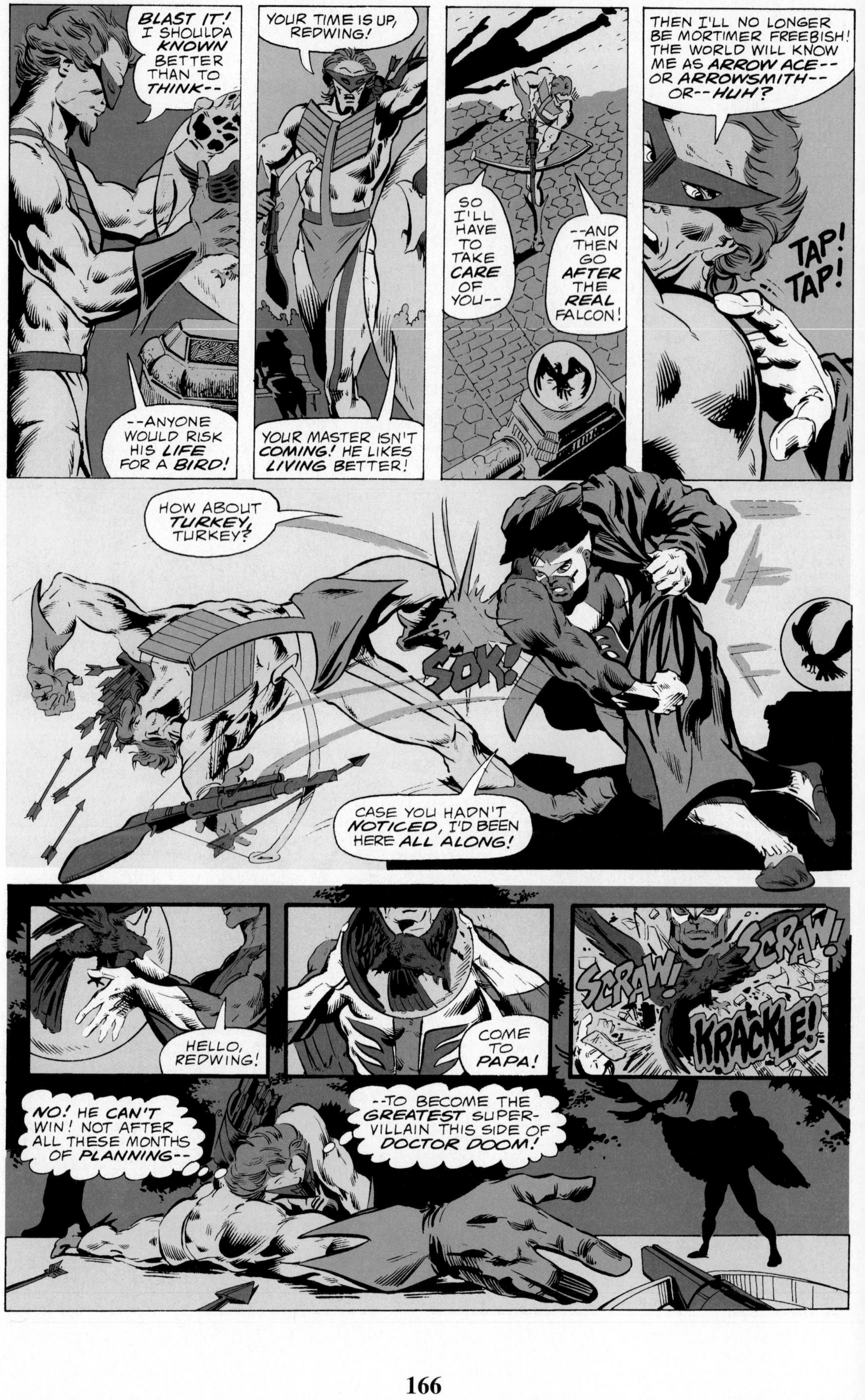

BLAST IT! I SHOULDA KNOWN BETTER THAN TO THINK--
--ANYONE WOULD RISK HIS LIFE FOR A BIRD!
YOUR TIME IS UP, REDWING!
YOUR MASTER ISN'T COMING! HE LIKES LIVING BETTER!
SO I'LL HAVE TO TAKE CARE OF YOU--
--AND THEN GO AFTER THE REAL FALCON!
THEN I'LL NO LONGER BE MORTIMER FREEBISH! THE WORLD WILL KNOW ME AS ARROW ACE--OR ARROWSMITH--OR--HUH?
TAP! TAP!
HOW ABOUT TURKEY, TURKEY?
SOK!
CASE YOU HADN'T NOTICED, I'D BEEN HERE ALL ALONG!
HELLO, REDWING!
COME TO PAPA!
SCRAW! SCRAW!
KRACKLE!
NO! HE CAN'T WIN! NOT AFTER ALL THESE MONTHS OF PLANNING--
--TO BECOME THE GREATEST SUPER-VILLAIN THIS SIDE OF DOCTOR DOOM!

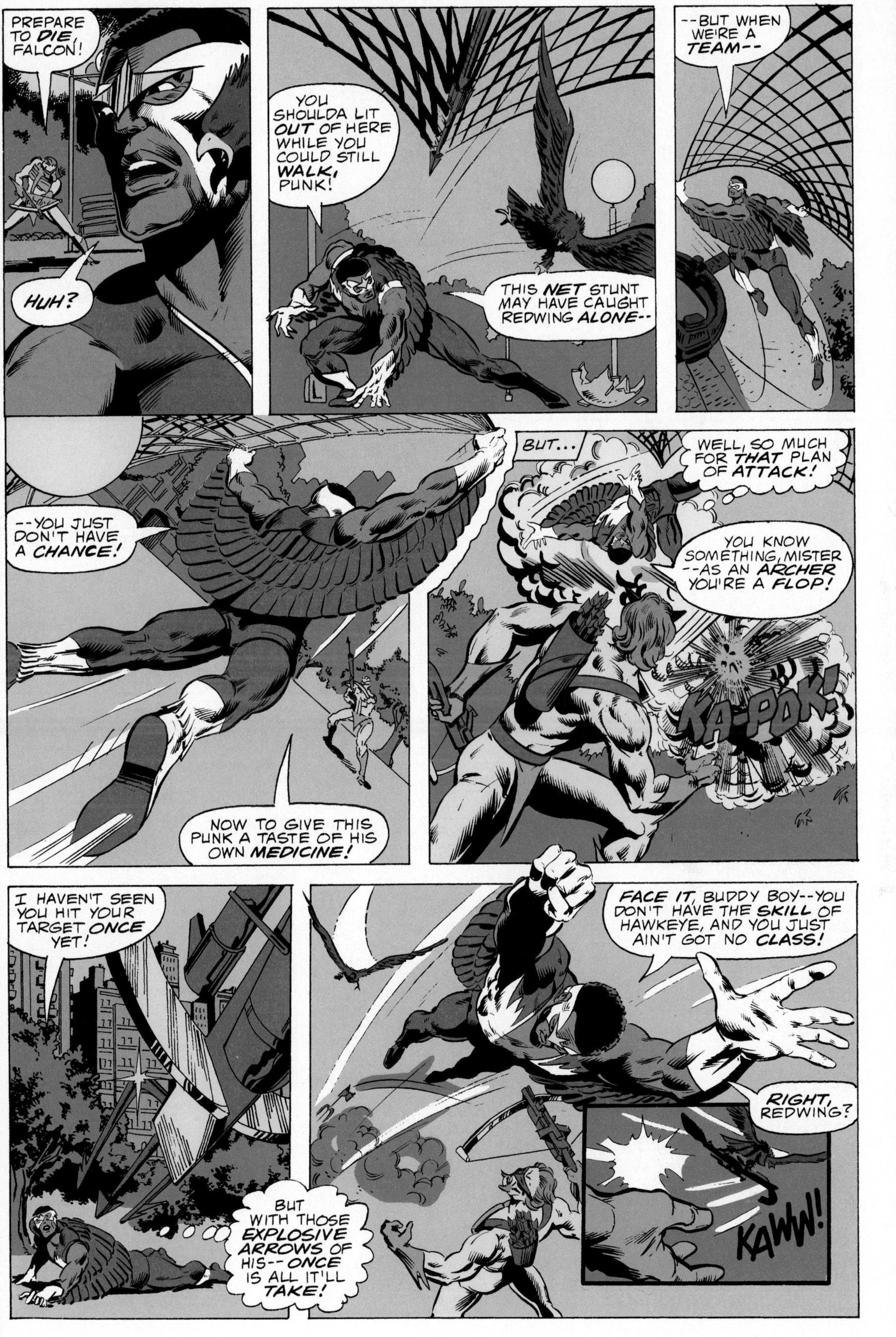
PREPARE TO DIE, FALCON!
HUH?
YOU SHOULDA LIT OUT OF HERE WHILE YOU COULD STILL WALK, PUNK!
THIS NET STUNT MAY HAVE CAUGHT REDWING ALONE--
--BUT WHEN WE'RE A TEAM--
--YOU JUST DON'T HAVE A CHANCE!
NOW TO GIVE THIS PUNK A TASTE OF HIS OWN MEDICINE!
BUT...
WELL, SO MUCH FOR THAT PLAN OF ATTACK!
YOU KNOW SOMETHING, MISTER --AS AN ARCHER YOU'RE A FLOP!
KA-POK!
I HAVEN'T SEEN YOU HIT YOUR TARGET ONCE YET!
BUT WITH THOSE EXPLOSIVE ARROWS OF HIS--ONCE IS ALL IT'LL TAKE!
FACE IT, BUDDY BOY--YOU DON'T HAVE THE SKILL OF HAWKEYE, AND YOU JUST AIN'T GOT NO CLASS!
RIGHT, REDWING?
KAWW!

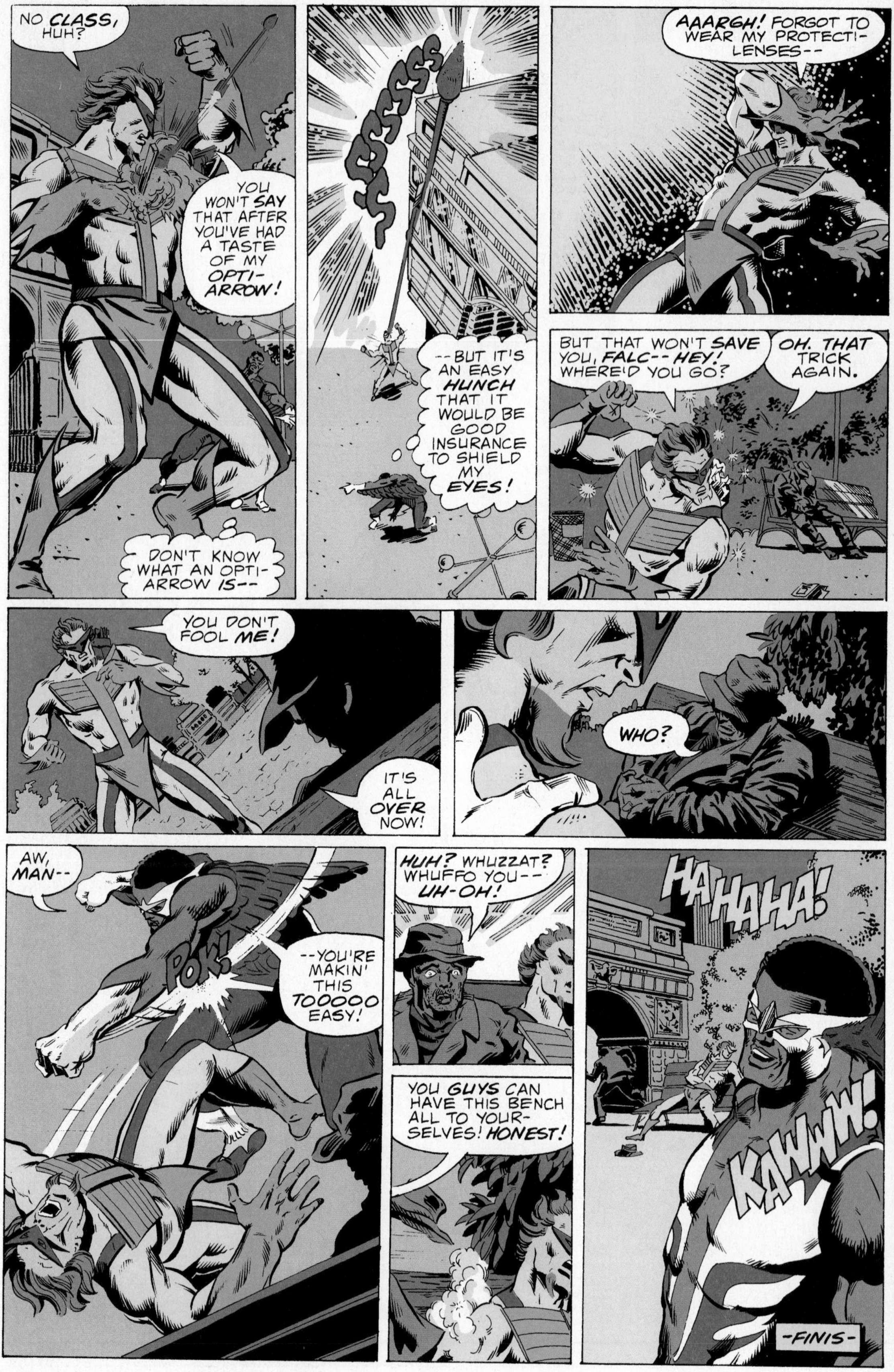

NO CLASS, HUH?
YOU WON'T SAY THAT AFTER YOU'VE HAD A TASTE OF MY OPTI-ARROW!
DON'T KNOW WHAT AN OPTI-ARROW IS--
SSSSSSS
--BUT IT'S AN EASY HUNCH THAT IT WOULD BE GOOD INSURANCE TO SHIELD MY EYES!
AAARGH! FORGOT TO WEAR MY PROTECTI-LENSES--
BUT THAT WON'T SAVE YOU, FALC--HEY! WHERE'D YOU GO?
OH. THAT TRICK AGAIN.
YOU DON'T FOOL ME!
IT'S ALL OVER NOW!
WHO?
AW, MAN--
POK!
--YOU'RE MAKIN' THIS TOOOOO EASY!
HUH? WHUZZAT? WHUFFO YOU-- UH-OH!
YOU GUYS CAN HAVE THIS BENCH ALL TO YOUR-SELVES! HONEST!
HAHAHA!
KAWWW!
-FINIS-

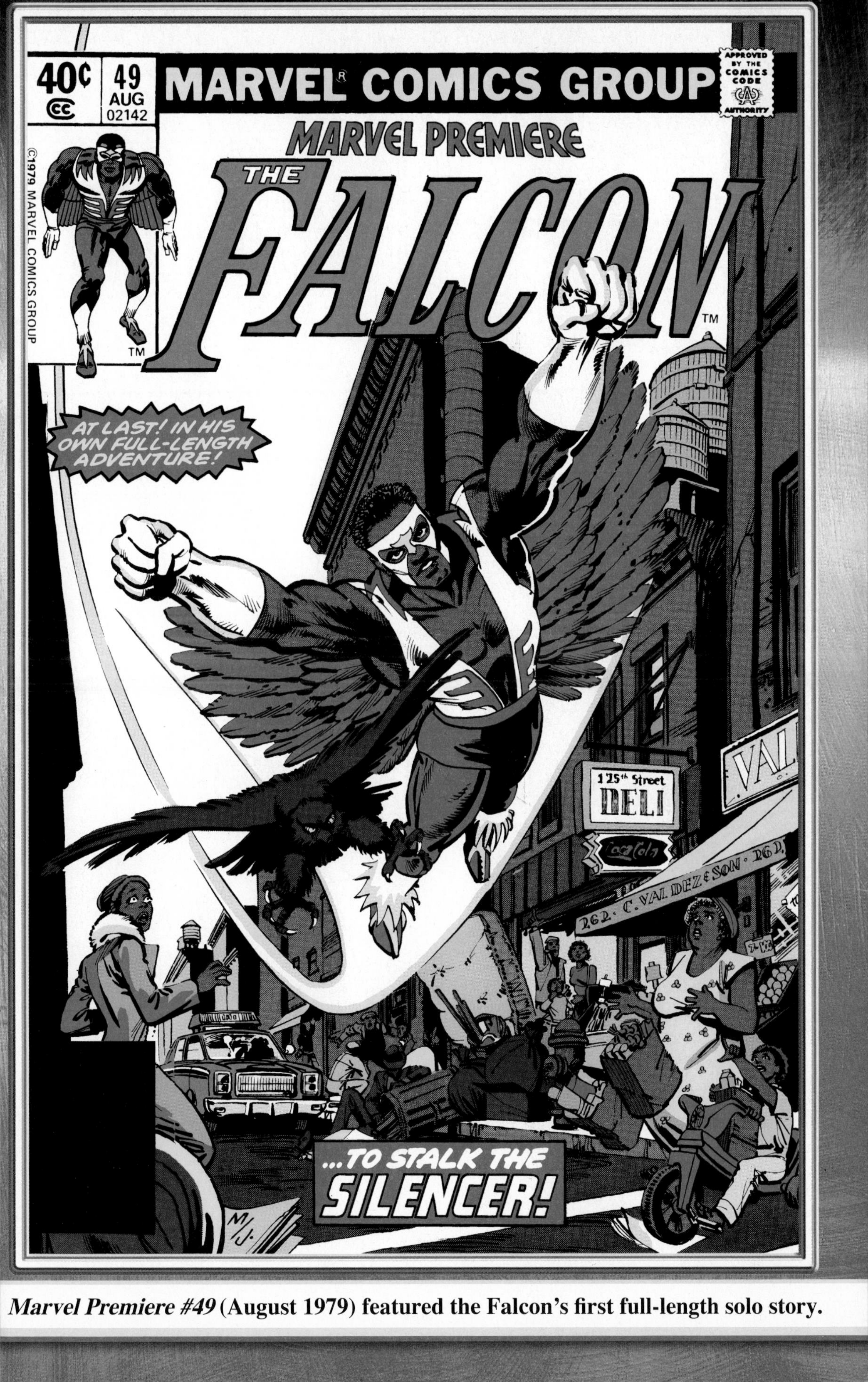
40¢
49
AUG
02142
MARVEL COMICS GROUP
APPROVED BY THE COMICS CODE AUTHORITY
MARVEL PREMIERE
THE FALCON
©1979 MARVEL COMICS GROUP
AT LAST! IN HIS OWN FULL-LENGTH ADVENTURE!
125th Street DELI
C. VALDEZ & SON
...TO STALK THE SILENCER!

Marvel Premiere #49 (August 1979) featured the Falcon's first full-length solo story.

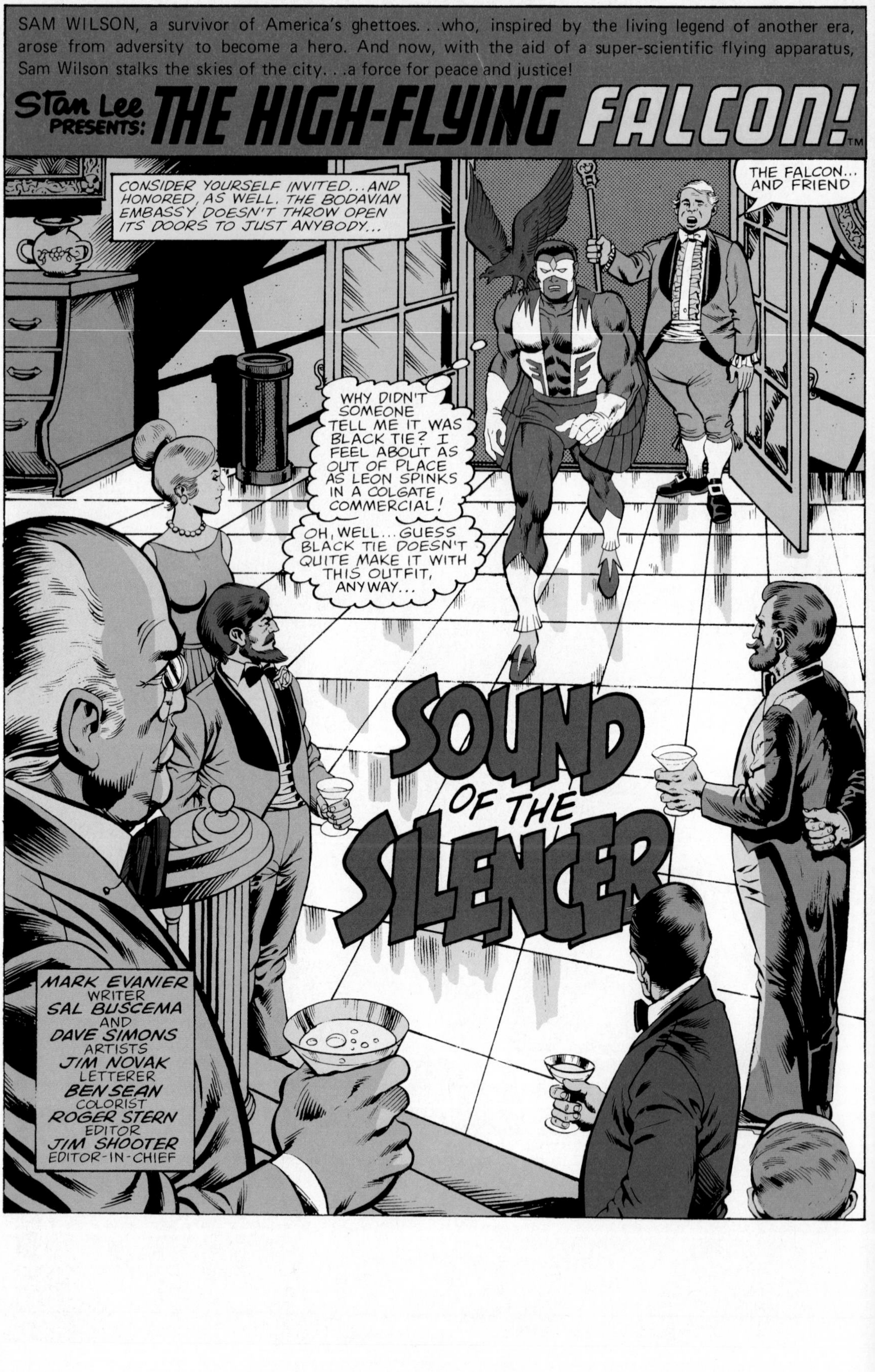

SAM WILSON, a survivor of America's ghettoes...who, inspired by the living legend of another era, arose from adversity to become a hero. And now, with the aid of a super-scientific flying apparatus, Sam Wilson stalks the skies of the city...a force for peace and justice!
Stan Lee PRESENTS: THE HIGH-FLYING FALCON! TM
CONSIDER YOURSELF INVITED...AND HONORED, AS WELL. THE BODAVIAN EMBASSY DOESN'T THROW OPEN ITS DOORS TO JUST ANYBODY...
THE FALCON... AND FRIEND
WHY DIDN'T SOMEONE TELL ME IT WAS BLACK TIE? I FEEL ABOUT AS OUT OF PLACE AS LEON SPINKS IN A COLGATE COMMERCIAL!
OH, WELL...GUESS BLACK TIE DOESN'T QUITE MAKE IT WITH THIS OUTFIT, ANYWAY...
SOUND OF THE SILENCER
MARK EVANIER WRITER
SAL BUSCEMA AND DAVE SIMONS ARTISTS
JIM NOVAK LETTERER
BEN SEAN COLORIST
ROGER STERN EDITOR
JIM SHOOTER EDITOR-IN-CHIEF

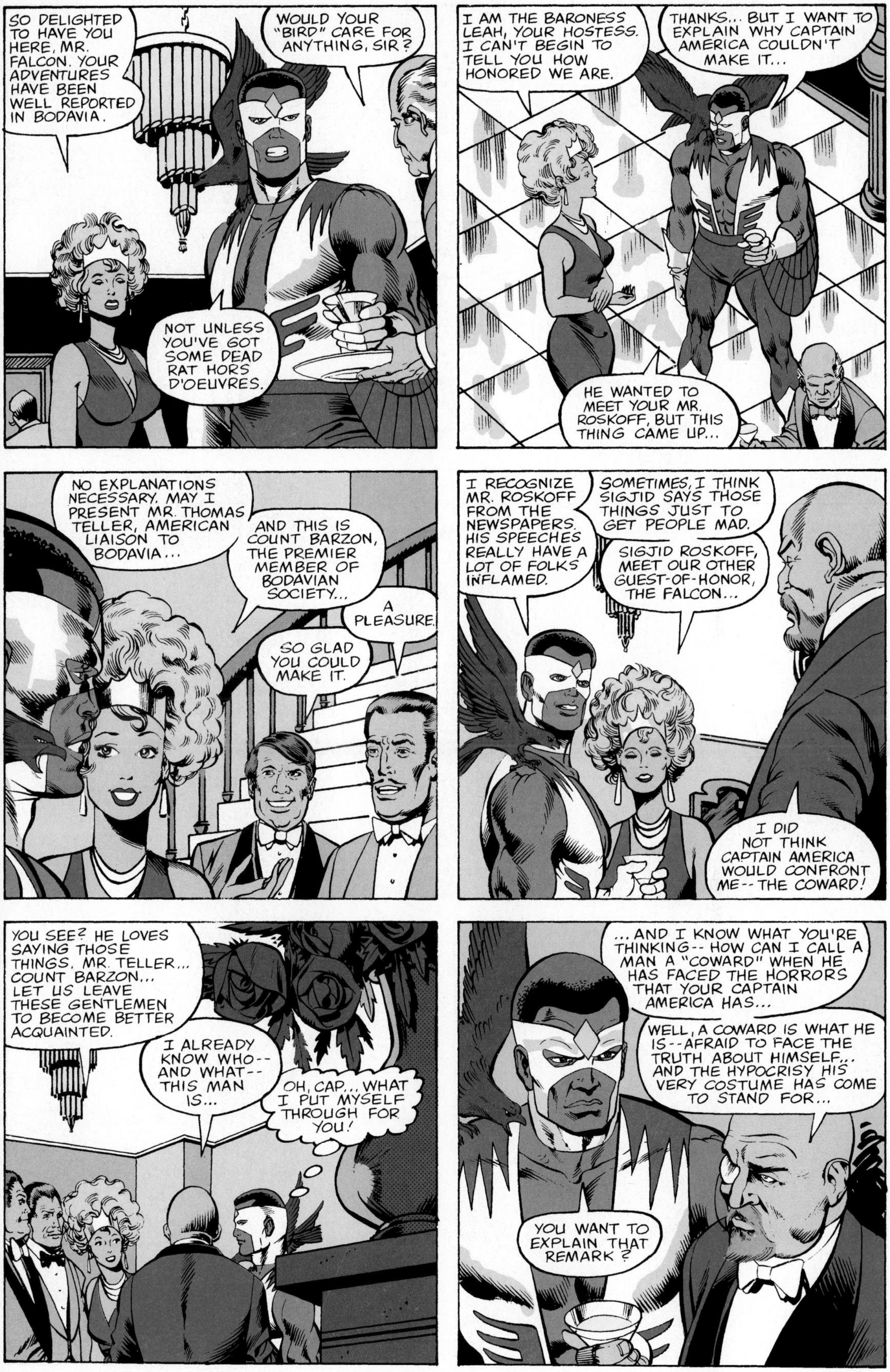
SO DELIGHTED TO HAVE YOU HERE, MR. FALCON. YOUR ADVENTURES HAVE BEEN WELL REPORTED IN BODAVIA.
WOULD YOUR "BIRD" CARE FOR ANYTHING, SIR?
NOT UNLESS YOU'VE GOT SOME DEAD RAT HORS D'OEUVRES.
I AM THE BARONESS LEAH, YOUR HOSTESS. I CAN'T BEGIN TO TELL YOU HOW HONORED WE ARE.
THANKS... BUT I WANT TO EXPLAIN WHY CAPTAIN AMERICA COULDN'T MAKE IT...
HE WANTED TO MEET YOUR MR. ROSKOFF, BUT THIS THING CAME UP...
NO EXPLANATIONS NECESSARY. MAY I PRESENT MR. THOMAS TELLER, AMERICAN LIAISON TO BODAVIA...
AND THIS IS COUNT BARZON, THE PREMIER MEMBER OF BODAVIAN SOCIETY...
A PLEASURE.
SO GLAD YOU COULD MAKE IT.
I RECOGNIZE MR. ROSKOFF FROM THE NEWSPAPERS. HIS SPEECHES REALLY HAVE A LOT OF FOLKS INFLAMED.
SOMETIMES, I THINK SIGJID SAYS THOSE THINGS JUST TO GET PEOPLE MAD.
SIGJID ROSKOFF, MEET OUR OTHER GUEST-OF-HONOR, THE FALCON...
I DID NOT THINK CAPTAIN AMERICA WOULD CONFRONT ME--THE COWARD!
YOU SEE? HE LOVES SAYING THOSE THINGS, MR. TELLER... COUNT BARZON... LET US LEAVE THESE GENTLEMEN TO BECOME BETTER ACQUAINTED.
I ALREADY KNOW WHO--AND WHAT--THIS MAN IS...
OH, CAP... WHAT I PUT MYSELF THROUGH FOR YOU!
...AND I KNOW WHAT YOU'RE THINKING--HOW CAN I CALL A MAN A "COWARD" WHEN HE HAS FACED THE HORRORS THAT YOUR CAPTAIN AMERICA HAS...
WELL, A COWARD IS WHAT HE IS--AFRAID TO FACE THE TRUTH ABOUT HIMSELF... AND THE HYPOCRISY HIS VERY COSTUME HAS COME TO STAND FOR...
YOU WANT TO EXPLAIN THAT REMARK?

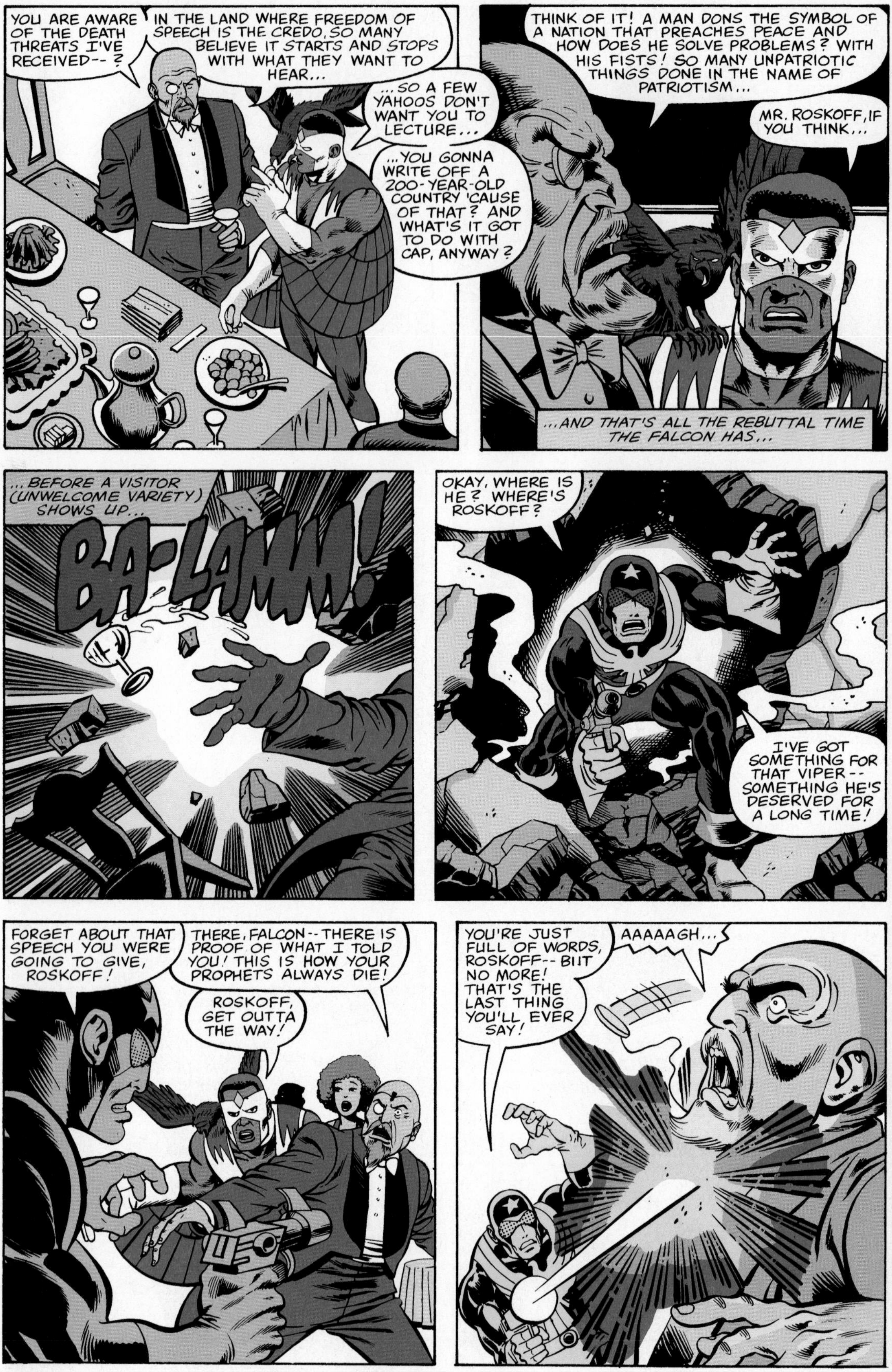
YOU ARE AWARE OF THE DEATH THREATS I'VE RECEIVED-- ?
IN THE LAND WHERE FREEDOM OF SPEECH IS THE CREDO, SO MANY BELIEVE IT STARTS AND STOPS WITH WHAT THEY WANT TO HEAR...
...SO A FEW YAHOOS DON'T WANT YOU TO LECTURE...
...YOU GONNA WRITE OFF A 200-YEAR-OLD COUNTRY 'CAUSE OF THAT? AND WHAT'S IT GOT TO DO WITH CAP, ANYWAY?
THINK OF IT! A MAN DONS THE SYMBOL OF A NATION THAT PREACHES PEACE AND HOW DOES HE SOLVE PROBLEMS? WITH HIS FISTS! SO MANY UNPATRIOTIC THINGS DONE IN THE NAME OF PATRIOTISM...
MR. ROSKOFF, IF YOU THINK...
...AND THAT'S ALL THE REBUTTAL TIME THE FALCON HAS...
...BEFORE A VISITOR (UNWELCOME VARIETY) SHOWS UP...
BA-LAMM!
OKAY, WHERE IS HE? WHERE'S ROSKOFF?
I'VE GOT SOMETHING FOR THAT VIPER-- SOMETHING HE'S DESERVED FOR A LONG TIME!
FORGET ABOUT THAT SPEECH YOU WERE GOING TO GIVE, ROSKOFF!
THERE, FALCON--THERE IS PROOF OF WHAT I TOLD YOU! THIS IS HOW YOUR PROPHETS ALWAYS DIE!
ROSKOFF, GET OUTTA THE WAY!
YOU'RE JUST FULL OF WORDS, ROSKOFF-- BUT NO MORE! THAT'S THE LAST THING YOU'LL EVER SAY!
AAAAAGH...

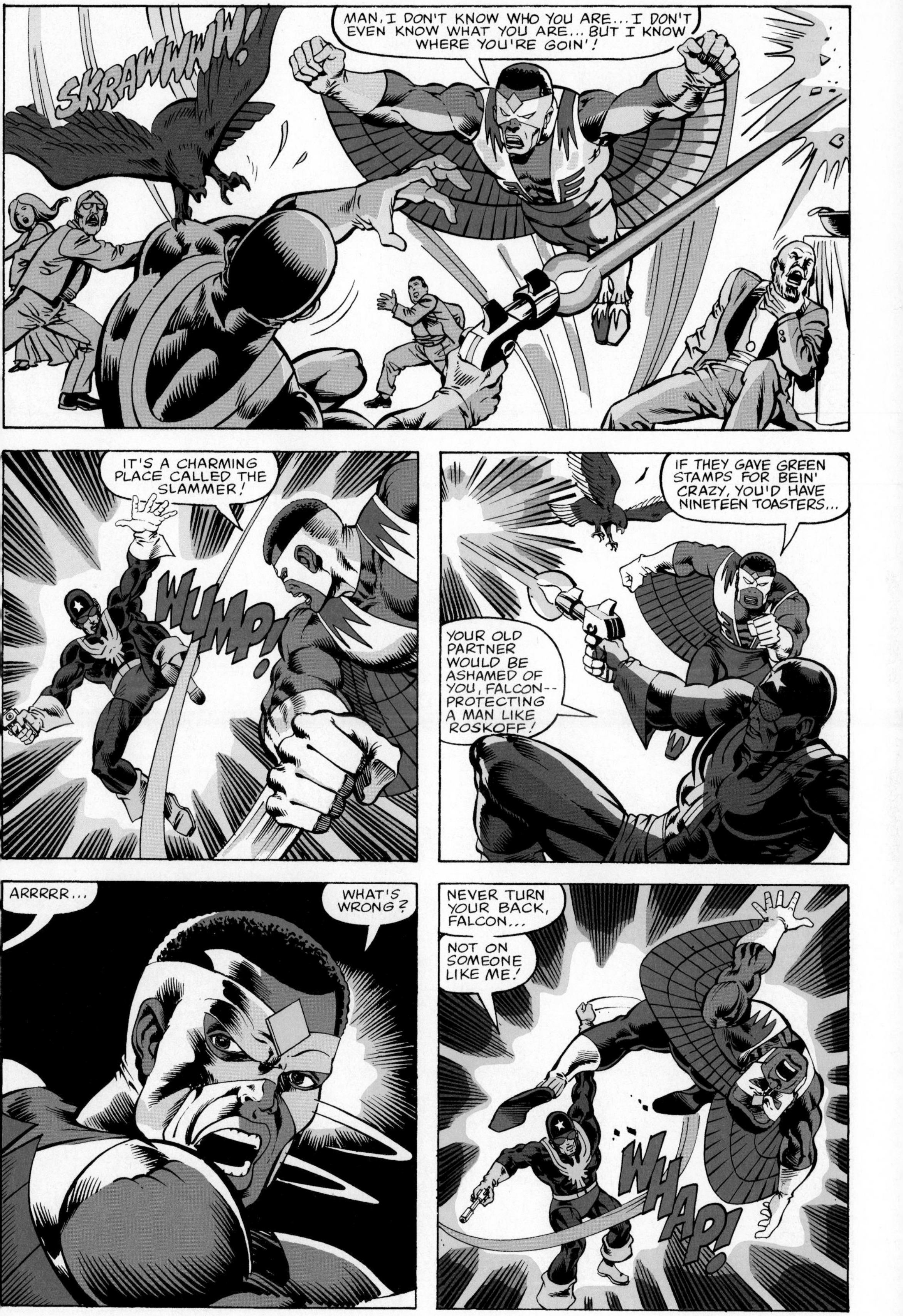
SKRAWWWW!
MAN, I DON'T KNOW WHO YOU ARE... I DON'T EVEN KNOW WHAT YOU ARE... BUT I KNOW WHERE YOU'RE GOIN'!
IT'S A CHARMING PLACE CALLED THE SLAMMER!
WUMP!
IF THEY GAVE GREEN STAMPS FOR BEIN' CRAZY, YOU'D HAVE NINETEEN TOASTERS...
YOUR OLD PARTNER WOULD BE ASHAMED OF YOU, FALCON-- PROTECTING A MAN LIKE ROSKOFF!
ARRRRR...
WHAT'S WRONG?
NEVER TURN YOUR BACK, FALCON...
NOT ON SOMEONE LIKE ME!
WHAP!

HAVING TROUBLE TALKING, ROSKOFF? CAN'T MAKE ANY MORE OF YOUR INSIDIOUS SPEECHES?

NOW YOU KNOW WHY THEY CALL ME THE SILENCER!

ARRRRRRR...

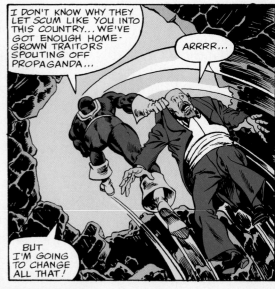

I DON'T KNOW WHY THEY LET SCUM LIKE YOU INTO THIS COUNTRY... WE'VE GOT ENOUGH HOME-GROWN TRAITORS SPOUTING OFF PROPAGANDA...

ARRRR...

BUT I'M GOING TO CHANGE ALL THAT!

GO AFTER THEM! HE TOOK MR. ROSKOFF! YOU'VE GOT TO SAVE HIM!

LADY, I FIGURE ON DOIN' JUST THAT!

WAY TO GO, REDWING! YOU CHECKED OUT WHICH WAY THEY WERE HEADED, DIDN'T YOU?

NOW, LEAD THE WAY!

THAT SILENCER DUDE'S REALLY ASKIN' FOR IT!

AND SO FALCON FOLLOWS FALCON ACROSS TOWN... STUPID, STUPID, STUPID, MAN-- LETTING HIM PUNCH YOU OUT LIKE THAT...

NOW, HE PROBABLY PLANS TO USE ROSKOFF FOR HIS OWN PROPAGANDA AND...

UH-OH...

LOOKS LIKE I'M ABOUT A MINUTE AND A HALF TOO LATE.

"I, SIGJID ROSKOFF DO HEREBY RENOUNCE MY PAST POSITIONS... BLAH BLAH BLAH... APOLOGIZE FOR STATEMENTS AGAINST THE U.S. ... BLAH BLAH BLAH..."

THE SILENCER WROTE THIS OUT AND MADE ROSKOFF SIGN IT BEFORE HE KILLED HIM...

REALLY MEANINGFUL.

WHAT'S THIS--?

THERE ARE TINY LITTLE *DOTS* UNDER CERTAIN LETTERS. ROSKOFF MUST HAVE PUT THEM THERE! HMM...

"O...T...T...F...F...S...S... E...N"... I GET THE FEELING THIS MEANS SOMETHING. ONLY WISH I KNEW WHAT IT WAS.

I, Sigjrd Roskoff, do hereby renounce my past position on the issues of in and apologize for statemen against the U.S. which none of the followin

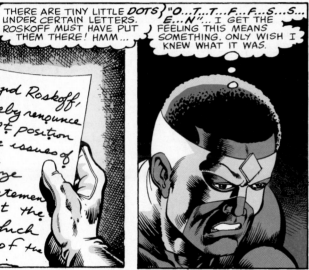

BEFORE THE DAY IS OUT, THE DRAMA SHIFTS TO THE LOCAL POLICE PRECINCT...

AUTOPSY'S JUST IN, IF YOU'RE INTERESTED!

5TH PRECINCT

ROSKOFF WAS SHOT POINT-BLANK WITH SOME SORT OF NERVE RAY! A MILDER DOSE FROM THE RAY CAUSED HIS VOCAL PARALYSIS EARLIER!

YOU LISTENING, FALCON?

YEAH... I'M STILL LOOKING AT THIS NOTE.

I CAN'T GET OVER THE IDEA THAT IF I FIGURE OUT WHAT "OTTFFSSEN" MEANS, I'LL...

THERE HE IS, BARONESS-- THAT'S WHAT PASSES FOR A "HERO" IN THIS COUNTRY!

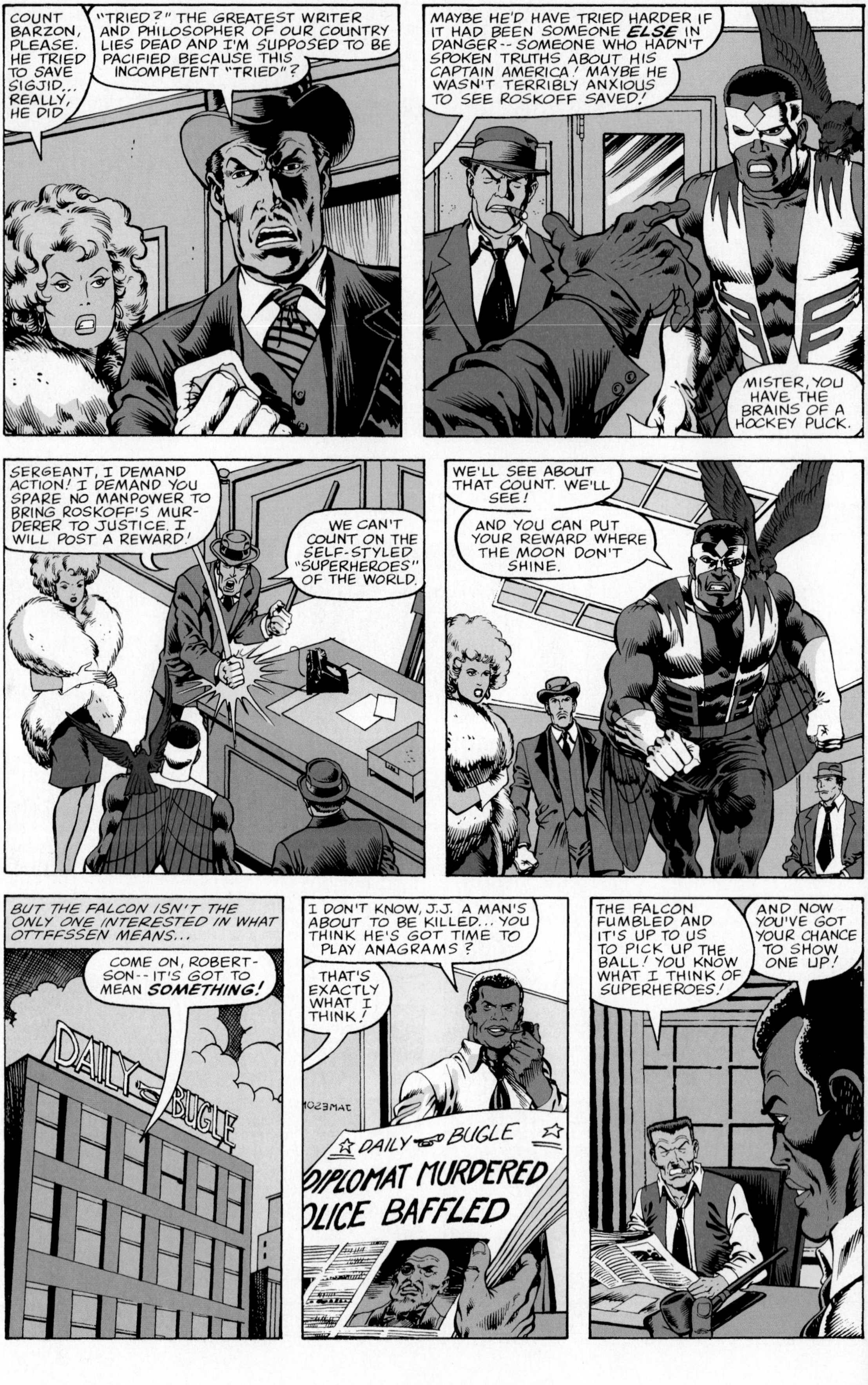
COUNT BARZON, PLEASE. HE TRIED TO SAVE SIGJID... REALLY, HE DID
"TRIED?" THE GREATEST WRITER AND PHILOSOPHER OF OUR COUNTRY LIES DEAD AND I'M SUPPOSED TO BE PACIFIED BECAUSE THIS INCOMPETENT "TRIED"?
MAYBE HE'D HAVE TRIED HARDER IF IT HAD BEEN SOMEONE ELSE IN DANGER -- SOMEONE WHO HADN'T SPOKEN TRUTHS ABOUT HIS CAPTAIN AMERICA! MAYBE HE WASN'T TERRIBLY ANXIOUS TO SEE ROSKOFF SAVED!
MISTER, YOU HAVE THE BRAINS OF A HOCKEY PUCK.
SERGEANT, I DEMAND ACTION! I DEMAND YOU SPARE NO MANPOWER TO BRING ROSKOFF'S MURDERER TO JUSTICE. I WILL POST A REWARD!
WE CAN'T COUNT ON THE SELF-STYLED "SUPERHEROES" OF THE WORLD.
WE'LL SEE ABOUT THAT COUNT. WE'LL SEE!
AND YOU CAN PUT YOUR REWARD WHERE THE MOON DON'T SHINE.
BUT THE FALCON ISN'T THE ONLY ONE INTERESTED IN WHAT OTTFFSSEN MEANS...
COME ON, ROBERTSON-- IT'S GOT TO MEAN SOMETHING!
DAILY BUGLE
I DON'T KNOW, J.J. A MAN'S ABOUT TO BE KILLED... YOU THINK HE'S GOT TIME TO PLAY ANAGRAMS?
THAT'S EXACTLY WHAT I THINK!
JAMESON
DAILY BUGLE
DIPLOMAT MURDERED
OLICE BAFFLED
THE FALCON FUMBLED AND IT'S UP TO US TO PICK UP THE BALL! YOU KNOW WHAT I THINK OF SUPERHEROES!
AND NOW YOU'VE GOT YOUR CHANCE TO SHOW ONE UP!

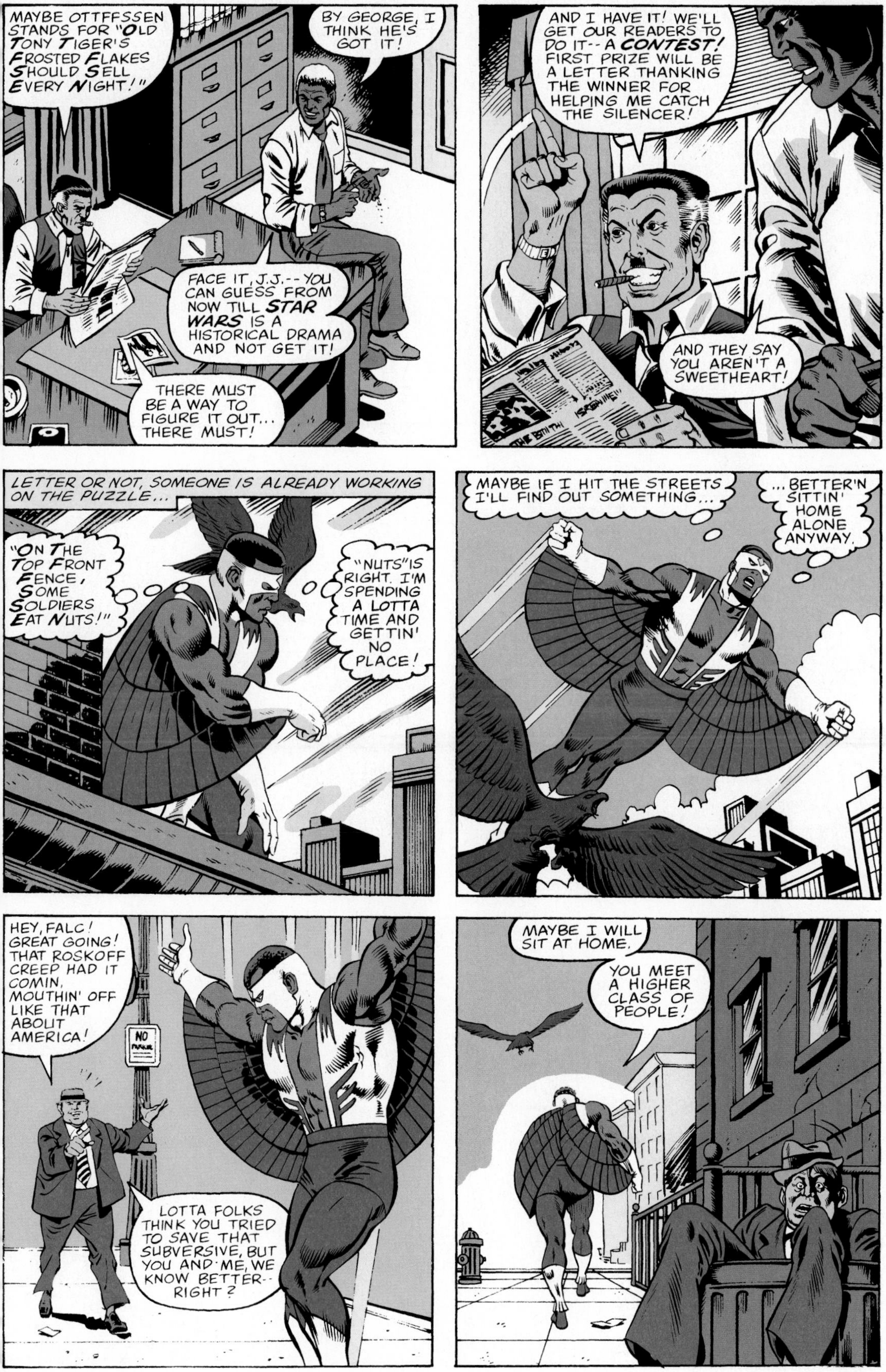

MAYBE OTTFFSSEN STANDS FOR "OLD TONY TIGER'S FROSTED FLAKES SHOULD SELL EVERY NIGHT!"
BY GEORGE, I THINK HE'S GOT IT!
FACE IT, J.J.-- YOU CAN GUESS FROM NOW TILL STAR WARS IS A HISTORICAL DRAMA AND NOT GET IT!
THERE MUST BE A WAY TO FIGURE IT OUT... THERE MUST!
AND I HAVE IT! WE'LL GET OUR READERS TO DO IT-- A CONTEST! FIRST PRIZE WILL BE A LETTER THANKING THE WINNER FOR HELPING ME CATCH THE SILENCER!
AND THEY SAY YOU AREN'T A SWEETHEART!
LETTER OR NOT, SOMEONE IS ALREADY WORKING ON THE PUZZLE...
"ON THE TOP FRONT FENCE, SOME SOLDIERS EAT NUTS!"
"NUTS" IS RIGHT. I'M SPENDING A LOTTA TIME AND GETTIN' NO PLACE!
MAYBE IF I HIT THE STREETS I'LL FIND OUT SOMETHING...
...BETTER'N SITTIN' HOME ALONE ANYWAY.
HEY, FALC! GREAT GOING! THAT ROSKOFF CREEP HAD IT COMIN, MOUTHIN' OFF LIKE THAT ABOUT AMERICA!
NO
LOTTA FOLKS THINK YOU TRIED TO SAVE THAT SUBVERSIVE, BUT YOU AND ME, WE KNOW BETTER-- RIGHT?
MAYBE I WILL SIT AT HOME.
YOU MEET A HIGHER CLASS OF PEOPLE!

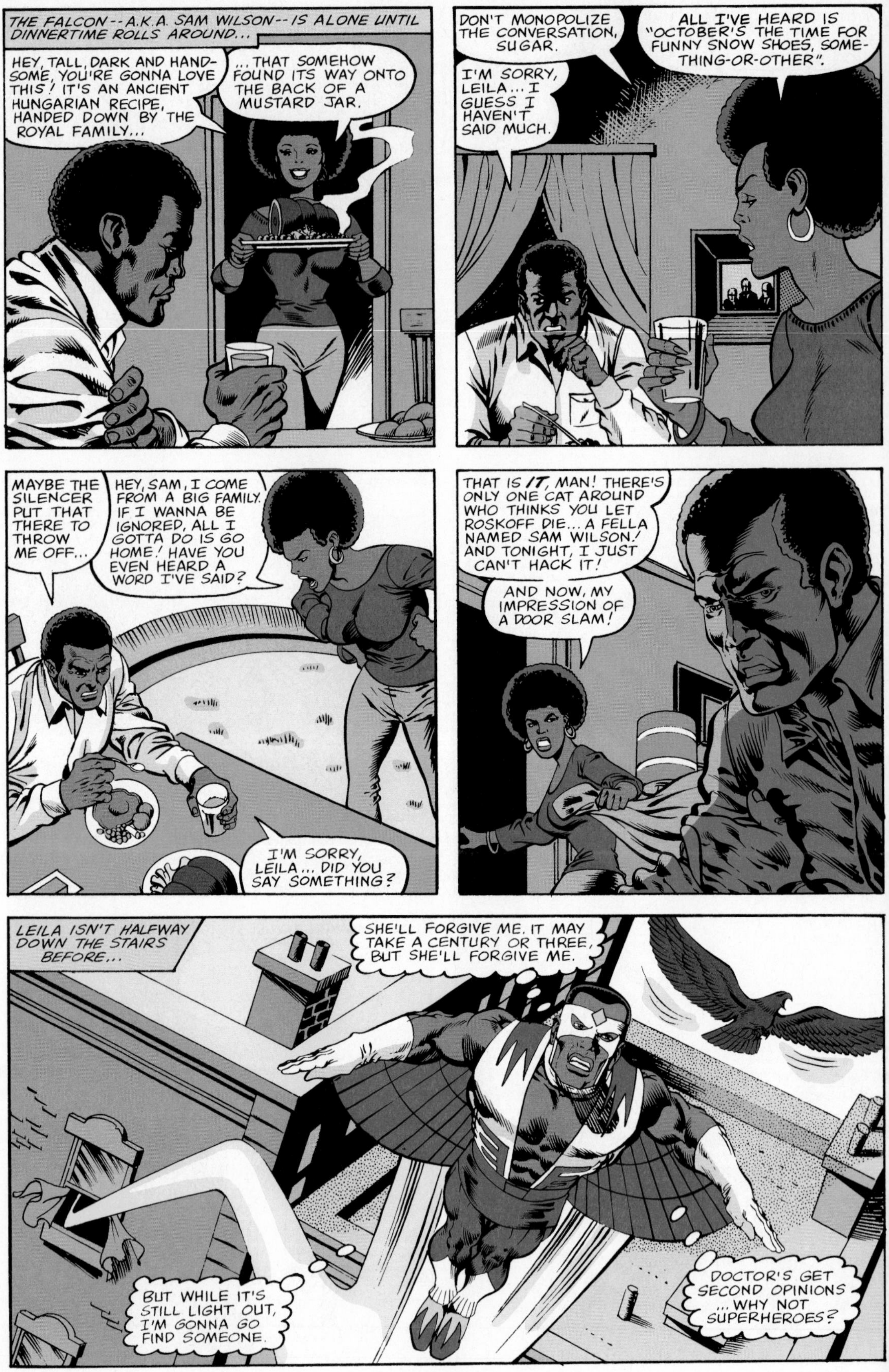
THE FALCON--A.K.A. SAM WILSON--IS ALONE UNTIL DINNERTIME ROLLS AROUND...
HEY, TALL, DARK AND HANDSOME, YOU'RE GONNA LOVE THIS! IT'S AN ANCIENT HUNGARIAN RECIPE, HANDED DOWN BY THE ROYAL FAMILY...
...THAT SOMEHOW FOUND ITS WAY ONTO THE BACK OF A MUSTARD JAR.
DON'T MONOPOLIZE THE CONVERSATION, SUGAR.
I'M SORRY, LEILA... I GUESS I HAVEN'T SAID MUCH.
ALL I'VE HEARD IS "OCTOBER'S THE TIME FOR FUNNY SNOW SHOES, SOMETHING-OR-OTHER".
MAYBE THE SILENCER PUT THAT THERE TO THROW ME OFF...
HEY, SAM, I COME FROM A BIG FAMILY. IF I WANNA BE IGNORED, ALL I GOTTA DO IS GO HOME! HAVE YOU EVEN HEARD A WORD I'VE SAID?
I'M SORRY, LEILA... DID YOU SAY SOMETHING?
THAT IS IT, MAN! THERE'S ONLY ONE CAT AROUND WHO THINKS YOU LET ROSKOFF DIE... A FELLA NAMED SAM WILSON! AND TONIGHT, I JUST CAN'T HACK IT!
AND NOW, MY IMPRESSION OF A DOOR SLAM!
LEILA ISN'T HALFWAY DOWN THE STAIRS BEFORE...
SHE'LL FORGIVE ME. IT MAY TAKE A CENTURY OR THREE, BUT SHE'LL FORGIVE ME.
BUT WHILE IT'S STILL LIGHT OUT, I'M GONNA GO FIND SOMEONE.
DOCTOR'S GET SECOND OPINIONS ...WHY NOT SUPERHEROES?

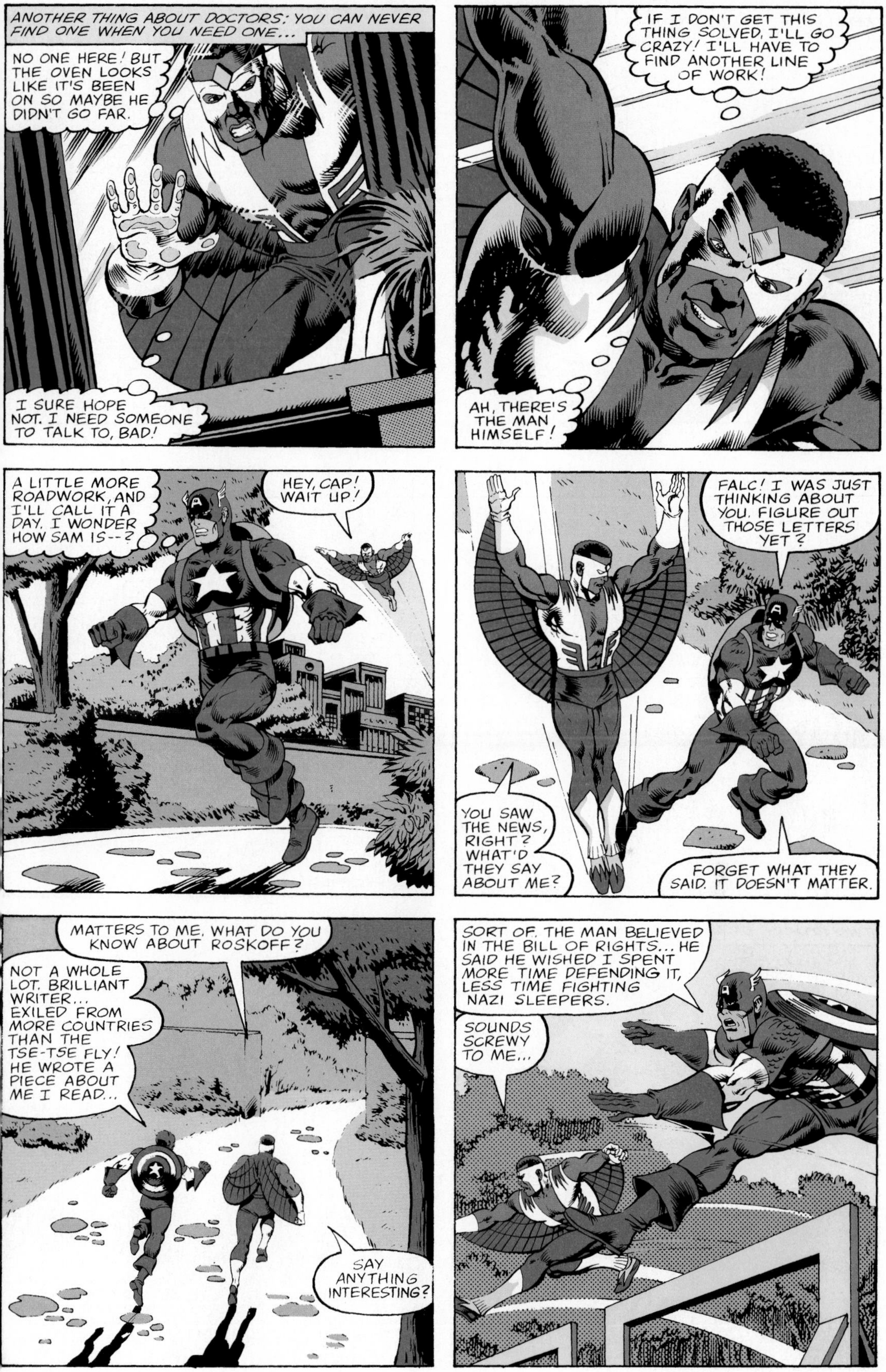
ANOTHER THING ABOUT DOCTORS: YOU CAN NEVER FIND ONE WHEN YOU NEED ONE...
NO ONE HERE! BUT THE OVEN LOOKS LIKE IT'S BEEN ON SO MAYBE HE DIDN'T GO FAR.
I SURE HOPE NOT. I NEED SOMEONE TO TALK TO, BAD!
IF I DON'T GET THIS THING SOLVED, I'LL GO CRAZY! I'LL HAVE TO FIND ANOTHER LINE OF WORK!
AH, THERE'S THE MAN HIMSELF!
A LITTLE MORE ROADWORK, AND I'LL CALL IT A DAY. I WONDER HOW SAM IS--?
HEY, CAP! WAIT UP!
FALC! I WAS JUST THINKING ABOUT YOU. FIGURE OUT THOSE LETTERS YET?
YOU SAW THE NEWS, RIGHT? WHAT'D THEY SAY ABOUT ME?
FORGET WHAT THEY SAID. IT DOESN'T MATTER.
MATTERS TO ME. WHAT DO YOU KNOW ABOUT ROSKOFF?
NOT A WHOLE LOT. BRILLIANT WRITER... EXILED FROM MORE COUNTRIES THAN THE TSE-TSE FLY! HE WROTE A PIECE ABOUT ME I READ...
SAY ANYTHING INTERESTING?
SORT OF. THE MAN BELIEVED IN THE BILL OF RIGHTS... HE SAID HE WISHED I SPENT MORE TIME DEFENDING IT, LESS TIME FIGHTING NAZI SLEEPERS.
SOUNDS SCREWY TO ME...

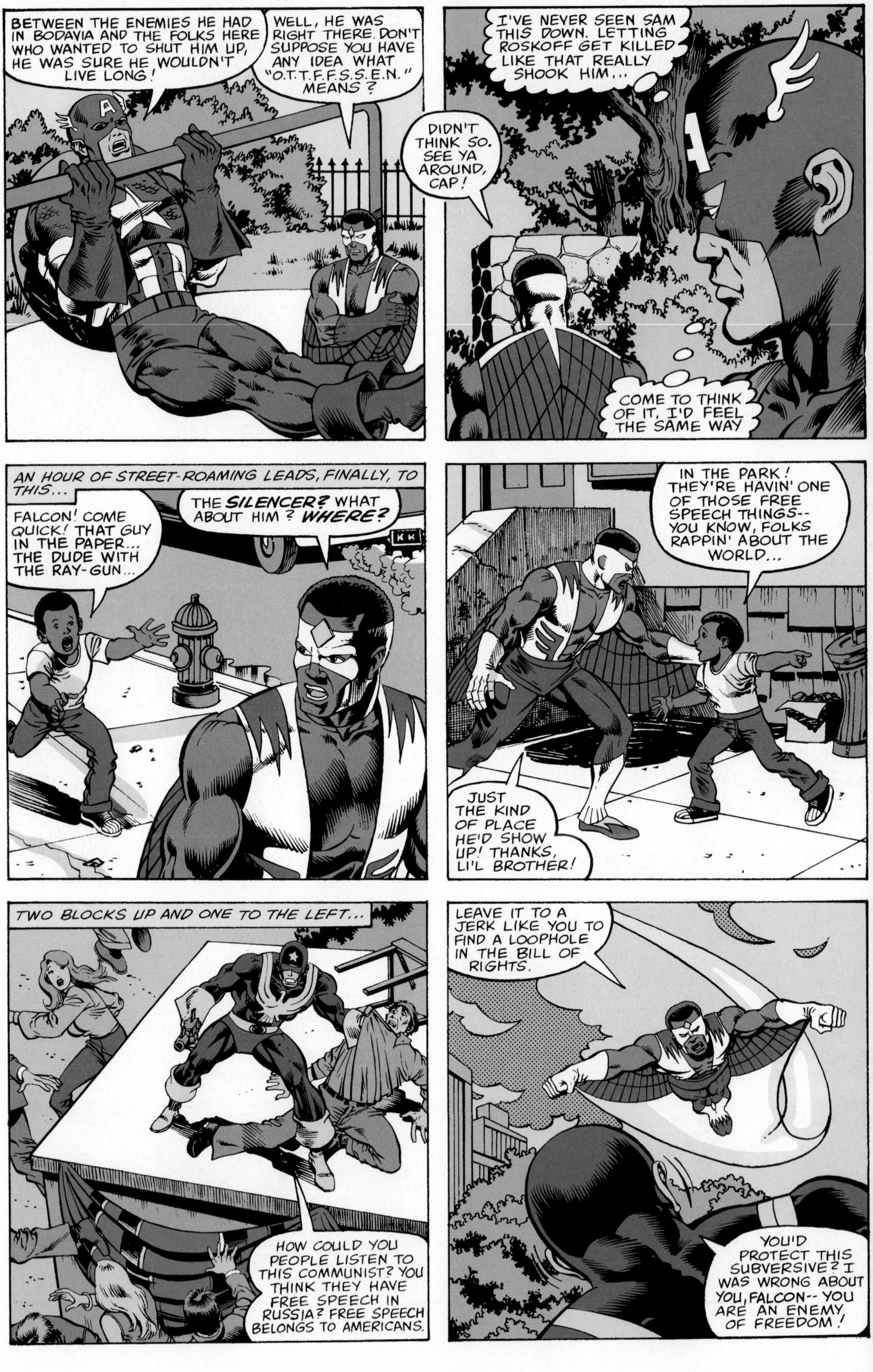

BETWEEN THE ENEMIES HE HAD IN BODAVIA AND THE FOLKS HERE WHO WANTED TO SHUT HIM UP, HE WAS SURE HE WOULDN'T LIVE LONG!
WELL, HE WAS RIGHT THERE. DON'T SUPPOSE YOU HAVE ANY IDEA WHAT "O.T.T.F.F.S.S.E.N." MEANS?
I'VE NEVER SEEN SAM THIS DOWN. LETTING ROSKOFF GET KILLED LIKE THAT REALLY SHOOK HIM...
DIDN'T THINK SO. SEE YA AROUND, CAP!
COME TO THINK OF IT, I'D FEEL THE SAME WAY
AN HOUR OF STREET-ROAMING LEADS, FINALLY, TO THIS...
FALCON! COME QUICK! THAT GUY IN THE PAPER... THE DUDE WITH THE RAY-GUN...
THE SILENCER? WHAT ABOUT HIM? WHERE?
IN THE PARK! THEY'RE HAVIN' ONE OF THOSE FREE SPEECH THINGS-- YOU KNOW, FOLKS RAPPIN' ABOUT THE WORLD...
JUST THE KIND OF PLACE HE'D SHOW UP! THANKS, LI'L BROTHER!
TWO BLOCKS UP AND ONE TO THE LEFT...
HOW COULD YOU PEOPLE LISTEN TO THIS COMMUNIST? YOU THINK THEY HAVE FREE SPEECH IN RUSSIA? FREE SPEECH BELONGS TO AMERICANS.
LEAVE IT TO A JERK LIKE YOU TO FIND A LOOPHOLE IN THE BILL OF RIGHTS.
YOU'D PROTECT THIS SUBVERSIVE? I WAS WRONG ABOUT YOU, FALCON-- YOU ARE AN ENEMY OF FREEDOM!

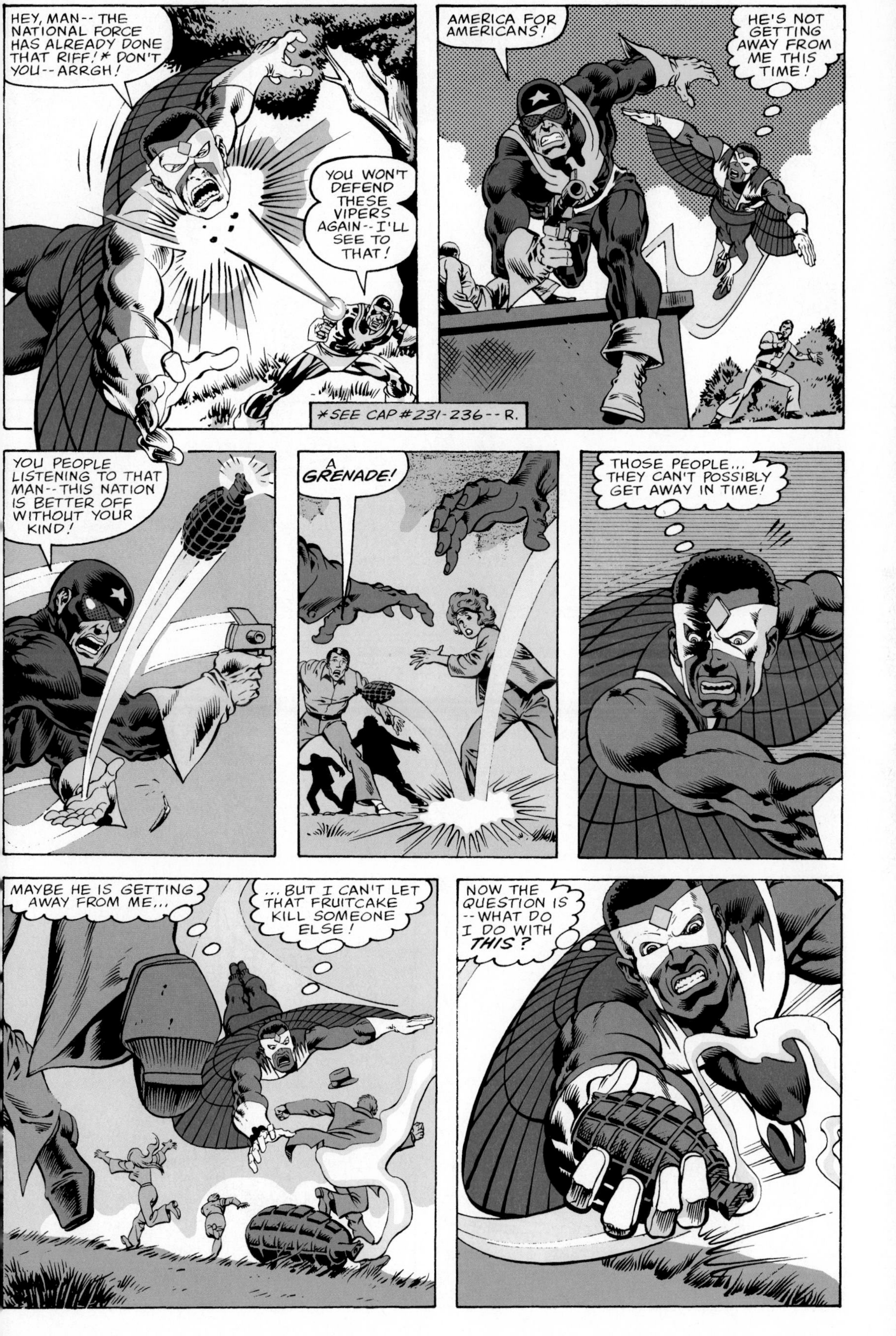
HEY, MAN-- THE NATIONAL FORCE HAS ALREADY DONE THAT RIFF! * DON'T YOU--ARRGH!
YOU WON'T DEFEND THESE VIPERS AGAIN--I'LL SEE TO THAT!
*SEE CAP #231-236--R.
AMERICA FOR AMERICANS!
HE'S NOT GETTING AWAY FROM ME THIS TIME!
YOU PEOPLE LISTENING TO THAT MAN--THIS NATION IS BETTER OFF WITHOUT YOUR KIND!
A GRENADE!
THOSE PEOPLE... THEY CAN'T POSSIBLY GET AWAY IN TIME!
MAYBE HE IS GETTING AWAY FROM ME...
...BUT I CAN'T LET THAT FRUITCAKE KILL SOMEONE ELSE!
NOW THE QUESTION IS --WHAT DO I DO WITH THIS?

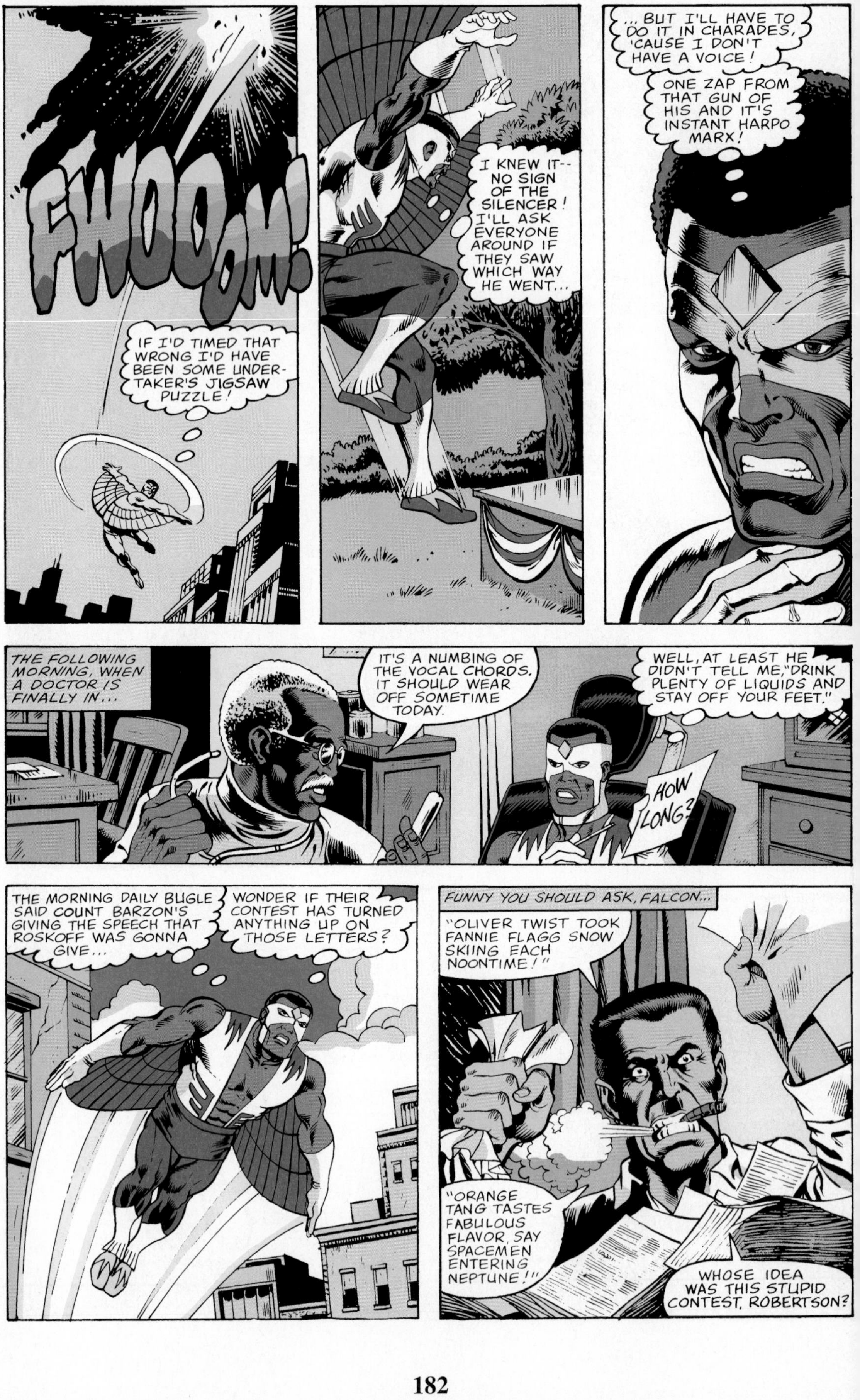
FWOOOM!
IF I'D TIMED THAT WRONG I'D HAVE BEEN SOME UNDERTAKER'S JIGSAW PUZZLE!
I KNEW IT-- NO SIGN OF THE SILENCER! I'LL ASK EVERYONE AROUND IF THEY SAW WHICH WAY HE WENT...
... BUT I'LL HAVE TO DO IT IN CHARADES, 'CAUSE I DON'T HAVE A VOICE!
ONE ZAP FROM THAT GUN OF HIS AND IT'S INSTANT HARPO MARX!
THE FOLLOWING MORNING, WHEN A DOCTOR IS FINALLY IN...
IT'S A NUMBING OF THE VOCAL CHORDS. IT SHOULD WEAR OFF SOMETIME TODAY.
HOW LONG?
WELL, AT LEAST HE DIDN'T TELL ME, "DRINK PLENTY OF LIQUIDS AND STAY OFF YOUR FEET."
THE MORNING DAILY BUGLE SAID COUNT BARZON'S GIVING THE SPEECH THAT ROSKOFF WAS GONNA GIVE...
WONDER IF THEIR CONTEST HAS TURNED ANYTHING UP ON THOSE LETTERS?
FUNNY YOU SHOULD ASK, FALCON...
"OLIVER TWIST TOOK FANNIE FLAGG SNOW SKIING EACH NOONTIME!"
"ORANGE TANG TASTES FABULOUS FLAVOR, SAY SPACEMEN ENTERING NEPTUNE!"
WHOSE IDEA WAS THIS STUPID CONTEST, ROBERTSON?

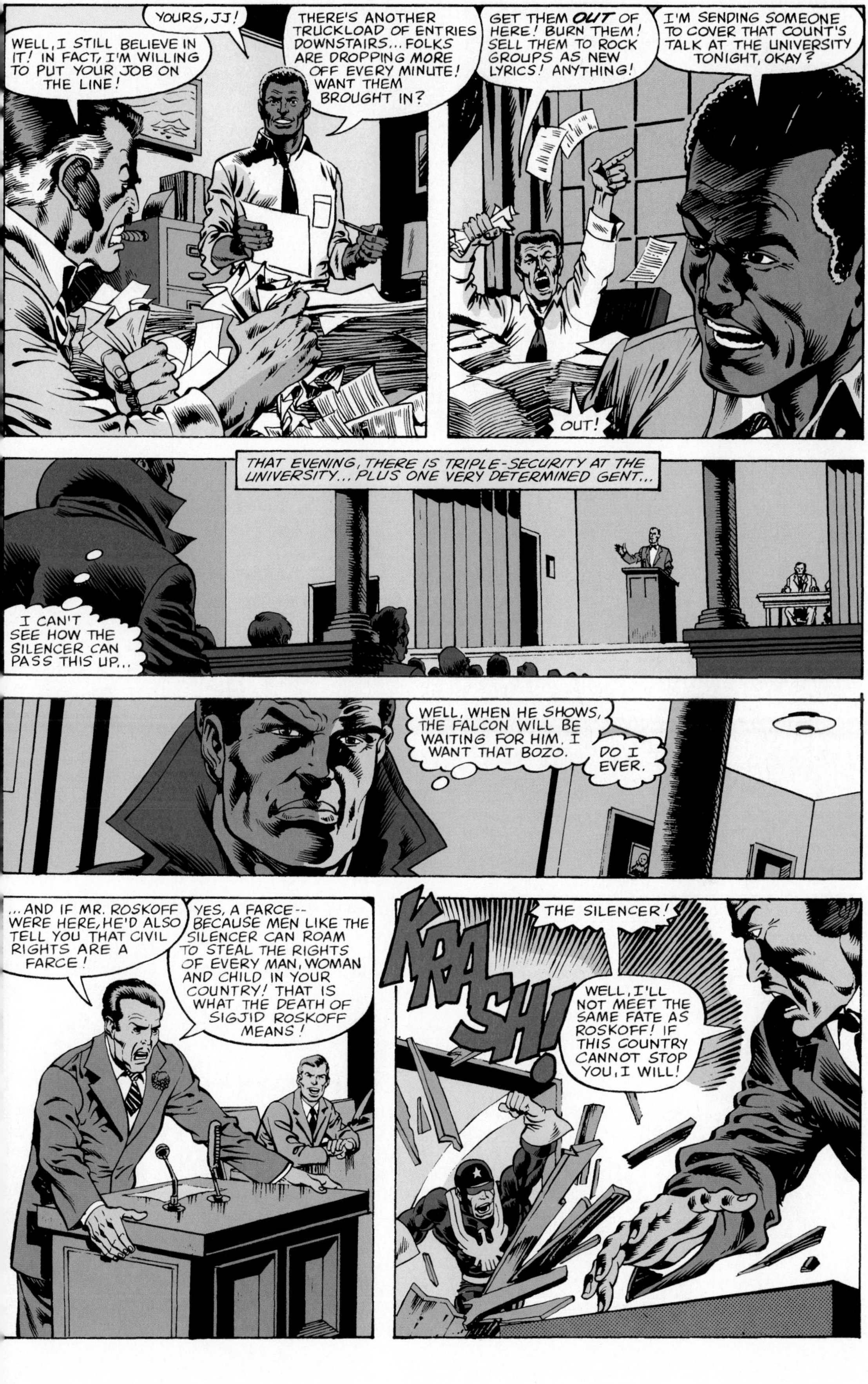

YOURS, JJ!
WELL, I STILL BELIEVE IN IT! IN FACT, I'M WILLING TO PUT YOUR JOB ON THE LINE!
THERE'S ANOTHER TRUCKLOAD OF ENTRIES DOWNSTAIRS... FOLKS ARE DROPPING MORE OFF EVERY MINUTE! WANT THEM BROUGHT IN?
GET THEM OUT OF HERE! BURN THEM! SELL THEM TO ROCK GROUPS AS NEW LYRICS! ANYTHING!
OUT!
I'M SENDING SOMEONE TO COVER THAT COUNT'S TALK AT THE UNIVERSITY TONIGHT, OKAY?
THAT EVENING, THERE IS TRIPLE-SECURITY AT THE UNIVERSITY... PLUS ONE VERY DETERMINED GENT...
I CAN'T SEE HOW THE SILENCER CAN PASS THIS UP...
WELL, WHEN HE SHOWS, THE FALCON WILL BE WAITING FOR HIM. I WANT THAT BOZO.
DO I EVER.
...AND IF MR. ROSKOFF WERE HERE, HE'D ALSO TELL YOU THAT CIVIL RIGHTS ARE A FARCE!
YES, A FARCE-- BECAUSE MEN LIKE THE SILENCER CAN ROAM TO STEAL THE RIGHTS OF EVERY MAN, WOMAN AND CHILD IN YOUR COUNTRY! THAT IS WHAT THE DEATH OF SIGJID ROSKOFF MEANS!
KRAASH!
THE SILENCER!
WELL, I'LL NOT MEET THE SAME FATE AS ROSKOFF! IF THIS COUNTRY CANNOT STOP YOU, I WILL!

UH-OH--THE COUNT'S OUT FOR BLOOD...

...AND I WANT THAT TURKEY ALIVE!

THE DEATH OF SIGJID ROSKOFF IS AVENGED! JUSTICE BE DONE.

BAM!

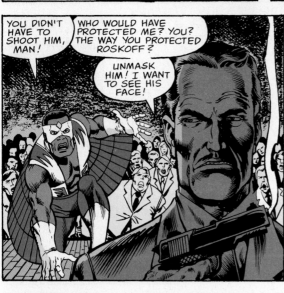

YOU DIDN'T HAVE TO SHOOT HIM, MAN!

WHO WOULD HAVE PROTECTED ME? YOU? THE WAY YOU PROTECTED ROSKOFF?

UNMASK HIM! I WANT TO SEE HIS FACE!

RECOGNIZE HIM, FALCON?

NOPE. BUT THE COPS'LL FIGURE OUT WHO HE IS, SOMEONE GIVE 'EM A BUZZ.

IT TAKES THREE HOURS TO MATCH A NAME TO THE CORPSE...

NAME'S HAL DOERNER--NO WANTS, NO WARRANTS... STRICTLY SMALL TIME. YOUR BASIC TWO-BIT THUG.

YOU GONNA HOLD COUNT BARZON?

WHAT FOR? IN A WAY, THE MAN DID US A FAVOR--WHICH IS MORE THAN I CAN SAY FOR SOMEONE ELSE!

MAN'S ABOUT AS SUBTLE AS A TAP-DANCING RHINOCEROS.

5th PRECINCT POLICE

I GET THE MESSAGE:"YOU BLEW IT, FALC... THREE CHANCES YOU HAD AT THAT FASCIST, AND, THREE TIMES, YOU BLEW IT."

JUST ONE THING BOTHERS ME...

184

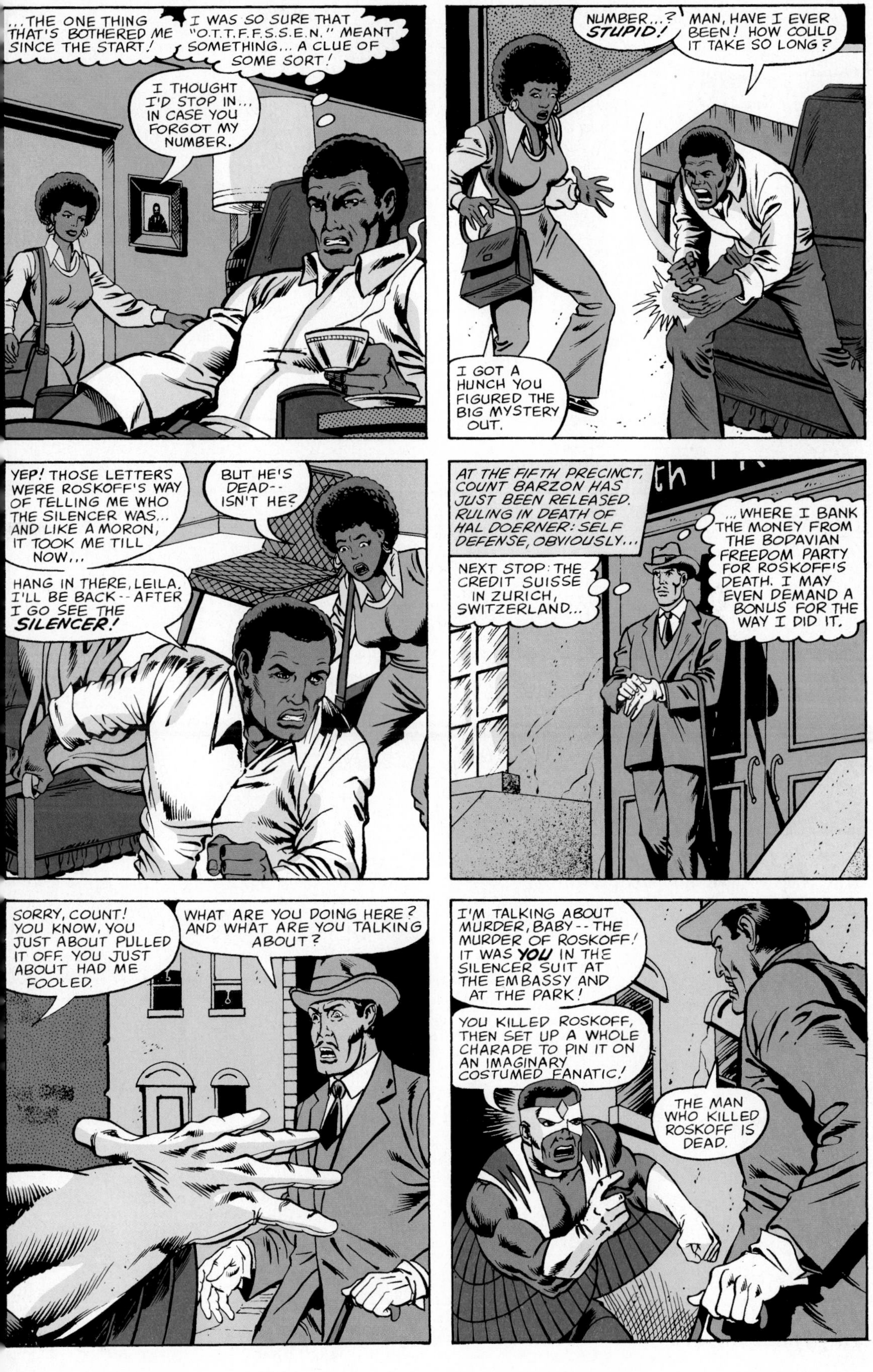
...THE ONE THING THAT'S BOTHERED ME SINCE THE START!
I WAS SO SURE THAT "O.T.T.F.F.S.S.E.N." MEANT SOMETHING... A CLUE OF SOME SORT!
I THOUGHT I'D STOP IN... IN CASE YOU FORGOT MY NUMBER.
NUMBER...? STUPID!
MAN, HAVE I EVER BEEN! HOW COULD IT TAKE SO LONG?
I GOT A HUNCH YOU FIGURED THE BIG MYSTERY OUT.
YEP! THOSE LETTERS WERE ROSKOFF'S WAY OF TELLING ME WHO THE SILENCER WAS... AND LIKE A MORON, IT TOOK ME TILL NOW...
BUT HE'S DEAD-- ISN'T HE?
HANG IN THERE, LEILA. I'LL BE BACK--AFTER I GO SEE THE SILENCER!
AT THE FIFTH PRECINCT, COUNT BARZON HAS JUST BEEN RELEASED. RULING IN DEATH OF HAL DOERNER: SELF DEFENSE, OBVIOUSLY...
NEXT STOP: THE CREDIT SUISSE IN ZURICH, SWITZERLAND...
...WHERE I BANK THE MONEY FROM THE BODAVIAN FREEDOM PARTY FOR ROSKOFF'S DEATH. I MAY EVEN DEMAND A BONUS FOR THE WAY I DID IT.
SORRY, COUNT! YOU KNOW, YOU JUST ABOUT PULLED IT OFF. YOU JUST ABOUT HAD ME FOOLED.
WHAT ARE YOU DOING HERE? AND WHAT ARE YOU TALKING ABOUT?
I'M TALKING ABOUT MURDER, BABY--THE MURDER OF ROSKOFF! IT WAS YOU IN THE SILENCER SUIT AT THE EMBASSY AND AT THE PARK!
YOU KILLED ROSKOFF, THEN SET UP A WHOLE CHARADE TO PIN IT ON AN IMAGINARY COSTUMED FANATIC!
THE MAN WHO KILLED ROSKOFF IS DEAD.

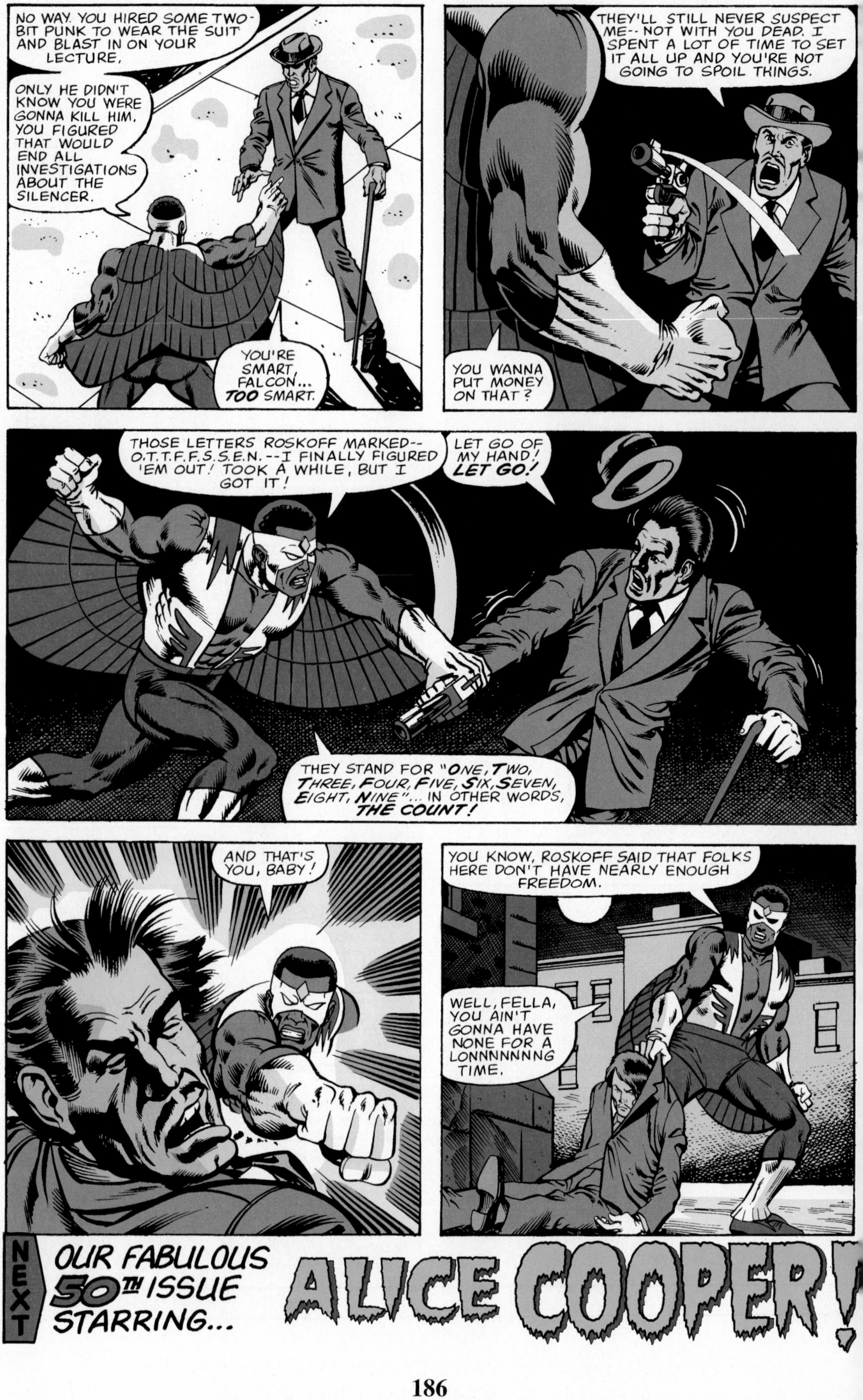
NO WAY. YOU HIRED SOME TWO-BIT PUNK TO WEAR THE SUIT AND BLAST IN ON YOUR LECTURE,
ONLY HE DIDN'T KNOW YOU WERE GONNA KILL HIM. YOU FIGURED THAT WOULD END ALL INVESTIGATIONS ABOUT THE SILENCER.
YOU'RE SMART, FALCON... TOO SMART.
THEY'LL STILL NEVER SUSPECT ME-- NOT WITH YOU DEAD. I SPENT A LOT OF TIME TO SET IT ALL UP AND YOU'RE NOT GOING TO SPOIL THINGS.
YOU WANNA PUT MONEY ON THAT?
THOSE LETTERS ROSKOFF MARKED-- O.T.T.F.F.S.S.E.N. --I FINALLY FIGURED 'EM OUT! TOOK A WHILE, BUT I GOT IT!
LET GO OF MY HAND! LET GO!
THEY STAND FOR "ONE, TWO, THREE, FOUR, FIVE, SIX, SEVEN, EIGHT, NINE"... IN OTHER WORDS, THE COUNT!
AND THAT'S YOU, BABY!
YOU KNOW, ROSKOFF SAID THAT FOLKS HERE DON'T HAVE NEARLY ENOUGH FREEDOM.
WELL, FELLA, YOU AIN'T GONNA HAVE NONE FOR A LONNNNNNNG TIME.
NEXT
OUR FABULOUS 50TH ISSUE STARRING...
ALICE COOPER!

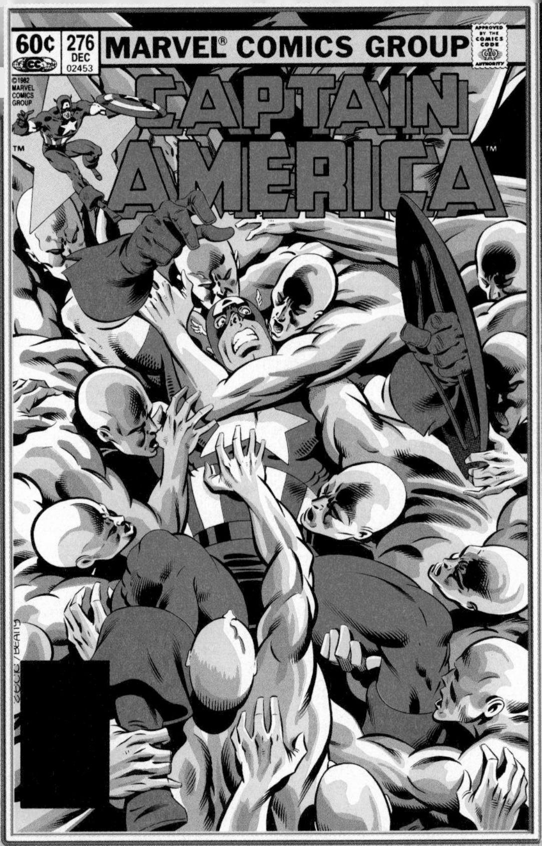
60¢
276
DEC
02453
MARVEL® COMICS GROUP
APPROVED BY THE COMICS CODE AUTHORITY
©1982 MARVEL COMICS GROUP
CAPTAIN AMERICA

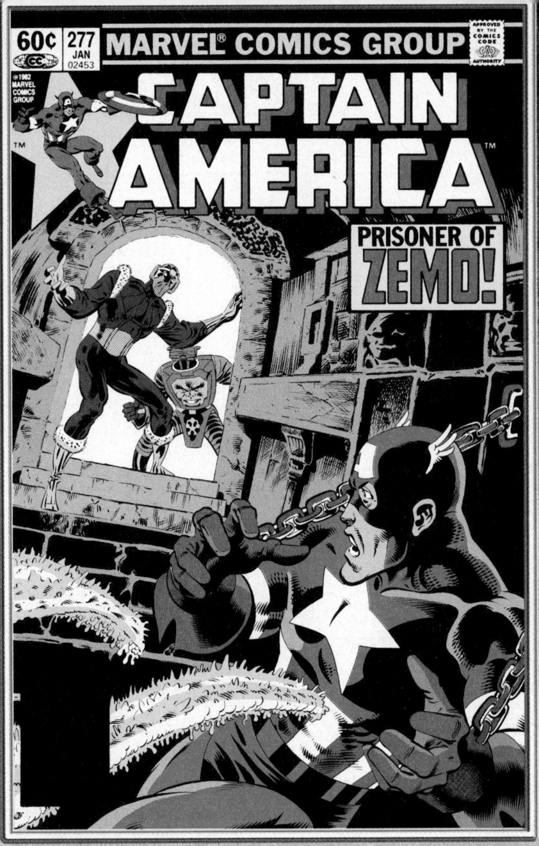
60¢
277
JAN
02453
MARVEL® COMICS GROUP
APPROVED BY THE COMICS CODE AUTHORITY
©1982 MARVEL COMICS GROUP
CAPTAIN AMERICA
PRISONER OF ZEMO!

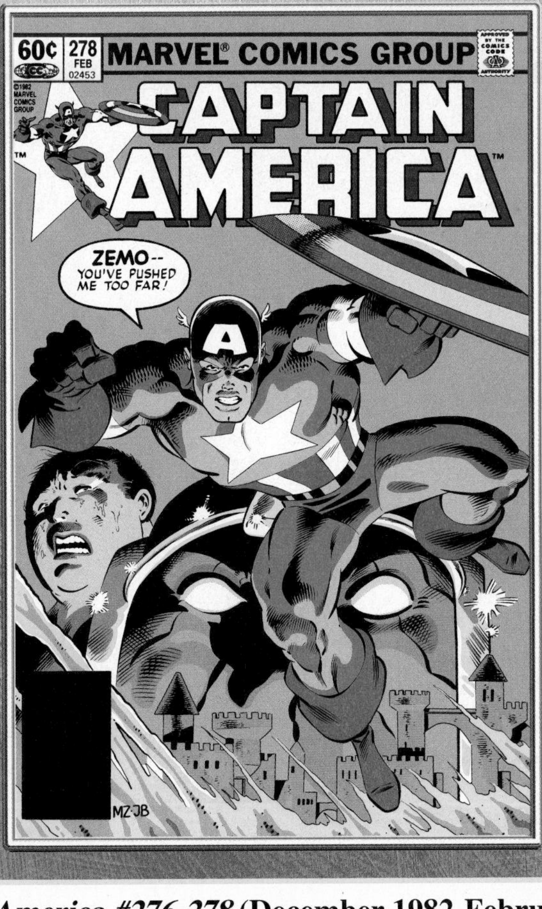
60¢
278
FEB
02453
MARVEL® COMICS GROUP
APPROVED BY THE COMICS CODE AUTHORITY
©1982 MARVEL COMICS GROUP
CAPTAIN AMERICA
ZEMO-- YOU'VE PUSHED ME TOO FAR!
MZ·JB

***Captain America #276-278* (December 1982-February 1983) featured a three-part Falcon backup story.**

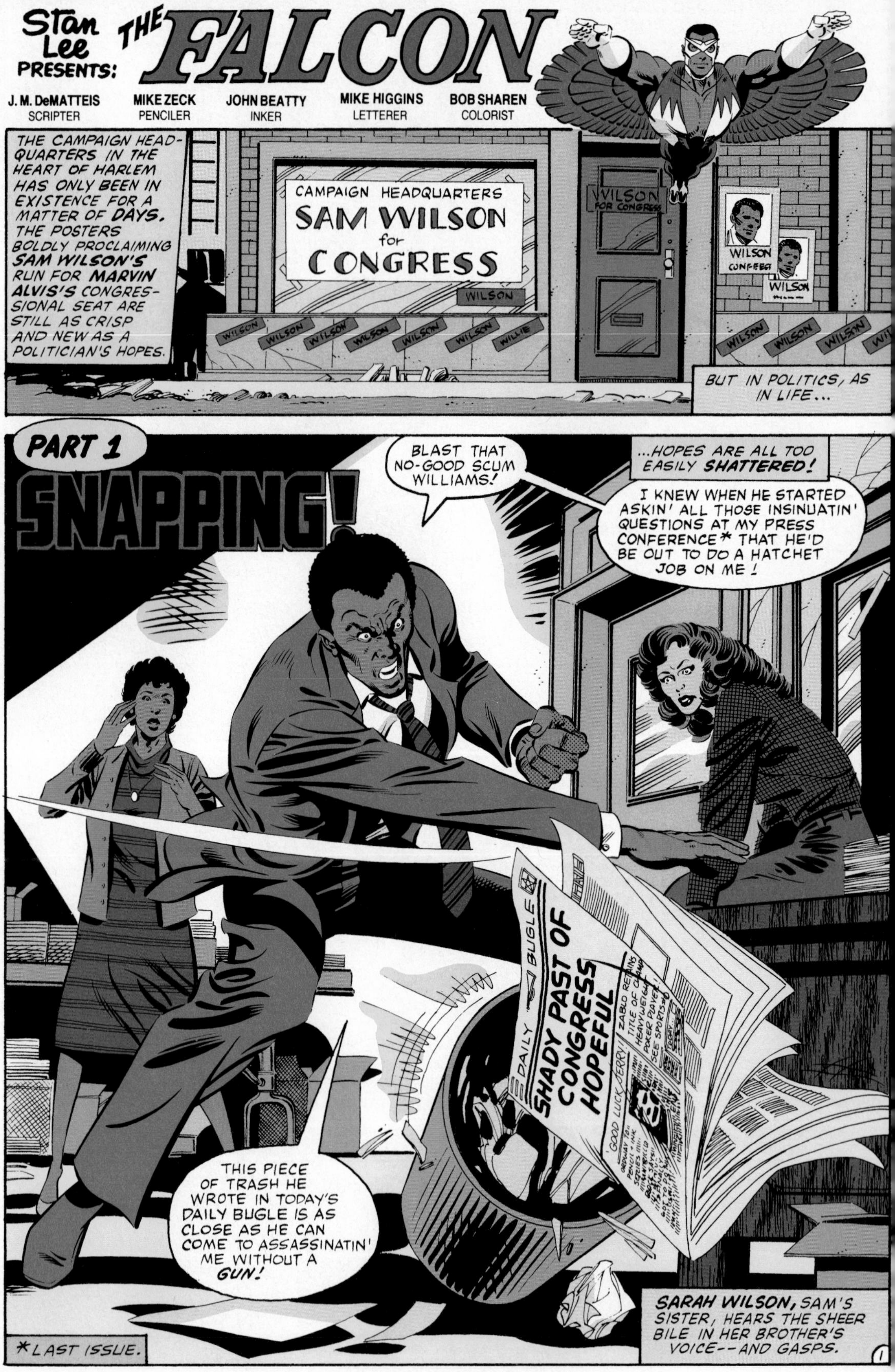
Stan Lee PRESENTS: THE FALCON
J. M. DeMATTEIS SCRIPTER
MIKE ZECK PENCILER
JOHN BEATTY INKER
MIKE HIGGINS LETTERER
BOB SHAREN COLORIST
THE CAMPAIGN HEADQUARTERS IN THE HEART OF HARLEM HAS ONLY BEEN IN EXISTENCE FOR A MATTER OF DAYS. THE POSTERS BOLDLY PROCLAIMING SAM WILSON'S RUN FOR MARVIN ALVIS'S CONGRESSIONAL SEAT ARE STILL AS CRISP AND NEW AS A POLITICIAN'S HOPES.
CAMPAIGN HEADQUARTERS SAM WILSON for CONGRESS
WILSON FOR CONGRESS
BUT IN POLITICS, AS IN LIFE...
PART 1
SNAPPING!
BLAST THAT NO-GOOD SCUM WILLIAMS!
...HOPES ARE ALL TOO EASILY SHATTERED!
I KNEW WHEN HE STARTED ASKIN' ALL THOSE INSINUATIN' QUESTIONS AT MY PRESS CONFERENCE* THAT HE'D BE OUT TO DO A HATCHET JOB ON ME!
DAILY BUGLE
SHADY PAST OF CONGRESS HOPEFUL
THIS PIECE OF TRASH HE WROTE IN TODAY'S DAILY BUGLE IS AS CLOSE AS HE CAN COME TO ASSASSINATIN' ME WITHOUT A GUN!
SARAH WILSON, SAM'S SISTER, HEARS THE SHEER BILE IN HER BROTHER'S VOICE--AND GASPS.
*LAST ISSUE.
1

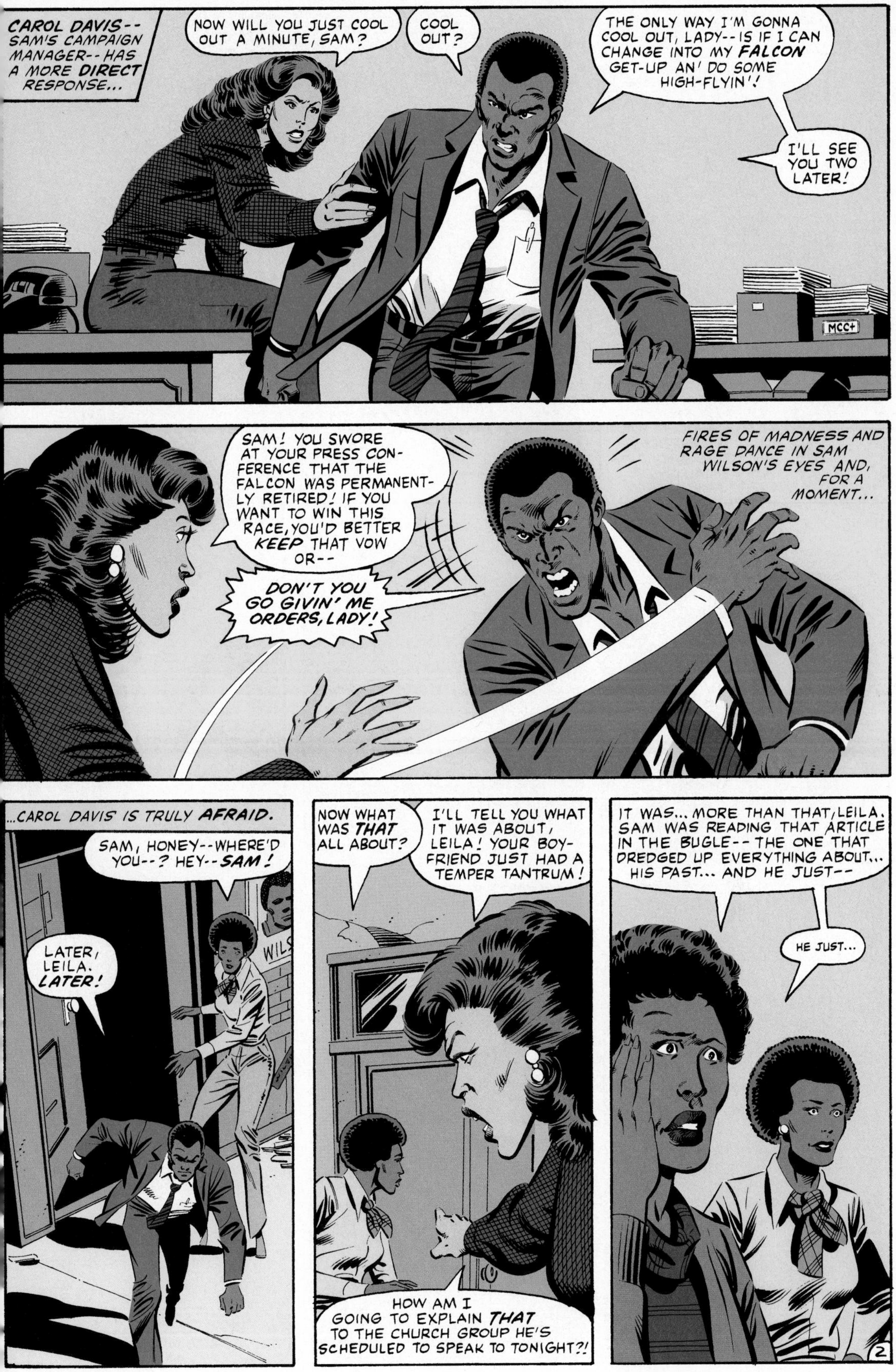
CAROL DAVIS-- SAM'S CAMPAIGN MANAGER-- HAS A MORE DIRECT RESPONSE...
NOW WILL YOU JUST COOL OUT A MINUTE, SAM?
COOL OUT?
THE ONLY WAY I'M GONNA COOL OUT, LADY-- IS IF I CAN CHANGE INTO MY FALCON GET-UP AN' DO SOME HIGH-FLYIN'!
I'LL SEE YOU TWO LATER!
MCC+
SAM! YOU SWORE AT YOUR PRESS CONFERENCE THAT THE FALCON WAS PERMANENTLY RETIRED! IF YOU WANT TO WIN THIS RACE, YOU'D BETTER KEEP THAT VOW OR--
DON'T YOU GO GIVIN' ME ORDERS, LADY!
FIRES OF MADNESS AND RAGE DANCE IN SAM WILSON'S EYES AND, FOR A MOMENT...
...CAROL DAVIS IS TRULY AFRAID.
SAM, HONEY-- WHERE'D YOU--? HEY-- SAM!
LATER, LEILA. LATER!
WILS
NOW WHAT WAS THAT ALL ABOUT?
I'LL TELL YOU WHAT IT WAS ABOUT, LEILA! YOUR BOYFRIEND JUST HAD A TEMPER TANTRUM!
HOW AM I GOING TO EXPLAIN THAT TO THE CHURCH GROUP HE'S SCHEDULED TO SPEAK TO TONIGHT?!
IT WAS... MORE THAN THAT, LEILA. SAM WAS READING THAT ARTICLE IN THE BUGLE-- THE ONE THAT DREDGED UP EVERYTHING ABOUT... HIS PAST... AND HE JUST--
HE JUST...
2

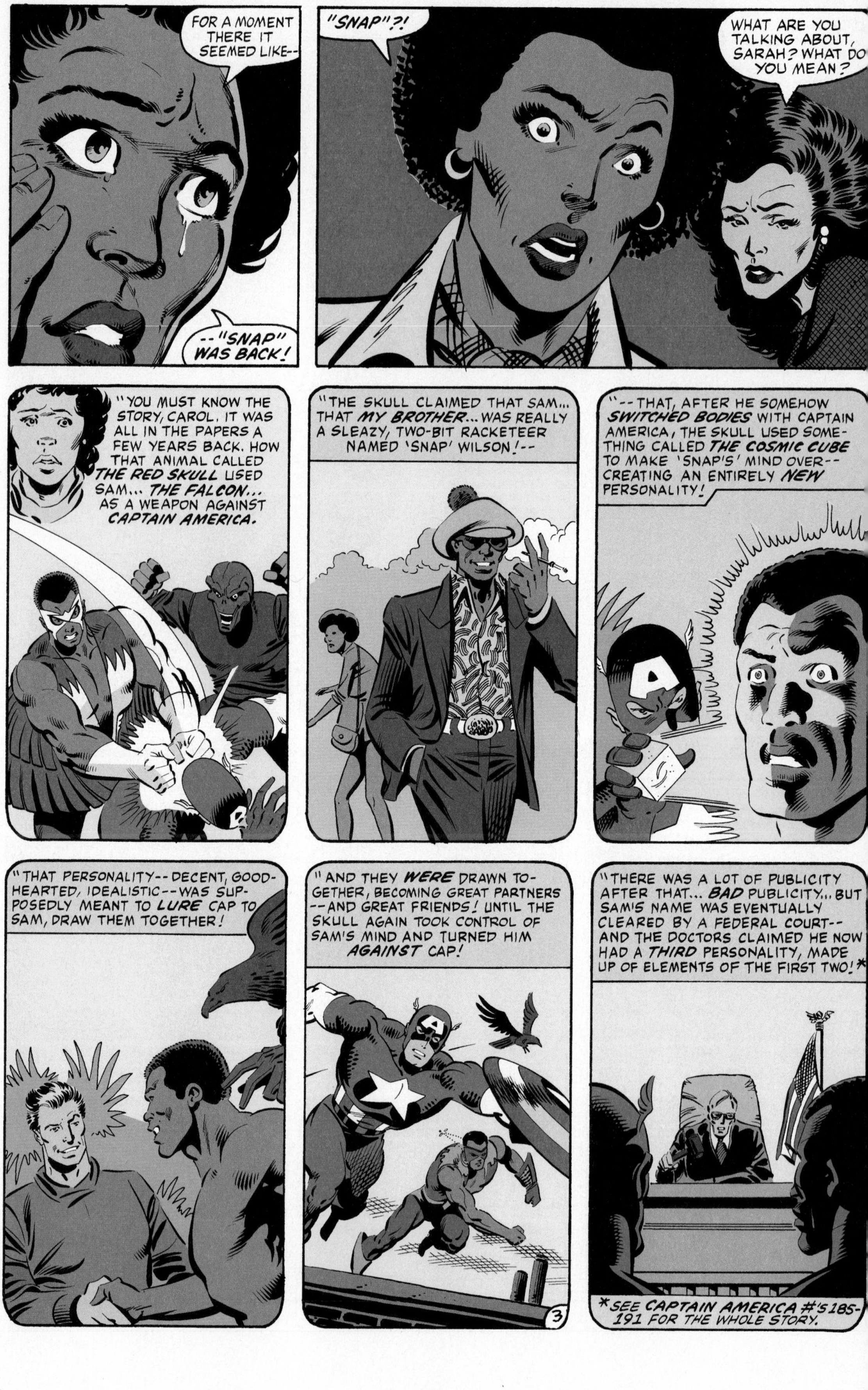
FOR A MOMENT THERE IT SEEMED LIKE--
--"SNAP" WAS BACK!
"SNAP"?!
WHAT ARE YOU TALKING ABOUT, SARAH? WHAT DO YOU MEAN?
"YOU MUST KNOW THE STORY, CAROL. IT WAS ALL IN THE PAPERS A FEW YEARS BACK. HOW THAT ANIMAL CALLED THE RED SKULL USED SAM... THE FALCON... AS A WEAPON AGAINST CAPTAIN AMERICA.
"THE SKULL CLAIMED THAT SAM... THAT MY BROTHER... WAS REALLY A SLEAZY, TWO-BIT RACKETEER NAMED 'SNAP' WILSON!--
"--THAT, AFTER HE SOMEHOW SWITCHED BODIES WITH CAPTAIN AMERICA, THE SKULL USED SOMETHING CALLED THE COSMIC CUBE TO MAKE 'SNAP'S' MIND OVER--CREATING AN ENTIRELY NEW PERSONALITY!
"THAT PERSONALITY--DECENT, GOOD-HEARTED, IDEALISTIC--WAS SUPPOSEDLY MEANT TO LURE CAP TO SAM, DRAW THEM TOGETHER!
"AND THEY WERE DRAWN TOGETHER, BECOMING GREAT PARTNERS --AND GREAT FRIENDS! UNTIL THE SKULL AGAIN TOOK CONTROL OF SAM'S MIND AND TURNED HIM AGAINST CAP!
3
"THERE WAS A LOT OF PUBLICITY AFTER THAT... BAD PUBLICITY... BUT SAM'S NAME WAS EVENTUALLY CLEARED BY A FEDERAL COURT-- AND THE DOCTORS CLAIMED HE NOW HAD A THIRD PERSONALITY, MADE UP OF ELEMENTS OF THE FIRST TWO!*
*SEE CAPTAIN AMERICA #'S 185-191 FOR THE WHOLE STORY.

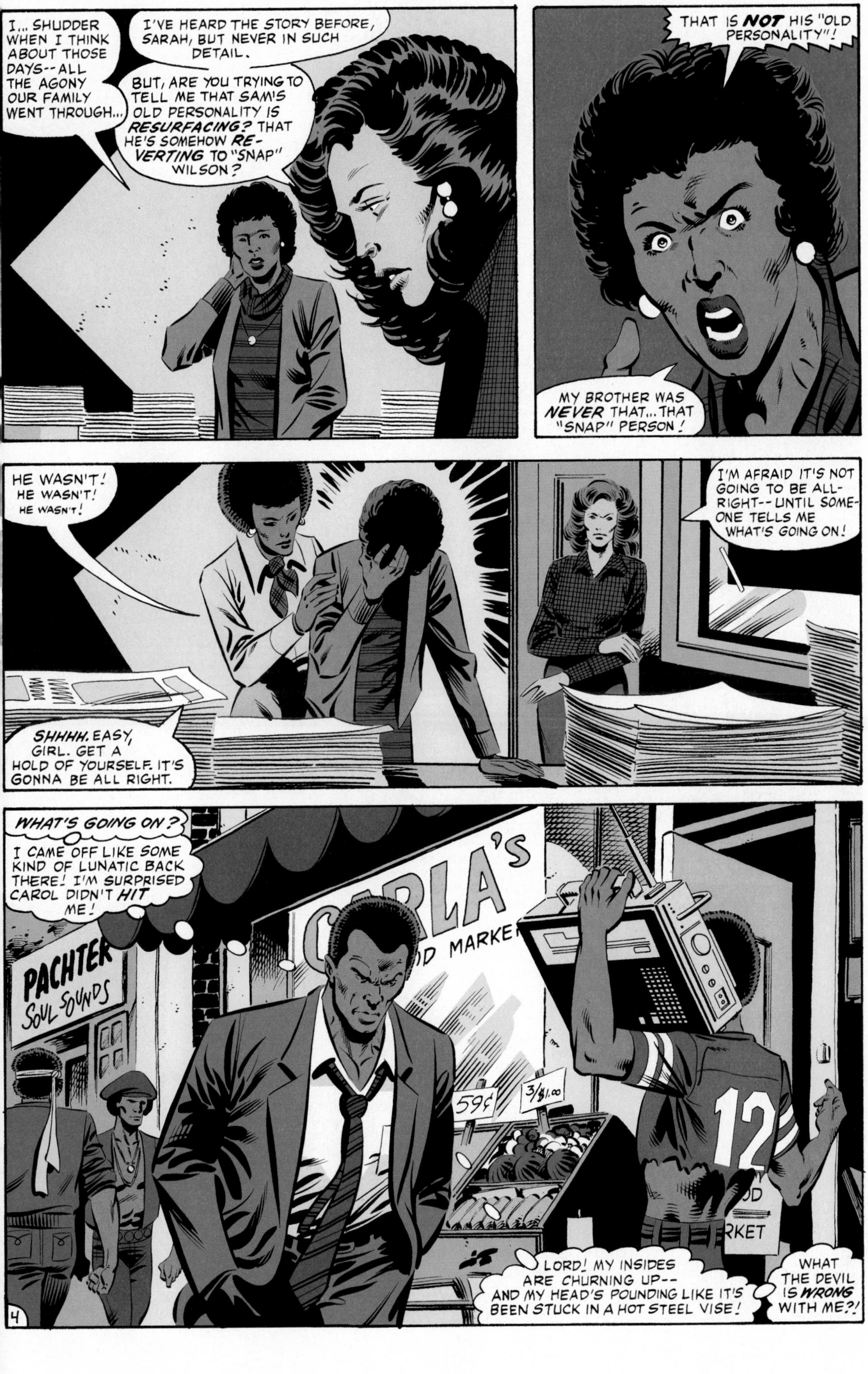
I... SHUDDER WHEN I THINK ABOUT THOSE DAYS--ALL THE AGONY OUR FAMILY WENT THROUGH...
I'VE HEARD THE STORY BEFORE, SARAH, BUT NEVER IN SUCH DETAIL.
BUT, ARE YOU TRYING TO TELL ME THAT SAM'S OLD PERSONALITY IS RESURFACING? THAT HE'S SOMEHOW RE-VERTING TO "SNAP" WILSON?
THAT IS NOT HIS "OLD PERSONALITY"!
MY BROTHER WAS NEVER THAT... THAT "SNAP" PERSON!
HE WASN'T! HE WASN'T! HE WASN'T!
SHHHH. EASY, GIRL. GET A HOLD OF YOURSELF. IT'S GONNA BE ALL RIGHT.
I'M AFRAID IT'S NOT GOING TO BE ALL-RIGHT--UNTIL SOME-ONE TELLS ME WHAT'S GOING ON!
WHAT'S GOING ON?
I CAME OFF LIKE SOME KIND OF LUNATIC BACK THERE! I'M SURPRISED CAROL DIDN'T HIT ME!
PACHTER
SOUL SOUNDS
59¢
3/$1.00
LORD! MY INSIDES ARE CHURNING UP-- AND MY HEAD'S POUNDING LIKE IT'S BEEN STUCK IN A HOT STEEL VISE!
WHAT THE DEVIL IS WRONG WITH ME?!
4

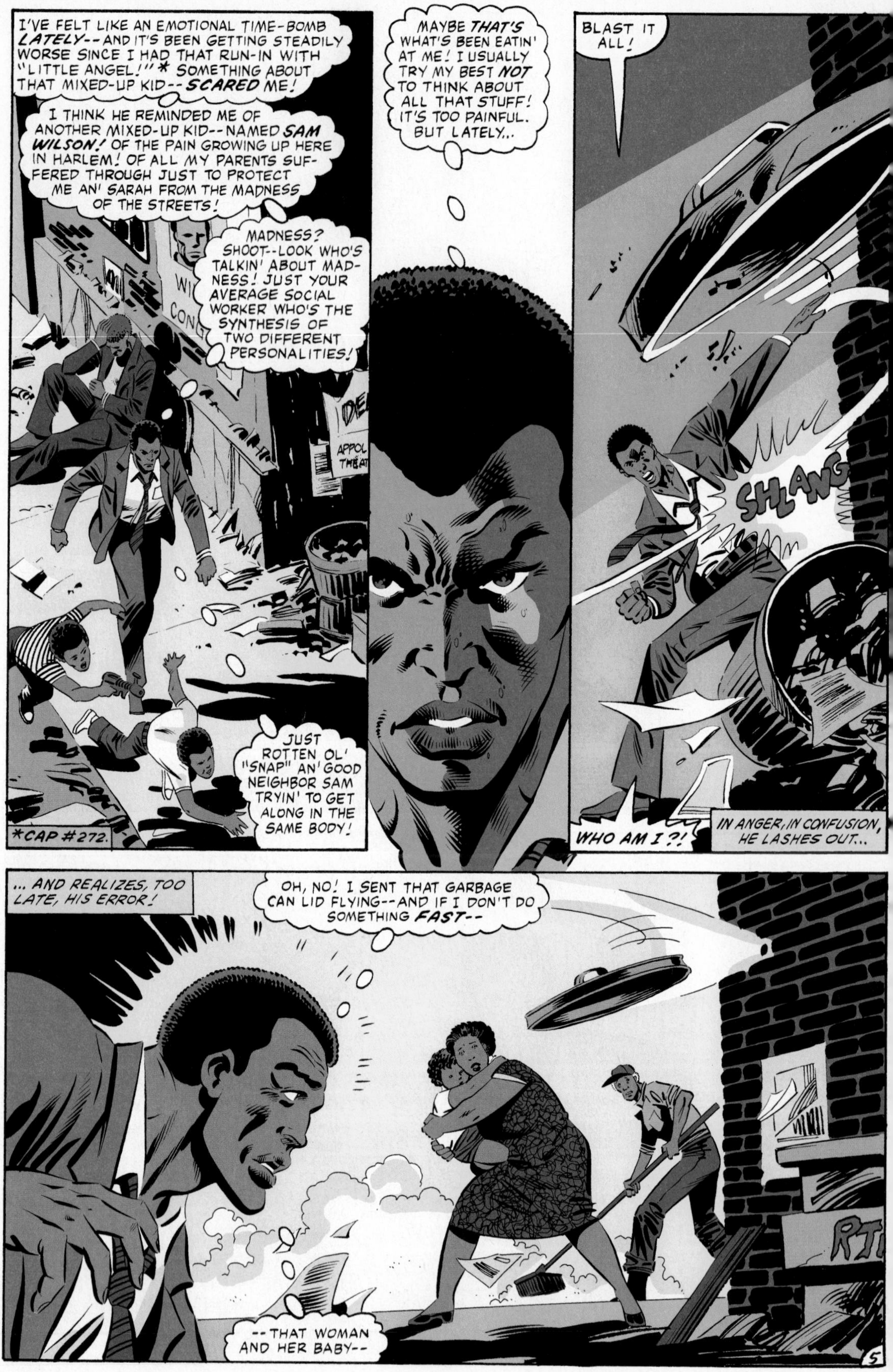
I'VE FELT LIKE AN EMOTIONAL TIME-BOMB LATELY--AND IT'S BEEN GETTING STEADILY WORSE SINCE I HAD THAT RUN-IN WITH "LITTLE ANGEL!"* SOMETHING ABOUT THAT MIXED-UP KID--SCARED ME!
I THINK HE REMINDED ME OF ANOTHER MIXED-UP KID--NAMED SAM WILSON! OF THE PAIN GROWING UP HERE IN HARLEM! OF ALL MY PARENTS SUFFERED THROUGH JUST TO PROTECT ME AN' SARAH FROM THE MADNESS OF THE STREETS!
MADNESS? SHOOT--LOOK WHO'S TALKIN' ABOUT MADNESS! JUST YOUR AVERAGE SOCIAL WORKER WHO'S THE SYNTHESIS OF TWO DIFFERENT PERSONALITIES!
JUST ROTTEN OL' "SNAP" AN' GOOD NEIGHBOR SAM TRYIN' TO GET ALONG IN THE SAME BODY!
*CAP #272.
MAYBE THAT'S WHAT'S BEEN EATIN' AT ME! I USUALLY TRY MY BEST NOT TO THINK ABOUT ALL THAT STUFF! IT'S TOO PAINFUL. BUT LATELY...
BLAST IT ALL!
SHLANG
WHO AM I?!
IN ANGER, IN CONFUSION, HE LASHES OUT...
... AND REALIZES, TOO LATE, HIS ERROR!
OH, NO! I SENT THAT GARBAGE CAN LID FLYING--AND IF I DON'T DO SOMETHING FAST--
--THAT WOMAN AND HER BABY--
5

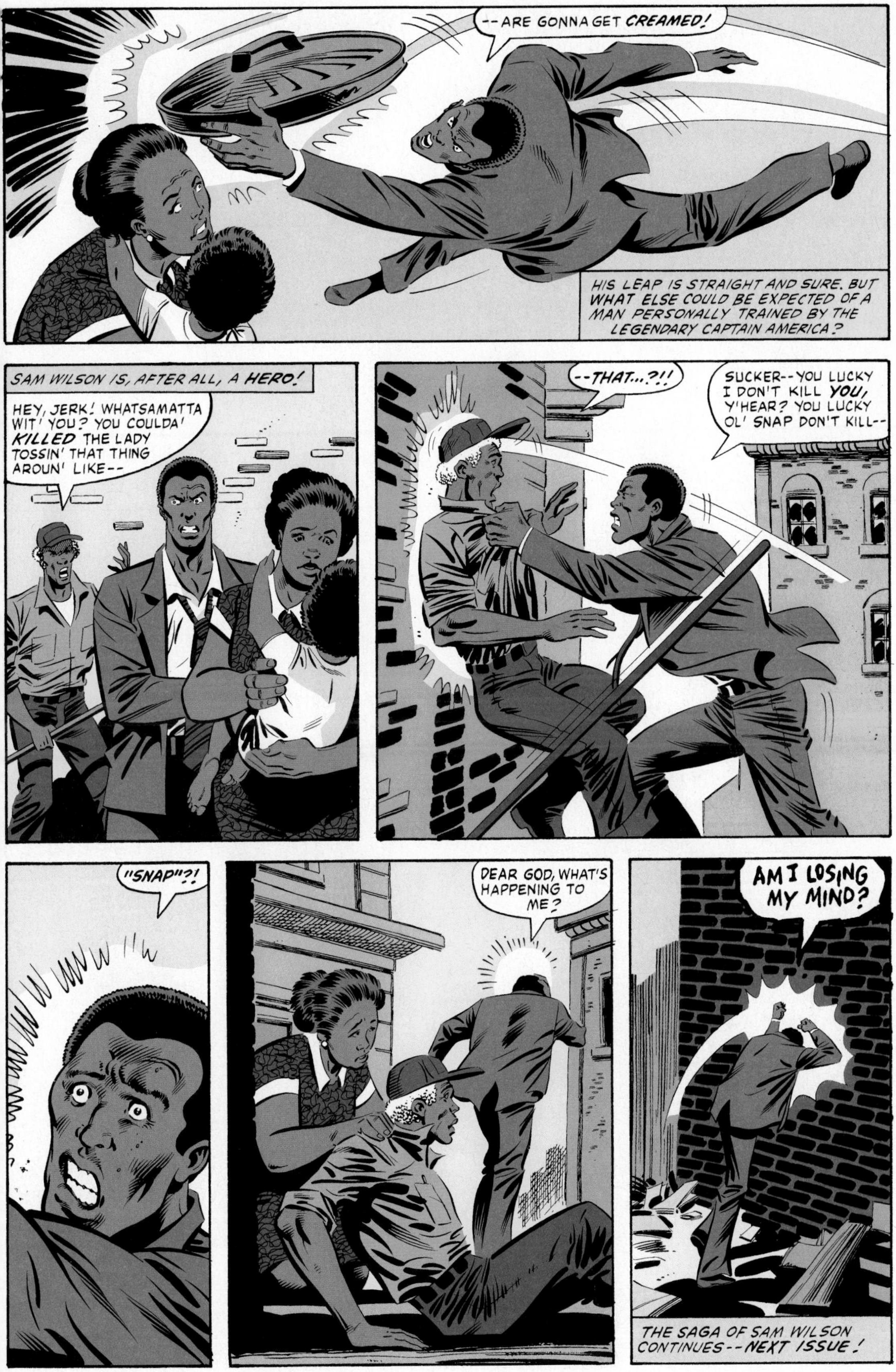
--ARE GONNA GET CREAMED!
HIS LEAP IS STRAIGHT AND SURE. BUT WHAT ELSE COULD BE EXPECTED OF A MAN PERSONALLY TRAINED BY THE LEGENDARY CAPTAIN AMERICA?
SAM WILSON IS, AFTER ALL, A HERO!
HEY, JERK! WHATSAMATTA WIT' YOU? YOU COULDA' KILLED THE LADY TOSSIN' THAT THING AROUN' LIKE--
--THAT...?!!
SUCKER--YOU LUCKY I DON'T KILL YOU, Y'HEAR? YOU LUCKY OL' SNAP DON'T KILL--
"SNAP"?!
DEAR GOD, WHAT'S HAPPENING TO ME?
AM I LOSING MY MIND?
THE SAGA OF SAM WILSON CONTINUES--NEXT ISSUE!

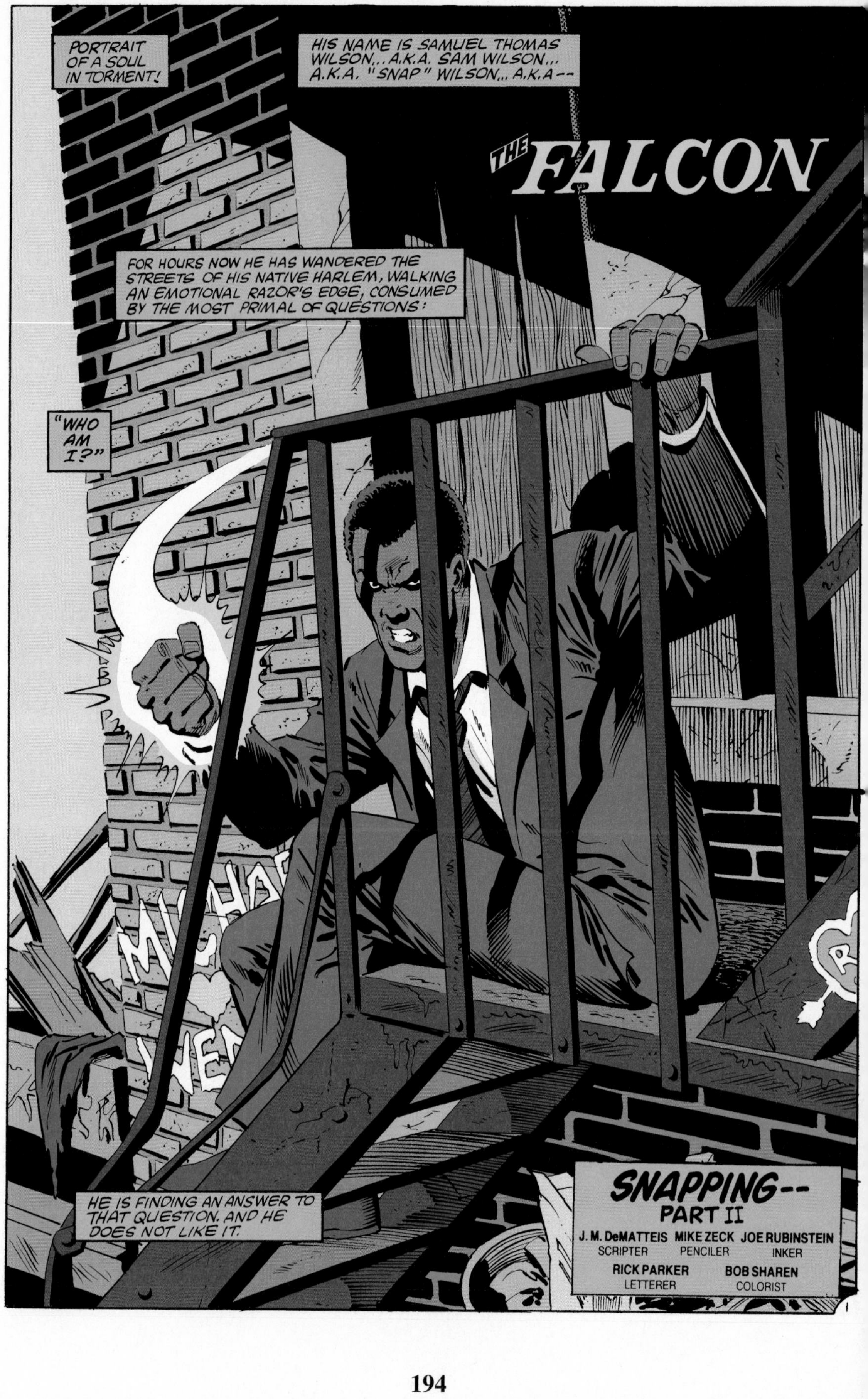
PORTRAIT OF A SOUL IN TORMENT!
HIS NAME IS SAMUEL THOMAS WILSON... A.K.A. SAM WILSON... A.K.A. "SNAP" WILSON... A.K.A--
THE FALCON
FOR HOURS NOW HE HAS WANDERED THE STREETS OF HIS NATIVE HARLEM, WALKING AN EMOTIONAL RAZOR'S EDGE, CONSUMED BY THE MOST PRIMAL OF QUESTIONS:
"WHO AM I?"
HE IS FINDING AN ANSWER TO THAT QUESTION. AND HE DOES NOT LIKE IT.
SNAPPING-- PART II
J. M. DeMATTEIS SCRIPTER
MIKE ZECK PENCILER
JOE RUBINSTEIN INKER
RICK PARKER LETTERER
BOB SHAREN COLORIST

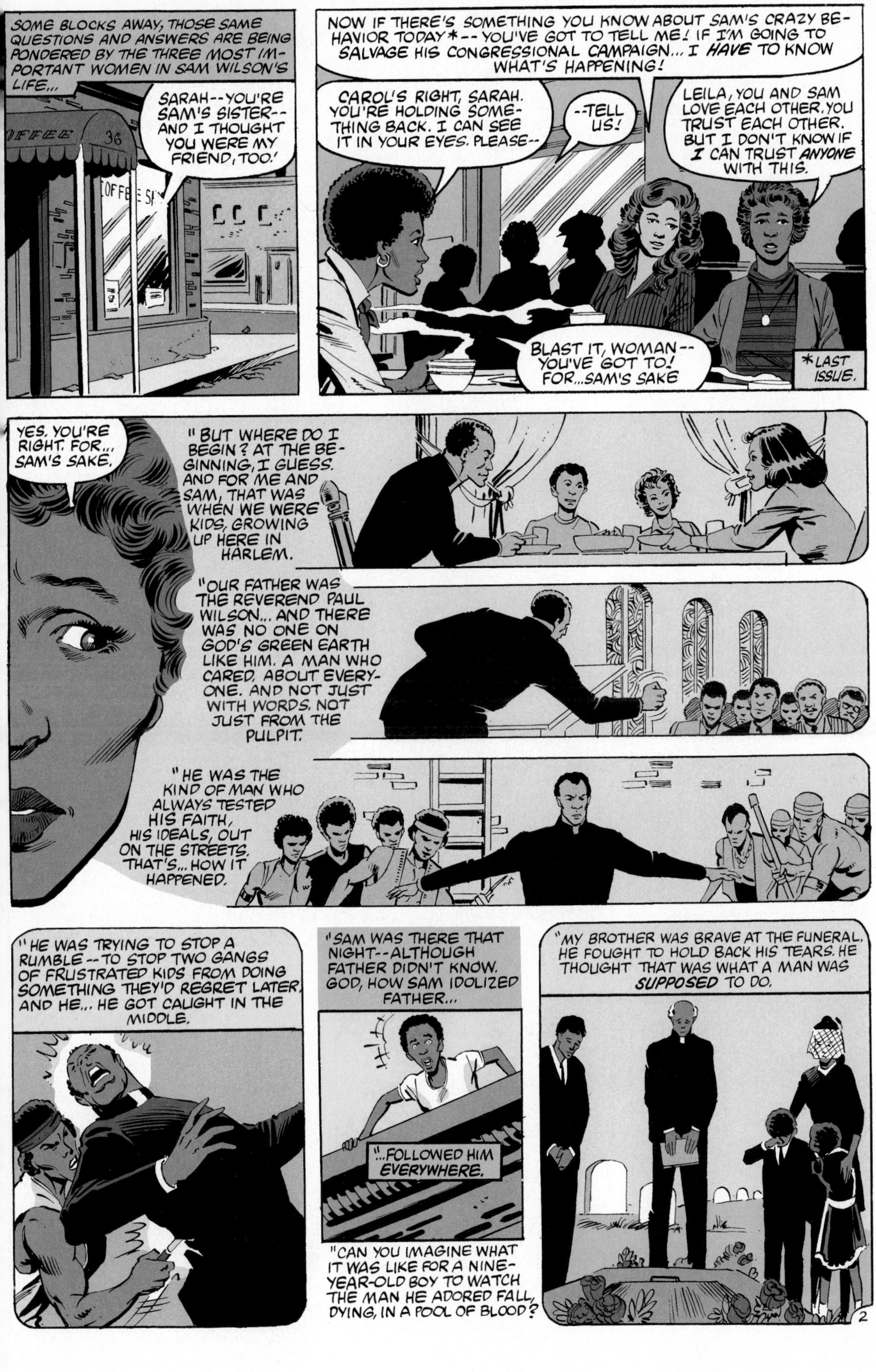
SOME BLOCKS AWAY, THOSE SAME QUESTIONS AND ANSWERS ARE BEING PONDERED BY THE THREE MOST IMPORTANT WOMEN IN SAM WILSON'S LIFE...
SARAH--YOU'RE SAM'S SISTER--AND I THOUGHT YOU WERE MY FRIEND, TOO!
NOW IF THERE'S SOMETHING YOU KNOW ABOUT SAM'S CRAZY BEHAVIOR TODAY* -- YOU'VE GOT TO TELL ME! IF I'M GOING TO SALVAGE HIS CONGRESSIONAL CAMPAIGN... I HAVE TO KNOW WHAT'S HAPPENING!
CAROL'S RIGHT, SARAH. YOU'RE HOLDING SOMETHING BACK. I CAN SEE IT IN YOUR EYES. PLEASE--
--TELL US!
LEILA, YOU AND SAM LOVE EACH OTHER. YOU TRUST EACH OTHER. BUT I DON'T KNOW IF I CAN TRUST ANYONE WITH THIS.
BLAST IT, WOMAN--YOU'VE GOT TO! FOR... SAM'S SAKE
*LAST ISSUE.
YES. YOU'RE RIGHT. FOR... SAM'S SAKE.
"BUT WHERE DO I BEGIN? AT THE BEGINNING, I GUESS. AND FOR ME AND SAM, THAT WAS WHEN WE WERE KIDS, GROWING UP HERE IN HARLEM.
"OUR FATHER WAS THE REVEREND PAUL WILSON... AND THERE WAS NO ONE ON GOD'S GREEN EARTH LIKE HIM. A MAN WHO CARED ABOUT EVERYONE. AND NOT JUST WITH WORDS. NOT JUST FROM THE PULPIT.
"HE WAS THE KIND OF MAN WHO ALWAYS TESTED HIS FAITH, HIS IDEALS, OUT ON THE STREETS. THAT'S... HOW IT HAPPENED.
"HE WAS TRYING TO STOP A RUMBLE -- TO STOP TWO GANGS OF FRUSTRATED KIDS FROM DOING SOMETHING THEY'D REGRET LATER, AND HE... HE GOT CAUGHT IN THE MIDDLE.
"SAM WAS THERE THAT NIGHT--ALTHOUGH FATHER DIDN'T KNOW. GOD, HOW SAM IDOLIZED FATHER...
"...FOLLOWED HIM EVERYWHERE.
"CAN YOU IMAGINE WHAT IT WAS LIKE FOR A NINE-YEAR-OLD BOY TO WATCH THE MAN HE ADORED FALL, DYING, IN A POOL OF BLOOD?
"MY BROTHER WAS BRAVE AT THE FUNERAL. HE FOUGHT TO HOLD BACK HIS TEARS. HE THOUGHT THAT WAS WHAT A MAN WAS SUPPOSED TO DO.
2

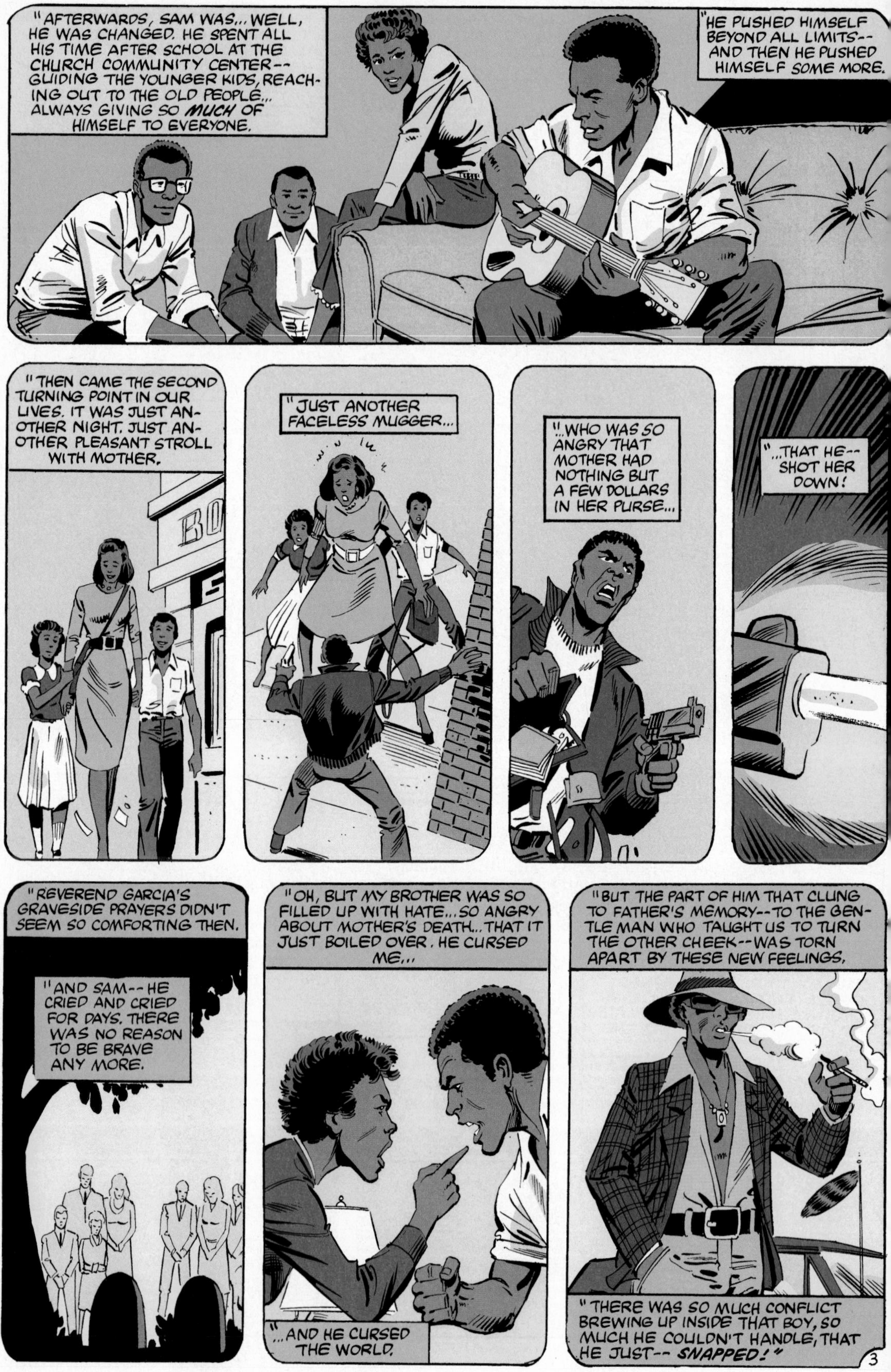
"AFTERWARDS, SAM WAS... WELL, HE WAS CHANGED. HE SPENT ALL HIS TIME AFTER SCHOOL AT THE CHURCH COMMUNITY CENTER--GUIDING THE YOUNGER KIDS, REACHING OUT TO THE OLD PEOPLE... ALWAYS GIVING SO MUCH OF HIMSELF TO EVERYONE.
"HE PUSHED HIMSELF BEYOND ALL LIMITS--AND THEN HE PUSHED HIMSELF SOME MORE.
"THEN CAME THE SECOND TURNING POINT IN OUR LIVES. IT WAS JUST ANOTHER NIGHT. JUST ANOTHER PLEASANT STROLL WITH MOTHER.
"JUST ANOTHER FACELESS MUGGER...
"...WHO WAS SO ANGRY THAT MOTHER HAD NOTHING BUT A FEW DOLLARS IN HER PURSE...
"...THAT HE--SHOT HER DOWN!
"REVEREND GARCIA'S GRAVESIDE PRAYERS DIDN'T SEEM SO COMFORTING THEN.
"AND SAM--HE CRIED AND CRIED FOR DAYS. THERE WAS NO REASON TO BE BRAVE ANY MORE.
"OH, BUT MY BROTHER WAS SO FILLED UP WITH HATE... SO ANGRY ABOUT MOTHER'S DEATH... THAT IT JUST BOILED OVER. HE CURSED ME...
"...AND HE CURSED THE WORLD.
"BUT THE PART OF HIM THAT CLUNG TO FATHER'S MEMORY--TO THE GENTLE MAN WHO TAUGHT US TO TURN THE OTHER CHEEK--WAS TORN APART BY THESE NEW FEELINGS.
"THERE WAS SO MUCH CONFLICT BREWING UP INSIDE THAT BOY, SO MUCH HE COULDN'T HANDLE, THAT HE JUST-- SNAPPED!"
3

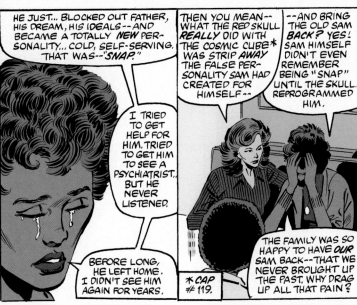

HE JUST... BLOCKED OUT FATHER, HIS DREAM, HIS IDEALS--AND BECAME A TOTALLY *NEW* PERSONALITY... COLD, SELF-SERVING. THAT WAS--*"SNAP."*

I TRIED TO GET HELP FOR HIM. TRIED TO GET HIM TO SEE A PSYCHIATRIST... BUT HE NEVER LISTENED.

BEFORE LONG, HE LEFT HOME. I DIDN'T SEE HIM AGAIN FOR YEARS.

THEN YOU MEAN-- WHAT THE RED SKULL *REALLY* DID WITH THE COSMIC CUBE* WAS STRIP *AWAY* THE FALSE PERSONALITY SAM HAD CREATED FOR HIMSELF--

*CAP #119.

--AND BRING THE OLD SAM *BACK?* YES! SAM HIMSELF DIDN'T EVEN REMEMBER BEING "SNAP" UNTIL THE SKULL REPROGRAMMED HIM.

THE FAMILY WAS SO HAPPY TO HAVE *OUR* SAM BACK--THAT WE NEVER BROUGHT UP THE PAST. WHY DRAG UP ALL THAT PAIN?

I--I WOULD'VE COME FORWARD AT THE FALCON'S TRIAL*--BUT SAM'S CONFRONTATION WITH THE STILT MAN CLEARED HIS NAME... AND AGAIN I WAS SPARED THE PAIN.

BUT IF IT'S HAPPENED AGAIN, CAROL...I-IF "SNAP" HAS REALLY COME BACK, I--

COFFEE SHOP

--DON'T KNOW WHAT TO DO!

I'VE NEVER FELT SO... MIXED UP IN ALL MY LIFE!

CAW!

HUH? *REDWING!* HEY, OLD BUDDY-- HOPE YOU'RE FEELIN' BETTER THAN I AM!

SKRAW!

I'M WITH YOU, FELLA! I NEED TO GET UP ABOVE IT ALL--

--MAYBE GET A DOSE OF PERSPECTIVE!

SO TELL ME, REDWING--HOW STUPID COULD I HAVE BEEN TO THINK ALL THAT STUFF WITH THE SKULL WAS BEHIND ME? I'VE BEEN PRETENDIN' IT NEVER HAPPENED... DENYING REALITY... FOR YEARS NOW!

DIDN'T WORK, DID IT?

THERE'S SO MUCH I WANT TO REMEMBER-- AND SO MUCH I *CAN'T* REMEMBER!

CAN YOU IMAGINE WHAT KIND OF CONGRESSMAN I'D MAKE? SHOOT! THEY'D KICK ME, BUTT-FIRST, RIGHT OFF CAPITOL HILL!

4

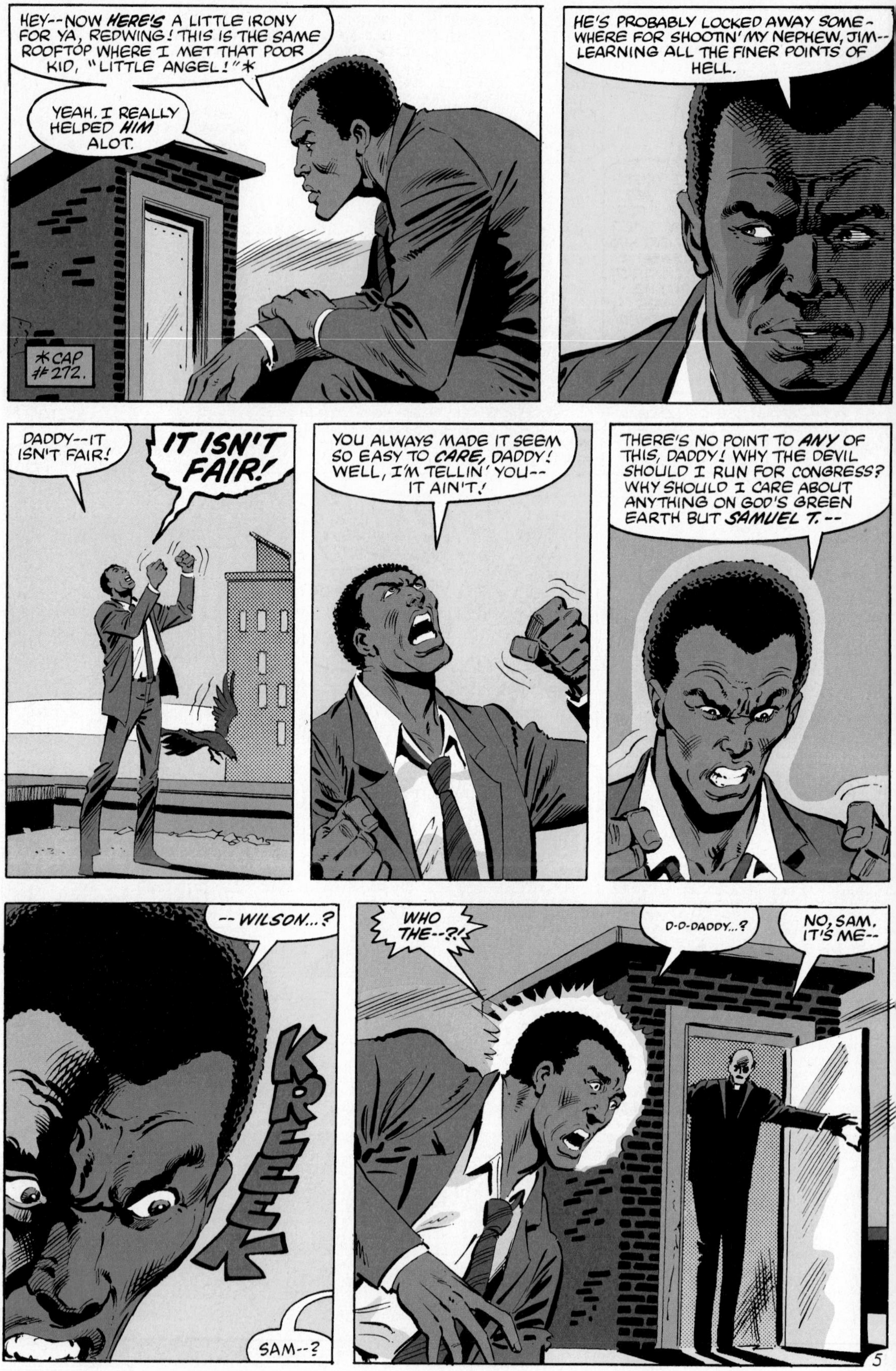
HEY--NOW HERE'S A LITTLE IRONY FOR YA, REDWING! THIS IS THE SAME ROOFTOP WHERE I MET THAT POOR KID, "LITTLE ANGEL!"*
YEAH. I REALLY HELPED HIM ALOT.
*CAP #272.
HE'S PROBABLY LOCKED AWAY SOMEWHERE FOR SHOOTIN' MY NEPHEW, JIM--LEARNING ALL THE FINER POINTS OF HELL.
DADDY--IT ISN'T FAIR!
IT ISN'T FAIR!
YOU ALWAYS MADE IT SEEM SO EASY TO CARE, DADDY! WELL, I'M TELLIN' YOU-- IT AIN'T!
THERE'S NO POINT TO ANY OF THIS, DADDY! WHY THE DEVIL SHOULD I RUN FOR CONGRESS? WHY SHOULD I CARE ABOUT ANYTHING ON GOD'S GREEN EARTH BUT SAMUEL T.--
--WILSON...?
KREEEK
SAM--?
WHO THE--?!
D-D-DADDY...?
NO, SAM. IT'S ME--
5

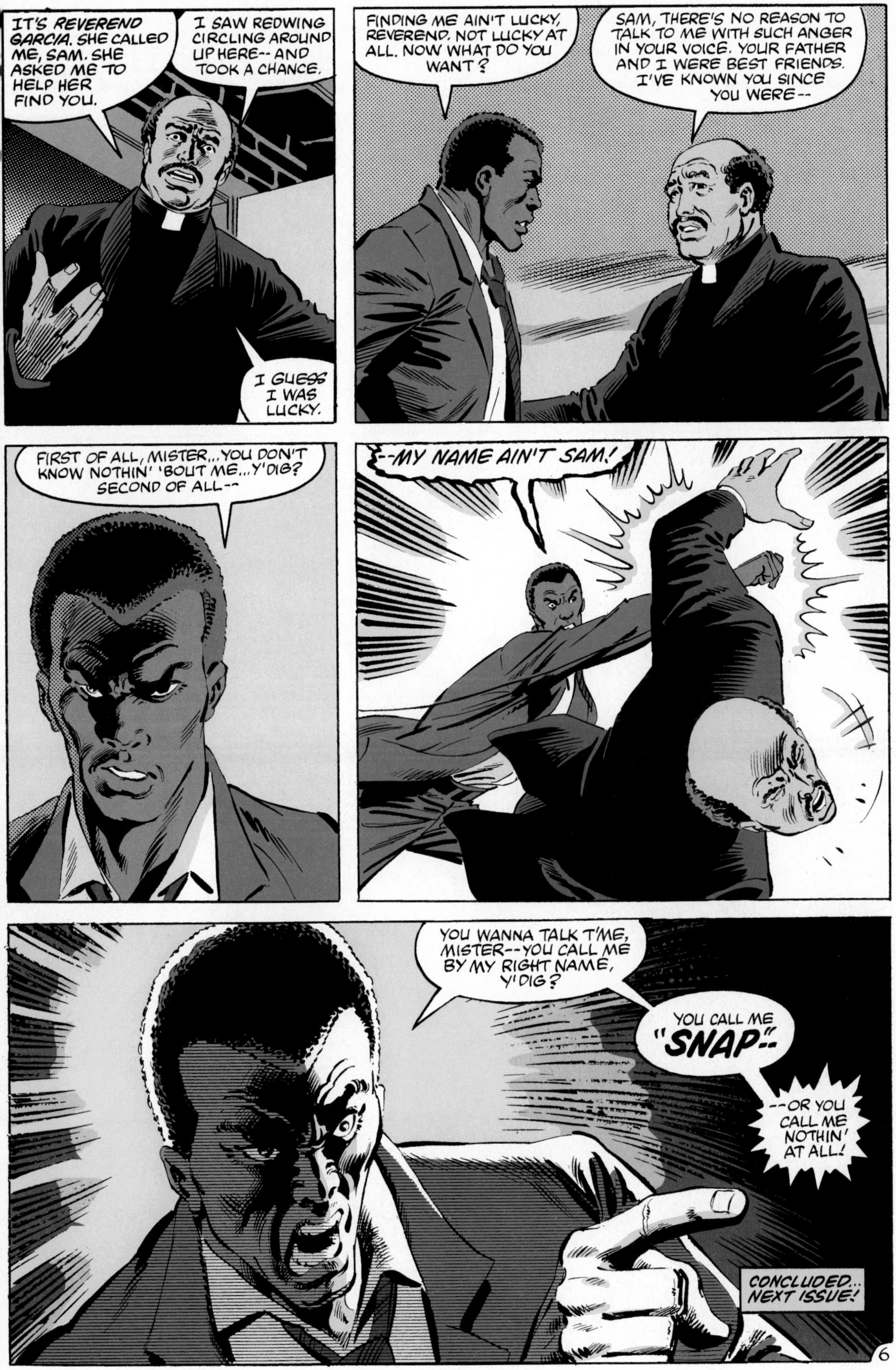

IT'S REVEREND GARCIA. SHE CALLED ME, SAM. SHE ASKED ME TO HELP HER FIND YOU.
I SAW REDWING CIRCLING AROUND UP HERE-- AND TOOK A CHANCE.
I GUESS I WAS LUCKY.
FINDING ME AIN'T LUCKY, REVEREND. NOT LUCKY AT ALL. NOW WHAT DO YOU WANT?
SAM, THERE'S NO REASON TO TALK TO ME WITH SUCH ANGER IN YOUR VOICE. YOUR FATHER AND I WERE BEST FRIENDS. I'VE KNOWN YOU SINCE YOU WERE--
FIRST OF ALL, MISTER... YOU DON'T KNOW NOTHIN' 'BOUT ME... Y'DIG? SECOND OF ALL--
--MY NAME AIN'T SAM!
YOU WANNA TALK T'ME, MISTER--YOU CALL ME BY MY RIGHT NAME, Y'DIG?
YOU CALL ME "SNAP"--
--OR YOU CALL ME NOTHIN' AT ALL!
CONCLUDED... NEXT ISSUE!
6

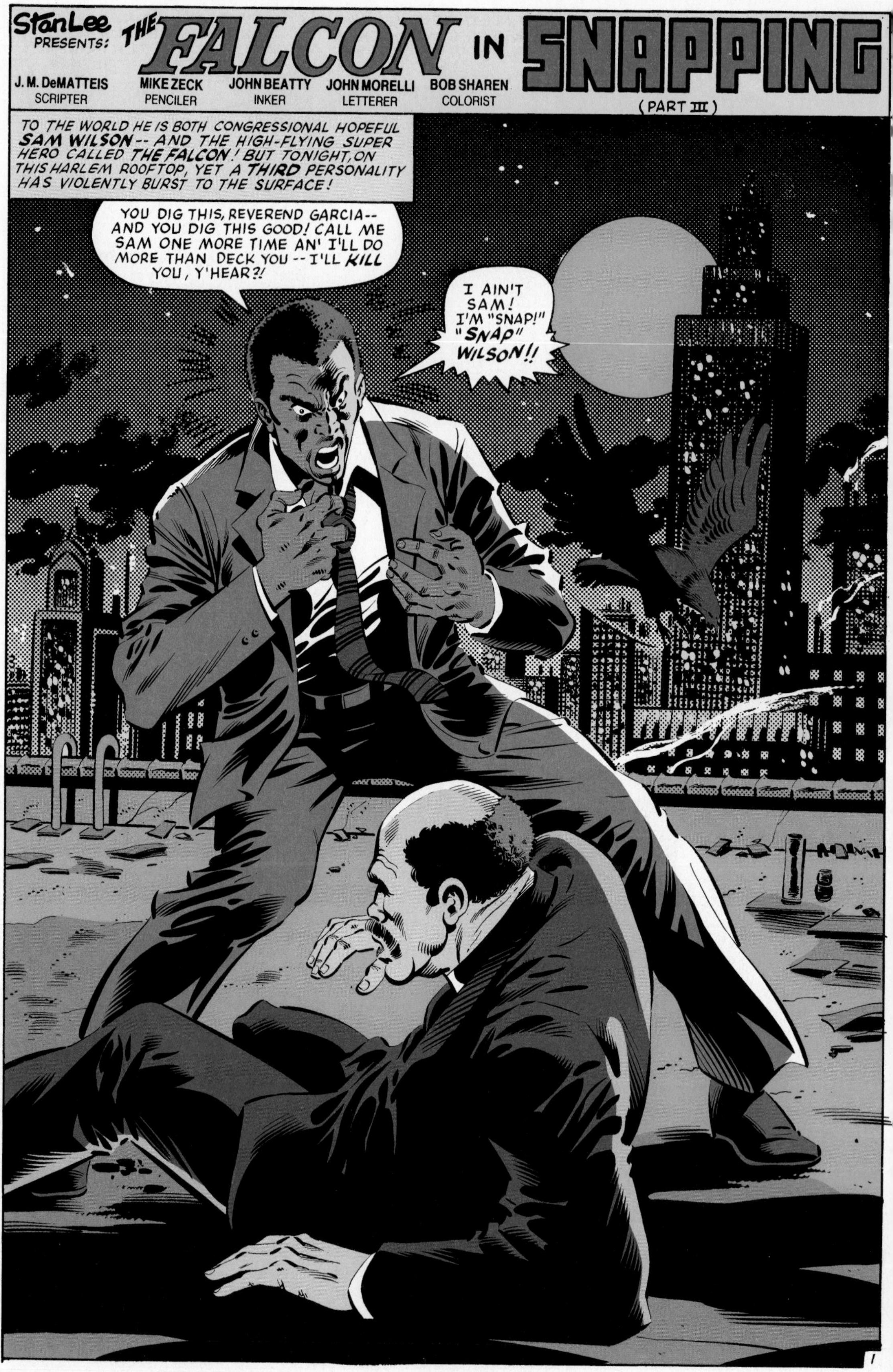
Stan Lee PRESENTS: THE FALCON IN SNAPPING
J. M. DeMATTEIS SCRIPTER
MIKE ZECK PENCILER
JOHN BEATTY INKER
JOHN MORELLI LETTERER
BOB SHAREN COLORIST
(PART III)
TO THE WORLD HE IS BOTH CONGRESSIONAL HOPEFUL SAM WILSON -- AND THE HIGH-FLYING SUPER HERO CALLED THE FALCON! BUT TONIGHT, ON THIS HARLEM ROOFTOP, YET A THIRD PERSONALITY HAS VIOLENTLY BURST TO THE SURFACE!
YOU DIG THIS, REVEREND GARCIA-- AND YOU DIG THIS GOOD! CALL ME SAM ONE MORE TIME AN' I'LL DO MORE THAN DECK YOU -- I'LL KILL YOU, Y'HEAR?!
I AIN'T SAM! I'M "SNAP!" "SNAP" WILSON!!
1

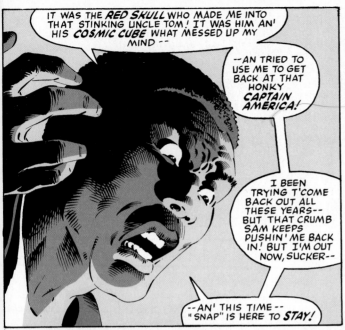

IT WAS THE *RED SKULL* WHO MADE ME INTO THAT STINKING UNCLE TOM! IT WAS HIM AN' HIS *COSMIC CUBE* WHAT MESSED UP MY MIND --

--AN' TRIED TO USE ME TO GET BACK AT THAT HONKY *CAPTAIN AMERICA!*

I BEEN TRYING T'COME BACK OUT ALL THESE YEARS-- BUT THAT CRUMB SAM KEEPS PUSHIN' ME BACK IN! BUT I'M OUT NOW, SUCKER--

--AN' THIS TIME -- "SNAP" IS HERE TO *STAY!*

NO. YOU ARE NOT THIS... "SNAP." IF THERE IS ANYTHING I KNOW FOR SURE-- IT IS THAT.

YOU...*CREATED* "SNAP"-- OUT OF PAIN... OUT OF FEAR ... WHEN FIRST YOUR FATHER, THEN YOUR MOTHER, WERE TAKEN FROM YOU BY SENSELESS ACTS OF VIOLENCE.

BUT THAT IS *NOT* WHO YOU ARE, SAM!

GARCIA--

--YOU TALKIN' CRAZY!!

SMAK

DID THAT GIVE YOU SATISFACTION, SAM? DID THAT MAKE YOU FEEL ANY BETTER?

2

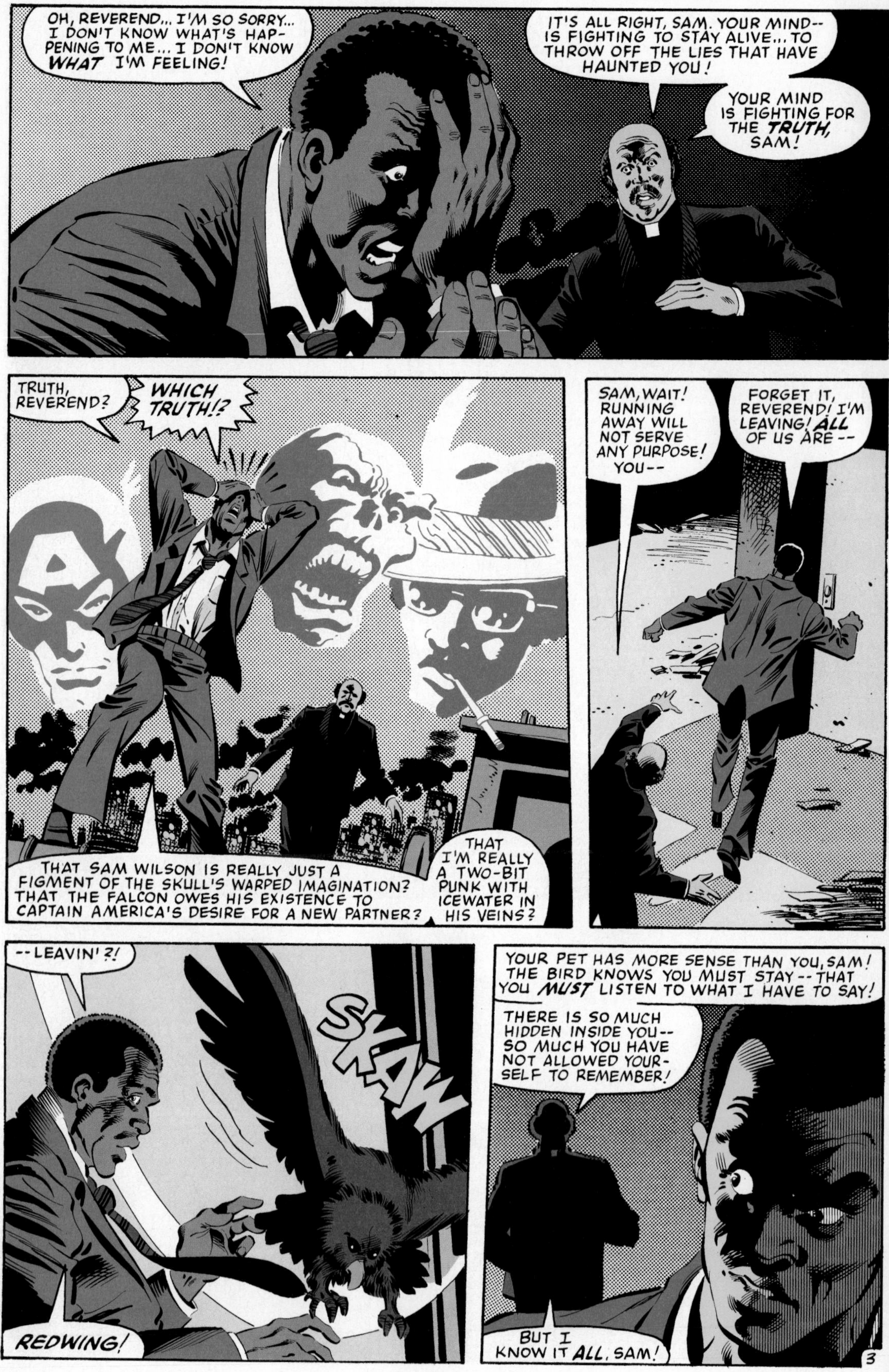
OH, REVEREND... I'M SO SORRY... I DON'T KNOW WHAT'S HAPPENING TO ME... I DON'T KNOW WHAT I'M FEELING!
IT'S ALL RIGHT, SAM. YOUR MIND-- IS FIGHTING TO STAY ALIVE... TO THROW OFF THE LIES THAT HAVE HAUNTED YOU!
YOUR MIND IS FIGHTING FOR THE TRUTH, SAM!
TRUTH, REVEREND?
WHICH TRUTH!?
THAT SAM WILSON IS REALLY JUST A FIGMENT OF THE SKULL'S WARPED IMAGINATION? THAT THE FALCON OWES HIS EXISTENCE TO CAPTAIN AMERICA'S DESIRE FOR A NEW PARTNER?
THAT I'M REALLY A TWO-BIT PUNK WITH ICEWATER IN HIS VEINS?
SAM, WAIT! RUNNING AWAY WILL NOT SERVE ANY PURPOSE! YOU--
FORGET IT, REVEREND! I'M LEAVING! ALL OF US ARE --
--LEAVIN'?!
SKAW
REDWING!
YOUR PET HAS MORE SENSE THAN YOU, SAM! THE BIRD KNOWS YOU MUST STAY -- THAT YOU MUST LISTEN TO WHAT I HAVE TO SAY!
THERE IS SO MUCH HIDDEN INSIDE YOU-- SO MUCH YOU HAVE NOT ALLOWED YOURSELF TO REMEMBER!
BUT I KNOW IT ALL, SAM!
3

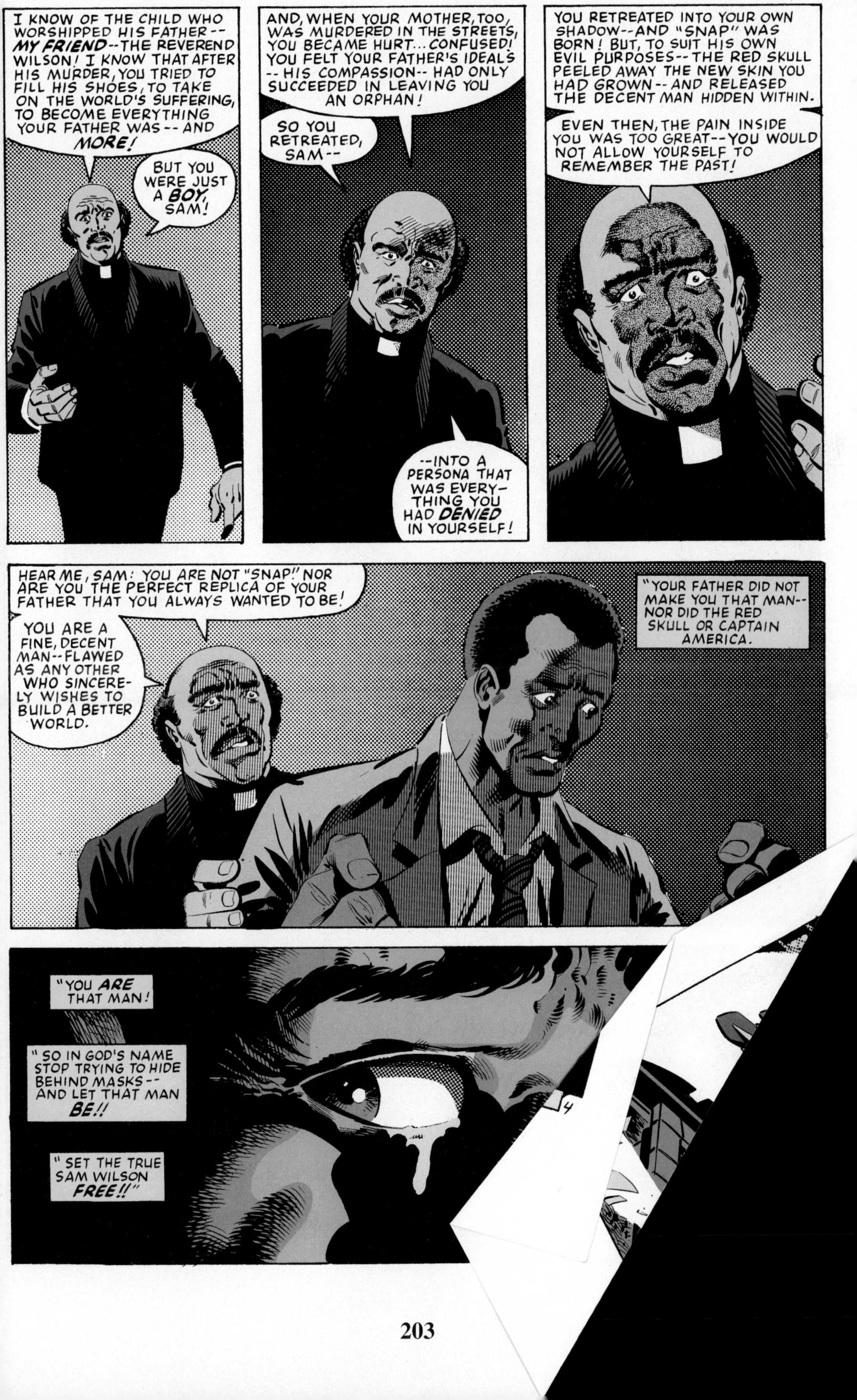

I KNOW OF THE CHILD WHO WORSHIPPED HIS FATHER -- MY FRIEND -- THE REVEREND WILSON! I KNOW THAT AFTER HIS MURDER, YOU TRIED TO FILL HIS SHOES, TO TAKE ON THE WORLD'S SUFFERING, TO BECOME EVERYTHING YOUR FATHER WAS -- AND MORE!
BUT YOU WERE JUST A BOY, SAM!
AND, WHEN YOUR MOTHER, TOO, WAS MURDERED IN THE STREETS, YOU BECAME HURT... CONFUSED! YOU FELT YOUR FATHER'S IDEALS -- HIS COMPASSION -- HAD ONLY SUCCEEDED IN LEAVING YOU AN ORPHAN!
SO YOU RETREATED, SAM --
--INTO A PERSONA THAT WAS EVERYTHING YOU HAD DENIED IN YOURSELF!
YOU RETREATED INTO YOUR OWN SHADOW -- AND "SNAP" WAS BORN! BUT, TO SUIT HIS OWN EVIL PURPOSES -- THE RED SKULL PEELED AWAY THE NEW SKIN YOU HAD GROWN -- AND RELEASED THE DECENT MAN HIDDEN WITHIN.
EVEN THEN, THE PAIN INSIDE YOU WAS TOO GREAT -- YOU WOULD NOT ALLOW YOURSELF TO REMEMBER THE PAST!
HEAR ME, SAM: YOU ARE NOT "SNAP!" NOR ARE YOU THE PERFECT REPLICA OF YOUR FATHER THAT YOU ALWAYS WANTED TO BE!
YOU ARE A FINE, DECENT MAN -- FLAWED AS ANY OTHER WHO SINCERELY WISHES TO BUILD A BETTER WORLD.
"YOUR FATHER DID NOT MAKE YOU THAT MAN -- NOR DID THE RED SKULL OR CAPTAIN AMERICA.
"YOU ARE THAT MAN!
"SO IN GOD'S NAME STOP TRYING TO HIDE BEHIND MASKS -- AND LET THAT MAN BE!!
"SET THE TRUE SAM WILSON FREE!!"

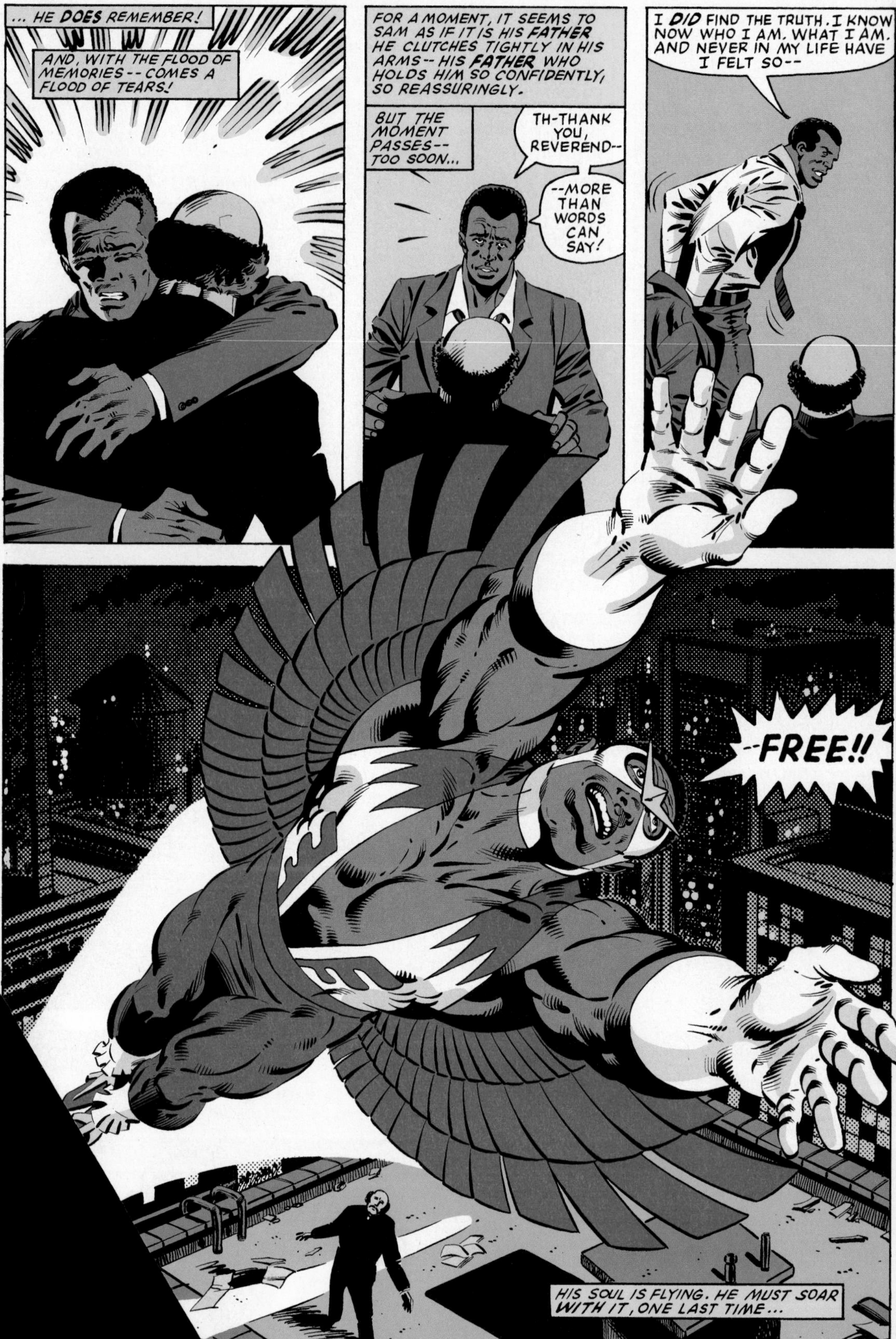
... HE DOES REMEMBER!
AND, WITH THE FLOOD OF MEMORIES -- COMES A FLOOD OF TEARS!
FOR A MOMENT, IT SEEMS TO SAM AS IF IT IS HIS FATHER HE CLUTCHES TIGHTLY IN HIS ARMS -- HIS FATHER WHO HOLDS HIM SO CONFIDENTLY, SO REASSURINGLY.
BUT THE MOMENT PASSES -- TOO SOON...
TH-THANK YOU, REVEREND--
--MORE THAN WORDS CAN SAY!
I DID FIND THE TRUTH. I KNOW NOW WHO I AM. WHAT I AM. AND NEVER IN MY LIFE HAVE I FELT SO--
--FREE!!
HIS SOUL IS FLYING. HE MUST SOAR WITH IT, ONE LAST TIME...
... HE MUST SOAR WITH IT.
5

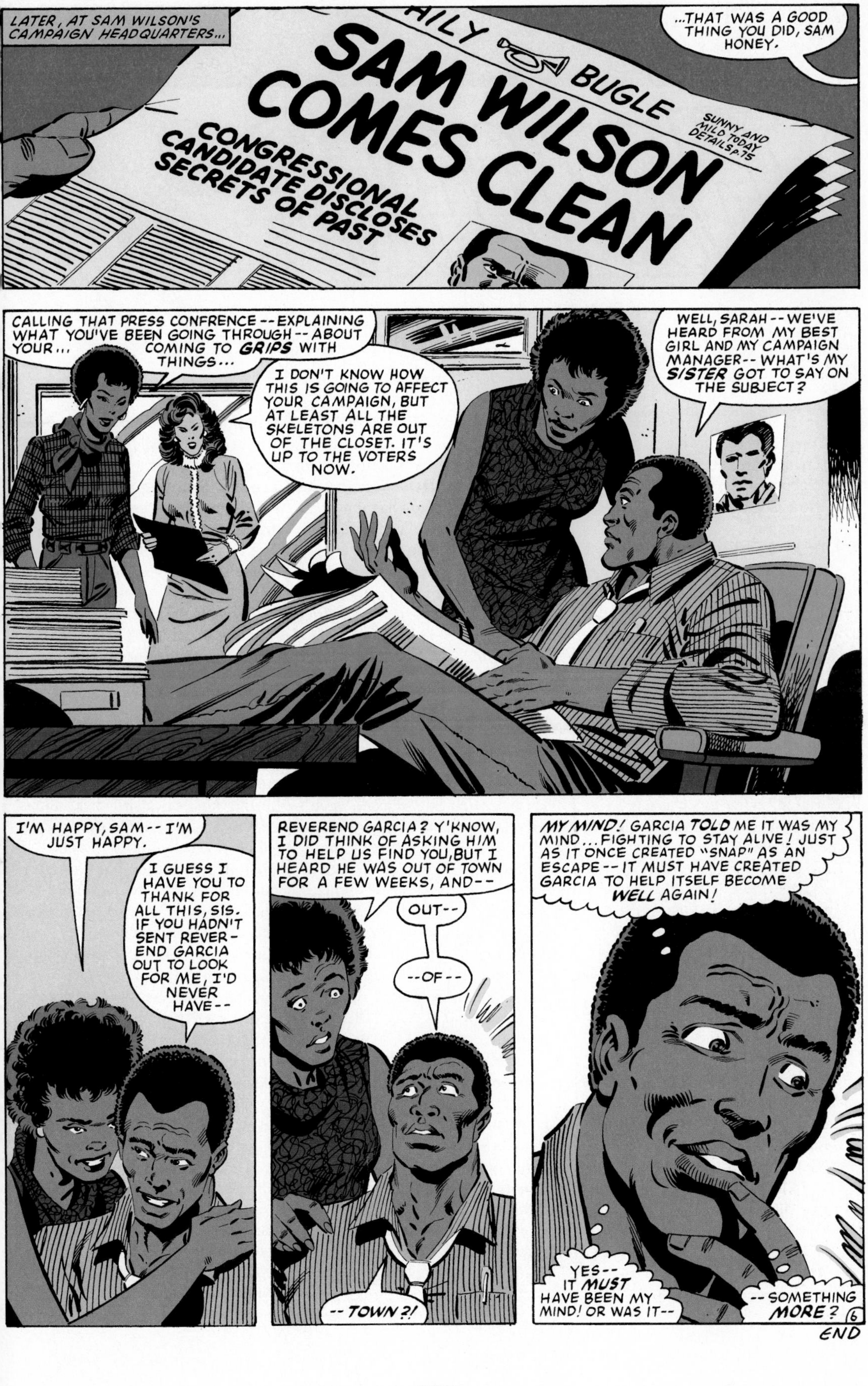
LATER, AT SAM WILSON'S CAMPAIGN HEADQUARTERS...
HILY BUGLE
SAM WILSON COMES CLEAN
CONGRESSIONAL CANDIDATE DISCLOSES SECRETS OF PAST
SUNNY AND MILD TODAY DETAILS P. 75
...THAT WAS A GOOD THING YOU DID, SAM HONEY.
CALLING THAT PRESS CONFRENCE -- EXPLAINING WHAT YOU'VE BEEN GOING THROUGH -- ABOUT YOUR... COMING TO GRIPS WITH THINGS...
I DON'T KNOW HOW THIS IS GOING TO AFFECT YOUR CAMPAIGN, BUT AT LEAST ALL THE SKELETONS ARE OUT OF THE CLOSET. IT'S UP TO THE VOTERS NOW.
WELL, SARAH -- WE'VE HEARD FROM MY BEST GIRL AND MY CAMPAIGN MANAGER -- WHAT'S MY SISTER GOT TO SAY ON THE SUBJECT?
I'M HAPPY, SAM -- I'M JUST HAPPY.
I GUESS I HAVE YOU TO THANK FOR ALL THIS, SIS. IF YOU HADN'T SENT REVER-END GARCIA OUT TO LOOK FOR ME, I'D NEVER HAVE--
REVEREND GARCIA? Y'KNOW, I DID THINK OF ASKING HIM TO HELP US FIND YOU, BUT I HEARD HE WAS OUT OF TOWN FOR A FEW WEEKS, AND--
OUT--
--OF--
--TOWN?!
MY MIND! GARCIA TOLD ME IT WAS MY MIND... FIGHTING TO STAY ALIVE! JUST AS IT ONCE CREATED "SNAP" AS AN ESCAPE -- IT MUST HAVE CREATED GARCIA TO HELP ITSELF BECOME WELL AGAIN!
YES-- IT MUST HAVE BEEN MY MIND! OR WAS IT--
--SOMETHING MORE?
6
END

CREATING A NEW LIMITED SERIES

THE FALCON

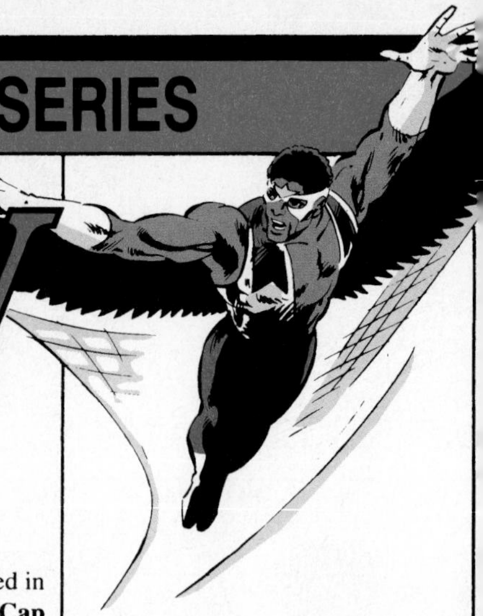

by Jim Owsley

In the ghetto
You're on your own
Dying is easy
Nobody cares, and
No one will save you...
...but him.

Dick Gregory, a well-known black comedian and political activist, once said he'd gone to dine at a racist restaurant in the south. When the waiter brought him his meal, a roast chicken, Dick found himself surrounded by several local citizens of the redneck persuasion. These gentlemen told Dick that whatever he did to that chicken on his plate, they would in turn do to him. He said, "You gentlemen mean to tell me that whatever I do to this chicken," I'm paraphrasing here, "no matter what it is, you'll do the same to me?" The redneck gentlemen reaffirmed their statement. Well, this presented Dick with a unique opportunity; one that doesn't present itself very often. Here was a solid opportunity for Dick to make a bold statement and leave a solid impression on these people. Without another word, Dick picked up the succulent bird in both hands, and kissed it.

The Falcon has long been a mainstay of the Marvel Universe. Created in 1969 by **Stan Lee** and **Gene Colan, the Falcon** made a name for himself within the pages of CAPTAIN AMERICA. For nine years, **the Falcon** teamed with **Cap** against the likes of **the Red Skull, Dr. Faustus, Batroc the Leaper,** and even **Spider-Man**. For over a hundred issues (CAPTAIN AMERICA #117-222) **the Falcon** shared in **Cap's** many adventures, until **Cap** left **Falcon** in charge of a fledgling group of super heroes, and took off to explore his past. Aside from short stints in both **the Defenders** and **the Avengers, the Falcon** has almost retired from the Marvel Universe. That is, of course, until now.

The Falcon's real name is **Sam Wilson**. Sam is a social worker who lives and works in the Harlem district of Manhattan, N.Y. To me, there's a whole world of possibilities presented within just those two sentences. Harlem is full of life and energy. It's not the den of iniquity cum enter-if-you-dare-kill-whitey type of place some people seem to think it is. Likewise, black people (especially black women) aren't nearly as loud, rude, angry, and/or violent as some people may think. I've been to Harlem, and I know more than my fair share of black people, so take it from me. I look at this series as my chance, my unique opportunity to try to explode a few of the many ridiculous stereotypes some people have placed on entire segments of our society. This is an opportunity that doesn't often present itself; a chance to take Marvel readers into **the Falcon's** world.

There's obviously more to the man than meets the eye. The truth is, **the Falcon** is a social worker in costume as well as out of it. He cares. That's the entire key to **the Falcon's** character; he cares. He cares about his friends, his neighbors, kids in trouble; anybody who needs help. The street people are his people. The young kids strung out on booze or drugs or running with gangs – those whom society would prefer to just ignore or wish away – are his prime concern. Sam Wilson is a well-educated man. He doesn't have to be a social worker, and he doesn't have to live in a poor neighborhood. But he stays. He stays because he's chosen to.

Living in the ghetto means always wanting to get out. Ask anyone who lives in a ghetto what their long range plans are. Nobody likes living in a ghetto. Living in a ghetto usually means your parents were poor and you were born poor. You grow up poor, live poor, and will probably die poor. Blacks in particular struggle on in this kind of environment almost like a society within a society. Unemployment in the U.S. may be officially listed at 10%, but the figures for blacks read more like 28%. The unemployment rate for black teenagers is an incredible 49%. Each summer schools in poor neighborhoods turn a mass of teenaged youths out onto the streets who have nothing to do. All day, all night. Nothing to do. Just waiting. I know about this first hand; I lived through it. This sort of living can give you an intense feeling of hopelessness and despair. A lot of these kids feel the need for some kind of escape. Some turn to crime. Some turn to drugs. Some try suicide.

These are the people **the Falcon** is out to save. Ever the idealist, **Falcon** refuses to admit there's no hope and likewise refuses to allow his young contemporaries to do so. Don't give

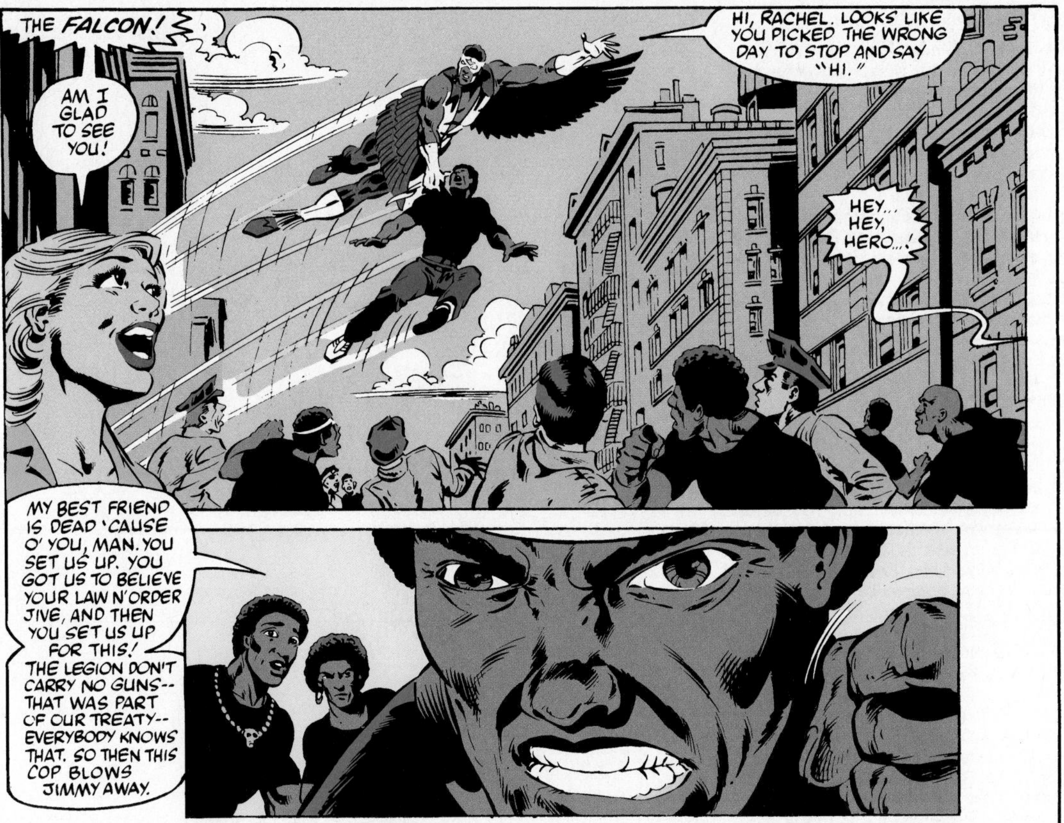
THE FALCON!
AM I GLAD TO SEE YOU!
HI, RACHEL. LOOKS LIKE YOU PICKED THE WRONG DAY TO STOP AND SAY "HI."
HEY... HEY, HERO...!
MY BEST FRIEND IS DEAD 'CAUSE O' YOU, MAN. YOU SET US UP. YOU GOT US TO BELIEVE YOUR LAW N' ORDER JIVE, AND THEN YOU SET US UP FOR THIS! THE LEGION DON'T CARRY NO GUNS-- THAT WAS PART OF OUR TREATY-- EVERYBODY KNOWS THAT. SO THEN THIS COP BLOWS JIMMY AWAY.

Here's a sizzling sample of the dramatic dialogue and drawing from the second issue of THE FALCON (Limited Series).

up. Both as Sam Wilson and as **the Falcon**, our hero works within this atmosphere every day, trying to keep these kids straight. **Falc's** identity is public record, thanks to a much-publicized trial, so he's accessible to these people 24 hours a day. If they're not jamming his office at the U.S Department of Social Services, then they're waiting for him on his fire escape at home. The Falcon has played a broad, no-holds-barred role in gaining the confidence and trust of the local residents, especially the kids. He's paid some heavy dues to win this trust.

In this series, you'll see just how heavy those dues were. Through no fault of his own, **Falc** fails to keep a promise to one of the local youth gangs and, as a result, one of their members is killed. The bond is broken. The trust is gone. Gang hostilities towards the police and local citizens escalate to the point where the president of the United States becomes involved. Touring Harlem on a "fact-finding" mission, the president is kidnapped by the street gang who call themselves **The Legion. The Falcon** is then placed in the no-win situation of having to not only rescue the president, but regain the Legion's trust amidst a sea of federal agents all looking to have these kids' collective head on a platter. Pressure like this would most certainly do in a half-baked writer like me, but the **Falcon**... well, let's just say that he doesn't believe in no-win situations.

I'm real happy about this issue. I'm really happy **Paul Smith** penciled the first issue. Paul is a remarkably talented guy who imbued the first issue with tons of atmosphere and characters who literally lept off the page, grabbed by pen, and wrote their own lines. And all this from an L.A. fair-haired beach bum, no less. When Paul could no longer find time in his schedule to continue penciling this series (he'd signed on to do the **X-Men**), I found lightning does strike twice.

Mark Bright wandered into **Jim Shooter's** office with a proposal for a **Falcon** Limited Series, and Shooter quickly hustled him down the hall to me. The rest is magic. Mark and I really had a lot of fun putting this series together. I'm confident that Mark is going to be a very hot property in the comics business in a very short time. Mark's already made a name for himself among science fiction paperback book publishers for his stunning cover paintings. He has a keen sense of storytelling with a flair for the dramatic. He adds little "bits" to my plot outlines (I love artists who make me look good), gives me grief about artistic detail, and generally puts about 900% into this series.

This, then, is my golden opportunity. That once in a lifetime chance to make a bold statement and leave a solid impression on your peers. Like Dick Gregory's chicken. I can only hope that my performance was as admirable in its own way as his. Cluck. Cluck.

FALCON

Real Name: Samuel Wilson
Occupation: Social worker, adventurer
Identity: Publicly known
Legal status: American citizen with criminal record
Former aliases: "Snap" Wilson
Place of birth: Harlem, New York
Marital status: Single
Known relatives: Paul (father, deceased), Darlene (mother, deceased), Sarah Casper (sister), Jody Casper (nephew), Jim nephew)
Group affiliation: Former Avenger, former partner of Captain America
Base of operations: New York City
First appearance: CAPTAIN AMERICA #117
Origin: CAPTAIN AMERICA #117, 186
History: Sam Wilson is the son of a dedicated and influential minister in Harlem who died trying to stop a street fight. Sam idolized his father and tried to emulate his selfless humanitarianism after his death. But when his mother was killed by a mugger two years later, Sam's grief and anger consumed him. Severely depressed, Sam Wilson's personality changed. No longer was he a concerned community volunteer, but a self-serving racketeer who called himself "Snap." En route from a mob assignment in Rio de Janeiro, Wilson's plane crashed on the Caribbean island run by the Exiles, a band of professional killers who were accomplices of the Red Skull (see *Deceased: Red Skull, Appendix: Exiles*). The Skull used the powers of the Cosmic Cube to transform "Snap" back into Sam, in order to use him as a pawn against Captain America, who was at that time trapped on the island (see *Captain America, Appendix: Cosmic Cube*). The Skull reasoned that Wilson's former idealism would appeal to the Captain enough that he would train him as a partner. Then, at some later date, the Skull could use him against his enemy if his current attack failed.

Wilson had always had a remarkable talent for handling birds, especially Redwing, a hunting falcon that he acquired in Rio. The Skull used the Cosmic Cube to strengthen their rapport into a permanent supernormal mental link, giving Wilson yet another qualification for being Captain America's partner. With the Captain's assistance and training, Wilson defeated the Exiles and assumed the costumed identity of the Falcon. Returning to Harlem, Wilson's "Snap" identity remained submerged until some years later when he recalled his criminal past while undergoing shock therapy at SHIELD headquarters (see *SHIELD*). Later still, Wilson underwent an identity crisis while running for Congress and came to terms with his ignominious past.

The Falcon had been solely a rooftop-swinging athlete until the Black Panther, king of the African nation of Wakanda, provided him with Wakandan technology that enabled him to fly (see *Black Panther*). The Falcon is currently one of Harlem's staunchest crimefighters.

Height: 6′ 2″ **Weight:** 240 lbs
Eyes: Brown **Hair:** Black
Strength level: The Falcon possesses the normal human strength of a man of his age, height, and build who engages in intensive regular exercise.
Known superhuman powers: None.

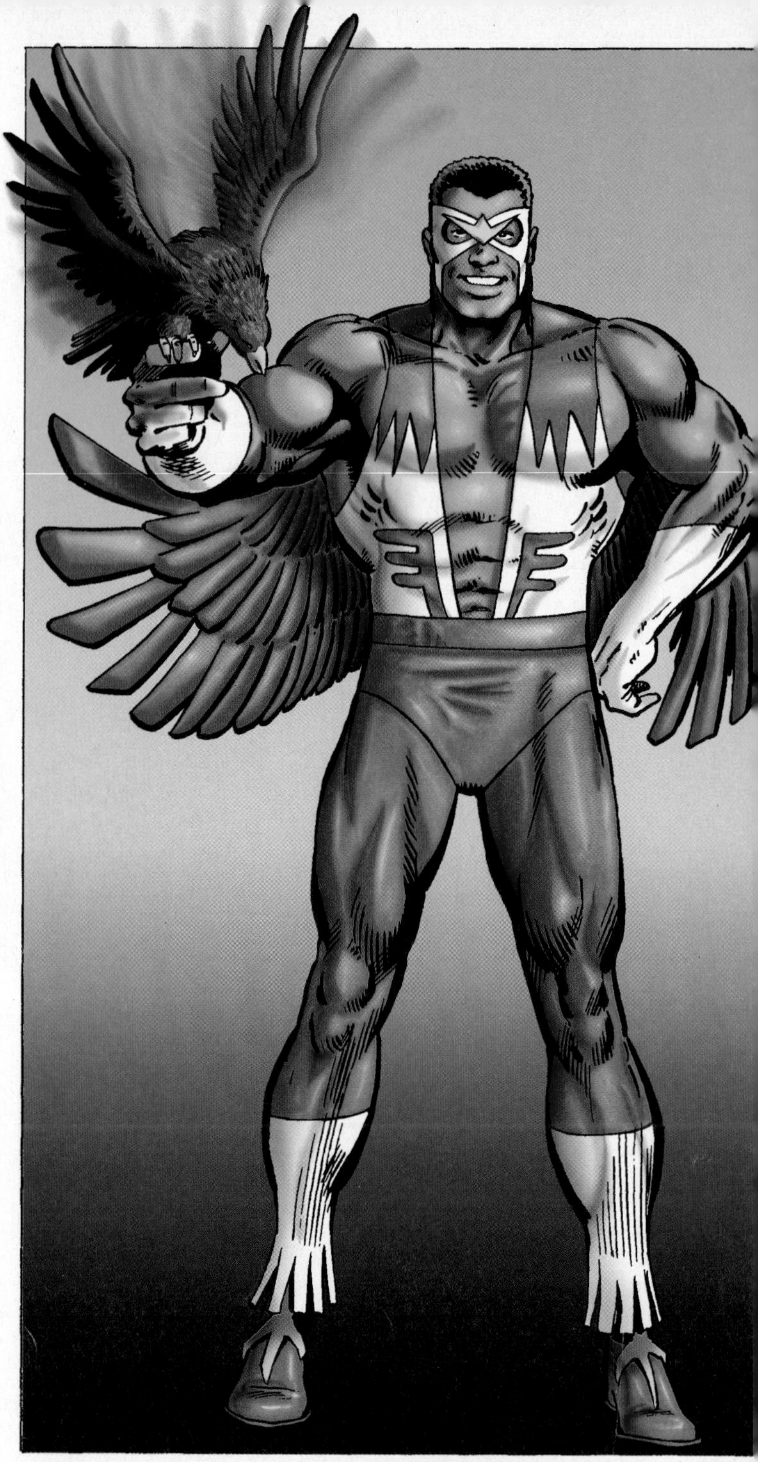

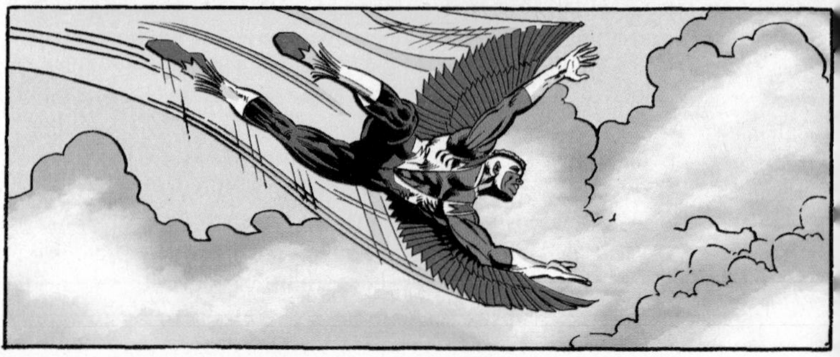

Official Handbook of the Marvel Universe: Deluxe Edition #4 profile

bilities: The Falcon is an excellent trainer f wild birds and has developed an almost-mpathic relationship with his hunting alcon Redwing.

The Falcon is a natural athlete and un-rmed combatant who has been trained by aptain America in gymnastics and martial rts.

araphernalia: The Falcon can fly by eans of his jet-powered glider wings hich extend beneath his arms from his rists to his waist. Made of lightweight anium ribbing and mylar, the wings are overed with wafer-thin, high-efficiency olar power receptors which convert sunght into electricity that power an array of miniature high-speed electric turbine fans. These engines are arranged along the edge of the Falcon's secondary "feathers" and are incorporated in his boots. The entire system is linked by cybernetic circuitry on the inside of his mask, giving him mental control over the operation of the jets. Thus, the Falcon can control his speed and flight attitude by throttling clusters of engines. The aerodynamic configuration of both his glider-wings and his own body also aid in his maneuverability. The solar-cells constantly operate in the presence of sunlight and charge a series of exotic, high-capacity micro-batteries that line several glider-wing struts. The batteries have a useful output over an 11.8 hour period, meaning the Falcon could fly for up to 11.8 hours on stored energy before it was depleted.

The maximum speed the powered glider-wing assembly can attain is about 250 miles per hour while the maximum practical speed at which the Falcon can still breathe is about 140 miles per hour. With a constant solar input, the solar-cell / charger / micro turbo-fan system could run indefinitely, with its only limitations being wear and tear on engine parts and the Falcon's extended arms having to resist the airstream. The maximum altitude the Falcon can reach and still breathe unaided is 24,000 feet. ■

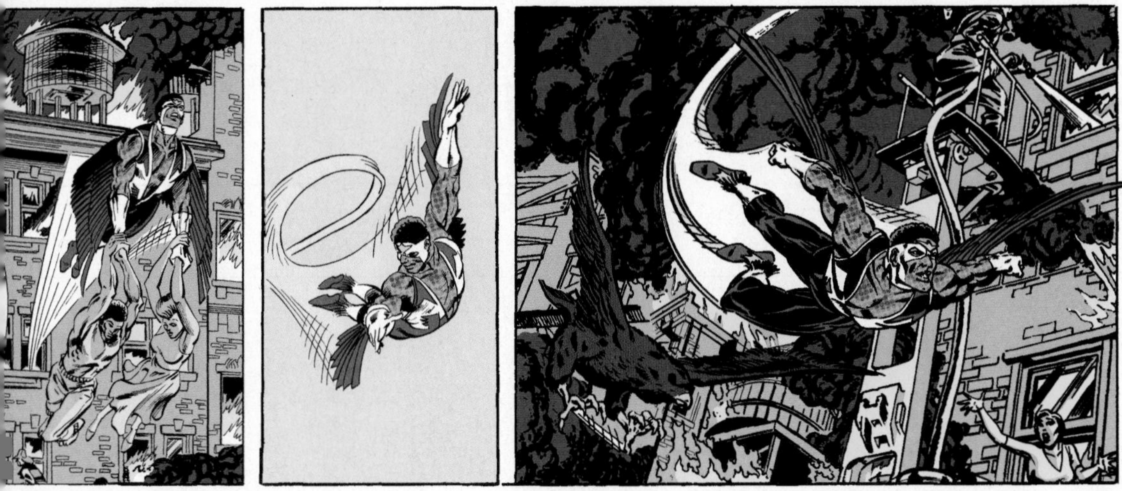

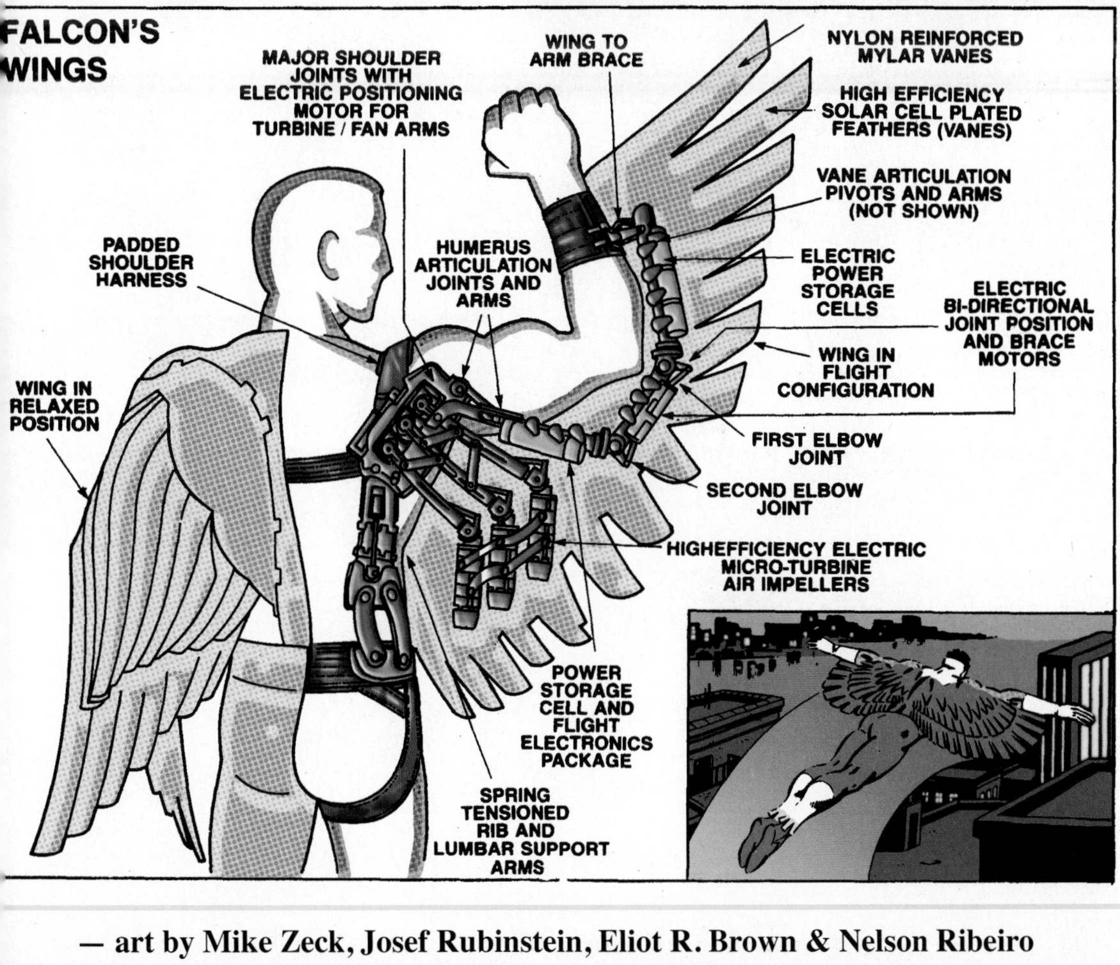

FALCON'S WINGS
MAJOR SHOULDER JOINTS WITH ELECTRIC POSITIONING MOTOR FOR TURBINE / FAN ARMS
WING TO ARM BRACE
NYLON REINFORCED MYLAR VANES
HIGH EFFICIENCY SOLAR CELL PLATED FEATHERS (VANES)
VANE ARTICULATION PIVOTS AND ARMS (NOT SHOWN)
PADDED SHOULDER HARNESS
HUMERUS ARTICULATION JOINTS AND ARMS
ELECTRIC POWER STORAGE CELLS
ELECTRIC BI-DIRECTIONAL JOINT POSITION AND BRACE MOTORS
WING IN FLIGHT CONFIGURATION
WING IN RELAXED POSITION
FIRST ELBOW JOINT
SECOND ELBOW JOINT
HIGHEFFICIENCY ELECTRIC MICRO-TURBINE AIR IMPELLERS
POWER STORAGE CELL AND FLIGHT ELECTRONICS PACKAGE
SPRING TENSIONED RIB AND LUMBAR SUPPORT ARMS

— art by Mike Zeck, Josef Rubinstein, Eliot R. Brown & Nelson Ribeiro

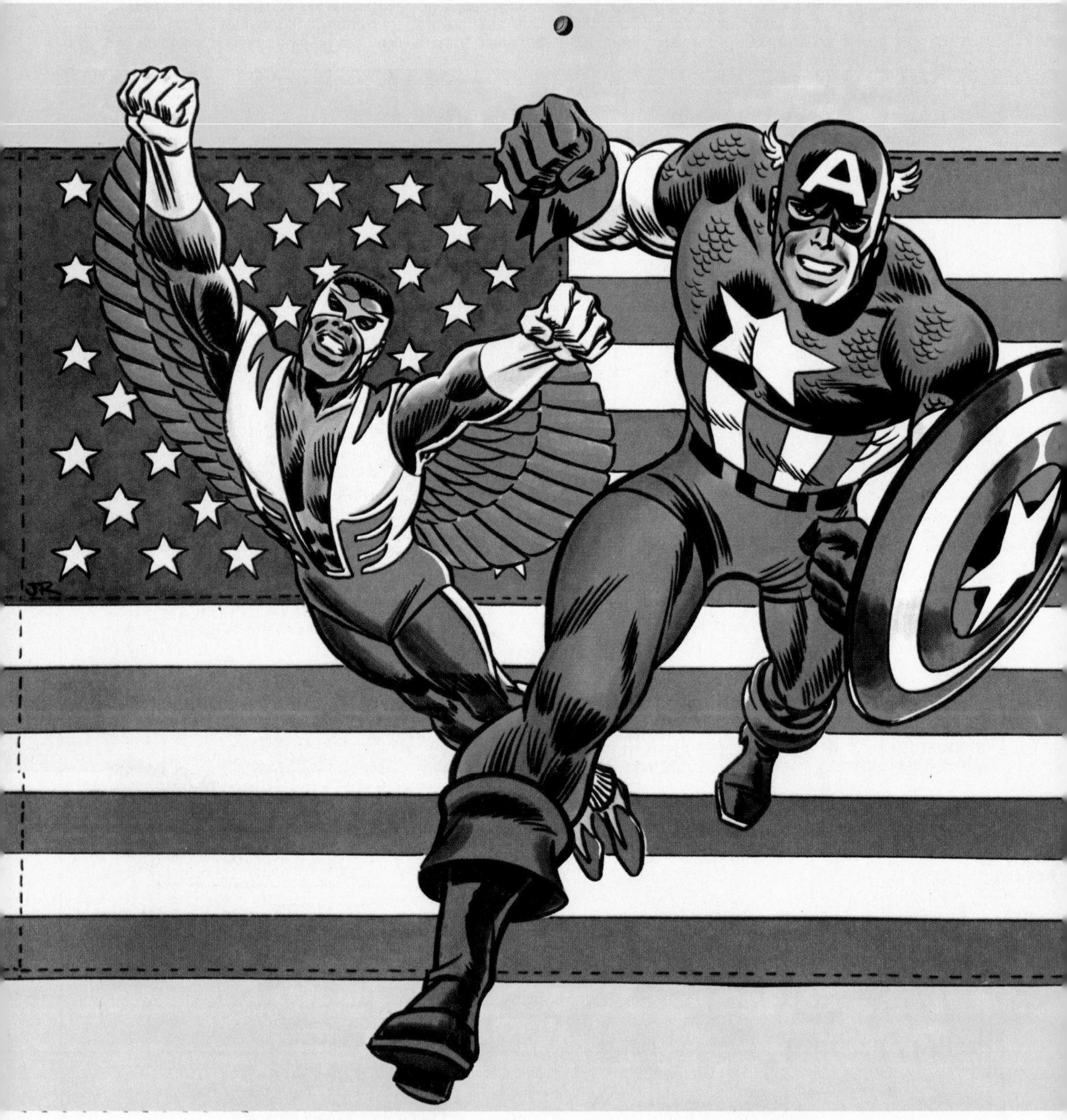
JR

Mighty Marvel Calendar 1975 **art by John Romita Sr.**

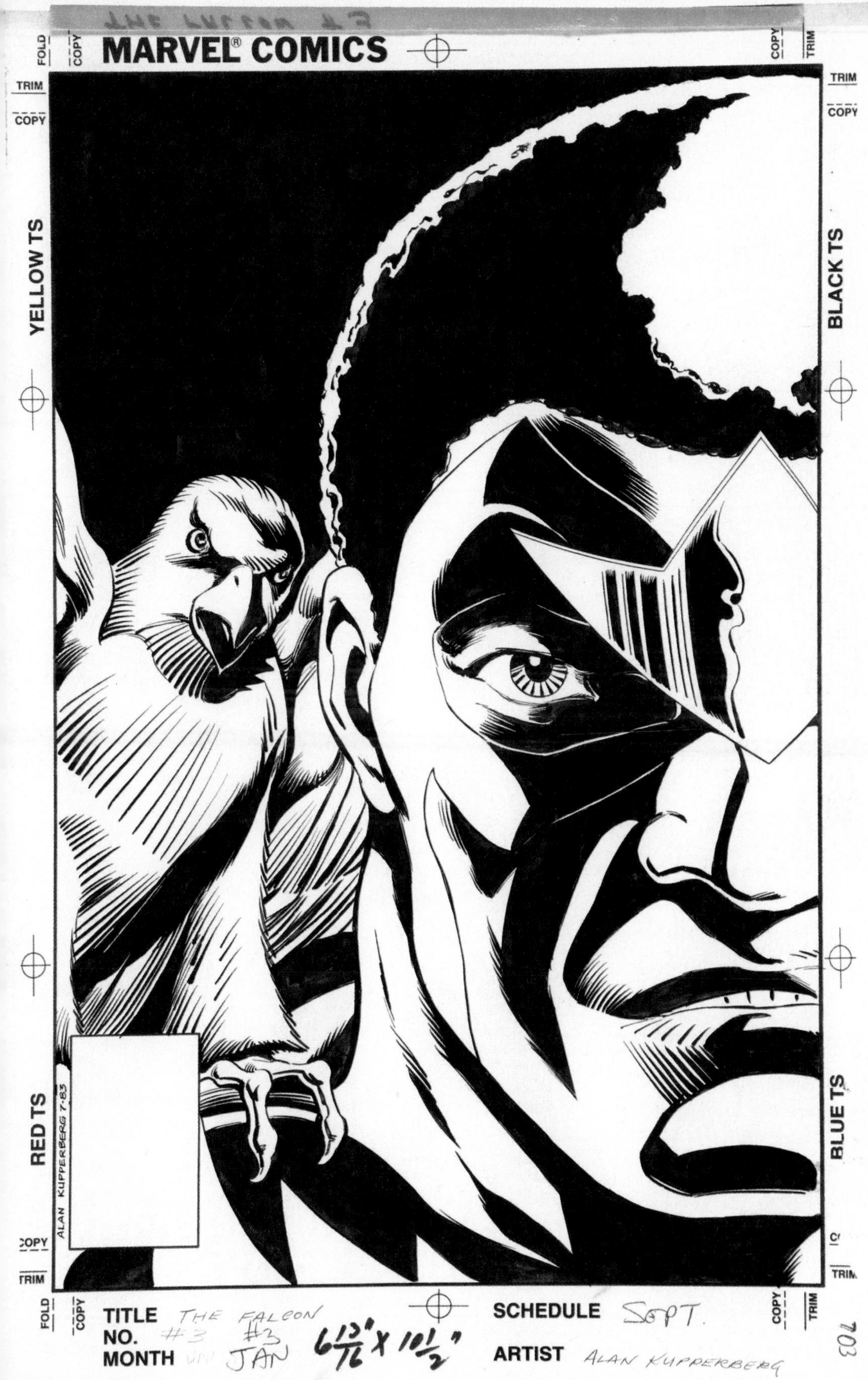
MARVEL® COMICS
FOLD
COPY
TRIM
YELLOW TS
BLACK TS
RED TS
BLUE TS
ALAN KUPPERBERG 7-83
TITLE THE FALCON
NO. #3 #3
MONTH JAN
6 13/16" x 10 1/2"
SCHEDULE SEPT.
ARTIST ALAN KUPPERBERG

Falcon #3 **cover art by Alan Kupperberg**

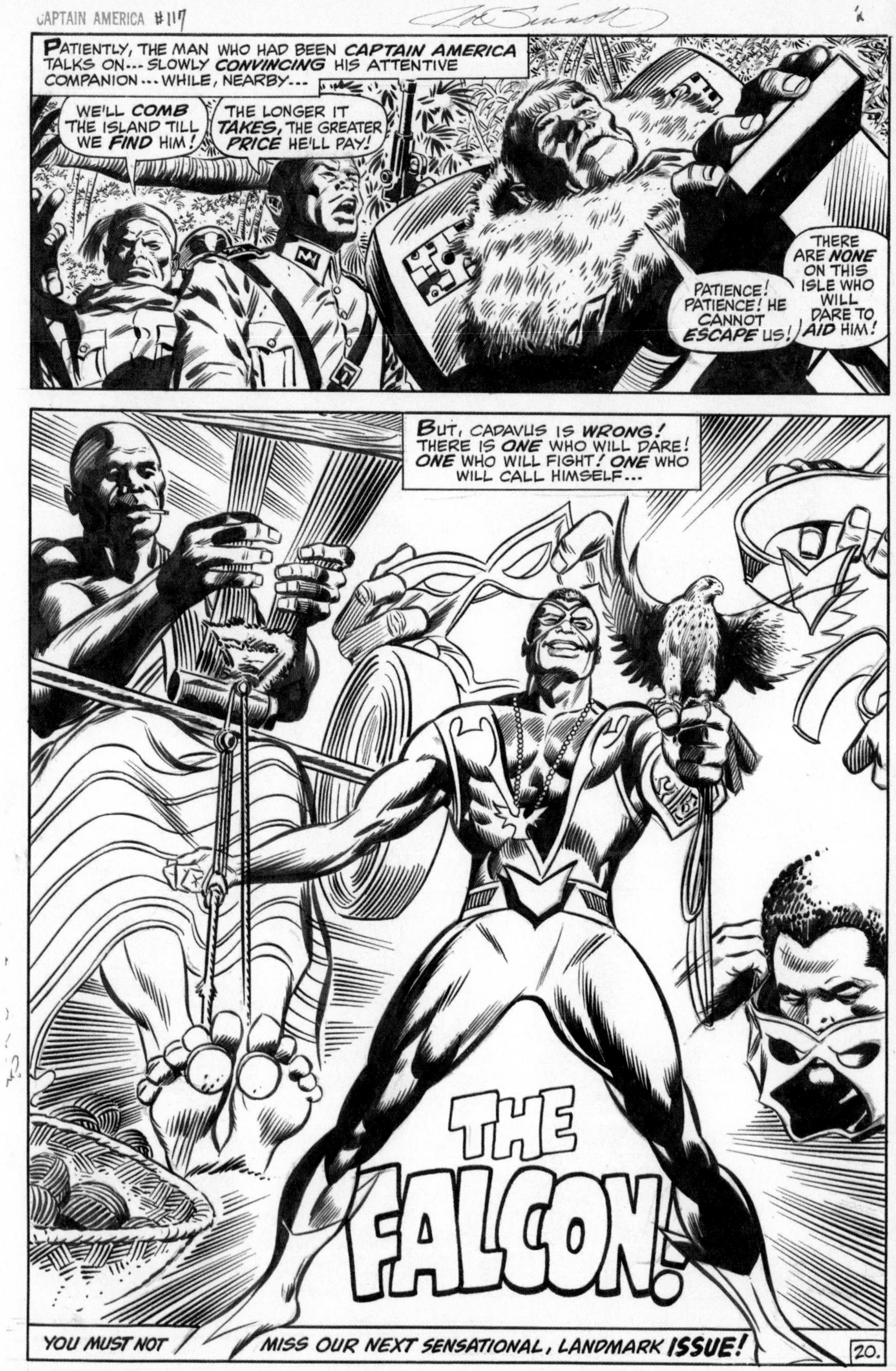
CAPTAIN AMERICA #117
PATIENTLY, THE MAN WHO HAD BEEN CAPTAIN AMERICA TALKS ON... SLOWLY CONVINCING HIS ATTENTIVE COMPANION... WHILE, NEARBY...
WE'LL COMB THE ISLAND TILL WE FIND HIM!
THE LONGER IT TAKES, THE GREATER PRICE HE'LL PAY!
PATIENCE! PATIENCE! HE CANNOT ESCAPE US!
THERE ARE NONE ON THIS ISLE WHO WILL DARE TO AID HIM!
BUT, CADAVUS IS WRONG! THERE IS ONE WHO WILL DARE! ONE WHO WILL FIGHT! ONE WHO WILL CALL HIMSELF...
THE FALCON!
YOU MUST NOT MISS OUR NEXT SENSATIONAL, LANDMARK ISSUE!
20.

***Captain America #117*, page 20 art by Gene Colan & Joe Sinnott**

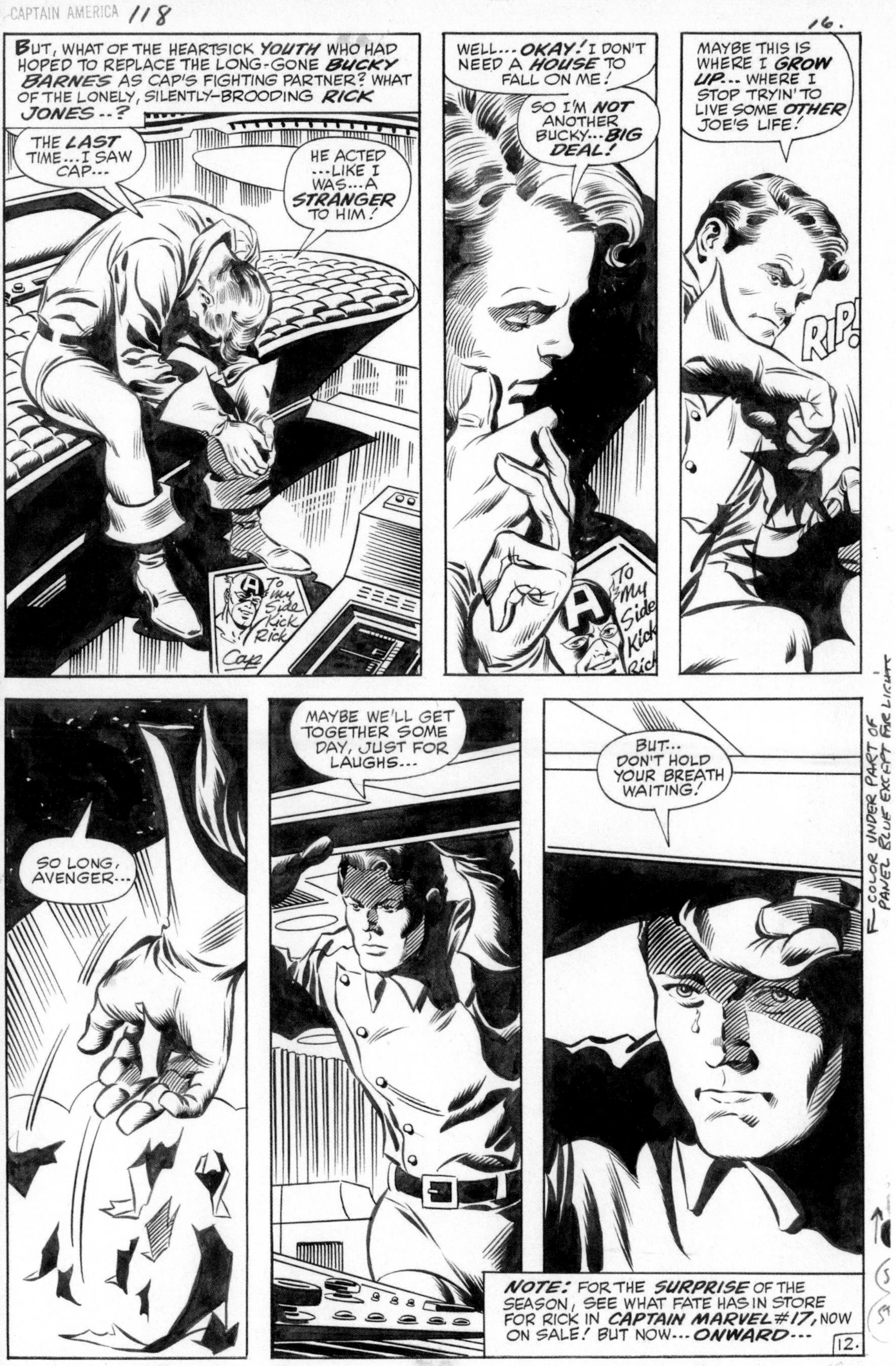
CAPTAIN AMERICA 118
16.
BUT, WHAT OF THE HEARTSICK YOUTH WHO HAD HOPED TO REPLACE THE LONG-GONE BUCKY BARNES AS CAP'S FIGHTING PARTNER? WHAT OF THE LONELY, SILENTLY-BROODING RICK JONES--?
THE LAST TIME...I SAW CAP...
HE ACTED ---LIKE I WAS...A STRANGER TO HIM!
To my Side Kick Rick
Cap
WELL...OKAY! I DON'T NEED A HOUSE TO FALL ON ME!
SO I'M NOT ANOTHER BUCKY...BIG DEAL!
MAYBE THIS IS WHERE I GROW UP... WHERE I STOP TRYIN' TO LIVE SOME OTHER JOE'S LIFE!
RIP!
SO LONG, AVENGER...
MAYBE WE'LL GET TOGETHER SOME DAY, JUST FOR LAUGHS...
BUT... DON'T HOLD YOUR BREATH WAITING!
NOTE: FOR THE SURPRISE OF THE SEASON, SEE WHAT FATE HAS IN STORE FOR RICK IN CAPTAIN MARVEL #17, NOW ON SALE! BUT NOW...ONWARD...
12.
COLOR UNDER PART OF PANEL BLUE EXCEPT FOR LIGHT

Captain America #118, page 12 art by Gene Colan & Joe Sinnott

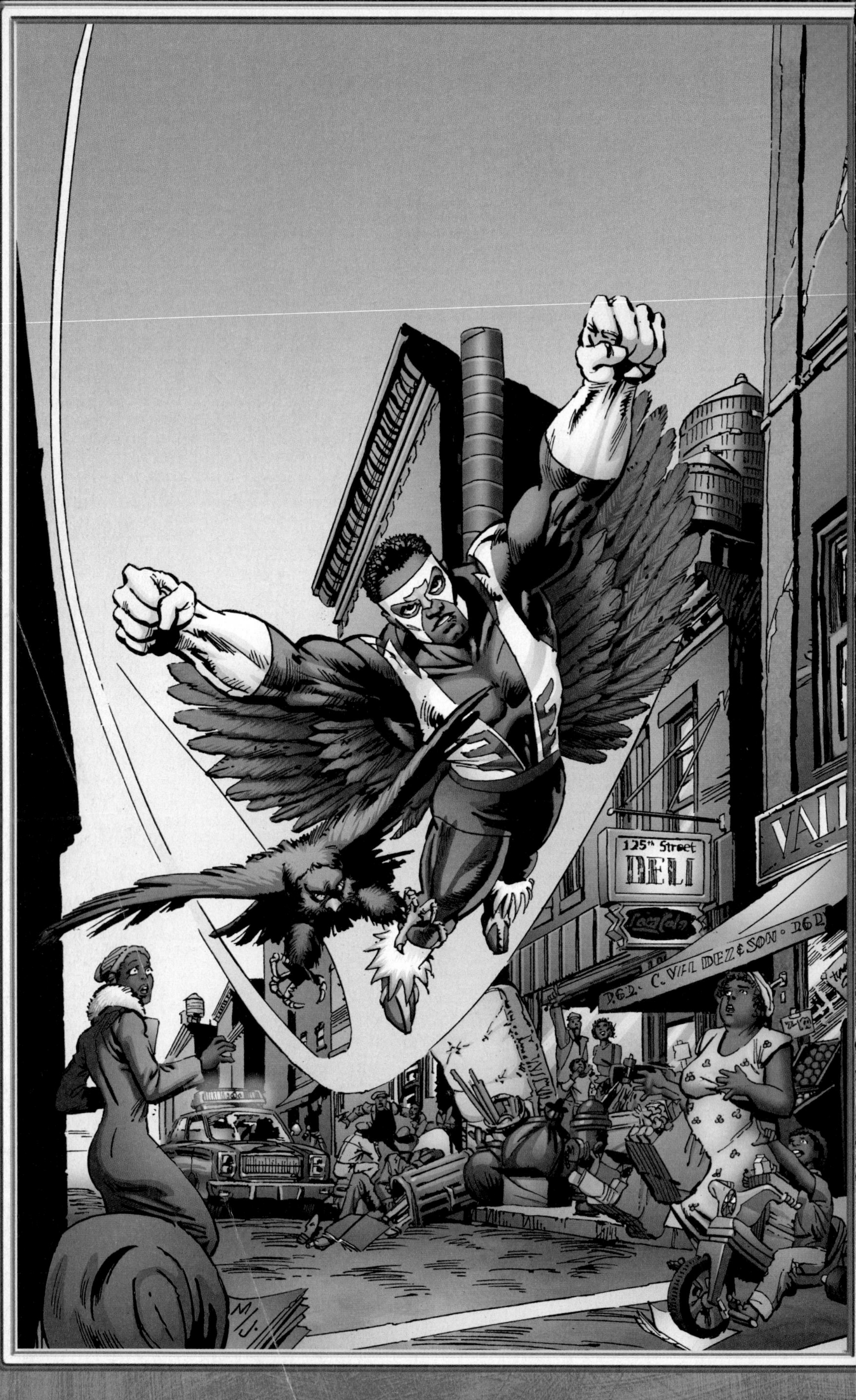
125th Street
DELI
VAL
D.G.D. C. VALDEZ & SON · D.G.D.

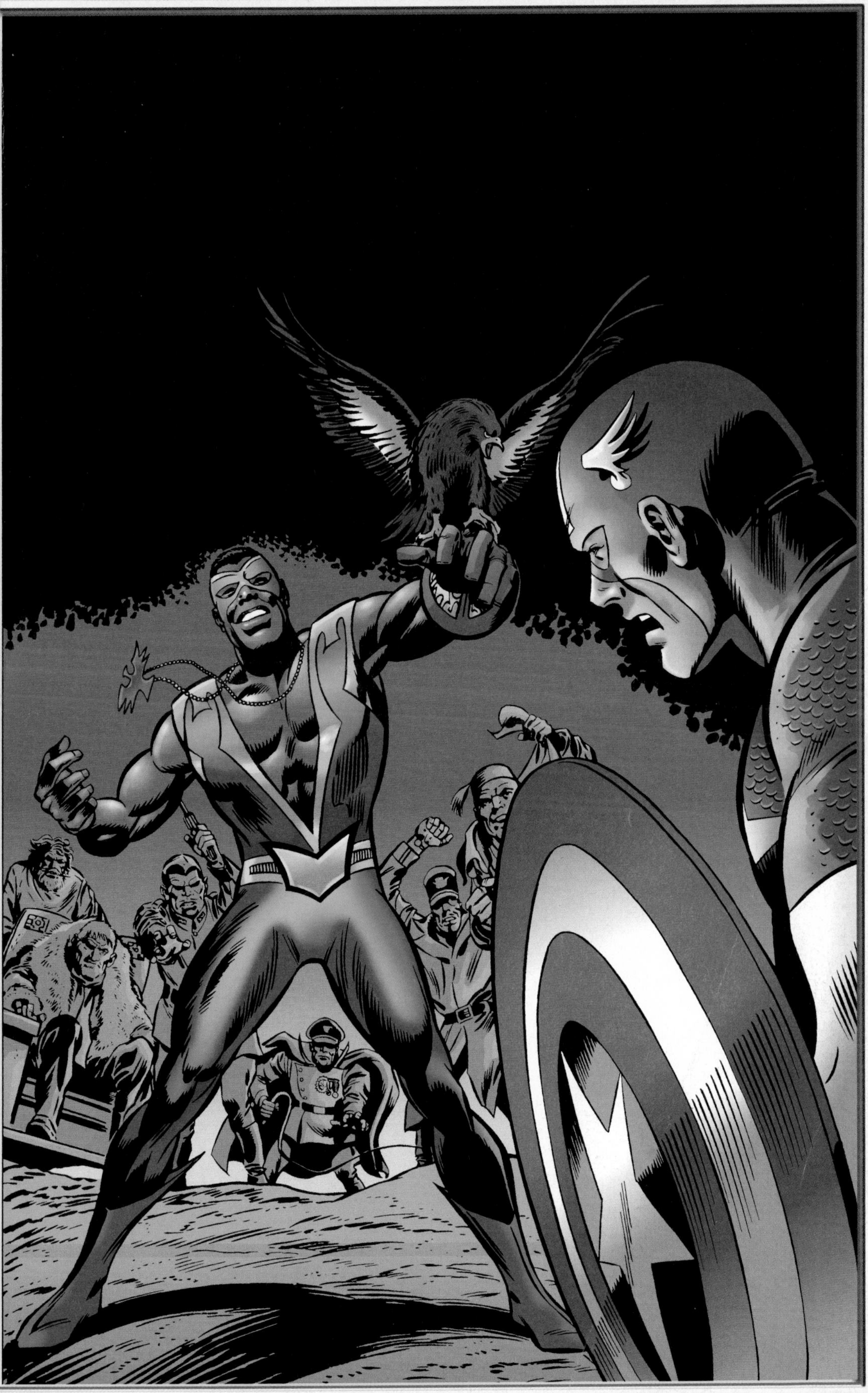

FALCON

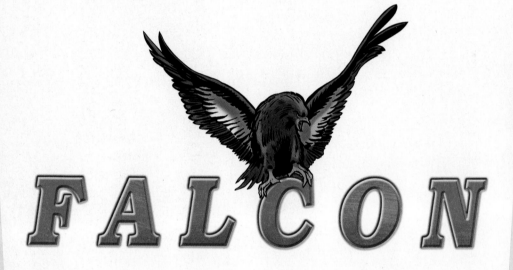